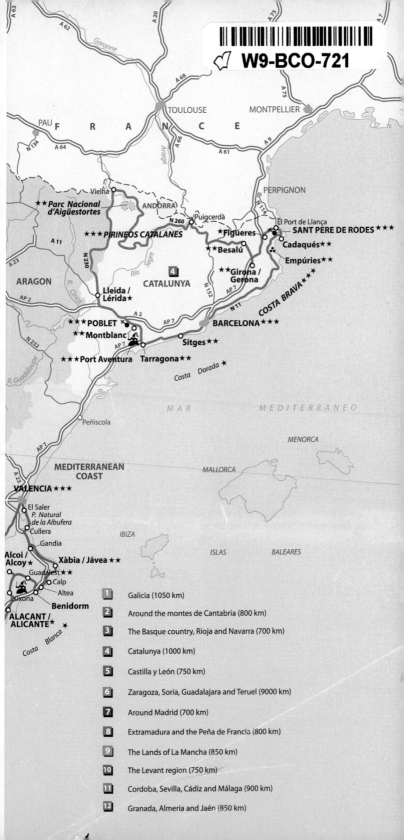

W9-BCO-721

1	Galicia (1050 km)
2	Around the montes de Cantabria (800 km)
3	The Basque country, Rioja and Navarra (700 km)
4	Catalunya (1000 km)
5	Castilla y León (750 km)
6	Zaragoza, Soria, Guadalajara and Teruel (9000 km)
7	Around Madrid (700 km)
8	Extramadura and the Peña de Francia (800 km)
9	The Lands of La Mancha (850 km)
10	The Levant region (750 km)
11	Cordoba, Sevilla, Cádiz and Málaga (900 km)
12	Granada, Almeria and Jaén (850 km)

The**Green**Guide
Spain

Teatre-Museu Dalí, Figueres, Catalunya ©Turespaña

General Manager   Cynthia Clayton Ochterbeck

THE GREEN GUIDE **SPAIN**

Editor	Alison Coupe
Principal Writers	Paul Murphy, Glenn Harper
Production Manager	Natasha G. George
Cartography	John Dear
Photo Editor	Yoshimi Kanazawa
Proofreader	Karolin Thomas
Interior Design	Chris Bell
Cover Design	Chris Bell, Christelle Le Déan
Layout	Nicole D. Jordan, Therese Schneider
Cover Layout	Michelin Apa Publications Ltd.

Contact Us   The Green Guide
                           Michelin Maps and Guides
                           One Parkway South
                           Greenville, SC 29615
                           USA
                           www.michelintravel.com

                           Michelin Maps and Guides
                           Hannay House
                           39 Clarendon Road
                           Watford, Herts WD17 1JA
                           UK
                           ✆01923 205240
                           www.ViaMichelin.com
                           travelpubsales@uk.michelin.com

Special Sales   For information regarding bulk sales,
                           customized editions and premium sales,
                           please contact our Customer Service
                           Departments:
                           USA   1-800-432-6277
                           UK   01923 205240
                           Canada 1-800-361-8236

HOW TO USE THIS GUIDE

PLANNING YOUR TRIP

The blue-tabbed PLANNING YOUR TRIP section at the front of the guide gives you **ideas for your trip** and **practical information** to help you organise it. You'll find tours, practical information, a host of outdoor activities, a calendar of events, information on shopping, sightseeing, kids' activities and more.

INTRODUCTION

The orange-tabbed INTRODUCTION section explores Spain's **Nature** and geology. The **History** section spans the Carthaginians through Napoleon to the modern day. The **Art and Culture** section covers architecture, art, literature and music, while **Spain Today** delves into modern Spain.

DISCOVERING

The green-tabbed DISCOVERING section features Principal Sights by region, featuring the most interesting local **Sights**, **Walking Tours**, nearby **Excursions** and detailed **Driving Tours**. Admission prices shown are normally for a single adult.

ADDRESSES

We've selected the best hotels, restaurants, cafés, shops, nightlife and entertainment to fit all budgets. See the Legend on the cover flap for an explanation of the price categories. See the back of the guide for an index of where to find hotels and restaurants.

Sidebars

Throughout the guide you will find blue, orange and green-coloured text boxes with lively anecdotes, detailed history and background information.

A Bit of Advice

Green advice boxes found in this guide contain practical tips and handy information relevant to the sight in the Discovering section.

STAR RATINGS ★★★

Michelin has given star ratings for more than 100 years. If you're pressed for time, we recommend you visit the ★★★, or ★★ sights first:

★★★ **Highly recommended**

★★ **Recommended**

★ **Interesting**

MAPS

- National Driving Tours
- Principal Sights map.
- Region maps.
- Maps for major cities and villages.
- Local tour maps.

All maps in this guide are oriented north, unless otherwise indicated by a directional arrow. The term "Local Map" refers to a map within the chapter or Tourism Region. A complete list of the maps found in the guide appears at the back of this book.

PLANNING
YOUR TRIP

E. Baret/MICHELIN

INTRODUCTION
TO SPAIN

DISCOVERING
SPAIN

CONTENTS

Welcome to Spain

If this is your first trip to Spain welcome to a land that is, by European standards, vast and, by any measure, varied, boasting many different cultures and languages, virtually every landscape, and a treasure trove of heritage and history. Whether you opt for beach or mountains, city or countryside, the choices are enormous. If you are a returning visitor, you'll probably note, with delight, how rapidly Spain's major cities are reinventing themselves for foreign visitors, and how many resorts also offer new levels of comfort and luxury. Meanwhile, the countryside and mountains remaining reassuringly unchanged.

Town of Carmona, near Sevilla, Andalucía

©Turespaña

ANDALUCÍA *(pp100–187)*

Andalucía is the popular picture-postcard Spain of bullfighting, flamenco, *pueblos blancos* (white villages) and the teeming built-up Costa del Sol of sun, sand and sangria; there are also plenty of smaller seaside hideaways. In Granada, Cordóba and Sevilla Andalucía boasts three of Spain's greatest Moorish cities.

ARAGÓN *(pp188–209)*

This little-known landlocked region offers magnificent mountain scenery in the Aragonese Pyrennees, and burgeoning culture in Zaragoza, site of Expo 2008. Its other must-see sight is Teruel for its lavish Mudéjar towers.

ASTURIAS AND CANTABRIA
(pp210–231)

This long Atlantic coastline is part of "Green Spain", steep and rolling with more in common, topographically and climatically, with northern Europe than central or southern Spain. The **Picos de Europa** is a spectacular area popular with walkers; the coastline is cut by *rías* (flooded river valleys).

CASTILLA-LEÒN *(pp232–281)*

Castille is the land of Castles, where medieval Spanish history and early kingdoms were forged by heroes such as El Cid. Large swathes are empty and unwelcoming but in the great monumental cities of León, Burgos and Salamanca the sense of history and grandeur is very tangible.

CASTILLA-LA MANCHA
(pp282–303)

The great central tableland of Spain is famous for Don Quixote, Manchego cheese. and La Mancha wines. This windswept arid area will never be an important tourist region but if you are passing through, or want to take time out of Madrid, pick up the Don Quixote trail to see the kind of landscapes and villages that have changed little in the 400 years since Miguel Cervantes wrote about Spain's famous knight.

CATALUNYA AND ANDORRA
(pp304–369)

Catalunya is home to Barcelona – Europe's favourite city, if not in visitor numbers, then in terms of image and all-round popularity. Whether you're a culture vulture, night owl, beach bum or football fan this is the only city in Europe that truly has it all. Catalunya and neighbouring Andorra offer landscapes as varied as anywhere in Spain, with sunbathing one day on the beautiful Costa Brava, skiing the next day in the Pyrenees.

Galician hórreo (granary) near Lugo, Galicia

M. C. Martinez Castellano/Michelin

EXTREMADURA *(pp370–383)*

A combination of geographic, geological and historical factors meant that Extremadura was dealt the worst hand of all the Spanish regions and for much of its history, a rich Roman period aside, it has been a neglected, isolated, empty zone. Out of such adversity came adventurers – *Conquistadores* – who were to discover and plunder the New World, bringing back great riches to found new towns and monuments in their homeland.

GALICIA *(pp384–409)*

Galicia is a land of misty green hills, bagpipes, and a spectacular rocky coastline of a thousand coves, where some of Europe's finest seafood is landed and freshly cooked. It is also home to one of Spain's most historic and certainly its most pious city, Santiago de Compostela – though you don't need to be a pilgrim to enjoy it.

MADRID *(pp410–447)*

Madrid possesses none of Spain's popular icons nor imagery. It is too hot (in summer) and too busy (year-round), to ever become a favourite short-break destination. However, for art lovers and visitors who want a Spanish history lesson it is home to some of the world's finest art galleries and palaces from where a vast Empire was once ruled.

NAVARRA, PAÍS VASCO, LA RIOJA *(pp448–481)*

Spain's northeastern regions are best known for their wine and food. Basque cuisine is the best in Spain and the resort of San Sebastian is as popular with gourmets as with families. Bilbao's Guggenheim Museum has been the biggest boost to regional tourism since the Camino de Santiago.

THE MEDITERRANEAN COAST *(pp482–509)*

Spain's central and southern eastern coastline is a huge holiday zone that has encouraged many north Europeans to stay permanently. Alicante province, including Benidorm is the busiest and most mature in terms of tourism. Murcia is a relative newcomer, though its arid land is now dotted with golf courses and *urbanizaciónes*. Valencia has become one of Spain's most exciting cities.

THE ISLANDS *(pp510–561)*

The Canary Islands and the Balearics are loved by Spaniards and north Europeans. Floating in the mid-Atlantic, the geography and indigenous culture of the volcanic-born Canaries have little in common with the rest of Spain. The Balearics are more typically Spanish: Mallorca and Ibiza are famous for their party lifestyle but away from the crowds is peace and beauty.

Serving Txacolí in a bar, Donostia-San Sebastian, País Vasco
©Philippe Roy/hemis.fr/Photoshot

Michelin Driving Tours

Refer to the Driving Tours Map on the inside back cover and to Michelin maps nos. 571, 572, 574, 577 and 578 in order to make the most of the following driving tours.

1 GALICIA

Round trip of 1 031km/644mi from A Coruña/La Coruña – This tour provides an insight into a region with magnificent towns and cities, verdant landscapes, an indented coastline and villages full of character and charm, known in ancient times as *finis terra*, or "end of the world". Galicia is also renowned for its delicious seafood. After visiting **A Coruña/La Coruña**, with its old quarter and attractive seafront promenade *(avenida de la Marina)*, head south to **Santiago de Compostela**, one of Spain's finest cities, to marvel at the spectacular plaza del Obradoiro, dominated by the impressive cathedral – the final destination for thousands of pilgrims every year. The tour continues along the **Rías Baixas/Rías Bajas** via **Pontevedra** to the mouth of the Miño, forming a natural border with Portugal. Along this magnificent stretch of coastline, with the scenic fishing village of **Combarro** and the summer resort of **Baiona**, the sea has created a series of beautiful inlets. Having followed the Miño as far as

the historic town of **Tui**, continue by motorway to **Ourense**. After visiting the town, the itinerary continues along the spectacular **Gargantas de Sil**, before following the same road into the province of León, and the town of Ponferrada, the gateway to the magical landscapes of **Las Médulas**. Heading back into Galicia, make your way to **Lugo**, which has managed to preserve its exceptional Roman walls. Continue north to the coast, driving along the **Rías Altas** before returning to A Coruña/ La Coruña.

2 AROUND THE MONTES DE CANTABRIA

Round trip of 764km/477mi from Santander – The Cantabrian mountains form a natural boundary between Castilla y León and the autonomous communities of Cantabria and Asturias. To the north, the highest summits of the Picos de Europa rise up close to the stunning coast, while in the lands of Castilla to the south you won't want to miss some of the towns and villages along the Way of St James, or two outstanding jewels of Gothic art, the cathedrals of León and Burgos. Leaving behind the seigniorial town of **Santander**, with its superb location on the **Costa de Contabria**, head west to the charming medieval town of **Santillana del Mar**, making sure you visit the replica of the **Cuevas de Altamira**, a masterpiece of prehistoric cave art. Continue along the same road to the picturesque pueblo of **Comillas**, before reaching the seaside resort of **San Vicente de la Barquera**. From here, the tour heads into the mountains, passing through the northern section of the **Parque Nacional de los Picos de Europa** and the exquisite panorama from the **Mirador del Fito**, before driving along the **Costa Verde** to the coastal city of Gijón, renowned for its extensive beach, and then south to nearby **Oviedo**, with its well maintained historical centre

Picos de Europa

J. Malburet/ MICHELIN

containing some outstanding examples of Asturian architecture. Continue inland to visit the historic city of **León**, and then east across the Meseta towards Burgos along the Way of St James, visiting Villalcázar de Sirga, Carrión de los Condes and **Frómista** en route, the latter famous for the Iglesia de San Martín, a masterpiece of Romanesque architecture. Having spent time exploring **Burgos** and its magnificent religious heritage, the tour continues towards Aguilar de Campoo, overseen by its castle, and from here to Reinosa, at the foot of the Montes Cantábricos, an ideal departure point for an excursion to the **Pico de Tres Mares**; alternatively, make your way back to Santander, stopping at **Puente Viesgo** to admire the wall paintings in the Cueva del Castillo.

③ THE BASQUE COUNTRY, RIOJA AND NAVARRA
Round trip of 696km/435mi from Bilbao – This tour combines stunning coastline dotted with picturesque villages, the delightful inland landscapes of northern Spain and the Way of St James, as well as charming towns and cities renowned for their wonderful gastronomy.

The tour starts with an obligatory visit to the Guggenheim Museum in **Bilbao** before following the indented **Costa Vasca** eastwards through quaint fishing villages to **Donostia-San Sebastián**, with its majestic setting on one of Spain's most breathtaking bays. From here, continue the short distance to **Hondarribia/Fuenterrabía**, a pleasant resort and fishing port with an attractive old quarter, close to the French border. The magnificent **Valle del Bidasoa** provides the backdrop as you head inland to **Pamplona**, a medieval town built around its imposing cathedral and famous for the annual running of the bulls. The route then heads deeper into Navarra, past monasteries and important staging-posts on the **Way of St James**

(**Leyre**, **La Oliva**, **Sangüesa/Zangoza** and **Puente la Reina**) and historic towns such as Sos del Rey Católico and Olite, before reaching **Estella**, one of the most important stops along the famous pilgrimage route. After visiting the nearby Monasterio de Irache, the pilgrims' path continues west to Logroño, the capital of La Rioja, known for its cathedral and old streets, and then through the extensive vineyards for which this region is justifiably renowned; the most famous halts on this section of the path are undoubtedly **Nájera** and **Santo Domingo de la Calzada**. Between the two, nestled in a delightful valley, is the village of **San Millán de la Cogolla**, the cradle of the written Castilian language. Before returning to the Basque Country via the capital of the province of Álava, **Vitoria-Gasteiz**, with its atmospheric old quarter and several museums of interest, take time to visit Haro and the Museo del Vino de La Rioja. Return to Bilbao via the motorway, which winds its way through an impressive mountain landscape.

④ CATALUNYA
Round trip of 1 020km/637mi from Barcelona – This driving tour through Catalunya is characterised by high Pyrenean peaks, rugged coasts with charming coves, long sandy beaches, picturesque villages, exquisite Romanesque churches, impressive monasteries, and towns and cities overflowing with history.

Once you've spent time in the region's capital, **Barcelona**, a city with a fascinating mix of modernity and history, begin your tour along the **Costa Brava**, a beautiful stretch of coastline dotted with authentic fishing villages and summer resorts. After visiting the old Roman colony of **Empúries**, the picture-postcard small town of **Cadaqués**, the **Monasterio de Sant Pere de Rodes** and El Port de Llançà, head inland to **Figueres**, home of the Dalí Theatre and Museum, and **Girona/Gerona**, a city that still retains the vestiges of its Roman, Jewish, Moorish and Christian past. From here, the tour climbs up into the **Pirineos Catalanes**, a land of spectacular mountain roads, beautiful valleys and charming villages of **Besalú**, with its Romanesque architecture, and Puigcerdà. After passing the **Parc Nacional d'Aigüestortes**, the itinerary abandons the mountains via Vielha to reach **Lleida/Lérida**, watched over by the remains of its former Moorish fortress and by the city's cathedral (Seo). The journey back to the Mediterranean provides an opportunity to visit **Poblet**, the most famous Cistercian monastery in Spain, as well as the walled town of **Montblanc**, before arriving in **Tarragona**, capital of Tarraconensis under the Romans. Have a fun day out at the **Port Aventura** theme park before heading back to Barcelona. The final leg of the tour runs past the attractive resort town of **Sitges** on the **Costa Dorada**.

5 CASTILLA Y LEÓN

Round trip of 756km/472mi from Salamanca – Historic towns and lofty castles dominate this tour through the lands of old Castile. If your trip coincides with Holy Week, head for Zamora or Valladolid to witness their solemn Semana Santa processions. After spending time exploring **Salamanca**, a lively university city teeming with sumptuous monuments, head north to **Zamora** to admire

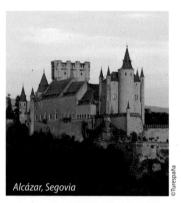

Alcázar, Segovia

©Turespaña

the scallop tiling on the cupola of the cathedral. The road east towards Valladolid passes through **Toro**, where the dome of the town's collegiate church is similar in style to the cupola of Zamora's cathedral, and Tordesillas, where the famous treaty dividing the lands of the New World between Spain and Portugal was signed. In **Valladolid**, renowned for fine examples of Isabelline art, it is well worth visiting the National Sculpture Museum (*Museo Nacional de Escultura*). Continue your journey through an extensive landscape of cereal crops, passing through Medina de Rioseco en route to **Palencia**, with its magnificent cathedral. Heading east into the province of Burgos, the itinerary takes in charming small towns and villages such as Lerma and **Covarrubias**. One of the highlights of this tour is the **Monasterio de Santo Domingo de Silos**, the cloisters of which are a masterpiece of Romanesque art. From here, the itinerary heads south, skirting along the banks of the Duero, to visit a series of castles built to defend the lands conquered by Christians from the Moors, such as the ruined fortress at **Peñaranda de Duero**; the impressive castle at **Peñafiel**; **Cuéllar**; and the more unusual castle at **Coca**, in Mudéjar style. The tour continues to **Segovia**, famous for its aqueduct and fairytale castle, and on to **Ávila**, a city of convents and churches, encircled by its famous walls. Before completing your circuit, it is well worth making a last stop in the small town of Alba de Tormes.

6 ZARAGOZA, SORIA, GUADALAJARA AND TERUEL

Round trip of 869km/543mi from Zaragoza – This tour travels across several inland provinces, passing through impressive mountain land-scapes, villages crowned by old castles and towns full of character and charm. The journey begins from **Zaragoza** with a foray into Navarra to visit **Tudela**, with its interesting examples of Mudéjar architecture and its fine cathedral. Returning to the province of Zaragoza, head for Tarazona, famous for its old quarter and cathedral, and the **Monasterio de Veruela**, which is well worth a visit. From Tarazona, continue to **Soria**, a quiet provincial capital embellished with impressive churches, on the banks of the Duero. The itinerary then continues southwest, passing through Calatañazor, a picturesque village overlooked by a medieval castle, to **Burgo de Osma**, yet another charming town, renowned for its magnificent cathedral. Head across country to Berlanga de Duero, the site of another castle built to defend the Duero, and on to San Baudelio de Berlanga, a hermitage with an unusual 11C Mozarabic chapel. Once past Atienza, crowned by the ruins of its castle, continue to historic **Sigüenza**, whose highlights include the fortified cathedral with its impressive array of sculptures, and the castle (now a parador). Join up with the fast highway heading east towards Zaragoza, passing through attractive scenery along the banks of the Jalón, crossing the river briefly to visit the magnificent **Monasterio de Santa María de Huerta**, built in sober Cistercian style with a number of Renaissance additions. As the road passes Ateca, head directly south past La Tranquera Reservoir to the **Monasterio de Piedra**, to enjoy a stroll through its delightful park. The tour continues via Molina de Aragón, with yet another castle, before entering the Sierra de **Albarracín** en route to the charming medieval village of the same name. The next stop on the itinerary is **Teruel**, a town which enjoys a superb location, and adorned with a number of interesting examples of Mudéjar architecture. To complete the tour, head north to **Daroca**, with its 4km/2.5mi of walls, before joining the motorway for the final leg back to Zaragoza.

⑦ AROUND MADRID

Round trip of 689km/431mi from Madrid – The area around the Spanish capital is home to several towns of major interest, a number of royal palaces and the scenic, mountainous landscapes of the Sierra de Gredos and Sierra de Guadarrama.

One of the closest towns to **Madrid** is **Alcalá de Henares**, the birthplace of Miguel de Cervantes, where the major attraction are the university buildings. From here, the route passes through **Chinchón**, with one of the country's prettiest main squares, and on to **Aranjuez**, nestled in a verdant setting on the banks of the Tagus. After visiting the royal palace and pavilions and strolling through the delightful gardens here, continue your journey southwest to the historic city of **Toledo**, magnificently perched in a loop of the Tagus, with the sumptuous vestiges of its rich past. Continue your journey west to Talavera de la Reina, famous for its ceramics, and then north along a mountain road through the **Sierra de Gredos** en route to Ávila, visiting along the way the **Cueva del Águila**, a cave 4km/2.5mi from the main road via an unsurfaced track. Ávila, a city of churches and convents, and the cradle of St Teresa, has pre-served intact its magnificent 11C walls. From Ávila, the tour heads east to the **Monasterio de El Escorial**, an immense monastery built by order of Philip II. On the way to Segovia, you may wish to branch off to the **Valle de los Caídos**, or Valley of the Fallen, impressively situated amid the stunning landscapes of the Sierra de Guadarrama. In **Segovia**, admire the incredible Roman aqueduct, the city's Romanesque churches and the exotic Alcázar. Close to the city, at the foot of the Sierra de Guadarrama, are the palace and magnificent gardens of **La Granja de San Ildefonso**, built by Philip IV, the grandson of Louis XIV, in nostalgia for the Versailles of his childhood. Return to the mountains, and after crossing the Navacerrada Pass, head northeast through a valley to the **Monasterio de El Paular**. A twisting road farther north traverses the Navafría Pass, before descending into **Pedraza de la Sierra**, a seigniorial town full of charm. Before returning by motorway to Madrid via the Somosierra Pass, the small town of Sepúlveda is worth a visit to admire its impressive site overlooking a deep gorge of the River Duratón.

8 EXTREMADURA AND THE PEÑA DE FRANCIA

Round trip of 780km/487mi from Plasencia – This tour through the region of Extremadura has a strong historic focus because of its links with the Romans, the great conquistadors and Emperor Charles V. The tour ends with the Peña de Francia, in the province of Salamanca.

After visiting the cathedral and old quarter of **Plasencia**, the tour starts in the verdant Valle de La Vera, the setting for the **Monasterio de Yuste**, to which Charles V withdrew following his abdication, and the 15C castle in Jarandilla de la Vera (now a parador). Leaving the valley along a country road that crosses the Valdecañas Reservoir, you come to the village of **Guadalupe**, huddled around its magnificent monastery. Following a visit to this shrine, continue westwards to the monumental town of **Trujillo**, the birthplace of several of the famous conquistadors, including Francisco Pizarro, and the site of one of Spain's most impressive and original main squares. From Trujillo, the tour then heads southwest by fast highway to **Mérida** to admire the city's Roman remains and the Museo Nacional de Arte Romano, which bears witness to Mérida's importance during this period. The next stops on the itinerary are **Cáceres**, a monumental town with a stunning and superbly preserved old town where time seems to have stopped in the 16C and 17C, and **Alcántara**, whose main sights of interest are a monastery, the seat of the military order of the same name, and an exceptional Roman bridge

spanning the Tagus. Head northeast to Coria to visit its cathedral, and then into the province of Salamanca, to **Ciudad Rodrigo**, a pleasant small town with several buildings of interest hidden behind its walls. The tour ends with a visit to the **Peña de Francia**, a crag rising to 1 723m/5 655ft, and the Sierra de Béjar, with its typical mountain village of the same name.

9 THE LANDS OF LA MANCHA

Round trip of 849km/531mi from Cuenca – For many, La Mancha conjures up a scene of seemingly endless fields of cereal crops and vines, interspersed with the occasional village or town and the evocative silhouette of a windmill or castle. Yet it is also an area of impressive mountains and landscapes that have little in common with this image. **Cuenca**, with its spectacular position between the ravines of the Júcar and Huécar rivers, is the starting-point for this tour, which begins with a drive through the **sierra** of the same name, famous for sights such as the **Ciudad Encantada** (with its unusual stone formations), the source of the River Cuervo, and the **Beteta** Ravine *(Hoz)*. Returning to Cuenca, the itinerary then heads out along the flat lands-capes to the southwest to **Belmonte**, with its castle and interesting colle-giate church, and Campo de Criptana, a typical La Mancha village, whose houses are framed by the silhouette of its windmills. After passing through Alcázar de San Juan, the largest town in the area, continue on to **Consuegra**, where the castle and line of windmills on a hill overlooking the town offers one of the region's most enduring sights. From here, head south for a visit to the Parque Nacional de las Tablas de Daimiel, a wetland area at the confluence of the River Guadiana and River Cigüela. The next stop on the itinerary is in **Almagro**, a historic town that has preserved its delightful old quarter, including a magnificent main square and the

Corral de Comedias, a 16C theatre. A short distance to the southeast stands Valdepeñas, the capital of La Mancha's wine industry. Continuing east, the tour passes through **Villanueva de los Infantes**, containing several fine examples of Renaissance and Baroque architecture, and the village of **Alcaraz**, with its outstanding main square lined by elegant buildings, protected by the mountain range in which the River Mundo has its source. The next stop is the city of Albacete, home to a provincial museum with an interesting archaeology section. From here, head north to **Alarcón**, impressively situated on a hill almost completely encircled by the River Júcar and crowned by an imposing medieval castle (now a parador), before returning to Cuenca.

1 0 THE LEVANTE REGION

Round trip of 715km/447mi from Valencia – This tour running along the coast and inland through the provinces of Valencia, Alicante and Murcia is characterised by long sandy beaches and charming villages and towns with a fascinating artistic and architectural heritage.

Having spent time exploring **Valencia**, start the tour along the Mediterranean, visiting El Saler, with its extensive sandy beaches, and the nearby Parque Natural de la Albufera, a large freshwater lake and important rice growing area. The itinerary then passes through a series of large resorts such as Cullera, Gandía, home to the former palace of the Dukes of Borja, and Denia, watched over by its castle. **Xàbia/Jávea**, with its picturesque old quarter, is just a few miles north of the Cabo de la Nao headland, offering spectacular views of the coast, and Calp/Calpe, located close to the impressive Penyal d'Ifac rock. **Altea**, the next resort to the south, is one of the area's most attractive coastal towns with its steep and narrow streets. Continue along the coast to Benidorm, where the backdrop to the beach is a mass of high-rise hotels

and apartment buildings, and from here to the **Terra Mítica** theme park. The tour then heads inland through the mountains to visit **Guadalest**, in a spectacular location on a rocky ridge, Alcoi/Alcoy, nestled in a fertile river valley, and to the south, Xixona, famous for its nougat, and reached via the Carrasqueta Pass. Returning to the coast, the next major city on the itinerary is **Alicante**, a pleasant and relaxed provincial capital overlooked by an imposing fortress, the Castillo de Santa Bárbara. The itinerary continues southwards, skirting the resorts of Guardamar del Segura and Torrevieja, before arriving at Mar Menor, a shallow lagoon separated from the sea by a long sandbar, at the southern tip of which stands the resort of La Manga del Mar Menor. After a visit to Cartagena, on the curve of a deep bay, leave the coast for the town of **Murcia**, whose main sights are its fine cathedral and the Museo Salzillo, a museum dedicated to the 18C sculptor Francisco Salzillo. Continue northeast to **Orihuela**, a tranquil town with numerous churches of interest, and then to **Elx/Elche**, famous for its palm grove. From here the itinerary heads farther inland by dual carriageway to Villena, protected by its imposing castle. The final stop on this driving tour is **Xàtiva**, the town of a thousand fountains and birthplace of two popes. Situated on a fertile plain, the town has preserved a number of buildings of architectural interest.

1 1 CÓRDOBA, SEVILLA, CÁDIZ AND MÁLAGA

Round trip of 890km/556mi from Córdoba – This tour takes in some of the finest cities of inland Andalucía, the delightful whitewashed villages (pueblos blancos) in the provinces of Cádiz and Málaga, and the famous Costa del Sol resorts.

Córdoba, one of the three emblems of Andalucía, along with Sevilla and Granada, is one of Spain's most beautiful cities with monuments such as the Mezquita, typical whitewashed streets and a history influenced by the Christian, Muslim and Jewish faiths. From here, head west to **Écija**, the so-called "frying pan" of Andalucía, a town of churches, convents, palaces and numerous bell towers. Farther west stands the breathtaking city of **Sevilla**, a name that conjures up passion and colour, where several days are needed to explore it to the full. The itinerary then heads towards the Atlantic, pausing in the elegant town of **Jerez de la Frontera**, famous for its sherry, equestrian history, and delightful architecture, before arriving in **Cádiz**, reached via an impressive causeway. This charming provincial capital and port is one of Spain's best-kept secrets, with its 18C architecture, historic squares, impressive monuments and super beaches. Chiclana de la Frontera, to the south, is the closest town to the Playa de la Barrosa, a magnificent, and seemingly endless sandy beach. From here, the tour heads inland to **Medina Sidonia**, one of the oldest towns in Europe, steeped in history with a medieval quarter perched on a hill with expansive views of the surrounding area. The white-washed town of **Arcos de la Frontera**, the next stop, has an even more out-standing location, straddling a ridge above a gorge of the River Guadalete. Arcos is one of the region's famous *pueblos blancos*, which include **Ronda**, renowned for its dramatic location, stunning architecture and tradition of bullfighting. From Ronda, the itinerary winds its way through stunning mountain scenery down to the coast, dominated by the impressive Rock of **Gibraltar**. The coast road east to Málaga passes through some of the **Costa del Sol**'s most famous resorts (**Estepona**, **Marbella**, Fuengirola, Benalmádena, etc.), with their luxury developments, hotels and apartments. From **Málaga**, follow the fast highway inland to **Antequera**, the ideal base from which to explore local nature, and from here to **Estepa**, crowned by the remains of a fortress. The hilltop

town of **Osuna**, the last stage on the journey, has preserved an interesting architectural heritage with numerous palaces and noble mansions amid its old whitewashed centre. From Osuna, return directly to Córdoba.

①② GRANADA, ALMERÍA AND JAÉN

Round trip of 835km/522mi from Granada – This tour through the eastern half of Andalucía is characterised by historic towns and cities with an outstanding artistic heritage, magnificent deserted beaches, breathtaking mountain scenery and a landscape carpeted with olive trees as far as the eye can see. For many, a visit to the Alhambra, overlooking **Granada**, is the highlight of a trip to Spain. It marks the starting-point for this driving tour, which begins with a journey across the spectacular **Alpujarras** mountain range, passing through verdant valleys and pictures-que whitewashed small towns and villages to reach **Almería**, a provincial capital overlooked by a Moorish fortress perched on a hill above the city. The itinerary continues through the **Parque Natural de Cabo de Gata-Níjar** and along the Almerian coast, an area of luminous skies, sand dunes, wild beaches and impressive desert landscapes that conjure up images of nearby Africa; **Mojácar**, perched on a hill, is the most attractive town in this area. From here, follow the fast highway north, cutting inland to the area known as Los Vélez, in the foothills of the Sierra de María, and the town of Vélez Blanco, overlooked by its unusual Renaissance castle. Once you have crossed the Sierra de María, a cross-country route leads to Pontones, in the province of Jaén, at the heart of the **Parque Natural de las Sierras de Cazorla, Segura y las Villas**. The tour through the park as far as **Cazorla** passes through impressive mountain landscapes cut by deep ravines, rivers and streams. Following a restorative sojourn at the heart of nature, the tour continues to **Úbeda** and **Baeza**, two monumental towns renowned for their magnificent Renaissance architecture. The last leg of the tour traverses extensive olive groves before reaching **Jaén**, spread out at the foot of the Cerro de Santa Catalina, a hill crowned by the city's imposing Arab fortress. Apart from the castle, the other major sights of interest in Jaén are its sumptuous cathedral and the Arab baths in the Palacio de Villardompardo.

Local Driving Tours

Listed below are the sights within the *Discovering Spain* section of the guide, where you can find local driving tours not listed on the Driving Tours Map.

- Pico de Tres Mares
- Cuevas de Canalobre and Jijona
- Sierra de Béjar and Sierra de Candelario
- East from Almería
- Desfiladero de los Gaitanes
- The Ribagorza
- Monte Hacho
- Sierra de Andía and Sierra de Urbasa
- The Alpujarras
- Los Mallos de Riglos
- Sierra de Loarre
- Serrablo
- Monasterio de San Juan de la Peña
- Valle de Hecho
- Roncal and Ansó Valleys
- Cistercian Monasteries of Catalunya
- Río Sil
- Valle del Bidasoa
- Upper Valley of the Ter
- La Cerdanya
- Vall del Segre
- Vall del Noguera Pallaresa
- La Vall d'Arán
- Vall del Noguera Ribagorçana
- Rías Bajas
- East of Vitoria-Gasteiz: Medieval Paintings
- Mallorca's Rocky Coast
- Mallorca's East Coast and Caves
- Tenerife, Canaries
- Lanzarote, Canaries
- La Palma, Canaries
- La Dehesa, El Hierro, Canaries

When and Where To Go

WHEN TO GO
SEASONS

As a guideline, the best two seasons to visit Spain are spring and autumn, when temperatures across the country are generally pleasant.

Spring is the best time to explore Extremadura, Castilla-La Mancha and Andalucía, which in summer are the hottest regions in Spain.

Late spring is also a good time to visit the Mediterranean and Balearic Islands, as the sea temperature starts to warm up.

In **summer**, the country's north coast comes into its own, offering a pleasant climate for sightseeing and relaxing on the beach without the oppressive heat of other parts of the country. This time of year is also ideal for discovering the magnificent mountain landscapes of the Pyrenees, Picos de Europa, and the Sierra de Gredos, Sierra de Guadarrama and Sierra Nevada ranges.

Autumn is a generally pleasant season across most of Spain.

In **winter**, skiing enthusiasts can head for the Pyrenees or the Sierra Nevada, while those preferring to escape the cold wet winter in northern Europe can travel south to the Canary Islands for some winter sunshine.

For up-to-date information on **weather** in Spain, log onto the Spanish Meteorological Office website at www.inm.es.

WHAT TO PACK

Since Spain has so many days of sunshine and its temperatures are generally warmer than many other European countries, pack as few clothes as possible. Unless you

Temperature chart (°C)

Maximum temperatures in black.
Minimum temperatures in red.

Month	Jan	Feb	Mar	Apr	May	Jun	Jul	Aug	Sep	Oct	Nov	Dec
	13	14	16	18	21	25	28	28	25	21	16	13
Barcelona	6	7	9	11	14	18	21	21	19	15	11	7
	9	11	15	18	21	27	31	30	26	19	13	9
Madrid	1	2	5	7	10	14	17	17	14	9	5	2
	12	12	15	15	17	20	22	22	21	18	15	12
Santander	7	6	8	9	11	14	16	16	15	12	9	7
	15	17	20	23	26	32	36	36	32	26	20	16
Sevilla	6	6	9	11	13	17	20	20	18	14	10	7
	15	16	18	20	23	26	29	29	27	23	19	16
Valencia	5	6	8	10	13	16	19	20	17	13	9	6

choose to visit in winter, lightweight clothing is usually an ideal choice. It's a good idea to pack a sturdy pair of walking shoes, or even hiking boots. An umbrella, rainwear, a lightweight jacket and suntan lotion are good to have with you. Try to pack everything in one suitcase and a carry-on bag. Take an extra tote bag for bringing new purchases back home.

IDEAS FOR YOUR VISIT
SPAIN'S COASTLINES
Mediterranean Coast

Spain has thousands of miles of beautiful coastline, with the Mediterranean continuing to attract millions of Spanish and foreign visitors every year to its delightful waters and magnificent beaches.

The rugged and indented **Costa Brava**, or Wild Coast, with its charming coves and lively resorts, extends from north of Barcelona as far as the French border.

The **Levante** coast, characterised by long sandy beaches and built-up resorts such as Benidorm, Cullera and Gandía, continues to be as popular as ever. This area is also favoured by Spanish families, and is occupied by a large number of second homes.

The **Costa del Sol**, in particular the famous stretch between Málaga and Estepona, is a succession of luxury developments and golf courses. Marbella is considered the leading resort here, reinforced by its reputation as the playground of the international jet-set.

The remainder of the Andalucían coast is generally quieter, attracting mainly Spanish visitors.

The **Balearic Islands** are one of the country's most popular tourist desti-nations. Of the three main islands, Mallorca and Ibiza attract large num-bers of Spanish and foreign (particularly German) visitors, who come here to enjoy their magnificent landscapes and beaches and lively nightlife. Menorca tends to be quieter, finding popularity with those in search of a more relaxing holiday.

Atlantic Coast

Spain's North Atlantic coast stretches from the Basque Country in the east to Galicia in the west. In general, its resorts are popular with Spanish visi-tors attracted by the temperate climate, delightful beaches, excellent fish and seafood, impressive landscapes and fascinating towns and cities, including renowned resorts such as Donostia-San Sebastián and San-tander. With the exception of a few places, the coast of northern Spain has escaped the frenetic development of the Mediterranean, and as such

Windsurfing in Tarifa, Costa de la Luz

©Nick Stubbs/Bigstockphoto.com

has managed to preserve its natural beauty. Although less popular with foreign visitors, the **Costa de la Luz** (Coast of Light), stretching between the south-ernmost tip of Spain and the Portuguese border, has some of the country's finest beaches, dotted with charming family resorts and historic cities such as Cádiz, the oldest in Spain.

Canary Islands

The Canary Islands come into their own in winter, when thousands of visitors flock here to escape the cold of northern Europe. High season in the Canaries runs from November to April. The main tourist centres on the archipelago can be found in the south of Gran Canaria (Maspalomas, Playa del Inglés and Playa de San Agustín) and on Tenerife (Playa de las Américas to the south, and Puerto de la Cruz to the north).

NATIONAL PARKS

Spain is a country that acts as a bridge between Europe and Africa, and as such has a wealth of different landscapes including salt marshes, conifer forests, high mountains, desert areas and Mediterranean woodland. The country's national parks protect those areas of major ecological interest to ensure their continuing survival. The main aim of these parks is to preserve their unique flora and fauna and to control public access. In total, Spain has fourteen national parks – nine on the mainland and five spread across the islands.

For many animal and plant species, Spain's mountain parks provide the most southerly habitat in Europe.

MOUNTAIN PARKS

The country's first national park was the Parque de Montaña de Covadonga, established in 1918. In 1995, this protected area was significantly extended (from 16 925ha/41 822 acres to 64 600ha/159 626 acres) and became known as the **Parque Nacional de los Picos de Europa**. This magnificent park is characterised by breathtaking landscapes with glacial lakes and extensive forests of beech (between 800m/2 624ft and 1 500m/4 920ft) as well as chestnut and oak, where water, in the shape of rivers, streams, lagoons and lakes, is an ecological factor of great importance. In terms of fauna, the main species found here are chamois, mountain cats, polecats, foxes, otters, squirrels, imperial eagles and partridges, with the occasional sighting of the brown bear. The main types of fish found in the park's rivers are trout and salmon.

The **Parque Nacional de Ordesa y Monte Perdido**, at the heart of the Pyrenees in the province of Huesca, covers an area of 15 608ha/38 567 acres, and was also established in 1918. The park is spread across four valleys, in which the landscape is dominated by bubbling mountain rivers and streams, waterfalls, impressive precipices and forests of mountain pine, beech and fir, inhabitated by polecats, wild boar, foxes, pine martens, otters, etc.

The present-day appearance of the **Parc Nacional d'Aigüestortes i Estany de Sant Maurici**, covering 9 851ha/24 342 acres in the province of Lleida, in the Catalan Pyrenees, was created by the ice that invaded this area during the Quaternary era. The park's varied landscape includes lakes, forests of mountain pine, fir and Alpine meadows, populated by a variety of fauna, including wild boar, ermine, pine martens, dormice, imperial eagles and partridge.

The **Sierra Nevada** (90 000ha/ 222 390 acres) is a mountain park with several summits over 3 000m/9 840ft, including Mulhacén, the highest peak on mainland Spain at 3 478m/11 413ft. This range is also renowned for the variety of its flora and fauna, which is the result of the unique climatic and topographical features that exist here.

Tablas de Daimiel
©Turespaña

The **Parque Nacional Monfragüe** (18 118ha/44 770 acres) runs westward along the River Tagus in Extremadura. The landscape varies from scrubland to mountainous ridges populated by eagles and the Iberian Lynx.

Flatland Park

The **Parque Nacional de Cabañeros** is spread across a flatland area between two rocky formations in the Montes de Toledo. This protected national park covering some 40 000ha/98 840 acres is characterised by a Mediterranean-style wooded landscape abundant with deer, wild boar and birds of prey, in particular black and griffon vultures.

Wetland Parks

The Tablas de Daimiel and the Parque Nacional de Doñana are of vital ecological importance due to the protection they offer flora and fauna in danger of extinction, and their role as a breeding, migration and wintering area for numerous species of birds.

The **Tablas de Daimiel**, in the province of Ciudad Real is the smallest of Spain's national parks, with an area of just 1 928ha/4 764 acres. The flooding of the Cigüela and Guadiana rivers has resulted in the formation of areas of shallow bodies of water ideal for the creation of typical marshland vegetation that has been colonised by various species of birds, some of which migrate here for the winter or to nest (grey herons, lesser egrets, red-crested pochard, etc.).

The extraordinary wealth of species in the **Parque Nacional de Doñana** (50 720ha/125 329 acres) is the result of its three distinct habitats: the coastal dunes, the salt marshes, and the former hunting grounds or cotos. Its strategic location on the southern tip of Europe, almost within sight of the coast of Africa, has resulted in its development as an important wetland for migratory birds. Various birds and animals in danger of extinction can still be found here, such as the lynx, ichneumon and imperial eagle.

Parks On The Spanish Islands

The **Parque Nacional Marítimo-Terrestre de Las Islas Atlánticas de Galicia** comprises the four archipelagos of Cíes, Ons, Sálvora and Cortegada, which lie off the coast of Pontevedra. The **Cabrera archipelago**, in the Balearics, stretches across an area of some 10 000ha/ 24 700 acres. The remaining four parks not on the Spanish mainland are found in the Canary Islands: the **Parque Nacional del Teide**, on Tenerife; the **Caldera de Taburiente**, on the island of La Palma; **Timanfaya**, on Lanzarote; and **Garajonay**, on the island of La Gomera.

OVER THE BORDER

If you're staying close to Spain's national borders, you may wish to consider a day trip into southwest France or Portugal to visit a number of sights of interest within easy distance. *The Green Guide* collection covers these areas (*Atlantic Coast; Languedoc Roussillon Tarn Gorges; and Portugal*), in addition to the **Michelin Guide France**, the **Michelin Guide España & Portugal**, and a comprehensive range of maps and plans to enhance your touring itineraries.

PLACES OF INTEREST CLOSE TO THE SPANISH BORDER

France

Across the border from the province of **Guipúzcoa**, the Basque Country of France boasts some of the country's most beautiful and most famous resorts such as St Jean de Luz, Biarritz and Bayonne.

Less than 30km/18.6mi from **Roncesvalles** (Navarra) is the town of St-Jean-Pied-de-Port, a famous staging-post on the Way of St James. From various places in the **Pirineos Aragoneses**, such as Somport and the Portalet Pass, it is possible to drive into the Parc National des Pyrénées, a protected area within the French Pyrenees. From the **Pirineos Catalanes**, it is also easy to cross

Parque Nacional de Garajonay, La Gomera
©Turespaña

the border to admire the impressive landscapes on the French side of the range.

From **Cerbère** (Girona), the coast road winds its way north to the delightful village of Collioure, where the poet Antonio Machado died, and then inland to Perpignan, the capital of French Catalunya.

Portugal

Opposite the Galician town of **Tui/Tuy** and linked by a bridge designed by Gustave Eiffel over the River Miño, stands Valença do Minho, where you can ascend Monte do Faro to enjoy a magnificent view.

To the south lies **Puebla de Sanabria**, in the province of Zamora. It is well worth visiting the historic Portuguese city of Braganza, while from **Ciudad Rodrigo** you may wish to explore the fortified town of Almeida.

From **Cáceres**, the N 521 runs directly west into Portugal and the attractive mountain landscapes of the Serra de São Mamede, including the fortified town of Marvão and Castelo de Vide. The walled town of Elvas is located just across the border from **Badajoz**, with Estremoz and its attractive old quarter some 50km/31mi further west.

Ayamonte, the closest town to Portugal in southern Spain, is the perfect starting-point from which to explore the summer playground of the Algarve, with its beautiful beaches, lively resorts and quaint fishing villages.

23

What to See and Do

OUTDOOR FUN

As a result of its climate and varied landscapes, Spain is able to offer a whole range of activities for nature-lovers and outdoor sports enthusiasts.

WINTER SPORTS

There are thirty five ski resorts in Spain including nineteen in the Pyrenees, six in the Cordillera Cantábrica, four in the Cordillera Central, three in the Cordillera Ibérica, two in the Sierra Nevada (near Granada) and one indoor ski slope in Madrid. Information on these is available from the **Federación Española de Deportes de Invierno** (Avenida de los Madroños 36, 28043 Madrid; ℘913 76 99 30; www.rfedi.es), or from **ATUDEM** (Asociación Turística de Estaciones de Esquí y Montaña, Calle Padre Damián 43, 1°, office 11, 28036 Madrid; ℘913 59 15 17; snow conditions: ℘913 50 20 20; www.esquiespana.org). Maps and brochures showing the major resorts, including their altitude and facilities (ski-lifts, downhill and cross-country runs), are available from tourist offices.

GOLF

There are 398 golf courses across the country, a number that is steadily growing, particularly in coastal areas. For further information, contact the **Real Federación**

Playing golf in Jávea

B. Kaufmann/ MICHELIN

Española de Golf (calle Provisional Arroyo del Fresno Dos, 5°, 28035 Madrid; ℘915 55 26 82; www.golfspainfederacion.com).
A map of golf courses is also available from tourist offices.
Golf courses and their telephone numbers are also listed in the current edition of the **Michelin Guide Portugal Madeira** under the nearest town or city.

HUNTING

Spain boasts the largest hunting area of any European country, populated by large game including wild boar, deer and moufflon, and smaller prey such as partridge, pheasant, rabbits, hare and duck. The hunting season generally runs from September to February, although this varies from species to species.
Hunting and fishing permits can be obtained from local autonomous community authorities. For further details, as well as information on the official hunting calendar, contact the **Real Federación Española de Caza** (Calle Francos Rodríguez 70, 2°, 28039 Madrid; ℘913 11 14 11; www.fecaza.com).

FISHING

Spain's 76 000km/47 235mi of river courses provide a wealth of options for freshwater fishing enthusiasts, although seasons can vary from one region to another. Fishing permits are issued by the Environment Agency (Ministerio de Medio Ambiente; www.marm.es) in the relevant autonomous community.
For further information on sea and freshwater fishing, contact the **Federación Española de Pesca y Casting** (Calle Navas de Tolosa 3, 1°, 28013 Madrid; ℘915 32 83 53; www.fepyc.es).

SAILING

The waters of the Mediterranean and Atlantic are one of Spain's major attractions. As a result, hundreds of sailing clubs and pleasure marinas have been established along the coastlines. For further information, apply to the **Royal Sailing Federation** (*Real Federación de Vela Calle, Luis de Salazar 9, 28002 Madrid; ℰ915 19 50 08; www.rfev.es*).

SCUBA-DIVING

The Spanish coast, in particular the waters of the Mediterranean, is becoming increasingly popular with scuba-divers, with the development of diving sites such as the Cabo de Gata, the Islas Medes, on the Costa Brava, and resorts in the Balearic and Canary islands. For further information, contact the **Spanish Scuba-Diving Federation** (*Federación Española de Actividades Subacuáticas, Calle Santaló 15, 3° 1ª, 0821 Barcelona; ℰ932 00 67 69; www.fedas.es*).

HIKING AND MOUNTAINEERING

Hiking is becoming increasingly popular across Spain. For information on hiking routes and paths, as well as mountaineering, contact the **Spanish Mountaineering Federation** (*Federación Española de Deportes de Montaña y Escalada, Calle Floridablanca 84, 08015 Barcelona; ℰ934 26 42 67; www.fedme.es*).

HORSE RIDING

A wide choice of options is available to horse-riding enthusiasts, ranging from short excursions to treks lasting several days. Every autonomous community has a large number of companies and organisations offering equestrian activities. For further information, contact the **Spanish Horse Riding Federation** (*Federación Hípica Española; calle Monte Esquinza 28, 3°, 28010 Madrid; ℰ914 36 42 00; www.rfhe.com*).

OTHER SPORTS

Information on clubs offering paragliding, hang-gliding, microlight flying, rafting, etc. is available from local tourist offices.

SPAS

The hectic pace of modern life has resulted in an increasing number of people visiting the country's spa resorts for a few days in which to relax, recharge their batteries and help ease certain illnesses and ailments through treatments that are based on the medicinal qualities of the resorts' mineral-rich waters.

Generally speaking, spa complexes are found in areas of outstanding beauty where visitors and patients are also able to enjoy the surrounding nature and leisure facilities available. In Spain, there are a number of spa resorts dotted around the country, inheriting a tradition that has been passed down from the Greeks, Romans and Moors. For information on the treatments and facilities available at individual spas, contact the **National Spa Resort Association** (*Asociación Nacional de Balnearios, Calle Rodríguez San Pedro 56, 3°, 28015 Madrid; ℰ915 49 03 00; www.balnearios.org*).

ACTIVITIES FOR CHILDREN

In this guide, sights of particular interest to children are indicated with a KIDS symbol (👧👦). Some attractions may offer discounted fees for children. In recent years, the number of leisure attractions popular with families has increased dramatically with the opening of several major theme and water parks. The following are just a few examples of places that will guarantee a fun day out for children and their parents alike.

The country's best-known theme parks are **Port Aventura** (*near Reus Airport, Tarragona; www.portaventura. co.uk*), **Terra Mítica** (*Benidorm; www. terramiticapark.com*), **Isla Mágica** (*Sevilla; www.islamagica.es*) and **Warner Bros. Park** (*on the outskirts of Madrid; www.parquewarner.com*). Wildlife parks, such as the **Parque de la Naturaleza de Cabárceno** (*near Santander; www.parquedecabarceno. com*), zoos and aquariums (Barcelona, Madrid, Benidorm, Donostia-San Sebastián, and O Grove, in

Port Aventura
©Turespaña

loroparque.com) and Cactus and Animal Park
(all on Tenerife); Palmitos Park, on Gran Canaria; and Tropical Park, on Lanzarote.

The Spanish coastline, particularly the Mediterranean, boasts numerous **water parks**, which are invariably full throughout the summer.

Interactive science museums, such as those in Valencia, Granada and A Coruña, offer an interesting and educational alternative to the leisure options above, as does a visit to the **Parque Minero de Riotinto** (*near Huelva; www.parquemineroderiotinto. com*), where visitors are transported by miners' train to discover this fascinating site.

Lastly, for those families on holiday close to Almería, a visit to **Oasys**, a desert park where many of the early Spaghetti Westerns were filmed, is an absolute must for young and old alike.

Galicia), continue to be popular with youngsters of all ages, as do the bird and animal parks in the Canary Islands, including the Parque Ecológico Las Águilas del Teide, **Loro Parque** (*www.*

Calendar of Events

Spain's major festivals are mentioned in the list below. In order to confirm exact dates and times, which may vary slightly, contact the relevant local tourist office, which will be able to provide an up-to-date calendar of events. During the summer months, practically every small town and village in the country hosts a fiesta in honour of its own patron saint.

WEEK BEFORE ASH WEDNESDAY
Carnival festivities
Cádiz (*www.carnavaldecadiz.com*)
Santa Cruz de Tenerife
(*www.santacruzmas.com*)

1ST SUNDAY IN MARCH
International Vintage Car Rally
Sitges (*www.rallyesitges.com*)

3RD SUNDAY IN LENT
Feast of the Magdalen bullfights, processions
Castellón de la Plana
(*http://fiestasmagdalena.es/blog*)

12–19 MARCH
Las Fallas Festival
Valencia
(*www.fallasfromvalencia.com*)

HOLY WEEK
Processions
Cartagena, Cuenca, Málaga, Murcia, Sevilla, Valladolid, Zamora

FIRST WEEK AFTER EASTER
Spring Festival
Murcia (*www.murciaciudad.com/ ingles/fiestas*)

APRIL
April Fair
Sevilla (*http://feriadesevilla. andalunet.com*)

22–24 OR 24–26 APRIL
St George's Festival: "Moors and Christians"
Alcoi *(www.ajualcoi.org/festes)*

LAST SUNDAY IN APRIL
Romería (pilgrimage) to the Virgen de la Cabeza
Andújar *(www.ayto-andujar.es)*

LATE APRIL–EARLY MAY
Horse Fair
Jerez de la Frontera
(www.webjerez.com)

LATE APRIL–EARLY MAY
Las Cruces Festival
Córdoba
(www.turismodecordoba.org)

WEEK OF 15 MAY
San Isidro Festival
Madrid *(www.las-ventas.com)*

WHITSUN
Pilgrimage to the Nuestra Señora del Rocío shrine
El Rocío *(www. hermandadmatrizrocio.org)*
La Caballada Festival
Atienza *(www.atienza.es)*

2ND SUNDAY AFTER WHITSUN: CORPUS CHRISTI CELEBRATION
Streets carpeted with flowers; competitions; processions
Puenteareas *(www.riasbaixas. depo.es)*
Sitges *(www.sitgestour.com)*
Toledo *(www.toledo-turismo.com)*

24 JUNE
"Hogueras" St John Festival
Alicante *(www.hogueras.org)*.
Midsummer's Day Festival
Ciutadella
(http://santjoan.ajciutadella.org)

1ST SUNDAY IN JULY
"A Rapa das Bestas" Festival
A Estrada
(www.riasbaixas.depo.es)

6–14 JULY
San Fermín Festival, the running of the bulls
Pamplona *(www.bullrunning. info/eng)*

1ST SATURDAY IN AUGUST
Kayak races on the River Sella
Arriondas y Ribadesella
(www.descensodelsella.com)

14–15 AUGUST
Elche Mystery Play
Elche *(www.misteridelx.com)*

LAST WEDNESDAY IN AUGUST
La Tomatina
Buñol *(www.latomatina.es)*

7–17 SEPTEMBER
Fair (Feria)
Albacete *(http://feria-de-albacete. albacity.org)*

21 SEPTEMBER
St Matthew's Festival
Oviedo *(www.ayto-oviedo.es)*

20–26 SEPTEMBER
La Rioja Wine Harvest Festival
Logroño *(www.logro-o.org)*

24 SEPTEMBER
Festival of Our Lady of Mercy (Virgen de la Merced)
Barcelona
(www.barcelonaturisme.com)

8 OCTOBER
Procession of the Virgin
Guadalupe *(www. monasterioguadalupe.com)*

WEEK OF 12 OCTOBER
Pilar Festival
Zaragoza *(www.zaragoza.es)*

CULTURAL FESTIVALS

HOLY WEEK
Sacred Music Festival
Cuenca *(www.juntacsemanasanta cuenca.com)*

LATE JUNE–MID-JULY
International Music and Dance Festival
Granada
(*www.granadafestival.org*)

JULY
International Classical Theatre Festival
Almagro
(*www.festivaldealmagro.com*)

MID-JULY
Jazz Festival
Vitoria (*www.jazzvitoria.com*)

LAST WEEK OF JULY
Jazz Festival
Donostia-San Sebastián
(*www.donostia.org*)

LATE JULY–LATE AUGUST
Classical Theatre Festival
Mérida
(*www.festivaldemerida.es*)
Castell de Perelada Festival
Peralada
(*www.festivalperalada.com*)

LAST FORTNIGHT IN SEPTEMBER
San Sebastián International Film Festival
Donostia-San Sebastián
(*www.sansebastianfestival.com*)

FIRST FORTNIGHT IN OCTOBER
Catalunya International Film Festival
Sitges
(*www.cinemasitges.com*)

LAST WEEK IN OCTOBER
Seminci (International Film Week) Valladolid
(*www.seminci.com*)

MID-NOVEMBER
Ibero-American Film Festival
Huelva (*www.festicinehuelva.com*)

SHOPPING

Spain has a rich tradition of arts and crafts reflecting the character of each region as well as the influence of the civilisations – Iberian, Roman, Visigothic and Muslim – that have marked the country's history. Traditional wares such as pottery, ceramics, basketwork and woven goods are produced countrywide.

POTTERY AND CERAMICS

The difference between pottery and ceramics is that pottery has been baked just once. In Castilla, pottery is mainly made by women who use a primitive technique. Among their specialities are kitchen utensils, jars and water pitchers. The basic items of crockery used in farmhouses – dishes, soup tureens and bowls made of glazed earthenware (*barro cocido*) – appear in villages and on stalls in every market. Many of the techniques (metal lustre, *cuerda seca*, decorative motifs, and colour) used in ceramics have been influenced by Islamic traditions. There are two large pottery centres in the Toledo region. The first, **Talavera de la Reina**, is famous for its blue, green, yellow, orange and black ceramics, while the second, **El Puente del Arzobispo**, mainly uses shades of green. Pottery from **La Bisbal d'Empordà** in Catalunya has a yellow background with green decorative motifs. The Mudéjar tradition is evident in Aragón and the Levante region where blue and white pottery is made in **Muel**, green and purple ceramics in **Teruel** and lustreware in **Manises** (in the province of Valencia). Most of the figurines used as decoration for cribs at Christmas are produced in **Murcia**. Spain's richest pottery region is Andalucía, with workshops in **Granada** (glazed ceramics with thick green and blue strokes), **Guadix** (red crockery), **Triana** in Sevilla (polychrome animal figures, glazed and decorated), **Úbeda** in Jaén, **Andújar** (jars with cobalt blue patterns) and in **Vera** (white pottery with undulating shapes). In Galicia, porcelain and earthenware goods with contemporary shapes and designs have been factory-made since 1806 at the **Sargadelos** centre in the province of A Coruña, but there is also a craft industry at **Niñodaguia** in Ourense (where the yellow glaze only partially covers the pottery) and at **Bruño** (where yellow motifs set off a dark brown background). Mention should be made of the famous *xiurels*, whistles decorated in red and green from the Balearic Islands.

LACE, WOVEN AND EMBROIDERED GOODS

The textile industry prospered under the Muslims and several workshops still thrive today. Brightly coloured blankets and carpets are woven in the Alpujarras region, La Rioja, the area around Cádiz (Grazalema) and at Níjar near Almería (where *tela de trapo* carpets are made from strips of cloth). Blankets from Zamora, Palencia and Salamanca are well known.

The village of **El Paso**, on the island of La Gomera, in the Canary Islands, is the only place in Spain that still produces silk fabrics.

In some villages in the province of Ciudad Real (particularly in **Almagro**) female lacemakers may still be seen at work in their doorways with bobbins and needles. Lacework from **Camariñas** in Galicia is also widely known. The most popular craft, however, is embroidery, often done in the family. The most typical, geometrically patterned embroideries come from the Toledo region (**Lagartera** and **Oropesa**). Embroidery has been raised to the level of a veritable art in two thoroughly Spanish domains: firstly, in the ornaments used for *pasos* during Holy Week and secondly, in the bullfighters' costume, *traje de luces*.

METALWORK

Iron forging, a very old practice in Spain, has produced outstanding works of art such as the wrought-iron grilles and screens that adorn many churches. Blacksmiths continue to make the grilles for doors and windows so popular in architecture in the south of Spain (La Mancha, Extremadura and Andalucía). **Guadalupe**, in Extremadura, is an important centre for copper production (boilers, braziers, etc.). Damascene weapons (steel inlaid with gold, silver and copper) are still produced, in **Eibar** (País Vasco) and in **Toledo** particularly, according to pure Islamic tradition. The best switchblades and knives in Spain are produced in **Albacete**, Las Palmas de Gran Canaria and Taramundi (Asturias).

Gold- and silver-smithing were developed in antiquity and throughout the Visigothic period and have retained some traditional methods. One example is filigree ornamentation (soldered, intertwined gold and silver threads) crafted in **Córdoba** and **Toledo**. Salamanca, Cáceres and Ciudad Rodrigo specialise in gold jewellery. **Santiago de Compostela** is the world's leading centre for black amber ornaments.

LEATHERWORK

Leather-making has always been an important trade, especially in Andalucía, and has become industrialised in some areas. The town of **Ubrique** (in the province of Cádiz) is the leading producer of leatherwork in Spain, followed by the Alicante area and the Balearic Islands. The production of famous **Córdoba** leather, including embossed polychrome leatherwork, continues to the same high standards.

Workshops specialising in the manufacture of harnesses and horse-riding and hunting accessories are predominantly found in Andalucía (Jerez de la Frontera, Alcalá de los Gazules, Villamartín, Almodóvar del Río and Zalamea la Real) .

Typically Spanish gourds and wineskin containers are made in the provinces of Bilbao, Pamplona and Burgos and in other wine-growing areas. The wineskins produced in Valverde del Camino (Huelva) are known throughout Spain.

BASKETWORK

Basket-making remains one of the most representative of Spanish crafts. Although carried out countrywide, it is particularly rich on the Mediterranean coast and in the Balearic Islands.

The type of product and the material used vary from region to region. Baskets, hats and mats are made of reeds, willow, *esparto* grass, strips of olive-wood and birch and chestnut bark, while furniture may be rush or wickerwork. Willow is used in Andalucía and in the Levante, hazel and chestnut in Galicia and in Asturias, and straw and *esparto* grass on the island of Ibiza.

SIGHTSEEING

Opening times and entrance fees for monuments, museums, churches, etc. are included in the *Discovering Spain* section of this guide. This information is given as a guideline only, as times and prices are liable to change without prior warning.

Prices shown are for individual visitors and do not take into account discounts for groups, who may also benefit from private visits. As many monuments require frequent maintenance and restoration, it is advisable to phone ahead to avoid disappointment. Information for churches is only given if the interior contains a sight of particular interest with specific opening times or if an entrance fee is payable. In general, religious buildings should not be visited during services, although some only open for Mass, in which case visitors should show appropriate respect.

BOOKS

Biography

Franco. Paul Preston (1994; 2004). A definitive life of the man who shaped Spain for decades, and whose Spain was unshaped on his demise.

Reference

Barcelona. Robert Hughes (1992; 2001). An enthusiastic and scholarly celebration of the coming-out of Catalunya's distinct culture after Franco.

History

Moorish Spain. Richard Fletcher (1992; 2001). An illumination through literature and history of the culture that was expelled from Spain but never expurgated.

Homage to Catalonia. George Orwell (1938; 2003). An inside look at the Spanish Civil War from the Republican side, and the Communist purges that engulfed Barcelona in 1937.

Fiction

Don Quixote de La Mancha. Miguel de Cervantes Saavedra (1605; 2008). The classic novel of Castille and of Spanish character.

Southern Seas. Manuel Vázquez Montalbán (1979; 1999). An acclaimed episode of the author's Pepe Carvalho series, involving murder, lust and nouvelle cuisine, set amid Barcelona.

The Shadow of the Wind. Carlos Ruiz Zafón (2001; 2005). A contemporary allegory of post-Civil War Barcelona infused with Latin American magical realism.

Travel

Death in the Afternoon. Ernest Hemingway (1932; 2007). A terse take on tauromarchy, tradition, and the Spanish soul.

Iberia. James A Michener (1968; 1989). Vintage Michener in a ramble through vintage Spain in the throes of entering modern Europe.

Driving over Lemons. Chris Stewart (1999). An account of unconventional living in rural Granada.

South from Granada. Gerald Brenan (1957; 2008). A literary and folkloric account of Spain in the last century.

Spain. Jan Morris (1970; 2008). The Morris take on Spain: history, encounters and pleasures.

The Way of St James. Alison Raju (2000; 2008). A modern guide to one of the first tourist routes.

Art

Picasso. Timothy Hilton (1976). An attempt to define the Spanish master's place in world art.

FILMS

Un Chien Andalou (*An Andalusian Dog*, 1929). The surrealist masterpiece by Luis Buñuel and Salvador Dalí.

Las Hurdes (*Land Without Bread*, 1933). Buñuel charts the hard lives of peasants of an Extremaduran *comarca*.

Surcos (*Furrows*, 1951). A neo-realist drama by José Antonio Nieves Conde about the disintegration of a family unit in Franco's Madrid.

La Caza (*The Hunt*, 1966). A thriller by Carlos Saura about war veterans whose reunion turns to violence.

Cría Cuervos (*Raise Ravens*, 1976). A symbolic criticism of the Franco regime by Saura, with a haunting soundtrack by Jeanette.

Mujeres al Borde de un Ataque de Nervios (*Women on the Verge of a Nervous Breakdown*, 1988). Pedro Almodóvar's feminist comedy, marking his international breakthrough.

Jamón, Jamón (Ham, Ham; 1992). Bigas Luna's satire on Iberian machismo starring Penélope Cruz and Javier Bardem.

Los Amantes del Círculo Polar (*The Lovers of the Arctic Circle*, 1998). An homage to love and fate by Julio Medem.

Land and Freedom (1995). A Liverpudlian's experience of fighting for the Republic in the Civil War, with a narrative comparable to Orwell's *Homage to Catalonia*.

Hable con Ella (*Talk to Her*, 2002). An Oscar winner by Almodóvar about two men and their devotion to the comatose women that they love.

Mar Adentro (*The Sea Inside*, 2004). Amenábar's Oscar-winning biopic about Ramón Sampedro and his struggle with disability.

El Laberinto del Fauno (*Pan's Labyrinth*, 2006). In post-Civil War Spain, a young girl embraces her fantasy world, sumptuously brought to life by Guillermo del Toro.

Vicky Cristina Barcelona (2008). A Woody Allen comedy about two friends on a holiday in Spain and their entanglement with Javier Bardem's painter.

Know Before You Go

USEFUL WEBSITES

www.spain.info
The official site of the Spanish Tourist Board, providing comprehensive information on all aspects of the country, including transport, accommodation, sport and leisure activities.

www.tourspain.co.uk
The Spanish Tourist Board's site for visitors from the UK.

www.okspain.org
The Spanish Tourist Board's site for visitors from the US.

www.tourspain.toronto.on.ca
The Spanish Tourist Board's site for Canadian visitors.

www.fco.gov.uk
The British Government's Foreign and Commonwealth Office website provides up-to-date information on travel.

www.state.gov
American visitors may check the US State Department website for travel advice.

www.fac-aec.gc.ca
Website of Foreign Affairs Canada with relevant travel updates.

www.tourspain.es
The business-to-business site of the
Spanish Tourist Board is useful for
travel professionals.

TOURIST OFFICES

London
2nd floor, 79 New Cavendish Street
London W1W 6XB
☏ (020) 7317 2010

New York
35th Floor, 666 Fifth Avenue
New York, NY 10103
☏ 212 265 8822

Chicago
Water Tower Place, Suite 915 East
845 North Michigan Avenue
Chicago, IL 60611
☏ 312 642 1992

Los Angeles
8383 Wilshire Blvd, Suite 960
Beverly Hills, CA 90211
☏ 323 658 7195

Miami
1395 Brickell Avenue,
Miami, FL 33131
☏ 305 358 1992

Toronto
2 Bloor St West, Suite 3402
Toronto, Ontario M4W 3E2
☏ 416 961 3131

INTERNATIONAL VISITORS
EMBASSIES AND CONSULATES

US Embassy
Serrano 75, 28006 **Madrid**
☏ 91 587 22 00 (emergencies
☏ 91 587 22 40)
www.embusa.es

US Consulates
Paseo Reina Elisenda de
Montcada 23, 08034 **Barcelona**
☏ 93 280 22 27
In addition there are consular
agencies in
Málaga ☏ 952 47 48 91
Sevilla ☏ 954 21 87 51

Valencia ☏ 963 51 69 73
Las Palmas ☏ 928 27 12 59
A Coruña ☏ 981 21 32 33
Palma de Mallorca ☏ 971 40 37 07

Australian Embassy
Torre Espacio, Paseo de la
Castellana, 259D, Planta 24,
28046 Madrid
☏ 913 53 66 00
www.embaustralia.es

British Embassy
Calle Fernando el Santo 16
28010 Madrid
☏ 917 00 82 00
www.ukinspain.fco.gov.uk

British Consulate-General
Paseo de Recoletos 7–9, 4o
28004 Madrid
☏ 91 524 97 00

British Consular Offices
Alicante ☏ 965 21 60 22
Barcelona ☏ 933 66 62 00
Bilbao ☏ 944 15 77 22
Granada ☏ 669 89 50 53
Ibiza ☏ 971 30 18 18
Las Palmas, Canary Islands
☏ 928 26 25 08
Málaga ☏ 952 35 23 00
Palma de Mallorca, Mallorca
☏ 971 71 24 45
**Santa Cruz de Tenerife, Canary
Islands** ☏ 922 28 68 63

Canadian Embassy
Calle Núñez de Balboa 35
28001 Madrid
☏ 914 23 32 50
www.espana.gc.ca

Canadian Consulate
Barcelona ☏ 934 12 72 36
Málaga ☏ 952 22 33 46

Embassy of Ireland
Ireland House, Paseo de la
Castellana 46, 4ª
28046 Madrid ☏ 914 36 40 93

Honorary Irish Consulates
Alicante ☏ 965 10 74 85

Barcelona ℰ934 91 50 21
Bilbao ℰ944 23 04 14
El Ferrol ℰ904 24 42 67
Lanzarote ℰ928 81 52 62
Las Palmas, Canary Islands
ℰ928 29 77 28
Málaga ℰ952 47 51 08
Palma de Mallorca ℰ971 72 25 04
Sevilla ℰ954 69 06 89
Santa Cruz de Tenerife ℰ922
24 56 71

DOCUMENTS

Visitors must be in possession of a
valid **passport**. Holders of British,
Irish and US passports do not need a
visa for a visit of up to 90 days. Visitors
from some Commonwealth countries
or those planning to stay longer than
90 days should enquire about visa
requirements at their local Spanish
consulate. **US citizens** should view
Tips for Traveling Abroad online *(http://
travel.state.gov/travel/tips/brochures/
brochures_1225.html)* for general information on visa requirements, customs
regulations, medical care, etc.

CUSTOMS REGULATIONS

In the UK, **HM Revenue and Customs**
(www.hmrc.gov.uk; ℰ0845 010 9000)
publishes *A Guide for Travellers* on

customs regulations and duty-free
allowances. **US Customs and Border
Protection** *(www.cbp.gov/xp/cgov/
travel/vacation/kbyg; ℰ(877) CBP-5511)*
offer a free publication *Know Before
You Go* for download.

HEALTH

British and Irish citizens should
apply for the European Health
Insurance Card *(UK: ℰ0845 606 2030;
www.ehic.org.uk or at a post office;
Ireland: www.ehic.ie or at a local health
office)* to obtain free or reduced-cost
treatment in the EU. All visitors should
consider insurance for uncovered
medical expenses, lost luggage,
theft, etc.
Pets (cats and dogs) – A general
health certificate and proof of rabies
vaccination should be obtained from
your local vet before departure.

ACCESSIBILITY

Information on facilities for the
disabled within Spain is available
from Polibea, Ronda de la Avutarda 3,
28043 Madrid, ℰ917 59 53 72
www.polibea.com/turismo

Getting There

BY PLANE

A number of Spanish and international
airlines operate direct scheduled
services to airports across Spain.
These include:

Iberia Airlines:
ℰ902 400 500. www.iberia.
com. Reservations within the UK:
ℰ0870 609 0500; within the US
and Canada: ℰ800 772 4642

British Airways:
ℰ0844 493 0787. www.ba.com.
Reservations within the US and
Canada: ℰ800 247 9297

Aer Lingus:
ℰ0818 365 000. www.aerlingus.
com. Reservations within the UK:
ℰ0870 876 2020

A number of low-cost airlines also
offer inexpensive flights to several
Spanish cities from the UK. Some
airlines only allow bookings to be
made online, while others offer small
discounts for internet bookings:

Bmibaby: www.bmibaby.com
Clickair: www.clickair.com
EasyJet: www.easyjet.com
Flybe: www.flybe.com
Ryanair: www.ryanair.com

Hundreds of weekly charter flights also operate from the UK to Spanish cities, particularly along the Mediterranean coast and in the Balearic and Canary islands.

BY SHIP

Brittany Ferries and P&O Ferries both operate services to northern Spain from the UK.

Brittany Ferries runs a ferry service from Plymouth (20hr journey time) and from Portsmouth to Santander (24hr journey) from mid-March to mid-November; for reservations, contact:

- **Brittany Ferries:**
  ☏0871 244 0744 (UK);
  ☏942 36 06 11 (Santander)
  www.brittany-ferries.com.

- **P&O Portsmouth** offers a twice-weekly crossing from Portsmouth to Bilbao from March to January; journey time: approx. 35hr. For reservations:☏08716 645 645; ☏902 02 04 61 (Spain) www.poferries.com.

BY TRAIN

Eurostar (☏08705 186 186; www.eurostar.com) operates high-speed passenger trains to Paris, from where overnight train-hotel services operate to Madrid and Barcelona, with onward connections to destinations across the country. Services from Paris, as well as train tickets within Spain, can be booked through the Spanish State Railway Network's (RENFE) UK agent, the Spanish Rail Service: ☏(020) 7725 7063; www.spanish-rail.co.uk. Alternatively, log-on to the official **RENFE** website at www.renfe.es.

BY COACH/BUS

Regular long-distance bus services operate from London to all major towns and cities in Spain. For information, contact:
Eurolines UK: ☏08717 818 181
www.eurolines.co.uk.

Getting Around

BY PLANE

Spain has over 45 commercial airports, including 12 on the islands. Information on any of these is available from **AENA** (Aeropuertos Españoles y Navegación Aérea): ☏902 40 47 04; www.aena.es. The largest airports in the country are as follows:

- **Madrid-Barajas**
- **Barcelona**
- **Palma de Mallorca**
- **Málaga**
- **Gran Canaria**
- **Alicante**
- **Tenerife Sur-Reina Sofía**
- **Valencia**
- **Girona-Costa Brava**

MAJOR AIRLINE COMPANIES

Iberia: Serviberia
☏902 400 500 (information and bookings)
www.iberia.com
Air Europa: ☏902 40 15 01
www.aireuropa.com
Spanair: ☏902 13 14 15
www.spanair.com

BY SHIP

Several ferry companies operate services between the Spanish mainland and the Balearics, Canaries, Italy and North Africa.
Trasmediterránea – Services between: Valencia to the Balearics; Barcelona to the Balearics, Livorno & Rome (Civitavecchia); Cádiz to the Canary Islands; Algeciras to Tanger & Ceuta; and Almeria to Nador & Ghazaouet.

Information and reservations

📞902 45 46 45

www.trasmediterranea.es

Regional offices:

◆ **Madrid** – Avenida Europa 10, Parque Empresarial La Moraleja, 28108 Madrid. 📞914 23 85 00.

◆ **Alicante** – Terminal MTMA del Sureste, 03001 Alicante. 📞965 20 08 41.

◆ **Barcelona** – Estació Marítima, Muelle San Beltrán, 08039 Barcelona. Fax 932 95 91 34.

Cádiz – Estación Marítima Muelle Alfonso XIII, 11006 Cádiz. Fax 956 22 20 38.

Baleària – Baleària operates services to and from the Balearics and from island to island. 📞902 160 180.www.balearia.com.

Regional offices:

◆ **Madrid** – Calle O'Donnell 38, 28009 Madrid. 📞914 09 14 42;

◆ **Barcelona –** Estació Marítima Drassanes, 08039 Barcelona. 📞933 24 89 80.

◆ **Denia (Alicante)** – Estación Marítima, 03700 Denia. 📞966 42 86 00.

BY TRAIN 🚃

RENFE 📞902 24 02 02; www.renfe.es.

AVE (*Alta Velocidad Española; www. renfe.es/ave)* high-speed trains run from Madrid to:

Sevilla (2hr30min)

Valladolid (1hr)

Barcelona (2hr45min)

Huesca (2hr15min)

Málaga (2hr45min)

and from Barcelona to:

Sevilla (5hr40min)

Málaga (5hr45min)

"Green" railway stations – Fifty stations are so designated *(estaciones verdes)* due to their location near nature reserves, or because of their suitability for hikers, mountain-bikers or for nature lovers wishing to discover the beauty of rural Spain. Information about attractions near designated stations is available online at www.renfe.es/comunicacion/mundotren/medio_ambiente/index.html (Spanish).

TOURIST TRAINS

El Transcantábrico – This narrow-gauge train journeys from León to Santiago de Compostela via the shores of the Bay of Biscay.

The trip lasts eight days and combines rail and bus travel. The service operates from April to October.

📧Prices start from 2 600€. 📞902 55 59 02. www.transcantabrico.com.

El Tren de la Fresa – The Strawberry Train operates vintage cars between Madrid and Aranjuez (hr), from May to July from Atocha station.

📧25€. 📞902 24 02 02. www.renfe.es/trenfresa (Spanish Railways).

BY METRO/TRAM

Eight cities in Spain host their own metro or light rail network and more are being constructed at the present time. The cities with networks are as follows: Alicante, Bilbao, Madrid, Valencia, Palma de Mallorca, Parla and Santa Cruz de Tenerife.

BY COACH/BUS

The Spanish bus network is a comfortable, modern and relatively inexpensive way of travelling across the country. Numerous companies offer local and long-distance services. Information on routes, timetables and prices can be obtained from local bus stations.

Two of the companies with the largest networks are:

Alsa – Extensive routes across the country, particularly in the northwest, centre, and along the Mediterranean. 📞913 27 05 40. www.alsa.es.

Avanzabus – Madrid-based company providing nationwide services. www.avanzabus.com.

BY CAR
ROAD NETWORK

Spain has over 343 000km/213 130mi of roads, including 9 000km/5 592mi of divided highways and expressways. **Speed limits** in Spain are as follows:

- ◆ 120kph/75mph on expressways and divided highways;
- ◆ 100kph/62mph on the open road (with a hard shoulder of at least 1.5m/5ft);
- ◆ 90kph/56mph on the open road (without a hard shoulder);
- ◆ 50kph/31mph in built-up areas.

DOCUMENTS

In general, motorists need only have a current driving licence from their country of origin and valid papers (vehicle documentation and valid insurance) to drive in Spain, although in certain situations an International Driving Permit may be required. If in doubt, visitors should check with the AA *(www.theaa.com)* or RAC *(www.rac.co.uk)* in the United Kingdom or with the AAA *(www.aaa.com)* in the US.

DRIVING REGULATIONS

The minimum driving age is 18. Traffic drives on the right. It is compulsory for passengers in both front and rear seats to wear **seat belts**. Motorcyclists (on all sizes of machine) must wear safety helmets. It is now a legal requirement for motorists to carry

Please note

In Spain, the word *calle* (Castilian) or *carrer* (Catalan) for street is not generally denoted on maps or in addresses. Therefore, in the *Discovering* section, you will see street names without *calle* or *carrer* preceding them. However, *av.* *(avenida – avinguda* in Catalan), *ctra (carretera), pl. (plaza – plaça* in Catalan), *pso (paseo)* and *pas. (passeig – passatage* in Catalan) *are* indicated.

two red warning triangles, in addition to a spare tyre and a set of replacement bulbs.

Motorists should note that it is illegal to use a **cell/mobile phone** when driving, unless the vehicle is fitted with a hands-free unit. Heavy on-the-spot fines are frequent for those caught using hand-held phones.

INSURANCE

Those motorists entering Spain in their own vehicles should ensure that their insurance policy includes overseas cover. Visitors are advised to check with their respective insurance company prior to travel. Motorists are also advised to take out adequate **accident** and **breakdown** cover for their period of travel overseas. Various motoring organisations (AA, RAC, etc.) will be able to provide further details on options available. Bail bonds are no

Driving on Sa Calobra Road, Mallorca

R. Pérousse/MICHELIN

longer necessary, although travellers may wish to take this precaution (consult your insurance company). Members of the AAA should obtain the free brochure *Offices to Serve You Abroad*, which gives details of affiliated organisations in Spain. If the driver of the vehicle is not accompanied by the owner, he or she must have written permission from the owner to drive in Spain.

ROAD INFORMATION

The **National Traffic Agency** (Dirección General de Tráfico) is able to provide information in English on road conditions, driving itineraries, regulations, etc. ℘900 12 35 05. www.dgt.es.

TOLLS

Tolls are payable on some sections of the Spanish highway network. On Michelin maps, these sections are indicated by kilometre markers in red; toll-free sections are marked in blue.

MAPS AND PLANS

Michelin's España & Portugal spiral **road atlas** and general **road maps** will assist you in the planning of your journey. These are listed in the **Maps and plans** section at the back of this guide.

MOTORING ORGANISATIONS

RACE (Royal Automobile Club of Spain) ℘902 40 45 45; 902 30 05 05 (roadside assistance). www.race.es.

CAR HIRE

Vehicles in Spain can be hired through the offices of all major international car hire companies around the world. Alternatively, cars can be hired at major airports, train stations, large hotels and in all major towns and cities around the country:

- **Avis** ℘902 18 08 54. www.avis.com.
- **Europcar** ℘902 10 50 30. www.europcar.com.
- **Hertz** ℘913 72 93 00. www.hertz.com.

Visitors should bear in mind that although the legal driving age in Spain is 18, most companies will only rent out vehicles to drivers over the age of 21.

Where to Stay and Eat

Hotel and Restaurant recommendations are located in the Addresses sections of individual principal sights in the *Discovering Spain* section of this guide. For coin ranges and for a description of the symbols used in the Addresses, see the Legend on the cover flap.
Hotel and Restaurant listings fall within the description of each region in order to enhance your stay and enable you to make the most of your holiday. These have been recommended for their location, comfort, value for money and, in some cases, for their charm. We have

Parador in Hondarribia, Costa Vasca
©Paradores

Tapas bar in Andalucia

R. Mattes/ MICHELIN

also made a conscious effort to cover all budgets, although some regions (for example the Costa Brava, Costa del Sol and the Balearic Islands) are more expensive than others, and prices in Madrid and Barcelona can be as high as in other major cities in Europe.
As a general rule, restaurants serve lunch from 1.30pm to 3.30pm and dinner from 9pm to 11pm.

FINDING A HOTEL

This section lists a selection of hotels, *hostales* and *pensiones* based on the price of a double room in high season and generally excluding breakfast and VAT, unless otherwise indicated. The difference in rates between high and low season can be significant, particularly on the coast and islands, so it is always advisable to receive confirmation of prices in writing at the time of booking.

PARADORS

Almost all of the state-run network of luxury hotels are in restored historic monuments (castles, palaces, monasteries, etc.) in magnificent locations. For more information, contact **Paradores de Turismo de España** (*calle Requena 3, 28013 Madrid; ℘915 16 67 00; www.parador.*

es). The official UK representative is **Keytel International** (*402 Edgware Road, London W2 1ED; ℘(020) 7616 0300; www.keytel.co.uk*). In the US, contact **PTB Hotels** (*℘1 800 634 1188; http://petrabax.com*). Special weekend offers are often available, in addition to a five-night "go as you please" accommodation card.

RURAL ACCOMMODATION

The number of visitors to Spain who wish to stay in rural accommodation is steadily increasing. Most autonomous communities publish a practical guide listing details of every type of accommodation available, including rooms in private houses, hostels for groups, entire houses for rent, and farm campsites. Contact local tourist offices listed within the Principal Sights for further details, or www.ecoturismorural.com.

CAMPSITES

The Secretaría General de Turismo publishes an annual campsite guide. Further details on camping and caravanning are supplied by the Federación Española de Campings (*calle Valderribas 48, Esc 3, 1º C, 28007 Madrid; ℘914 48 12 34; www.fedcamping.com*). Book in advance for popular resorts during summer.

YOUTH HOSTELS

Spain's 160 youth hostels are open to travellers with an **international card**, available from international youth hostelling offices and youth hostels themselves. For further information, contact the **Spanish Youth Hostel Network** (*Red Española de Albergues Juveniles, Castello 24, 28001 Madrid; ℘915 22 70 07; www.reaj.com*).

SPECIAL OFFERS

Many chains and hotels catering to business travellers often offer reduced rates at weekends. It is also possible to purchase vouchers for one or several nights at advantageous prices. For further information on these special offers, contact the following:

NH Hoteles 📞902 11 51 16. www. nh-hoteles.es. ⊜Sleep and Go rates for 18–30 year olds for 50€.

Bancotel 📞902 87 78 77. 00 800 1001 1002 (from Europe). www.bancotel. com/ing/index.htm. Bancotel sells the *Bancotel checkbook* worth 150€ or 250€ for use in affiliated hotels throughout the country. Good discounts on standard rates.

Halcón Viajes 📞807 22 72 22. (information and reservations) www.halcon-viajes.es. Individual vouchers (for a one-night stay for one or two people) with a discount on the official rate.

Hoteles Meliá 📞902 14 44 40. www.solmelia.com. Discounts and special weekend offers available via the MAS rewards card.

DON'T FORGET THE MICHELIN GUIDE

The red-cover **Michelin Guide España & Portugal** is revised annually and is an indispensable complement to this guide with additional information on hotels and restaurants including category, price, degree of comfort and setting.

WHERE TO EAT

The restaurants listed in the Addresses in this guide have been chosen for their surroundings, ambience, typical dishes or unusual character. Coin symbols (◔*see the Legend on the cover flap*) correspond to average cost of a meal and are given as a guideline only.

TAPAS

Given the country's reputation for tapas, we have also included a list of tapas bars where visitors can enjoy an aperitif or meal throughout the day and late into the evening. Prices of tapas are often not listed, although as a general rule the cost of a reasonably priced tapas lunch or supper should not exceed 14€.

TAKING A BREAK, SHOPPING AND NIGHTLIFE

These headings, which appear periodically in Address Books throughout the guide, include a variety of addresses from cafés and bars to shops and theatres, as well as nightclubs and concert venues. Some may be quiet cafés during the day, transforming themselves into lively bars at night.

Useful Words and Phrases

The following phrases denote translations between English and **Castilian**, the official language of Spain and better known as Spanish in the wider world. Yet, there are also four other languages officially recognised in various regions of Spain: **Catalan** (Catalonia, Valencia and the Balearics); Basque (Basque Country); **Galician** (Galicia); and **Aranes** (northwest Catalonia). These languages are widespread in these areas and many inhabitants see Castilian as their second language.

Common words

	Translation
Yes, No	Sí, No
Good Morning	Buenos Días
Good Afternoon	Buenas Tardes
Goodbye	Hasta Luego, Adiós
Please	Por Favor
How Are You?	¿Qué Tal?
Thank You (Very Much)	(Muchas) Gracias
Excuse Me	Perdone
I Don't Understand	No Entiendo
Sir, Mr; You	Señor; Usted
Madam, Mrs	Señora
Miss	Señorita

Time

	Translation
When?	¿Cuándo?
What Time?	¿A Qué Hora?
Today	Hoy
Yesterday	Ayer
Tomorrow	Mañana

Shopping

	Translation
How Much?	¿Cuánto (Vale)?
(Too) Expensive	(Demasiado) Caro
A Lot, Little	Mucho, Poco
More, Less	Más, Menos
Big, Small	Grande, Pequeño
Credit Card	Tarjeta De Crédito
Receipt	Recibo

Correspondence

	Translation
Postbox	Buzón
Postcard	(Tarjeta) Postal
Post Office	Correos
Telephone	Teléfono
Letter	Carta
Stamp	Sello
Telephone Call	Llamada
Tobacco Shop	Estanco, Tabaquería

On the road, In town

	Translation
Coche, Auto	Car
Gasolina	Petrol, Gasoline
A La Derecha	On the right
A La Izquierda	On the left
Obras	Roadworks
Peligro, Peligroso	Danger, Dangerous
Cuidado	Beware, Take care
Después De	After, Beyond

Numbers

	Translation
0	cero
1	uno/una
2	dos
3	tres
4	cuatro
5	cinco
6	seis
7	siete
8	ocho
9	nueve
10	diez
20	veinte
50	cincuenta
100	cien
1 000	mil

Food and drink

	Translation
Aceite, Aceitunas	Oil, Olives
Agia con/sin gas	Sparkling/ still Water
Ajo	Garlic
Tengo Alergia a...	I'm allergic to...
Arroz	Rice
Azúcar	Sugar
Café con leche	Coffee with hot milk
Café solo	Black coffee
Carne	Meat
Cebolla	Onion
Cerdo	Pork
Cerveza	Beer
Crema	Cream
Ensalada	Salad
Gambas	Prawns
Helado	Ice cream
Huevo	Egg
Jamón	Ham
Lactosa	Lactose
Leche	Milk
Legumbres	Vegetables
Limón	Lemon
Mantequilla	Butter
Manzana	Apple
Mariscos	Seafood, shellfish
Naranja	Orange
Nuez (Nueces)	Nut(s)
Pan	Bread
Patatas	Potatoes
Pescados	Fish
Pimienta (Negra)	(Black) pepper
Plátano	Banana
Postre	Dessert
Potaje	Soup
Queso	Cheese
Sal	Salt
Salchichas	Sausages
Setas/hongos	Mushrooms
Soja	Soya
Tortilla	Omelette
Trigo	Wheat
Vaca/buey	Beef
Vegetariano/a	Vegetarian
Vino Blanco/rosado /tinto	White/rosé/ Red wine

Out and about

Also See architectural terms in the Introduction.

	Translation
Where is?	¿Dónde Está?
May one visit?	¿Se Puede Visitar?
Key	Llave
Light	Luz
Guide	Guía
Porter, Caretaker	Guarda, Conserje
Open, Closed	Abierto, Cerrado
No Entry, Not allowed	Prohibido
Entrance, Exit	Entrada, Salida
Wait	Esperar
Beautiful	Hermoso/a
Storey, Stairs, Steps	Piso, Escalera
Alcázar	Muslim Palace
Alrededores	Outskirts
Alto	Pass, High Pass
Audiencia	Audience, Court
Ayuntamiento	Town Hall
Balneario	Spa
Barranco	Gully, Ravine
Barrio	Quarter
Bodega	Wine Cellar/store
Cabo	Cape, Headland
Calle	Street
Calle Mayor	Main street
Camino	Road, Track
Campanario	Belfry
Capilla	Chapel
Carretera	Main Road
Casa	House
Casa Consistorial	Town Hall
Castillo	Castle
Ciudad	Town, City
Claustro	Cloisters
Colegio, Colegiata	College, Collegiate Church
Collado	Pass, High Pass
Convento	Monastery, Convent
Cruz	Cross
Cuadro	Picture
Cueva, Gruta, Cava	Cave, Grotto
Desfiladero	Defile, Cleft
Embalse	Reservoir, Dam
Ermita	Hermitage, Chapel
Estación	Station
Excavaciones	Excavations
Finca	Property, Domain
Fuente	Fountain
Gargantas	Gorges
Gruta	Cavern, Grotto
Huerto, Huerta	Vegetable/ Market Garden

Iglesia	Church
Imagen	Religious Statue/ Sculpture
Isla	Island, Isle
Lago	Lake
Mezquita	Mosque
Mirador	Belvedere, Viewpoint, Lookout Point
Monasterio	Monastery
Monte	Mount, Mountain
Museo	Museum
Nacimiento	Source, Birthplace
Palacio (Real)	(Royal) Palace
Pantano	Artificial Lake
Paseo	Avenue, Promenade
Plaza	Square
Plaza Mayor	Main Square
Plaza De Toros	Bullring
Pórtico	Portal, Porch
Presa	Dam
Pueblo	Village, Market Town
Puente	Bridge
Puerta	Door, Gate, Entrance
Puerto	Pass, Harbour, Port
Ría	Estuary
Río	River, Stream
Santuario	Church
Siglo	Century
Talla	Carved Wood
Tapices	Tapestries
Techo	Ceiling
Tesoro	Treasury, Treasure
Torre	Tower, Belfry
Torreón	Keep
Vidriera	Stained-glass Window
Vista	View, Panorama

Jamón

H. Champollion/MICHELIN

Basic Information

BUSINESS HOURS

Shops are generally open 10am–2pm, 5–8.30pm, although an increasing number of larger stores and shopping centres do not close for lunch. The majority of shops close on Sundays, and some on Saturday afternoons.

DISCOUNTS

Consult the website of the **Instituto de la Juventud** *(Calle Marqués de Riscal 16, 28010 Madrid; ℰ913 63 78 49; www.injuve.mtas.es)* for links to youth-orientated travel services.

The **Oficina Nacional de Turismo e Intercambio de Jóvenes y Estudiantes (TIVE)** *(Calle José Ortega y Gasset 71, 28006 Madrid; ℰ913 47 77 00)* arranges hostel reservations, discounted transportation and language study, and sells certain student cards. There are offices in other major cities.

The **EURO<26 Card**, issued by student organisations in 27 countries, entitles young people between the ages of 14 and 25 to a whole series of discounts on travel, cultural events, accommodation, etc. In Spain, some 50 000 outlets participate in the scheme. For information, see www.eyca.org. In Spain, ℰ91 363 76 85 or at TIVE offices *(see above)*.

The **Student Card**, available to those aged 12 and over, also provides numerous discounts on a variety of services.

Senior citizens aged 65 and over qualify for significant discounts on transport, entrance fees to monuments, and events and shows. Many museums offer half-price entry, with free entrance to many national monuments.

ELECTRICITY

220V AC (some older establishments may still have 110V). Plugs are two-pin.

EMERGENCIES

ℰ112 connects with all emergency services in Spain, when in Spain.

Police: ℰ091(national), 092 (local)
Medical emergencies: ℰ061
Fire: ℰ080, 085
Civil Guard: ℰ062
Mossos d'Esquadra (Catalan police): ℰ088
Directory Enquiries: ℰ11818
International Directory Enquiries: ℰ11825

PUBLIC HOLIDAYS

Municipalities may declare a maximum of 14 public holidays per year, up to 9 of which are selected by the national government. Therefore, the following list represents those public holidays that are taken throughout the country:

PUBLIC HOLIDAYS	
1 January	New Year's Day
6 January	Epiphany
2nd day before Easter	Good Friday
1 May	Labour day
15 August	Labour Day
12 October	Assumption of the Virgin
1 November	Hispanic Day
6 December	All Saints Day
8 December	Immaculate Conception
25 December	Christmas Day

MAIL/POST

Post offices *(correos; www.correos.es)* are open Mon–Fri 8.30am–2.30pm and Sat 9.30am–1pm.

Stamps *(sellos)* can also be purchased at tobacconists *(estancos)*. The red-cover **Michelin Guide España & Portugal** gives the postcode for every town and city covered.

MONEY

The unit of currency in Spain is the **euro** (€). Coin denominations are: 1, 2, 5, 10, 20 and 50 cents and 1 and 2 euro. Notes come in 5, 10, 20, 50, 100, 200 and 500 values. There are no restrictions on the amount of currency foreigners may bring into Spain.

CHANGING MONEY

Traveller's cheques and foreign cash can be exchanged at banks and exchange offices *(cambios)*. International credit cards are accepted in most shops, hotels and restaurants. Visitors can also obtain cash from bank machines using credit and debit cards; a pin number will be required.

Banks

Banks are generally open Mon–Fri 8.30am–2pm and Sat (Oct–May) 9am–1pm. Selected branches may also open on weekdays 4–5.30pm.

Credit Cards

In the event of a **lost or stolen credit card**, contact the relevant issuer as soon as possible:
Mastercard: ℘900 97 12 31.
Visa: ℘900 99 11 24.
American Express: ℘902 37 56 37.
Diners Club: ℘902 40 11 12.

SMOKING

The Spanish anti-smoking law came into effect on 1 January 2006: smoking is prohibited in offices, shops, schools, hospitals, cultural centres and on public transport, including at airports. Restaurants and bars larger than 100sq m/119.6sq yd have partitioned separate areas for clients who wish to smoke; smaller premises are only required to denote whether they are smoke free, meaning that a majority of establishments still allow smoking. Around a quarter of the population smoke, in a culture where smoking has been ingrained since Rodrigo de Jerez, a crew member of Columbus, became the first credited European smoker more than 500 years ago.

Souvenir shop in Pampaneira

H. Champollion/MICHELIN

TELEPHONES

For **international calls** from Spain, dial 00, then dial the country code (44 for the UK, 353 for Ireland, 1 for the US and Canada), followed by the area code (minus the first 0 of the STD code when dialling the UK), and then the number.

- For calls **within Spain**, dial the full 9-digit number of the person you are calling.
- When calling Spain **from abroad**, dial the international access code, followed by 34 for Spain, then the full 9-digit number.

For more information, call ℘1004 (in Spain) or visit www.telefonica.com.

TIME

Spain is 1hr ahead of GMT. The Spanish keep different hours from either the British or North Americans: as a general rule, restaurants serve lunch from 1.30pm to 3.30pm and dinner from 9pm to 11pm.

TIPPING

Restaurants and other establishments in Spain usually include both taxes and service in prices. It is customary to leave an additional cash tip of from 5 to 10 per cent of a restaurant cheque or taxi fare. Tip porters 1€ per bag for assistance, and chambermaids 1€ per day. Guides may be tipped 3 to 5€ per day at your discretion.

CONVERSION TABLES

Weights and Measures

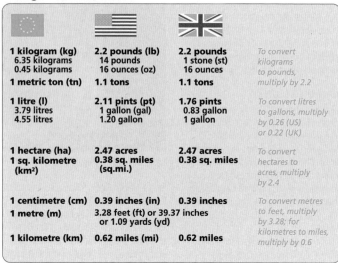

1 kilogram (kg) 6.35 kilograms 0.45 kilograms	**2.2 pounds (lb)** 14 pounds 16 ounces (oz)	**2.2 pounds** 1 stone (st) 16 ounces	*To convert kilograms to pounds, multiply by 2.2*
1 metric ton (tn)	**1.1 tons**	**1.1 tons**	
1 litre (l) 3.79 litres 4.55 litres	**2.11 pints (pt)** 1 gallon (gal) 1.20 gallon	**1.76 pints** 0.83 gallon 1 gallon	*To convert litres to gallons, multiply by 0.26 (US) or 0.22 (UK)*
1 hectare (ha) **1 sq. kilometre (km²)**	**2.47 acres** 0.38 sq. miles (sq.mi.)	**2.47 acres** 0.38 sq. miles	*To convert hectares to acres, multiply by 2.4*
1 centimetre (cm) **1 metre (m)**	**0.39 inches (in)** 3.28 feet (ft) or 39.37 inches or 1.09 yards (yd)	**0.39 inches**	*To convert metres to feet, multiply by 3.28; for kilometres to miles, multiply by 0.6*
1 kilometre (km)	**0.62 miles (mi)**	**0.62 miles**	

Clothing

Women					Men			
		35	4	2½			40	7½	7
		36	5	3½			41	8½	8
		37	6	4½			42	9½	9
Shoes		38	7	5½	Shoes		43	10½	10
		39	8	6½			44	11½	11
		40	9	7½			45	12½	12
		41	10	8½			46	13½	13

Women					Men			
		36	6	8			46	36	36
		38	8	10			48	38	38
Dresses		40	10	12	Suits		50	40	40
& suits		42	12	14			52	42	42
		44	14	16			54	44	44
		46	16	18			56	46	48

Women					Men			
		36	06	30			37	14½	14½
		38	08	32			38	15	15
Blouses &		40	10	34	Shirts		39	15½	15½
sweaters		42	12	36			40	15¾	15¾
		44	14	38			41	16	16
		46	16	40			42	16½	16½

Sizes often vary depending on the designer. These equivalents are given for guidance only.

Speed

KPH	10	30	50	70	80	90	100	110	120	130
MPH	6	19	31	43	50	56	62	68	75	81

Temperature

Celsius (°C)	0°	5°	10°	15°	20°	25°	30°	40°	60°	80°	100°
Fahrenheit (°F)	32°	41°	50°	59°	68°	77°	86°	104°	140°	176°	212°

To convert Celsius into Fahrenheit, multiply °C by 9, divide by 5, and add 32.
To convert Fahrenheit into Celsius, subtract 32 from °F, multiply by 5, and divide by 9.
NB: Conversion factors on this page are approximate.

UNESCO WORLD HERITAGE SITES

In 1972, the United Nations Educational, Scientific and Cultural Organization (UNESCO) adopted a Convention for the preservation of cultural and natural sites. Over 800 sites "of outstanding universal value" are now on the World Heritage List. The protected cultural heritage may be monuments (buildings, sculptures, archaeological structures, etc.) with unique historical, artistic or scientific features; groups of buildings (such as religious communities, ancient cities); or sites (human settlements, examples of exceptional landscapes, cultural landscapes) which are the combined works of man and nature of exceptional beauty. Natural sites may be a testimony to the stages of the earth's geological history or to the development of human cultures and creative genius or represent significant ongoing ecological processes, contain superlative natural phenomena or provide a habitat for threatened species. Spain has over 35 World Heritage Sites; those mentioned in the guide are below.

Alcalá de Henares: University and historic quarter
Aranjuez: Cultural landscape
Atapuerca (Burgos): Prehistoric remains
Ávila: Old town and extra-muros churches
Barcelona: Parc Güell; Palau Güell; Casa Milà; Palau de la Música Catalana; Hospital de Sant Pau
Burgos: Cathedral
Cáceres: Old town
Córdoba: Historic centre
Cuenca: Historic fortified town
Doñana: National Park
Elx/Elche: El Palmeral palm grove
El Escorial: Monastery
La Gomera: Garajonay National Park
Granada: Alhambra; Generalife; Albaicín
Guadalupe: Monasterio Real de Santa María
Ibiza: Biodiversity and culture
Lugo: Roman walls
Mérida: Archaeological site
Oviedo: Monuments in the city; kingdom of Asturias
Poblet: Monastery
Salamanca: Old town
San Millán de la Cogolla: Monasterio de Yuso; Monasterio de Suso
Santiago de Compostela: Old town; Way of St James
Segovia: Old town; aqueduct
Sevilla: Cathedral; Alcázar; Archivo de Indias
Tarragona: Roman town (Tarraco)
Tenerife: San Cristóbal de la Laguna; Parque Nacional del Teide
Teruel: Mudéjar architecture
Toledo: Historic city
Úbeda & Paeza: Renaissance monumental ensembles
Valencia: La Lonja de la Seda
Vall de Boí (Lleida): Romanesque churches

Equestrian statue of Philip III, Plaza Mayor, Madrid
E. Baret/MICHELIN

PLAZA
MAYOR

RESTAURAD
AÑO
MDCCLXXXI

Spain Today

Spain is living testimony that countries can change profoundly and permanently: from a closed society where views were rarely expressed in public to one where people speak their minds; from economically backward to a dynamic economy that attracts immigrants; from a centralised government to a land that thrives on regional diversity; from a repressive state to one whose prosecutors relentlessly pursue human rights abuses worldwide. And yet all this transformation has come about while maintaining essential values and the Spanish way of life. Elsewhere, the penetration of worldwide brands and fashion and slang will make the visitor feel at times as if he or she has never left home. But when you are in Spain, it is clear that you are nowhere else.

GOVERNMENT AND ADMINISTRATION

The Spanish Constitution, which was approved by referendum on 6 December 1978, defines the political status of the Spanish State as a constitutional monarchy in which sovereignty rests with the Spanish people. This political system can be broken down as follows: a **Head of State**, in the shape of the King, the **Cortes Generales** (Parliament) and a **Government**. The **Cortes** are elected by universal suffrage every four years. They are divided into two chambers: the **Congreso de los Diputados** and the **Senado**. The Government (*Gobierno*) performs executive functions and comprises a head of government (*Presidente del Gobierno* or prime minister), vice-presidents and ministers. Judicial power is an independent authority administered by judges and magistrates. The Supreme Court acts as the highest tribunal in the land.

Spain can be broken down into the following administrative divisions:

Autonomous Communities: Spain is divided into 17 *Comunidades Autóno-mas*, in addition to two autonomous cities (Ceuta and Melilla, in North Africa). These communities may compose a single province or several provinces. The leading political figure in these is the *Presidente de la Comunidad*, who is elected by universal suffrage every four years. The transfer of decision-making to autonomous bodies has yet to be fully achieved; however, the system of autonomy developed in Spain is one of the most advanced in Europe.

The Basque Country is designated as a historical region in Spain for its independent sense of identity. Extremists known as the **Euskadi Ta Askatasuna** (Basque Homeland and Freedom) or ETA have fought a violent campaign of murders and kidnappings since 1959 to press for an independent country. The devolved nature of these Autonomous Communities has allowed parties such as the **Euzko Alderdi Jeltzalea** (Basque National Party) to campaign for Basque autonomy through democratic and peaceful means.

Catalunya has developed a separate identity since the Middle Ages, with its own language (Catalan) and culture epitomised by its centre of Barcelona. This came to a nadir during Franco's dictatorship, when the use of Catalan was forbidden in print and banned in public events. It is now an official language, taught publicly in schools and thrives alongside Spanish.

Other Autonomous Communities such as Galicia, Valencia and Andalucía have also identified themselves as nationalities and promoted their own languages and regional administrations.

Provinces: The need for greater administrative efficiency led the governments under Isabel II (19C) to establish an initial division of the country into provinces. At present, Spain has 50 provinces.

Municipalities: This is the smallest territorial division, comprising a town council (*ayuntamiento*) headed by a mayor (*alcalde*).

Given the administrative system now operating within Spain, communities and municipalities are able to administer their territories, in one of the most decentralised countries in Europe.

A WAY OF LIFE

Whenever foreigners conjure up an image of Spain, their thoughts inevitably turn to a leisurely lifestyle, plentiful sunshine, noisy and lively towns and cities, and an extroverted, friendly people whose daily timetable is impossible to comprehend!

Yet, irrespective of the crazy rhythms imposed by the demands of modern life, the Spanish always attempt to extract the very maximum from life; the maxim that most applies to them is that of having to work to live rather than living for work.

Despite the differences that exist between the north and south, the coast and inland areas, and towns and cities, it can be said that a common bond exists among all Spaniards in the manner in which they approach life.

LIFE IN THE STREET

There's no doubt that the excellent climate enjoyed by most parts of the country is one of the main reasons

The **Iberian Peninsula**, which is separated from the rest of Europe by the Pyrenees, is made up of continental Spain and Portugal. Spain covers an area of 504 030sq km/194 364sq mi, including the Canary Islands and Balearic Islands, and is the second largest country on Western Europe after France. It has over 4 000km/2 500mi of coastline lapped by the waters of the Mediterranean and Atlantic. The country's population currently stands at over 46 000 000.

for the Spaniards' "passion" for living outdoors; there are of course others, of lesser or equal importance. Spain is a country of informal get-togethers and social gatherings, in bars, cafés, restaurants, at work, and of chance meetings of a couple of friends – any excuse is good enough to indulge in a friendly chat or animated discussion. This affection for going out as a group, meeting friends for dinner, or enjoying an aperitif or drink, is to the Spanish a

Plaza Mayor, Madrid

J. Malburet/MICHELIN

sign of identity, irrespective of their age or social standing. Nor is it uncommon for Spaniards to have a relaxed drink with friends or colleagues before heading home after a long day's work.

DAILY SCHEDULE

The daily schedule of the Spanish is completely different from that of the rest of Europe and as such is the major characteristic that distinguishes the country from its European neighbours. Spaniards don't usually have lunch before 2pm or 2.30pm, or dinner before 9.30pm, a custom that results in long mornings and afternoons and provides ample time for them to indulge in their passion for a leisurely stroll, shopping or meeting up for a snack with friends and work acquaintants.

TAPAS AND APERITIF TIME

This gastronomic pastime is one of the most deeply rooted traditions in Spain, with youngsters, couples and entire families heading for bars to *tapear*, either standing at the counter or, if time allows, sitting down in a café terrace. An aperitif can be a frugal affair, although by ordering a number of tapas you can quite easily create an alternative to lunch or dinner.

These traditional appetisers come in many guises, ranging from the small tapa itself to larger portions known as a *media ración* or *ración*. Choose a *media ración* of Manchego cheese or

Jabugo cured ham, a *ración* of chorizo sausage, or a selection of vegetarian, fish, seafood or meat dishes – washed down perhaps with a glass of draught beer *(una caña)* or a glass of fino sherry *(una copa de fino)*. Every region has its own specialities and its own way of presenting tapas, yet whether you're in the Basque Country, Andalucía or in the middle of the Meseta, tapas are appreciated the length and breadth of the country.

BARS

There are literally tens of thousands of bars in Spain, including in the smallest and most remote hamlets and villages. They act as a focal point for locals, who congregate here with friends or family in the evening and at weekends. During the afternoon and early evening in smaller towns and villages you're bound to come across locals playing cards or indulging in a game of dominoes over a coffee or something stronger. The mornings are busy in bars as well, with regulars stopping by for a pastry and coffee for breakfast.

TERRACES

With the onset of fine weather, terraces spring up across Spain – outside restaurants, cafés, bars and ice-cream parlours, on pavements and patios and in gardens and narrow alleyways. During the warmer months, it is pleasant at any time of day to take the weight off your feet for a short while and watch the world go by in front of your table.

In summer, many of the most crowded bars and clubs, particularly those by the sea, provide outdoor terraces for their customers.

BEACH BARS

These typical features of resorts along the Spanish coast come in various guises, ranging from the cheap and cheerful to the expensive and luxurious. These *chiringuitos*, as they are known, have grown in popularity, particularly given that customers can enjoy a drink or have a meal wearing only their swim suits. In the more popular tourist areas they have become a meeting-point for locals and visitors alike, with some also open for dinner.

NIGHTLIFE

The lively character of Spanish towns and cities and summer resorts is often a cause of great surprise to visitors. Nowadays, the choice of venues is often overwhelming, with something to suit every budget and taste: quiet cafés for a drink and a chat with friends; lively bars packed to the rafters, with dance floors and music played at full volume; clubs offering a variety of shows; and nightclubs ranging from holes-in-the-wall to mega-venues where the pace doesn't stop until late the next morning. On Thursday and Friday nights and on weekends, as well as in summer and during holidays, the action is almost constant, with nightclubbers migrating from one club or bar to the next – don't be surprised if you get stuck in a traffic jam at three or four in the morning! An example of this is on the Paseo de la Castellana, in Madrid, with its numerous outdoor bars open until the small hours.

THE SIESTA

Although the demands of modern life prevent most people from perpetuating this healthy custom, most Spaniards long to have an afternoon nap and will make sure that they take a restorative siesta on weekends and when they're on holiday. Although less common nowadays, those Spaniards whose work schedule allows them three hours off from 2–5pm will try to make it home for lunch and a short sleep.

THE FAMILY

In line with other Latin countries, the family remains the bedrock of Spanish life, and is a determining factor in the behaviour and many of the habits of Spanish society at large. Without a solid family base, it would be hard to understand how a country with a high rate of unemployment and one in which children continue to live with their parents until their late-20s and even early-30s could prosper without too many problems. It should also be added that numerous Spanish celebrations and fiestas are based upon these close family ties.

THE WORK ETHIC

Those foreigners who have chosen to live in Spain soon realise that the old image of Spain as a country where very little work is done – a view perpetuated by the country's way of life and daily schedule, and the Spaniards' well-documented liking for enjoying themselves to the full – is far removed from modern reality. Nowadays, the work ethic in Spain is similar to that in any other European country. Visitors may wonder how this is possible, given the unusual lifestyle. The answer is simple: the Spanish sleep less. Working hours are little different from those in the rest of Europe, but from an early age the Spanish are brought up used to sleeping less during the week and trying to catch up on lost sleep at the weekend.

TRADITIONS AND FOLKLORE

Spain has kept alive its old traditions, as can be witnessed by the huge number of fiestas fervently celebrated around the country throughout the year. These unique and varied outpourings of religious sentiment and joy are a clear demonstration of Spain's rich cultural heritage and diversity.

Los Sanfermines de Pamplona

©Turespaña

a huge firework rocket or *chupinazo*. For an entire week the city is the backdrop for a non-stop celebration that enjoys its most spectacular moments during the morning running of the bulls *(encierros)* and at the early-evening bullfights. This ends at midnight on 14 July, with the candlelit singing of *Pobre de Mí* (Poor Me).

Las Fallas de Valencia, held in March in honour of San José, are renowned for firework displays. This begins every day of the festival at 8am with *la despertà* (the wake-up call), a heady mix of brass bands and firecrackers. This culminates in the *Nit del foc* (Night of Fire), when the impressive *ninots* (pasteboard figures) dotted around the city are set alight.

A LAND OF FIESTAS AND TRADITIONS

Numerous fiestas are celebrated across Spain. Unbridled joy, pomp and ceremony, and a sense of theatre are just some of the characteristics associated with these traditional aspects of Spanish life.

🕭 *A detailed list of major festivals in Spain can be found in the Planning Your Trip section of this guide.*

Major festivals

To a greater or lesser degree, every Spanish town and city celebrates one main festival every year, normally in honour of its patron saint. These celebrations, many of which take place over the summer months, attract the entire local population, as well as inhabitants from outlying villages and rural areas. Typical events will include religious celebrations and processions, bullfights and bull-running, while many will attend just to indulge in animated discussions with friends until the early hours, or to enjoy rides on the fairground attractions that are traditional features of these events.

The most important festivals in Spain include:

Los Sanfermines de Pamplona, in honour of San Fermín (7 July), which starts on 6 July with the setting-off of

Andalucían fiestas

Sevilla's *Feria de Abril* (April Fair) is the most famous of these festivals, with a reputation that has stretched far beyond the borders of Spain. Andalucían fiestas are renowned for their exciting atmosphere, colourful costumes and spontaneous dance, with mountains of tapas consumed, accompanied by a glass or two of chilled dry sherry *(fino)* such as *manzanilla*. The streets of the fairground area are a mass of colour as Andalucían women parade up and down on foot or on horseback dressed in the breathtaking flamenco dresses *(faralaes)* for which the region is famous.

Romerías

Romerías (pilgrimages) are an important aspect of religious life in Spain. Although each of these colourful events has its own specific characteristics, the basic principle is the same: a pilgrimage on foot, and occasionally on horseback, to a hermitage or shrine to venerate a statue. Usually, this religious peregrination will also include a procession, music, dancing and a festive meal in the countryside.

The pilgrimage to El Rocío (Almonte, Huelva) is the most extravagant and popular *romería* in the whole of Spain, attracting around one million pilgrims every year. Others of note include the St. John of the Mountain Festival in Miranda de Ebro dating from the 14C and the

Festival of the Virgen de la Cabeza in Andújar, Jaén.

Semana Santa

Holy Week processions are another vivid expression of the Spanish character. Numerous villages, towns and cities around the country participate in these outpourings of religious fervour, which see thousands of people taking to the streets to accompany the passion of Christ and the pain of his mother. Semana Santa tends to be a more sober affair in Castilla, and more festive in Andalucía, although across Spain the beauty of the statues (often works of art in their own right), the solemnity of the processions, some of which take place against a magnificent backdrop, and the fervour of those involved, create an atmosphere that will impress believers and non-believers alike.

Although Holy Week in Sevilla is undoubtedly the most famous, the processions in Valladolid, Málaga, Zamora and Cuenca are also worthy of particular note.

Carnival

Carnival celebrations in Spain are generally extravagant affairs where the imagination is stretched to its limits and joy is unbounded. They often involve many months of hard work during which performances are rehearsed and costumes made.

In the Canaries, particularly on Tenerife, Carnival is an important aspect of island tradition, involving a procession of floats and the election of the Carnival queen – events that bring the island to a standstill. The Carnival in Cádiz, which is known for its groups of musicians and folk dancers, is the liveliest on mainland Spain.

Christmas

The Christmas period in Spain is traditionally a time for family celebration. At home, where the Christmas tree and crib are essential decorative features, families congregate for dinner either on Christmas Eve or on Christmas Day, depending on the custom of their region. An equally traditional aspect of Christmas is the procession of the Kings: as a prelude to the most eagerly awaited night of the year, the Three Wise Men and their pages ride through the streets of towns and cities on the night of 5 January, handing out sweets to excited children lining their path.

Bullfighting festivals

It is impossible to broach the subject of fiestas without mentioning bullfighting – a subject that raises passions and criticism in equal measure. Bullfighting festivals are, indeed, just as much a part of Spanish culture as Holy Week processions; it is also true that the bullfighting world is indelibly linked with the major festivals around the country, and it is rare to find a town in which bullfighting is not present in some shape or form.

Very few cultural events are as regimented as a bullfight; consequently, a basic understanding of the various moves and stages of the contest is required to make any attempt to appreciate the spectacle.

The bullfighting season runs from the spring to the autumn, and the most important festivals are those in Sevilla, held during the April Fair, and the San Isidro festival in Madrid.

FOLKLORE

Andalucía

Flamenco, derived from gypsy and Arab sources, is a befitting expression of the Andalucían soul. It is based on the *cante jondo*, or deep song, which describes the performer's profound emotions in ancient poetic phrases. The rhythm is given by hand-claps, heel-clicks and castanets. The **Sevillana**, from Sevilla, is a more popular type of dance and song. Sevilla and Málaga are the best places to see **tablaos** or performances of Andalucían music.

Flamenco and the Sevillana owe much of their grace to the Andalucían costume of brilliantly coloured flounced dresses for women and close-fitting short jacketed suits, wide flat hats and heeled boots for men.

Flamenco performance

R. Mattès/MICHELIN

Aragón

No general rejoicing here goes without a **jota**, a bounding, leaping dance in which couples hop and whirl to the tunes of a *rondalla* (group of stringed instruments), stopping only for the occasional brief singing of a *copla* by a soloist.

Catalunya and the Comunidad Valenciana

The **sardana** dance is still very popular in Catalunya where it is performed in a circle in main squares on Sundays. The **Castells**, who form daring human pyramids, may be seen in festivals at El Vendrell and Valls. In the Levante, the rich local costume notable for its colour and intricate embroidery is worn during lively, colourful festivals. Valencia's **Fallas** in March are a veritable institution which Alicante's **Fogueres** try to rival.

La Tomatina, which takes place in the Valencian town of Buñol every August, has become a renowned food fight festival, where participants from all over the world come to throw overripe tomatoes in the streets, in honour of the town's patron saints. Lastly, the **Moros y Cristianos** festivals – those of Alcoy (22–24 April) are the best known – give a colourful replay of the confrontations between Moors and Christians during the Reconquest, where *filaes* (organised companies) represent the different legions with colouful medieval

uniforms in a background of fireworks and music.

Galicia, Asturias and Cantabria

Romerías in Asturias and Galicia are always accompanied by the shrill tones of the **gaita**, a type of bagpipe, and sometimes by drums and castanets. The *gaita* is played during events in honour of cowherds, shepherds, sailors and others who work in the country's oldest occupations. The most typical festivals are those held in summer for *vaqueiros*, or cowherds, in Aristébano and others for shepherds near the Lago de Enol. Common dances in Galicia include the *muñeira* or dance of the miller's wife, the sword dance performed only by men, and the *redondela*.

Bowls *(bolos)* is a very popular game, supposedly brought to the region by pilgrims on the Way of St James.

País Vasco and Navarra

The Basque Country and Navarra have preserved many of their unusual traditions. Men dressed in white with red sashes and the famous red berets dance in a ring accompanied by **zortzikos** (songs), a **txistu** (flute) and a *tamboril*. The most solemn dance, the *aurresku*, is a chain dance performed by men after Mass on Sundays. The **espata-dantza**, or sword dance, recalls warrior times while others, like the spinners' dance or another in which brooms are used, represent daily tasks. The Basques love contests, such as tug-of-war, trunk cutting, stone lifting and pole throwing. But by far the most popular sport is *pelota*, played in different ways: with a **chistera**, or wickerwork scoop, or with the very similar **cesta punta** in an enclosed three-walled court *(jai alai)*, or with a wooden bat or *pala* or, finally, simply with the hand, **a mano**. There is a famous pelota university at Markina in Vizcaya.

Castilla

Few regions in Spain are as mystical or have such sober customs as Castilla. Traditional dances include the **seguidilla**, originating from La Mancha region, and

Castells forming a human pyramid in Valls

©Turespaña

the **paloteo**, also known as the **danza de palos**, which is accompanied by flute, tambourine, and sometimes by a bass drum or the most typical of Castilian instruments, the local reed-pipe, or **dulzaina**. Peasant costumes around Salamanca are richly embroidered with precious stones, silk thread and sequins.

Balearic Islands

Mallorca's traditional dances include the *copeo*, the *jota*, the *mateixes* and the *bolero*. Dances and festivals are accompanied by a *xeremía* (local bagpipes) and a tambourine. In Menorca, a festival, dating back to medieval times and calling for about 100 horsemen in elegant costumes, is held at Ciutadella on Midsummer's Day (The Feast of St John or *Sant Joan*, on 23–24 June). Popular dances in Ibiza have a poetical accompaniment to guide the performers' movements.

Canary Islands

The folklore of the Canaries shows influences from the Spanish mainland, Portugal and South America (the last as a consequence of the strong links created by emigration); these in turn have become intertwined with local traditions. The **isa**, the **malagueña**, the *folía* and the *tajaraste* are the four best-known types of dance from the islands.

The *timple* is a type of small guitar which is typical of the archipelago. The *salto del pastor* (shepherd's leap) is a traditional folk sport throughout the islands involving long pole vaults known as *garrotes*.

FOOD AND DRINK

Spanish food is distinctively Mediterranean: it is cooked with an olive oil base, seasoned with aromatic herbs and spiced with hot peppers. It nevertheless varies enormously from region to region. Among dishes served throughout the country are garlic soup, *cocido* (a type of stew accompanied by beans or chickpeas), omelettes with potatoes, like the famous tortilla, typical pork meats like chorizo (a kind of spicy sausage), savoury rice dishes and delicious lean *serrano* hams. Fish and seafood are also used in a great many dishes.

No description of Spanish food should be complete without mentioning the ubiquitous tapas – the hors d'oeuvres which appear on the counters of most bars and cafés just before lunch and dinner. This often vast array of colourful appetisers comes in two different forms: tapas (small saucer-size amounts) or *raciones*, more substantial portions. A selection of two or three tapas or one or two *raciones* makes for a very pleasant lunch accompanied by a glass (*caña*) of draught beer.

The country is also renowned for its magnificent wines, which include famous appellations such as Rioja and Penedès, and the sherries of the Jerez region.

GALICIA

Galicia's cuisine owes its delicacy to the quality of its **seafood**: octopus, hake, gilthead, scallops (*vieiras*), mussels (*mejillones*), goose-barnacles (*percebes*), prawns (*gambas*), king prawns (*langostinos*) and mantis shrimps (*cigalas*). There is also el **caldo gallego**, a local soup, **lacón con grelos** (hand of pork with turnip tops) and another common traditional recipe, **pulpo gallego** (Galician-style octopus), often served as a tapa or *ración*. All these dishes may be accompanied by local wines such as red or white Ribeiro or white Albariño. The region's desserts include *tarta de Santiago*, an almond-flavoured tart, and *filloas*, a type of sweet fritter.

ASTURIAS AND CANTABRIA

In Asturias, fish and seafood are also important but the main speciality is a casserole dish called **fabada** made with white beans, pork, bacon and spicy sausages. As far as cakes and pastries are concerned, mention should be made of **sobaos**, delicious biscuits which originated in Cantabria and are cooked in oil. Cider is often drunk at meals.

PAÍS VASCO

Cooking in the Basque Country has been raised to the level of a fine art and requires laborious preparation. Meat is mostly served roasted, grilled or cooked in a sauce, while fish such as cod or hake is often accompanied by a green parsley sauce (*salsa verde*) or by peppers. *Chipirones en su tinta* is a dish of baby squid in their own ink. *Marmitako*, a typical fishing village dish, is composed of tuna fish, potatoes and hot red peppers, and is often served with a good *txacolí*, a tart white wine.

NAVARRA AND LA RIOJA

Navarra and La Rioja are the regions for game, excellent market-garden produce and the best Spanish wines, especially reds. The food is varied and refined, with partridge, quail and woodpigeon competing with trout for pride of place in local dishes. Navarra has noteworthy rosés and fruity white wines. Delicious Roncal cheese is made in the valleys from ewe's milk.

ARAGÓN

Aragón is the land of **chilindrón**, a stew made with meat or poultry and peppers, and of **ternasco** (roast kid or lamb). These dishes may be washed down with heavy red Cariñena wines.

CATALUNYA

Catalunya has a typically Mediterranean cuisine. Look out in particular for *pan con tomate* (bread rubbed with a cut tomato and occasionally garlic and sprinkled with olive oil), red peppers cooked in oil, and wonderful fish dishes with a variety of sauces such as *all i oli* (crushed garlic and olive oil) and *samfaina* (tomatoes, peppers and aubergines).

Among pork meats are **butifarra** sausages, various kinds of slicing sausage and the *fuet* sausage from Vic. Dried fruit is used in a great many dishes or may be served at the end of a meal. The most widespread dessert is **crema catalana**, a kind of crème brûlée. Catalunya is also home to *cava*, a sparkling wine. Excellent light wines are made in the Empordà region, fruity whites in Penedès and reds in Priorato.

CASTILLA AND EXTREMADURA

Castilian specialities from local produce include roast lamb **(cordero asado)**, suckling-pig (**cochinillo tostón** or **tostado**) and the ubiquitous **cocido**, all of which may be accompanied by a light fresh Valdepeñas red.

Rueda wines from the province of southern Valladolid are fresh fruity whites, while those from Ribera del Duero are generally acidic reds.

Castilla is also known for its cheeses, with a ewe's milk speciality from Burgos and many varieties of Manchego, Spain's best-known cheese, which is best served with *dulce de membrillo*, a sweet spread made from quince paste. Among local sweets are the famous marzipans *(mazapán)* from Toledo.

Extremadura enjoys an excellent reputation for its hams, such as those from Guijuelo (Salamanca) and Montánchez (Cáceres).

LEVANTE

The Levante is the kingdom of rice dishes, including the famous **paella**, which is cooked with a saffron rice base and chicken, pork, squid, mussels, shrimps and king prawns. As for sweets, **turrón** (made of almonds and honey or castor sugar, rather like nougat) is a Levantine speciality.

A traditional drink of *horchata de chufas*, made from tiger-nuts, water and sugar, makes for a pleasantly refreshing summer drink.

BALEARIC ISLANDS

Soups are specialities in the Balearics; Mallorca's Mallorquina has bread, leeks and garlic, while other soups are made with fish. **Tumbet** is a well-known casserole of potatoes, onions, tomatoes, courgettes and peppers. **Sobrasada**, a spicy sausage, flavours many local dishes. **Cocas**, pastries with sweet or savoury fillings, and **ensaimadas**, light spiral rolls, make delicious desserts.

THE CANARY ISLANDS

Canarian specialities include **papas arrugadas**, small and wrinkly potatoes with a dry, salty coating, best served with *mojo*, a red or orange sauce made from garlic, paprika and cumin.

Stoneground flour made from roasted maize, called *gofio*, is added to many foods or made into dough-like balls called *pella*.

The Canary Islands are also known for their wine, made from malvasia grapes and for *ronmiel* (literally "honey rum").

ANDALUCÍA

The region's best-known dish is **gazpacho**, a cold cucumber and tomato soup made with oil and vinegar and flavoured with garlic. Andalucíans love food fried, especially seafood. Pigs are reared in the Sierra Nevada and Sierra de Aracena for the exquisite *serrano* ham. Among local desserts, *tocino de cielo* is as sweet as an Oriental pastry.

The region is especially well known for its dessert wines: the famous **Jerez** or sherries, **Montilla-Moriles** and **Málaga**.

History

Modern Spain represents the culmination of centuries of crossbreeding, political union, exclusion and division. The country's history is a complex one, enlivened by myths and legends, and punctuated by significant historical and cultural landmarks. A heady mix of Carthiginian, Roman, Visigothic, Moorish and Christian imprints have blended to form a culture that has made a profound impact on world history. From the flourishing of arts and literature in the Spanish Golden Age; the colonization and identity of much of Latin America; to the establishment of a democratic and constitutional monarchy, Spanish culture and influence have combined to create a unique and proud people.

TIME LINE
FROM ANTIQUITY TO THE VISIGOTHIC KINGDOM

BC

11C–5C – Phoenician and Greek trading posts founded on the eastern and southern coasts of Spain, inhabited by **Iberians** and **Tartessians** respectively. In the 9C BC, the central-European Celts settle in west Spain and on the Meseta, intermingling with the Iberians (forming **Celtiberians**).

3C–2C – The **Carthaginians** take over the southeast after conquering the Greeks and Tartessians. The capture of Sagunto by Hannibal leads to the Second Punic War (218–201 BC). Rome expels the Carthaginians and begins the conquest of peninsular Spain (with resistance at **Numancia**).

THE CHRISTIAN RECONQUEST OF THE IBERIAN PENINSULA

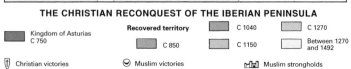

Kingdom of Asturias C 750

Recovered territory

C 850

C 1040

C 1150

C 1270

Between 1270 and 1492

Christian victories

Muslim victories

Muslim strongholds

1492

If there were only one important date to remember in Spanish history, it would be 1492. That year, after 781 years of Muslim occupation, the Reconquest ended with the fall of Granada on 2 January. This was also the year that the Jews were expelled, the Spaniard Roderic de Borja (Borgia) became Pope Alexander VI and on 12 October, Christopher Columbus landed in the Americas.

Christopher Columbus (Cristóbal Colón) (1451–1506) and the discovery of America – Born in Genoa, the son of a weaver, Columbus began his seafaring career at an early age. He travelled to Lisbon in 1476 where he developed a passion for map-making on discovering Ptolemy's Geography and Pierre d'Ailly's Imago Mundi. Convinced that the Indies could be reached by sailing west, he submitted a navigation plan to João II of Portugal and to the Kings of France and England. He ultimately managed to gain the support of the Duke of Medinaceli and that of the Prior of the Monasterio de La Rábida, Ximenes de Cisneros, who was Isabel the Catholic's confessor. The Catholic Monarchs agreed to finance his expedition and, if he succeeded, to bestow upon him the hereditary title of Admiral of the Ocean Sea and the viceroyship of any lands discovered.

On 3 August 1492, heading a fleet of three caravels (the *Santa María*, under his command, and the *Pinta* and the *Niña* captained by the Pinzón brothers), he put out from Palos de la Frontera. On 12 October, after a difficult crossing, San Salvador (Bahamas) came into sight and a short time later Hispaniola (Haiti) and Cuba were discovered. On his return to Spain on 15 March 1493, Christopher Columbus was given a triumphant welcome and the means with which to organise new expeditions. This marked the beginning of the Spanish and European colonisation of the New World.

1C BC–1C AD – Cantabria and Asturias are finally pacified in AD 19. Spain is now known as Iberia or Hispania.

AD

1C – Christianity reaches the Iberian Peninsula and begins to spread.

5C–6C – Early Suevi (Swabian) and Vandal invasions are followed by those of the **Visigoths** (415), who establish a powerful monarchy with Toledo as capital. The peninsula unites under King Leovigild (584–85).

MUSLIM SPAIN AND THE RECONQUEST

8C – Moors invade and annihilate the Visigothic Kingdom after the **Battle of Guadalete** in c 711. Pelayo's victory at **Covadonga** in 722 heralds an 800-year-long Christian War of Reconquest. The first Muslim invaders are subjects of the Umayyad Caliphate in Damascus. **Abd ar-Rahman I** breaks with Damascus by founding an independent emirate at Córdoba in 756.

9C – Settlement of uninhabited land by Christians.

10C – Golden age of the emirate of Córdoba, which is raised to the status of a caliphate (929–1021) by **Abd ar-Rahman III**. A period of great prosperity ensues during which the expansion of Christian kingdoms is checked. Fortresses are built in the north along the Duero river.

11C – Christian Spain now includes the Kingdoms of León, Castilla, Navarra and Aragón, and the County of Barcelona. On the death of Al-Mansur in 1002, the Caliphate of Córdoba disintegrates into about 20 *taifa* (faction) kingdoms

(1031). Alfonso VI of Castilla conquers Toledo (1085), and the area around the Tajo river is resettled by Christians. The *taifa* kings call upon the **Almoravids** (Saharan Muslims) for assistance and in a short time the tribe overruns a large part of Spain. Pilgrims begin to tread the Way of St James of Compostela. **El Cid** conquers Valencia (1094).

12C – Dissension stemming from a second age of *taifa* kingdoms assists the Reconquest, especially in the Ebro Valley (Zaragoza is taken in 1118, Tortosa in 1148 and Lleida in 1149), but after Yakub al-Mansur's victory in Alarcos (1195), the **Almohads** (who routed the Almoravids) recover Extremadura and check Christian expansion towards the Guadiana and Guadalquivir rivers. Sevilla, with Córdoba under its control, enjoys great prosperity.

Great military orders are founded (Calatrava, Alcántara and Santiago).

Unification of the kingdoms of Aragón and Catalunya (1150).

13C – The *taifa* kingdoms enter their third age. The decline of the Muslims begins with the **Battle of Las Navas de Tolosa** (1212). Muslim influence is reduced to the Nasrid Kingdom of Granada (modern provinces of Málaga, Granada and Almería), which holds out until its capture in 1492. Unification of Castilla and León under St Ferdinand III (1230).

The crown of Aragón under James I the Conqueror (1213–76) gains control over considerable territory in the Mediterranean.

THE CATHOLIC MONARCHS (1474–1516) AND THE UNIFICATION OF SPAIN

1474 – Isabella, wife of Ferdinand, succeeds her brother Henry IV to the throne of Castilla. She has to contend with opposition from the supporters of her niece Juana la Beltraneja until 1479.

1478–79 – The court of the **Inquisition** is instituted by a special Papal Bull and **Tómas de Torquemada** is later appointed Inquisitor-General. The court, a political and religious institution directed

El Cid

Rodrigo Díaz de Vivar was born to a noble family around 1040 in Vivar, near Burgos. Having served under two kings in the Reconquista, during which time he earned the honorific title of 'El Campeador' for his forward thinking and leadership, prompting jealousy amongst his peers. He was exiled by King Alfonso VI in 1079 for insubordination. The bloody Christian defeat at the Battle of Sagrajas (1086) prompted King Alfonso repeal his decision, and El Cid was welcomed back. El Cid then raised an army and beseiged Valencia, finally conquering the city in May 1094. Though officially ruling in the name of King Alfonso, Valencia became his own independent Christian fiefdom. His legend has led him to be considered as Spain's national hero.

El Cid has inspired everything from epic poems ('The Song of the Cid') to Hollywood films (El Cid, 1961, starring Charlton Heston). His grave now lies as the centerpiece of Burgos Cathedral. Tizona, his legendary sword, can be found at the Museo de Burgos (*see BURGOS*).

against Jews, Moors and later Protestants, survives until the 19C.

Ferdinand becomes King of Aragón in 1479 and Christian Spain is united under one crown.

1492 – Fall of Granada marks the end of the Reconquest. Expulsion of Jews.

12 Oct 1492 – Christopher Columbus lands in the Americas.

1494 – The **Treaty of Tordesillas** divides the New World between Spain and Portugal.

1496 – Joanna, daughter of the Catholic Monarchs, marries Philip the Handsome (Felipe el Hermoso), son of Holy Roman Emperor Maximilian I of the Habsburgs.

1504 – Death of Isabel. The kingdom is inherited by her daughter, Joanna the Mad (Juana la Loca) but Ferdinand governs as regent until Joanna's son Charles (1500–1558), future Emperor Charles V, comes of age.

1512 – The Duke of Alba conquers Navarra, thus bringing political unity to Spain.

THE HABSBURGS (1516–1700) AND THE CONQUEST OF AMERICA

1516 – **The apogee: Charles I** (1516–56) and **Philip II** (1556–98). On the death of Ferdinand, his grandson becomes Charles I (Carlos I) of Spain. Through his mother, Charles inherits Spain, as well as Naples, Sicily, Sardinia and American territories. Cardinal Cisneros governs until the new king arrives for the first time in Spain in 1517.

1519 – On the death of Maximilian of Austria, Charles I is elected Holy Roman Emperor under the name of **Charles V** (Carlos V). He inherits Germany, Austria, the Franche-Comté and the Low Countries.

A Life Less Ordinary

Miguel de Cervantes Saavedra was born in poverty at Alcalá de Henares in 1547, yet he went on to lead a life of adventure. From being a valet in Renaissance Rome, Cervantes would later fight against the Ottomans in the Battle of Lepanto (1571). He then spent five years in slavery in Algiers, before returning to Madrid as a purveyor and tax collector for the Spanish Armada. While being imprisoned for debts in La Mancha, it is said that he had the idea for his famous literary work, **Don Quixote de La Mancha**, now considered to be one of the greatest novels of all time. He died peacefully in 1616, having settled in Madrid and ending his wayfaring lifestyle.

1520–22 – The Spanish, incensed by Charles V's largely Flemish court advisers and the increasing number of taxes, rise up in arms. The emperor quells **Comuneros** and **Germanías** revolts.

1521–56 – Charles V wages five wars against France in order to secure complete control of Europe. In the first four he conquers Francis I (imprisoned at Pavia in 1525) and in the fifth he routs the new French king, Henri II, and captures Milan.

The Conquistadores move across America. **Vasco Núñez de Balboa** discovers the Pacific; **Hernan Cortés** seizes Mexico in 1521; **Francisco Pizarro** and **Diego de Almagro** subdue Peru in 1533; **Francisco Coronado** explores the Colorado river in 1535; **Hernando de Soto** takes possession of Florida in 1539; and **Pedro de Valdivia** founds Santiago de Chile in 1541.

1555 – Charles V signs the Peace of Augsburg with the Protestants

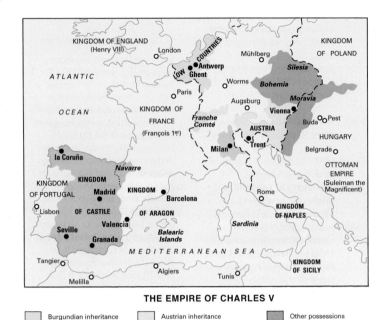

THE EMPIRE OF CHARLES V

- Burgundian inheritance
- Spanish inheritance
- Austrian inheritance
- Charles V's conquests
- Other possessions
- – – – The Holy Roman Empire

in Germany after failing to suppress the Reformation.

1556 – Charles V abdicates in favour of his son and retires to a monastery in Yuste. **Philip II** becomes king, inheriting Spain and its colonies, the kingdom of Naples, Milan, the Low Countries and the Franche-Comté, but not Germany and Austria which are left by Charles to his brother Ferdinand I of Austria. Philip II turns his attention to Spain and the defence of Catholicism. He chooses Madrid as his de facto capital in 1561. Spain goes through a serious economic crisis.

1568–70 – Revolt of the Moriscos (Muslims who converted to Christianity) in Granada.

1571 – The Turks are defeated in the **Battle of Lepanto** by a fleet of ships sent by the Pope, the Venetians and the Spanish, under the command of **Don John of Austria**, the king's natural brother. The victory seals Spain's mastery of the Mediterranean.

1580 – The King of Portugal dies without an heir. Philip II asserts his rights, invades Portugal and is proclaimed king in 1581.

1588 – Philip II sends the **Invincible Armada** against Protestant England, which supports the Low Countries. The destruction of the fleet marks the end of Spain as a sea power.

1598 – Philip II dies, leaving a vast kingdom which, in spite of huge wealth from the Americas, is crippled by debt after 70 years of almost incessant war and monumental building projects like El Escorial.

1598–1621 – **The decline** – The last Habsburgs, **Philip III** (Felipe III, 1598–1621), **Philip IV** (Felipe IV, 1621–65) and **Charles II**

(Carlos II, 1665–1700), lack the mettle of their forebears. Paradoxically, Spain enjoys a **golden age** of art and culture. Philip III entrusts the affairs of state to the Duke of Lerma, who advises him to expel the Moriscos in 1609. 275 000 Moors leave Spain with disastrous consequences for agriculture.

1640 – Under Philip IV (Felipe IV), the Count-Duke of Olivares adopts a policy of decentralisation which spurs Catalunya and Portugal to rebellion. The Portuguese proclaim the Duke of Braganza King John IV, but their independence is not recognised until 1668.

1618–48 – Spain wastes her strength in the **Thirty Years' War**. In spite of victories like that of Breda (1624), the defeat in the Netherlands at Rocroi (1643) signals the end of Spain as a European power. The **Treaty of Westphalia** gives the Netherlands independence.

1659 – The **Treaty of the Pyrenees** ends war with France. Philip IV arranges the marriage of his daughter María Teresa to Louis XIV of France.

1667-97 – Spain loses strongholds in Flanders to France during the **War of Devolution** (1667–68). The Dutch Wars (1672–78) end with the **Treaty of Nijmegen**. The **Treaty of Ryswick** (1697) concludes the war waged by the Confederation of Augsburg (Spain is a member) against France (1688–97).

THE BOURBONS, NAPOLEON AND THE WAR OF INDEPENDENCE (1808–14)

1700 – Charles II dies without issue. He wills the crown to Philip, Duke of Anjou, grandson of his sister María Teresa and Louis XIV. Emperor Leopold, who had renounced his rights to the Spanish throne in favour of his son, the Archduke Charles, is displeased, but the appointment of the Bourbons to the Spanish throne stabilises the balance of power in Europe.

1702–14 – **War of the Spanish Succession** – England, the Netherlands, Denmark and Germany support the Archduke of Austria against France and Philip of Anjou. Catalunya, Valencia and Aragón also side with the Archduke and war spreads throughout Spain (1705). By the **Treaty of Utrecht**, Spain forfeits Gibraltar and Menorca (taken by the English) and many of her Italian possessions. **Philip V** (Felipe V) is proclaimed King of Spain (1683–1746).

1759–88 – The reign of **Charles III** (Carlos III), an enlightened despot, is the most brilliant of those of the Bourbons. He is assisted by competent ministers (Floridablanca and Aranda) who draw up important economic reforms. Expulsion of the Jesuits in 1767.

1788 – **Charles IV** (Carlos IV) succeeds to the throne. A weak-willed king, he allows the country to be governed by his wife María Luisa and her favourite, Manuel de Godoy.

1793 – On the death of Louis XVI, Spain declares war on France (then in the throes of the Revolution).

1796–1805 – Spain signs an alliance with the French Directorate against England (Second Treaty of San Ildefonso, 1796). **Napoleon** enters Spain with his troops on the pretext that he is going to attack Portugal. The renewed offensive against England in 1804 ends disastrously with the **Battle of Trafalgar** the following year.

1805–08 – Napoleon takes advantage of the disagreement between Charles IV and his son Ferdinand to engineer Charles IV's abdication and appoint his own brother, Joseph, King of Spain. The Aranjuez Revolt takes place in March 1808.

2 May 1808 – The Madrid uprising against French troops marks the beginning of the **War of Independence** (The Peninsular War), which lasts until Napoleon is exiled by Wellington in 1814. During the war there are battles at Bailén (1808), Madrid, Zaragoza and Girona.

1812 – The French are routed by Wellington in the Arapiles Valley; King Joseph flees from Madrid. Valencia is taken by the French General Suchet.
Spanish patriots convene the Cortes (parliament) and draw up the liberal **Constitution of Cádiz.**

1813–14 – Anglo-Spanish forces expel Napoleon after successive victories.
Ferdinand VII (Fernando VII) returns to Spain, repeals the Constitution of Cádiz and so reigns as an absolute monarch until 1820. Meanwhile, the Latin American colonies struggle for independence.

THE DISTURBANCES OF THE 19C

1820–23 – The liberals oppose the king's absolute rule but their uprisings are all severely quelled. The 1812 constitution is reinstated after a liberal revolt led by **General Riego** in Cádiz in 1820, but only for three years.
In 1823 Ferdinand VII appeals to Europe for assistance and 100 000 Frenchmen are sent in the name of St Louis to re-establish absolute rule (which lasts until 1833).

1833–39 – On the death of Ferdinand VII, his brother Don Carlos disputes the right to the throne of his niece Isabel II, daughter of the late king and Queen María Cristina. The traditionalist Carlists fight Isabel's liberal supporters, who, after six years, win the **First Carlist War** (Convention of Vergara). In 1835, the government minister **Mendizábal** has a series of decrees passed which do away with religious orders and confiscate their property (desamortización).

1840 – A revolutionary junta forces the regent María Cristina into exile. She is replaced by General Espartero.

1843–68 – Queen Isabel II comes of age. The **Narváez** uprising forces Espartero to flee. A new constitution is drawn up in 1845. The Second Carlist War (1847–49) ends in victory for Isabel II but her reign is troubled by a succession of uprisings on behalf of progressives and moderates. The 1868 revolt led by General Prim puts an end to her reign. Isabel leaves for France and General Serrano is appointed leader of the provisional government.

1869 – The Cortes passes a progressive constitution which, however, envisages the establishment of a monarchy. Amadeo of Savoy is elected king.

1873 – The Third Carlist War (1872–76). The king abdicates on finding himself unable to keep the peace. The National Assembly proclaims the **First Spanish Republic**.

1874 – General Martínez Campos leads a revolt. The head of the government, Cánovas de

Castillo, proclaims Isabel's son **Alfonso XII** King of Spain. The Bourbon Restoration opens a long period of peace.

1885 – Death of Alfonso XII (at 28). His widow María Cristina (who is expecting a baby) becomes regent.

1898 – Cuba and the Philippines rise up with disastrous losses for Spain.

The United States, which supports the rebel colonies, occupies Puerto Rico and the Philippines, marking the end of the Spanish Empire.

1902 – **Alfonso XIII** (born after the death of his father Alfonso XII) assumes the throne at 16.

THE FALL OF THE MONARCHY AND THE SECOND REPUBLIC (1931–36)

1914–18 – Spain remains neutral throughout the First World War. A general strike in 1919 is severely put down.

1921 – Insurrection in Morocco; General Sanjurjo occupies the north (1927).

1923 – General **Miguel Primo de Rivera** establishes a dictatorship with the king's approval. Order is restored, the country grows wealthier but opposition increases among the working classes.

1930 – In the face of hostility from the masses, Primo de Rivera is forced into exile and General Berenguer is appointed dictator.

1931 – April elections bring victory to the Republicans in Catalunya, the País Vasco, La Rioja and the Aragonese province of Huesca. The king leaves Spain and the Second Republic is proclaimed.

Jun 1931 – A constituent Cortes is elected with a socialist Republican majority; a Constitution is promulgated in December. Don Niceto Alcalá Zamora is elected President of the Republic. Agrarian reforms, such as compulsory purchase of large properties, meet strong right-wing opposition.

1933 – The **Falange Party**, which opposes regional separation, is founded by **José Antonio Primo de Rivera**, son of the dictator. The army plots against the régime.

Oct 1934 – Catalunya proclaims its autonomy. Miners in Asturias spark off a revolt against the right-wing government and are brutally repressed.

Feb 1936 – The Popular Front wins the elections, precipitating a revolutionary situation. Radicals hit the streets and the right promptly retaliates.

THE CIVIL WAR (1936–39)

17 Jul 1936 – The Melilla uprising triggers the Civil War. The army takes control and puts an end to the Second Republic. Nationalist troops based in Morocco and led by General Franco cross the Straits of Gibraltar and make their way to Toledo, which is taken at the end of September. Franco is proclaimed Generalísimo of the armed forces and Head of State in Burgos. Nationalists lead an unsuccessful attack against Madrid.

While Madrid, Catalunya and Valencia remain faithful to the Republicans, the Conservative agricultural regions – Andalucía, Castilla and Galicia – are rapidly controlled by the Nationalists. These regions out-supply the Republicans and the Republicans themselves are torn by dissension between the Anarchist CNT party, the Communist PCE and the Marxist POUM. They do, however, receive assistance from International Brigades.

1937 – Industrial towns in the north are taken by Nationalist supporters in the summer (on 26 April, Gernika is bombed by German planes). The Republican Government is moved to Barcelona in November. In the battle of Teruel in December, the Republicans try to breach the Nationalist front in Aragón and thereby relieve surrounded Catalunya. Teruel is taken by the Republicans and recaptured by the Nationalists soon after.

1938 – The Nationalist army reaches the Mediterranean, dividing Republican territory into two parts. The **Battle of the Ebro** lasts from July to November: Franco launches an offensive against Catalunya, which is occupied by the Nationalists in February 1939.

1 Apr 1939 – The war ends with the capture of Madrid.

THE FRANCO ERA

1939–49 – Spain is declared a monarchy with Franco as regent and Head of State and remains neutral in the Second World War. Period of diplomatic isolation.

1952 – Spain joins UNESCO.

1955 – Spain becomes a member of the United Nations.

1969 – Prince Juan Carlos is named as Franco's successor.

20 Dec 1973 – Prime Minister Carrero Blanco is assassinated.

20 Nov 1975 – Death of Franco. **Juan Carlos I** becomes King of Spain.

DEMOCRACY

15 Jun 1977 – General elections – **Adolfo Suárez** is elected prime minister. A new constitution is passed by referendum in 1978. Statutes of autonomy are approved for Catalunya, the País Vasco (Euskadi) and Galicia.

1981 – The Prince of Asturias Awards are established to honour public achievements.

1981–82 – Suárez resigns. There is an attempted military coup on 23 February 1981. The Socialist Party gains power and **Felipe González** becomes prime minister after winning general elections.

1 Jan 1986 – Spain joins the **European Economic Community**.

12 Mar 1986 – Spain's continued membership in NATO is voted by referendum.

11 Jun 1986 – Felipe González is re-elected prime minister.

1992 – Barcelona hosts the 1992 Summer Olympics, and Sevilla hosts Expo 1992.

3 Mar 1996 – **José María Aznar** of the Popular Party becomes prime minister.

3 Oct 1997 – The Guggenheim Museum in Bilbao is opened to the public.

1 Jan 2002 – Spain adopts the **Euro**.

11 Marh 2004 – The **Madrid train bombings** by terrorists leave countless dead and injured.

14 Mar 2004 – **José Luis Rodríguez Zapatero** of the Socialist Party becomes prime minister.

22 May 2004 – The Prince of Asturias, heir to the Spanish crown, marries Letizia Ortiz Rocasolano, a journalist and divorcée.

31 Oct 2005 – Princess Leonor is born in Madrid to the crown prince and princess.

29 Apr 2007 – Princess Sofia is born, the second child of the crown prince.

11 Apr 2008 – Prime Minister Zapatero is re-elected.

29 Jun 2008 – Spain unites in celebration as Spain wins the **UEFA Euro 2008** Football Championships.

Art and Culture

ARCHITECTURE AND THE VISUAL ARTS

Over the centuries, Spain has amassed countless artistic and architectural treasures across the length and breadth of the country, ranging from diminutive Romanesque chapels, lofty Gothic cathedrals and exuberant Baroque churches to awe-inspiring Hispano-Moorish monuments, imposing castles, magnificent paintings and outstanding sculptures.

FROM PREHISTORY TO THE MOORISH CONQUEST

Prehistoric art

Prehistoric inhabitants of the Iberian Peninsula have left some outstanding examples of their art. The oldest are the Upper Palaeolithic (40 000–10 000 BC) cave paintings in Cantabria (Altamira and Puente Viesgo), Asturias (El Pindal, Ribadesella and San Román) and the Levante region (Cogull and Alpera). Megalithic monuments like the famous Antequera dolmens were erected during the Neolithic Era (7 500–2 500 BC), or New Stone Age, while in the Balearic Islands strange stone monuments known as **talaiots** and *navetas* were built by a Bronze Age people (2 500–1 000 BC).

First Millennium BC

Iberian civilisations produced gold and silverware (treasure of Carambolo in the Museo Arqueológico in Sevilla), and fine sculpture. Some of their work, such as the Córdoba lions, the Guisando bulls and, in the Museo Arqueológico in Madrid, the *Dama de Baza* and the *Dama de Elche*, is of a remarkably high standard. Meanwhile, Phoenician, Carthaginian and in turn Greek colonisers introduced their native art: Phoenician sarcophagi in Cádiz, Punic art in Ibiza and Greek art in Empúries.

Roman Spain (1C BC–5C AD)

Besides roads, bridges, aqueducts, towns and monuments, Roman legacies include the Mérida theatre, the ancient towns of Italica and Empúries, and the Segovia aqueduct and Tarragona triumphal arch.

The Visigoths (6C–8C)

Christian Visigoths built small stone churches (Quintanilla de las Viñas, San Pedro de la Nave) adorned with friezes carved in geometric patterns with plant motifs. The apsidal plan was square and the arches were often horseshoe-shaped. The Visigoths were outstanding gold and silversmiths who made sumptuous jewellery in the Byzantine and Germanic traditions. Gold votive crowns (Guarrazar treasure in Toledo), fibulae and belt buckles adorned with precious stones or *cloisonné* enamel were presented to churches or placed in the tombs of the great.

HISPANO-MOORISH ARCHITECTURE (8C–15C)

The three major periods of Hispano-Moorish architecture correspond to the reigns of successive Arab dynasties over the Muslim-held territories in the peninsula.

Caliphate or Córdoba architecture (8C–11C)

This period is characterised by three types of building: **mosques**, built to a simple plan consisting of a minaret, a courtyard with a pool for ritual ablutions

Dama de Elche

©Photoolasson/Dreamstime.com

ARCHITECTURE A–Z

Words in italics are Spanish.

Ajimez paired window or opening separated by a central column.

Alfarje wooden ceiling, usually decorated, consisting of a board resting on cross-beams (a feature of the Mudéjar style).

Alfiz rectangular surround to a horseshoe-shaped arch in Muslim architecture.

Alicatado section of wall or other surface covered with sheets of ceramic tiles *(azulejos)* cut to form geometric patterns. Frequently used to decorate dados (a Mudéjar feature).

Aljibe Arab word for cistern.

Altarpiece also retable. Decorative screen above and behind the altar.

Apse far end of a church housing the high altar; can be semicircular, polygonal or horseshoe-shaped.

Apsidal or radiating chapel small chapel opening from the apse.

Arch *See illustrations*

Horseshoe (Moorish)

R. Corbel/MICHELIN

Archivolt ornamental moulding on the outer edge of an arch.

Artesonado marquetry ceiling in which raised fillets outline honeycomb-like cells in the shape of stars. This decoration,

which first appeared under the Almohads, was popular throughout the country, including Christian Spain, in the 15C and 16C.

Ataurique decorative plant motif on plaster or brick which was developed as a feature of the Caliphate style and was subsequently adopted by the Mudéjar.

Azulejos glazed, patterned, ceramic tiles.

Barrel vaulting vault with a semicircular cross-section. *See illustrations*

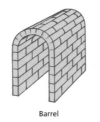

Barrel

R. Corbel/MICHELIN

Cabecera the east or apsidal end of a church.

Caliphate the architectural style developed in Córdoba under the Caliphate (8C–11C) of which the finest example is the mosque in that city.

Camarín a small chapel on the first floor behind the altarpiece or retable. It is plushly decorated and very often contains a lavishly costumed statue of the Virgin Mary.

Capilla mayor the area of the high altar containing the *retablo mayor* or monumental altarpiece, which often rises to the roof.

Coro a chancel in Spanish canonical churches often built in the middle of the nave. It contains the **stalls**

(sillería) used by members of religious orders. When placed in a tribune or gallery it is known as the *coro alto*.

Churrigueresque in the style of the Churrigueras, an 18C family of architects. Richly ornate Baroque decoration.

Crucero transept. The part of a church at right angles to the nave which gives the church the shape of a cross.

Estípite pilaster in the shape of a truncated inverted pyramid.

Gargoyle projecting roof gutter normally carved in the shape of a grotesque animal.

Girola (also *deambulatorio*): ambulatory. An extension to the aisles forming a gallery around the chancel and behind the altar.

Groined vaulting vault showing lines of intersection of two vaults or arches (usually pointed).

Grotesque typical Renaissance decoration combining vegetation, imaginary beings and animals.

Kiblah sacred wall of a mosque from which the mihrab is hollowed, facing towards Mecca.

Lacería geometric decoration formed by intersecting straight lines making star-shaped and polygonal figures. Characteristic of Moorish architecture.

Lombard bands decorative pilaster strips typical of Romanesque architecture in Lombardy.

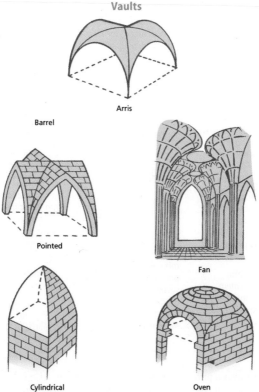

Arches

Pointed horseshoe

Raised

Ogee

Basket-handle

Rampant

Vaults

Arris

Barrel

Pointed

Fan

Cylindrical

Oven

R. Corbel/MICHELIN

Lonja commodity exchange building.

Mihrab richly decorated prayer-niche in the sacred wall (kiblah) in a mosque.

Minaret tower of the mosque (*mezquita*), from which the muezzin calls the faithful to prayer.

Minbar pulpit in a mosque.

Mocárabes decorative motifs of Muslim architecture formed by assembled prisms ending in concave surfaces. They resemble stalactites or pendants

69

Tympanum

H. Chomet/MICHELIN

and adorn vaults and cornices.

Mozarabic the work of Christians living under Arab rule after the Moorish invasion of 711. On being persecuted in the 9C, they sought refuge in Christian areas bringing with them Moorish artistic traditions.

Mudéjar the work of Muslims living in Christian territory following the Reconquest (13C–14C).

Mullion slender column or pillar dividing an opening in a door or window.

Naveta megalithic monument found in the Balearic Islands, which has a pyramidal shape with a rectangular base, giving the appearance of an upturned boat.

Plateresque term derived from *platero* (i.e. silversmith); used to describe the early style of the Renaissance characterised by finely carved decoration.

Predella the lower part of an altarpiece.

Presbiterio the space in front of the altar (the presbytery is known as the *casa del cura*).

Púlpito pulpit.

Sagrario chapel containing the Holy Sacrament. May sometimes be a separate church.

Sebka type of brick decoration developed under the Almohads consisting of an apparently endless series of small arches forming a network of diamond shapes.

Seo cathedral.

Sillería the stalls.

Soportales porticoes of wood or stone pillars supporting the first floor of houses. They form an open gallery around the plaza mayor of towns and villages.

Star vault vault with a square or polygonal plan formed by several intersecting arches.

Stucco type of moulding mix consisting mainly of plaster, used for coating surfaces. It plays a fundamental role in wall decoration in Hispano-Muslim architecture.

Talayot: megalithic monument found in the Balearic Islands, which takes the form of a truncated cone of stones.

Taula (*mesa* in the Mallorcan language) megalithic monument found in the Balearic Islands, which consists of a monolithic horizontal stone block placed on top of a similar vertical stone block.

Trasaltar back wall of the *capilla mayor* in front of which there are frequently sculptures or tombs.

Trascoro the wall, often carved and decorated, which encloses the *coro*.

Triforium arcade above the side aisles which opens onto the central nave of a church.

Tympanum inner surface of a pediment. This often ornamented space is bounded by the archivolt and the lintel of the doors of churches.

Venera scallop-shaped moulding frequently used as an ornamental feature. It is the symbol of pilgrimages to Santiago de Compostela.

Yesería plasterwork used in sculptured decoration.

---

and finally a square prayer room with a mihrab (prayer-niche marking the direction of Mecca); **alcázares** (palaces), built around attractive patios and surrounded by gardens and fountains; and **alcazabas** (castle fortresses), built on high ground and surrounded by several walls crowned with pointed merlons – one of the best examples of these can be found in Málaga. The most famous monuments from this period are in Córdoba (the Mezquita and the Medina Azahara palace) and in Toledo (Cristo de la Luz) where, besides the ubiquitous horseshoe arch which virtually became the hallmark of Moorish architecture, other characteristics developed incl-uding ornamental brickwork in relief,

Hispano-Moorish art

CÓRDOBA – Mezquita: Puerta de Alhakem II (10C)

Eight centuries of Moorish rule in Spain had a fundamental influence on Spanish art.

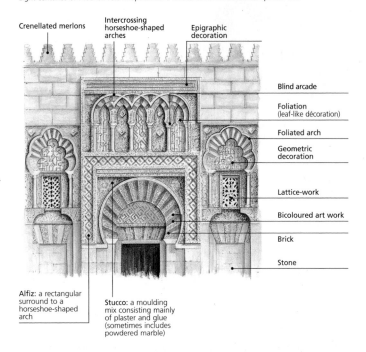

Crenellated merlons

Intercrossing horseshoe-shaped arches

Epigraphic decoration

Blind arcade

Foliation (leaf-like décoration)

Foliated arch

Geometric decoration

Lattice-work

Bicoloured art work

Brick

Stone

Alfiz: a rectangular surround to a horseshoe-shaped arch

Stucco: a moulding mix consisting mainly of plaster and glue (sometimes includes powdered marble)

cupolas supported on ribs, turned modillions, arches with alternating white stone and red-brick voussoirs, **multifoil arches** (⌖ *see illustration*) and doors surmounted with blind arcades. These features subsequently became popular in Mudéjar and Romanesque churches.

The Umayyads brought a taste for profuse decoration from Syria. As the Koran forbids the representation of human or animal forms, Muslim decoration is based on calligraphy (Cufic inscriptions running along walls), geometric patterns (polygons and stars made of ornamental brickwork and marble) and lastly plant motifs (flowerets and interlacing palm leaves).

Almohad or Sevilla architecture (12C–13C)

The religious puritanism of the Almohad dynasty, of which Sevilla was the capital, was expressed in architecture by a refined, though sometimes rather austere, simplicity. One of the

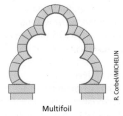

Multifoil

R. Corbel/MICHELIN

The Decorative Arts

Extremely rich and varied decorative artefacts from the Almohad period include geometric wood strapwork, brocades, weapons, ceramics with *esgrafiado* decoration and small ivory chests.

GRANADA – La Alhambra (14C)

Mocárabes: decorative motifs of Muslim architecture formed by assembled prisms ending in concave surfaces. Used to adorn vaults, arches and cornices

A panel of *azulejos* with epigraphic and geometric decoration

R. Corbel/MICHELIN

H. Choimet/MICHELIN

Pointed

characteristics of the style consisted of brickwork highlighted by wide bands of decoration in relief, without excessive ornamentation (the Giralda tower in Sevilla is a good example). The style was later used in the Mudéjar architecture of Aragón. Other features that emerged at this time include *artesonado* ceilings and *azulejos*. Arches of alternate brick and stonework disappeared, the horseshoe arch became **pointed** and the multifoil arch was bordered by a curvilinear festoon (ornament like a garland) as in the Aljafería in Zaragoza. Calligraphic decoration included cursive (flowing) as well as Cufic script to which floral motifs were added to fill the spaces between vertical lines.

Nasrid or Granada architecture (14C–15C)

This period of high sophistication, of which the **Alhambra** in Granada (see illustration) is the masterpiece, produced less innovation in actual architectural design than in the decoration, whether stucco or ceramic, that covered the walls. Surrounds to doors and windows became focal points for every room's design and the spaces between them were filled by perfectly proportioned panels. Arch outlines were simplified – the stilted round arch became widespread – while detailed lacework ornamentation was used as a border.

Mudéjar architecture

This is the name given to work carried out by Muslims while under the Christian yoke, yet executed in the Arab tradition. It was fashionable from the 11C to the 15C in different regions depending on the area recovered by the Reconquest, although some features, like *artesonado* ceilings, continued as decorative themes for centuries.

Court Mudéjar, developed by Muslim artists (in buildings ordered by Peter the Cruel in Tordesillas and Sevilla, and in synagogues in Toledo), was an extension of the Almohad or contemporary Nasrid style. Popular Mudéjar, on the other hand, was produced by local Muslim workshops and reflects marked regional taste: walls were decorated with blind arcades in Castilla (Arévalo, Sahagún and Toledo) and belfries were faced with *azulejos* (see illustration) and geometric strapwork in Aragón.

PRE-ROMANESQUE AND ROMANESQUE ART AND ARCHITECTURE (8C–13C)

Asturian architecture

A highly sophisticated style of court architecture, characterised by sweeps of ascending lines, developed in the small kingdom of Asturias between the 8C and the 10C.

Asturian churches (Naranco, Santa Cristina de Lena) followed the precepts of the Latin basilica in their rectangular plan with a narthex, a nave and two aisles separated by **semicircular arches** (see illustration), a vast transept and an east end divided into three. Decoration inside consisted of frescoes, and borrowings from the East including motifs carved on **capitals** (strapwork, rosettes and monsters, see illustration) and ornamental openwork around windows. Gold and silversmiths in the 9C and 10C produced rich treasures, many of which may be seen in the Cámara Santa in Oviedo Cathedral.

Mozarabic architecture

This term is given to work carried out by Christians living under Arab rule after the Moorish invasion of 711. Churches built in this style, especially in Castilla (San Miguel de Escalada, San Millán de la Cogolla), brought back Visigothic traditions (horseshoe arches) enriched by Moorish features such as ribbed cupolas and turned modillions.

Illuminated manuscripts provide the earliest known examples of Spanish medieval painting (10C). They were executed in the 10C and 11C by Mozarabic monks and have Moorish features such as horseshoe arches and Arab costumes. They portray St John's Commentary on the Apocalypse written in the 8C by the

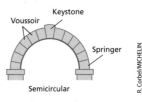

Keystone
Voussoir
Springer
Semicircular

R. Corbel/MICHELIN

monk **Beatus de Liébana**, after whom the manuscripts were named.

Catalunya, home of the earliest Romanesque style in Spain

Catalunya had intimate links with Italy and France and consequently developed an architectural style strongly influenced by Lombardy from the 11C to the 13C. This evolved in the Pyrenean valleys, isolated from the more travelled pilgrim and trade routes. Sober little churches were built often accompanied by a separate bell tower decorated with Lombard bands. Interior walls in the 11C and 12C were only embellished with frescoes which, in spite of their borrowings from Byzantine mosaics (heavy black outlines, rigid postures, and themes like Christ in Glory portrayed within a mandorla), proved by their realistic and expressive details to be typically Spanish. Altar fronts of painted wood, executed in bright colours, followed the same themes and layout.

European Romanesque art along the pilgrim routes

Northwest Spain opened its gates to foreign influence during the reign of Sancho the Great of Navarra early in the 11C. Cistercian abbeys were founded and French merchants allowed to settle rate free in towns (Estella, Sangüesa and Pamplona). Meanwhile, the surge of pilgrims to Compostela and the fever to build along the routes brought about the construction of a great many religious buildings in which French influence was clearly marked (characteristics from Poitou in Soria and Sangüesa, and from Toulouse in Aragón and **Santiago de Compostela** (see illustration). The acknowledged masterpiece of this style is the Santiago de Compostela Cathedral.

Romanesque

SANTIAGO DE COMPOSTELA – Cathedral: Interior (11C-13C)

Santiago cathedral is a typical example of a Spanish pilgrimage church and shows clear French influence.

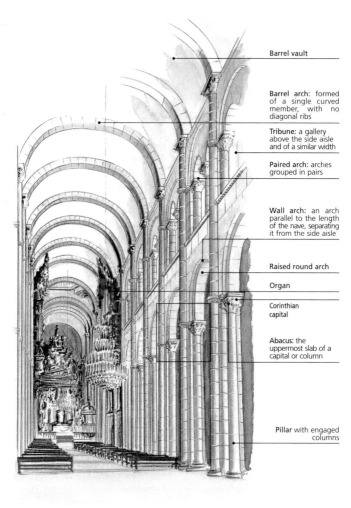

Barrel vault

Barrel arch: formed of a single curved member, with no diagonal ribs

Tribune: a gallery above the side aisle and of a similar width

Paired arch: arches grouped in pairs

Wall arch: an arch parallel to the length of the nave, separating it from the side aisle

Raised round arch

Organ

Corinthian capital

Abacus: the uppermost slab of a capital or column

Pillar with engaged columns

H. Chalmet/MICHELIN

In Aragón, Romanesque art was particularly evident in sculpture. The artists who carved capitals in the manner of their leader, the Maestro de San Juan de la Peña, had a seemingly clumsy style because their emphasis was more on symbolism than realistic portrayal. Disproportionate faces with bulging eyes were the means by which the sculptor illustrated the soul, while gestures such as outstretched hands conveyed religious meaning.

In the early 12C, reform of the **Cistercian Order** with emphasis on austerity brought an important change to architecture. The transitional style which heralded the Gothic (intersecting ribbed vaulting, squared apses) was introduced and the profusion of Romanesque decoration disappeared. Examples of this style may be seen in the monasteries of Poblet, Santes Creus, La Oliva and Santa María de Huerta.

THE GOTHIC PERIOD (FROM THE 13C)

The early stages

French Gothic architecture made little headway into Spain except in Navarra where a French dynasty had been in power since 1234. The first truly Gothic buildings (Roncesvalles church, Cuenca and Sigüenza cathedrals) appeared in the 13C. Bishops in some of the main towns in Castilla (**León** (*see illustration*), Burgos, Toledo) sent abroad for cathedral plans, artists and masons. An original style of church, with no transept, a single nave (aisles, if there were any, would be as high as the nave), and pointed stone arches or a wooden roof resting on diaphragm arches, developed in **Valencia**, **Catalunya** and the **Balearic Islands**. The unadorned walls enclosed a large, homogeneous space in which there was little carved decoration, and purity of line supplied a dignified elegance.

Civil architecture followed the same pattern and had the same geometrical sense of space, used with rare skill particularly in the *lonjas* or commodity exchanges of Barcelona, Palma, Valencia and Zaragoza.

The Gothic style develops

During the 14C and 15C in Castilla, the influence of artists from the north, such as **Johan of Cologne** and **Hanequin of Brussels**, brought about the flowering of a style approaching Flamboyant Gothic. As it adapted to Spain, the style developed simultaneously in two different ways: in one, decoration proliferated to produce the Isabelline style; in the other, structures were simplified into a national church and cathedral style, which remained in favour until the mid-16C (Segovia and **Salamanca**, *see illustration*).

The last of the Gothic cathedrals

Following the example of Sevilla, the dimensions of Gothic cathedrals became ever more vast. Aisles almost as large as the nave increased the volume of the building, while pillars, though massive, retained the impression of thrusting upward lines. A new plan emerged in which the old crescendo of radiating chapels, ambulatory, chancel and transept was superseded by a plain rectangle. Gothic decoration accumulated around doors, on pinnacles and in elaborate star vaulting; a style echoed in some Andalucían cathedrals.

Painting

Artists in the Gothic era worked on polyptyches and altarpieces which sometimes reached a height of more than 15m/49ft.

The Primitives, who customarily painted on gold backgrounds, were influenced by the Italians (soft contours), the French and the Flemish (rich fabrics with broken folds and painstaking detail). Nonetheless, as they strove for expressive naturalism and lively anecdotal detail, their work came across as distinctively Spanish.

There was intense artistic activity in the states attached to the Crown of Aragón, especially in Catalunya. The Vic, Barcelona and Valencia museums contain works by **Jaume Ferrer Bassá** (1285–1348) who was influenced by the Sienese **Duccio**, paintings by his successor **Ramón Destorrents** (1346–91), and by the **Serra** brothers, Destorrents' pupils. Among other artists were **Luis Borrassá** (c. 1360–c. 1425), who had a very Spanish sense of the picturesque, **Bernat Martorell**, who gave special importance to landscape, **Jaime Huguet** (1412–92), who stands out for his extreme sensitivity and is considered to be the undisputed leader of the Catalan School, and finally **Luis Dalmau** and **Bartolomé Bermejo** (c. 1440–c. 1498), both influenced by Van

Gothic

LEÓN – Cathedral: side façade (13C-14C)

In Gothic architecture, light was considered the essence of beauty and the symbol of truth. León cathedral is the brightest and most delicate of all the major Spanish cathedrals and is viewed as the best example of this concept. The beauty and magnificence of its stained glass attracts the admiration of its many thousands of visitors every year. French influence is clearly evident in its ground plan (Reims) and sculptures (Chartres).

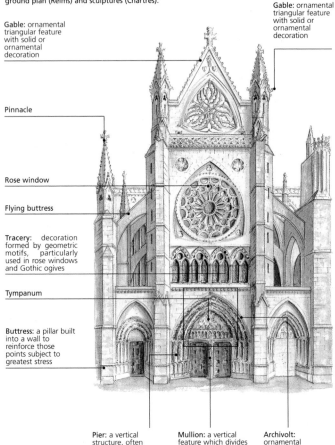

Gable: ornamental triangular feature with solid or ornamental decoration

Gable: ornamental triangular feature with solid or ornamental decoration

Pinnacle

Rose window

Flying buttress

Tracery: decoration formed by geometric motifs, particularly used in rose windows and Gothic ogives

Tympanum

Buttress: a pillar built into a wall to reinforce those points subject to greatest stress

Pier: a vertical structure, often finely decorated, supporting a door or a wall

Mullion: a vertical feature which divides in two the opening or span of a portal or window

Archivolt: ornamental moulding on the outer edge of an arch

H. Choimet/MICHELIN

Eyck (who accompanied a mission sent to Spain by the Duke of Burgundy).

In Castilla, French influence predominated in the 14C and Italian in the 15C until about 1450 when Flemish artists like **Roger van der Weyden** arrived. By the end of the 15C, **Fernando Gallego** had become the main figure in the Hispano-Flemish movement in which **Juan de Flandes** was noted for his appealingly delicate touch.

Sculpture

Gothic sculpture, like architecture, became more refined. Relief was more accentuated than in Romanesque carving, postures more natural and details more meticulous. Decoration grew increasingly abundant as the 15C progressed and faces became individualised to the point where recumbent funerary statues clearly resembled the deceased. Statues were

Isabellin style - Capilla del Condestable in Burgos Cathedral by Simone of Cologne

©World Illustrated/Photoshot

surmounted by an openwork canopy, while door surrounds, cornices and capitals were decorated with friezes of intricate plant motifs. After being enriched by French influence in the 13C and 14C and Flemish in the 15C, sculpture ultimately developed a purely Spanish style, the **Isabelline**.

Portals showed a French influence. Tombs were at first sarcophagi decorated with coats of arms, sometimes surmounted by a recumbent statue in a conventional posture with a peaceful expression and hands joined. Later, more attention was paid to the costume of the deceased; with an increasingly honed technique marble craftsmen were able to render the richness of brocades and the supple quality of leather. In the 15C, sculptors produced lifelike figures in natural positions, kneeling for instance, or even in nonchalant attitudes like that of the remarkable Doncel in Sigüenza Cathedral. Altarpieces comprised a predella or plinth, surmounted by several levels of panels and finally by a carved openwork canopy. Choir stalls were adorned with biblical and historical scenes or carved to resemble delicate stone tracery.

The Isabelline style

At the end of the 15C, the prestige surrounding the royal couple and the grandees in the reign of Isabel the Catholic (1474–1504) provided a favourable context for the emergence of a new style in which exuberant decoration covered entire façades of civil and religious buildings. Ornamentation took the form of supple free arcs, lace-like carving, heraldic motifs and every fantasy that imagination could devise. The diversity of inspiration was largely due to foreign artists: **Simon of Cologne** (son of Johan) – San Pablo in Valladolid, Capilla del Condestable in Burgos; **Juan Guas** (son of the Frenchman Pierre) – San Juan de los Reyes in Toledo; and **Enrique Egas** (nephew of Hanequin of Brussels) – Capilla Real in Granada.

THE RENAISSANCE (16C)

In the 16C, at the dawn of its Golden Age, Spain was swept by a deep sense of its own national character and so created a style in which Italian influence became acceptable only when hispanicised.

Architecture

Plateresque was the name given to the early Renaissance style because of its finely chiselled, lavish decoration reminiscent of silverwork (*platero*: silversmith). Although close to the Isabelline style in its profusion of carved forms extending over entire façades, the rounded arches and ornamental themes (grotesques, foliage, pilasters, medallions and cornices) were Italian. The Plateresque style was brought to a

Plateresque

SALAMANCA – University: façade (16C)

Although the exuberant decoration used to cover the entire façade is somewhat Gothic in style, the motifs used are Classical.

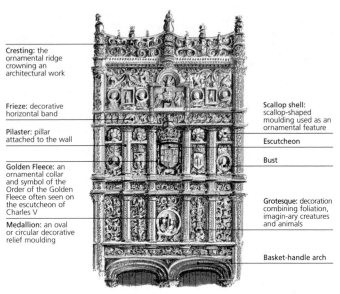

Cresting: the ornamental ridge crowning an architectural work

Frieze: decorative horizontal band

Pilaster: pillar attached to the wall

Golden Fleece: an ornamental collar and symbol of the Order of the Golden Fleece often seen on the escutcheon of Charles V

Medallion: an oval or circular decorative relief moulding

Scallop shell: scallop-shaped moulding used as an ornamental feature

Escutcheon

Bust

Grotesque: decoration combining foliation, imagin-ary creatures and animals

Basket-handle arch

H. Chômet/MICHELIN

climax in **Salamanca** in the **façade of the Universidad** (*see illustration*) and that of the Convento de San Esteban.

Among architects of the time were **Rodrigo Gil de Hontañón**, who worked at Salamanca (Palacios de Monterrey and Fonseca) and at Alcalá de Henares (university façade), and **Diego de Siloé**, the main architect in Burgos (Escalera de la Coronería). Together with **Alonso de Covarrubias** (1488–1570), who worked mainly in Toledo (Alcázar and Capilla de los Reyes Nuevos in the cathedral), Diego de Siloé marked the transition from the Plateresque style to the Classical Renaissance. **Andrés de Vandelvira** (1509–75) was the leading architect of the Andalucían Renaissance (Jaén Cathedral). His work introduces the austerity which was to characterise the last quarter of the century.

The Renaissance style drew upon Italian models and adopted features from Antiquity such as rounded arches, columns, entablatures and pediments. Decoration became of secondary impor-

tance after architectonic perfection. **Pedro Machuca** (c. 1490–1550), who studied under Michelangelo, designed the palace of Charles V in Granada, the most classical example of the Italian tradition. Another important figure, **Bartolomé Bustamante** (1500–70), built the **Hospital de Tavera** in **Toledo** (*see illustration*).

The greatest figure of Spanish Classicism was **Juan de Herrera** (1530–93), who gave his name to an architectural style characterised by grandeur and austerity. He was the favourite architect of Philip II. The king saw in him the sobriety that suited the Counter-Reformation and in 1567 entrusted him with the task of continuing work on El Escorial, his greatest achievement.

Sculpture

Sculpture in Spain reached its climax during the Renaissance. In the 16C, a great many choir stalls, mausoleums and **altarpieces** (also known as **retables**: *see illustration*) were still being made

Renaissance

TOLEDO - Hospital Tavera: patio (16C)

The sense of proportion, visible on both the ground and first floors surrounding the double patio of this hospital, is a typical feature of pure Renaissance style.

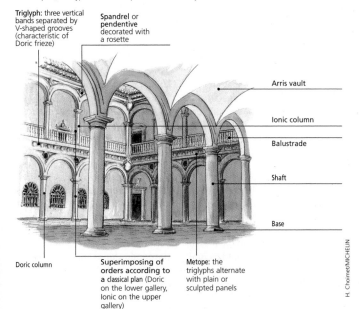

Triglyph: three vertical bands separated by V-shaped grooves (characteristic of Doric frieze)

Spandrel or **pendentive** decorated with a rosette

Arris vault

Ionic column

Balustrade

Shaft

Base

Doric column

Superimposing of orders according to a classical plan (Doric on the lower gallery, Ionic on the upper gallery)

Metope: the triglyphs alternate with plain or sculpted panels

H. Choimet/MICHELIN

of alabaster and wood. These latter were then painted by the *estofado* technique in which gold leaf is first applied, then the object is coloured and finally delicately scored to produce gold highlights. Carved altarpiece panels were framed by Corinthian architraves (epistyles) and pilasters.

The sculptures of **Damián Forment** (c. 1480–1540), who worked mainly in Aragón, belong to the transition period between Gothic and Renaissance styles. The Burgundian **Felipe Vigarny** (c. 1475–1542) and the architect **Diego de Siloé**, who was apprenticed in Naples, both worked on Burgos Cathedral.

Retable or altarpiece

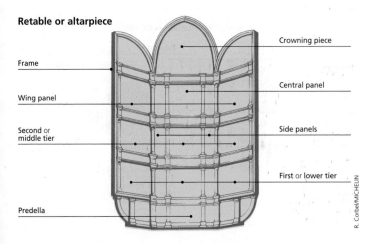

Frame

Wing panel

Second or middle tier

Predella

Crowning piece

Central panel

Side panels

First or lower tier

R. Corbel/MICHELIN

Bartolomé Ordóñez (c. 1480–1520) studied in Naples and carved the *trascoro* (choir screen) in **Barcelona Cathedral** (see illustration) and the mausoleums of Joanna the Mad, Philip the Handsome (Capilla Real in Granada) and Cardinal Cisneros (Alcalá de Henares).

The home of the Renaissance School moved from Burgos to Valladolid in the mid-16C by which time the Spanish style had absorbed foreign influences and Spain's two great Renaissance sculptors had emerged. The first, **Alonso Berruguete** (c. 1488–1561), who studied in Italy under Michelangelo, had a style which drew closely on the Florentine Renaissance and reflected a strong personality. He sought strength of expression rather than formal beauty and his tormented fiery human forms are as powerful as those of his master (statue of San Sebastián in the Museo de Valladolid). The second, **Juan de Juni** (c. 1507–77), a Frenchman who settled in Valladolid, was also influenced by Michelangelo and founded the Catalan School of sculpture. His statues, recognisable by their beauty and the fullness of their forms, anticipated the Baroque style through the dramatic postures they adopted to express sorrow. Many of his works, such as the famous Virgen de los Siete Cuchillos (Virgin of the Seven Knives) in the Iglesia de las Angustias in Valladolid

and the Entombments in the Museo de Valladolid and Segovia Cathedral, were subsequently copied.

Most of the finely worked wrought-iron grilles closing off chapels and *coros* (chancels) were carved in the 15C and 16C. Members of the **Arfe** family, Enrique, Antonio and Juan, stand out in the field of gold and silversmithing. They made the monstrances of Toledo, Santiago de Compostela and Sevilla Cathedrals respectively.

Painting

Under Italian Renaissance influence, Spanish painting in the 16C showed a mastery of perspective, a taste for clarity of composition and glorification of the human body. These features found their way into Spanish painting mainly through the Valencian School where **Fernando Yáñez de la Almedina** and **Hernando Llanos** introduced the style of Leonardo da Vinci, while **Vicente Macip** added that of Raphael and his son **Juan de Juanes** produced Mannerist works. In Sevilla, **Alejo Fernández** painted the famous *Virgin of the Navigators* in the Alcázar. In Castilla, the great master of the late 15C was **Pedro Berruguete** (c. 1450–1503), whose markedly personal style drew upon all the artistic influences in the country. His successor, **Juan de Borgoña**, specialised particularly in landscape,

Ground plan

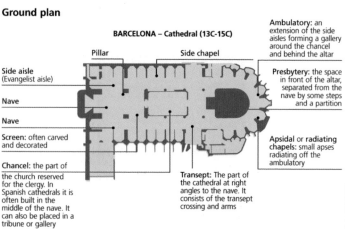

BARCELONA – Cathedral (13C-15C)

Ambulatory: an extension of the side aisles forming a gallery around the chancel and behind the altar

Pillar

Side chapel

Side aisle (Evangelist aisle)

Presbytery: the space in front of the altar, separated from the nave by some steps and a partition

Nave

Nave

Screen: often carved and decorated

Apsidal or radiating chapels: small apses radiating off the ambulatory

Chancel: the part of the church reserved for the clergy. In Spanish cathedrals it is often built in the middle of the nave. It can also be placed in a tribune or gallery

Transept: The part of the cathedral at right angles to the nave. It consists of the transept crossing and arms

R. Corbel/MICHELIN

architecture and decorative motifs. Another artist, **Pedro de Campaña** from Brussels, used *chiaroscuro* to dramatic effect while **Luis de Morales** (c. 1520–86), a Mannerist, gave his work a human dimension through the portrayal of feelings. Ordinary people with religious sentiments responded favourably to the spiritual emotion expressed in his paintings. At the end of the 16C, Philip II sent for a great many Italian or Italian-trained artists to paint pictures for El Escorial. During his reign he introduced portrait painting under the Dutchman **Antonio Moro** (c. 1519–c. 1576), his cohort **Alonso Sánchez Coello** (1531–88) and **Juan Pantoja de la Cruz** (1553–1608). **El Greco** (1541–1614), on the other hand, was scorned by the court and settled in Toledo.

BAROQUE (17C–18C)

Spanish art reached its apogee in the mid-17C. Baroque met with outstanding success in its role as an essentially religious art in the service of the Counter-Reformation and was particularly evident in Andalucía, then enriched by trade with America.

Architecture

Architects in the early 17C were still under the influence of 16C Classicism and the Herreran style to which they added decorative details. Public buildings proliferated and many continued to be built throughout the Baroque period. Public buildings of the time in Madrid include the plaza Mayor by **Juan Gómez de Mora**, built shortly before the *ayuntamiento* (town hall), and the most significant building of all, the present Ministerio de Asuntos Exteriores (Ministry of Foreign Affairs) by **Juan Bautista Crescenzi**, the architect of the Panteón de Reyes at El Escorial. Church architecture of the period showed greater freedom from Classicism. A style of Jesuit church, with a cruciform plan and a large transept that served to light up altarpieces, began to emerge. Madrid has several examples including the Iglesia de San Isidro by the Jesuits **Pedro**

Virgin and the Child (16C) by Luis de Morales, Museo Nacional del Prado

Photo ©White Images/Photo Scala, Florence

Sánchez and **Francisco Bautista**, and the Real Convento de la Encarnación by **Juan Gómez de Mora**. In the middle of the century, architects adopted a less rigid style, changing plans and façades, breaking up entablatures and making pediments more elaborate. A good example of this Italian Baroque style is the Iglesia Pontificia de San Miguel (18C) in Madrid. A new feature, the **camarín**, was introduced: at first simply a passage behind the high altar leading to the retable niche containing a statue venerated by the faithful, it developed into a highly ornate chapel. Decoration of this kind may be seen in Zaragoza's Basílica de Nuestra Señora del Pilar designed by **Francisco Herrera el Mozo** (1622–85). The Clerecía in Salamanca is a magnificent Baroque creation with a patio that anticipates the audacity and superabundant decoration characteristic of the Churrigueresque style.

The Churrigueresque style

In this style, named after the Churriguera family of architects (late 17C), architecture became no more than a support for dense concentrations of ornament covering entire façades. The style is typified by the use of *salomónicas*, or barley sugar columns entwined with vines, and *estípites*, or pilasters arranged in an inverse pyramid.

Baroque

MADRID – Museo Municipal (Antiguo Hospicio): portal (18C)

The Baroque retable or altarpiece, which reached new architectural heights in Spain, was occasionally created on the façade of a building, rather than inside it.

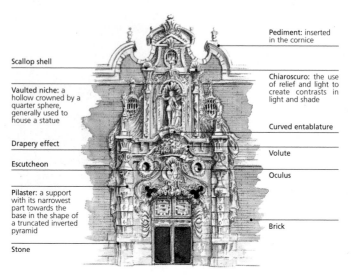

Scallop shell

Vaulted niche: a hollow crowned by a quarter sphere, generally used to house a statue

Drapery effect

Escutcheon

Pilaster: a support with its narrowest part towards the base in the shape of a truncated inverted pyramid

Stone

Pediment: inserted in the cornice

Chiaroscuro: the use of relief and light to create contrasts in light and shade

Curved entablature

Volute

Oculus

Brick

H. Choimet/MICHELIN

Early examples of this extravagance, the altarpiece of the Convento de San Esteban in Salamanca and the palace in Nuevo Baztán near Madrid, were by **José de Churriguera** (1665–1725), who was the instigator of the style but did not make any architectural changes. His brothers **Joaquín** (1674–1724) and especially **Alberto** (1676–1750), who designed the plaza Mayor in Salamanca, took greater liberties in their work. **Pedro de Ribera** (1681–1742), a Castilian architect who worked mainly in Madrid, surpassed the Churriguera brothers in decorative delirium. The other great Castilian, **Narciso Tomé**, is remembered for the façade of the Universidad de Valladolid (1715) and particularly for the *Transparente* in Toledo Cathedral (1721–32).

Regional variations

The popularity of the Baroque spread countrywide, differing from province to province. In **Galicia**, where the hardness of the granite precluded delicate carving, Baroque took the form of softer lines and decorative mouldings. The best example of the style was by **Fernando de Casas Novoa**, who designed the Obradoiro façade of Santiago de Compostela Cathedral (1750) at the end of his life. In **Andalucía**, Baroque attained its utmost splendour, especially in decoration. Undulating surfaces characterised the façades of palaces (Écija), cathedrals (Guadix) and the doorways of countless churches and mansions (Jerez) in the 18C. As well as sculptor and painter, **Alonso Cano** was the instigator of Andalucían Baroque and designed the façade of Granada Cathedral. The major exponent of the style was, however, **Vicente Acero**, who worked on the façade of Guadix Cathedral (1714–20), designed Cádiz Cathedral and built the tobacco factory in Sevilla. Mention should also be made of **Leonardo de Figueroa** (1650–1730) for the Palacio de San Telmo in Sevilla and **Francisco Hurtado** (1669–1725) and **Luis de Arévalo** for La Cartuja in Granada; Hurtado worked on the monastery's tabernacle and Arévalo on the sacristy, the most exuberant Baroque works in Andalucía.

Las Meninas (1656) by Diego Velázquez, Museo Nacional del Prado

©World Illustrated/Photoshot

In the **Levante**, Baroque artists used polychrome tiles to decorate church cupolas and spires like that of Santa Catalina in Valencia. In the same town, the Palacio del Marqués de Dos Aguas by **Luis Domingo** and **Ignacio Vergara** is reminiscent of façades by Ribera, although its design is more like French Rococo. The cathedral in Murcia has an impressive façade by **Jaime Bort y Meliá**.

The golden age of Spanish painting

This was characterised by the rejection of the previous century's Mannerism and the adoption of Naturalism. The starting point was Caravaggio's tenebrism, powerful contrasts of light and shade, and his stern realism. Painters took up portraiture and still life *(bodegón)*, while allegories on the theme of *vanitas* (still-life paintings showing the ephemerality of life) reflected a philosophical purpose by juxtaposing everyday objects with symbols of decay to illustrate the transience of wealth and the things of this world and the inevitability of death. Among 17C artists were two from the Valencian School – **Francisco Ribalta** (1565–1628), who introduced tenebrism into Spain, and **José de Ribera** (1591–1652), known for his forceful realism. Some of the greatest Baroque artists worked in Andalucía. One was **Francisco de Zurbarán** (1598–1664), master of the Sevilla School; light in his paintings springs from within the subjects themselves. Other artists included **Bartolomé Esteban Murillo** (1617–82), who painted intimate, mystical scenes, and **Valdés de Valdés Leal** whose powerful realism clearly challenged earthly vanities. **Alonso Cano** (1601–67),

83

architect, painter and sculptor, settled in Granada and painted delicate figures of the Virgin.

The Castilian painters of the century, **Vicente Carducho** (c. 1576–1638) and the portraitists **Juan Carreño de Miranda** (1614–85) and **Claudio Coello** (1642–93), all excellent artists, nonetheless pale beside **Diego Velázquez** (1599–1660). His aerial perspective and outstanding sense of depth are beyond compare.

Sculpture

Spanish Baroque sculpture was naturalistic and intensely emotive. The most commonly used medium was wood, and while altarpieces continued to be carved, *pasos* or statues specially made for Semana Santa processions proved a great novelty.

The two major schools of Baroque sculpture were in Castilla and Andalucía. **Gregorio Hernández**, Juni's successor, worked in Valladolid, the Castilian centre. His style was a lot more natural than that of his master, and his Christ Recumbent for the Convento de Capuchinos in El Pardo was widely copied. Sevilla and Granada were the main centres for the Andalucían School. **Juan Martínez Montañés** (1568–1649) settled in Sevilla and worked exclusively in wood, carving a great many *pasos* and various altarpieces. **Alonso Cano** became

Detail of Mary Magdalene (17C) by Pedro de Mena, Museo Nacional Colegio de San Gregorio, Valladolid

Photo Scala, Florence

famous for the grace and femininity of his Immaculate Conceptions while his best-known disciple, **Pedro de Mena**, produced sculptures of great dramatic tension which contrasted with his master's understated style. The statue of Mary Magdalene (Museo Nacional de Escultura Policromada, Valladolid), St Francis (Toledo Cathedral) and the Dolorosa (Monasterio de las Descalzas Reales, Madrid) are telling examples of his work.

The 18C saw the rise to prominence of the great Murcian, **Francisco Salzillo**, whose dramatic sculptures were inspired by Italian Baroque.

Churrigueresque excess in sculpture took the form of immense altarpieces which reached the roof. These huge constructions took on such grand proportions that they began to be designed by architects. Their statues seemed smothered by decoration, lost in an overabundance of gilding and stucco.

BOURBON ART

Austrian imperialism was succeeded by enlightened Bourbon despotism which resulted in artistic as well as political change in the 18C. Henceforth the rules of art were to be governed by official bodies like the Academia de Bellas Artes de San Fernando.

Architecture

During the first half of the century architecture still bore the stamp of Spanish Baroque, itself influenced at the time by French Rococo. The king and queen had palaces built in a moderate Baroque style (El Pardo, Riofrío, La Granja and Aranjuez) and began work on Madrid's Palacio Real modelled on Versailles. These buildings sought to ally French Classical harmony with Italian grace, and to this end most of the work was entrusted to Italian architects who generally respected the traditional quadrangular plan of *alcázares*, so typically Spanish. The vast gardens were given a French design.

Excavations of Pompeii and Herculaneum contributed to the emergence

Neo-Classical

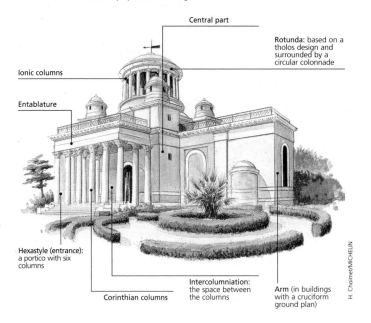

MADRID - Observatório Astronómico (18C)

This small building designed by Juan de Villanueva is a model of simplicity and purity which shows clear Palladian influence in its proportions and design.

Central part

Rotunda: based on a tholos design and surrounded by a circular colonnade

Ionic columns

Entablature

Hexastyle (entrance): a portico with six columns

Corinthian columns

Intercolumniation: the space between the columns

Arm (in buildings with a cruciform ground plan)

H. Choimet/MICHELIN

of a new, Neoclassical style which flourished between the second half of the 18C and 19C. It repudiated Baroque excess and aspired to Hellenistic beauty through the use of Classical orders, pediments, porticoes and cupolas. The Kings of Spain, Charles III in particular, set about embellishing the capital by building fountains (Cibeles, Neptune), gates (Alcalá and Toledo), and planting botanic gardens.

The first Spanish Neoclassical architect, **Ventura Rodríguez** (1717–85), who was actually apprenticed in Italian Baroque, quickly developed an academic Neoclassical style. His works include the façade of Pamplona Cathedral, the paseo del Prado in Madrid and the Basílica de Nuestra Señora del Pilar in Zaragoza. **Francesco Sabatini** (1722–97), whose style developed along similar lines, designed the Puerta de Alcalá and the building that now houses the Ministerio de Hacienda (Ministry of Finance) in Madrid. The leading

architect was without doubt **Juan de Villanueva** (1739–1811), schooled in Classical principles during a stay in Rome. He designed the façade of the *ayuntamiento* in Madrid, the Casita del Príncipe at El Escorial and most importantly, the **Museo del Prado**. Two notable town planners emerged during the 19C: **Ildefonso Cerdá** in Barcelona and **Arturo Soria** (1844–1920) in Madrid.

Painting

Bourbon monarchs took pains to attract the greatest painters to court and grant them official positions. In 1752 Ferdinand VI founded the Academia de Bellas Artes de San Fernando where it was intended that students should learn official painting techniques and study the Italian masters. Leading artists of the time were **Anton Raphael Mengs** (1728–79) from Bohemia and the Italian **Giambattista Tiepolo** (1696–1770), both of whom decorated the Palacio

The Third of May (1814) by Francisco de Goya, Museo Nacional del Prado

©Imagestate/Tips Images

Real. There was also **Francisco Bayeu** (1734–95) from Aragón, who painted a great many tapestry cartoons, as did his brother-in-law **Francisco de Goya** (1746–1828). Goya's work, much of which may be seen in the Prado, Madrid, was to dominate the entire century.

Painters working in the post-Goya period did not follow in the master's footsteps as academic Neoclassical influences and Romanticism took over; Goya's legacy was not taken up until the end of the 19C. The following stand out among artists of the academic Romantic trend: **Federico de Madrazo**, representative of official taste in royal portraits and historical scenes, **Vicente Esquivel**, portrait-painter, and lastly **Leonardo Alenza**, and **Eugenio Lucas Velázquez**, the spokesmen for **Costumbrismo**, which had attained full status as a genre. (This was a style of painting illustrating scenes of everyday life which gradually developed from the simply anecdotal to a higher calling, the evocation of the Spanish soul.) Historical themes became very popular in the 19C with works by **José Casado del Alisal**, **Eduardo Rosales** and **Mariano Fortuny**.

Impressionist features began to appear in naturalist paintings by **Ramón Martí Alsina** and in post-Romantic landscapes by **Carlos de Haes**. The style secured a definitive hold in the works of **Narciso Oller**, **Ignacio Pinazo Camarlench**, the best Valencian Impressionist, **Darío de Regoyos** and lastly, **Joaquín Sorolla**, who specialised in light-filled folk scenes and regional subjects.

The Basque artist **Ignacio Zuloaga** (1870–1945) expressed his love for Spain in brightly coloured scenes of everyday life at a time when Impressionism was conquering Europe.

The Decorative Arts

Factories were built under the Bourbons to produce decorative material for their royal palaces. In 1760, Charles III founded the Buen Retiro works, where ceramics for the famous Salones de Porcelana in the royal palaces of Aranjuez and Madrid were made. The factory was destroyed during the Napoleonic invasion.

In 1720, Philip V opened the Real Fábrica de Tapices de Santa Bárbara (in Madrid), the equivalent of the French Gobelins factory in Paris. Some of the tapestries were of Don Quixote while others depicted scenes of everyday life based on preparatory cartoons by Bayeu and Goya.

20C ART

From Modernism to Surrealism

The barren period that Spanish art in general experienced at the end of the 19C was interrupted in Catalunya by a vast cultural movement known as **Modernism**. This was particularly strong

Modernist

BARCELONA –Casa Batlló (Antoni Gaudí: 1905-07)

Modernism is a colourful, decorative and sensual style which recreates organic forms in a world dominated by curves and reverse curves.

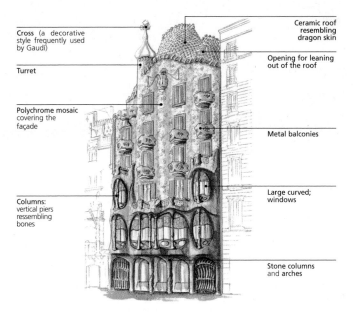

Cross (a decorative style frequently used by Gaudí)

Turret

Polychrome mosaic covering the façade

Columns: vertical piers ressembling bones

Ceramic roof resembling dragon skin

Opening for leaning out of the roof

Metal balconies

Large curved; windows

Stone columns and arches

Mediterranean Rationalist

BARCELONA – Fundació Joan Miró (JL Sert: 1972-75)

The building consists of a series of interrelated architectural features and open spaces in which natural light plays a fundamental role.

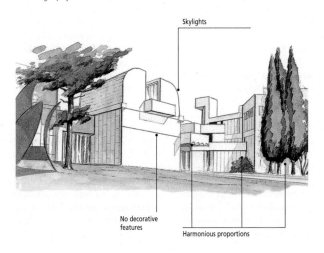

Skylights

No decorative features

Harmonious proportions

F. Vidal/MICHELIN

Inverted cupola of polychrome glass in the concert hall, Palau de la Música Catalana in Barcelona, designed by Domènech i Montaner

in architecture, with outstanding work by **Antoni Gaudí**, **Lluís Domènech i Montaner** and **Josep Maria Jujol**.

In the field of sculpture, **Pablo Gargallo** broke new ground through the simplicity of his shapes, the attention he gave to volume and the use of new materials like iron.

Painting was varied and prolific. The following stand out among the many artists of the time: **Ramón Casas**, the best Spanish Impressionist, whose works are suffused with an atmosphere of grey melancholy, **Santiago Rusiñol**, **Isidro Nonell**, instigator of Spanish Expressionism, and **Pablo Picasso** (1881–1973), the dominant figure whose innovations were to mark the entire history of 20C painting.

Picasso's attention was first devoted to academic Naturalism *(Science and Charity)*. He subsequently became a Modernist and social Expressionist. Later, once he had moved to Paris (1904), his style developed through the successive blue and rose periods to Cubism *(Les Demoiselles d'Avignon)*, Surrealism and Expressionism *(Guernica)*, which in turn led to a totally personal and subjective lyrical style *(La Joie de Vivre)*.

In the 1920s a movement began to emerge that was influenced by Cubism and, more particularly, by Surrealism. Its sculptors were **Ángel Ferrant**, **Victorio Macho**, **Alberto Sánchez Pérez** and lastly **Julio González**, who strove towards Abstract Expressionism through the use of iron and simple shapes. Painters of the movement included **Daniel Vázquez Díaz**, Juan Gris, Joan Miró and Salvador Dalí. **Juan Gris** (1887–1927), the most faithful analytical Cubist, worked in Paris. The works of **Joan Miró** (1893–1983), champion of Surrealism, are characterised by childlike spontaneity and an original attitude to everyday objects. Miró used very bright colours and magic symbols in all his paintings; today the Fundació Joan Miró in Barcelona houses her works (see illustration). **Salvador Dalí** (1904–89), a quasi-Surrealist, dreamed up his own creative method which he called the paranoic critical. Some of his best paintings were a result of his interest in the subconscious and his vision of a dream world. All his works attest to an excellent drawing technique and many show an attention to detail worthy of the best miniaturists.

Post-war art

Spanish art was crucially affected by the Civil War in two ways: firstly, the fact that several artists went into exile meant that the country suffered cultural loss, and secondly, official taste in architecture developed a penchant for the monumental. This is clearly apparent in a number of colossal edifices. Many government buildings, all in Madrid, were designed in the manner of El Escorial, including the Ministerio del Aire, the Museo de América, the Arco del Triunfo and the Consejo de Investigaciones Científicas. The most striking example is the monument of the Valle de los Caídos (Valley of the Fallen) outside Madrid. However, among exponents of the Nationalist style, there were several innovative architects like **Miguel Fisac**.

In 1950 the first signs of a new style, based on rational and functional criteria, began to emerge. Examples abound in Barcelona, including the Vanguardia building by **Oriol Bohigas** and **José María Martorell**, the residential block by **Ricardo Bofill Leví** in carrer de Nicaragua, and in Madrid, the Colegio Monfort by **Antonio Fernandez Alba**, the Maravillas secondary school (*gimnasio*) by **Alejandro de la Sota** and the Torres Blancas (White Towers) by **Francisco Javier Sáenz de Oíza**.

Post-war sculpture and painting are basically academic but there are some notable artists such as **José Gutiérrez Solana**, whose paintings are full of anguish, and the landscape painters **Benjamín Palencia**, who glorifies the country and light of Castilla, and **Rafael Zabaleta**, who is more interested in painting the region's country folk.

Avant-Garde painters also began to emerge after the war. The first post-war Surrealists are members of a group called **Dau al Set** including **Modest Cuixart**, **Antoni Tàpies** and **Joan-Josep Tharrats**. Tàpies is a veritable pioneer, one of the major abstract artists.

New artistic trends

In the 1950s two abstract groups, with different qualities but with the common aim of artistic innovation, were formed: the **El Paso** group in Madrid with **Antonio Saura**, **Manolo Millares**, **Rafael Canogar**, **Luis Feito**, **Manuel Viola** and **Martín Chirino**, all representatives of what was known as action painting; and the **Equipo 57** group in Cuenca with **Ángel Duarte**, **Agustín Ibarrola**, **Juan Serrano** and

José Duarte, who were more interested in drawing. The movement's sculptors included **Jorge Oteiza**, **Andreu Alfaro** and lastly **Eduardo Chillida**, who worked in iron and wood and stripped his sculptures of any figurative suggestion.

SPANISH GARDENS

The gardens of Spain are a further example of the country's rich culture, and bear witness to an enviable ability to adapt to a varied climate. Although Spanish landscape gardening has inherited many of its traditions from within Europe, particularly from the Greco-Roman era, the long period of Moorish occupation added a completely new dimension to the country's landscape.

THE GENERALIFE (14C), GRANADA

The Moors were truly gifted gardeners. The Generalife is *the* Moorish garden par excellence, despite the alterations it has undergone over the centuries. As a result of its extraordinary position it is a magnificent balcony, but above all it has been able to preserve an intimate, sensual character which was such a feature of Muslim gardens.

El Generalife, Granada

H. Le Gac/MICHELIN

A Moorish garden is always an evocation of paradise; it is a feast for the senses and a harmonious whole which avoids grandiloquence. Nothing has been left to chance: the colour of the plants and flowers, their scent, and the omnipresence of water combine to create a serene ambience full of intimate charm. The Generalife has been laid out on several levels to ensure that the trees in one garden do not interfere with the views from another. In fact, the Generalife is a series of landscaped areas and enclosures each with its own individuality yet part of an overall design. The garden's architectural features and vegetation, reflected in the water channels, blend together to create a perfect whole.

LA GRANJA (18C), LA GRANJA DE SAN ILDEFONSO, SEGOVIA

Once he came to the Spanish throne, Philip V, the grandson of Louis XIV, chose a beautiful spot in the Segovian countryside at the foot of the Sierra de Guadarrama to create these magnificent Baroque gardens. They bring to mind those of Versailles, where the monarch spent his childhood. Philip V was to make La Granja his personal retreat.

Although the Versailles influence is clearly evident, the differences are also obvious. Because of its position, hemmed in by the mountains, the grandiose perspectives of Versailles are not to be found at La Granja.

The rigidity of the French garden is also lost here as there is no clear central axis; instead, La Granja consists of a succession of parts each with a certain independence, thus adopting hints of Moorish design. Although the gardeners brought with them a variety of species from France, they were able to adapt perfectly to the features of the local landscape and to preserve the somewhat wild appearance which gives it an undoubted charm. Magnificent fountains and sculptures scattered in small squares and along avenues add a theatrical touch.

PAZO DE OCA (18C–19C), LA ESTRADA, LA CORUÑA

A *pazo* is a Baroque-style manor typically found in Galicia. These large rustic residences are built on plots of land which generally comprise a recreational garden, a kitchen garden and cultivated farmland.

The Pazo de Oca garden, the oldest in Galicia, is a magnificent example of a garden in the wet part of Spain. What comes as a complete surprise is its perfect integration into its surroundings, where the damp climate has enabled vegetation to grow on rocks, creating an intimate relationship between its architectural and vegetal features.

Jardín La Granja de San Ildefonso, Segovia

©Fotosearch

Pazo de Oca, La Coruña

B. Brillon/MICHELIN

Water plays a vital role, appearing in basins or fountains or trickling through the garden. The most attractive part, with its two ponds, is hidden behind a parterre. A delightful bridge, with benches enabling visitors to enjoy this enchanting spot, separates the two sections, overcoming the difference in height between them. The lower pond contains the *pazo*'s most representative and famous feature: the stone boat, with its two petrified sailors, planted with hydrangeas.

The combination of both climate and vegetation gives the site an unquestionably romantic air.

JARDÍN BOTÁNICO DE MARIMURTRA (20C), BLANES, GIRONA

Carlos Faust, the German impresario who settled on the Costa Brava, created this botanical garden in 1921 for research purposes to enable scientists to carry out studies on flora, and to catalogue and preserve plants threatened with extinction. It is situated in a delightful spot between the sea and the mountains and offers visitors magnificent views of the coast.

Marimurtra is a fine example of a contemporary Mediterranean garden, although a number of exotic species from every continent have also adapted perfectly here. It contains an interesting cactus garden, an impressive aquatic garden, as well as a collection of medicinal, toxic and aromatic plants. The scientific aims of the garden have not interfered in any way with the

aesthetic direction it has taken. The only architectural feature with a purely decorative function is the small temple built at the end of the steps running down to the sea.

At present, 5ha/12 acres of Marimurtra is open to the public.

LITERATURE

Errant knights, Don Juan characters, mystics and highwaymen occupy a hallowed place in Spanish letters. Spanish literature reached its peak during the Golden Age of the 16C and 17C, and has enjoyed a renewed period of acclaim since the beginning of the 20C, through the works of a new generation of writers from within Spain and across the Spanish-speaking world.

Roman Spain produced great Latin authors such as **Seneca the Elder** or the Rhetorician, his son **Seneca the Younger** or the Philosopher, Quintilian the Rhetorician, and the epic poet **Lucan**. In the 8C, the monk **Beatus** wrote the Commentary on the Apocalypse, which gave rise to a series of outstanding illuminated manuscripts known as Beatus. Arab writers won renown during the same period. Works written in Castilian began to emerge only in the Middle Ages.

Jardín Botánico de Marimurtra, Blanes, Girona

©Turespaña

Statues of Don Quixote, Sancho Panza and Miguel de Cervantes, Plaza de España, Madrid

THE MIDDLE AGES

The first milestone of Spanish literature appeared in the 12C in the form of *El Cantar del Mío Cid*, an anonymous Castilian poem inspired by the adventures of El Cid. In the 13C, the monk **Gonzalo de Berceo**, drawing on religious themes, won renown through his works of *Mester de Clerecía*, the learned poetry of clerics and scholars. **Alfonso X the Wise**, an erudite king who wrote poetry in Galician, decreed that in his kingdom, Latin should be replaced as the official language by Castilian, an act subsequently followed throughout Spain except in Catalunya where Catalan remained the written language.

In the 14C, **Don Juan Manuel** introduced the use of narrative prose in his moral tales while **Juan Ruiz, Archpriest of Hita**, wrote a brilliant satirical verse work titled *El Libro de Buen Amor*, which later influenced the picaresque novel.

THE RENAISSANCE

In the 15C, lyric poetry flourished under Italian influence with poets such as **Jorge Manrique** and the **Marquis of Santillana. Romanceros**, collections of ballads in an epic or popular vein, perpetuated the medieval style until the 16C when *Amadís de Gaula* (1508) set the model for a great many romances or tales of chivalry. In 1499, *La Celestina*, a novel of passion in dialogue form by **Fernando de Rojas**, anticipated modern drama in a subtle, well-observed tragicomic intrigue.

THE GOLDEN AGE (SIGLO DE ORO)

Spain enjoyed its greatest literary flowering under the Habsburgs (1516–1700), with great lyric poets such as **Garcilaso de la Vega**, disciple of Italian verse forms, **Fray Luis de León** and above all **Luis de Góngora y Argote** (1561–1627) whose obscure, precious style won fame under the name of Gongorism. Pastoral novels became popular with works by Cervantes and Lope de Vega. The **picaresque** novel, however, was the genre favoured by Spanish writers at the time. The first to appear in 1554 was *Lazarillo de Tormes*, an anonymous autobiographical work in which the hero, an astute rogue (*pícaro* in Castilian), casts a mischievous and impartial eye on society and its woes. There followed **Mateo Alemán**'s *Guzmán de Alfarache* with its brisk style and colourful vocabulary, and *La Vida del Buscón*, an example of the varied talents of **Francisco de Quevedo** (1580–1645), essayist, poet and satirist. The genius of the Golden Age, however, was **Miguel de Cervantes** (1547–1616), with his masterpiece, the universal **Don Quixote** (1605). **Lope de Rueda** paved the way for *comedia*, which emerged at the end of the 16C. Dramatists proliferated, among them the master **Lope de Vega** (1562–1635), who perfected and enriched the art form. This "phoenix of the mind" wrote more than 1 000 plays on the most diverse subjects. His successor, **Pedro Calderón de la Barca** (1600–81), wrote historical and philosophical plays (*La vida es sueño* or *Life's a Dream* and *El alcalde de Zalamea* or *The Mayor of Zalamea*) in which he brilliantly reflects the mood of Spain in the 17C. **Tirso de Molina** (1579–1648) left his interpretation of Don Juan for posterity while **Guillén de Castro** wrote *Las Mocedades del Cid (Youthful Adventures of the Cid)*. Mention should also be made of works on the conquest of America by **Cortés** and **Bartolomé de las Casas** among others. Finally, the moralist **Fray Luis de Granada** and the mystics **Santa Teresa de Ávila** (1515–82) and **San Juan de la Cruz** (St John of the Cross) (1542–91) wrote theological works.

18C AND 19C

The critical mode found expression in the works of essayists such as **Benito Jerónimo Feijoo** and **Jovellanos**, while elegance dominated the plays of **Moratín**. The great romantic poet of the 19C was **Bécquer** (1836–70) from Sevilla, while **Larra** was a social satirist, **Menéndez Pelayo** a literary critic and **Ángel Ganivet** a political and moral analyst. Realism was introduced to the Spanish novel by **Alarcón** *(The Three-Cornered Hat)* and **Pereda** *(Peñas arriba)* who concentrated on regional themes. By the end of the 19C, the best realist was **Pérez Galdós** whose prolific, lively work *(National Episodes)* is stamped with a great sense of human sympathy.

20C

A group of intellectuals known as the Generation of '98, saddened by Spain's loss of colonies like Cuba, pondered over the future and character of their country and, more generally, the problems of human destiny. The atmosphere was reflected in the work of essayists such as **Miguel de Unamuno** (1864–1936) who wrote *El Sentimiento trágico de la vida (The Tragic Sense of Life)*, and **Azorín**, as well as the philologist **Menéndez Pidal**, the novelist **Pío Baroja** and the aesthete **Valle Inclán**, who created an elegant poetic prose style. Among their contemporaries were **Jacinto Benavente** (winner of the 1922 Nobel Prize for literature), who developed a new dramatic style, and the novelist **Vicente Blasco Ibáñez**. Henceforth Spain opened up to literary contributions from abroad.

Some great poets began to emerge, including **Juan Ramón Jiménez** (Nobel Prize 1956), who expressed his feelings through simple unadorned prose poems *(Platero y Yo)*, **Antonio Machado** (1875–1939), the bard of Castilla, and **Rafael Alberti**. **Federico García Lorca** (1898–1936) equally great as both poet and dramatist *(Bodas de Sangre)*, was Andalucían through and through. His work was, perhaps, the most fascinating reflection of a Spain whose mystery **José Ortega y Gasset** (1883–1955), essayist and philosopher, spent his life trying to fathom.

POST-WAR WRITING

Several years after the Civil War, writing rose from its ashes with works by essayists **(Américo Castro)**, playwrights **(Alfonso Sastre)** and, above all, novelists such as **Miguel Delibes**, **Camilo José Cela** *(La Familia de Pascual Duarte)* who won the Nobel Prize for Literature in 1989, **Juan Goytisolo**, **Ramón Sender** and **Antonio Ferres**, all preoccupied with social issues.

Among contemporary authors, mention should be made of novelists **Juan Benet**, **Juan Marsé**, **Manuel Vázquez Montalbán**, **Terenci Moix**, **Javier Marías** and **Eduardo Mendoza**, and playwrights **Antonio Gala**, **Fernando Arrabal** and **Francisco Nieva**.

©The Bettmann Archive/Corbis

Luis Buñuel

CINEMA AND MUSIC

Over the centuries, Spain has produced countless musicians and thespians of world renown. In more recent times, the genius of film directors such as **Luis Buñuel**, **Juan Antonio Bardem** and **Pedro Almodóvar**, composers such as **Manuel de Falla**, and classical guitarists such as **Antonio Segovia**, have thrilled audiences the world over.

CINEMA

Spanish cinema dates back to a short film in 1897 which shows people leaving the Basílica de Nuestra Señora del Pilar in Zaragoza after Mass. Studios for silent movies were later set up in Barcelona. In the 1920s, several Surrealists tried their hand at the new art form. Among them were **Dalí** and above all **Luis Buñuel**, a master of Spanish cinema, who made *Un chien Andalou (An Andalusian Dog)* in 1928 and *Âge d'Or (The Golden Age)* in 1930. When talking films appeared in the 1930s, Spain was in the throes of a political and economic crisis and so her studios lacked the means to procure the necessary equipment.

At the end of the 1930s, when films like *Sor Angélica (Sister Angelica)* by **Francisco Gargallo** tended to address religious themes, Juan Piqueras launched a magazine called *Nuestro Cinema*, which was strongly influenced by Russian ideas, and gave star billing to films such as *Las Hurdes (Land Without Bread)* by Buñuel in 1932, depicting poverty in a remote part of Spain.

During the Civil War and the ensuing Franco era, films were heavily censored and the cinema became one of the major vehicles for the ideology of the time, with historical and religious themes glorifying death and the spirit of sacrifice. One such success was *Marcelino Pan y Vino (The Miracle of Marcelino)* by Ladislao Vajda in 1955. Change came with works by Juan Antonio Bardem like *Muerte de un Ciclista (Death of a Cyclist)* and with Berlanga's *Bienvenido Mister Marshall (Welcome Mr Marshall*, 1953) and *El Verdugo (The Executioner*, 1963).

The 1960s enjoyed a period of renewal with directors like **Carlos Saura**, whose first film, *Los Golfos (The Delinquents)*, came out in 1960. More than ever before, the 1970s saw a new wave in Spanish cinema with outstanding directors and films. These were mainly concerned with the problems of childhood and youth marked by the Franco régime. Saura's *Cría Cuervos (Raise Ravens*, 1976) shows two orphans reflecting on the death of their parents personify the all-powerful hold of the army and religion during the Franco era. Mention should also be made of Saura's *Ana y los Lobos (Anna and the Wolves*, 1973); *El Espíritu de la colmena (The Spirit of the Beehive*, 1973) and *El Sur (The South*, 1983) both by **Víctor Erice**; *La Colmena (The Beehive*, 1982) by **Mario Camus**, and films by **Manuel Gutiérrez Aragón** such as *Demonios en el jardín (Demons in the Garden*, 1982) and *La Mitad del cielo (Half of Heaven*, 1986) which illustrate the economic changes between Spain under Franco and Spain as a democracy. **Pedro Almodóvar** breaks with this serious, nostalgic type of cinema so critical of the Franco era. His films are of a completely different, modern Spain is shown in a comic light, but not without an edgy criticism, as in *Mujeres al Borde de un Ataque de Nervios (Women on the Verge of a Nervous Breakdown*, 1988), *Carne trémula (Live Flesh*, 1997) and *Hable con ella (Talk to Her;* 2002).

Four Spanish films have won the Oscar for Best Foreign Film: *Volver a empezar (To Begin Again*, 1982), directed by **José Luis Garci**; **Fernando Trueba's** *Belle epoque (The Age of Beauty*, 1992); *Todo sobre mi madre (All About My Mother*, 1999), by **Pedro Almodóvar**; and *Mar adentro (The Sea Inside*, 2004) by **Alejandro Amenábar**.

There has been a resurgence in Spanish cinema in recent years with directors such as **Bigas Luna** (*Jamón, Jamón*, 1992), **Alejandro Amenábar** (*Tesis*, 1996 and *Abre los ojos*, 1997), **Julio Medem** (*Los Amantes del Círculo Polar*, 1998; *Tierra*, 1996), **Icíar Bollaín** (*Te doy mis ojos, 2003) and **Isabel Coixet** (*La Vida secreta de las Palabras*, 2005). This development has resulted in huge box office triumphs, such as *El Perro del hortelano* (*The Dog in the Manger*, 1996) by the late **Pilar Miró**, and *Secretos del Corazón* (*Secrets of the Heart*, 1997) by **Montxo Armendáriz**. Other successful films of recent years include *Barrio* (1998) by **Fernando León de Aranoa**, *Solas* (*Alone*, 1999) by **Benito Zambrano**, *El Laberinto del Fauno* (*Pan's Labyrinth*, 2006) by the Mexican director Guillermo del Toro, and *La Soledad* (*Solitary Fragments*, 2007) by **Jaime Rosales**.

MUSIC

Alongside its folk music, Spain has developed an extraordinarily rich musical repertory since the Middle Ages, marked by a large number of influences including Visigothic, Arabic, Mozarabic and French. Polyphonic chants were studied in the 11C and the oldest known piece for three voices, the *Codex calixtinus*, was composed at Santiago de Compostela c. 1140. During the Reconquest, the church encouraged great musical creativity in the form of liturgical chants, plays *(autos)* like the *Elche Mystery* which is still performed today, and poetry like the 13C Cantigas de Santa María by **Alfonso the Wise**.

At the end of the 15C, the dramatist **Juan de la Encina** composed secular songs, thus proving that he was also an excellent musician. Music, like the other arts, however, reached its climax in the second half of the 16C, under the protection of the early Habsburgs. **Tomás Luis de Victoria** (1548–1611) was one of the most famous composers of polyphonic devotional pieces, while among his contemporaries, **Francisco de Salinas** and **Fernando de las Infantas** were learned musicologists and **Cristóbal de Morales** and **Francisco Guerrero** were accomplished religious composers. As for instruments, the organ became the invariable accompaniment to sacred music, while a favourite for profane airs

was the *vihuela*, a sort of guitar with six double strings, which was soon replaced by the lute and eventually by the five-string Spanish guitar. In 1629, **Lope de Vega** wrote the text for the first Spanish opera. **Pedro Calderón de la Barca** is credited with creating the **zarzuela**, a musical play with spoken passages, songs and dances, which, since the 19C, has based its plot and music on popular themes. The major composer of religious and secular music in the 18C was **Padre Antonio Soler**, a great harpsichord player.

In the 19C, the Catalan **Felipe Pedrell** brought Spanish music onto a higher plane. He opened the way for a new generation of musicians and was the first to combine traditional tunes with classical genres. At the beginning of the century, while works by French composers (Ravel's *Bolero*, Bizet's *Carmen*, Lalo's *Symphonie Espagnole* and Chabrier's *España*) bore a pronounced Hispanic stamp, Spanish composers turned to national folklore and traditional themes: **Isaac Albéniz** (1860–1909) wrote *Iberia*, **Enrique Granados** (1867–1916) became famous for his *Goyescas* and **Joaquín Turina** (1882–1949) for his *Sevilla Symphony*. This popular vein culminated in works by **Manuel de Falla** (1876–1946) including *Nights in the Gardens of Spain*, *El Amor Brujo* and *The Three-Cornered Hat*.

Among the best-known contemporary classical guitar players are **Andrés Segovia** (1893–1987), **Joaquín Rodrigo** (1901–99), famous for his *Concierto de Aranjuez*, and **Narciso Yepes** (1927–97), have shown that this most Spanish of instruments can interpret a wide variety of music. Another Spaniard, **Pablo Casals** (1876–1973), was possibly the greatest cellist of all time. Spain holds a leading position in the world of opera with singers such as **Victoria de los Ángeles** (1923–2005), **Montserrat Caballé**, **Plácido Domingo**, **Alfredo Kraus** (1927–99), **José Carreras** and **Teresa Berganza**.

Nature

Because of its geographical location, Spain acts as a bridge between two continents – Europe and Africa. The country has myriad natural attractions, ranging from long sandy beaches, sheltered coves and steep cliffs to breathtaking mountain landscapes characterised by high peaks and enclosed valleys. By contrast, the centre of Spain, known as the Meseta, is marked by seemingly endless expanses of flat terrain.

LANDSCAPE

Relief – The average altitude in Spain is 650m/2 100ft above sea level and one sixth of the terrain rises to more than 1 000m/3 300ft. The highest peak on the Spanish mainland is Mulhacén (3 422m/11 427ft) in the Sierra Nevada. The highest point in Spain, however, is Mount Teide on the Canary Islands, rising to a height of 3 718m/12 195ft. The dominant feature of the peninsula is the immense plateau at its centre. This is the **Meseta**: a Hercynian platform between 600m/1 968.5ft and 1 000m/3 281ft high, which tilts slightly westwards. The Meseta is surrounded by long mountain ranges which form barriers between the central plateau and the coastal regions. All these ranges, the **Cordillera Cantábrica** in the northwest (an extension of the Pyrenees), the **Cordillera Ibérica** in the northeast and the **Sierra Morena** in the south, were caused by Alpine folding. Other mountains rising here and there from the Meseta are folds of the original, ancient massif. They include the **Sierras de Somosierra**, **Guadarrama** and **Gredos**, the **Peña de Francia** and the **Montes de Toledo**.

The highest massifs in Spain, the **Pyrenees** (Pirineos) in the north and the **Sierras Béticas**, including the **Sierra Nevada**, in the south, are on the country's periphery, as are Spain's greatest depressions, those of the Ebro and Guadalquivir rivers.

CLIMATE

Although most of Spain enjoys 300 days of sunshine a year, the great diversity of its landscapes is partly due to the country's wide variety of climates.

The **Meseta** accounts for 40 per cent of the surface area of Iberia and includes Castilla y León, Castilla-La Mancha, Madrid and Extremadura. It has a continental climate with extremes of temperature ranging from scorching hot in summer to freezing cold in winter. These excesses are combined with modest and irregular rainfall to form an arid landscape, that complements the seemingly infinite horizons in this part of Spain. The masiff of the adjoining Pyrenees has a colder, alpine climate.

Mallorca

J. Malburet/MICHELIN

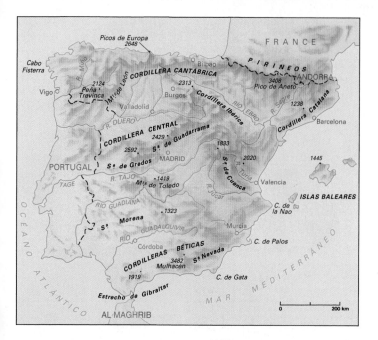

This is also prevalent in the Sierra Nevada (Snowy Range) in Andalucía.

The northern coast, which runs from Galicia to the País Vasco, is nicknamed **España verde** (Green Spain) due to its mild and very humid climate, with rainfall being much higher than in the heartlands of northern Europe. This is in stark contrast to the perceived image of Spain as being one of an entirely dry country.

The Levante has a Mediterranean climate with rainfall being restricted mainly to autumn and spring and warm temperatures in the winter giving way to high temperatures between July and August. This humidity is tempered by the Levante, the cool wind by which this eastern coast, from Almería in the south to Catalunya in the east, is named.

A semi-arid or desert climate affects **Almería**, in southeastern Andalucía, with low rainfall to an extent that the Cabo de Gata near Almería is known as the driest region in Europe. The remaining coastline of **Andalucía** shares traits of a Mediterranean and subtropical region lending it a mild and sunny climate.

The climate of the **Balearic Islands** (Mallorca, Menorca, Ibiza, Formentera) in the Mediterranean Sea is characterised by mild and tempestuous winters, in between hot and bright summers.

The **Canary Islands** (Tenerife, Gran Canaria, Lanzarote, Fuerteventura, La Palma, La Gomera, El Hierro, *see Discovering the Islands*) are characterised by a subtropical climate, due to its latitude in the Atlantic Ocean. It is well known for its year-round pleasant temperatures and low rainfall, making it a haven for winter sun-seekers.

Sierra Nevada

©Turespaña

97

Mezquita, Córdoba
©mtrommer/Fotolia.com

ANDALUCÍA

Andalucía is picture-postcard Spain. Inland, set among the olive groves are dazzling white villages, their red-roofed houses decked with geraniums and black iron-grilles. On the coast there's sun, sea and sand, and tanning holidaymakers. Southernmost Spain is the spiritual home of flamenco, bullfighting, gazpacho, sherry and sultry dark-eyed Carmen-lookalikes. This is both quintessential Spain and a pastiche of itself. Holidaymakers can do and see most things here, from an African wildife safari to skiing the snowy slopes of the Sierra Nevada.

Highlights

1 Walking between the 856 columns of the Mezquita in **Cordóba** (p115)

2 Spotting flamingos in the **Parque Nacional de Doñana** (p124)

3 Contemplating *Death in the Afternoon* in the Bullring **Ronda** (p162)

4 Enjoying a tipple in a sherry bodega in **Jerez** (p147)

5 Stolling the picture-perfect alleyways of the Barrio Santa Cruz in **Sevilla** (p175)

Sol, Spain's frenetic holiday playground. A few miles inland lie some of Spain's prettiest *pueblos blancos* (white villages) and quintessentially Andalucán towns, such as Antequera and Ronda, the home of bullfighting. Gibraltar is a Little England in deepest Spain, but worth a visit for its scenic Rock and dramatic historical sites. Dolphins skit reliably across sightseeing boats in the waters between here and North Africa where the port of Ceuta awaits curious explorers.

- **Antequera**
- **Costa del Sol**
- **Gibraltar**
- **Málaga**
- **Ronda**

Southwestern Andalucía

Cadiz and Huelva provinces attract Spanish holidaymakers with most north European tourists found among the surfers who have colonised the windy beaches of the Costa de la Luz. Cádiz is a characterful very Spanish city which hosts relatively few visitors. Jerez de la Frontera, by contrast, is the home of sherry bodegas and Andalucían horsemanship, both of which attract coachloads of holidaymakers. Aracena's Cave of Marvels is a popular day trip though only the most determined make it as far inland as the Aracena Mountains; their reward is stunning scenery and quiet picturesque villages

- **Aracena**
- **Cádiz**
- **Costa de la Luz**
- **Jerez de la Frontera**

Southern Andalucía

The recently revitalised and thoroughly Spanish city of Málaga is the gateway to Málaga Province and the Costa del

Southeast Andalucía

Granada is the glistening focus of this region with a fabulous natural setting and, in the Alhambra, one of the greatest palaces ever built. Despite its honeypot nature the city has an earthy atmosphere and more than its share of attractions besides.

Literally just beyond (actually above) the city is the snow-capped Sierra Nevada range. It is quite possible to ski here in the morning and sunbathe on the beach in the afternoon, perhaps on the sands of the Almería coastline, the latest of Spain's costas to be fashionably developed for sun-starved north Europeans. Although this is the driest part of Spain, it grows huge amounts of fruit and vegetables, mostly under giant swathes of huge plastic, which deface the landscape.

- **Almería**
- **Granada**
- **Guadix**

Puente Nuevo over the ravine, Ronda

R. Mattès/MICHELIN

Central Andalucía

If the Alhambra is the pinnacle of Moorish Andalucía, the architectural riches of Sevilla and Córdoba lie very close to the peak and Sevilla is one of Spain's most beautiful all-round cities with a vibrant atmosphere. Córdoba too is a lively city with more to offer than just its, admittedly stunning, Mezquita mosque-cathedral. Few foreigners have even heard of Osuna, even though its monumental centre is one of the region's finest, or Priego de Córdoba, a Baroque gem, far from the main roads.

- **Córdoba**
- **Osuna**
- **Priego de Córdoba**
- **Sevilla**

Northeast Andalucía

Jaén province is easily the most overlooked part of Andalucía which is possibly a bonus for independent travellers as its majestic scenery, magnificent castles and historic paradors make it perfect unspoiled touring country, with little in the way of tourist fripperies. Baeza and Úbeda are two of Andalucías architectural treasures and either make a good touring base. Jaén is famous for its cathedral and Moorish Baths. Away from the monumental buildings and history, a driving excursion and walk in the hills of the Sierras de Cazorla, Spain's largest nature reserve, is highly recommended.

- **Baeza**
- **Sierras de Cazorla**
- **Jaén**
- **Úbeda**

Almería

Almería is a swathe of white between the Mediterranean and a fortress-crowned hill. Its magnificent climate – hills shelter it from winds – has made it a major tourist destination. Life bustles in the city centres on the Paseo de Almería, a tree-lined avenue. Another oasis, the parque de Nicolás Salmerón, stretches along the harbour. Houses in La Chanca, the fishermen's quarter, are built into rock.

A BIT OF HISTORY

The city was founded by Abd ar-Rahman III of Córdoba in 955, and played an important role in the 11C when it was the capital of a taifa kingdom. It was captured by Alfonso VII in 1147; however, upon his death, ten years later, it fell into Moorish hands once more. Almería formed part of the Nasrid kingdom of Granada until 1489, the year in which it was reconquered by the Catholic Monarchs.

In the last third of the 20C, the development of advanced agricultural techniques and the opening-up of modern infrastructures have placed this provincial capital at the forefront of Spanish agriculture.

SIGHTS
Alcazaba★

▲▲ ⊙Open Tue–Sun Nov–Apr 9am–6.30pm; May–Oct 9am–8.30pm. ⊕1.50€; free for EU citizens. ℘950 17 50 00. www.juntadeandalucia.es/cultura/museos/CMAAL.

Abd ar-Rahman III ordered this fortress built in the 10C. Almotacín built a splendid palace, enlarged by the Catholic Monarchs. Its crenellated, ochre walls dominate Almería. A section of old ramparts links the fort to San Cristóbal hill, once crowned by a castle.

Attractive **gardens** are laid out in the first walled enclosure where rivulets spring from fountains. The bell in the Muro de la Vela, a wall separating the enclosures, once warned of pirates. In the third enclosure, the keep (torre del

▶ **Population:** 187 521
⚙ **Michelin Map:**
124 COSTA DEL SOL
🅸 **Info:** Plaza del Bendicho. ℘950 62 11 17. www.almeria-turismo.org.
▶ **Location:** Almería lies on the southern coast on the Mediterranean.
🚆Plaza de la Estación
🏛 **Don't Miss:** The Alcazaba of Almería, the Moorish castle that overlooks the city.
🕐 **Timing:** Take a half day at least for the fortress and a stroll.
▲▲ **Kids:** Kids always love castles.

homenaje), with incredibly thick walls, looks down on the Christian alcázar. The **view**★ from the battlements takes in the town, surrounding hills and sea.

Catedral★

Pl. de la Catedral. ⌛Guided tours Mon–Fri 10am–5pm, Sat 10am–1pm. ⊙Closed festive holidays. ⊕2€. ℘609 57 58 02.

The cathedral was built in 1524, fortified against raids by Barbary pirates. It has two well-designed **portals**★ and, at the east end, a **delicately carved sunburst**★. The high altar and pulpits of inlaid marble and jasper are 18C, the choir stalls are from 1560 and the jasper trascoro with three alabaster statues is 18C. A chapel in the ambulatory houses a statue of the Cristo de la Escucha.

Aljibes de Jayrán

Tenor Iribarne. ⊙Open Mon–Fri 11am–1pm, 6–8pm. ℘950 27 30 39.
The Moorish cisterns that once supplied the city.

Iglesia de Santiago

Tiendas. ℘950 23 71 20.
This 16C church on one of the city's main shopping streets (calle de las Tiendas) has a fine **Renaissance doorway**★ similar to the cathedral's.

Museo de Almería

Ctra de Ronda 91. ⏱*Open Tue 2.30–8.30pm, Wed–Sat 9am–8.30pm, Sun and public holidays 9am–2.30pm.* *1.50€; free for EU citizens (on presentation of ID).* *950 17 55 10.*
Museum exhibits cover prehistory through the Islamic era, with pieces from sites in the province, notably the El Argar and Los Millares cultures.

🚗 DRIVING TOURS

The East Coast★
Approx. 240km/150mi.

▶ *Take the airport road and turn right after 14.5km/9mi.*

Parque Natural de Cabo de Gata-Níjar★★
950 16 04 35.
www.cabodegata-nijar.com.
South of the volcanic Cabo de Gata mountains, past the Acosta salt flats, this park is a haven of wild, unspoiled beaches. The lighthouse faces Mermaid Reef, popular for underwater fishing. On the other side of the mountain is the small summer resort of San José with two beautiful beaches; los **Genoveses**★ and **Monsul**★ (about 2km/1.2mi from the centre of the town).

▶ *Take the AL 12; turn at Venta del Probe.*

ADDRESSES

🛏STAY

🛏 **Hotel Costasol** – *Pas. de Almería 58.* *950 23 40 11. www.hotelcostasol. com. 55 rooms.* *6.30€.* The Costasol is housed in a 1960s-style building on Almería's busiest shopping street, although the rooms are spacious and comfortable, some with a balcony.

Agua Amarga
Agua Amarga is a pleasant seaside complex with an attractive beach.

▶ *Follow the coast road to Mojácar (32km/20mi).*

The road twists upward, offering views of the coast, a 17C fortified tower and a 13–14C Moorish watchtower.

Mojácar★
The village stands on a splendid **site**★ on an outcrop with **views** of the coast (2km/1.2mi away) and a plain broken by odd rock formations. The steep, narrow village streets are clearly Moorish.

▶ *Follow the AL 12 back towards Almería, turning off at Níjar.*

Níjar
This one-time Arab village carries on the craft of weaving *jarapas* (blankets), using strips of material *(trapos)*.

The Road Northeast
55km/34mi along the N 370.
Sand dunes stretching from Benahadux to Tabernas were used as a desert film location for such films as *Lawrence of Arabia*. Film sets are open to the public at **Oasys**, a desert theme park. ⏱*Open Apr–Oct daily 10am–8pm; Nov–Mar Sat–Sun & public holidays 10am–7pm. t950 36 52 36.*
Beyond Tabernas, the land is red and barren; pottery-making is the main occupation. **Sorbas** has an amazing **setting**★. Its houses cling to a cliff, circled below by a river loop.

🛏 **Las Salinas de Cabo de Gata** – *Barriada La Almadraba de Monteleva, Las Salinas, 04150 El Cabo de Gata.* *950 37 01 03. www.lasalinascabodegata.com. 20 rooms.* *5€. Closed Oct.* The hotel's tranquil location in Parque Natural de Cabo de Gata makes this an ideal base from which to enjoy a number of excursions. All the rooms offer views of the bright-white salt pans or the beach.

⟨/EAT

⊜⊜⊜ **La Gruta** – *5km/3mi W of the city on the Aguadulce road (N 340a). ℘950 23 93 35. www.asadorlagruta.com. Dinner only. Closed 2nd fortnights in Feb & Oct and Sun.* The enormous caves of a former quarry are the setting of this unusual restaurant specialising in grilled meats and high-quality ingredients.

TAPAS

Casa Puga – *Jovellanos 7 (old quarter). ℘950 23 15 30. www.barcasapuga. es. Closed 3 weeks Sept, public holidays and Sun.* Almería is teeming with tapas bars, of which Casa Puga is the oldest, with a choice of tapas, excellent wines and sausages, and friendly patrons.

Antequera★

In whitewashed Antequera, set in a fertile valley, the new and venerable co-exist. Cobblestone alleys, grilled windows, and the churches and fine Mudéjar brick belfry of San Sebastián are the essence of Andalucía.

- ▶ **Population:** 45 037
- ⚙ **Michelin Map:** 578 U 16
- ℹ **Info:** Plaza de San Sebastián 7. ℘952 70 25 05. www.antequera.es.
- ▶ **Location:** Antequera lies in southern Andalucía, inland from the Costa del Sol. ⟺Plaza de la Estación
- ⊙ **Don't Miss:** Ancient dolmens (burial chambers).

SIGHTS

Alcazaba
⊙*Open Tue–Sat 10am–2pm, 3.30–6pm, Sun and public holidays 10am–2pm. Contact tourist office for further details.*
This was the first fortress taken by the Christians during the reconquest of the kingdom of Granada (1410), but it was soon lost again. Today, its walls shelter a pleasant garden and its towers offer a fine **view**★ over Antequera.

Real Colegiata de Santa María★
Pl. de Santa María. ⊙*Open Tue–Fri 10am–1.30pm, 4.30–6.30pm, Sat 10am–1.30pm, Sun and public holidays 11am–1.30pm. ℘952 84 61 43.*
Access this church, at the foot of the castle gardens, by the 16C **Arco de los Gigantes** (Arch of Giants). Built in

1514, it has one of the earliest Renaissance façades in Andalucía. The adjacent observation point looks out on 1C Roman baths.

Iglesia del Carmen
Pl. del Carmen. ⊙*Open Tue–Fri 10am–2pm, 4.30–6pm, Sat–Sun and public holidays 10.30am–1.30pm. ⊜2€.*
The central nave of the church boasts a Mudéjar artesonado ceiling and a magnificent Churrigueresque altarpiece.

Museo Municipal
Palacio de Nájera, Pl. del Coso Viejo. ⊙*Open Tue–Fri 10am–1.30pm, 4.30–6.30pm, Sat 10am–1.30pm, Sun 11am–1.30pm.* ⊙*Closed public holidays. ⊜3€. ℘95 270 40 21.*
The museum in this 17C palace exhibits archaeological pieces. The most outstanding item is the **Ephebus of Antequera**★, a 1C bronze Roman sculpture.

A Bit of Advice

Given the dangerous nature of the defile and to ensure the safety of visitors, we recommend that you go no farther than the metal bridge suspended high above the El Chorro defile.

Dolmen de Menga y Viera★

*Avenida de Málaga 1.   To the left
of the Antequera exit on the A 354,
towards Granada.* ◐*Open Tue–Wed,
Sat and public holidays 9am–6pm, Sun
9.30am–2.30pm.* ℘ *952 71 22 06.*
Dating from 2500 to 2200 BC, these are
enormous funerary chambers beneath
great stone slabs. Menga, the older and
larger, is oblong, divided by pillars supporting stone slabs.

◖ *Continue along the A 354 and turn
left onto the N 331.*

Dolmen de El Romeral★

*Cerro Romeral. Antigua CN 232 towards
Córdoba.* ◐*Open same hours as
dolmens menga y viera.*
This is the most recent chamber (1800
BC), consisting of small flat stones laid
to create a trapezoidal section.

EXCURSIONS
Parque Natural de El Torcal★

*14km/8.7mi SE. Take the C 3310 towards
Villanueva de la Concepción; go right at
the* **Centro de Recepción "El Torcal"**
signpost. ◐*Open daily 10am–5pm.*
℘*952 70 25 05.*
The park, spread over 12ha/30 acres, has
some of Spain's most unusual eroded
karst scenery. Two signposted paths
(1hr and 3hr) lead to strangely shaped
limestone rocks.

TOUR TO THE DESFILADERO DE LOS GAITANES★★
50km/31mi SW.

◖ *Take the A 343 to Álora.*

After the Abdajalís Valley, the road zig-
zags through superb mountain scenery
up to **Álora**★, an attractive village of
twisting alleyways overlooking the
Guadalhorce river.

◖ *Take the MA 444 from Álora. Leave
your car at the El Chorro campsite.
Continue on foot along a tarmac
track (30min there and back) up to a
metal bridge with magnificent canyon
viewsaaa.*

FROM ANTEQUERA TO MÁLAGA★
*62km/39mi S by the A 45, C 356
and C 345.*
These pleasant roads, within sight of
majestic hills, afford splendid **views**★★
beyond the Puerto del León (Lion Pass,
960m/3 150ft) of Málaga and the sea.

Aracena★

Aracena rises in tiers up a hillside,
crowned by the remains of a Templars' castle, its whitewashed houses
adorned with ornate grilles.

⛉ Gruta de las Maravillas (Cave of Marvels) ★★★

Pozo de la Nieve. ◔⛏*Guided tours
(45min) daily 10am–1.30pm, 3–6pm.*
◐*Closed 24, 25, 31 Dec.* ◉*8€.* ℘*959 12
83 55 (* ◉ *advance booking from tourist
office recommended).*
Rivers below the castle formed vast
caves with limpid pools. Formations

▸ **Population:** 7 468
◔ **Michelin Map:** 578 S 10
▤ **Info:** Calle Pozo de la Nieve.
  ℘663 93 78 77.
  www.aracena.es.
◖ **Location:** Aracena is in
  west-central Andalucía.
⛉ **Kids:** Kids might love the
  Cave of Marvels.

include draperies and pipes coloured
by iron and copper oxide or brilliant
white calcite crystal as in the **Salón de
la Cristalería de Dios**★★ (God's Crystal-

Gruta de las Maravillas

©Turespaña

ware Chamber). Here also is the **Museo Geológico Minero** (🕐 *open daily 10am–1.30pm, 3–6pm;* 🚫*no charge*), a geological and mining museum.

Castillo e Iglesia del Mayor Dolor

🕐*Open daily Sept–Jun 10am–5.30pm; Jul–Aug 10am–7pm.* 🚫*No charge.*
The castle was built in the 9C over an Almohad fortress. Note the decoration on the north side of the tower next to the church, similar to that of the Giralda in Sevilla.

ADDRESSES

EXCURSIONS
Parque Natural de la Sierra de Aracena y Picos de Aroche★★
The cool forests of this park are punctuated by slender peaks and picturesque villages such as whitewashed **Alájar**★, and **Almonaster la Real**★ *(www. almonasterlareal.com)*, concealed amid chestnut, eucalyptus, cork and holm oak, which has a rare intact **mosque**★ (🕐 *open Sat–Sun and public holidays 11am–7pm; www.sierradearacena.net)*. Nearby **Jabugo** *(www.jabugo.es)* is justifiably famous for its delicious cured hams.

Minas de Riotinto★★
35km/22mi S.
The mining tradition of this area dates back to Antiquity.
Parque Minero de Riotinto★★
📞*959 59 00 25. www.parqueminerode riotinto.com.*
This mining theme park takes in the mining and railway museum, the **Museo Minero y Ferroviario**★ (🕐*open daily Oct–early Jul 10.30am–3pm, 4–7pm; late Jul–Sept 10.30am–3pm, 4–8pm;* 🚫*4€)*, the spectacular open-cast mines of **Corta Atalaya**★★★ and **Cerro Colorado**★★, and a **tourist train** *(call for schedule* 📞*959 59 00 25;* 🚫*10€)* along a 19C line built by the Río Tinto Company.

Baeza★★

Noble Baeza stretches across a hill above olive groves and grain fields. Renaissance-style churches and mansions witness a bygone importance.

WALKING TOUR
MONUMENTAL CENTRE★★★
Route marked on town plan – allow half a day.

Plaza del Pópulo★
In the small, irregular square is the **Fuente de los Leones** (Lion Fountain), built with fragments from Cástulo. The Renaissance building to the left, bearing the coat of arms of Charles V, was, surprisingly, the **carnicería** (abattoir). The **Casa del Pópulo** (now the tourist office), at the end of the square, has Plateresque windows and medallions. Six doors once opened on six notaries' offices; court hearings were held upstairs. A balcony projects onto the **Puertó de Jaén**, which, along with the Villalar arch, honoured Charles V. The Jaén gate marked the emperor's visit on his way to Sevilla to marry

▶ **Population:** 16 197
⚙ **Michelin Map:** 578 S 19
🛈 **Info:** Plaza del Pópulo.
  𝒞 953 74 04 44.
  www.andalucia.org.
▶ **Location:** With nearby Úbeda, Baeza is in the green centre of Jaén province, near Parque Natural de Cazorla (to the east). ▬▬Linares Baeza (17km/10.5mi)
🗺 **Don't Miss:** The heritage plazas.
🕓 **Timing:** Take half a day for the old quarter.

Isabel of Portugal in 1526. The **Arco de Villalar** was erected in submission to the king after his victory, in 1521, over the Comuneros, whom the town had supported.

Plaza de Santa María
The walls of the 17C **Seminario de San Felipe Neri** bear inscriptions – traditionally done in bull's blood upon gradua-

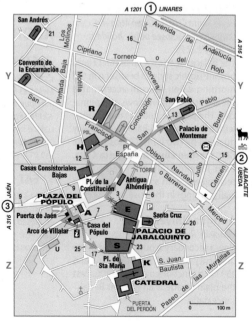

tion. Behind the **Fuente de Santa María**, an arch adorned with atlantes, is the Gothic façade of the **Casas Consistoriales Altas**, with the coats of arms of Juana the Mad and Philip the Fair. Also in the plaza is the **Iglesia de San Andrés**, notable for the **Gothic paintings**★ in the sacristy.

Catedral★

Pl. de Santa María. ⏱*Museum is open daily 10.30am–1pm, 4–6pm.* ∞*2€.* ☎*953 74 41 57.*

The **interior**★★ was remodelled by Vandelvira and his followers in the 16C. The outstanding Capilla Dorada (Gold Chapel) bears Italianate relief; St James' chapel has a fine Antique setting and St Joseph's is flanked by caryatids. The sacristy door has scrollwork and angels' heads. A monumental iron grille by Bartolomé closes the first bay in the nave; a pulpit of painted metal (1580) is in the transept. In the **Capilla del Sagrario**, to one end on the right, is a Baroque silver monstrance carried in procession on the feast of Corpus Christi.

In the cloisters are four Mudéjar chapels with *atauriques,* inscribed in Arabic.

Palacio de Jabalquinto★

Pl. de Santa Cruz. ⏱*Open Mon–Fri 9am–2pm.* ⏱*Closed public holidays.* ☎*953 74 27 75.*

The palace **façade**★★, in perfect Flamboyant-Gothic style, is best seen in the morning when the sun accentuates the decoration of windows and pinnacles. The **patio** (c. 1600) is more sober, with a monumental Baroque stairway guarded by two lions. Opposite is the Romanesque **church of Santa Cruz**, built immediately after the town's reconquest, with a Gothic chapel and wall paintings in the apse.

Antigua Universidad

Conde de Romanones.

Now a secondary school, the seat of the university was built between 1568 and 1593 and functioned until the 19C. Past the plain façade is an elegant Renaissance patio.

Plaza del Mercado Viejo (or Plaza de la Constitución)

This busy square is lined by bars and cafés. Fronting it are the **Antigua Alhóndiga** (former corn exchange), with porticoed façade (1554), and the **Casas Consistoriales Bajas** (1703) as a gallery for officials to view celebrations.

Ayuntamiento★ (Town Hall)

Pj Cardenal Benavides. www.baeza.es. The old law courts and prison has a Plateresque façade and ornate balconies.

Ruinas de San Francisco

San Francisco.

Only the vast transept, apse and majestic stone altarpieces remain of the beautiful 16C church that once stood here. It is now an auditorium.

Palacio de Los Salcedo (Palace of the Counts of Garcíez)

San Pedro 18. ☎*953 74 72 00. www.palaciodelossalcedo.com. Beautiful Gothic windows and a Plateresque patio adorn this early-16C palace, now a hotel. Along the street is the* **Iglesia de San Pablo***, with its Renaissance façade.*

ADDRESSES

⌂ STAY

◓ᐁ **Puerta de la Luna** – *Canónigo Melgares Raya 7.* ☎*953 74 70 19. www. hotelpuertadelaluna.com. 44 rooms.* ⊟*13€. Restaurant* ◓ᐁ. This 16C palace by the cathedral perfectly melds contemporary service with the tranquillity of another era.

⊘ EAT

◓ᐁ **Vandelvira** – *San Francisco 14.* ☎*953 74 81 72. www.vandelvira. es. Closed Jan; Sun eve & Mon.* This elegant restaurant occupies part of the 16C Monasterio de San Francisco.

Cádiz★★

Surrounded by water on three sides, Cádiz has attracted mariners for over 3 000 years. It is also one of Andalucía's most delightful provincial capitals, with charming squares, narrow alleyways and a quiet air, broken only by the exuberant Carnival, the best on the Iberian Peninsula.

THE CITY TODAY

Despite its location and the fine beaches on either side of the town, Cádiz has never embraced costa-style tourism. In summer Spanish holidaymakers and, to a lesser degree, cruise ship day trippers make up most of its visitors. At other times of year its fishing and shipbuilding ports make it a hive of activity with all nationalities passing through, adding a dash of colour to the cobbled streets, and custom to the many excellent fish restaurants of its old town.

A BIT OF HISTORY

Oldest city in Europe – Cádiz was founded by the Phoenicians in 1100 BC. It was conquered by the Romans in 206 BC, and in turn by the Visigoths and Moors. Alfonso X reconquered the city in 1262. During the 16C, Cádiz was attacked by English corsairs, and partially destroyed by the Earl of Essex in 1596. In the 18C, Cádiz became a great port.

Constitution of Cádiz – During the French siege of 1812, patriots convened the Cortes which promulgated Spain's first liberal constitution.

Watchtowers – Between the 16C and 18C, merchants in Cádiz built over 160 towers to watch over the arrival and departure of their ships.

SIGHTS

Museo Catedralicio★

Pl. Fray Félix. ⏰*Open Tue–Fri 10am–1.30pm, 4.30–7pm, Sat 10.30am–1pm.* ⊙*3€ (includes visit to the cathedral).* ℘*956 25 98 12.*

This medieval complex around a fine 16C **Mudéjar patio**★ holds liturgical objects

> **Population:** 127 200
> **Michelin Map:** 578 W 11
> **Info:** Paseo de Canalejas. ℘956 24 10 01. www.cadizturismo.com.
> **Location:** This coastal city is positioned with the Atlantic to the south and west, the Bahía de Cádiz to the north and east. 🚋Plaza de Sevilla 1
> **Parking:** It's difficult in the old quarter.
> **Don't Miss:** A wander within the walls.

and art, including the 16C **Custodia del Cogollo**★, a gold-plated monstrance attributed to Enrique Arfe, and the 18C **Custodia del Millón**.

Oratorio de la Santa Cueva★

Rosario. ⏰*Open Tue–Fri 10am–1pm, 4.30–7.30pm, Sat–Sun 10am–1pm.* ⊙*2€.* ℘*956 22 22 62.*

Three **canvases**★★ in this elliptical oratory were painted by Goya in 1795.

Museo de Cádiz★

Pl. de Mina. ⏰*Open Tue 2.30–8.30pm, Wed–Sat 9am–8.30pm, Sun and public holidays 9am–2.30pm.* ⊙*1.50€; free for EU citizens.* ℘*956 20 33 77.*

The city's museum is in a small mid-19C Neoclassical palace. The collection includes vases, oil lamps and jewellery, including two 5C BC Greek **anthropoidal sarcophagi**★★ based on Egyptian models. Paintings include nine **panels**★ by Zurbarán from the Carthusian monastery in Jerez.

Torre Tavira★

Marqués del Real Tesoro 10. ⏰*Open daily Oct–May 10am–6pm; Jul–Sept 10am–8pm.* ⏰*Closed 25 Dec, 1 Jan.* ⊙*4€.* ℘*956 21 29 10.*

The first 18C watchtower houses the first **camera obscura** in Spain, a device capturing real-time images of the city.

The Battle of Trafalgar

On 21 October 1805, Admiral de Villeneuve sailed out of Cádiz harbour with his Franco-Spanish fleet to confront the English under Nelson off the Cabo de Trafalgar headland. The ships were ill equipped and poorly manned; after some heroic combat Villeneuve's fleet was destroyed and he was taken prisoner. Nelson had been mortally wounded during the course of the battle but England's supremacy at sea was established.

Oratorio de San Felipe Neri

Santa Inés. ⏱*Open Mon–Sat 10am–1.30pm.* 🎫*1.20€.* 📞*956 21 16 12.*
In this elliptical Baroque church the Cortes proclaimed the liberal Constitution of Cádiz in 1812. The **Immaculate Conception** was painted by Murillo in 1680 shortly before his death.

Museo de las Cortes de Cádiz

⏱*Open Tue–Fri 9am–1pm, 4–7pm, Sat–Sun 9am–1pm.* ⏱*Closed public holidays.* 📞*956 22 17 88.*
The museum's main exhibit is a **model**★ of Cádiz in the reign of Charles III.

EXCURSIONS
San Fernando

9km/5.5mi SE along the CA 33. 📞*956 94 42 26.*
This town has been a naval base since the 18C. The main monuments are all have Royal grants *(Real)*: the town hall, Iglesia del Carmen, and the Museo Histórico Municipal. The main civil building is the Neoclassical **Observatorio Astronómico de la Marina** *(Cecilio Pujazón;* 👣*guided tours (1hr)* 📞*956 59 93 67),* from 1753.

Medina Sidonia★

44km/27mi E on CA 33, A 48 and A 390. 📞*956 41 24 04. www.turismomedina sidonia.com.*
The **Iglesia Mayor Santa María la Coronada**★ *(pl. de la Iglesia Mayor);* a 15C Gothic church, holds an exquisite Plateresque **altarpiece**★ by Juan Bautista Vázquez el Viejo. The **Torre de Doña Blanca**, a tower next to the church, provides access to the remains of the alcázar and the old quarter, with its 16C houses. The descent to the modern town passes under the Arco de la Pastora, to reach the **Conjunto Arque-**ológico **Romano**, a Roman complex with 30m/98ft of underground galleries from the 1C AD. *(Espíritu Santo 3;* ⏱*Open 10am–1.30pm, 4.30–6.30pm (Apr–Jun 8pm; Jul–Oct 5–9.30pm);* 🎫*3.10€;* 📞*956 41 24 04).*
The *cardo maximus* was the main street in Roman days. On the plaza de España lies the 18C Neoclassical **town hall**.

🐾 WALKING TOURS

1 AROUND SANTA MARÍA AND THE PÓPULO DISTRICT
Plaza de San Juan de Dios

This 16C square is the most popular in the city. On one side stands the Neoclassical façade of the 1799 **town hall** *(ayuntamiento)*, by Torcuato Benjumeda, beside the Baroque tower of the Iglesia de San Juan de Dios. The tourist office is in an attractive Neoclassical building.

▷ *Take Sopranis, to the left of the Iglesia de San Juan de Dios.*

Calle Sopranis

The street contains some of the best Baroque civil architecture in Cádiz, particularly the houses at nos. 9, 10 and 17. At the end of the street note the 19C iron-and-brick former **tobacco factory**, and the **Convento de Santo Domingo** (⏱ *open Mon–Sat 8.45am–noon, 7–8.45pm, Sun 8am–noon, 7–8pm;* 🎫*no charge).*

▷ *Continue along Plocia as far as Concepción Arenal.*

Cárcel Real★

Concepción Arenal.
The 1792 royal jail, by Torcuato Benjumeda, is one of the most important Baroque civil buildings in Andalucía.

The façade with triumphal-arch entry bears the escutcheon of the monarchy. It houses the city's law courts.

Iglesia de Santa María
Santa María.
The spire on the belfry of this 17C Mannerist church is adorned with *azulejos.*

▷ *Continue along Santa María, past the 18C Casa Lasquetty to the left; cross Félix Soto towards the 13C Arco de los Blancos.*

Casa del Almirante
Pl. de San Martín. ⚊*Closed to the public.*
The outstanding feature of this 17C Baroque palace is the double-section Italian marble **doorway**★★, with Tuscan and Solomonic columns.

Iglesia de Santa Cruz★
Pl. Fray Féliz. ⏱*Open Tue–Sat 10am–2pm, 5-8pm, Sun 10am–2pm.* ⏱*Closed mornings in Aug.* ⚏*No charge.* ✆*956 28 77 04.* ✆*956 28 77 04.*
The old cathedral was rebuilt following the sacking by the Earl of Essex in 1596. Robust Tuscan columns define spaces. The church museum **(Museo Catedralicio)** is alongside in the Casa de la Contaduría (⚭ *see Sights*).

Catedral★★
Pl. de la Catedral. ⏱*Open Tue–Fri 10am–1.30pm, 4.30–7pm, Sat 10am–1pm.* ⚏*3€ (includes museum).* ✆*956 25 98 12.*
Work on the new cathedral began in 1722 and lasted over a century. The result is Baroque in character with the occasional Neoclassical feature. The **façade**★ is flanked by two lofty towers.

Façade, Catedral de Cádiz

B. Kaufmann/ MICHELIN

The triple-aisle interior is surprisingly light and spacious. The crypt holds the remains of the composer **Manuel de Falla** (1876–1946).

② FROM PLAZA SAN JUAN DE DIOS TO THE CATHEDRAL

▷ *Follow Nueva to Pl. San Juan de Dios. Turn left into Cristóbal Colón.*

Casa de las Cadenas
This Baroque mansion has a Genoese marble **doorway**★ and Solomonic columns.

▷ *Continue along calles Cristóbal Colón and Cobos to pl. de la Candelaria; return to Nueva. Past pl. de San Agustín, take Rosario, to the Oratorio de la Santa Cueva (⚭ see Sights).*

The Order of Alcántara

The Knights of San Juan de Pereiro became the Order of Alcántara when entrusted with the defence of the town in 1218. Like the other great orders of chivalry in Spain its aim was to free the country from the Moors. Each order, founded as a military unit under the command of a master, lived in a community under Cistercian rule. These religious militias, always prepared for combat and capable of withstanding long sieges, played a major role in the Reconquest.

CÁDIZ STREET INDEX

SIGHS ON MAP

CÁDIZ

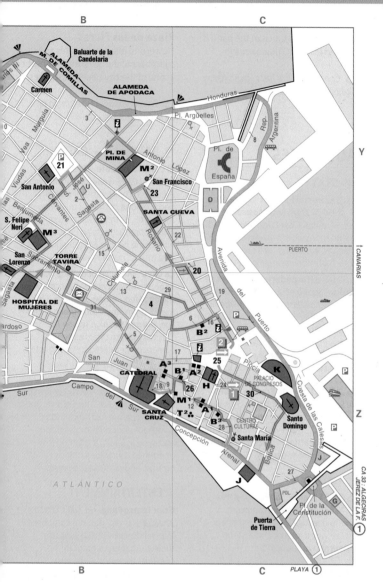

Plaza de San Francisco

This charming plaza, under the Baroque tower of the Iglesia de San Francisco, is lined by lively bars and cafés.

Plaza de Mina★★

Once the kitchen garden of the Convento de San Francisco, this verdant square is imbued with a colonial feel. Fine examples of Isabelline buildings around the square include the **Museo de Cádiz** (*see Sights*).

▶ *Head down de San José to the Oratorio de San Felipe Neri. The oratory stands alongside the Museo Iconográfico e Histórico de las Cortes y Sitio de Cádiz (see Sights).*

Hospital de Mujeres★

Hospital de Mujeres. Open Mon–Sat 10am–1.30pm. 0.80€. 956 22 36 47. This Baroque building is planned around two patios linked by an extraordinary Imperial-style **stair-**

way★★. The Vía Crucis in the patio is created from 18C Triana *azulejos*.

▶ *Continue to the Torre Tavira (&see Sights) on Sacramento.*

ADDRESSES

🏠 STAY

▢▢▣▣ **Hostal Fantoni** – *Flamenco 5.* ☎*956 28 27 04. www.hostalfantoni. net. 12 rooms. Closed Dec–mid-Feb.* Why spend more when you can stay in this pleasant *hostal*? Try for a room with en-suite bathroom facing a pedestrian lane.

▢▢▣▣ **Hospedería Las Cortes de Cádiz** – *San Francisco 9.* ☎*956 22 04 89. www.hotellascortes.com. 36 rooms.* Rooms in this 19C home in the old quarter are well equipped, set around a covered patio. individually decorated, and dedicated to a local event or personality. Attractive outside areas.

▢▢▣▣ **Hotel de Francia y París** – *Pl. de San Francisco 6.* ☎*956 21 23 19. www. hotelfrancia.com. 57 rooms. ☑7.25€.* An early 20C hotel with pleasant rooms fronting an attractive small square in the centre of the city.

🍴 EAT

▢▢▣ **El Faro** – *San Félix 5.* ☎*902 21 10 68. www.elfarodecadiz.com.* This fine restaurant-tapas bar offers a cozy wood interior and a menu that emphasizes local fare.

TAPAS

Aurelio – *Zorrilla 1.* ☎*956 22 10 31. Closed Mon in Aug–Jun.* This popular seafood bar is one of the places for tapas in Cádiz. Its only drawback is its small size – it soon fills up. A good central location close to Plaza de Mina.

Joselito – *San Francisco 38.* ☎*956 25 22 51. Closed Sun.* Choose either entry, one with a covered terrace. The dining room serves fish, paella and stews.

Plaza de las Flores

Flower and plant stalls, cafés and shops contribute to the delightful atmosphere in one of the city's liveliest squares.

▶ *Take Compañía to return to pl. de la Catedral.*

🍷 BARS AND 🍸/CAFÉS

El Café de Levante – *Rosario 35.* ☎*956 22 02 27. www.cafelevante.com.* A quiet café with tasteful modern décor on one of the old quarter's most typical streets. Its relaxed atmosphere attracts an eclectic crowd who come here to enjoy a quiet chat. Live music Thursday evenings.

La Cava – *Antonio López 16.* ☎*956 21 18 66. www.flamencolacava.com. Closed Jan and Mon.* 🎭*show and drink 22€ from 9.30pm (low season shows are on Tue, Thu and Sat; high season Tue–Sat).* This cosy tavern offers authentic flamenco interpreted by young artists.

FESTIVALS

Carnaval de Cádiz – *www.carnavalde cadiz.com. Early Feb.* This Carnival on the week before Ash Wednesday, is without doubt the most famous and lively in Spain. It is famed for uniformed *chirigotas* (comedy groups), and poetical *comparsas*.

🎭 ENTERTAINMENT

Gran Teatro Falla – *Pl. Falla.* ☎*956 22 08 34.* Named after the composer Manuel de Falla (1876–1946), this theatre organises a programme of events throughout the year.

The city's **cultural centres** – **El Palillero** (pl. Palillero; ☎*956 22 65 16*), **El Bidón** (Alcalde Juan de Dios Molina 23; ☎*956 26 15 02*), **La Viña** (av. Campo Del Sur 38; ☎*956 22 51 04*), and **La Lechera** (pl. Argüelles 2; ☎*956 22 06 28*) host a wide range of exhibitions, workshops etc, as well as flamenco concerts at the fifth venue, the **Baluarte de la Candelaria** (Alameda Marqués de Comillas; ☎*956 22 14 42*).

Córdoba★★★

Córdoba owes its fame to the brilliance of the Roman, Moorish, Jewish and Christian civilisations that have endowed its rich and varied history. The Mezquita, the city's most precious jewel, dominates the old section whose narrow, whitewashed streets and charming small squares are embellished with wrought-iron grilles and flower-filled patios.

THE CITY TODAY

The city is on the same well-trodden "Moorish Treasures" sightseeing trail as Seville and Granada, though due to its distance from the coast it receives fewer visitors. However, Córdoba is not just a preserved tourist theme park, as beyond the medieval core lies a lively modern sophisticated centre with buzzing bars and nightlife.

A BIT OF HISTORY

The Roman city – Córdoba was the birthplace of **Seneca the Rhetorician** (55 BC–AD 39), and his son **Seneca the Philosopher** (4 BC–AD 65). A noted early bishop was **Ossius** (257–359), counsellor to Emperor Constantine.

Of Roman Córdoba only the mausoleum in the Jardines de la Victoria, the ruins of a 1C temple, and the bridge linking the old section with the Torre de la Calahorra remain.

The Córdoba Caliphate – Emirs from Damascus established themselves in Córdoba as early as 719. In 756 **Abd ar-Rahman I**, sole survivor of the **Umayyads**, founded the dynasty which was to rule Muslim Spain for three centuries. In 929 **Abd ar-Rahman III** proclaimed himself Caliph of Córdoba. In the 10C a university was founded. Christians, Jews and Muslims lived side by side and enriched each other intellectually and culturally. On the accession, in 976, of the feeble **Hisham II**, power fell into the hands of the ruthless **Al-Mansur** (the Victorious). Al-Andalus fragmented into warring kingdoms, the **reinos de taifas**. Córdoba became part of the Kingdom of Sevilla in 1070. However, intellectual

▶ **Population:** 325 453
⏱ **Michelin Map:** 578 S 15
▯ **Info:** Estación Ave Renfe. ℘902 20 17 74. www.turismodecordoba.org.
◉ **Location:** Córdoba lies along the Guadalquivir river in Andalucía, between ranchland and olive country. The A4 highway runs to Écija (52km/32mi SW) and Sevilla (143km/89mi SW). ▭Glorieta de las Tres Culturas
Ⓟ **Parking:** Park outside the old city and walk Córdoba's lanes and alleys.
◉ **Don't Miss:** The Mezquita.
🕐 **Timing:** See the Mezquita, followed by the Jewish quarter.

life flourished. **Averroës**, physicist, astrologer, mathematician and doctor, brought the learning of Aristotle to the West. The Jew **Maimónides** (1135–1204) was famed in medicine, theology and philosophy, but fled in order to escape persecution.

Reconquered in 1236, Córdoba declined until the 16C and 17C, when its tooled leatherwork became fashionable.

SIGHTS

THE MEZQUITA AND THE JUDERÍA★★★
Mezquita-Catedral★★★ (Mosque-Cathedral)

Torrijos. &Ⓞ*Open Mon–Sat 8.30am–7pm, Sun and public holidays 8.30–10am, 2–7pm.* ▭*8€.* ℘*957 47 05 12.*

The Mezquita

The traditional Muslim crenellated square encloses the Patio de los Naranjos (Orange Tree Court) with a **Basin of Al-Mansur (1)** for ritual ablution, a hall for prayer and a minaret.

The first Muslims in Córdoba shared the Visigothic church of St Vincent with the Christians. Soon Abd ar-Rah-

The Sephardic Jews

Maimónides

©Corbis

No history of Spain is complete without a mention of the *Sefardíes* whose presence may still be felt in *juderías* (old Jewish quarters) and synagogues. The main Jewish towns in the past were Córdoba, Toledo and Granada.

The Sephardic Jews (*Sepharad* is the Hebrew word for Spain) came to the Iberian Peninsula in Antiquity at the same time as the Greeks and Phoenicians. In the 8C, during the Arab occupation, they welcomed the Muslims, who regarded them as sympathetic allies. The Muslims put them in charge of negotiating with the Christian community. As merchants, bankers, craftsmen, doctors and scholars, Jews played an important economic role and influenced the domains of culture and science. Some became famous, like the Torah scholar Maimónides of Córdoba (1135–1204).

The Jews were particularly prosperous under the Caliphate of Córdoba (929–1031). However, at the end of the 11C, Jews from Andalucía moved to Toledo and Catalunya, especially Girona, as a result of intolerance and persecution under the Almohads. They were often persecuted by Christians during the Reconquest (a royal decree forced them to wear a piece of red or yellow cloth). The Alhambra Decree was proclaimed in 1492 by the Catholic Monarchs to expel them. Some chose to convert, others (known as *Marranos*), in spite of having publicly converted, continued practising their Jewish faith in hiding, while most emigrated to other parts of the Mediterranean.

Today, Sephardic Jews account for up to 20 per cent of the total Jewish population in the world and most of them have kept their language, Ladino, which is derived from 15C Castilian.

man I (731–788) purchased part of the site. He razed the church and around the year 780 began the construction of a splendid mosque with 11 aisles each opening onto the Patio de los Naranjos. Marble pillars and Roman and Visigothic stone were re-used. The mosque became famous for an innovation: the superimposition of two tiers of arches to add height and spaciousness. After the reconquest, Christians built chapels in the west nave, including the 17C **Capilla de la Purísima Concepción (2)**, completely covered with marble.

In 848 Abd ar-Rahman II had the mosque extended to the present-day Capilla de Villaviciosa (Villaviciosa Chapel). In 961 El Hakam II built the *mihrab*, and in 987, Al-Mansur added eight aisles (with red-brick floors).

Interior

Enter by the Puerta de las Palmas. The interior is a forest of columns (about 850) and the horseshoe-shaped arches. The wide main aisle off the doorway has a beautiful *artesonado* ceiling. It leads to the **kiblah** wall, where the faithful prayed, and the **mihrab**★★★, normally a simple niche, but here a sumptuous room preceded by a triple **maksourah (3)** (enclosure) reserved for the caliph. Its three ribbed domes rest on unusual apparently interweaving multifoil arches. Alabaster plaques and ornate stucco arabesques and palm-leaf motifs sometimes framed by Cufic script enhance the architecture.

In the 13C, Christians walled off the aisles from the court. A few columns were removed and pointed arches substituted for Moorish ones when the first **cathedral (4)** was built. Alfonso X was responsible for the chancel in the

Capilla de Villaviciosa or **Lucernario** (5), and built the **Capilla Real** ★ (6) decorated in the 13C with Mudéjar stucco. Chapels were built in the western nave, including the fine marble-faced 17C **Purísima Concepción** (2).

Catedral

In the 16C the canons cut away the centre of the mosque to erect loftier vaulting. Emperor Charles V was far from pleased: "You have destroyed something unique," he said, "to build something commonplace." The roof is a mix of 16C and 17C styles (Hispano-Flemish, Renaissance and Baroque). Additional enrichments are the Baroque **choir stalls** ★★ (8) by Pedro Duque Cornejo (c. 1750) and two **pulpits** ★★ (7) of marble, jasper and mahogany.

Tesoro

The treasury, built by the Baroque architect Francisco Hurtado Izquierdo, in the **Capilla del Cardenal** (Cardinal's Chapel) (9), includes a large 16C **monstrance** ★ by E Arfe and an exceptional Baroque figure of Christ in ivory.
Exterior features include the **minaret**, enveloped by a 17C Baroque tower. Giving onto the street is the 14C Mudéjar **Puerta del Perdón** (Pardon Doorway) faced with bronze. Further on is the small chapel of the **Virgen de los Faroles** (Virgin of the Lanterns) (10).

The Alcázar of the Umayyads stood in magnificent gardens facing the mosque where the Palacio Episcopal (Bishop's Palace) now houses the **Museo Bellas Artes** *Pz(a del Potro;* ○*open Tue 2.30–8.30pm, Wed–Sat 9am–8.30pm, Sun and public holidays 9am–2.30pm.* ⊚*1.50€, Free for EU citizens;* ☏*957 35 55 50).*

Judería★★ (Old Jewish Quarter)

NW of the Mezquita. Narrow streets, flower-draped walls, cool patios, and lively nightlife characterise the quarter from which Jews were expelled.

Sinagoga

Judíos. ♿○*Open Tue–Sat 9.30am–2pm, 3.30–5.30pm, Sun and public holidays 9.30am–1.30pm.* ⊚*0.30€; free for EU citizens.* ☏*957 20 29 28.*
Built in the early 14C, this synagogue is a small square room with a balcony for the women. The upper walls are covered in Mudéjar stucco.

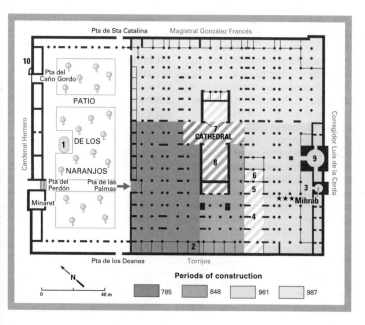

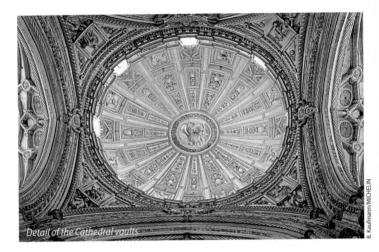

Detail of the Cathedral vaults

B. Kaufmann/MICHELIN

Nearby is the **Zoco Municipal** (souk) where craftsmen work around a large patio, a setting for flamenco dancing in summer. In the 16C Casa de las Bulas is the **Museo Taurino** (*Bullfighting Museum; pl. Maimónides; ☛ closed for renovation; ✆957 20 10 56*).

Palacio de Viana★★

Pl. de Don Gome 2. ☛Guided tours (1hr) Tue–Fri 10am–7pm, Sat–Sun 10am–3pm. ⓞClosed public holidays. ⊛6€ (3€ patios only, no tour). ✆957 49 67 41.

This fine example of 14C–19C Córdoban civil architecture has 12 patios and an attractive garden, outstanding in a city famous for its beautiful patios.

On the ground floor are collections of porcelain, 17C–19C side-arms and tapestries. The staircase to the first floor has a beautiful Mudéjar *artesonado* ceiling of cedar. The most interesting areas are the Córdoban leather room; tapestries made in the royal workshops from cartoons by Goya; the library; and the main room with a rich *artesonado* ceiling and tapestries illustrating the Trojan War and Spanish tales.

Museo Arqueológico★★

Pl. Jerónimo Páez. ⓞOpen Tue 2.30–8.30pm, Wed–Sat 9am–8.30pm, Sun 9am–2.30pm. ⊛1.50€; free for EU citizens. ✆957 35 55 31.

The archaeological museum is in the 16C Palacio de los Páez, a palace designed by Hernán Ruiz. Displayed here are prehistoric Iberian objects, Visigothic remains and, in particular, the **Roman collection**★ (reliefs, capitals, sarcophagi and mosaics). There are also Muslim ceramics, capitals, and the outstanding 10C **stag**★ (*cervatillo*) from Medina Azahara.

Alcázar de los Reyes Cristianos★

Caballerizas Reales. ⓞOpen Tue–Fri 8.30am–7.30pm, Sat 9.30am–4.30pm, Sun 9.30am–2.30pm. ⊛4€ (includes Museo Julio Romero), 2€ for the baths; free on Wed. ✆957 42 01 51.

This 14 C complex, later expanded, retains attractive Moorish patios with ornamental basins and pools, baths, rooms with Roman **mosaics**★ and a fine 3C **sarcophagus**★. The towers afford garden and city **views**. The **gar-**

SIGHTS ON MAP							
Caballerizas Reales	AZ	A	Facultad de Filosofía y Letras	AZ	U	Museo Julio Romero de Torres	BZ	M7
Casa de los Luna	BY	B	Monumento a Manolete	BY	F	Museo Municipal Taurino	AZ	M9
Convento de Santa Isabel	BY	C	Museo de Bellas Artes	BZ	M3	Palacio de los Villalones	BY	N
			Museo Diocesano de Bellas Artes	ABZ	M5	Posada del Potro	BZ	E
						Triunfo de San Rafael	BZ	V

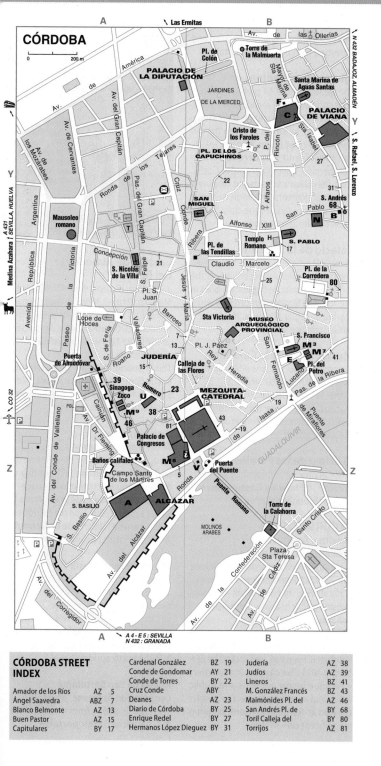

dens★, in Arabic style, are terraced and refreshed with pools and fountains.

Iglesias Fernandinas★

The beauty of the 14 parish churches built soon after the reconquest by Ferdinand in 1236 can still be seen today, particularly in **Santa Marina** (pl. del Conde de Priego), **San Miguel** (pl. de San Miguel) and **San Lorenzo** (pl. de San Lorenzo). Built in a primitive Gothic style, they show a sober beauty in purely structural elements. The single trumpet-shaped doorways are the only lighter aspect of the architecture.

Palacio de la Merced★

Pl. de Colón.
The provincial Parliament building is the former Convento de la Merced, built in the 18C. The façade is graced by a white marble Baroque doorway. Inside are a patio, staircase and church.

Museo Torre de la Calahorra

Puente Romano. ◐Open daily 10am–6pm. ◌4.50€. ℘957 29 39 29.
In the 14C Moorish fortress a museum traces the caliphate using audio and video. There is also a fine **model**★ of the mosque as it was in the 13C.

El Cristo de los Faroles

The Calvary surrounded by lanterns (faroles) in **Plaza de Capuchinos**★ is known throughout Spain.

EXCURSIONS

Medina Azahara★★

▶Leave Córdoba on the A 431 (W of plan). After 8km/5mi bear right. ◐Open Tue–Sat mid-Sept–Apr Tue–Sat 10am–6.30pm; May–mid-Sept 10am–8.30pm, Sun and public holidays 10am–2pm. ◌1.50€; free for EU citizens. ℘957 35 55 14.
This sumptuous city, built by Abd ar-Rahman III from 936, was sacked by Berbers in 1013. The city rose in three tiers – mosque below, gardens and public areas, and an alcázar above. The jewel is the **Abd ar-Rahman III room**, featuring magnificent carved stone.

Abd ar-Rahman III room, Medina Azahara
©Turespaña

Castillo de Almodóvar del Río★★

25km/15mi W along the A 431. ◐Open Mon–Fri 11am–2.30pm, 4–7pm (8pm in summer); Sat–Sun 11am–7pm (8pm in summer). ◐Closed 25 Dec, 1 Jan. ◌5€. ℘957 32 82 17. www.castillodeal modovar.com.
This imposing 14C eight-towered Gothic **castle** dominates town and countryside. Stroll the path behind the parapet, parade ground and towers.

Andújar★

76km/47mi E along the A 4.
Andújar retains many 15–16C houses and churches. On the last Sunday of April, a popular romería (pilgrimage) is held to the Santuario de la Virgen de la Cabeza (32km/20mi N on the J 5010), set in the **Parque Natural de la Sierra de Andújar**★, with pasture and ravines.

Iglesia de Santa María

Pl. Santa María. ℘953 50 01 39.
The 15C–17C Church of St Mary holds El Greco's Christ in the Garden of Olives★★, set in a chapel enclosed by a fine **grille**★ by Master Bartolomé.
An Assumption of the Virgin by Pacheco is in the north apsidal chapel.

Iglesia de San Bartolomé

Corredera San Bartolomé. ℘953 50 01 11.
This church, dating from the end of the 15C, has three **Gothic portals**★.

ADDRESSES

🏠 STAY

🛏 **Hostal La Milagrosa** – *Rey Heredia 12.* *℘957 47 33 17. 8 rooms (doubles only).* Good central location near the Mezquita. Attractive features are the plant-filled typically Córdoban patio and well-kept, large, cool guest rooms with full bathrooms.

🛏🛏 **Hostal El Triunfo** – *Corregidor Luis de la Cerda 79.* *℘957 49 84 84. www.hostaltriunfo.com. 58 rooms. ⊇5€. Restaurant⊇. Closed 24–25 Dec.* Most of the rooms look onto the Mezquita, just across a narrow street. Stay on the top floor if you can to make use of the huge terrace. All rooms have a TV.

🛏🛏 **Hostal Séneca** – *Conde y Luque 7.* *℘957 47 32 34. 12 rooms. Closed fortnight in Aug.* The Seneca is a quiet *hostal* near the Mezquita with typical Andalucían décor and a flower-filled patio. Despite the rooms being fairly basic (some without a bathroom), the hotel is often full so advance booking is recommended.

🛏🛏🛏 **Hotel González** – *Manríquez 3.* *℘957 47 98 19. www.hotel-gonzalez.com. 20 rooms. ⊇3.50€. Restaurant⊇🛏🛏* The rooms in this 16C palace, in the triangle of the Mezquita, the Judería and the gardens of the Alcázar, are spacious and well appointed. The Moorish-inspired dining room doubles as the hotel restaurant.

🛏🛏🛏🛏 **Hotel Casa de los Azulejos** – *Fernando Colón 5.* *℘957 47 00 00. www.casadelosazulejos.com. 8 rooms. Closed 24–25 Dec.* This charming hotel is a traditional Andalucían house with a colonial flavour. Outstanding features include a lovely interior garden with plants, and magnificent large rooms with period furnishings, iron headboards, original floors and colourful designer baths.

🛏🛏🛏🛏 **Hotel Posada de Vallina** – *C. del Corregidor Luis de la Cerda 83.* *℘957 49 87 50. www.hhposadadevallina.es. 24 rooms. ⊇6€.* Elegance and comfort are the main features of this small hotel in a tastefully restored Córdoban house, whose windows open out onto the Mezquita. The pleasant restaurant on the ground floor is particularly popular.

🍴 EAT

🍽 **Taberna los Faroles** – *Velázquez Bosco 1.* *℘957 486 876. Closed Sat–Sun.* This tavern is named for the lanterns that illuminate its attractive patio. Specialities here include local dishes such as salmorejo (a variant of gazpacho), aubergine with honey and *rabo de toro* (braised oxtail). A cool, pleasant atmosphere is enhanced by the *azulejos* on the walls.

🍽 **Paseo de la Ribera** – *Pl. Cruz del Rastro 3.* *℘957 47 15 30. www.paseoribera.com.* One of the best places for Córdoban cuisine. The dining room, between stone arches, brings to mind a Romanesque church. The terrace, on Pas. de la Ribera, overlooks the Guadalquivir river. Specialities are rice dishes and oxtail.

🍽🍽 **El Rincón de Carmen** – *Romero 4.* *℘957 29 10 55. Closed Mon in low season and Sun in high season.* The patio provides an escape from the frenzied tourist activity in the Judería. Plenty of alternatives to the traditional gazpacho and an interesting wine list.

🍽🍽🍽 **Almudaina** – *Pl. Campo Santo de los Mártires 1.* *℘957 47 43 42. www.restaurantealmudaina.com. Closed Sun eve.* An attractive restaurant in a plaza, near the Alcázar. High point is the painstaking regional décor, with dining on two levels around a pleasant covered patio. The excellent food is a good introduction to Córdoban cuisine.

🍽🍽🍽 **Casa Palacio Bandolero** – *Torrijos 6.* *℘957 47 64 91. www.restaurantebandolero.com.* The Bandolero is superbly located opposite the Mezquita and is popular with locals. Home-made tapas are served in the bar, in addition to local cuisine and a long wine list in the medieval-style dining room and on the flower-decked patio.

TAPAS

Córdoba does full justice to Andalucía's great tapas tradition with a wide range of bars offering a huge selection of local specialities such as *salmorejo* (a type of local gazpacho), *rabo de toro* (braised oxtail), *embutidos* (sausage) and sherries (*finos, amontillados, olorosos*).

Patio in Córdoba

B. Kaufmann/ MICHELIN

Taberna Casa Pepe de la Judería – *Romero 1. ℘957 20 07 44. Reservations recommended.* This bar opened in 1928 and the counter dates from this period. Several rooms around an attractive patio offer tapas, with an Andalucían restaurant upstairs. **Taberna Salinas** – *Tundidores 3. ℘957 48 01 35. www. tabernasalinas.com. Closed Aug, Sun.* Open for more than a century, this welcoming bar consists of a counter, two rooms decorated with *azulejos* and photos of celebrities, and a small patio.

Taberna San Miguel-Casa El Pisto – *Pl. San Miguel 1. ℘957 47 01 66. Closed Sun and Aug.* Founded in 1886, the Taberna San Miguel, opposite the church of the same name, is popular choice for tapas. The traditional décor is enhanced by the bullfight posters and photos on the walls.

♥ BARS AND ♥ CAFÉS

Cafetería Siena – *Pl. de las Tendillas. ℘957 47 30 05. Closed Sun.* A long-established café in Córdoba's main square, with one of the city's most popular outdoor terraces. A perfect venue for a morning coffee or an evening drink.

Málaga Café – *Málaga 3. ℘957 47 62 98.* A quiet café with classical décor and comfortable sofas and armchairs near the plaza de las Tendillas in the centre of the city. Highly recommended for evening drinks with friends.

Sojo – *Benito Pérez Galdós 3. ℘957 48 39 98. Closed Sun.* Popular with the over-25s, this avant-garde bar is open from breakfast time to late at night. The Sojo also organises concerts by soloists, as well as art, photography and video exhibitions. Highly recommended, whatever the hour.

☺ NIGHTLIFE

El Puentecillo – *Poeta Emilio Prados. Closed Fri in low season.* A small venue on the way to the El Brillante district. Warm and inviting décor inside and on the small patio. Tends to be frequented by an older, quieter crowd. Popular for drinks early in the evening.

⇛ SHOPPING

The city's traditional craftwork includes embossed leather and cordovans, in addition to gold and silver filigree. Another good buy is the local wine, **Montilla-Moriles** *(www.montilla-moriles.org)*, produced to the south of Córdoba in the area around Montilla, Puente Genil, Lucena and Baena. The excellent wines and brandies from Montilla-Moriles are similar in style to those of Jerez.

FESTIVALS

Festival of the Crosses (Cruces de Mayo) – At the beginning of **May**, the central squares of the city (San Basilio, Santa Marina and San Augustín) are adorned with over 80 large crosses made of flowers with a prize for the best. Also in early May Córdoba is famous for its glorious **patios**, **with** many of these opened up to the public for a close look. As with the Crosses, many compete in the Concurso de Patios Córdobes for the title of town's best patio. Ask at the *turismo* for a map, or simply browse the Old Town, particularly on and around Calle San Basilio, looking out for *Patio* signs. The ever-popular **Feria** is held at the end of the month with the usual Andalucían equestrian events, fireworks, flamenco and revelries.

Costa de la Luz★

The southwestern coast in the provinces of Huelva and Cádiz is edged with beaches interrupted by the mouths of major rivers – the Guadiana, Tinto and Guadalquivir. Several resorts are being developed beside the dazzling white sand and translucent skies that make this the Coast of Light.

🚗 DRIVING TOURS

The Huelva Coast★
Ayamonte to the Parque Nacional de Doñana – 135km/84mi – allow one day.

Ayamonte★
This fishing port at the mouth of the Guadiana is a lively border town of cobbled streets and whitewashed and brightly coloured houses. In the old quarter are the 16C colonial-style Iglesia de las Angustias, the Convento de San Francisco, with its elegant bell tower and magnificent *artesonado* work, and the 13C Iglesia del Salvador.

Boat service is available to Vila Real de Santo António in Portugal.

Coastal resorts between Ayamonte and Huelva include **Isla Canela, Isla Cristina** (www.islacristina.es), **La Antilla** (www.lepe.es) and **Punta Umbría** (www.ayto-puntaumbria.es). This area also includes the marshland of the **Marismas del Río Piedras y Flecha de El Rompido**★, the Portil lagoon, and the Enebrales de Punta Umbría, a landscape dominated by juniper trees.

Huelva★
🚏 *Avenida de Italia 36.*
In the 15C and 16C, the estuary formed by the Tinto and Odiel rivers saw the departure of numerous expeditions to the New World, notably those led by Columbus. A large monument to these explorers, the **Monumento a Colón** (1929), stands near the harbour at Punta del Sebo.

In Huelva, see the unusual **Barrio Reina Victoria**★, an English-style district

🛈 **Michelin Map:** 578 U 7-8-9-10, V 10, W 10-11, X 11-12-13 – *ANDALUCÍA (Huelva, Cádiz)*

📋 **Info:** El Puerto de Santa María: Luna 22. ℘956 54 24 13; Huelva: Plaza Alcalde Coto Mora 2. ℘959 65 02 00; Sanlúcar de Barrameda: Avenida Calzada Del Ejército. ℘956 36 61 10; Tarifa: Paseo de la Alameda. ℘956 68 09 93. www.andalucia.org.

🧭 **Location:** The Costa de la Luz extends from Ayamonte, at the mouth of the Guadiana, to Tarifa, the most southerly town on mainland Spain.

named after Queen Victoria; the **Catedral de La Merced** (*pl. de la Merced; ℘959 24 30 36*), with its Renaissance façade and sculpture of the Virgen de la Cinta, the town's patron saint, by Martínez Montañés; and paintings by Zurbarán in the **Iglesia de la Concepción** (*Concepción*) and the **Museo** (*Alameda Sundheim 13; ⚊closed for renovation; ℘959 25 93 00*).

Paraje Natural de las Marismas del Odiel★★
2km/1.2mi SE. 🚗*Exit Huelva along Avenida Tomás Domínguez (Cto de Recepción La Calatilla, Carretera del Dique Juan Carlos I; ⚙activities require advance booking ℘954 50 90 11.*
This marshland (*marisma*) of outstanding beauty, at the mouth of the Tinto and Odiel rivers, close to an industrial chemical facility, is a **World Biosphere Reserve**. It provides a habitat for over 200 bird species. Visited by **canoe** or small boat.

La Rábida★
10km/6.2mi SE of Huelva off N 442.
In 1484, the Prior of the **Monasterio de Santa María** (*Camino del Monasterio;* 🕐*open Sept–Jul Tue–Sat 10am–1pm, 4–*

6pm, Sun and public holidays 10.45am–
1pm, 4–7pm; Aug daily 10am–1pm,
4.45–8pm; ⌨2.50€, audioguide 1.50€;
✆959 35 04 11), Juan Pérez, believed
Columbus' claim that the world was
round and interceded to obtain the
support of the Catholic Monarchs.

The **church**★ preserves old frescoes,
wooden *artesonado* work and the delicate 14C alabaster statue of the **Virgen
de los Milagros**★ (Virgin of Miracles), in
front of which Columbus is said to have
prayed prior to setting sail. A small room
displays a **mapamundi**★, by Juan de la
Cosa, which outlined the coast of America for the first time.

Full-scale replicas of Columbus' three
caravels are moored at the **Muelle de las
Carabelas**★ (◐open Tue–Sun 1–7pm;
⌨3.10€; ✆959 53 05 97), a modern dock
and museum on the Tinto Estuary.

Palos de la Frontera★
13km/8mi SE of Huelva by A 5026.

This picturesque town on the left bank
of the Río Tinto was the birthplace of
the Pinzón brothers, who sailed with
Columbus. The **Casa-Museo de Martín
Alonso Pinzón** (⚬━closed for renovation; ✆959 35 01 99) and the *azulejos*
dotted around the town provide a
reminder of the first voyage. The 15C
Iglesia de San Jorge is fronted by an
interesting Gothic-Mudéjar doorway.

Moguer★
20km/12.4mi NE of Huelva off A 494.

Expeditions left this tranquil town with
its elegant houses for points unknown.
The verses of **Juan Ramón Jiménez**
(1881–1958), Moguer's most illustrious
son and winner of the Nobel Prize for
Literature in 1956, adorn *azulejo* panelling dotted around the town centre. His
home is a museum, the **Casa-Museo
Juan Ramón Jiménez**★ (*Juán Ramón
Jimenez 10;* ⚬━closed until further notice;
✆959 37 21 48).

The **town hall** (*ayuntamiento*) has a fine
Renaissance **façade**★. Head along the
pedestrianised **calle Andalucía**★, lined
by interesting buildings, including the
Archivo Histórico Municipal and Biblioteca Iberoamericana; and the 15C Con-

vento de San Francisco, with its Mannerist cloisters, Baroque altarpiece and
lofty belfry. The **tower**★ of the Iglesia de
Nuestra Señora de la Granada recalls
the Giralda in Sevilla.

Convento de Santa Clara★
☁Guided tours (40min) Tue–Sat 11am
–12.30pm and 5–7pm. ◐Closed public
holidays. ⌨2€. ✆959 37 01 07.

The church of this Gothic-Mudéjar
monastery houses the Renaissance-style
marble **tombs of the Portocarrero
family**★, noteworthy **tombs**★ at the
high altar, and some quite exceptional
14C **Nasrid-Mudéjar choir stalls**★★.

▶ *Return to the C 442, which follows
the coast.*

Parque Nacional de Doñana★★★
This park, at the crossroads of continents
and of the Atlantic and the Mediterranean, acts as a rest stop for African and
European migratory birds. Doñana is
Spain's largest wildlife reserve with a
protected area (inner and outer park)
of 73 000ha/180 387 acres. The **salt
marshes** are the larger part of the park
and are the ideal habitat for birds which
migrate to Europe over the winter. **Sand
dunes** are grouped in formation parallel
to the Atlantic and advance inland at a
rate of 6m/19.6ft per year. The stabilised
sands or **cotos** are dry, undulating areas
covered with heather, rockrose, rosemary
and thyme, and trees such as cork oak
and pine.

The Doñana is home to lynx, wild boar,
deer and a wide variety of birds, including Spanish imperial eagles, flamingos,
herons, wild ducks and coots.

El Rocío
65km/40.4mi E of Huelva, along A 483.

This small village is famous as the site
of the **Santuario de Nuestra Señora
del Rocío** (*Sanctuary of the Virgin of the
Dew;* ✆959 44 24 25), to which Spain's
most popular religious pilgrimage
(*romería*) is made during Whitsun weekend every year.

The Cádiz Coast★
From Sanlúcar de Barrameda to Tarifa
160km/99.4mi – allow one day

Sanlúcar de Barrameda★
The fishing port of Sanlúcar, at the mouth of the Guadalquivir, is the home town of *manzanilla*, a sherry matured like Jerez *fino* but which has a special flavour thanks to the sea air. The bodegas (cellars) are in the old quarter on the hill around the massive **Castillo de Santiago** (*Cava de Castillo*).
The **Iglesia de Nuestra Señora de la O** (*pl. de la Paz*) close by has a fine Mudéjar **doorway**★★ and a 16C **Mudéjar artesonado ceiling**★.
In the modern town, pass the **Palacio de Orleans y Borbón** (*Cuesta de Belén*), a 19C palace built in neo-Moorish style, and now Sanlúcar's town hall, and the **covachas**★, a mysterious series of five ogee arches decorated with Gothic tracery. The lower town has two main churches: the **Iglesia de la Trinidad** (*pl. de San Roque*), with its magnificent 15C Mudéjar **artesonado**★★; and the **Iglesia de Santo Domingo** (*Santo Domingo*), with the noble proportions of a Renaissance building. The **Centro de Visitantes Fábrica de Hielo** (◷*open daily 9am–7pm (8 or 9pm in summer); ℘956 38 65 77)*, a visitor centre in Bajo de Guía, near the mouth of the Guadalquivir, provides information on the Parque Nacional de Doñana across the river. Park excursions also depart from here.

Rota
23km/14mi S of Sanlúcar off A 491.
The **old town**★ inside the ramparts is laid out around the **Castillo de la Luna** (*Avenida Mancomunidad Bajo Guadalquivir 3; ℘956 84 62 88*) and the **Iglesia de Nuestra Señora de la O**★ (*Luis Vázquez 2; ℘956 81 00 84*). Rota is known for beaches such as the **Playa de la Costilla**★. A large naval base is on the outskirts of the town.

El Puerto de Santa María★
24km/15mi SE of Sanlúcar, off A 491.
The harbour, in Cádiz Bay, played an active role in trade with the New World.

Today, fishing, the export of sherry and tourism (beaches and golf courses) are important. A palm-shaded promenade overlooking the quays along the north bank leads to the 12C **Castillo de San Marcos**, a castle which was the seat of the Dukes of Medinaceli. The late 15C **Iglesia Mayor Prioral** (*Pagador 8*) stands in the centre of the town. The **Portada del Sol**★, or Sun Gateway, in plaza de España, is a mix of Plateresque and Baroque styles. The **Fundación Rafael Alberti** (*Santo Domingo 25; ◷open Tue–Sun 11am–2.30pm; ◷4€. ℘956 85 07 11; www.rafaelalberti.es*) nearby shows photos, letters and manuscripts by the poet. The **Casa-Museo de Pedro Muñoz-Seca** (1879–1936), author of *La Venganza de Don Mendo*, is also here (*Nevería 48; ◷open Tue–Sun 11am–2.30pm; ◷1.20€; ℘956 85 17 31*).

Cádiz★★ ◒See CÁDIZ
52km/32mi S of Sanlúcar.
South of Cádiz, there are good beaches at **La Barrosa**★★, Chiclana de la Frontera and **Conil de la Frontera** (**Playa de la Fontanilla** and **Playa de los Bateles**).

Vejer de la Frontera★
57km/35mi SE of Cádiz along E 5.
Vejer, perched on a crag, is one of the prettiest white villages of Andalucía. The best approach is along the hillside road from the south. The **Iglesia del Divino Salvador** has a three-aisle **interior**★ a mix of Romanesque and Gothic features. The road on to Tarifa runs through the Baetic foothills. The **Parque Natural La Breña y Marismas de Barbate**★ (*℘956 27 48 42*), with spectacular cliffs and picturesque coves, such as the **Cala de los Caños de Meca**★★, is 10km/6mi from Vejer.

Ruinas Romanas de Baelo Claudia★
◷*Open Sun 9am–2pm; Tue–Sat Jun–Sept 9am–8pm, Mar–May & Oct 9am–7pm, Nov–Feb 9am–6pm.*
◷*Closed 24, 25, 31 Dec, 1 & 6 Jan.*
◷*1.50€; free for EU citizens.*
℘956 10 67 97.

The remains of the Roman city of Baelo Claudia date back to the 2C BC, when a salting factory specialising in the production of *garum* (a sauce made from the remains of fish) was established here. Vestiges of the basilica, forum and theatre are still visble.

Tarifa

105km/65mi S of Cádiz, along E 5.
Spain's southmost point, a major centre for windsurfing and kitesurfing. The **Castillo de Guzmán el Bueno**, taken by the Christians in 1292, was commanded by Guzmán el Bueno who accepted the execution of his sons by the Moors rather than surrender.

ADDRESSES

STAY

Hotel Convento de San Francisco – *La Plazuela, Vejer de la Frontera. ℘956 45 10 01. 25 rooms. ☐3.70€. Restaurant.* This former convent for Poor Clares dating from the 17C is situated in Vejer's old quarter. Although soberly decorated, the rooms are pleasant, with high ceilings and exposed beams. The hotel also has a good restaurant.

Hotel Toruño – *Pl. del Acebuchal 22, El Rocío. ℘959 44 23 23. 30 rooms.* At the edge of Parque Nacional de Doñana, this traditional great house blends perfectly into the village of El Rocío. Some rooms have lovely marsh views. Prices soar for the pilgrimage.

Posada de Palacio – *Caballeros 11 (Barrio Alto), Sanlúcar de Barrameda. ℘956 36 48 40. www. posadadepalacio.com. 30 rooms. ☐8€. Closed 8 Jan–Feb.* This family-run hotel is in an 18C mansion opposite the town hall *(ayuntamiento)* in the upper section of Sanlúcar. The rooms, laid out around an attractive patio, are simply yet tastefully decorated with antique furniture.

EAT

Casa Bigote – *Bajo de Guía 10, Sanlúcar de Barrameda. ℘956 36 26 96. www.restaurantecasabigote.com. Closed Nov, Sun.* This old tavern in the river district of Bajo Guía has developed into a famous gastronomic landmark. Run by the same family for the past 50 years,
it is decorated with old photos, fishing mementoes and antique objects. Pride of place on the extensive menu is given to the excellent local fish and prawns.

Trafalgar – *Pl. de España 31, Vejer de la Frontera. ℘956 44 76 38. Closed Jan, Sun, Mon (except Jun–Aug).* This welcome culinary surprise, on the attractive plaza de los Pescaítos, specialises in delicious fresh fish. Tapas are also served at the entrance. Guests can dine on the terrace in summer.

SIGHTSEEING

Because of the park's fragile ecology, entry to the **Doñana** is rigorously controlled. The El Acebuche visitor centre *(pl. Acebuchal, 22 El Rocío, Huelva; ℘959 448 711)* co-ordinates all park activities. **River trips** (4hr) are also available if booked in advance *(℘956 36 38 13)*. Contact the administrative centre for more information: *℘959 448 640*.

GUIDED TOURS

Several types of excursions are possible within the park and leave from El Acebuche visitor centre in Huelva:

By Jeep – These tours should be booked in advance. Two visits per day Tue–Sun at 8.30am and 3pm (5pm in high season). Itineraries vary according to the time of year.

On foot – A number of paths depart from the four information centres where details are available on the level of difficulty and duration of the walks.

On horseback – Excursions are available by horseback or horse-drawn carriage. Further information can be obtained from the visitor centres.

Costa del Sol★

Sheltered by the Sierra Nevada, Spain´s Sun Coast enjoys mild winters and hot summers. Millions of visitors are attracted by sandy beaches, whitewashed towns and villages and a variety of leisure activities. In summer, beaches are packed, and the nightlife continues until dawn.

 DRIVING TOURS

Tour of the Western Coastline★★

From Estepona to Málaga
139km/86mi – allow one day

Estepona★
The **old quarter**★ retains its Andalucían charm. Its attractions are the **plaza de las Flores**, the ruins of the castle and the 18C **Iglesia de los Remedios** (*pl. San Francisco*).

In the hills above is **Selwo Aventura Park** (○*open mid-Feb–Oct daily; Nov Fri–Sun, 4–8 Dec from 10am; see website for closing times;* ∞*24.50€, child 17€;* ✆*902 19 04 82; www.selwo.es*) where open-sided lorries takes visitors on safari spotting rhinos, giraffes, zebras, lions and tigers roaming freely in large enclosures which give the illusion of natural surroundings.

- **Michelin Map:** 578 V16-22, W 14-15-16. Local map, *see* 124 COSTA DEL SOL
- **Info:** Estepona: Av. San Lorenzo 1. ✆952 80 20 02; Marbella: Glorieta de la Fontanilla. ✆952 77 14 42; Nerja: Carmen 1. ✆952 52 15 31; Salobreña: Plaza de Goya. ✆958 61 03 14. www.visitcostadelsol.com.
- **Location:** The Costa del Sol stretches along the Mediterranean from the Straits of Gibraltar to east of Almería.
- **Parking:** You´ll have to search in beach towns, so get there early.
- **Kids:** Selwo Aventura Park.

Casares★, 24km/15mi inland along the A 377 and MA 539, is a charming much photographed whitewashed town of Moorish origin with a maze of narrow streets, clinging to a rock in the Sierra de Crestenilla.

San Pedro de Alcántara
22km/14mi E of Estepona, off E 15.
Archaeological sites close to the beach include **Las Bóvedas** (*thermal baths dating from the 3C AD*) and the palaeo-Christian basilica of Vega del Mar (*guided tours (1hr45min);* ∞*no charge;* it is

Puerto Banús

J. Malburet/MICHELIN

advisable to reserve a day ahead; ℘952 78 13 60)
For a description of the road from Ronda, see RONDA.

Puerto Banús★★
4km/2.5mi E of San Pedro along A 7.
This magnificent marina attracts some of the world's most luxurious sailing craft. Its many restaurants, bars and boutiques are hugely popular on summer evenings.

Marbella★★
8km/5mi E of Puerto Banús along N 340.
The long-established capital of the Costa del Sol is still an international jet-set destination.

Old quarter★
Whitewashed old buildings stand beside shops, bars and restaurants along a maze of streets and lanes.
The enchanting **plaza de los Naranjos★**, named for its orange trees, is lined by the 16C town hall, the 17C Casa del Corregidor, and a small 15C chapel, the Ermita de Nuestro Señor Santiago. Other sights in the old quarter are the 17C Iglesia de Santa María de la Encarnación and the **Museo del Grabado Español Contemporáneo★** (ⓞopen 22 Sept–15 Jun Mon & Sat 9am–2pm, Tue–Fri 9am–9pm; 16 Jun–21 Sept Mon and Sat 9am–2pm, Tue–Fri 9am–2pm, 6–9pm; ₃€, free on Sat; ℘952 76 57 41) devoted to contemporary prints, in a 16C former hospital.
Marbella also has a marina, luxury accommodations, excellent beaches, a long promenade, designer boutiques, health spas and golf courses.

Fuengirola
35km/22mi E of Marbella off E 15.
The Castillo de Sohail, a castle of Moorish origin, dominates this large resort. The remains of some Roman baths and villas are in the Santa Fe district.

▶ Head N for 9km/5.6mi towards Mijas.

Mijas★
Views★ from this picturesque white-washed town in the sierra encompass much of the coast. It is well worth strolling narrow, winding streets dotted with tiny squares and charming nooks and crannies. Highlights are sections of the old Moorish wall, and the 16C Iglesia de la Inmaculada Concepción, crowned by a Mudéjar tower. Shops display Andalucían arts and crafts (pottery, basketwork and textiles). Mijas also has an unusual miniatures museum, known as the **Carromato de Max** (Avenida del Compás; ⓞopen daily 10am–7pm (10pm in summer) ₃€; ℘952 48 58 20).

Benalmádena
8km/5mi E of Mijas along A 7.
Benalmádena stands several kilometres inland from the resort of Benalmádena Costa. Its main historical sights include several 16C watchtowers and a small **archaeological museum** (ⓞopen late-Sept–Jun Tue–Sat 9.30am–1.30pm; Jul–early Sept Tue–Sat 9.30am–1.30pm, 5–7pm; Sun and public holidays 10am–2pm; ⓞclosed 1 and 6 Jan, Good Fri, 1 May, 24, 25, 31 Dec; ℘952 44 85 93).

Torremolinos
12km/7.4mi NE of Benalmádena, off E 15. www.ayto-torremolinos.org.
The promenade and the long beach are the main attractions of this onetime fishing village, now a huge resort.

Málaga★ (See MÁLAGA)
17km/10.5mi NE from Torremolinos off A 7. ▭Explanada de la Estación.

Tour of the Eastern Coastline★
From Málaga to Almería
204km/127mi – allow one day.
This beautiful coast is punctuated by the ruins of Moorish towers – defences built after the Reconquest against attacks by Barbary pirates.

Nerja★
53km/33mi E of Málaga along E 15.
Nerja, a large resort, overlooks the Mediterranean from the top of a prom-

ontory. The **Balcón de Europa**★ is a magnificent mirador offering views of this dramatic coastline and occasional glimpses of North Africa.

Cuevas de Nerja★★

4.5km/2.7mi E along the Motril road.
🕐 *Open daily 10am–2pm, 4–6.30pm.*
🎫 *8.50€.* ✆ *952 52 95 20.*

In this cave were found paintings, weapons, jewels and bones, indicating habitation in the Palaeolithic era. Its size and stalactites and stalagmites are both impressive. An annual festival of music and dance is held in the Sala de la Cascada (Cascade Chamber) the second and third weeks of July.

The Road from Nerja to La Herradura★

The scenic road snakes along a mountainside with delightful **views**★★.

Almuñécar

23km/14mi E of Nerja along N 340.
Bananas, medlars, pomegranates and mangoes are grown on the small alluvial plain *(hoya)* behind this resort. The **Cueva de los Siete Palacios** houses an archaeological museum *(🕐open Tue–Sat 10.30am–1.30pm, 6.30–9pm, Sun 10.30am–1.30pm; 🎫2€; ✆958 63 11 25).* The **Castillo de San Miguel** is also open to the public *(San Miguel; 🕐open*

Cueva de Nerja

H. Champollion/MICHELIN

Tue–Sat 10.30am–1.30pm, 5–7.30pm, Sun 10.30am–2pm; 🎫2.30€).

Salobreña★

13km/8mi E of Almuñécar along E 15.
Salobreña, prettiest town on this coast, spreads across a hill, a white blanket punctuated by purple splashes of bougainvillea. An imposing Moorish **fortress** converted into a palatial residence by Nasrid kings in the 14C stands above *(🕐 open daily 9.30am–2pm, 4–6.30pm; 🎫1.80€; ✆958 61 03 14).*

The Road from Calahonda to Castell de Ferro★

The road hugs the rocky coast, offering mountain and sea views. After Balanegra the N 340 turns inland through an immense sweep of greenhouses around El Ejido, where flowers, vegetables and tropical fruit are grown.

Almería 🕮 *See ALMERÍA*

Town of Salobreña with its castle

©Philip Lange/Bigstockphoto.com

ADDRESSES

🛏 STAY

ALMUÑÉCAR

⊖🍽🛏 **Hotel Casablanca** – *Pl. San Cristóbal 4*. ☎*958 63 55 75*. *http://hotel casablancaalmunecar.com*. *35 rooms.* ⊐*2.50€*. *Restaurant*⊖🍽. With its cupola, raspberry-coloured façade and arches that imitate the architecture of Moroccan palaces, the Casablanca is a visual experience not to be missed! Once inside your room, the crystal chandeliers and marble décor add a decidedly Oriental touch. Make sure you book in advance.

BENALMÁDENA

⊖🍽🛏 **Hotel La Fonda** – *Santo Domingo 7*. ☎*952 56 83 24*. *26 rooms.* A charming hotel in the Sierra de Castillejos, overlooking the Mediterranean. Spacious rooms, indoor pool, flower-filled patios and terraces with views of the hills and sea. Very reasonably priced given the standard.

ESTEPONA

⊖🍽 **Hostal El Pilar** – *Pl. de las Flores 10*. ☎*952 80 00 18*. *www.hostalelpilar.es*. *17 rooms.* Time would appear to have stopped in this charming *hostal* on the main square. The interior, decorated with black and white family photos, has an impressive staircase leading up to the basic but pleasant rooms.

MARBELLA

⊖🍽🛏 **Hotel La Morada Más Hermosa** – *Montenebros 16*. ☎*952 92 44 67*. *www. lamoradamashermosa.com*. *7 rooms.* Find this hotel on a plant-bedecked alley right in the old part of town. The charming rooms have been decorated with care by the owner in a personal country Andalucían style with colonial details. Ask for room 2 with its pleasant terrace or wood-panelled room 5.

⊖🍽🛏🛏 **Marbella Club** – *Bulevar Príncipe Alfonso von Hohenlohe*. ☎*952 82 22 11*. *www.marbellaclub.com*. *135 rooms.* ⊐*35€*. *Six restaurants*⊖🍽🛏🛏 One of the best hotels along the coast, built in the middle of a superb garden planted with palm trees. The bungalow accommodation here frequently hosts the rich and famous. The Marbella Club is the perfect place to unwind and enjoy the magnificent sports facilities available (swimming pool, beach, tennis, golf, spa, etc.).

NERJA

⊖🍽 **Hostal San Miguel** – *San Miguel 36*. ☎*952 52 18 86*. *www. hostalsanmiguel.com*. *12 rooms.* ⊐*4.50€*. This hotel is in a recently restored town house near the centre, with modest but comfortable rooms. There's a bar-coffee shop, and a special feature is the top-floor terrace with small pool and sea and mountain views.

⊖🍽🛏 **Hostal Marissal** – *Pas. Balcón de Europa 3*. ☎*952 52 01 99*. *www.hostalmarissal.com*. *22 rooms.* ⊐*3€*. *Restaurant*⊖🍽. In a privileged location, at the entry to the famed Balcony of Europe, with fine views to the passage from some rooms. Coffee shop and restaurant.

OJÉN

⊖🍽🛏 **La Hostería de Don José** – *Pas. del Nacimiento*. ☎*952 88 11 47*. *www.lahosteriadedonjose.com*. *6 rooms.* A charming small hotel on the top of a hill overlooking the town. At the Don José everything you need for a comfortable stay is on hand: comfort, simple yet cosy furnishings, a friendly welcome and unforgettable views of Ojén's whitewashed houses set against the backdrop of the Mediterranean.

🍴 EAT

MARBELLA

⊖🍽 **El Balcón de la Virgen** – *Remedios 2*. ☎*952 77 60 92*. *www.hosteleriamalaga.com/ elbalcondelavirgen*. *Closed Tue.* In an attractive street lined by an endless succession of restaurant terraces.

Plaza de los Naranjos, Marbella
©Turespaña

The restaurant, recognisable by the image of the Virgin Mary on its attractive façade, is mainly popular with tourists. Andalucían cuisine.

Casa de la Era – *Finca El Chorraero. 1km/0.6mi N. ℘952 77 06 25. www.casadelaera.com. Closed Mon–Thu (except Aug) for dinner, Aug for lunch, Sun.* In a typical chalet house, this restaurant affords superb views of the mountain range, to go with the Andalucían and Morrocan cuisine.

MIJAS

La Alcazaba de Mijas – *Pl. de la Constitución. ℘952 59 02 53. www.rest-laalcazabademijas.com. Closed Mon. Reservations recommended.* Perched on the Arab walls of Mijas with fine vistas and careful decoration, La Alcazaba's best feature is its timeless *Mozarabic* dining room, with flowing detailing and two venerable horseshoe arches framing an endless landscape.

El Olivar – *Av. Virgen de la Peña, edificio El Rosario. ℘952 48 61 96. Closed Feb, Sat.* This country restaurant offers fine sierra views through its large windows and finer views from its terrace.

NERJA

Marisquería La Marea – *Pl. Cantarero. ℘952 52 57 78. Reservations recommended.* A good address for fish and seafood. The scallops and clams on display at the bar are grilled fresh when you order them and served either in the bar itself or in the nautically decorated restaurant.

Pepe Rico – *Almirante Ferrándiz 28. ℘952 52 02 47. www.peperico.info. Closed 3 weeks in Jan, Sun.* On a pedestrianised street, this is a cosy, Swedish-run eatery with fireplace, ceiling fans, and oil paintings on its walls. Specialities include duck cooked in wine and suckling pig. Holiday flats are available around a patio ().

Udo Heimer – *Pueblo Andaluz 27. ℘952 52 00 32. www.udoheimer.net. Closed Jan, Mon–Wed and Sun for dinner. Reservations required.* An arresting variety of textures and flavours epitomises the cuisine of this establishment, with locally sourced produce.

OJÉN

Mesón Lorente – *Junquillo 32. ℘952 88 11 74. Closed 2nd half of Jan and Jul, Thu. Reservations recommended.* Many Andalucíans and tourists looking for a breather from the coast head for this restaurant, which is well known for its home cooking. The greenhouse looks onto the liveliest street in the town.

TAPAS

The pedestrianised district of **La Carihuela**, alongside the beach, is the most attractive part of Torremolinos, with dozens of bars, restaurants, hotels and shops. Two of the best restaurants are **Casa Juan** (*pas. Marítimo 28; ℘952 38 56 56*), which has been specialising in seafood for more than 30 years, and **La Jábega** (*Mar 17; ℘952 38 63 75*), overlooking the promenade.

🛒 SHOPPING

Marbella is one of the best places for shopping on the Costa del Sol with all the top names in international fashion represented here.
Most of these stores are concentrated in Puerto Banús, where there is an impressive nucleus of modern, designer boutiques, and in the centre of Marbella, particularly along avenida Ricardo Soriano and calle Ramón y Cajal. The best indoor shopping centre on the Costa del Sol is also found in Puerto Banús.
Markets are an important feature of life on the Costa del Sol. The one in Marbella takes place on Saturday mornings next to the Nueva Andalucía bullring (*pl. de Toros*) near Puerto Banús.

La Carihuela

B. Kaufmann/ MICHELIN

Granada★★★

Granada enjoys a glorious setting★★★ on a fertile plain overlooked by three hills and the majestic peaks of the Sierra Nevada. Watching over the modern Christian city stands the breathtaking Alhambra, one of the most magnificent monuments ever created by man and for many, the highlight of Spain.

THE CITY TODAY

Granada has an undoubtedly glorious past and a bright present too. The vast majority of visitors see little beyond the Alhambra and perhaps the picturesque cobbled labyrinth that is the Albaicín district. The city beyond is young and vibrant, from the earthy Gypsy clubs of Sacromonte to its crammed tapas bars and hip nightclubs driven by a high student population.

A BIT OF HISTORY

Granada gained importance in the 11C as Córdoba declined. It became capital of the Almoravids, who were ousted a century later by the Almohads. In the 13C, Muslims from Córdoba, fleeing the Christians in 1236, sought refuge, enriching the city. In 1238, the new **Nasrid** *ruler, Mohammed ibn Nasr, submitted to the authority of Ferdinand III, thus ensuring peace, and the kingdom flourished.*

The fall of Granada – In the 15C, the Catholic Monarchs turned their attention to Granada. By 2 January 1492, after a six-month siege, the city fell. Boabdil, the last Nasrid king, delivered the keys of the city and went into exile. As he looked back, his mother is said to have scolded him: "You weep like a woman for what you could not hold as a man."

Granada flourished again in the Renaissance, but its fortunes suffered during the ruthless suppression of the Las Alpujarras revolt in 1570.

Modern Granada – The old quarters east of **plaza Nueva**, havens of peace and greenery on the Alhambra and Albaicín hills, contrast with the noisy, bustling lower town and the pedestrian

▸ **Population:** 236 988
⚲ **Michelin Map:** 578 U 19 (town plan) map 124 COSTA DEL SOL
🛈 **Info:** Central Tourist Reception Centre: Virgen Blanca 9. ℘902 40 50 45; Info points: Plaza Bib-Rambla; Plazade Mariana Pineda 10; Avenida Generalife; Plaza de Santa Ana. www.granadatur.com.
◗ **Location:** Granada is in southern Andalucía, separated from the sea by the Sierra Nevada. The A 44 and other highways link with major cities in the region. 🚍Avenida de los Andaluces
🅿 **Parking:** Space is limited in the Albaicín; there is visitor parking at the Alhambra.
⊘ **Don't Miss:** The Alhambra.
🕑 **Timing:** Organise your stay around your visit to the Alhambra, fitting other sights as time allows.
👪 **Kids:** Take the little ones to Parque de las Ciencias.

quarter around the Cathedral between the **Gran Vía de Colón** and **Calle de los Reyes Católicos**.

SIGHTS
The Alhambra and the Generalife★★★

Real de la Alhambra 🕑*Open daily Mar–Oct 8.30am–8pm; Nov–Feb 8.30am–2pm, 2–6pm. Night-time visits Mar–Oct Tue–Sat 10–11.30pm; Nov–Feb Fri–Sat 8–9.30pm.* 🕑*Closed 1 Jan, 25 Dec.* ⊘*12€, advance purchase from any branches of the BBV bank in Spain. One ticket covers the entire Alhambra and Generalife gardens and specifies entry time to the Nasrid Palace. 6€ for gardens only.* ℘*902 44 12 21. www.alhambra-patronato.es.*

Nasrid architecture was the ultimate expression of a civilisation in decline.

Alhambra

B. Kaufmann/MICHELIN

Nasrid princes built for the moment: beneath fabulous decoration lie ill-assorted bricks and rubble, so it is surprising how little time has diminished this masterpiece.

Decoration was the main concern. Walls and ceilings everywhere reveal an art without equal. **Stuccowork** is worked in patterns in a low relief of flat planes to catch the light; another type of decoration was made by cutting away layers of plaster to form stalactites *(mocárabes)*. This type of ornament, painted and even gilded, covered capitals, cornice mouldings, arches, pendentives and entire cupolas.

Ceramic tiles provided geometric decoration for walls: *alicatados* formed a colourful marquetry, with lines of arabesque motifs making star designs; *azulejos* gave colour, different hues separated by a thin raised fillet or a black line *(cuerda seca)*. **Calligraphy** employed elegant Andalucían cursive; the more decorative Cufic was reserved for religious aphorisms in scrollwork.

The Alhambra★★★

The Calat Alhambra (Red Castle) must be one of the most remarkable fortresses ever built. It commands views of the town, the Sacromonte heights,

hillsides and the gardens of the Albaicín. Enter through the Puerta de Las Granadas (Pomegranate Gateway) built by Emperor Charles V; a paved footpath then leads through to the **shrubbery**★.

Palacios Nazaríes★★★ (Nasrid Palace)

The 14C Nasrid Palace was built around the Patio de los Arrayanes and Patio de los Leones. Its richness and the originality of its decoration defy description. In the **Mexuar**, used for government and judicial administration, a frieze of *azulejos* and an epigraphic border cover the walls. An oratory stands at one end. Cross the **Patio del Cuarto Dorado** (1). The south wall, protected by a remarkable carved wood cornice, exemplifies Granada art: windows are surrounded by panels covered with every variety of stucco and tile decoration. The **Cuarto Dorado** (Golden Room) has tiled panelling, fine stuccowork and a beautiful wooden ceiling. The delightful **view**★ extends over the Albaicín.

Adjoining is the beautiful oblong **Patio de los Arrayanes** (Myrtle Courtyard). A pool banked by myrtles reflects the **Torre de Comares** (Comares Tower) which contrasts with slender porticoes

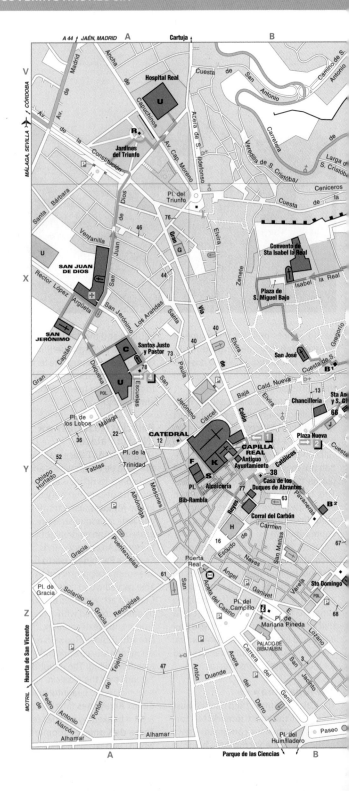

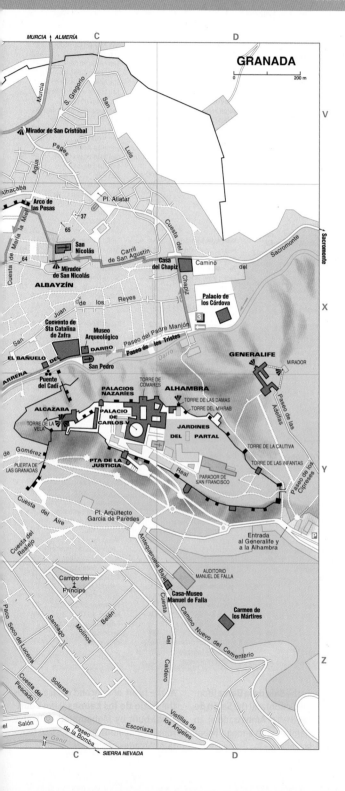

GRANADA

0   200 m

GRANADA STREET INDEX

SIGHTS ON MAP

that give onto the **Sala de la Barca** (from *barakha*, benediction) and the **Salón de Embajadores** (Hall of Ambassadors), an audience chamber with a magnificent domed cedar ceiling.

At the heart of a second palace stands the **Patio de los Leones** (Lion Courtyard) built by Mohammed V. Twelve rough stone lions support a low fountain. Arcades of slender columns lead to the main state apartments. The **Sala de los Abencerrajes** (named for the family massacred here) has a splendid star-shaped *mocárabe* cupola.

The vaulting of alcoves at the end of the **Sala de los Reyes** (Kings' Chamber) is atypically painted to illustrate pastimes of Moorish and Christian princes – possibly done after the Reconquest.

The **Sala de las Dos Hermanas** (Hall of the Two Sisters), named for two marble slabs in the pavement, is renowned for honeycomb cupola vaulting. Beyond are the resplendent **Sala de los Ajimeces** and the **Mirador de Lindaraja**. Past a room once occupied by Washington Irving is a gallery with views of the Albaícin. *Descend to the Patio de la Reja* (2).

▶ *Cross the Patio de Lindaraja to the Partal Gardens.*

Gardens and perimeter towers★★

The terraced Jardines del Partal descend to the 14C porticoed **Torre de las Damas** (Ladies' Tower). The Torre de Mihrab (*right*) is a former oratory. The Torre de la Cautiva and Torre de las Infantas (Captive's and Infantas' towers) are sumptuously decorated inside.

▶ *Enter the Palacio de Carlos V.*

Palacio de Carlos V★★ (Emperor Charles V's Palace)

In 1526, Pedro Machuca was commissioned to design a palace to be financed by a tax on the Moors. The 1568 uprising delayed construction. It is one of the most successful Renaissance creations in Spain. Although in comparison with the Nasrid Palaces the building may at first appear lacking, its grandeur becomes apparent, in its perfect lines, its dignity, and its simple plan of a circle within a square.

Museo de la Alhambra★

Palacio de Carlos V. ◷*Open Tue–Sat 9am–2pm.* ◷*Closed public holidays.* ☞*No charge.*

This museum is devoted to Hispano-Moorish art: ceramics, woodcarvings, panels and more. Outstanding are the famous 14C **blue** (or **gazelle**) **amphora**★ and the Pila de Almanzor, decorated with lions and deer.

Museo de Bellas Artes (Fine Arts Museum)

Palacio de Carlos V. ◷*Open Mar–Oct Tue 2.30–8pm, Wed–Sat 9am–8pm, Sun and public holidays 9am–2.30pm; Nov–Feb Tue 2.30–6pm, Wed–Sat 9am–6pm, Sun and public holidays 9am–2.30pm.* ◷*Closed 1, 6 Jan, 1 May, 24–25, 31 Dec.* ☞*1.50€; free for EU citizens.* ✆*958 57 54 50.*

Religious sculpture and paintings of the 16C to the 18C predominate: works by Diego de Siloé, Pedro de Mena, Vicente Carducho and Alonso Cano, and a magnificent still life, *Thistle and Carrots*★★, by Brother Juan Sánchez Cotán.

Alcazaba★

The two towers of this austere fortress on the Plaza de los Aljibes (Cistern Court) date to the 13C. The Torre de la Vela (Watchtower) commands a fine **panorama**★★ of the palace, gardens, Sacromonte and the Sierra Nevada.

Puerta de la Justicia★

The massive Justice Gateway is built into a tower in the outer walls. On the façade, a strip of delightful 16C *azulejos* bears an image of the Virgin and Child.

The Generalife★★

The **water gardens** are one of the most enjoyable parts of the 14C Generalife, the summer palace. The Patio de los Cipreses (Cypress Alley) and Patio de las Adelfas (Oleander) lead in. The nucleus is the **Patio de la Acequia** (Canal Court), a pool with fountains, a pavilion at either end, and a *mirador* in the middle. The pavilion to the rear contains the Sala Regia, with fine stuccowork.

The upper gardens contain the famous **escalera del agua**, or water staircase.

CATHEDRAL QUARTER
Capilla Real★★ (Chapel Royal)

Oficios 3. ◐*Open Apr–Oct Mon–Sat 10.30am–1pm, 4–7pm, Sun 11am–1pm, 4–7pm; Nov–Mar Mon–Sat 10.30am–1pm, 3.30–6.30pm, Sun 11am–1pm, 3.30–6.30pm.* ◐*Closed 1, 2 Jan, Good Friday, 12 Oct (morning), 25 Dec.* ⊗*3€.* ☏*958 22 78 48. www.capillareal granada.com.*

The **Catholic Monarchs** commissioned this Isabelline Gothic chapel by Enrique Egas. To enter *(by the south door)*, cross the courtyard of the old **Lonja** (Exchange), also by Egas. The south front has an elegant Renaissance façade of superimposed arcades with turned columns. Every conceivable decoration of the Isabelline style is seen inside: ribbed vaulting, coats of arms, the yoke and fasces (revived in 1934 by the Falange), monograms, and the eagle of St John. In the chancel, closed by a gilded **screen★★★** by Master Bartolomé, are the **mausoleums★★★** of the Catholic Monarchs on the right, and of Philip the Handsome and Juana the Mad, the parents of Charles V, on the left. The first was carved by Fancelli in Genoa in 1517, the second, magnificent in scale and workmanship, by Bartolomé Ordóñez (the sarcophagi are in the crypt). The high altar **retable★** (1520) by Felipe Vigarny shows great movement and expression. The lower register of the predella depicts the siege of Granada and the baptism of the Moriscos.

Sacristía-Museo

Among objects on display are **Queen Isabel's sceptre and crown**, **King Ferdinand's sword**, and outstanding **paintings★★** by Flemish (Rogier Van der Weyden), Italian (Perugino, Botticelli) and Spanish (Bartolomé Bermejo, Pedro Berruguete) artists. The central section of the *Triptych of the Passion* was painted by the Fleming Dirk Bouts. Two sculptures of the Catholic Monarchs at prayer are by Felipe Vigarny.

Opposite are the 18C Baroque-style former **town hall** *(ayuntamiento)*, and just below, the **Centro de Arte José Guerrero**, dedicated to modern art, especially Granada's José Guerrero (1914–91) *(Oficios 8;* ◐*open mid-Sept–May Tue–Sat and public holidays 10.30am–2pm, 4–9pm, Sun 10.30am–2pm; Jun–mid-Sept Tue–Sat and public holidays 11am–2pm, 5–9pm, Sun 10.30am–2pm;* ◐*closed 1 Jan, 24–25, 31 Dec;* ⊗*1€, free on Wed;* ☏*958 22 01 09; www.centroguerrero.org).*

Catedral★

Gran Vía de Colón 5. ◐*Open Apr–Oct Mon–Sat 10.45am–1.30pm, 4–8pm, Sun and public holidays 4–8pm; Nov–Mar Mon–Sat 10.45am–1.30pm, 4–7pm, Sun and public holidays 4–7pm.* ⊗*3.50€.* ☏*958 22 29 59.*

Construction started in 1518. Diego de Siloé introduced the Renaissance style to the design of Enrique Egas. The façade (1667) is by Alonso Cano.

The **Capilla Mayor★** is surprising. Siloé designed a rotunda circled by an ambulatory, cleverly linked to the basilica. The rotunda combines superimposed orders, the uppermost with paintings by Alonso Cano of the Life of the Virgin and beautiful 16C stained glass. Marking the rotunda entrance are figures of the Catholic Monarchs by Pedro de Mena and, in a medallion by Alonso Cano, Adam and Eve.

The **organ★** from about 1750 is by Leonardo of Ávila. The finely carved Isabelline doorway in the south transept is

Façade,Catedral de la Encarnación de Granada

©Ken Sorrie/iStockphoto.com

ALHAMBRA

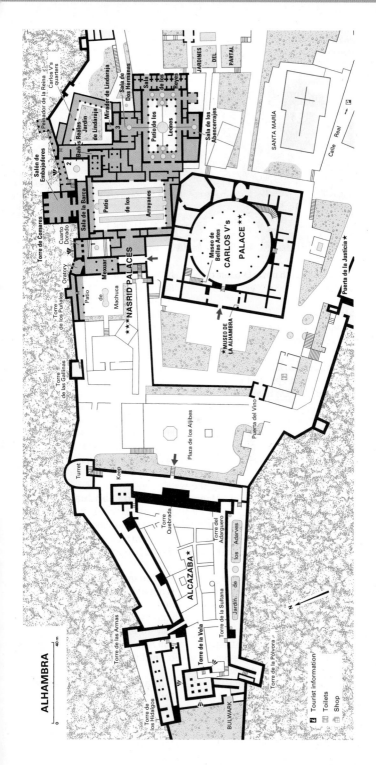

0 — 40 m

Torre de los Hidalgos
Torre de las Armas
Torre de la Vela
Torre de la Sultana
Jardín de los Adarves
Torre del Adarguero
ALCAZABA ★
Torre Quebrada
Torre de la Pólvora
BULWARK
Torre de los Puñales
Torre de las Gallinas
Keep
Turret
Plaza de los Aljibes
Puerta del Vino
Puerta de la Justicia ★

★★★ NASRID PALACES
Patio de Machuca
Oratory
Mexuar
Cuarto Dorado
Patio de los Arrayanes
Sala de la Barca
Torre de Comares
Salón de Embajadores
Baños Reales
Jardín de Lindaraja
Peinador de la Reina
Carlos V's quarters
Mirador de Lindaraja
Sala de Dos Hermanas
Sala de los Reyes
Patio de los Leones
Sala de los Abencerrajes

JARDINES DEL PARTAL

CARLOS V's PALACE ★★
Museo de Bellas Artes
★ MUSEO DE LA ALHAMBRA

SANTA MARÍA
Calle Real

N

🅘 Tourist information
🚻 Toilets
🛍 Shop

139

View of Albaicin district from the Alhambra

©Christina Hanck/iStockphoto.com

the original **north portal**★ of the older Capilla Real.

Alcaicería

The area, with craft and souvenir shops, was a silk market in Moorish times.

Corral del Carbón

Mariana Pineda. ⊘*Open Mon–Fri 9am–7pm, Sat–Sun 10am–2pm.* ⊜*No charge.*

This 14C former Moorish storehouse has an arched doorway with *alfiz* surround and panels of *sebka* decoration.

ALBAICÍN★★

This quarter covers a slope facing the Alhambra. It was here that the Moors lived after the Reconquest.

Alleys are lined by white-walled houses. Walls enclose luxuriant gardens of *cármenes* (town houses). Go to the **Iglesia de San Nicólas** *(plaza de San Nicólas)* at sunset, for a **view**★★★ of the Alhambra and the Generalife. The Sierra Nevada beyond is spectacular under snow in winter.

Baños Árabes★ (El Bañuelo)

Car. del Darro 31. ⊘*Open Tue–Sat 10am–2pm.* ⊘*Closed public holidays.* ⊜*No charge.* ℘*958 22 97 38.*

These 11C baths with star-pierced vaulting are the best preserved in Spain.

Monasterio de San Jerónimo★

Rector López Argüeta. ⊘*Open daily Oct–Mar 10am–1.30pm, 3–7.30pm; Apr–Sept 10am–1.30pm, 4–7.30pm.* ⊜*3€.* ℘*958 27 93 37.*

This 16C monastery was principally designed by Diego de Siloé. Plateresque and Renaissance doorways lead to harmonious cloisters. The **church**★★, with the tomb of Gonzalo Fernández de Córdoba, the Gran Capitán, has a rich Renaissance apse, and superb coffers and vaulting adorned with saints, angels and animals. The **retable**★★ is a jewel of the Granadine School. The paintings are from the 18C.

Basílica de San Juan de Dios★

San Juan de Dios 23. ⊶*Guided tours (50min) Sept–Jul Mon–Sat 10am–1pm; open afternoons by prior arrangement.* ⊘*Closed public holidays.* ℘*958 27 57 00.*

The Baroque Church of St John of God is noted for its richness and stylistic uniformity. Behind a massive Churrigueresque altarpiece of gilded wood is a lavish *camarín* with the funerary urn of **San Juan de Dios**, founder of the Order of Knights Hospitallers.

Monasterio de la Cartuja★

Pas. de la Cartuja. ⊘*Open Apr–Oct 10am–1pm, 4–8pm; Nov–Mar daily 10am–1pm, 3.30–6pm.* ⊜*3€.* ℘*958 16 19 32.*

Go in through the cloisters. The church is exuberantly decorated with Baroque stucco. At the back of the apse is the early 18C Sancta Sanctorum, a *camarín* decorated with multi-hued marble; beneath the cupola, painted in false relief, a marble Sagrario contains the Tabernacle.

The outstanding Late Baroque **sacristy**★★ (1727–64) is called the Christian Alhambra for its intricate stuccowork. The door and cedarwood furnishings, inlaid with tortoiseshell, mother-of-pearl and silver, are by a Carthusian monk, José Manuel Vásquez.

👥 Parque de las Ciencias★

Av. de la Ciencia. 🕐*Open Mon–Sat 10am–7pm; Sun and public holidays 10am–3pm.*🕐*Closed 1 Jan, 1 May, 25 Dec.* 💶*5.50€ (child 4.50€), 2.50€ planetarium (child 2€).* 📞*958 13 19 00. www.parqueciencias.com.*

This science park comprises an interactive museum, planetarium, observatory and tropical butterfly collection.

Museo Arqueológico

Carrera del Darro 43. 🕐*Open Tue 2.30–8.30pm, Wed–Sat 9am–8.30pm, Sun and public holidays 9am–2.30pm.* 🕐*Closed 1, 6 Jan, 1 May, 1 Nov, 24–25, 31 Dec.* 💶*1.50€; free for EU citizens.* 📞*958 57 54 08.*

The archaeological museum is in Casa Castril, a Renaissance palace with a fine **Plateresque doorway**★. It exhibits Egyptian alabaster vases found in a necropolis in Almuñecar, a bull figure from Arjona and Roman and Moorish decorative art.

Sacromonte

The hillside opposite the Generalife is the Gypsy quarter where flamenco performances are given in troglodyte dwellings. At then end of camino del Sacromonte is the 17C–18C abbey for which the hill is named *(Barranco de los Negros;* 🕐 *museum open Apr–Oct Tue–Sun 10am–2pm, 5–9pm; Nov–Mar Tue–Sun 10am–2pm, 4–7pm;* 💶*4€ vantage point; 1€ other areas;* 📞*958 21 51 20; www.sacromontegranada.com).*

Hospital Real

Cuesta del Hospicio.

The royal hospital, now the university rectorate, was founded by the Catholic Monarchs. The plan, similar to those in Toledo and Santiago de Compostela, is of a cross within a square. Four Plateresque windows adorn the façade.

Fundación Rodríguez-Acosta★

Callejón Niños del Rollo 8. 🕐*Open Wed–Sun 10am–2pm (Tue for pre arranged bookings only).* 🕐*Closed public holidays.* 💶*4€; 6€ with cave, library tour.* 📞*958 22 74 97. www.fundacion rodriguezacosta.com.*

This foundation houses the legacies of painter José María Rodríguez-Acosta (1886–1941) and archaeologist Manuel Gómez-Moreno (1870–1970), in a fine *carmen* built between 1914 and 1928. Gómez-Moreno's personal collection includes Romanesque and Gothic pieces, and canvases by Zurbarán, Ribera, Alonso Cano and others, as well as Aztec and Chinese items.

Carmen de los Mártires

Pas. de los Mártires. 🕐*Open Nov–Mar Mon–Fri 10am–2pm, 4–6pm, Sat–Sun and public holidays 10am–6pm; Apr–Jul Sept–Oct Mon–Sat 10am–2pm, 6–8pm, Sun and public holidays 10am–8pm.* 💶*No charge.* 📞*958 22 79 53.*

The romantic terraced **gardens**★ of this Carmelite monastery on the Alhambra hill are embellished with fountains and sculptures.

🚶 WALKING TOURS

🔖*Suggested routes are marked on the plan.*

EXCURSIONS

Fuente Vaqueros

Federico García Lorca, poet and dramatist, was born 20km/12.4mi from Granada in this village in 1898. The house museum **Huerta de San Vicente** *(*🕐*open Tue–Sun Oct–Mar 10am–1pm, 4–6pm; Apr–Jun and Sept 10am–1pm, 5–7pm; Jul–Aug 10am–2pm;* 💶*3€;* 📞*958 51 69 62; www.museogarcialorca.org)* offers admirers an insight into his life.

The Alpujarran Uprising

In 1499 the Arabs who did not wish to leave Spain were forced to renounce their religion and to convert to Christianity. They were known as Moriscos. In 1566 Philip II forbade them their language and traditional dress, which sparked off a serious uprising, especially in Las Alpujarras where the Moriscos proclaimed as king Fernando de Córdoba under the name Abén Humeya. In 1571 Philip II sent in the army under Don Juan of Austria, who crushed the rebellion. However, a tense feeling of unrest remained, and in 1609 Philip III ordered the expulsion of all the Moriscos (who numbered about 275 000) from Spain.

SIERRA NEVADA★★

The Sierra Nevada between the Costa del Sol and Granada is massive, beautiful, and often snow-capped. There is skiing at **Solynieve**★★, with over 60km/37mi of slopes, 45 runs and 20 ski lifts. Lodging is at **Pradollano**.
Vehicular access to the **national park** is restricted; the best way to tour is on foot. The most interesting routes are the ascents to the Laguna de la Yeguas, **Mulhacén** (3 482m/11 424ft) and **Veleta** (3 394m/11 132ft). Contact **El Dornajo Visitor Centre** (◷ *open 9am–2pm (2.30pm in summer), 4.30–6pm (7pm in summer);* ☏*958 34 06 25*).

Alhama de Granada★

60km/37mi SW on the A 92 and A 335.
Alhama de Granada is a village of white-washed houses and narrow streets above a deep gorge, dominated by the **Iglesia de la Encarnación**★, a well-proportioned church built of golden stone. The stunning **view**★ from the belvedere behind the Iglesia del Carmen encompasses the canyon of the Alhama River. Baths on the outskirts date from the Roman period. A Moorish **cistern**★ survives.

🚗 DRIVING TOUR

THE ALPUJARRAS★★
90km/56mi – allow one day.
This isolated region stretches across the southern slopes of the Sierra Nevada.

From Lanjarón to Valor
The High Alpujarras encompass the valley of the Guadalfeo river. Houses typically have a flat roof terrace, a *terrao*.

Lanjarón
This resort is famous for its medicinal mineral water and spa. The 16C castle affords fine valley views.

▷ *9km/5.6mi from Lanjarón, before Órgiva, take the GR 421, a narrow mountain road.*

Pampaneira★★
Of the villages in the **Poqueira Valley**★★, Pampaneira best preserves its traditional architecture, including the 17C Iglesia de Santa Cruz.
Bubión, a centre of Morisco resistance in 1569, is 5km/3mi further along. In **Capileira** is the **Museo de Artes y Costumbres Populares**, a museum re-creating 19C Alpujarran life through its popular arts and customs (*Casa de la Cultura;* ◷*open Mon–Fri 11.30am–2.30pm, Sat 4–7pm (8pm in summer);* ☏*958 76 30 51*).

▷ *Return to the GR 421. The road enters the Trevélez Valleya.*

Trevélez★
Trevélez, the highest municipality in Spain (1 600m/5,248ft), is famous for cured hams and dried sausages. Behind the village rises **Mulhacén**, Spain's highest peak (3 482m/11 424ft). Beyond Trevélez, the valley opens and the verdant landscape gives way to drier terrain planted with the occasional vineyard.
Yegen owes it fame to the Englishman Gerald Brenan, the author of *South from Granada*.
Abén Humeya (👆*see The Alpujarran Uprising sidebar*) was born and lived in Válor, the next village after Yegen. Its 16C church, like many in the region, is built in Mudéjar style.

ADDRESSES

🛏 STAY

🍽🍽 **Hotel Los Tilos** – *Pl. Bib Rambla 4. ℰ958 26 67 12. www.hotellostilos.com. 30 rooms. ☕7€.* This no-frills hotel fronts a charming square filled with flower stalls, just a few metres from the Cathedral. Although on the basic side, the rooms are comfortable, some with the bonus of a view over the plaza.

🍽🍽 **Hotel Maciá Plaza** – *Pl. Nueva 5. ℰ958 22 75 36. www.maciahoteles. com. 44 rooms. ☕7€.* A four-storey building with an attractive façade in a central square at the foot of the Alhambra. Standard-quality rooms with carpets and wicker furniture.

🍽🍽🍽 **Hotel América** – *Real de la Alhambra 53. ℰ958 22 74 71. www.hotel-americagranada.com. 17 rooms. ☕8€. Restaurant 🍽. Closed Dec–Feb.* A small, family-run hotel superbly located within the confines of the Alhambra. A warm welcome and friendly service are the trademarks of the América, which also has a pleasant patio.

🍽🍽🍽 **Hotel Palacio de Santa Inés** – *Cuesta de Santa Inés 9. ℰ958 22 23 62. www.palaciosantaines.com. 35 rooms. ☕10€.* This 16C Mudéjar-inspired building is situated in the Albaicín district, with several rooms enjoying views of Granada's number one attraction. In the charming colonnaded patio, you can still make out what's left of the building's original Renaissance frescoes.

🍴 EAT

🍽🍽 **La Ermita en la Plaza de Toros** – *Av. Doctor Olóriz 25 (at the bullring). ℰ958 29 02 57. www.ermitaplazadetoros. com. Closed 24, 31 Dec for dinner.* Its unusual location within the confines of the city's bullring and its tasteful decoration of exposed brickwork, wooden tables, rustic-style chairs and bullfighting memorabilia on the walls have made this a popular restaurant in which to enjoy typical Andalucían cuisine. The restaurant is on the first floor, and a tapas bar on the ground floor.

🍽🍽🍽 **Chikito** – *Pl. Campillo 9. ℰ958 22 33 64. www.restaurantechikito.com. Closed Wed. Reservations recommended.* A hugely popular restaurant and bar with locals and visitors alike, and renowned for serving local specialities and superb cured hams. It was here that artists and intellectuals such as García Lorca used to meet in the 1930s.

🍽🍽🍽 **Mirador de Morayma** – *Pianista García Carrillo 2. ℰ958 22 48 12. www.alqueriamorayma.com. Closed Sun July–Aug, Sun eve rest of year.* This restaurant in the Albaicín district has one of the best settings of any in the city. Rustic décor, a plant-filled terrace and magnificent views of the Alhambra. Private-label wines, flamenco show Tue evening.

TAPAS

Bodegas Castañeda – *Almireceros 1. ℰ958 22 32 22. Closed Sun.* The bar and tables in this typical bodega, its décor enhanced by the myriad bottles on display, are often full with customers enjoying the delicious hot and cold tapas and regional specialities. A good central location just a few metres from Plaza Nueva.

Casa Enrique – *Acera del Darro 8. ℰ958 25 50 08. Closed Sun and fortnight in Aug.* This tavern dates from 1870 and has become a symbol of the city. Its small size and careful decoration make it a good meeting-point. Outstanding wine cellar, Iberian ham and local cheeses.

Pilar del Toro – *Hospital de Santa Ana 12. ℰ958 22 54 70. www.pilardeltoro.es.* Housed in an old 17C house, the Pilar del Toro is notable for its distinctive architecture alone. The iron gate leads to the bar with a small counter to the left and a large Andalucían patio to the right, with an attractive restaurant upstairs and enchanting rooms as well.

La Trastienda – *Pl. Cuchilleros 11. ℰ958 76 33 29. Closed Aug.* Founded in 1836. Once through the small entrance door, head down some steps to the former grocery store, which has retained its original counter, where you can enjoy excellent chorizo and tapas, either at the bar or in the small room to the rear.

🍷 BARS AND 🍴 CAFÉS

El Tren – *Carril del Picón 22.* This unusual bar has a warm and friendly atmosphere and an extensive choice of teas, coffees and cakes. The bar has an electric train running on tracks suspended from the ceiling, hence the name. A varied clientele which changes according to the time of day.

Teterías – *Calderería Nueva.* Calle Calderería Nueva, between the city centre and the Albaicín, is a typical example of a street found in the Moorish quarter of any city. The small and cosy *teterías* are typical cafés which give a welcoming feel to this particular street. Two are worth mentioning: the quiet and pleasant **Pervane** *(no 24)*, with its huge selection of teas, coffees, milkshakes and cakes; and **Kasbah** *(no 4)*, decorated with cushions and rugs on the floor in true Moorish coffee shop style.

🎭 NIGHTLIFE

El Camborio – *Camino de Sacromonte 47.* 📞*958 22 12 15.* One of Granada's oldest and most established nocturnal haunts, El Camborio has been open for the past 30 years. Best approached by car or taxi as it is located in one of the city's least salubrious districts. The venue itself is quite unique with four interconnected caves and with good dance music. Popular with an eclectic crowd, though

predominantly frequented by students. A good place to end the night.

La Fontana – *Carrera del Darro 19.* 📞*958 22 77 59.* Housed in an old residence at the foot of the Alhambra and Albaicín hills, this inviting antique-adorned café is an ideal place for a quiet drink in an atmosphere dominated by lively conversation. An excellent choice of coffees, herbal teas and cocktails.

Sala Príncipe – *Campo del Príncipe 7.* 📞*958 22 80 08.* This large venue is the place to be seen for the city's in-crowd, hosting regular concerts by leading Spanish groups. Always crowded with a mix of ages.

El Tercer Aviso – *Real Maestranza 1, Pl. de Toros.* 📞*958 20 60 42. Open Sun–Wed.* A surprising location inside the bullring, where its spacious design combines with modern, tasteful décor. The café is located on several floors, and from each floor it is possible to look down onto the floors below. Good chart music popular with the 25–45 crowd, and also quiet areas for those wanting to enjoy a chat.

FIESTAS

The city's religious festivals are lively, colourful events, especially those held in Holy Week and at Corpus Christi. The city also holds an annual **music and dance festival** *(www.granadafestival. org)* in June and July in the delightful surroundings of the Generalife gardens.

Guadix★

Guadix, an ancient farming centre, became important under the Romans and the Visigoths as a strategic road junction. It flourished under the Moors and up to the 18C, a period of artistic splendour. Guadix is known for one of the largest complexes of cave dwellings in Spain.

SIGHTS
Catedral★
Santa María del Buen Aire 2. 🕐*Open Apr–Sept Mon–Sat 10.30am–1pm, 5–7pm; Oct–Mar Mon–Fri 10.30am– 1pm, 4–6pm.* 🕐*Closed public holidays.*

▶ **Population:** 20 326
🕐 **Michelin Map:** 578 U 20
ℹ **Info:** Avenida Mariana Pineda. 📞958 66 26 65. www.guadix.es.
🧭 **Location:** Guadix, at the centre of a basin in southern Spain, is 57km/35mi from Granada along the A 92, and a good base for exploring the Alpujarras (Puerto de la Ragua is just 30km/18.6mi to the south). 🚃Avenida de la Estació

Castillo de La Calahorra
B. Morandi/MICHELIN

3€ *(with museum); no charge Thu.*
℘958 66 50 89.
The east end is by Diego de Siloé; the 17C Renaissance tower and Baroque **façade**★ (1713) are additions. Gothic naves lead to the Renaissance apse with a large lantern above the transept.

Plaza de la Constitución
Admire the 17C town hall, built during the reign of Philip III.

Barrio de Santiago★
Monuments in this typical district include the **Iglesia de Santiago** *(Santiago)*, its lovely Plateresque **doorway**★ leading to a pleasant square; and mansions such as the **Palacio de Peñaflor** *(Barradas)*. The Moorish **alcazaba** *(enter via the seminary, Barradas;* ⏰ *open Tue–Sat 11am–2pm, 4–6.30pm;* 1.20€; ℘958 66 93 00) affords fine views to the troglodyte quarter.

Barrio de las Cuevas★ (Troglodyte Quarter)
Walk toward the Iglesia de Santiago.
Beyond the church are dwellings hollowed out of the soft tufa hillside, with conical chimneys. These unique dwellings maintain a stable temperature. One is a **museum** *(pl. Ermita Nueva;* ⏰ *open Jul–Sept Mon–Fri 10am–2pm, 5–7pm, Sat and public holidays 10am–2pm; Oct–Jun Mon–Fri 10am–2pm, 4–6pm,*

Sat and public holidays 10am–2pm; 2.50 €; ℘958 66 55 69; www.escreativa.com).

EXCURSIONS
Purullena
6km/3.7mi NW.
The **road**★★ winds to the **troglodyte village** of Purullena, where pottery is made. Beyond, the Granada road winds upwards, to offer plateau and canyon **views**★, to the **Puerto de Mora** (Mora Pass) at 1 390m/4 560ft.

La Calahorra★
18km/11mi SE along the A 92.
La Calahorra is dominated by a **castillo**★★ (⏰*guided tours Wed 10am–1pm, 4–6pm;* ℘958 67 70 98) so austere that the graceful interior is completely unexpected. Park in the village and walk up. A heavy door opens onto a Renaissance **patio**★★, a masterpiece of refinement. The arcades and balustrade, Italian window surrounds and **staircase**★ bespeak an elegant style of life.

The River of Life
It was the Moors who gave this old Roman camp the poetic name of Guadh-Haix, which translates as "the river of life".

Jaén

Jaén is known for its imposing fortress, and is famous for the oil produced from its olive trees. The name derives from *geen* (on the caravan route). Its heritage includes Moorish remains and Renaissance buildings, many designed by Vandelvira.

▶ **Population:** 116 417
◔ **Michelin Map:** 578 S 18
ℹ **Info:** Calle Ramón y Cajal 4. ℘953 31 32 81. www.turjaen.org.
◗ **Location:** Jaen is at the base of the Sierra de Jabalcuz. The A 44 heads south to Granada (94km/59mi S) past the Parque Natural de la Sierra Mágina.

SIGHTS

Catedral★★

Pl. Santa María. ◔*Open Mon–Sat 8.30am–1pm, 4–7pm, Sun 9am–1.30pm, 5–7pm (Sept–May).* ◎*3€ (sacristry and museum).* ℘*953 23 42 33. www.catedraldejaen.org.*

The Cathedral looms over the historical quarter. It was built in the 16C and 17C by **Andrés de Vandelvira**, master of Andalucían Baroque. The façade with statues, balconies and pilasters resembles that of a palace.

The triple-nave **interior**★★ is crowned by fine ribbed vaulting and an imposing cupola above the transept. Behind the Renaissance altarpiece with its Gothic image of the **Virgen de la Antigua**★, a chapel holds the **Reliquía del Santo Rostro**★ – believed to be the cloth used by St Veronica to wipe Christ's face. The **choir stalls**★★ are carved in the Ber-

ruguete style. The sacristy, also by Vandelvira, houses the **museum** (*museo*), which includes two canvases by Ribera, a Flemish *Virgin and Child*, large bronze candelabra by Master Bartolomé, and miniature choir books.

Baños Árabes★★

These Moorish baths are the largest in Spain (470sq m/5 059sq ft). They lie beneath the 16C **Palacio de Villardompardo** and have been restored to their 11C appearance *(pl. de Santa Luisa de Marillac;* ◔*open Tue–Fri 9am–8pm, Sat–Sun 9.30am–2.30pm;* ◔*closed public holidays;* ℘*953 24 80 00).*

Castillo de Santa Catlina★

Carretera del Neveral 5. ◔*Open Tue–Sun 16 May–31 Oct 10am–2pm, 5–9pm; 1 Nov–15 May 10am–2pm, 3.30–7.30pm.* ◔*Closed 1 Jan, 24–25, 31 Dec.* ◎*3€.* ℘*953 12 07 33.*

On a ridge to the west of Jaén stands the Castillo de Santa Catalina (Castillo de Jaén), built during a period of Arab rule in the early 13C. It was captured in 1246 by Ferdinand III and extended to hold out against the repeated attacks by the Moors over the next two hundred years. The castle was rebuilt and extended to form the parador, which opened in 1968, though you can visit the castle and parador wing quite separately. There is a magnificent 360° panorama from here.

Baños Árabes

H. Belmenouar/MICHELIN

Jerez de la Frontera★★

Jerez looks out at fertile countryside. A provincial capital, it springs into life at fiesta time, sharing its tradions of wine, horsemanship, and flamenco.

THE CITY TODAY

Modern Jerez was built around 150 years ago on its Anglo-Spanish sherry wealth and retains its elegant, aristocratic, rather staid air. Relatively few visitors stay overnight but those that do can enjoy authentic flamenco (the town has a large *gitano* population) and may also like to seek out the lively bars just north of the Alcázar.

A BIT OF HISTORY

Jerez was one of the first towns to be founded by the Moors on the Iberian Peninsula. A number of vestiges remain from the Moorish "Sahrish", including sections of the old walls, the fortress (*alcazaba*) and a mosque. In 1264, Jerez was conquered by the troops of Alfonso X, and developed into a settlement of strategic importance as well as a leading commercial centre. The economic resurgence experienced by the province of Cádiz in the 18C left its mark on Jerez, with the construction of fine Baroque buildings and its famous wine cellars, some of which can still be seen today.

SIGHTS

Bodegas Domecq

San Luis. Guided tours by arrangement Mon–Fri 11am–12.30pm, 12.30–2pm. 5€ weekday mornings (7€ afternoons, Sat–Sun and public hols). 956 33 96 34. www.alvaro domecq.com.

The visit to the oldest Jerez bodega includes storehouses where a host of celebrities have signed their names.

Bodegas González Byass

Manuel María González 12. Guided tours Oct–Jun Mon–Sat 11am, noon, 1pm, 2pm, 4pm, 5pm and 6pm, Sun at

> ▶ **Population:** 205 364
> ⊚ **Michelin Map:** 578 V 11
> 🗏 **Info:** Alameda Cristina. 🎧956 33 88 74. www.turismojerez.com.
> ◖ **Location:** Jerez is in the Andalucían countryside, just 35km/22mi from the provincial capital, Cádiz and 90km/56mi from Sevilla. 🚃Plaza de la Estación
> ⊛ **Don't Miss:** A bodega tour.
> ◷ **Timing:** Take several hours to stroll the old quarters, with a stop at at least one bodega according to its hours

11am, noon, 1pm and 2pm; Jul–Sept Mon–Sat 11.30am, 12.30pm, 1.30pm, 2pm, 4.30pm, 5.30pm, 6.30pm, Sun 11.30am, 12.30pm, 1.30pm, 2pm. 8.50€. 902 44 00 77. www.gonzalezbyass.com.

The most famous storehouse is the spectacular La Concha bodega, designed by Gustave Eiffel in 1862.

Palacio del Tiempo★★

Cervantes 3. Open Tue–Sat 10am–2pm, 5–7pm, Sun 10am–2pm. Guided tours on the hour and at quarter past. Closed 24–25, 31 Dec. 6€ (9€ with Misterio de Jerez). 956 18 21 00. www.elmisteriodejerez.org.

This clock museum in the 19C Palacete de la Atalaya exhibits 300 18–19C timepieces in perfect working order. In the same gardens the **Misterio de Jerez** tells the story of Jerez wines (guided tour, same hours as Palacio del Tiempo; 5€).

Real Escuela Andaluza del Arte Ecuestre★

Av. Duque de Abrantes. Guided tour (30min) including facilities and training sessions Mon, Tue (Nov–Feb), Wed and Fri 11am–1pm; horse show Tue (Mar–Dec), Thu, Fri (Aug) at noon. Closed public holidays.

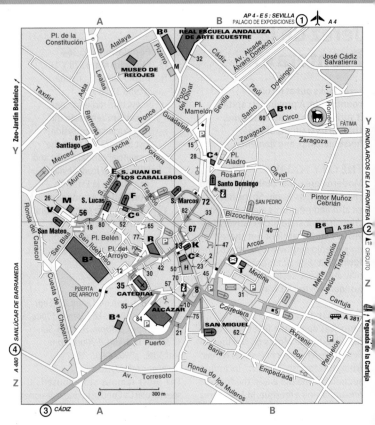

SIGHTS ON MAP								
Alcázar	AZ		Catedral	AZ		Iglesia de San Miguel	BZ	
Bodegas Domecq	AZ	B2	Centro Andaluz de Flamenco	AY	E	Museo Arqueológico de Jerez	AY	M
Bodegas González Byass	AZ	B4	Convento de Santa María de Gracia	AY	F	Museo de Relojes	AY	
Bodegas Harvey	BZ	B6	Convento de Santo Domingo	BY		Palacio de Riquelme	AY	V
Bodegas Sandeman	ABY	B8	Iglesia de San Dionisio	BZ	K	Palacio del Marqués de Bertemati	AZ	R
Bodegas Williams & Humbert	BY	B10	Iglesia de San Juan de los Caballeros	AY		Real Escuela Andaluza de Arte Ecuestre	BY	
Cabildo	BZ	C2	Iglesia de San Lucas	AY		Teatro Villamarta	BZ	T
La Cartuja	BZ		Iglesia de San Marcos	ABY		Yeguada de la Cartuja	BZ	
Casa de los Ponce de León	AY	C6	Iglesia de San Mateo	AZ		Zoo-Jardín Botánico	AY	
Casa Domecq	BY	C4						

8€; show: 18€ or 24€. ℮ *956 31 96 35. www.realescuela.org.*
The foundation in a 19C mansion by Charles Garnier, is dedicated to equestrian arts, including the training of horses. A **show**★★ in the main arena is not to be missed.

Museo Arqueológico de Jerez

Pl. del Mercado. ◔*Open Sept–mid-Jun Tue–Fri 10am–2pm, 4–7pm, Sat–Sun and public holidays 10am–2.30pm; mid-Jun–Aug daily 10am–2.30pm.* ⌖*1.75€.* ℮ *956 33 33 16. www.museoarqueologico.webjerez.com.*
The outstanding exhibit in the archaeological museum is a **Greek helmet**★.

◗◗◗ WALKING TOUR
THE OLD TOWN
Plaza del Mercado
The medieval market is now a tranquil square bordered by the **Palacio Riquelme**, with imposing Renaissance façade, the 15C **Iglesia de San Mateo**, and the **Museo Arqueológico**.

◗ *Take Cabezas to the **Iglesia de San Lucas**, then Ánimas de Lucas, plaza de Orbaneja and San Juan.*

Iglesia de San Juan de los Caballeros★

Pl. de San Juan. ℮ *956 32 43 41.*
This medieval church has a magnificent 14C **polygonal apse**★, topped by a ribbed cupola with jagged decoration.

◗ *Take Francos, then Canto to plaza de Ponce de León.*

Note the fine **Plateresque window**★★ on one of the corners.

◗ *Go along Juana de Dios Lacoste, cross Francos. Follow Compañía.*

Bodega González Byass

J. Malburet/MICHELIN

Iglesia de San Marcos

Pl. de San Marcos. 🖉 *956 34 18 97.*
This late 15C church has a beautiful 16C **star vault**. The apse is hidden by a 16C polygonal **altarpiece**★ showing strong Flemish influence.

▷ *From the square, Tonería leads to plaza de Plateros.*

Plaza de Plateros

The **Torre de Atalaya**, a 15C tower, is adorned with Gothic windows.

▷ *Head down José Luis Díez.*

Plaza de la Asunción★

The Renaissance façade of the **Casa del Cabildo**★★ (1575) is adorned with grotesque figures. The Gothic **Iglesia de San Dionisio** (🖉 *956 34 29 40*) shows Mudéjar influence.

▷ *Continue along José Luis Díez.*

Plaza del Arroyo

The **Palacio del Marqués de Bertemati**★ has fine Baroque balconies.

▷ *Continue on José Luis Díez and on to plaza del Arroyo, turn left at del Encarnación, then right at Manuel María González.*

Catedral★★

Pl. de la Encarnación.
🕐*Open Mon–Fri 11am–1pm.* 🚫*No charge.* 🖉 *956 34 84 82.*

Cartuja
©Turespaña

This monumental cathedral, with five aisles, combines Renaissance and Baroque features. The cupola bears bas-reliefs of the Evangelists. The annual wine harvest festival is held in front of the Cathedral.

▷ *Return to Manuel María González and head NE. Turn right at plaza Monti, left at Armas and right at plaza del Arenal.*

Alcázar★

Alameda Vieja. 🕐*Open daily May–mid-Sept 10am–8pm; mid-Sept–Apr 10am–6pm.* 🕐*Closed 1, 6 Jan, 25 Dec.* 🎫*3.35€ (with camera obscura), 1.35€ (baths, mosque and windmill).* 🖉 *956 14 99 55.*
From this 12C Almohad fortress, enjoy an excellent **view**★★ of the cathedral. Enter by the **Puerta de la Ciudad** (City Gateway). The prayer room in the **mosque**★★, located within the walls of the Alcázar, is covered by a delightful **octagonal cupola**. A **camera obscura** in the **Palacio de Villavicencio** provides a unique view of Jerez via its mirrors and lenses.

▷ *Head NE along Plaza del Arenal towards Caballeros, turn right at San Miguel and bear left towards the church.*

Iglesia de San Miguel★★

Pl. de San Miguel. 🖉 *956 34 33 47.*
Construction began in Gothic style in the late 16C; the Baroque tower dates from two centuries later.The older San José façade is a fine example of the Hispano-Flemish style. The Renaissance **altarpiece**★ is by Martínez Montañés.

EXCURSIONS
La Cartuja★

Carrera de Jerez a Algeciras, 6km/3.5mi SE. 🕐*Gardens and patio are open Mon–Sat 9.30am–11.15am, 12.45–6.30pm.* 🕐*Closed public holidays.* 🚫*No charge.* 🖉 *956 15 64 65.*
This Carthusian monastery, founded in 1477, has a Greco-Roman portal attributed to Andrés de Ribera. The Flamboyant Gothic church has a richly decorated Baroque **façade**★★★.

La Cartuja Stud Farm★ (Yeguada de la Cartuja)

At the Finca Fuente del Suero, 6.5km/4mi from Jerez on the Medina Sidonia road. 🚶Guided tours (2hr)

Sat, 11am–1pm. 🕐Closed 15 Dec–15 Jan. ☜12.50€; 7.50€ child. ☏956 16 28 09.
Visitors to the stud farm get a close look at the famous Cartujana horses.

ADDRESSES

🛏 STAY

🍽🛏 **Serit** – *Higueras 7.* ☏956 34 07 00. www.hotelserit.com. 37 rooms. ⊐7€. A central, family-run hotel, functional and up-to-date. Best rooms, in the annex, have wood floors and wrought-iron furniture.

🍽🛏🛏 **Hotel Doña Blanca** – *Bodegas 11.* ☏956 34 87 61. www.hoteldonablanca.com. 30 rooms. ⊐7€. This unpretentious hotel in an attractive Andalucían-style building has the great advantage of a superb location between the market and post office in the centre of Jerez. The bedrooms here are on the spacious side with all the usual creature comforts.

🍴 EAT

🍽🛏 **Gaitán** – *Gaitán 3.* ☏956 16 80 21. www.restaurantegaitan.es. Closed Sun. This well-respected restaurant serves good-quality, innovative regional cuisine. The small whitewashed dining room is long and narrow and abundantly embellished with decorative objects.

🍽🛏🛏 **La Taberna Flamenca** – *Angostillo de Santiago 3.* ☏956 32 36 93. www.latabernaflamenca.com. Closed Sun, Mon Nov–May. Reservations advised. This restaurant in an ex-wine storehouse offers meals with a *tablao flamenco* performance.

TAPAS

Juanito – *Pescadería Vieja 8–10.* ☏956 34 12 18. www.bar-juanito. com. Closed during Jerez fair. This Jerez classic in a pedestrianised street lined with outdoor terraces, has been serving its huge choice of tapas in Jerez for the past 50 years or more. The décor could not be more Andalucían, with its ceramic tiles and bullfighting-inspired pictures.

🍷 NIGHTLIFE

Bereber – *Cabezas 10.* ☏956 34 42 46. www.tablaodelbereber.com. Closed Sun. Reservations recommended. Bereber, in a Moorish palace, is the obligatory night-time stopping-point. Its spaces (café, bar, patios, dance floors in wine cellars and restaurant with flamenco) are variously decorated in impeccable Arabian and Andalucían style.

🎭 ENTERTAINMENT

The **Teatro Villamarta** *(pl. Romero Martínez;* ☏956 14 96 85; www.villamarta.com)* offers opera, music, dance and theatre, including flamenco. The city's best-known flamenco clubs *(peñas flamencas)* are the **Peña Tío José de Paula** *(Merced 11;* ☏956 32 01 96),* and the popular **Peña el Garbanzo** *(Santa Clara 9;* ☏956 33 76 67).

🤸 LEISURE

Baños Árabes Hammam Andalusí – *Salvador 6.* ☏956 34 90 66. www.hammamandalusi.com. Baths 10am–10pm in 2hr sessions (reserve). These re-created Moorish baths transport us to other times. The terrace and tea house look out to the Cathedral.

FIESTAS

Horses are as important as sherry in Jerez. In the 16C, the Carthusian monastery (Cartuja) crossed Andalucían, Neapolitan and German breeds, giving rise to the famous **Cartujana** horse. In **early May** there are racing, dressage and carriage competitions at the **Feria del Caballo** (Horse Fair). In **September** the **Fiesta de la Vendimia** (Wine Harvest Festival) showcases a cavalcade and a flamenco festival; the *cante jondo* is particularly alive and popular in Jerez, a town which is home to such famous singers as **Antonio Chacón** (1869–1929) and **Manuel Torres**.

Málaga★

Founded by Phoenicians, Málaga became a Roman colony and later, the main port of Moorish Granada. Today, it is the capital of the Costa del Sol, but it retains character-istic old houses and gardens that bespeak its importance as a 19C port. Beaches stretch eastwards from La Malagueta, at one end of the Paseo Marítimo, to **El Palo** *(5km/ 3mi E)*, a former fishermen's quarter.

THE CITY TODAY

Málaga may be the gateway to the Costa del Sol but unlike its resort neighbours it has retained its Spanishness and is well worth a day or two stopover before hit-ting the beaches.
Recently revitalised by the Museo Picasso and other development, it is now one of the region's liveliest cities, with Plaza de la Merced the focus of

▸ **Population:** 566 447
🖍 **Michelin Map:** 578 V 16 (town plan) map 124 COSTA DEL SOL
🛈 **Info:** Pasaje de Chinitas 4. ☏951 30 89 11. www. malagaturismo.com.
◔ **Location:** Málaga is 59km/37mi E of Marbella and 124km/77mi SW of Granada. Whitewashed Málaga is at the mouth of the Guadalmedina along the Mediterranean. ⛴ Explanada de la Estación
🅿 **Parking:** Park outside old quarter and walk.
◉ **Don't Miss:** Museo Picasso; Alcazaba.
◕ **Timing:** Head first for the Picasso Museum then to the castle and old quarter.

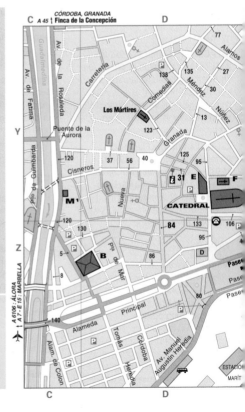

attention in town, while in summer the action also shifts to the beaches, particularly to Pedregalejo. Málaga is bidding to be European Capital of Culture 2016 so more cultural investment is in the pipeline.

SIGHTS
Museo Picasso (Picasso Museum)★★

San Agustín 8. Open Tue–Thu, Sun and public holidays 10am–8pm, Fri–Sat 10am –9pm. Closed 1 Jan, 25 Dec. 6€; free last Sun of month 3–8pm. 902 44 33 77. www.museopicassomalaga.org.

The 16C Palacio de Buenavista houses oils, sketches, engravings, sculptures and ceramics from the collections of Christine and Bernard Ruiz-Picasso, his daughter-in-law and grandson.

Among paintings are *Bust of Woman with Arms Crossed Behind Head* (1939), *Woman in an Armchair* (1946) and *Jacqueline Seated* (1954).

Alcazaba★

Alcazabilla 2. Open daily 30 Mar–26 Oct 9.30am–8pm; 27 Oct–29 Mar 8.30am–7pm. Closed last day in Feb. 2€. 952 12 20 20.

The ruins of a **Roman theatre** line the approach to this 11C Moorish fortress. Inside the final gateway are Moorish gardens. There is a **view**★ of the harbour and city from the ramparts. The former Nasrid palace is within.

Catedral★

Molina Lario. Open Mon–Fri 10am– 6pm, Sat 10am–5pm. Closed Sun and public holidays. 3.50€. 952 22 84 91.

Construction spanned three centuries (16C–18C); the south tower still lacks its full elevation. **Oven vaulting**★ covers the aisles. Classically ordered Corinthian columns, entablatures and cornices add a monumental appearance. **Choir stalls**★ bear figures by Pedro de Mena.

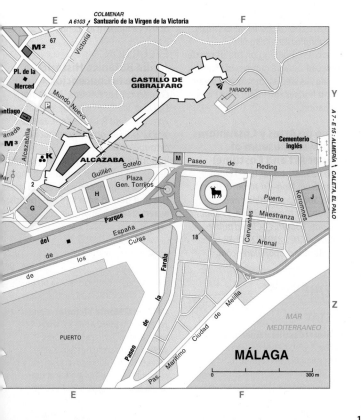

Málaga Wine

This aperitif or dessert wine is predominantly produced from Pedro Ximénez and Moscatel grapes. The main types are Málaga Negro, Lágrima and Color. Large quantities of currants are also produced in the Málaga area, mainly for export.

There is an impressive early 15C carved and painted **Gothic retable**★ in the ambulatory.

The 18C **Palacio Episcopal** (Episcopal Palace) on the square, in Baroque style, has a lovely marble façade.

El Sagrario, an unusual 16C rectangular church in the cathedral gardens, features a fine **north portal**★ in Isabelline Gothic style. The 18C interior is Baroque; a beautiful **Mannerist altarpiece**★★ is crowned by a well-preserved Calvary.

Casa-Museo Pablo Ruiz Picasso

Pl. de la Merced 15. 🕐 *Open daily 9.30am–8pm.* 🕐 *Closed public holidays.* 🖾*1€.* 🖉*952 06 02 15. http:// fundacionpicasso.malaga.eu.*

The mid-15C building on the **plaza de la Merced** shows a number of Picasso's drawings as well as photos and ceramics; and houses the Pablo Ruiz Picasso Foundation.

Museo de Artes y Costumbres Populares (Museum of Popular Art and Costume)

Pasillo de Santa Isabel 10. 🕐 *Open Oct–mid-Jun Mon–Fri 10am–1.30pm, 4–7pm, Sat 10am–1.30pm; mid-Jun– Sept Mon–Fri 10am–1.30pm, 5–8pm, Sat 10am–1.30pm.* 🕐*Closed public holidays.* 🖾*2€.* 🖉*952 21 71 37. www.museoartespopulares.com.*

The museum in a 17C inn displays objects once used for work on land or sea, as well as 18C and 19C costumes.

Santuario de la Virgen de la Victoria★

Pl. del Santuario. 🕐🖾*Guided tours (45min) Tue–Fri, Sun 10am–noon, 4.30– 7pm, Sat 10am–noon.* 🖉*952 25 26 47.*

The sanctuary was founded by the Catholic Monarchs. The church is dominated by a large 17C altarpiece at the centre of which stands the **camarín**★★, a Baroque masterpiece covered by stuccowork and presided over by a fine 15C German *Virgin and Child*.

Centro de Arte Contemporáneo de Málaga

Alemania s/n. 🕐 *Open Tue–Sun 25 Sept–Jun 10am–8pm; Jul–24 Sept 10am–2pm, 5–9pm.* 🕐 *Closed 1 Jan, 25 Dec.* 🖾*No charge.* 🖉*952 12 00 55. www.cacmalaga.org.*

The old wholesale market, a Rationalist building by Luis Gutiérrez Soto (1939), houses a modern art centre.

EXCURSION
Jardín Botánico Histórico Finca de la Concepción★

Carretera de Las Pedrizas, 7km/4.3mi N. 🕐 *Open Tue–Sun Oct–May 9.30am– 7pm; Jun–Sept 9.30am–4pm.* 🖾*4€.* 🖉*952 25 07 87. http://laconcepcion. ayto-malaga.es.*

Visitors will enjoy strolling through this delightful jungle, planted with more than 300 tropical and subtropical species and dotted with streams, ponds, waterfalls and Roman ruins.

ADDRESSES

🏠 STAY

🍽🍽 **Hotel Castilla y Guerrero** – *Córdoba 7.* 🖉*952 21 86 35. www. hotelcastillaguerrero.com. 40 rooms.* Plain but comfortable and well located, with everything needed for a good rest,

and adequate bathrooms. Go up the stairs to check in. Good for the price.

🍽🍽 **Hotel Monte Victoria** – *Conde de Ureña 58.* 🖉*952 65 65 25. www. hotelmontevictoria.com. 8 rooms.* 🛏*9€.* Quiet family hotel in a villa. Best assets are the garden terrace with impressive city views and the carefully kept rooms. Located on a narrow, climbing street where it's hard to park, though only 15min on foot from the Casco Viejo (Old quarter).

Hotel Don Curro – *Sancha de Lara 7.* *952 22 72 00. www.hoteldon curro.com. 118 rooms. 9€. Restaurant.* This slim tower is right downtown, with cosy, comfortable rooms and a game room that's always full.

EAT

El Chinitas – *Moreno Monroy 4–6.* *952 21 09 72. www.elchinitas.com.* Ceramic murals, photos and pictures of popular personalities and artists make this one of the most characteristic restaurants of Málaga. The terrace on a pedestrian street is pleasant, and there are dining areas on three floors.

Restaurante-Museo La Casa del Ángel – *Madre de Dios 29 (facing Teatro Cervantes).* *952 60 87 50. Closed Mon.* Ángel Garó captures the senses by conjuring up the best of Andalucían gastronomy in a unique artistic setting. Enjoy delicious cuisine while surrounded by original works by the likes of Picasso, Dalí, Miró, Sebastiano del Piombo and Julio Romero de Torres, master on canvas of the beauty of the Spanish woman.

TAPAS

Bar La Mesonera – *Gómez Pallete 11.* *952 22 59 65.* This small bar fills up with stars and the rich and famous before and after flamenco performances at the Teatro Cervantes opposite (and for shows right here on Mon and Wed evenings, 10€). Delicious tapas and a colourful, typically Andalucían atmosphere.

CAFÉS

Café Central – *Pl. de la Constitución 11.* *952 22 49 72. www.cafecentral-malaga.com.* One of Málaga's most typical and long-standing coffee houses, frequented by a faithful batch of regulars. Although the terrace on the square is particularly pleasant, the large tea room stands out as the café's most impressive feature.

Casa Aránda – *Herrería del Rey 3.* *952 22 28 12.* This lively, atmospheric café has taken over every building on this narrow street. A great place for a chat with friends over *chocolate con churros*.

NIGHTLIFE

El Pimpi – *Granada 62.* *952 22 89 90.* One of Málaga's most traditional locales, in the old city next to the Museo Picasso. Its old-time tavern décor is perfect for enjoying sweet wine and tapas. Leading luminaries have signed its casks and the walls display old bullfight posters.

Puerta Oscura – *Molina Lario 5.* *952 22 19 00. www.malaganet. com/puertaoscura.* Excellent for a cup of coffee or something stronger, while you listen to chamber music. The setting is classically elegant, intimate and distinguished. During Málaga's fiesta, the decorations of religious imagery transform the space.

Liceo – *Beatas 21.* *952 60 24 40.* This disco with a lively upstairs bar, in one of Málaga's old town houses, is popular with an international crowd, particularly those in their thirties. This old mansion with its 19C feel really comes to life at the weekend.

ENTERTAINMENT

Teatro Cervantes – *Ramos Marín near Pl. la Merced.* *952 22 41 00. www. teatrocervantes.com.* Teatro Cervantes, which first opened its doors in 1870, offers an extensive programme of theatre, concerts and dance, and hosts the Málaga Festival of Spanish Film.

FIESTAS

Málaga's major celebrations are **Holy Week** and the **Feria** *(the week of 15 August;* *952 21 94 82)*, which commemorates the Reconquest by the Catholic Monarchs in 1487. The festivities revolve around the *Cortijo de Torres*, *Plaza General Torrijos*, *Plaza de la Marina* and *Paseo del Parque*.

Osuna★★

This elegant town in the Sevillan countryside retains a beautiful monumental centre★ from its past as a ducal seat of the house of Osuna, one of the most powerful on the Iberian Peninsula.

SIGHTS

Zona Monumental★

▶ *Follow signs to Centro Ciudad (town centre) and Zona Monumental.*

Colegiata★

Pl. de la Encarnación. ⏣⏣Guided tours (45min) May–Sept Tue–Sat 10am–1pm, 4–7pm, Sun 10am–1pm; Oct–Apr Tue–Sun 10am–1.30pm, 3.30–6.30pm. ⏲Closed public holidays. ⏣2.50€. ☎954 81 04 44.

This 16C Renaissance-style collegiate church houses five **paintings**★★ by **José (Jusepe) de Ribera "El Españoleto"** (1591–1652), including *The Expiration of Christ*, in the side chapel off the Nave del Evangelio. The remainder are exhibited in the sacristy.

Panteón Ducal★★ (Ducal Pantheon)

The pantheon was built in Plateresque style in 1545 for the Dukes of Osuna. It is approached by a delightful patio. The chapel (1545) stands below the Colegiata's main altar and is crowned by a blue-and-gold polychrome coffered ceiling, now blackened by candle smoke. Another crypt, built in 1901, holds the tombs of the most important dukes.

Nearby stand the 16C **former university** (Antigua Universidad) and the 17C **Monasterio de la Encarnación**★ *(cuesta de San Antón 15; ⏲open same hours as colegiata; ⏣2€; ☎954 71 04 44)*, in which the highlight is the magnificent **dado**★ of 17C Sevillan *azulejos* in the patio. The nuns here produce and sell several types of delicious biscuits and pastries.

On the descent into the town centre, note the 12C–13C Torre del Agua, a former defensive tower now a small

archaeological museum *(pl. de la Duquesa; ⏲open same hours as colegiata; ⏣2€; ☎954 81 12 07).*

THE TOWN CENTRE

Mainly around Pl. del Duque and Pl. España.

Osuna's streets are lined by numerous Baroque **mansion houses and palaces**★★, whose massive wooden doors, darkly shining and copper nailed, reveal fine wrought-iron grilles and cool green patios. Of particular note are the **calle San Pedro**★ (Cilla del Cabildo, Palacio de los Marqueses de la Gomera), the Antigua Audencia (former Law Courts), the Palacio de los Cepeda, the former Palacio de Puente Hermoso, several fine churches (Santo Domingo, la Compañía) and the **belfry of the Iglesia de la Merced**★, built by the same architect as the **Cilla del Cabildo**.

EXCURSION

Écija★

34km/21mi N along the A 351.

The town lies in the Guadalquivir depression and is renowned for its lofty Baroque belfries decorated with ceramic tiles, such as the 18C **Torre de San Juan**★ *(pl. de San Juan; ⏲open Mon–Sat 10am–1pm, 6–9pm, Sun 10am–1pm; ⏣no charge; www.turismo ecija.com).* ▣ *Park in plaza de España.*

The **Ayuntamiento** (town hall) has two **Roman mosaic floors**★ and a *camera oscura* which offers lovely and surprising

▶ **Population:** 17 813
⏣ **Michelin Map:** 578 U 14
▮ **Info:** Carrera 82. ☎954 81 57 32. www.andalucia.org.
⏣ **Location:** Osuna rises to the south of the Guadalquivir Basin, near the A 92 highway linking Granada (160km/100mi E) with Sevilla. ⏣Avenida de la Estación
⏣ **Don't Miss:** The Ducal Pantheon and heritage buildings untouched by time.

perspectives of the city (*pl. de España 1;* ◯ *open daily 10am–1.30pm;* ◉ *2.50€;* ✆ *955 90 02 40*).

Écija has several delightful small squares, and houses adorned with decorative columns, coats of arms and charming patios. Along the streets adjoining avenida Miguel de Cervantes are several old palaces with fine **façades**★: the 18C Baroque **Palacio de Benamejí** (*pl. de la Constitución;* ◯ *open Oct–May Tue–Fri 10am–1.30pm, 4.30–6.30pm, Sat 10am–2pm, 5.30–8pm, Sun and public holidays 10am–3pm; Jun–Sept Tue–Fri 10am–2.30pm, Sat 10am–2pm, 8–10pm, Sun and public holidays 10am–3pm;* ◉ *no charge;* ✆ *954 83 04 31*); the concave and fresco-adorned **Palacio de Peñaflor** (*Emilio Castelar 26*), its portal built on columns; and the Plateresque-style **Palacio de Valdehermoso** (*Emilio Castelar 37*). Several churches are noteworthy: **Los Descalzos**, renowned for the exuberant decoration of its **interior**★; **Santa María** (*pl. de Santa María;* ◯ *open May–Sept Mon–Sat 10am–1pm, 6–9pm, Sun 10am–1pm; Oct–Apr Mon–Sat 10am–1pm, 5.30–7pm, Sun 10am–1pm;* ◉ *no charge;* ✆ *954 83 04 30*), crowned by an impressive tower; the Convento de los Marroquíes, with its lofty **bell tower**★, where the delicious *marroquíes* biscuits are still produced and sold by the nuns; and the **Iglesia de Santiago**★, which retains the Mudéjar windows of an earlier building and a Gothic **retable**★ at the high altar illustrating the Passion and the Resurrection. The outbuildings of the iglesia de Santa Cruz, following a restoration, house the **Museo de Arte Sacro** (sacred art museum) with 16C-19C works. (*pl. Virgen del Valle.* ◞ *guided tour (30 min) daily Oct–May 10am–1.30pm, 4.30–8pm; Jun–Sept 9.30am–1pm, 5–9pm;* ◉ *no charge;* ✆ *954 83 06 13; www.museosantacruz.com*).

Parque Natural de las Sierras de
Cazorla, Segura y Las Villas★★★

Spain's largest nature reserve extends over 214 300ha/529 535 acres at an altitude of between 600m/1 968ft and 2 017m/6 616ft. Steep cliffs, deep gorges and a complex of rivers and streams, including the source of the Guadalquivir, make up this park. The dense montane vegetation is similar to that found in Mediterranean regions. Deer, mountain goats, wild boar, golden eagles, griffon vultures and osprey abound.

⬤ **Michelin Map:** 578 S 20-21-22 R 20-21-22 Q 21-22

▯ **Info:** Carretera del Tranco, Km 48.3, Torre del Vinagre. ✆ 953 71 30 40; Juan Domingo 2, Cazorla. ✆ 953 72 01 15. www.acazorla.com.

▶ **Location:** The park lies in southeastern Spain, east of Úbeda.

◯ **Timing:** Allow a full day at least for the park.

⬤ DRIVING TOURS

◉ Before setting out, visit an **information point** at Torre del Vinagre, Cazorla, Segura de la Sierra or Siles. Mountain-bikers, horse-riders and hikers can follow the extensive network of forest tracks and marked footpaths.

From Tíscar to the Embalse del Tranco de Beas
92km/57mi – allow one day.

Tíscar★
The **Santuario de Tíscar** (◯ *open for worship daily Oct–May 11.30am–1pm, 4.30–6pm; Jun–Sept 11am–1pm, 5–7pm;*

Castillo de la Iruela and Sierra de Cazorla

B. Kaufmann/MICHELIN

953 71 36 06) enjoys a superb site enclosed by rocks. Below this place of pilgrimage is the impressive **Cueva del Agua**★, a cave formation where a torrent of water emerges from between the rocks.

◔ *Follow the C 323 as far as Quesada.*

Quesada

Quesada sits on the Cerro de la Magdalena hill, amid olive groves. A **museum** is dedicated to painter Rafael Zabaleta (1907–60) *(pl. Cesáreo Rodríguez Aguilera;* ○ *open Wed–Sun and public holidays May–Sept 10am–2pm, 5–8pm; Oct–Apr 10am–2pm, 4–7pm;* ○ *closed 1 Jan & 25 Dec;* ○ *6€;* ℘*953 73 30 25; www. museozabaleta.org).*

The Cañada de las Fuentes, a ravine on the outskirts, is the **source of the Guadalquivir river** *(access via a track off the A 315, to the N of Quesada).* Wall paintings from the Palaeolithic era can be viewed in Cerro Vitar and in the Cueva del Encajero, a short distance from the town.

◔ *Take the A 315 towards Peal de Becerro; bear right on the A 319.*

Cazorla★

Cazorla occupies an outstanding **site**★ below the Peña de los Halcones, dominated by the **Castillo de la Yedra**

(camino del Castillo; ℘*953 72 00 00),* its whitewashed houses adorned with balconies. At the centre of the plaza de Santa María stands a Renaissance fountain; the ruins of the Iglesia de Santa María *(pl. Santa María),* by Vandelvira, are now used as an auditorium.

◔ *Head 1.5km/1mi NE along the A 319; turn right at a signposted junction.*

La Iruela

The remains of a Templar castle offer superb **views**★★ *(camino del Castillo;* ◌*no charge)* of the Guadalquivir Valley. The Iglesia (church) de Santo Domingo was designed by Vandelvira.

The road from La Iruela to the Tranco Reservoir★

The first 17km/10.5mi stretch provides **spectacular views**★★. The Parador de **El Adelantado** is 8km/5mi along a branch road up through pine forests.

◔ *Follow the A 319 along the river.*

Torre del Vinagre

Carretera del Tranco, A 319. ○*Open daily 10am–2pm, 4–6pm (7pm in spring, 8pm in summer).* ○ *Closed 25 Dec.* ℘*953 71 30 40.*

This information centre contains a hunting museum as well as a botanical garden with species native to the park. Several routes start here.

A game reserve, **Parque Cinegético de Collado del Almendral**, 15km/9.3mi along the A 319, has lookouts for viewing deer, mouflons and mountain goats. *Information* ℘953 71 01 25.

Embalse del Tranco de Beas

⚠ Several camping areas and hotels are close to this reservoir. Water sports are available. Islands in the reservoir are Isla de Cabeza la Viña; and **Isla de Bujaraiza**, with the ruins of a Moorish castle. Both are seen from the **Mirador Rodríguez de la Fuente** viewpoint.

Santiago-Pontones to Siles

80km/50mi – allow half a day.

Santiago-Pontones

This municipality includes scattered mountain villages along with the **Cueva del Nacimiento**, a cave 9 000 years old, and the **Cuevas de Engalbo**, with their impressive wall art.

▶ *From Pontones, go NW on the A 317.*

Hornos

Fortress remains rise above a steep cliff from where there are some spectacular **views**★ of the reservoir and the Guadalquivir Valley.

ADDRESSES

🏠 STAY

⊜⊜⊜ **Molino La Fárraga** – *Cam. de la Hoz. ℘953 72 12 49. www.molinola farraga.com. 8 rooms. Closed 15 Dec–15 Feb.* In an 18C olive oil mill, whose machinery can still be seen under the house. Basic rooms, a garden with a small stream and a swimming pool with views of the castle and mountains.

▶ *Take the A 317, then bear right to Segura de la Sierra at a junction.*

Segura de la Sierra★

This picturesque village, birthplace of the 15C poet Jorge Manrique, is at an altitude of 1 240m/4 067ft in the shelter of its Mudéjar **castle** *(paraje del Castillo)*, with its sweeping **panorama**★★ of the Sierra de Segura. In the centre of the village are the **town hall** *(Regidor Juan de Isla 1; ℘953 48 02 80)* with its Plat_eresque doorway; the **parish church**, containing a delicate, polychrome statue of the Virgin Mary carved in Gothic style from alabaster, and a recumbent Christ attributed to Gregorio Hernández; and the **Moorish baths** *(baños árabes)*.

▶ *Follow the JV 7020 to Orcera.*

Orcera

The Iglesia de Nuestra Señora de la Asunción, with its sober Renaissance portal, and the Fuente de los Chorros, a 15C fountain, can be seen in the main square. Vestiges of the former Moorish fortress are on the outskirts of Orcera.

▶ *Continue along the JV 7020 beyond Benatae, then take the JV 7021.*

Siles

The village retains sections of its old walls. Nearby is the nature reserve of Las Acebeas.

🍴 EAT

CAZORLA

⊜⊜⊜ **La Sarga** – *Pl. de Andalucía 13. ℘953 72 15 07. www.lasarga.com. Closed Tue, second fortnights in Jan and Sept.* This well-run restaurant in the centre of town has impressive mountain views. Good-quality regional cuisine and attentive service.

Priego de Córdoba★★

This capital of Córdoban Baroque flourished with the silk industry in the 18C. Its fountains, churches and delightful old Moorish quarter are a pleasant surprise in this isolated part of Andalucía.

> ▶ **Population:** 23 309
> ⚲ **Michelin Map:** 578 T 17
> ▣ **Info:** Carrera de las Monjas 1. ℘957 70 06 25. www.turismodepriego.com.
> ◐ **Location:** Priego is on a plain in the Subbética Cordobesa range, away from major road and rail links.

SIGHTS

Fuentes del Rey y de la Salud★★ (Fountains of the King and of Health)

At the end of calle del Río.
These fountains surprise the visitor. The older, the **Fuente de la Salud**, is a 16C Mannerist frontispiece. The lavish **Fuente del Rey** was completed at the beginning of the 19C. Its dimensions and rich design evoke Baroque palace gardens. 139 jets spout water from masks. The central display represents Neptune's chariot.

Barrio de la Villa★★

This charming quarter, dating back to Moorish times, has narrow, winding streets and flower-decked houses.

©Turespaña

Houses with ornate wrought-iron grills in Priego de Córdoba

El Adarve★

This delightful viewpoint looks onto the Subbética range to the north.

Parroquia de la Asunción★ (Parish Church of the Assumption)

Abad Palomino. ⏰ *Open for Mass Mon–Tue and Thu–Sat 7.15–8pm, Sun 11.15am–noon.*
This 16C church was remodelled in Baroque style in the 18C. The presbytery is dominated by a carved and painted 16C Mannerist **altarpiece**.

El Sagrario★★

The chapel, which opens on to the Nave del Evangelio, is a masterpiece of Andalucían Baroque. An antechamber leads into an octagonal space. Light plays on the scene; intensified by white walls and ceiling, it shimmers over the extensive and lavish **yeserías**★★★ (plasterwork decoration), creating a magical atmosphere. In spite of excessive adornment, the effect is one of delicacy.

From the paseo del Abad Palomino view the remains of a Moorish **fortress** (⏰ *open Tue–Sat 11.30am–1.30pm, 4–6pm;* ⬤*no charge*), modified in the 13C and 14C.

Priego has numerous churches: the charming Rococo-style **Iglesia de las Angustias**; the **Aurora**, with a fine portal; and **San Pedro**, adorned with interesting statues. Also noteworthy amid this Baroque splendour is the 16C **royal abattoir** (*Carnicerías Reales, San Luis;* ⏰*open Tue–Sat 11.30am–1.30pm, 4–6pm, Sun 11.30am–1.30pm;* ⬤*no charge*), now an exhibition centre.

Ronda★★

Ronda stands above a deep ravine. Its isolation and legends of local highwaymen made it a place of pilgrimage for Romantic writers during the 19C. It retains cobbled streets, whitewashed houses and impressive mansions.

> ▶ **Population:** 36 532
> ⚭ **Michelin Map:** 578 V 14
> ▯ **Info:** Plaza de España 9. ☎952 87 12 72. www.turismoderonda.es.
> ▷ **Location:** Ronda lies in SE Spain, 60km/37mi inland and over the mountains from Marbella. ▭Avenida de la Victoria 31

SIGHTS

Museo de la Ciudad★★

Pl. Mondragón. ☐ *Open Mon–Fri 10am–6pm, Sat–Sun and public holidays 10am–3pm.* ☐*Closed 1 Jan, Good Friday, 25 Dec.* ▱*2€.* ☎*952 87 84 50.*

The charming **Mudéjar patio**★★ has the remains of *azulejos* and stuccowork between its arches. The collection includes an exhibition on the natural habitats of the Serranía de Ronda, and historical and ethnographic sections.

Plaza de Toros: Museo Taurino★

Virgen de la Paz. ☐ *Open daily 10am–6pm.* ▱*5€.* ☎*952 87 41 32. www.rmcr.org.*

Dating from 1785 and with a capacity for 6 000, this is one of Spain's oldest and most beautiful bullrings. Enter through an elegant gateway. Traditional *Corridas Goyescas*, fights in period costumes, are held annually. The museum contains sumptuous costumes and mementos of Ronda matadors.

Casa del Rey Moro

Cuesta de Santo Domingo. ☐ *Open daily 10am–7pm.* ▱*4€.* ☎*952 18 72 00.*

Inside are impressive Moorish steps, known as **La Mina**, which descend to the river. The **gardens**★ were laid out in 1912 by French landscapist **Jean-Claude Forestier**, who also designed María Luisa Park in Sevilla.

Museo del Bandolero

Armiñán 65. ☐ *Open daily 10.30am–7pm.* ▱*3€.* ☎*952 87 77 85.*

The Serranía de Ronda range was once frequented by bandits, brigands and outlaws. This museum provides insight into these legendary figures.

ADDITIONAL SIGHT

Templete de la Virgen de los Dolores★ (1734) *(Virgen de los Dolores).*

☙ WALKING TOUR

The River Guadalevín divides Ronda into two parts, connected by the 18C Puente Nuevo, offering a **view**★ of the El Tajo ravine: to the south, the **Ciudad**, the old quarter; and, to the north, the **Mercadillo**, the old market area. The Camino de los Molinos road provides views of cliffs and the **Tajo**★.

LA CIUDAD★★

☙*Guided tours (2hr). Depart from Puente Nuevo.*

Ronda – The Cradle of Bullfighting

Ronda is indelibly linked with the world of bullfighting. **Francisco Romero**, who was born here in 1700, laid down the rules of bullfighting, which until then had been only a display of audacity and agility. He became the father of modern bullfighting by his introduction of the cape and the **muleta**. His son Juan introduced the *cuadrillo*, or supporting team, and his grandson, **Pedro Romero** (1754–1839), became one of Spain's greatest bullfighters. He founded the **Ronda School**, known still for its classicism, strict observance of the rules and *estocada a recibir*.

RONDA STREET INDEX

SIGHTS ON MAP

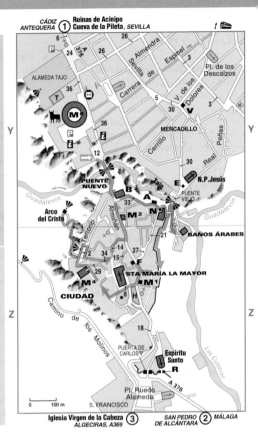

The old walled town, a vestige of Moorish occupation until 1485, is a picturesque quarter of alleys and whitewashed houses with wrought-iron balconies.

▶ *Cross the bridge and follow Santo Domingo.*

Casa del Rey Moro

This 18C building was erected in neo-Mudéjar style (👁 *see Sights*).

Palacio del Marqués de Salvatierra

This small mansion is graced with an exceptional Renaissance **portal**★★ and a wrought-iron balcony decorated with pre-Columbian-inspired statues.

▶ *From the Arco de Felipe V, by the Puente Viejo, a stone path leads to the Baños Árabes.*

The Adoration of Orson and Papa

Ronda's romantic landscape and link to bullfighting inspired both Ernest "Papa" Hemingway and Orson Welles, who now have *paseos* named in their honour. In *Death in the Afternoon* (1932), Hemingway states that Ronda "is where you should go if you ever go to Spain on a honeymoon". The ashes of Orson Welles are interred in the nearby farm of El Recreo (on the estate of Antonio Ordóñez, whom Hemingway wrote about in *The Dangerous Summer*). In Welles' own words "A man is not from where he is born, but where he chooses to die".

Baños Árabes★

San Miguel. Open Mon–Fri 10am–6pm, Sat–Sun and public holidays 10am–3pm. Closed 1 Jan, 24 Dec. 2€. 952 87 08 18.

Built at the end of the 13C in the artisans' and tanners' district, the Moorish baths comprise three rooms topped with barrel vaults and illuminated by star-shaped lunettes.

Follow a stone staircase parallel to the walls, then pass through a 13C gateway, the Puerta de la Acijara.

Minarete de San Sebastián★

This graceful minaret is the only one remaining from a 14C Nasrid mosque. A horseshoe arch frames the door.

Iglesia de Santa María la Mayor★

Pl. de la Duquesa de Parcent. Open daily 15 Jun–15 Sept 10am–8pm; 16 Sept–14 Jun 10am–7pm. 2€. 952 87 22 46.

The Collegiate Church of St Mary was built over the town's main mosque. Today, only a 13C horseshoe arch, decorated with *atauriques* and calligraphic motifs, and a minaret remain from the original building. The interior is divided into three distinct architectural styles: Gothic (aisles), Plateresque (high altar); and Baroque (choir stalls). On the exterior, note the double balcony used as a tribune by local dignitaries.

Continue along Manuel Montero.

Palacio de Mondragón

Two Mudéjar towers crown the Renaissance façade of the palace, now the **Museo de la Ciudad** (*see Sights*).

Iglesia Rupestre de la Virgen de la Cabeza★

2.7km/1.7mi along the A 369 towards Algeciras. Open Mon–Sat 10.30am–2pm. Closed 1 Jan, 24 Dec. 2€. 952 87 12 72.

This 9C Mozarabic monastery was excavated out of rock. The frescoes in the church were painted in the 18C. The **views**★★ of Ronda are impressive.

Ruinas de Acinipo

19km/11.8mi along the A 376 towards Sevilla. Open Tue–Sun 10am–5pm. Call to confirm hours. No charge. 951 04 14 00.

Known as Ronda la Vieja, the ruins of Acinipo retain a 1C AD theatre, with part of the stage and terraces.

Cueva de la Pileta★

20km/12.4mi SW. Take the A 376 towards Sevilla, then the MA 555 towards Benaoján. Bear onto the MA 561. Guided tours (1hr) daily 10am–1pm, 4–5pm (till 6pm 16 Apr–31 Oct). Closed 1 Jan, 24 Dec. 6.50€. 952 16 73 43. www.cueva delapileta.org.

The cave has over 2km/1.2mi of galleries. Red and black wall paintings predate those of Altamira, with figurative motifs from the Palaeolithic era (20 000 BC) and symbolic art and Neolithic animal drawings (goats, panthers, etc. 4 000 BC).

Ronda to San Pedro de Alcántara by road★★

49km/30mi SE on the C 339 – about 1hr.

For 20km/12.4mi the road crosses a bare mountain landscape; it then climbs steeply into a **corniche**★★ above the Guadalmedina valley. The route is deserted, there's not a single village.

DRIVING TOURS

Ronda to Algeciras★

118km/73mi SW on the C 341, C 3331 and A 7 – about 3hr.

The road climbs to overlook the Genal Valley, then winds around the foot of **Jimena de la Frontera** (*Juan de Dios 17*) perched on a hill and crosses the **Parque Natural de los Alcornocales**★, one of the largest forests of cork oaks in Spain.

After 22km/14mi, a narrow road leads *(right)* to **Castellar de la Frontera**★, a village of flower-filled alleyways huddled within the castle grounds.

Pueblos Blancos★★
(white towns of Andalucía)

To the west of Ronda, in often weirdly shaped mountains, are the remains of the *pinsapos* forest of pines dating from the beginning of the Quaternary era. The beauty of the countryside is set off by delightful white towns *(pueblos blancos)*, often perched on rocky crags or stretched along escarpments, their whitewashed houses dominated by a ruined castle or a church.

From Ronda to Arcos de la Frontera

By the northern route; 130km/81mi – about 4hr.
Take the MA 428 towards Arriate, then continue on the CA 4211.

Setenil de la Bodegas★

In this unique village, in the gorge of the Guadalporcún river, are a number of troglodyte dwellings built into the rock. Also of interest are the **tourist office** *(Villa 2; ℘956 13 42 61; www.setenil.com),* in an impressive building with a handsome 16C **artesonado ceiling**, the keep (torre del homenaje), and the Iglesia de la Encarnación.

Travel 16km/10mi NW.

Olvera

Olvera enjoys an impressive hillside **site**★★ amid olive groves, crowned by the keep of its triangular-shaped **castle** and the Iglesia de la Encarnación. Olvera is renowned for its superb olive oil *(pl. de la Iglesia; ⏲ open Tue–Sun 10.30am–2pm, 4–6.30pm; ⊚2€ with museum; ℘956 12 08 16).*

Take the A 384 towards Algodonales; turn off to the right onto the CA 531.

Zahara de la Sierra★

The village enjoys an extraordinary hilltop **setting**★★. Zahara was a defensive enclave for the Nasrids, and later for Christians. The outlines of the 12C **castle** and the 18C Baroque **Iglesia de Santa María de Mesa** stand out.

Return to the A 382 and continue towards Villamartín.

Villamartín

The **Alberite dolmen** *(℘956 73 35 55),* dating from around 4 000 BC, can be visited 4km/2.5mi to the south. A 20m/65ft gallery is formed by large stone slabs.

Bornos

The plaza del Ayuntamiento is fronted by the **Castillo-Palacio de los Ribera**★ *(pl. Alcalde José González; ℘956 72 82 64; www.bornos.es),* now the tourist office. Inside are a Renaissance-style **patio** and a 16C garden. Also on the square is the **Iglesia de Santo Domingo**, a Gothic church built in the late 15C.

Espera

10km/6.2mi NW of Bornos on the CA 402.
This village on a small outcrop is dominated by the ruins of a Moorish castle, the **Castillo de Fatetar** *(free access; ℘956 72 00 11).*

Arcos de la Frontera★★

Arcos has a remarkable **site**★★ atop a crag enclosed by a loop in the Guadalete river. The old town huddles against formidable crenellated castle walls and those of the two churches.

Park below the village in plaza de Andalucía. Ascend the cuesta de Belén, a hill which connects modern Arcos with the medieval town.

Note the 15C Gothic-Mudéjar **façade**★ of the **Palacio del Conde del Águila**.

Continue to the right along Nueva to plaza del Cabildo.

Plaza del Cabildo

Overhanging the precipice, one side of the plaza boasts a **view**★ that extends to a meander of the Guadalete. On the plaza are the town hall *(ayuntamiento),* parador (a former palace), and the castle (closed to visitors).

Basilica de Santa María★

Pl. del Cabildo. ⏰ *Open daily 10am–6.30pm.* ⏰ *Closed 1, 6 Jan, 25 Dec.* 🎫*3€.* 📞*956 70 00 06.*
This church was built around 1530. The **west façade★** is Plateresque. Don't miss the 17C **altarpiece** of the Ascension of the Virgin.
A charming maze of alleys leads to the other side of the cliff, where the Capilla de la Misericordia, the Palacio del Mayorazgo (now a music conservatory) and the **Iglesia de San Pedro** can be seen.

Iglesia de San Pedro

San Pedro. ⏰*Open Mon–Sat 10am–1pm, 4–7pm, Sun 10am–1.30pm.*
This church dates from the early 15C and boasts a façade crowned by an impressive Neoclassical bell tower.

From Arcos de la Frontera to Ronda

By the southern route; 102km/63mi – about 3hr.
Leave Arcos along the A 372 towards **El Bosque**. The Parque Natural Sierra de Grazalema visitor centre is here *(av. de la Diputación;* 📞*956 71 60 63).*

◐ *Leave El Bosque on the A 373.*

Ubrique

The **road★** enters the heart of the Sierra de Grazalema. Beyond the **plaza del Ayuntamiento**, is the 18C parish church of **Nuestra Señora de la O** (📞*956 46 49 00).*

◐ *From Ubrique, continue 10km/6.2mi E along the A 374.*

Villaluenga del Rosario

This village is the highest in Cádiz province. Its irregularly shaped **bullring** *(pl. de toros; Real 19;* 📞*956 46 00 01)* is built on top of a rock.

◐ *Head 15km/9.3mi NE on the A 374.*

Grazalema★★

Grazalema, one of Andalucía's most charming villages, is the wettest place in the whole of Spain. It retains its Moorish layout, as well as the tower of the **Iglesia de San Juan** *(José M Jiménez;* 📞*956 13 20 10).* The 18C **Iglesia de la Aurora** *(pl. de España 8)* is adorned with an unusual fountain. Grazalema is famous for its white and brown woollen blankets; a traditional **hand loom** operates at the entrance to the town.

◐ *Return to Ronda on the A 372.*

ADDRESSES

🏨 STAY

⊜⊜⊜ **Hotel San Gabriel** – *Marqués de Moctezuma 19.* 📞*952 19 03 92. www. hotelsangabriel.com. 22 rooms.* ⊑*6.50€. Closed 21 Dec–8 Jan and last week in Jul.* A delightful, magnificently decorated mansion dating from 1736. Some of the rooms look onto a charming patio. The hotel prides itself on its friendliness and attention to detail.

🍴 EAT

⊜⊜ **Doña Pepa** – *Pl. del Socorro 10.* 📞*952 87 47 77. www.dpepa.com. Closed 24, 31 Dec for dinner.* Try the best of Ronda cooking, such as *rabo de toro* (bull's tail), in a house with all the charm and style of Andalucia. The set menu is reasonably priced.

⊜⊜⊜ **Tragabuches** – *José Aparicio 1.* 📞*952 19 02 91. www.tragabuches. com. Closed Sun evening, Mon and three weeks in January.* This restaurant, considered by many locals to be the best in Ronda, is just a stone's throw from the parador and the bullring. Its kitchen offers guests modern cuisine in an avant-garde setting. *Reservations recommended.*

Sevilla★★★

Sevilla, set in the plain of the Guadalquivir, is capital of Andalucía and Spain's fourth largest city. To appreciate its many moods, take time to stroll the narrow streets of old quarters like Santa Cruz, or ride slowly through peaceful parks and gardens in a horse-drawn carriage. Sevilla is the centre of flamenco, famous for its bullfights, its 18C Maestranza bullring, and for its cafés and tapas bars.

THE CITY TODAY

If Spain had a beauty contest for its cities, or a contest for the most Spanish city in Spain, Sevilla would probably win both. It boasts more monumental set pieces and more pretty unspoiled corners than any other Andalucían city. It also claims the best tapas, the best nightlife, the best *ferias*, and is a stronghold for bullfighting and flamenco. Come here in spring when the orange blossom is in full fragrance, but avoid the heat of high summer.

A BIT OF HISTORY

Sevilla is summed up on the Puerta de Jerez (Jerez Gate): "Hercules built me; Caesar surrounded me with walls and towers; the King Saint took me." Sevilla was chief city of Roman Baetica and capital of the Visigothic kingdom before Toledo. In 712 the Moors arrived; in the 11C, it became capital of a kingdom

- ▶ **Population:** 699 759
- ⚙ **Michelin Map:** 578 T 11-12 (town plan)
- **Info:** Paseo de las Delicias 9. ☎954 23 44 65. www.turismosevilla.org.
- ▷ **Location:** Sevilla, in south-western Spain, is lined by motorways and dual carriageways to Huelva (92km/57mi W), Jerez de la Frontera (90km/56mi SW), Cádiz (123km/77mi SW) and Córdoba (143km/89mi NE). ▭Avenida Kansas City
- **P Parking:** Find a space in the centre, leave your car, and stroll the streets.
- ⊘ **Don't Miss:** The Giralda and the Alcázar.
- 🕓 **Timing:** Take at least a day for the marvels of central Sevilla, then enjoy quarters such as Santa Cruz, María Luisa park and sites nearby.
- 👪 **Kids:** Isla Mágica beckons for at least a day.

which prospered under the Almohads. In 1195 **Sultan Yacoub al-Mansur** (1184–99), builder of the Giralda, defeated the Christians at Alarcos. On 19 November 1248, **King Ferdinand III of Castilla**, the Saint, delivered the city from the Moors.

A Tradition of Fiestas

The great festivals, when vast crowds flock to the city from all over Spain and overseas, reveal the provincial capital in many guises. During **Semana Santa**, or **Holy Week**, *pasos* processions are organised nightly in each city quarter by rival brotherhoods. *Pasos* are great litters sumptuously bejewelled and garlanded with flowers on which are mounted religious, polychrome wood statues; these constructions are borne through the crowd on the shoulders of between 25 and 60 men. Accompanying the statues are penitents, hidden beneath tall pointed hoods; from time to time a voice is raised in a *saeta*, an improvised religious lament. During the **April Fair or Feria**, which began life in the middle of the 19C as an animal fair, the city becomes a fairground with horse and carriage parades. The women in flounced dresses and the men in full Andalucían costume ride up to specially erected canvas pavilions to dance *sevillanas*.

PRACTICAL INFORMATION

GETTING THERE

Airport – Aeropuerto de San Pablo, 8km/5mi towards Madrid on the N IV motorway, (*954 44 90 00; www.aena.es)*. A bus service operates from the airport to the railway station and city centre.

Trains – Estación de Santa Justa. The high-speed AVE (Tren de Alta Velocidad) departs from this station, taking just 45min to Córdoba and 2hr 15min to Madrid. For information and bookings, call *902 24 02 02 or visit www.renfe.com.

Inter-city buses – Sevilla has two bus stations: **Estación Plaza de Armas** *954 23 44 65; and **Estación del Prado de San Sebastián** *954 17 11 18.

Taxis – Radio Taxi *954 67 55 55. www.taxigiralda.es.

SIGHTSEEING

Publications – Two free bilingual publications (Spanish-English) are published for tourists every month. These brochures, **Welcome Olé** and **The Tourist**, can be obtained from major hotels and tourist sites around the city. Sevilla City Hall's Department of Culture **(NODO)** also publishes a monthly brochure listing all the city's cultural events. A monthly publication covering the whole of Andalucía, **El Giraldillo**, contains information on the region's fairs, exhibitions and theatres, as well as details on cinemas, restaurants and shops. www.elgiraldillo.es.

Horse-drawn carriages – It is well worth taking a trip in one of the numerous horse-drawn carriages operating in the city. They can normally be hired by the Cathedral, in front of the Torre del Oro and in the María Luisa park.

Boat trips on the Guadalquivir – Boat trips lasting 1hr during the day and 1hr 30min at night depart every half-hour from the Torre del Oro. *954 56 16 92.

The discoveries brought new prosperity. By 1503, Isabel the Catholic created the *Casa de contratación* or Exchange to control trade with America. This monopoly lasted until 1717.

Art and architecture in Sevilla – The northern ramparts, the Alcázar walls, the **Torre del Oro** (Golden Tower) and the Giralda were all built by the Moors. The **Mudéjar style**, a mix of Moorish and Christian, is testimony to the lasting influence of Arab design in the Alcázar and other monuments after the city's reconquest.

Golden Age painters of the **Seville School** corresponded to three reigns: under Philip III (1598–1621) **Roelas** and **Pacheco**; under Philip IV (1621–65) **Herrera the Elder** and **Zurbarán** (1598–1664), who portrayed figures with spiritual intensity. Finally under Charles II (1665–1700) **Murillo** (1617–82) created radiant Immaculate Conceptions and brilliant everyday scenes. The best

work of **Valdés Leal** (1622–90) can be seen in the Hospital de la Caridad. **Diego Velázquez** (1599–1660) was born in Sevilla.

Many statues are the work of 17C sculptor **Martínez Montañés**. Well-known are the **Cristo del Gran Poder** (Christ of Great Power) by **Juan de Mesa** and the **Cachorro** by Francisco Antonio Gijón in the **Capilla del Patrocinio** (calle Castilla). The **Macarena Virgin** is the most popular figure in Sevilla.

SIGHTS

The Giralda and Cathedral★★★ *Allow 1hr30min.*
Open Mon–Sat 11am–5pm (Cathedral Jul–Aug 9.30am–4pm), Sun and public holidays 2.30–6pm. Closed 1, 6 Jan, 20, 22 Mar, 26, 30 May, 15 Aug, 8, 25 Dec. Restricted opening times during Holy Week. 8€ including both sites. www.catedraldesevilla.es.

La Giralda★★★

Alemanes. ☏954 21 44 71.

When built in the 12C, the 98m/322ft minaret resembled the Koutoubia in Marrakesh. The top storey and Renaissance lantern were added in the 16C. Typically Almohad, it creates grandeur in harmony with the ideal of simplicity. A gently sloping ramp *(accessible from inside the cathedral)* leads to the top (70m/230ft) for excellent **views**★★★.

CATHEDRAL★★★

Av. de la Constitución. ☏954 21 49 71.

"Let us build a cathedral so immense that everyone, on beholding it, will take us for madmen", the chapter is said to have declared. Sevilla's cathedral is the third largest in Europe after St Peter's in Rome and St Paul's in London.

The late Gothic cathedral shows Renaissance influence. The main portals are modern. However, the Puerta de la Natividad (Nativity Doorway) and the Puerta del Bautismo (Baptism Doorway), right and left of the west door, include beautiful sculptures by Mercadente de Bretaña (c. 1460). Miguel Perrin (1520) used Renaissance perspective fully in the Renaissance tympana of the Puerta de los Palos and Puerta de las Campanillas *(east end doorways)*.

▷ *Enter by the Puerta de San Cristóbal.*

The **interior** is striking. Massive columns appear slender because they are so tall. Magnificent Flamboyant vaulting rises 56m/184ft above the transept crossing. A **mirror (1)** on the floor affords a striking view.

Capilla Mayor (Chancel)

Splendid Plateresque **grilles**★★ (1518–33) precede an immense Flemish **altarpiece**★★★, profusely carved

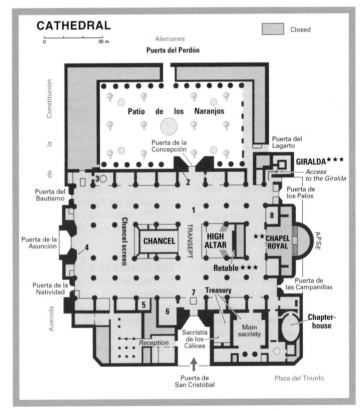

CATHEDRAL

0 ——— 30 m

Closed

Alemanes

Puerta del Perdón

Constitución

Patio de los Naranjos

Puerta del Lagarto

Puerta de la Concepción

GIRALDA★★★

Access to the Giralda

3

2

Puerta de los Palos

Puerta del Bautismo

1

Puerta de la Asunción

4

Chancel screen

CHANCEL

TRANSEPT

HIGH ALTAR

8

★★**CHAPEL ROYAL**

APSE

Puerta de la Natividad

Avenida

7

Retable★★★

Puerta de las Campanillas

5

6

Treasury

Chapter-house

Reception

Sacristía de los Cálices

Main sacristy

Puerta de San Cristóbal

Plaza del Triunfo

la

de

Catedral de Sevilla

G. Bludzin/MICHELIN

with scenes from the life of Christ and gleaming with gold leaf (1482–1525).

Tesoro (Treasury)

The **Sacristía de los Cálices** (Chalice Sacristy) contains canvases by Goya (*Santa Justa* and *Santa Rufina*), Valdés Leal, Murillo and Zurbarán, and a triptych by Alejo Fernández.

In the 16C **Sacristía Mayor** are a Renaissance **monstrance** by Juan de Arfe, 3.9m/13ft in height and weighing 475kg/1 045lb, and paintings by Zurbarán and Lucas Jordán.

Capilla Real★★ (Chapel Royal)

An elegant Renaissance dome is decorated with carved busts. On either side are the tombs of Alfonso X of Castilla (d. 1284) and his mother, Beatrice of Swabia. On the high altar is the robed

Chapels and Altars

Altar de Nuestra Señora de Belén (2) (Our Lady of Bethlehem): on the north side, to the left of the Puerta de la Concepción. A fine portrayal of the Virgin Mary by Alonso Cano.

Capilla de San Antonio (3): this chapel contains several interesting canvases dominated by Murillo's *Vision of St Anthony of Padua,* on the right-hand wall. Also worthy of note are *The Baptism of Christ,* also by Murillo, and two paintings of St Peter by Valdés Leal.

Altar del Santo Ángel (4) (at the foot of the Cathedral, to the left of the Puerta Mayor): this altar is dominated by a fine *Guardian Angel* by Murillo.

Capilla de San Hermenegildo (5) (next to the Capilla de San José): the 15C alabaster tomb of Cardinal Cervantes sculpted by Lorenzo Mercadante.

Capilla de la Virgen de la Antigua (6) (the next chapel): larger than the others and covered with an elevated vault. A fine 14C fresco of the Virgin adorns the altar.

19C funerary monument to Christopher Columbus (7): the explorer's coffin is borne by four pallbearers, each with the symbol of one of the kingdoms of Castilla, León, Navarra and Aragón on his chest.

Capilla de San Pedro (8): canvases by Zurbarán.

Virgen de los Reyes, patron of Sevilla, given by St Louis of France to St Ferdinand of Spain, who is buried in a silver gilt shrine below.

Patio de los Naranjos (Orange Tree Court) – This patio served as the ablutions area in the mosque.

Exit by the **Puerta del Perdón**, an Almohad arch decorated with stucco and two statues by Miguel Perrin.

NORTH OF THE CATHEDRAL
Museo de Bellas Artes★★★ (Fine Arts Museum)

Pl. del Museo 9. ⏰ *Open Tue 2.30–8.30pm, Wed–Sat 9am–8.30pm, Sun and public holidays 9am–2.30pm.* ⏰*Closed 1 & 6 Jan, 1 May, 24, 25, 31 Dec.* ✆*1.50€; free for EU citizens.* ✆*954 78 65 00.*

The Convento de la Merced (Merced Friary) was built in the 17C by Juan de Oviedo around three beautiful patios.

Sala I of the museum inside contains medieval art. **Room II** is dedicated to Renaissance art, in particular a fine sculpture of *St Jerome* by Pietro Torrigiani, a contemporary of Michelangelo.

Two magnificent portraits of *A Lady and a Gentleman* by Pedro Pacheco are the highlight in **Room III**.

Room V with Murillo's Immaculate Conception, Museo de Bellas Artes

B. Kaufmann/MICHELIN

In **Room V**★★★ walls decorated with paintings by the 18C artist Domingo Martínez are a stunning backdrop to outstanding work by Murillo and a Zurbarán masterpiece, *The Apotheosis of St Thomas Aquinas* (in the nave), with its skilful play of light and shade. **Murillo**'s monumental *Immaculate Conception*, with its energetic movement, is in the transept. On the right-hand side of the transept is a kindly *Virgen de la Servilleta* (note the effect of the Child approaching).

Upper Floor: Room VI displays a fine collection of saints. **Room VIII** is devoted to Baroque artist Valdés Leal. European Baroque is represented in **Room IX**. **Room X**★★ includes works of **Zurbarán**. In *Christ on the Cross*, the body of Christ appears as if sculpted. His *St Hugh and Carthusian Monks at Table* displays errors in perspective. The ceiling of the inner room should not be missed. In **Room XI** is Goya's *Portrait of Canon José Duato*.

Casa de Pilatos★★ (Pilate's House)

Pl. de Pilatos 1. ⏰*Open daily Apr–Oct 9am–7pm; Nov–Mar 9am–6pm.* ✆*8€ (5€ ground floor only).* ✆*954 22 52 98.*

The large Mudéjar patio of this 15C–16C palace displays fine stuccowork and magnificent lustre **azulejos**★★. *Artesonado* ceilings, the chapel with Gothic vaulting and *azulejo* and stucco decoration, and a remarkable wood **dome**★ over the grand **staircase**★★ illustrate the vitality of the Mudéjar style during the Renaissance. The gardens are open to the public.

Iglesia de San Luis de los Franceses★

San Luis 37. ⏰ *Open Tue–Thu 9am–2pm, Fri–Sat 9am–2pm, 5–8pm.* ✆*No charge.* ✆*954 55 02 07.*

This church, by Leonardo de Figueroa, is one of the best examples of the Sevillan Baroque. The exuberant **interior**★★ is a mix of outstanding murals, sumptuous retables and fine azulejos.

Convento de Santa Paula★

Santa Paula 11. ◷ *Open Tue–Sun 10.30am–1pm.* ◷ *Closed for certain religious ceremonies.* ✆*2€.* ✆*954 53 63 30.*

The church's breathtaking **portal**★ (1504) is adorned with ceramics. Despite its mix of styles, the overall effect is harmonious. **Inside**★, the nave is covered by a 17C roof and the chancel by a Gothic vault with attractive frescoes.

The **museum**★ *(entrance through nº11 on the plaza)* has works by Ribera, Pedro de Mena, Alonso de Cana and others. The gilded **Capilla de San José**★ **(St Joseph's Chapel)** gleams at night.

Palacio de la Condesa de Lebrija★

Cuna 8. ◷*Open Mon–Fri 10am–1.30pm, 5–8pm, Sat 10am–2pm.* ✆*6.60€ (3.60 € ground floor only).* ✆*954 21 81 83.*

This noble home is decorated with **Roman mosaics**★ from Itálica, Mudéjar *artesonado* ceilings, 16C–17C *azulejos*, and a sumptuous **stairway**★.

Iglesia del Salvador★

Pl. del Salvador. ◷*Open Sat–Sun and public holidays May–Sept 10am–1.30pm, 4–7.30pm; Oct–Apr 10am–1.30pm, 5–8.30pm.* ✆*2€ suggested donation.* ✆*954 59 54 05. www.colegialsalvador.org.*

It this 17C–18C church are some of the city's most impressive 18C **Baroque retables**★★.

Ayuntamiento (Town Hall)

Pl. Nueva 1. ◷ *Open with prior booking Sept–Jul Tue–Thu 5.30–6pm.* ✆*954 59 01 01.*

The attractive **east façade**★ (1527–34) is Renaissance in style and adorned with delicate scrollwork decoration.

AROUND THE CATHEDRAL
Iglesia de Santa María la Blanca★

Santa María la Blanca 5. ✆*No charge.* ✆*954 41 05 93.*

In the **interior**★ of this former synagogue, exuberant Baroque ceilings are balanced by pink marble columns.

The Cuarto Real Alto

An optional 30min guided tour enables visitors to view the King and Queen of Spain's official residence in Sevilla. The various rooms, with their fine *artesonado* ceilings, contain an impressive display of 19C furniture and clocks, 18C tapestries and French lamps. Of particular note are the **Capilla de los Reyes Católicos** (Chapel of the Catholic Monarchs) – an exquisite oratory with a ceramic font, by Nicola Pisano – and the Mudéjar **Sala de Audiencias**.

Hospital de la Caridad★ (Hospital of Charity)

Templado 3. ◷ *Open Mon–Sat 9am–1.30pm, 3.30–7.30pm, Sun and public holidays 9am–1pm.* ✆*4€.* ✆*954 22 32 32. www.santa-caridad.org.*

The hospital was founded in 1625. Great Sevillan artists decorated the **church**★★. Valdés Leal illustrated Death with a striking sense of the macabre. Murillo showed Charity in *The Miracle of the Loaves and Fishes, Moses Smiting Water from the Rock, St John of God* and *St Isabel of Hungary Caring for the Sick.* Pedro Roldan's **Entombment**★★ adorns the high altar.

Archivo General de Indias (Archives of the Indies)

Av. de la Constitución 3. ◷ *Open Mon–Sat 10am–4pm, Sun and public holidays 10am–2pm.* ◷ *Closed 25, 31 Dec.* ✆*No charge.* ✆*954 50 05 28. www.mcu.es.*

The building (1572), designed as an Exchange *(lonja)* by Juan de Herrera, houses priceless documents on America at the time of the Conquest, including maps and charts.

SOUTH OF THE CATHEDRAL
Parque de María Luisa★★

The vast **plaza de España**★ of this 19C park remains from the 1929 Ibero-American Exhibition. Each bench represents a province of Spain.

SEVILLA STREET INDEX

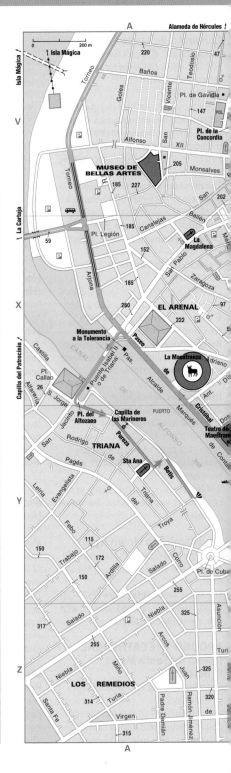

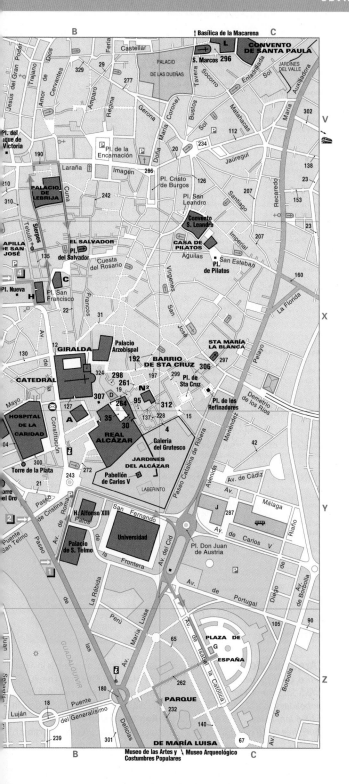

† Basílica de la Macarena

Febo	AY	Miño	AZ	San Jorge	AX
Feria	BV	Monsalves	AV	San José	CX
La Florida	CX	Monte Carmelo	AZ	San Juan de la Palma	BV 277
Francisco Carrión Mejías	CV 126	Murillo	AV 202	San Leandro Pl.	CV
Francos	BX	Museo Pl. del	AV 205	San Pablo	AX
Fray Ceferino González	BX 127	Navarros	CVX 207	San Pedro Pl.	BV 286
García de Vinuesa	BX 130	Niebla	AZ	San Sebastián Pl.	CY 287
Gavidia Pl. de la	AV	Nueva Pl.	BX	San Telmo Puente	BY
General Polavieja	BX 135	O'Donnell	BV 210	San Vicente	AV
Generalísimo Puente del	BZ	Padre Damián	AZ	Santa Cruz Pl. de	CX
Gerona	BCV	Pagés del Corro	AY	Santa Fe	AZ
Gloria	BXY 137	Palos de la Frontera	BY	Santa Isabel Pl. de	CV 296
Goles	AV	Pascual de Gayangos	AV 220	Santa María la Blanca	CX 297
Gonzalo Bílbao	CV 138	Pastor Landero	AX 222	Santa Marta Pl. de	BX 298
Hernán Cortés Av.	CZ 140	Pedro del Toro	AV 227	Santa Teresa	CX 299
Imagen	BV	Perú	BZ	Santander	BY 300
Imperial	CX	Pilatos Pl. de	CX	Santiago	CV
Isabel II o de Triana Puente	AX	Pimienta o Susona	BCY 228	Santiago Montoto Av.	BZ 301
Isabel la Católica Av. de	CZ	Pizarro Av.	CZ 232	Sierpes	BVX
Jaúregui	CV	Ponce de León Pl.	CV 234	Socorro	CV
Jesús de la Vera Cruz	AV 147	Portugal Av. de	CYZ	Sol	CV
Jesús del Gran Poder	BV	Presidente Carrero Blanco	BZ 239	Temprado	BY 304
José Laguillo Av.	CV 302	Puente y Pellón	BV 242	Teodosio	AV
José María Martínez		Puerta de Jerez	BY 243	Tetuán	BX
Sánchez Arjona	AY 150	Pureza	AY	Torneo	AV
Juan Ramón Jiménez	AZ	La Rábida	BY	Trabajo	AY
Juan Sebastián Elcano	BZ	Recaredo	CV	Trajano	BV
Julio César	AX 152	Refinadores Pl. de los	CX	Tres Cruces Pl. de las	CX 306
Júpiter	CV 153	Regina	BV	Triunfo Pl. del	CX 307
Laraña	BV	República Argentina Av.	AYZ 255	Troya	AY
Leiria	AY	Reyes Católicos	AX 260	Turia	AZ
Luis Montoto	CX 160	Rodrigo Caro Callejón de	BX 261	Velázquez	BV 310
Málaga Av.	CY	Rodrigo de Triana	AY	Venerables Pl. de los	BCX 312
Marcelino Champagnat	AY 172	Rodríguez Caso Av.	CZ 262	Virgen de África	AZ 314
María Auxiliadora	CV	Roma Av. de	BY	Virgen de Fátima	AZ 317
María Luisa Av.	BZ	Romero Morube	BX 264	Virgen de Loreto	AZ 320
Marineros Voluntarios		Rosario Cuesta del	BX	Virgen de los Reyes	
Glorieta	BZ 180	Salado	AYZ	Pl. de la	BX 324
Marqués de Paradas Av.	AVX 185	Salvador Pl. del	BX	Virgen de Luján	ABZ
Martín Villa	BV 190	San Eloy	AV	Virgen del Águila	AZ 315
Matahacas	CV	San Esteban	CX	Virgen del Valle	AZ 325
Mateos Gago	BX 192	San Fernando	BY	Virgenes	CX
Méndez Núñez	AX	San Francisco Pl.	BX	Viriato	BV 329
Menéndez Pelayo	CXY	San Gregorio	BY 272	Zaragoza	AX
Mesón del Moro	BX 197	San Jacinto	AY		

SIGHTS ON MAP

Alameda de Hércules	BU	Convento de Santa Isabel	CV	Museo de Artes y	
Archivo General de Indias	BXY A	Convento de Santa Paula	CV	Costumbres Populares	BCZ M2
Ayuntamiento	BX H	La Giralda	BX	Museo de Bellas Artes	AV
Barrio de Santa Cruz	BCX	Hospital de la Caridad	BY	Palacio Arzobispal	BX
Basílica de la Macarena	CV	Hospital de los Venerables	BX	Palacio de la Condesa	
Caja de Ahorros		Iglesia de la Magdalena	AX	de Lebrija	BV
San Fernando	BX C	Iglesia de San Marcos	CV	Palacio de San Telmo	CZ
Capilla de los Marineros	AY	Iglesia de Santa		Parque de María Luisa	CZ
Capilla del Patrocinio	AX	Maria la Blanca	CX	Parroquia de Santa Ana	AY
Capilla de San José	BX	Iglesia del Salvador	BX	Plaza de España	CZ
La Cartuja-Centro		Isla Mágica	AV	Real Alcázar	BXY
Andaluz de Arte		Itálica	AVX	Teatro de la Maestranza	AY
Contemporáneo	AVX	Jardines del Alcázar	BCY	Torre de la Plata	BY
Casa de Pilatos	CX	La Maestranza	AX	Torre del Oro	
Catedral	BX	Monumento a la		(Museo de la Marina)	BY
Convento de San Leandro	CVX	Tolerancia	AX	Triana	AY
		Museo Arqueológico		Universidad	BY
		de Sevilla	CZ		

Museo Arqueológico★

Pl. de América. ⏰*Open Tue 2.30–8.30pm, Wed–Sat 9am–8.30pm, Sun and public holidays 9am–2.30pm.* ⏰*Closed 1 & 6 Jan, 1 May, 24–25 & 31 Dec.* 🎟*1.50€; free for EU citizens.* ☎*954 78 64 74.*

The archaeological museum is in a palace on plaza de América. The 7C–6C BC **Carambolo Treasure**★ includes a statue with a Phoenician inscription. In the **Roman section**★ are statues and mosaics from Itálica (⏰*see Excursions*).

REAL ALCÁZAR★★★

Patio de Banderas. 🕐 *Open Oct–Mar Tue–Sat 9.30am–5pm, Sun and public holidays 9.30am–1.30pm; Apr–Sept Tue–Sat 9.30am–7pm, Sun and public holidays 9.30am–5pm.* 🕐 *Closed for official ceremonies.* ✆7€; top floor 4€. 𝒫 954 50 23 24.

All that remains of the 12C Almohad Alcázar are the **Patio de Yeso** and a courtyard wall. In the 13C, Alfonso X, the Wise, built a palace, known today as **Charles V's rooms**. Peter the Cruel (1350–69) erected the nucleus of the present building, known as **Peter the Cruel's Palace**, in 1362, using masons from Granada. It is one of the purest examples of the Mudéjar style.

Patio de las Doncellas, Real Alcázar

©Thomas Snaaijer/Dreamstime.com

Cuarto del Almirante (Admiral's Apartments)

Right side, the Patio de la Montería. In the Sala de Audiencias (Audience Chamber) the **Virgin of the Navigators**★ altarpiece (1531–36) is by Alejo Fernández.

Palacio de Pedro el Cruel★★★ (Palace of Peter the Cruel)

A passage leads to the **Patio de las Doncellas** (Court of the Maidens), a Moorish arched patio; the upper storey was added in the 16C. An elevated round arch leads to the **Dormitorio de los Reyes Moros** (Bedroom of the Moorish Kings), two rooms decorated with blue-toned stucco and a magnificent *artesonado* ceiling. Through a small room is the **Patio de las Muñecas** (Dolls' Court) with Granada-type decoration. The gallery on the upper floor dates from the 19C. The Catholic Monarchs' bedroom leads to the **Salón de Felipe II** (Philip II Salon), the **Arco de los Pavones** (Peacock Arch) and the **Salón de Embajadores** (Ambassadors Hall), the most sumptuous room, with a remarkable 15C half-orange cedarwood **cupola**★★★. The **Sala del Techo de Carlos V** (Charles V Room), the former chapel, has a magnificent ceiling.

▷ *Cross the Patio de la Montería and go down a vaulted passage (right).*

Palacio Gótico or Salones de Carlos V (Gothic Palace or Charles V's Rooms)

The palace, which was built in the reign of Alfonso X, houses magnificent **tapestries**★★ from the Real Fábrica de Tapices illustrating Charles V's conquest of Tunis in 1535.

Jardines★

Continue to the Mercurio pool and 17C **Galería del Grutesco**★ to view the magnificent Moorish gardens. The most enchanting parts are **Charles V's pavilion**, the maze and the English garden. The silhouette of the Giralda rises above the **Patio de Banderas** (Flag Court), bordered by elegant façades.

BARRIO DE SANTA CRUZ★★★ (SANTA CRUZ QUARTER)

The former Jewish quarter is replete with alleys, wrought-iron grilles and flower-filled patios. It is delightful in the evenings when cafés and restaurants overflow into the squares.

Hospital de los Venerables★

Pl. de los Venerables 8. 🔊 *Guided tours (15min) daily 10am–2pm, 4–8pm.* 🕐 *Closed 1 Jan, 25 Mar, 25 Dec.* ✆4.75€; free Sun afternoon. 𝒫 954 56 26 96. www.focus.abengoa.es.

This building, in lively plaza de los Venerables, is one of the best examples of

Street in the Barrio de Santa Cruz
©Turespaña

17C Sevillan Baroque. Its fine **church**★ is covered with frescoes by Valdés Leal and his son Lucas Valdés.

ISLA DE LA CARTUJA (LA CARTUJA ISLAND)
Isla Mágica★(Magic Island)

🕒 *Open Apr–Oct daily and Jun–Sept 11am–10pm (or midnight); check hours for rest of season and holidays.* 28€, *child 20€ during high season; 25€/18€ low season; 22€/16€ Christmas.* 902 16 17 16. *www.islamagica.es.*

This amusement park focuses on the Century of Discovery, with such theme areas as **Amazonia** and **The Pirates' Den**, live performances and rides such as **Rapids of the Orinoco**.

Centro Andaluz de Arte Contemporáneo

Av. de Américo Vespucio 2. 🕒 *Open Tue–Fri 10am–9pm (8pm Oct–Mar), Sat 11am–9pm, Sun and public holidays 10am–3pm.* 🕒 *Closed 1, 6 Jan, 1 May, 1 Nov, 24, 25, 31 Dec.* 3€; *free Tue for EU citizens.* 955 03 70 70. *Buses C 1 and C 2. www.caac.es.*

This modern art museum is in the former La Cartuja monastery; some **convent buildings**★ remain. The collection includes notable 20C artists (Miró and Chillida).

ADDITIONAL SIGHTS

Triana district★: Iglesia de la Magdalena (**interior**★); Iglesia de San Marcos (**Mudéjar tower**★)

WALKING TOURS
▷ *Follow routes on plan.*

EXCURSIONS
Ruinas de Itálica★

Av. de Extremadura 2, Santiponce. 9km/6mi NW on the N 630. 🕒 *Open Apr–Sept Tue–Sat 8.30am–8.30pm, Sun 9am–3pm; Oct–Mar Tue–Sat 9am–5.30pm, Sun 10am–4pm.* 🕒 *Closed public holidays.* 1.50€; *free for EU citizens.* 955 99 73 76.

This **Roman town** was the birthplace of emperors Hadrian and Trajan. Mosaics of birds and Neptune are in their original sites. The **Anfiteatro** (amphitheatre), seating 25 000, was one of the largest in the empire.

Carmona★★

40km/25mi W along the A 4.
Carmona, with its heritage buildings, overlooks the River Corbones.
🅿 *Park in the lower part of town.*

Old Town★

Note the **Baroque tower**★ of the **Iglesia de San Pedro**★ *(Arco de la Carne),* a church with a sumptuous sacrarium chapel (Capilla del Sagrario), and, further along, the **Convento de la Concepción** with its fine cloisters and Mudéjar church.

Through the **Puerta de Sevilla**★ is the 17C–18C **Iglesia de San Bartolomé** *(Prim 29).* The *capilla mayor* in the Mudéjar church of **San Felipe**★ *(San Felipe)* is covered with 16C ceramics.

The Baroque **town hall** *(ayuntamiento),* facing **Plaza de San Fernando** (entrance on calle de El Salvador), has a Roman mosaic. Next door, the 17C–19C **Iglesia del Salvador** is adorned with a magnificent Churrigueresque altarpiece (🕒 *open Mon, Thu, Fri 11am–2pm, 4–6pm, Sat–Sun 11am–2pm;* 1.20€; 954 14 12 70).

The 15C Gothic **Iglesia de Santa María la Mayor**★ is nearby. A monumental **Plateresque altarpiece**★ illustrates the Passion. The **Convento de las Descalzas**★ is a stunning example of 18C Sevillan Baroque. The Mudéjar church of the **Convento de Santa Clara** contains paintings by Valdés Leal.

The **Alcázar de Arriba** (Upper Fortress), a Roman structure, offers superb **views**★. It is now a parador.

ADDRESSES

🍽 STAY

Sevilla has a huge range of accommodation for visitors, but beware that during Holy Week and the Feria, prices are likely to double or even triple. If you're planning to stay in the city for these events, make sure you check the room rate carefully beforehand.

⊜⊜ **Hotel Amadeus Sevilla** – *Farnesio 6. ℘954 50 14 43. www.hotelamadeus-sevilla.com. 14 rooms. ⊒8€.* A family of musicians converted this typically Sevillan house with courtyard in the heart of the Santa Cruz district into a delightful small hotel, in which the décor enhances the building's original architectural features.

⊜⊜ **Hotel Londres** – *San Pedro Mártir 1. ℘954 50 27 45. www.londreshotel. com. 22 rooms.* Near the Museo de Bellas Artes. This centrally located hotel has basic but clean rooms, some with balcony. The best rooms have balconies and overlook the street. The hotel is slowly upgrading, while maintaining its traditional charm.

⊜⊜⊜ **Hotel Las Casas de la Judería** – *Callejón Dos Hermanas 7, Pl. de Santa María La Blanca. ℘954 41 51 50. www. casasypalacios.com. 175 rooms. ⊒17€. Restaurant⊜⊜⊜⊜.* A pleasant surprise in the city's old Jewish quarter. Elegant, traditional and full of colour, this charming, old hotel is housed in the former mansion of the Duke of Béjar.

Necrópolis Romana★

Av. de Jorge Bonsor 9, Carmona. ⓐ*Access to the Roman necropolis is indicated along the road to Sevilla.* ⓞ*Open 15 Jun–15 Sept Tue–Fri 8.30am–2pm, Sat 10am–2pm; 16 Sept–14 Jun Tue–Fri 9am–5pm, Sat–Sun 10am–2pm.* ⓞ*Closed public holidays.* ⓝ*No charge. ℘954 14 08 11.*

Of more than 300 1C tombs, mausoleums and crematoria, the most interesting are the large **Tumba del Elefante** and the huge **Tumba de Servilia**.

⊜⊜⊜ **Hotel Sevilla** – *Daóiz 5. ℘954 38 41 61. www.hotel-sevilla.org. 27 rooms.* An excellent location in a pleasant small square near the Palacio de la Condesa de Lebrija. A good option for those looking for basic comfort at budget prices. The faded décor here adds to the hotel's overall charm.

⊜⊜⊜ **Hotel Simón** – *García de Vinuesa 19. ℘954 22 66 60. www.hotel-simonsevilla.com. 29 rooms. ⊒4.75€.* This whitewashed mansion, arranged around a cool internal patio, seems to be from a different era, with corridors decorated with antique furniture and large mirrors. All the bedrooms are comfortable, with the best adorned with colourful *azulejos*. An excellent location close to the Cathedral.

⊜⊜⊜⊜ **La Casa del Maestro** – *Niño Ricardo 5. ℘954 50 00 07. www.lacasadel-maestro.com. 11 rooms.* A delightful hotel located in the birthplace of the famous flamenco guitarist Niño Ricardo (1904–72). A pleasant patio area and rooms decorated in yellow and earth red.

⊜⊜⊜⊜ **Hotel Alfonso XIII** – *San Fernando 2. ℘954 91 70 00. www. starwoodhotels.com. 147 rooms. ⊒20€.* Built in 1928 in neo-Mudéjar style, the Alfonso XIII is Sevilla's most luxurious and famous hotel. An excellent location opposite the gardens of the Alcázar.

⊜⊜⊜⊜ **Reyes Catolicos** – *Gravina 57. ℘954 21 12 00. www.hotelreyescatoli-cos.info. 29 rooms. ⊒9€. Restaurant⊜⊜⊜.* Centrally located close to the Plaza de Armas and the Isla Mágica theme park. Well-equipped rooms complemented by the restaurant.

♟/ EAT

◉◉ **Corral del Agua** – *Callejón del Agua 6. ☏954 22 48 41. www. corraldelagua.es. Closed Sun.* A pleasant, refreshing surprise awaits you in this quiet, atmospheric alley. The terrace, with its abundant vegetation, is delightful in the heat of summer. Classic Andalucían cuisine.

◉◉◉ **Bodegón La Universal** – *Betis 2 (Triana). ☏954 33 47 46. Closed Wed.* The terrace, cooled by the fresh air rising from the Guadalquivir, provides a great view of the city and bullring. Traditional cuisine and a pleasant place to eat either before or after exploring the Triana quarter.

◉◉◉◉ **Taberna del Alabardero** – *Zaragoza 20. ☏954 50 27 21. www. tabernadelalabardero.es. Closed Aug.* This 19C mansion houses one of the best restaurants in Sevilla, a high-class hotel with a dozen or so rooms, a very pleasant tea room and the city's school of hotel management. One of the best tables in Sevilla.

TAPAS

Bar Europa – *Siete Revueltas 35 (pl. del Pan). ☏954 22 13 54. www.bareuropa. info.* The Europa, in a street behind Plaza del Salvador, is a traditional bar that has retained its Belle Epoque feel. Popular with a young crowd who head here in the early evening for tapas and people-watching. Wines served at cellar temperature.

Bodeguita Romero – *Harinas 10. ☏954 22 95 56. Closed Mon and fortnight in Aug.* Held in high esteem by residents, its bar bursts with tapas and larger portions, all made with quality ingredients. The décor has a local flair.

Bodega San José – *Adriano 10. ☏954 22 41 05.* Given its location close to the Maestranza bullring, it's not surprising that this typical bodega is popular with aficionados of bullfighting and good fino sherry. The air of authen–ticity is enhanced

A typical tapas bar

R. Mattes/ MICHELIN

by the dirt floor and the aromas emanating from the huge barrels.

El Rinconcillo – *Gerona 40 y Alhóndiga 2. ☏954 22 31 83. www.elrinconcillo1670. com. Closed 3 weeks Jul–Aug.* One of the oldest and most attractive bars in Sevilla. Although it dates back to 1670, the décor is from the 19C, including the attractive *azulejo* panelling and the wooden ceiling and counter. Complete meals too at a modest price.

Sol y Sombra – *Castilla 151. ☏954 33 39 35. www.tabernasolysombra.com.* One of the most popular bars in the city. This bustling bar with its characteristic aromas of fine cheeses, cured hams and cigarette smoke, and walls covered with old and modern brightly coloured bullfighting posters is a must for visitors.

Las Teresas – *Santa Teresa 2 (Santa Cruz). ☏954 21 30 69.* This small, typically Sevillan tavern, whose doors open onto a picturesque narrow street, is one of the oldest in the Barrio Santa Cruz. Attractive early 19C décor; specialising in Iberian ham. Continue to Casa Plácido opposite for cold tapas.

♟/ CAFÉS

Confitería La Campana – *Sierpes 1. ☏954 22 35 70. www. confiterialacampana.com.* One of Sevilla's classic cafeterias. The Modernist décor creates a pleasant atmosphere in which to enjoy La Campana's pastries, which are famous throughout the city. Varied clientele ranging from the district's senior citizens to tourists passing through the centre.

Horno San Buenaventura – *Av. de la Constitución 16.* ☎*954 45 87 11. www. hornosanbuenaventura.com.* Part of a network of old furnaces over six centuries old. Particularly popular because of its proximity to the Cathedral and its spacious lounge on the top floor. Its cakes are justifiably famous.

🎭 NIGHTLIFE

Café de la Prensa – *Betis 8.* ☎*954 33 34 20.* This modern café with a young and intellectual ambience is located alongside the riverbank. Its outdoor tables offer a magnificent view of both the Guadalquivir and the monumental heart of the city. Perfect for whiling away the late afternoon or for a few drinks to start the evening.

La Carbonería – *Levíes 18 (pl. de las Mercaderías).* ☎*954 21 44 60.* One of Sevilla's institutions and the key to the culture of the city's alternative crowd. Housed in a former coal warehouse in the Jewish quarter (Judería), La Carbonería is split up into a number of different areas, where you can listen to a musical recital in intimate surroundings around a chimney or to authentic lively flamenco (live music every night). The venue also hosts art and photography exhibitions.

Paseo de las Delicias – This avenue is home to four venues (Chile, ☎954 23 52 58; Líbano, ☎954 23 34 77; Alfonso, ☎954 23 37 35; and Bilindo, ☎954 62 61 51). Although not open all year round, these venues become lively in summer, when they are perfect for those who prefer to move from bar to bar. On winter afternoons they are ideal for a quiet drink in the middle of the María Luisa park, surrounded by buildings used during the 1929 Ibero-American Exhibition, while in the summer, drinking and dancing outdoors into the early hours is more the scene. The age range is between 25 and 40, but varies from one venue to the next.

El Tamboril – *Pl. de Santa Cruz 1–12.* Tucked away in a corner of the Santa Cruz district, this taberna is always heaving with its faithful clientele, who occasionally burst into song

with an impromptu *sevillana* or *rumba*. Always busy until the early hours of the morning. The Salve Rociera, a prayer to Our Lady of El Rocío, is sung at midnight every day.

🎭 ENTERTAINMENT

El Patio Sevillano – *Pas. de Cristóbal Colón 11 A.* ☎*954 21 41 20. www.elpatiosevillano.com. Daily flamenco shows 7–8.30pm & 9.30–11pm.* 🎟*37€.* A long-running flamenco club catering to aficionados of the art form in its many variations, in a good location by the La Maestranza bullring, with public parking opposite.

Tablao El Arenal – *Rodó 7 (Arenal).* ☎*954 21 64 92. www.tablaoelarenal.com. Daily flamenco shows 8.30pm, 10.30pm.* Rated by those in the know as a place to enjoy flamenco in its pure form.

Teatro de la Maestranza – *Pas. de Cristobal Colón 22.* ☎*954 22 33 44. www.teatromaestranza.com.* This theatre offers a full season of theatre and dance, including performances by leading international stars, particularly in the field of opera.

🛍 SHOPPING

Most of the city's smartest shops and large department stores are located in and around **Sierpes**, O'Donnell and San Pablo streets. A less upmarket shopping area can also be found behind the Iglesia del Salvador. Antique lovers should wander the historic centre of the city, particularly the Santa Cruz district.

The **Jueves** (Thursday) is a weekly small market held along calle Feria.

Arts and crafts – Sevilla has a rich craft tradition. Potters can still be found in the Santa Cruz and **Triana** districts (in the latter on calle Alfarería, literally Pottery Street). The La Cartuja factory is heir to this tradition, which dates back to Roman times and the period of Moorish occupation of the city. Other products from Sevilla include inlaid woodwork, shawls, fans, wrought iron, harnesses, guitars and castanets.

Úbeda★★

Úbeda, set amid olive groves, is one of Andalucía's architectural treasures. It flourished in the 16C, when palaces, churches and fine squares were built.

⟳ WALKING TOUR
BARRIO ANTIGUO★★ (OLD QUARTER)

Allow one day

Plaza Vázquez de Molina★★

The square is lined with historic buildings, such as the **Palacio del Deán Ortega** (𝒞953 75 03 45), which serves as a parador.

Palacio de las Cadenas★ (House of Chains)

Pl. Vázquez de Molina.

Now the *ayuntamiento* (town hall), this mansion is named for the chains round the forecourt. It was designed in 1562 by Vandelvira, also responsible for the Jaén Cathedral. The majestic **façade★★**, relieved by bays and pilasters, is decorated with caryatids and atlantes.
The Renaissance patio is delightful. On the upper floor is the Archivo Histórico Municipal, with pleasant views of the square.
In the **Centro Municipal de Interpretación Turística** (tourist centre;

- ▶ **Population:** 34 462
- ⟳ **Michelin Map:** 578 R 19
- 🛈 **Info:** Calle Bajo del Marqués 4 (Palacio Marqués de Contadero). 𝒞953 77 92 04. www.ubedainteresa.com.
- ◐ **Location:** Úbeda is south of Madrid, between the Guadalquivir and Guadalimar rivers.

⟳ *open Mon–Sat 10am–2pm, 5–8pm (5.30–8.30pm during summer), Sun 10am–2pm)* downstairs, panels explain Úbeda's heritage, and craft items are displayed.

Colegiata de Santa María de los Reales Alcázares★

Pl. Vázquez de Molina. ⟳*Open daily 11am–noon.*

The church was built in the 13C on the site of a mosque and damaged in the Civil War. Note the harmonious façade; the main door; the late 16C Puerta de la Consolada *(left side)*; and the 16C Renaissance cloisters.
Several delightful **chapels★**, are adorned with sculptures and profuse decoration and enclosed by impressive **grilles★**, most the work of Master Bartolomé.

Casa del Deán Ortega - Parador de Úbeda (left) and Capilla del Salvador (right)

©Paradores

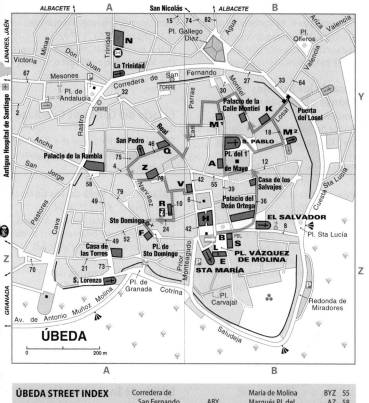

ÚBEDA

Capilla de El Salvador★★

Pl. Vázquez de Molina. Open Mon–Sat 10am–2pm, 5.30–7pm, Sun and public holidays 10.45am–2pm, 4.30–7pm. 3€. 953 75 81 50.
Diego de Siloé designed this sumptuous church in 1536. Its façade is ornamented with Renaissance motifs.

The **interior**★★ is frankly theatrical: the single nave, closed by a monumental grille, has vaulting outlined in blue and gold. The Capilla Mayor (chancel) forms a kind of rotunda. A huge 16C altarpiece includes a baldaquin with a sculpture by Berruguete of the Transfiguration (only the Christ figure remains).

The **sacristy**★★, by Vandelvira, is ornamented with coffered decoration, caryatids and atlantes with all the splendour of the Italian Renaissance style.

Casa de los Salvajes (House of the Savages)
Ventaja.
On the façade, two odd savages in animal skins support a bishop's crest.

Iglesia de San Pablo★
Pl. Primero de Mayo. 🕐 *Open for Mass Mon–Sat 7.30–8.30pm, Sun and public holidays 11.30am–1pm.* 🎟 *No charge.*
The church mixes a Gothic west door and the Isabelline style, in the **south door** (1511). The Capilla de las Calaveras (Skull Chapel) was designed by Vandelvira. The Isabelline Capilla de las Mercedes is enclosed by an extraordinary **grille**★★ – note the highly imaginative depiction of Adam and Eve.
The Palladian-influenced 17C former town hall is on plaza Primero de Mayo.

Convento de San Miguel
Carmen 13. 🕐 *Open Tue–Sun 11am–12.45pm, 5–6.45pm.* 🎟 *1.20€.* 📞 *953 75 06 15.*
The **Museo de San Juan de la Cruz** (St John of the Cross Museum) in this ex-convent traces the final days of this great mystical poet who died in Úbeda.

Palacio del Torrente
Pl. Primero de Mayo.
This early Renaissance palace has a monumental gate flanked by twisted columns.

Casa Mudéjar
Cervantes 6. 🕐 *Open 16 Oct–15 Jun Tue–Sat 10am–2pm, 4–7pm, Sun 10am–2pm; 15 Jun–16 Oct Tue–Sun* 9am–2pm. 🕐 *Closed public holidays.* 🎟 *No charge.* 📞 *953 75 37 02.*
In this restored 14C Mudéjar house is the **Museo Arqueológico**, displaying objects discovered in Úbeda and nearby).

Palacio del Conde de Guadiana
Real.
The early 17C Palace of the Count of Guadiana is crowned by a fine **tower**★ with angular balconies.

Palacio de la Vela de los Cobos
Juan Montilla. 📞 *953 75 00 34.*
The palace's façade is late 18C. A Renaissance appearance bears witness to the long survival of this style in Úbeda.

Palacio del Marqués del Contadero (Palace of the Marquis of Contadero)
Baja del Marqués 4. 🕐 *Open Mon–Fri 8am–3pm, 5–8pm, Sat–Sun 10am–2pm.* 📞 *953 75 08 97.*
The late 18C façade, crowned by a gallery, is also Renaissance in style.

Iglesia de Santo Domingo
Calle Escuelas.
The church's delicate south door is decorated with Plateresque reliefs.

ADDITIONAL SIGHTS
Antiguo Hospital de Santiago – *(av. Cristo Rey)*
Palacio de los Bussianos – *(Trinidad)*
Iglesia de la Trinidad – *(Corredera de San Fernando)*
Palacio de la Rambla – *(pl. del Marques 1)*
Casa de las Torres – *(pl. de San Lorenzo)*
Iglesia de San Lorenzo – *(pl. de San Lorenzo)*

ADDRESSES

🛏 STAY

🍴 **La Paz** – *Andalucía 1.* 📞 *953 75 08 48. www.hotel-lapaz.com. 40 rooms.* 🍽 *3.75€.* This is a small family-run hotel, with attentive service and impeccably clean rooms.

🍴🍴 **Palacio de la Rambla** – *Pl. del Marqués 1.* 📞 *953 75 01 96. www.palaciodelarambla.com. 8 rooms. Closed 16 Jul–10 Aug.* This fine 16C palace treats you like a family guest in a refined yet relaxed atmosphere. It has a magnificent Renaissance patio; on the façade are life-size warriors bearing weapons.

℉ EAT

🍴🍴 **Mesón Gabino** – *Fuente Seca.* 🕿*953 75 75 53. Closed Sun.* Set in the fortress walls, this traditional restaurant specialises in grilled meats and regional specialities (*andrajos* soup, pork loin, partridge).

FIESTAS

The nocturnal procession on Good Friday is known for its great solemnity. The town also hosts an international music and dance festival from May to early June *(www.festivaldeubeda.com)*.

Gibraltar★

One of the last outposts of the British Empire and a self-governing Crown Colony, the towering bulk of Gibraltar is impressive and distinctive, visible for miles. For many visitors, the first contact with Gibraltar is likely to be the incredible landing strip, crossed by the main road into town.

GEOGRAPHY

The **Rock of Gibraltar**★ is a gigantic monolith of Jurassic limestone which forms a craggy promontory connected with mainland Spain to the north and stretching south into the Strait. It covers an area of about 6.5km2/2.5sq mi (4.5km/3mi long and 1.4km/0.9mi at its widest), rising to 423m/1 388ft at its highest point, Mount Misery. The east face of the Rock drops sheer into the sea, while the less steep west face has been partially reclaimed at the water's edge and forms the site of the town.

A BIT OF HISTORY

Archaeological discoveries on Gibraltar testify to 100 000 years of human occupation, by Carthaginians, Phoenicians and even Neanderthal Man.
The Rock of Gibraltar, considered by the Ancient Greeks to be one of the **Pillars of Hercules**, was transformed into an Islamic citadel after the Moors invaded under **Tarik-ibn-Zeyad** in AD 711. Jebel Tarik (Tarik's Mountain, hence Gibraltar) was the site of a castle, now in ruins but still known as the Moorish Castle.

▶ **Population:** 28 875
🕐 **Michelin Map:** 578 X 13. British Crown Colony
🛈 **Info:** The Piazza, Main Street. 🕿350 74982 (956 77 49 50 from Spain); www.gibraltar.gi.
🌐 **Location:** Gibraltar lies at the southwest tip of Spain only 24km/15mi from North Africa.
🅿 **Parking:** Can be tight in town.
👁 **Don't Miss:** The Top of the Rock.
🕐 **Timing:** Take a morning drive from Spain.
👪 **Kids:** The Apes' Den.

Gibraltar was recaptured by Spain on 20 August 1462. During the War of Spanish Succession, Anglo-Dutch naval forces, under **Admiral Rooke**, captured the Rock in 1704. Gibraltar was ceded to Britain in the Treaty of Utrecht in 1713. The citadel guarding the Strait of Gibraltar has remained in British hands ever since. In the **Great Siege of 1779–83**, the garrison heroically resisted Spanish and French efforts to starve or bomb them into submission. The old city of Gibraltar was destroyed, but the Rock lived up to its reputation of being impregnable. Gibraltar became a British Crown Colony in 1830.
In 1967, Gibraltar's inhabitants voted resoundingly to retain their connection with Britain, by 12 138 votes to 44,

Upper Rock of Gibraltar

©Bernd Haak/Fotolia.com

in a referendum. In 1969, Spain closed the border and maintained a blockade until 1985. It is still not unusual for Spanish customs to delay vehicles. With its people descended from a variety of races, religions and cultures, their identity shaped by years of resisting sieges, Gibraltar is an excellent example of a harmonious, multicultural society.

Gibraltar's economy is based on financial services and tourism. The territory is a free port and trade is based on transit and refuelling.

The naval and commercial ports, as well as the town with its mixture of English- and Spanish-style houses, pubs and shops, lie against the west face of the Rock. Numerous examples of Moorish

Customs and other formalities – Gibraltar is a British Crown Colony. The border is open 24hr a day. Visitors must be in possession of a valid passport. Holders of UK passports and citizens of other EU countries do not need a visa. Other nationalities should check visa requirements with a British consulate, high commission, or embassy. Gibraltar is a VAT-free shopping area.

Travel and accommodation – There are daily scheduled flights from London Heathrow, Gatwick and Luton and a daily ferry service between Gibraltar and Morocco (℘350 78305). Regular flights also operate to and from North Africa. Hotel accommodation is available. There are no campsites.

Money matters – The currency is the Gibraltar pound, on a par with sterling. The Euro and credit cards are widely accepted.

Language – The official language spoken on the Rock is English, but most people speak some Spanish.

Time – Gibraltar is on European time (one hour ahead of GMT).

Motoring – Driving is on the right. Drivers must have a current licence, vehicle registration documents, evidence of insurance and nationality plates.

Telephoning – The international code for Gibraltar is 350 (from Spain, dial 9567 before the five-digit local number).

Tourist information – Further tourist information is available from the Gibraltar Government Office, Arundel Great Court, 179 Strand, London WC2R 1EH. ℘(020) 7836 0777; Gibraltar Information Bureau, 1156 15th St NW, Washington, DC 20005. ℘202 452 1108. www.gibraltar.gov.gi.

architecture are still to be found, notably in the cathedral which has the ground plan of a mosque.

SIGHTS
Tour of the Rock★
⏱Open daily 10am–6pm. Cable car Mon–Sat 9.30am–5.45pm. ⏱Closed 1 Jan, 25 Dec. ☎£8. ☎350 200 45957. ☎350 200 77826 (cable car). www.gibtaxi.com (private car).

The Top of the Rock can be reached on foot, by cable car and in official tour vehicles (*☞private cars are not allowed on the Upper Rock*). Go down Queensway and follow the signs to Upper Rock, a **nature reserve** and home to a number of Gibraltar's most interesting historical sites. The road leads first to **St Michael's Cave**, once inhabited by Neolithic man, which features some stalactites and stalagmites. From here, it is possible to walk to the Top of the Rock (*⏱1hr there and back),* from where there are excellent **views**★★ of both sides of the rock and of the Spanish and North African coasts. The road continues to the **Apes' Den**, home of the famous Barbary Apes.

Visitors interested in military history should not miss the **Great Siege Tunnels**, excavated in 1779 to mount guns on the north face of the Rock, creating a defence system still impressive for its ingenuity. A military heritage centre is housed in Princess Caroline's Battery. Finally there are the ancient ruins of the **Moorish Castle** and the northern defences dominating the hillside.

Gibraltar Museum
18/20 Bomb House Lane. ⏱Open Mon–Fri 10am–6pm, Sat 10am–2pm (last entry 30 min before closing). ☎£2. ☎350 200 74289. www.gib.gi/museum.
This museum contains extensive collections on local military and natural history. It also houses the well-preserved **Moorish Baths**.

The **Alameda Gardens** display interesting and exotic plants, including Canary Islands dragon trees, cacti, succulents and Mediterranean vegetation. Gibraltar is home to some 600 species of flowering plant, which flourish in the subtropi-

Neanderthal Man or Gibraltar Woman?
Eight years before the discovery in 1856 of a 60 000-year-old skeleton in the Neander Valley, east of Düsseldorf, Germany, a skull of the same age, thought to be that of a woman, was discovered on Gibraltar. However, delays in publicising the Gibraltar findings meant that Gibraltar Woman didn't gain the fame of Neanderthal Man.

cal climate, including a few unique to the Rock, such as its national flower, the Gibraltar Candytuft.

For those interested in seeing more examples of Gibraltar's plant and bird life, the **Mediterranean Steps**, leading from Jew's Gate (good view of the other Pillar of Hercules, Jebel Musa in Morocco) round the south of the Rock and up the east face of the Rock to the summit, make a rewarding walk (*🚶3hr walk from Jew's Gate, steep in parts; wear good boots).*

STRAITS OF GIBRALTAR
Michelin map 578 X 1; *Gibraltar: British Crown Colony. The A 7 motorway links the southernmost part of Spain to the Costa del Sol.*

The Straits, the gateway to the Mediterranean and a mere 14km/9mi wide, have always played a strategic role in the region. The Bay of Algeciras is surrounded by Algeciras and La Línea de la Concepción, and the British outpost of Gibraltar.

TOURING THE STRAITS
Fourteen species of cetaceans – whales, dolphins and porpoises – are to be found in the Straits so **whale- and dolphin-watching cruises** are consequently very popular, sailing from Gibraltar, Algeciras, La Línea and Tarifa. Reputable operators include Turmares Tarifa (*☎956 68 07 41; www.turmares.com)* and Whale Watch (*☎956 62 70 13; www.whalewatchtarifa.net).* The probability of seeing these beautiful creatures is very high (90%–95%) and some operators

Barbary Apes

The origin of the apes, one of Gibraltar's best-known attractions, is unknown. Legend has it that British rule will last as long as the apes remain in residence on the Rock. When it looked as if they might become extinct in 1942, Churchill sent a signal ordering reinforcements. The ape colony has since flourished – there are currently some 230 of them. They are renowned for their charm and highly inquisitive natures. The apes, in reality tailless monkeys, are the protégés of the Gibraltar Regiment.

©David Stanley/iStockphoto.com

will refund your money in the unlikely event of a "no-show".

While boats for larger groups may provide underwater viewing areas, small fast boats provide more thrills as they race along with the dolphins swimming in their wake and criss-crossing the bows. The 21km/13mi of road linking Tarifa to Algeciras provides stunning **views**★★★ of the North African coast. The best viewpoint is at the Mirador del Estrecho, 8km/5mi from Tarifa.

Tarifa ♺ See COSTA DE LA LUZ

Algeciras

Arabs arrived in al-Yazirat-al-jadra (Green Island, now joined to the mainland) in 711 and remained until 1344.

The Bahía de Algeciras is a safe anchorage and strategic vantage point overlooking the Straits.

Algeciras is Spain's busiest passenger port with crossings to Tangier and **Ceuta** several times a day. The main sights of interest are the the plaza Alta, the hub of the town, fronted by two churches: the 18C **Iglesia de Nuestra Señora de la Palma**, and the Baroque Iglesia de Nuestra Señora de la Aurora, and the **Museo Municipal** (Ortega y Gasset; ◷ open 27 Oct–30 Mar Mon–Fri 9am–2pm, 5–7pm; 1 Apr–26 Oct 9am–2pm; ◷ closed public holidays; ℘956 57 06 72; www.fmcjoseluiscano.com), displaying interesting exhibits on the **Siege of Algeciras** (1342–44).

View of mountains in Morocco across the Straits of Gibraltar from near Tarifa
©Panoramic Images/Getty Images

ACROSS THE STRAITS
Ceuta

Michelin map 742 folds 5 and 10 – North Africa. Population 78 320. **Trasmediterránea** *operates services between Algeciras and Ceuta. Journey time: 40min.* ℰ*902 45 46 45. www.trasmediterranea.es.*

Ceuta occupies a strategic position, dominating the Straits of Gibraltar. With its European architecture, it is situated on a narrow isthmus on the coast of North Africa. The closest African port to Europe, Ceuta was conquered by the Portuguese in 1415, and passed to Spain in 1580, when Philip II annexed Portugal.

Museo Municipal

Pas. de Revellín 30. ◔*Open Jun–Sept Tue–Sat 10am–2pm, 7–9pm, Sun and public holidays 11am–2pm; Oct–May Tue–Sat 10am–2pm, 5–8pm, Sun and public holidays 10am–2pm.* ◔*Closed 1 Jan, 25 Dec.* ⊜*No charge.* ℰ*956 51 73 98.*

This museum houses a white marble Roman sarcophagus, Punic and Roman amphorae, a collection of coins and old weapons and ceramic ware.

Parque Marítimo del Mediterráneo

Compañía del Mar. ◔*Open Sept–May daily 11am–8pm; Jun–Aug Mon, Thu 10am–8pm, Tue–Wed 10am–1am, Fri–Sun and public holidays 10am–8pm.* ⊜*1–5.50€, price varies by day and time.* ℰ*956 51 77 42.*

Palm trees, exotic plants, swimming pools, lakes, waterfalls and sculptures have all been perfectly integrated by César Manrique to create this spectacular leisure park on 56ha/138 acres facing the sea. Several restaurants, a nightclub and a casino operate inside the fort which dominates the park. A cinema complex is in the Poblado Marinero.

Other places of interest are the **Iglesia de Nuestra Señora de África** (Church of Our Lady of Africa; *pl. de África;* ℰ*956 51 77 32*), housing the statue of the town's patron saint, the 18C **Catedral** *(pl. de África;* ◔*open Tue–Sun 9am–1pm, 6.15–7.30pm;* ℰ*956 51 77 71)* and **Foso de San Felipe** (◔*open daily 11am–7pm;* ℰ*956 51 17 70)*, a Portuguese fort where San Juan de Dios, the founder of the Orden de los Hospitalarios (Order of the Hospitallers of St John), worked in 1530.

Monte Hacho★

Best visited in the morning.

Calle Independencia and calle Recintor Sur, parallel to the seafront, lead to the foot of Monte Hacho, which has a citadel at its summit. The corniche road encircling the peninsula offers beautiful **views** of the Western Rif coastline to the south and the Spanish coast and the Rock of Gibraltar to the north.

▷ *Before reaching the lighthouse (no entry), bear left.*

Ermita de San Antonio

◍*Leave your car in the car park.*

The wide flight of steps leads to a charming square fronted by the 16C Capilla de San Antonio (Chapel of St Anthony). The imposing **Fortaleza de Hacho** *(ctra. de circunvalación del Monte Hacho;* ⚲*guided tours available by booking beforehand;* ℰ*956 51 16 21)* stands atop a hill nearby.

From here there is a magnificent **view**★★ to the left, of the town spread out on its curving isthmus around the port, and to the right, the distant peninsula coastline.

ADDRESSES

♈/ EAT

⊜⊜⊜⊜ **Parador H La Muralla** – *Pl. Nuestra Señora de África 15.* ℰ*956 51 49 40. www.parador.es.* A good place to pause during your visit, an attractive dining area with lush tropical plants and exposed beams. The cooking is Andaucían with Arab influences.

ARAGÓN

One of Spain's least known and least visited regions, Aragón is over twice the size of Wales or New Jersey, but is a sparsely populated wild land with over half its 1.2 million population huddled into its only city, Zaragoza.

The very name Aragón evokes images of romantic medieval Spain and is well known in European history as its kingdom once held sway across Barcelona, Valencia and as far afield as Sardinia. The Crown of Aragón was disbanded after its union with Castile, however, and, by the early 18C, had reverted to its sleepy provincial role. Today it is largely a destination for lovers of the great outdoors.

Highlights

Zaragoza and Central Aragón

The tongue-twisting capital of Aragón – its present name supposedly derives from the Roman colony of Caesar Augusta – is a vibrant city.

At first sight it is unprepossessing with traffic-laden streets and unattractive modern buildings, many designed to accommodate the steady influx from the countryside over the last 50-or-so years, but at its heart is the historical old town (casco viejo) so typical of many Spanish cities.

The city, or at least its riverside, has recently been regenerated as a result of its hosting Expo 2008. The legacy of this international exposition is an assortment of new buildings and visitor attractions including the largest freshwater aquarium in Europe. Expo also helped put Zaragoza on the worldwide map and increased its vistor awareness and infrastructure. Indeed the city is now bidding (alongside Málaga) to become European Capital of Culture for 2016. It credentials are good; with strong links to the great artist Goya, and a 500-year-old university with around 50 000 students.

Outside the capital, much of central Aragón is flat and featureless. The main source of livelihood is farming around Huesca and stock-raising in the valleys.Huesca, the quiet capital of Upper Aragón, has an appealing historic centre while picturesque Alquézar has a wonderful isolated setting in an area famed for its sport of canyoning. Near here, Barbastro, boasting fine 16C architecture, makes a good base for exploring the Central Pyrenees and picturesque historic villages such as Roda de Isábena.

- Huesca
- Barbastro
- Zaragoza

Northern Aragón

The northernmost part of this area butts right up to the French border and is known as the Aragonese Pyrenees (Pirineos Aragoneses).

The highlight of this spectacular region is the Parque Nacional de Ordesa y Monte Perdido, the latter being one of three mountains in this range that tower (just) over 3 350m/11 000ft, making them the highest peaks in the central Pyrenees. The Ordesa Canyon is one of Spain's natural wonders and Europe's riposte to the Grand Canyon. its chasms, cliffs and gorges are home to a rich variety of flora and fauna including ibex, golden eagles and a goat-like antelope, known as an izard. The attractive village of Torla is the gateway to the park while the small town of Jaca also makes a central base for climbers

Teruel

©Turespaña

and walkers in the rest of the region. Near here the Monasterio de San Juan de la Peña occupies a spectacular location beneath overhanging rock.

In winter Spanish skiers arrive at resorts such as Formigal, which has a lively après-ski scene.

🚶 **Jaca**
🚶 **Parque Nacional de Ordesa y Monte Perdido**
🚶 **Pirineos Aragoneses**

Southern Aragón

The clay hills bordering the Ebro Basin in Bajo Aragón (Lower Aragón) around Daroca and Alcañiz are planted with vineyards and olive groves. Brick villages and ochre-coloured houses merge in with the tawny shade of the deeply scored hillsides. The jewel of Bajo (Lower) Aragón is Teruel, declared a UNESCO World Heritage site on account of its rich Mudéjar (Christian-Moorish) architecture, and famous in particular for its lavish ornate towers. From here there is a spectacular drive (38km/24mi) to Albarracín, a splendidly sited medieval hill town, set high on a cliff, which even draws coach tours from the coast.

Like Albarracín, Daroca was a fortress town and its battlemented wall once had over 100 towers. Its old quarter has many fine old buildings testifying

to an important part – today it is home to fewer than 3 000 people. The nearby Monastery of Piedra has long ceased to be monk's dwelling – it is now a private hotel, but is worth the detour for a walk in its popular park, with waterfalls and grottoes.

If you are in Southern Aragón during Holy Week then head for Alcañiz which is famous for its celebrations. The town also boasts some fine architecture including its 13C castle, now a parador.

🚶 **Alcañiz**
🚶 **Daroca**
🚶 **Monasterio de Piedra**
🚶 **Teruel**

189

Alcañiz

Alcañiz, set in olive groves, is the capital of Lower Aragón. The region is famous for Holy Week ceremonies.

SIGHTS
Plaza de España★
Two memorable façades meet on the square: the tall Catalan Gothic arcade of the **Lonja**, once a market, and the Renaissance town hall *(ayuntamiento)*. Both are crowned by an Aragón gallery with overhanging eaves.

Colegiata de Santa María la Mayor
Pl. de España. ⏱*Open daily 9am–1pm, 4–7pm.* ⊗*No charge.*

> ### Luis Buñuel (1900–1983)
> The great film director was from **Calanda**, 17km/10.5mi SW of Alcañiz.

▶ **Population:** 1 623
⛯ **Michelin Map:** 574 I 29
ℹ **Info:** Calle Mayor 1. ☎978 83 12 13. www.alcaniz.es.
▷ **Location:** Alcañiz is in the northeastern province of Teruel.

Vertical lines and curves and a Baroque **portal**★ mark the collegiate church, rebuilt in the 18C. Massive columns with composite capitals rise to a projecting cornice.

Castillo de los Calatravos
⏱*Open Sept–Jul Wed–Sun 10am–1.30pm; Aug daily 10am–1.30pm, 4–7pm.* ⊗*4.70€.*
The hilltop castle was the local seat of the Order of Calatrava in the 12C. The part used as a parador largely dates from the 18C. Note the Gothic chapel, with its aisle of equilateral arches, and in the keep, 14C wall paintings.

Barbastro

Barbastro's interesting architecture bears witness to its 16C importance. It is a base for excursions into the central Pyrenees and capital of the Somontano wine region.

SIGHTS
Catedral★
San José de Calasanz.
The cathedral is a standard hall-church with three elegant aisles beneath richly ornamented vaulting with gilded decoration, borne by slender columns.
The predella on the high altar **retable** is an important work by Damián Forment. Several side chapels are Churrigueresque; the first on the left-hand side holds a fine early 16C retable. The **Museo Diocesano** (⏱*open daily 10am–1pm, 6–8pm;* ⊗*suggested donation 2€;* ☎*974 31 16 82)* is open to the public.

▶ **Population:** 16 486
⛯ **Michelin Map:** 574 F 30 – Aragón (Huesca)
ℹ **Info:** Avenida de la Merced 64. ☎974 30 83 50. www.barbastro.org.
▷ **Location:** Barbastro is at the end of two Pyrenean valleys, one leading to Parque de Ordesa, the other to the Maladeta range, via the Congosto de Ventamillo canyon.

Complejo de San Julián y Santa Lucía
Av. de la Merced.
The former Hospital de San Julián houses the tourist office, a wine shop, and a **museum** dedicated to the excellent Somontano appellation.
The 16C Renaissance church of San Julián opposite houses the **Centro de**

Interpretación del Somontano★ (🕐 *open Mon–Sat 10am–2pm, 4.30–7.30pm;* 🕐 *closed 25 Dec;* 💶 *2€*), highlighting the area and its tourist sites via a short film.

EXCURSIONS
Alquézar★
23km/14mi NW on the A 1232, following the Río Vero.
Alquézar enjoys a magnificent isolated **setting**★★ amid red earth, appearing to cling to a rocky promontory in a loop of the river.

Old quarter
The medieval old quarter is a maze of uneven streets lined by houses adorned with rounded stone doorways and coats of arms. The arcaded main square is enchanting.
Colegiata★ – ✆*Guided tours Sept–Jul Wed–Mon 11am–1.30pm, 4–6pm; Aug 11am–1pm, 4.30–7.30pm.* 💶 *2€. www. somontano.org/alquezar.* A Moorish **alcázar** on the site fell to Sancho Ramírez, King of Aragón. In the late 11C and early 12C, the walls were constructed, along with a church (rebuilt in 1530). A beautiful Romanesque Christ dates from the 12C.
Cañón del río Vero★ – 🚶Allow a day to walk up and in some places wade or swim this spectacular canyon. Or hike only to the Roman bridge at Villacantal (*2hr round trip*) for an overview and to see impressive ochre and grey walls.

 DRIVING TOUR

Through the Ribagorza
85km/53mi– allow one day.
Follows the Esera and Isábena rivers, through the historic county of Ribagorza, in the pre-Pyrenees of Aragón.

▷ *Leave Barbastro on the N 123; after 16km/10mi go right onto the A 2211.*

Santuario de Torreciudad
🕐*Open Mon–Fri 10am–2pm, 4–7.30pm, Sat 10am–2pm, 4–8.30pm, Sun 9am–2pm, 4–8.30pm, except 1*

Alquézar

B. Brillion/MICHELIN

Jul–15 Sept Mon 7.30pm, 16 Sept–Apr 7pm. ✆*974 30 40 25. www.torreciudad. org.*
In 1804, an 11C Romanesque statue of Our Lady of Torreciudad was placed in a small shrine and locally venerated. In 1975 a pilgrimage church was built under the auspices of Monsignor José María Escrivá de Balaguer (now canonised), founder of Opus Dei (1928). Before the brick buildings, a vast esplanade affords beautiful **views**★ of the Pyrenees and the El Grado dam. The statue of Our Lady of Torreciudad is in the lower part of the altarpiece.

▷ *From Torreciudad, return to the A 2211, heading towards La Puebla de Castro, then take the N 123ª.*

Graus
The village huddles around the irregular **Plaza de España**, lined by old houses decorated with frescoes, carved beams and brick galleries. The 16C **Santuario de la Virgen de la Peña**★★ has a Renaissance doorway and single aisle crowned by pointed vaulting.

▷ *The A 1605 crosses the Esera river.*

Roda de Isábena★
26.5km/16.5mi from Graus.
This picturesque village perches on a promontory in a beautiful mountain

setting★. Construction of the impressive **cathedral**★ (━guided tours (30min); ⌖2.50€; please call to reserve on ✆974 54 45 35) began in the 11C. Most of the interior, basilical in plan with three aisles, was built in the 12C. In the central **crypt** is the **tomb of San Ramón**★★, with interesting polychrome low reliefs. A 13C fresco adorns a chapel off the cloisters.

▷ *Continue 16km/10mi N on A 1605.*

Monasterio de Santa María de Obarra

Only the 10C–11C church, built by Lombard masters, remains of this monastery. A 12C hermitage, the Ermita de San Pablo, stands to one side.

Daroca★

Daroca's battlemented walls★, originally with 100 towers and gateways, lie between two ridges. The **Puerta Baja** (Lower Gate) is flanked by square towers.

SIGHTS
Colegiata de Santa María

Pl. de España 8. ◷ *Open Tue–Sun 8am–1pm, 5.30–6.30pm.* ⌖*3€.* ✆*976 80 07 32.*

This Romanesque collegiate church, a repository for the holy cloths, was modified in the 15C and 16C. Beside the belfry is a Flamboyant Gothic portal.

The late Gothic nave includes a Renaissance cupola above the transept crossing.

The **south chapels** are partly faced with 16C *azulejos*. To the right of the entrance is a 15C **altarpiece**★ in multicoloured alabaster believed to have been carved in England. The 15C **Capilla de los Corporales**★ (Chapel of the Holy Relics) is on the site of the original Romanesque apse. The altar includes a shrine

▷ **Population:** 2 345
◷ **Michelin Map:** 574 I 25 – Aragón
▯ **Info:** Plaza de España 4. ✆976 80 01 29. www.daroca.org.
◷ **Location:** Daroca is in eastern Spain at the crossroads of the N 234 and N 330, close to Calatayud (40km/25mi N), Zaragoza (85km/53mi NE) and Teruel (96km/59.6mi S).

enclosing the holy altar cloths. Statues in delightful poses are carved of multicoloured alabaster. The painted Gothic **retable**★ is dedicated to St Michael.

Museo Parroquial★

Pl. de España. ◷ *Open Tue–Sun 11am–1pm, 6–8pm.* ⌖*3€.* ✆*976 80 07 61.*

Holdings include two rare though damaged 13C panels and **altarpieces** to St Peter (14C) and St Martin (15C), and

The Miracle of the Holy Altar Cloths

The miracle of the holy altar cloths took place in 1239, after the conquest of Valencia, when Christian troops in Daroca, Teruel and Calatayud were setting out to recover territory occupied by the Moors. Just as Mass was being celebrated, the Moors attacked and the priest had to hide the consecrated hosts between two altar cloths. Shortly afterwards, it was seen that the hosts had left bloodstained imprints on the linen. The three towns of Daroca, Teruel and Calatayud all claimed the precious relic. To settle the dispute the holy cloths were placed upon a mule which was then set free. It made straight for Daroca, dying, however, as it entered the Puerta Baja.

gold and silver plate mostly of local manufacture, as well as **chasubles**.

Iglesia de San Miguel
Pl. Colegial.
This fine church, outstanding for the purity of its Romanesque east end and its 12C portal, is restored to its original design. A short distance below is the restored Mudéjar-style belfry of the **Iglesia de Santo Domingo**.

Huesca★

The tranquillity of Huesca, capital of Alto Aragón (Upper Aragón), belies its turbulent past. The old town huddles around the top of a promontory crowned by an imposing cathedral.

A BIT OF HISTORY

Historical notes – Huesca was the capital of a Roman state, a Moorish stronghold until its reconquest by **Pedro I of Aragón** in 1096, and capital of Aragón until 1118.

The origins of a well-known Spanish saying – "Ringing like the bell of Huesca" – is a Spanish way to describe a dire event. In the 12C, King **Ramiro II** summoned his truculent nobles to watch the casting of a bell – and promptly had them beheaded.

SIGHTS
OLD QUARTER
Catedral★
Pl. de La Catedral. ○ *Open Mon–Fri 10.30am–1.30pm, 4–7pm, Sat 10.30am–1.30pm.* ◉*3€ (including Cathedral museum).* ☎*974 23 10 99.*
The 13C Gothic façade is divided unusually by a gallery and an Aragonese carved wood overhang. A gable encloses a rose window and the portal covings with weathered statues.
On the tympanum are the Magi and Christ before Mary Magdalene. The alabaster **altarpiece**★★ dates from 1533. In this masterpiece by Damián Forment, three scenes of the Crucifixion appear in high relief in the middle of Flamboyant canopy and frieze decoration.
Facing the Cathedral, the *ayuntamiento* (town hall) is a tastefully decorated Renaissance town house.

▶ **Population:** 51 117
◈ **Michelin Map:** 574 F 28 – local map – JACA
▦ **Info:** Plaza Luis López Allué. ☎974 29 21 70. www.huescaturismo.com.
◗ **Location:** Huesca is 72km/44.7mi N of Zaragoza, 91km/56.5mi S of Jaca and 123km/76.4mi NW of Lleida/Lérida, along the E 7 motorway. It is a good base for excursions into the Pyrenees). ▦José Gil Cávez 10

Museo de Huesca★
Pl. Universidad 1. ○ *Open Tue–Sat 10am–2pm, 5–8pm, Sun and public holidays 10am–2pm.* ○ *Closed 1, 6 Jan, 24, 25, 31 Dec.* ◉*No charge.* ☎*974 22 05 86.*
The museum is in the old university, built in 1690 around a fine octagonal patio incorporating parts of the royal palace (and notorious massacre site). The collection includes prehistoric artefacts and **Aragonese primitive paintings**★, several by the Maestro de Sigena (16C).

Iglesia de San Pedro el Viejo★
Pl. de San Pedro. ○*Open Mon–Sat 10am–1.30pm.* ☛*Guided tour* ◉*2€.* ☎*974 22 23 87.*
The 11C monastery's **cloisters**★, with their historiated capitals, are a jewel of Romanesque sculpture in Aragón. The tympanum of the cloister doorway has an unusual Adoration of the Magi with all the emphasis on movement. A Romanesque chapel holds the

Castillo de Loarre

M. Lemaire/MICHELIN

tombs of kings Ramiro II and Alfonso I, the Battler.

EXCURSION
Monasterio de Monte Aragón
5km/3mi E along the N 240.
The monastery was originally a fortress built by Sancho I Ramírez.

DRIVING TOUR

Tour through Los Mallos de Riglos – Sierra de Loarre

▷ *Take the A 132 to Ayerbe. Continue 9km/5.6mi, then turn left to Agüero.*

Agüero
The village is set against a spectacular background of *Mallos* (*see entry*). Before Agüero, a road leads *(right)* to the Romanesque **Iglesia de Santiago**. Three aisles of the church are covered by three separate stone roofs.

▷ *Take the A 132 towards Huesca, then the HU 310 left toward Riglos.*

Los Mallos de Riglos★★
The Río Gállego is banked by tall crumbling cliffs, red ochre in colour. **Los Mallos** are a formation of rose pudding-

stone, eroded into sugar loaf forms. The most dramatic group *(to the right)* dominates the village of **Riglos**.

▷ *Return to Ayerbe on the A 132, then turn left to Loarre along the A 1206.*

Castillo de Loarre★★
○ *Open daily Nov–Feb 11am–1.30pm, 3–5.30pm; 16 Jun–15 Sept 10am–2pm, 4–8pm; Mar–15 Jun 16 Sept–31 Oct 10am–2pm, 4–7pm.* ○ *Closed 1 Jan, 25 Dec.* ⊚*2€.* ✆*Guided tours ⊚1.50€.* ✆*974 34 21 66. www.castillodeloarre.org.*
In the 11C, Sancho Ramírez, King of Aragón and Navarra, had this castle-fortress built at an altitude of 1 100m/3 609ft. The walls, flanked by round towers, command a vast **panorama★★** of the Ebro Basin. After the massive keep and fine covered stairway, view the 12C church. The capitals are very beautiful.

▷ *Continue SE on the A 1206.*

Bolea
The main church **altarpiece** is a superb example of 15C Hispano-Flemish art.

▷ *Return to Huesca on the A 132.*

Jaca★

Jaca, the "pearl of the Pyrenees" stands strategically at the foot of the Pyrenees, under the Peña de Oroel. It was an important stop along the "Camino de Santiago", and became the capital of Aragón in the 9C.

SIGHTS

Catedral★

◷Open daily 11.30am–1.30pm, 4–8pm. ℘974 35 62 41.

Spain's oldest Romanesque cathedral, from the 11C, influenced craftsmen who worked on churches along the pilgrim route to Santiago de Compostela. Note the **historiated capitals**★ of the south porch and great detail in the south doorway figures.

Gothic vaulting covers unusually wide aisles. The apse and side chapels are decorated with sculpture but the cupola on squinches over the transept crossing has retained its simplicity.

Museo Diocesano (Diocesan Museum)

Pl. de San Pedro. ○━Closed for restoration. ℘974 35 63 78.

The cloisters and adjoining halls contain Romanesque and Gothic **wall paintings**★ from village churches in the area, and Romanesque paintings.

Castillo de San Pedro

Av. del Primer Viernes de Mayo.
◷ Open Dec–early Nov Tue–Sun 11am–2pm, 4–7pm. ◉10€ (includes toy soldier museum). ℘974 36 30 18.

Built in 1595 during the reign of Philip II as part of a network of castles and towers to guard the French border, this citadel is an outstanding example of 16C military architecture and has been declared a National Monument. Surrounded by a moat, the fortress has a perfect pentagonal plan, with defensive bulwarks at each vertex.

Inside is the **Museo de Miniaturas Militares** (www.museominiaturasjaca. es), which contains over 32 000 military figurines.

▶ **Population:** 13 193
 Michelin Map: 574 E 28
 Info: Plaza de San Pedro nº 11–13. ℘974 36 00 98. www.jaca.es.
 Location: Jaca is along the A 23, from Huesca to El Puerto de Somport, and the N 240, to Pamplona (111km/69mi NW).

🚗 DRIVING TOURS

1 TOUR THROUGH SERRABLO

54km/34mi – allow half a day.

▶ Leave Jaca on the A 23 towards Sabiñánigo.

This excursion includes extraordinary 10C and 11C Mozarabic churches.

Museo de Dibujo

In Larrés, 18km/11mi E of Jaca along the A 23. ◷ Open Nov–Mar Tue–Sat 11am–1pm, 3–6pm, Sun and public holidays 11am–1pm, 4–6pm; Apr–Jun Sept–Oct Tue–Sun and public holidays 11am–1pm, 4–7pm; Jul–Aug daily 10am–2.30pm, 4.30–9pm. ◉3€. ℘974 48 29 81. www.serrablo.org/museodibujo.

This museum, in the 14C Castillo de Larrés, displays sketches by Martín Chirino, Salvador Dalí and others. A section covers graphic humour.

▶ Return to the A 23. From Cartirana, take the N 260 to Puente Oliván. Follow signs to Oliván, then turn towards Orós Bajo. Follow directions below.

Mozarabic churches

The churches of the Serrablo are small and rectangular, with a semicircular apse. Walls are generally devoid of bays, while the arches are either horseshoe or semicircular; occasionally, doors are framed by an alfiz surround. The most impressive churches are in Orós Bajo, San Martín de Oliván, **San Juan**

Capitals of Monasterio de San Juan de la Peña

de Busa★ (with unfinished apse), **San Pedro de Lárrede**★ and Satué.

◉ *From Satué, head towards Sabiñánigo.*

Museo Ángel Oresanz y Artes de Serrablo★

San Nicolás 1, Sabiñánigo. In Puente de Sabiñánigo S of the town centre.
◔ *Open Oct–May Tue–Sun 10am–1pm, 3.30–6.30pm; Jun–Sept Tue–Sun 11am–2pm, 4–8pm (Jul–Aug daily).*
⊛2€. ℘974 48 42 61. www.serrablo. org/museoartespopulares.

The major ethnographic collection in the Huescan Pyrenees is in a wonderful traditional Serrablo house.

② MONASTERIO DE SAN JUAN DE LA PEÑA★★
25km/15.5mi – allow half a day.

◉ *Take the N 240 from Jaca. After 11km/6.8mi, turn off towards Santa Cruz de la Serós.*

Santa Cruz de la Serós★

Pl. Mayor. ◔*Open daily Sept–15 Oct 16 Mar–May 10am–2pm, 4–7pm; Jun 10am–2.30pm, 4–8pm; Jul–Aug 10am–2.30pm, 3.30–8pm; 16–31 Oct 10am–2pm, 4–5.30pm; Nov–15 Mar 11am–2pm, 4–5.30pm.* ◔*Closed 1 Jan, 25 Dec.* ⊛*4.50€.* ℘*974 35 51 19.*

This 10C convent, endowed by nobles and princesses, was abandoned in the 16C. Only the **Romanesque church**★, surrounded by small Aragonese houses,

remains. The stout belfry, crowned by an octagonal turret, abuts the lantern. The portal recalls Jaca Cathedral.

◉ *Beyond Santa Cruz de la Serós the road winds through the sierra.*

Monasterio de San Juan de la Peña★★

◔ *Open daily Nov–early Mar 10.30am–2pm, 3.30–5.30pm; Jun–early Jul 10am–2pm, 3–8pm, late Jul–Aug 10am–8pm; 6 Mar–May and Sept–Oct 10am–2pm, 3.30–7pm.* ◔ *Closed 25 Dec, 1 Jan.* ⊛*6€ (12€ including "Kingdom of Aragón" and Monastery Interpretation Centres). ℘974 35 51 19. www.monasteriosanjuan.com.*

The most spectacular feature of this monastery is its **setting**★★ in a hollow beneath overhanging rocks. The monastery was chosen as a pantheon for the kings and nobles of Aragón and Navarra, and expanded in the 12C.

The oldest features can be seen on the lower storey, where the Lower Church dates from the early Mozarabic monastery. The **Sala de Concilios** (Council Chamber) was built by King Sancho Garcés around the year 922.

In the 11C–14C **Panteón de Nobles Aragoneses** are niches with coats of arms, sacred monograms and in many cases a cross with four roses, the emblem of Iñigo Arista, founder of the Kingdom of Navarra.

The late 11C **Iglesia Alta** (Upper Church) comprises a single aisle, while the three apsidal chapels with blind arcades are hollowed out of the cliff. The **Panteón de Reyes** (Royal Pantheon) opens off the north wall.

The 12C **cloisters**★★, between precipice and cliff, are accessed by a Mozarabic door. Only two galleries and fragments of another remain. The **capitals**★★ exhibit a personal style and use of symbolism which influenced sculpture in the region for years.

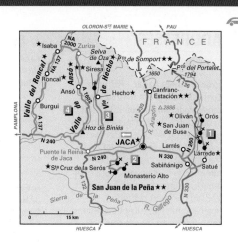

③ VALLE DE HECHO★
60km/37mi – allow one day.

▶ *Leave Jaca on the N 240. In Puente la Reina de Jaca, turn right on the A 176.*

The road follows the Aragón Subordán. The traditional houses of **Hecho**★ *(www.hecho.es)* have stone doorways, many with coats of arms. The **Museo de Escultura al Aire Libre**, by the tourist office, shows sculpture in the open. There is also a **Museo Etnológico** (☉*open Jul–mid-Sept 10.30am–1.30pm, 5–9pm;* ☞*1.20€;* ✆*974 37 55 05).*
2km/1.2mi to the north in Siresa is the **Iglesia de San Pedro**★★, once part of a monastery. It was visited by **St Eulogus of Córdoba**, martyred in 859. The 11C **church** has a fine elevation and walls with blind arcades and buttresses. The **altarpieces**★ are principally 15C. (☉ *open daily 11am–1pm, 3–5pm; summer 11am–1pm, 5–8pm;* ☞*1.50€).*

▶ *The road continues through a narrow valley towards Selva de Oza.*

④ TOUR THROUGH THE RONCAL AND ANSÓ VALLEYS
161km/100mi – allow one day.
These two high valleys have a self-sufficient economy based on sheep rearing in common pastures. Festivals are celebrated in traditional costume.

▶ *Leave Jaca on the N 240, heading W.*

For 47km/29mi the road runs along the River Aragón through clay hills.

▶ *Turn right onto the NA 137.*

The road goes up the green **Roncal Valley**★ watered by the River Esca. It crosses a narrow humpbacked bridge just before **Burgui**. **Roncal**★, famous for its cheese, has fine examples of noble architecture, and a museum dedicated to tenor **Julián Gayarre**. The road passes *(to the left)* the fortified tower of the Iglesia de Nuestra Señora de San Salvador de Urzainqui. **Isaba/Izaba**★ *(www.isaba.es)* is the major valley centre.

▶ *A little further N, take the NA 2000 towards the Zuriza tourist complex.*

Once in the **Ansó Valley**★, this spectacular **road**★ runs along the River Veral to **Ansó** *(✆974 37 02 25).* In the church, the Museo Etnológico is dedicated to local ways (⊶ *closed for renovation;* ✆*974 37 01 85).*

▶ *Return S along the narrow, winding A 1602 through the Veral Valley and the Hoz de Biniés gorge.*

ADDRESSES

🛏 STAY

🍽🍽🍽 **Conde Aznar** – *Pas. de la Constitución 3.* ☎*974 36 10 50. www. condeaznar.com. 34 rooms.* ☐*7.48€. Restaurant*🍽. A good location in an old house on the quiet Paseo de la Constitución, five minutes from the cathedral. Access to the hotel, furnished with antiques, is via a small terrace; an attractive wooden staircase leads to the guest bedrooms. The hotel also has two exceptional suites and a restaurant serving some of the best cuisine in the Pyrenees.

🍽 EAT

🍽🍽🍽 **Gaby-Casa Blasquico** – *Pl. La Fuente 1, Hecho.* ☎*974 37 50 07. www. casablasquico.com. Closed 1–15 Sept, 22–25 Dec.* This famous Pyrenean restaurant serves some of the best cuisine to be found in Huesca, with a successful fusion of traditional and innovative ideas. The dining room is small but attractive, plus there are six guest rooms and a plant-filled terrace.

🍽🍽🍽 **Lilium** – *Av. Primer Viernes de Mayo 8.* ☎*974 35 53 56. Closed fortnight in Oct, 24–25 Dec, Mon eve, Tue.* A restaurant noted for its fine Aragonese cuisine, upheld with great care by the proprietor, located in the heart of Jaca. The ground and first floors have a modern décor, whilst the basement has a rustic décor with a beautiful wooden ceiling.

Parque Nacional de
Ordesa y Monte Perdido★★★

The Ordesa canyon cuts through vast, layered limestone folds. Escarpments rise nearly 1 000m/ 3 280ft in grey and ochre strata, streaked in spring with cascades of snowmelt. Growing up the lower slopes are pines, larches, firs – some 25m/82ft tall – and a carpet of box, hawthorn and service trees. The park's valleys lie under such impressive peaks as Monte Perdido (3 355m/11 004ft).

- ♿ **Michelin Map:** 574 E 29-30
- 🅸 **Info:** Torla. ☎974 48 64 72; Ainsa. ☎974 50 07 67. http://reddeparques nacionales.mma.es.
- ▸ **Location:** This national park is 98km/61mi SE of Huesca in the central Pyrenees (with its twin on the French side) and can be approached from Torla to the west or Ainsa from the south east.

🥾 WALKING TOURS
VALLE DE ORDESA★★★

A viewpoint on the entry road offers a general panorama. A second point, near the road's end, overlooks 60m/197ft high **cascada de Tamborrotera** ① (waterfall). 🚶The rest of the park may only be visited on foot. The best route for inexperienced walkers or families with young children is the shaded path along the bottom of the canyon. *Allow a day from the car park to the end of the canyon and back.*
🚶*The walks to follow are feasible for experienced, well-equipped hikers.*

CIRCUITO DEL CIRCO DE SOASO (SOASO CIRQUE ROUTE)

🚶*Start from the Cadiera hut beyond the car park; 7hr. The walk to the valley floor is easy. The second part, via the Cola de Caballo (Horse's Tail), is only recommended to those who are well equipped and in good physical condition (steep climbs).*

Parque Nacional de Ordesa

©Turespaña

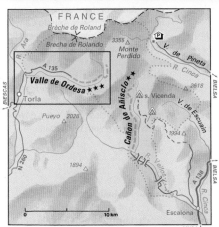

**PARQUE NACIONAL
DE ORDESA Y
MONTE PERDIDO**

– – –	Path described
– –	Other path
⌂	Refuge
✕	Restaurant
🛈	Tourist Information Centre
🅿	Car park
🄿	Parador

This walk provides the best and most complete tour of the Ordesa Valley. From the Circo de Soaso path several waterfalls can be seen including the **Gradas de Soaso** ②, or Soaso Steps, followed by the impressive, 70m/230ft high **Cola de Caballo** ③. The path continues along the **Faja de Pelay** overlooking the canyon to a depth of 2 000m/6 550ft at the foot of the Sierra de Cutas.

Continue on the **Senda de los Cazadores** (Huntsman's Path) ⑤ for a wonderful view of the canyon. The best panorama is from the **Mirador de Cal-**

199

The National Park

The Valle de Ordesa was declared a national park in 1918 and was expanded in 1982 to cover an area of 15 608ha/38 569 acres, including the Monte Perdido massif and the Ordesa, Añisclo, Escuain and Pineta valleys. The purpose of the park is to safeguard the region's outstanding natural beauty – the massif's limestone relief of canyons, cliffs and chasms – as well as the variety and richness of its flora and fauna (Pyrenean ibex, golden eagle and izard, a goat-like antelope of the Pyrenees). The National Park

cilarruego 🚴. The path back to the hut drops almost 1 000m/3 281ft.

CIRCO DE COTATUERO (COTATUERO CIRQUE)

🚶*Start from the restaurant; 4hr.*
On the park's northern border are the **Cotatuero** ⑥ and the **Copos de Lana**

(Tufts of Wool) *cascadas* (waterfalls) ⑦ with a drop of 250m/820ft.

CIRCO DE CARRIATA

🚶*From the Centro de Información; 4hr.*
The walk is worth doing although the *clavijas* (mountaineering peg track) is not for those who suffer from vertigo. A long hike is possible to Monte Perdido via the Goriz refuge; or to the Cirque de Gavarnie in France via the Brecha de Rolando (Roland Gap) *(ask at the Centro de Información).*

CAÑÓN DE AÑISCLO★★

Access from Escalona village on the Bielsa-Ainsa road – a 13km/8mi drive.
In the cool and lovely Añisclo Canyon, narrower than Ordesa, pine trees cling to the limestone walls.

WALK TO RIPARETA

🚶*Start from the San Urbez bridge. 5hr there and back.* A wide, well-defined path follows the enclosed Río Vellos down to its confluence with the Pardina.

Monasterio de Piedra★★

Hidden in a fold of this arid plateau is an oasis fed by the River Piedra. Approach the monastery via Ateca, across a parched landscape above the Tranquera Reservoir and past the village of Nuévalos.

A BIT OF HISTORY

The site was discovered by Cistercian monks, who generally chose pleasant surroundings. Monks from the Abbey of Poblet in Tarragona established a monastery in 1194. It was rebuilt several times. The buildings have been reconstructed as a hotel.

Park and Waterfalls★★

🕐*Open daily Apr–Nov 9am–8pm; Dec–Mar 9am–6pm.* ✎*12 €.* ✆*902 19 60 52. www.monasteriopiedra.com.*

- 🚲 **Michelin Map:**
  574 or 575 I 24
- ▶ **Location:** This magnificent area is 25km/15mi S of the N II-E 90 highway from Madrid to Zaragoza (104km/64.6mi).

Waterfalls and cascades are everywhere along the footpath through the forest *(follow red signposts to go, blue to return).* The paths, steps and tunnels laid out last century by **Juan Federico Muntadas** have transformed an impenetrable forest into a popular park. The first fall is the **Cola de Caballo** (Horse's Tail), a cascade of 53m/174ft. You come on it again at the end of your walk if you descend steep and slippery steps into the beautiful **Cueva Iris** (Iris Grotto). **Baño de Diana** (Diana's Bath) and **Lago del Espejo** (Mirror Lake), between tall cliffs, are both worth a halt.

Pirineos Aragoneses★★

The central Pyrenees, in the north of Huesca province, include the highest peaks: Aneto (3 404m/11 165ft), Posets (3 371m/11 060ft) and Monte Perdido (3 355m/11 004ft). The foothills are often ravined with sparse vegetation; at the heart of the massif, accessible up the river courses, valleys lead to mountain cirques well worth exploring.

A BIT OF HISTORY

Structure and relief – Vast longitudinal bands are clear in this region. The **axis of Palaeozoic terrain** comprises the Maladeta, Posets, Vignemale and Balaïtous massifs, where there are remains of Quaternary glaciers. In the **Pre-Pyrenees** (Monte Perdido), deep **Mesozoic limestone** is eroded into the canyons, gorges and cirques of the upper valleys. The limestone area, which extends in broken mountain chains to the Ebro Basin, is divided at Jaca by the long depression of the River Aragón. Tertiary sediment has accumulated into hills; some are bare of vegetation, in an unusual blue marl landscape like that around the **Yesa Reservoir**.

Life in the valleys – The upper valleys of the Kingdom of Aragón developed self-contained communities. Folk tradtions are still followed and native costume is worn in certain valleys. Emigration has led to the abandonment of a number of villages. Tourism is a major economic activity. Winter resorts include Candanchú, Astún, Canfranc, Panticosa, El Formigal and Benasque.

🚗 DRIVING TOURS

The following route described covers the Pirineos Aragoneses from east to west, divided into six separate drives.

1 FROM VIELHA TO BENASQUE
122km/76mi – allow about 3hr.

- **Michelin Map:** 574 D 28-32, E 29-32 and F 30-31 – Aragón (Huesca)
- **Info:** Avenida Pirenaica 1, Ainsa. ℘974 50 07 67. www.pirineos.com.
- **Location:** From Pamplona/Iruña follow the N 240 to Jaca (111km/69mi SE); from Huesca the N 330 to Jaca (91km/57mi N); from Barbastro the N 123 and the A 138 to Ainsa (52km/32.5mi N).
- **Don't Miss:** A hike in a spectacular canyon, and a surprising country repast.

Vielha *See PIRINEOS CATALANES*
The road cuts the Maladeta massif via the Vielha tunnel to the lonely upper valley of the Noguera Ribagorçana where the attractive hamlet of **Vilaller** huddles.

▷ *Take the N 260 to Castejón de Sos, a paragliding centre, then the A 139.*

Valle de Benasque★
Benasque (1 138m/3 734ft) lies in an open valley, lush and green, overshadowed by the Maladeta massif, a base for walkers, climbers (ascending the Aneto) and skiers (Cerler, 5km/3mi). Streets are lined with old mansions. **Anciles**, 1.6km/1mi away, is known for its attractive houses. 15km/9.3mi further north, just before the road ends, a turnoff leads to the Hospital de Benasque (*www.llanosdelhospital.com*), departure point for excursions into Parque Natural Posets-Maladeta.

2 FROM BENASQUE TO AINSA
180km/112mi – allow half a day.
The road south through the Esero Valley passes through Villanova (*www.villanova.es*), with its two 11C–12C Lombard-Romanesque-style churches. After Castejón de Sos, it follows the **Congosto de Ventamillo**★★, a 3km/1.8mi defile with sheer limestone rock walls.

Ainsa★

Ainsa, one of the prettiest towns in the Pyrenees, stands on a promontory still girded by a wall, commanding the juncture of the River Cinca and River Ara.

In the 11C it was the capital of the kingdom of Sobrarbe. Its arcaded **Plaza Mayor**★★ in the upper town, under the tower of a Romanesque church, is a gem of Aragonese architecture. The contemporary-style **Museo de Oficios y Artes Tradicionales**★ *(pl. San Salvador 10;* ○*open Fri–Sat 10am–2pm, 4–7.30pm, Sun 10am–2pm;* ⊛*2.50€;* ☏*974 51 00 75)* is a museum devoted to traditional arts and crafts.

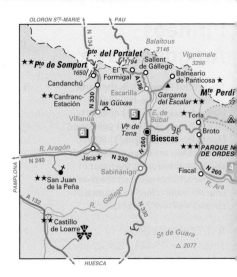

③ FROM AINSA TO MONTE PERDIDO

73km/45mi – allow about 4hr.

The A 138 follows the River Cinca northwards, through a dramatic landscape at the **Desfiladero de las Devotas**★.

Cañón de Añisclo★★ ⊙*See Parque Nacional de ORDESA Y MONTE PERDIDO*

Valle de Gistaín★

▶ *Exit the A 138 at Salinas de Sin.*

In this valley, also known as the Valle de Chistau, are some of the most picturesque villages in the Pyrenees, including **Plan**, **San Juan de Plan** and **Gistaín**.

Aínsa

M. Lemaire/MICHELIN

Parque Nacional de Ordesa y Monte Perdido★★★ 🚗 *see Parque Nacional de ORDESA Y MONTE PERDIDO*

⑤ THE PORTALET ROAD

52km/32.3mi – allow about 2hr.

The **Tena** Valley beyond Biescas widens out into the vast Búbal reservoir.

▶ *A short distance before Escarilla, bear right onto HU 610 for Panticosa.*

Garganta del Escalar★★ (Escalar Gorge)

The sun rarely penetrates this gorge. The road cuts down the west slope by ramps and hairpin bends to an austere mountain cirque, the setting for the **Balneario de Panticosa★** (✆902 25 25 22; www.panticosa.com), a spa with six sulphurous and radioactive springs, and a charming 19C air.

▶ *Return to Escarilla and continue to the Portalet Pass.*

The mountain town of **Sallent de Gállego**, at 1 305m/4 281ft, hosts a summer music festival and is renowned for trout fishing and mountaineering. **El Formigal** (alt 1 480m/4 856ft), further on, is a ski resort.

Carretera del Portalet

Alt 1 794m/5 886ft. The pass lies between Portalet peak and Aneu summit to the west. The view extends to the Aneu cirque and Pic du Midi d'Ossau in France (alt 2 884m/9 462ft).

⑥ FROM BIESCAS TO THE PUERTO DE SOMPORT

58km/36mi – allow about 2hr.

▶ *Continue S on the N 260 to Sabiñánigo – from here it is possible to follow the tour through the Serrablo (🚶see JACA – Excursions) – then take*

Bielsa and Valle de Pineta

19km/11.8mi NW of Plan, along A 138.
From the pleasant village of Bielsa, a narrow road climbs the valley of the Cinca River, traversing the impressive landscapes of the **Valle de Pineta★★** to the Parador de Bielsa, nestled in a spectacular glacial cirque.

④ FROM AINSA TO BIESCAS

81km/51mi – allow about 3hr

Between **Boltaña** (16C church; *www. boltana.es*) and **Fiscal** (medieval tower; *www.aytofiscal.es*), the river course reveals underlying strata. The church of **Broto** *(www.broto.es)* has an interesting Renaissance doorway.

Beyond Broto, the great mass of the Mondarruego (alt 2 848m/9 341ft), closing the Ordesa Valley, backdrops the spectacular **landscape★★** where the village of **Torla★** lies on the western slope of the Ara Valley.

The church, the Iglesia de San Salvador, houses noteworthy 18C altarpieces. The castle-abbey in Torla has an **ethnographic museum** *(for information, call town hall; ☞1€).*

the N330 to Jaca (&see JACA). From Jaca, the N 330 continues northwards.

The **Cueva de las Güixas**, a cave in Villanúa, has some 300m/330yd of galleries (*4.80€; ℘974 37 81 39; www. sargantana.info). Beyond Canfranc is the abandoned early 20C **Canfranc international resort**★★ (www.canfranc.es), an extraordinary example of early 20C architecture.

The **Puerto de Somport**★★ (alt 1 632m/ 5 354ft), beside the Somport tunnel (opened in 2003), is the only pass in the Central Pyrenees which generally remains snow-free all year.
Candanchú (www.candanchu.com), the best-known ski resort in Aragón, is less than 1km/0.6mi away.
Climb the mound to the right of the monument commemorating the building of the road for an extensive **panorama**★★ of the Spanish Pyrenees.

ADDRESSES

🛏 STAY

🛏 **Hostal Dos Rlos** – *Avda Central 2, Ainsa. ℘97450 01 06. www.hoteldosrios. com Closed Nov–25 Dec and 7 Jan–mid-Mar.* This *hostal* and the hotel of the same name are the best medium-priced options in Ainsa. From its location in the lower town, the main square is easily reached on foot or by car. Guest rooms are clean and perfectly adequate.

🛏 **Hotel-Restaurante Casa Frauca** – *Ctra de Ordesa, Sarvisé. ℘974 48 63 53. www.casafrauca.com. 12 rooms. ⌷6€. Restaurant⌷. Closed Jan–Feb.* Cosy rooms where wood floors and beams add to the atmosphere. The rustic-style restaurant has an extensive menu.

🛏 **H. Hospital de Benasque** – *Cam. Real de Francia, Benasque. 15km/9mi N of Benasque along the A 139. Follow a road to the right, signposted Los Llanos del Hospital. ℘974 55 20 12. www.llanosdelhospital.com. 52 rooms. Restaurant (⌷).* Wood and stone are the order of the day in this charming hotel established in a former pilgrims' hospital. The setting, at the foot of the Pico de Maladeta and close to the Pico de Aneto, is quite spectacular. Cosy, pleasantly decorated rooms.

🛏 **Hotel Pradas** – *Av. Ordesa 7, Broto. ℘974 48 60 04. www.hotelpradas. com. 24 rooms. Restaurant⌷. Closed Dec–Mar.* The stone façade is the first thing you notice as you approach this hotel on the main

road into Broto. Several rooms have their own lounge area, albeit with a more expensive price tag.

🛏 **Hotel Villa de Torla** – *Pl. Aragón 1, Torla. ℘974 48 61 56. www. hotelvilladetorla.com. 38 rooms. ⌷6€. Restaurant⌷. Closed 6 Jan–15 Mar.* The rooms in this recently renovated, attractive stone house in the centre of Torla are rustic, pleasant and comfortable. The swimming pool and terrace are welcome in summer.

🍴 EAT

🍴 **Bodegas del Sobrarbe** – *Pl. Mayor 2, Ainsa. ℘974 50 02 37. www. bodegasdelsobrarbe.com. Closed Jan–Feb.* Set on the main square of this medieval town this restaurant is decorated in traditional country style and serves excellent game and grilled steaks.

🍴 **Casa Ruba** – *Esperanza 18, Biescas. ℘974 48 50 01. www.hotelcasaruba.com. Closed Sun eve, Mon.* Set in a traditional house and with over a century of tradition this restaurant is locally renowned. It serves full meals plus tapas at the bar. 29 rooms (⌷) also available here. Highly recommended.

🍴 **Deth Gormán** – *Met Día 8, Vielha. ℘973 64 04 45. Closed 2nd fortnight in May, Tue.* A small restaurant in the village centre. The wooden front suggests the rustic, simple interior, where regional specialties are served, such as mountain snails.

Teruel★

Isolated amid rugged hills and deep ravines, Teruel has retained the charm of its narrow streets and splendid buildings which transport visitors back through the centuries. The smallest provincial capital, of Bajo (Lower) Aragón, it is a UNESCO World Heritage Site for its magnificent Mudéjar architecture.

▶ **Population:** 35 037
◔ **Michelin Map:** 574 K 26
▯ **Info:** Plaza de la Catedral 1. ℘978 61 99 03. http://turismo.teruel.net.
◖ **Location:** Teruel is at 916m/3 005ft directly east of Madrid on the Turia river.
▭ Camino de la Estación

SIGHTS

Plaza del Torico, the heart of the town, is lined with Rococo-style houses. It is named for a small statue of a bull calf.

Casa de la Comunidad-Museo Provincial★

Pl. Fray Anselmo Polanco 3. ◔ *Open Tue–Fri and public holidays 10am–2pm, 4–7pm, Sat–Sun 10am–2pm.* ◔*Closed 1 Jan, 1 May, 24,25, 31 Dec.* ⬤*No charge.* ℘978 60 01 50. www.dpteruel. es/museodeteruel/museodeteruel.htm.
The museum, in a mansion with an elegant Renaissance façade crowned by a gallery, displays ethnological and archaeological collections, including tools and everyday objects. Note the reconstitution of a forge and the 15C Gothic door knocker.
The first floor is given over to ceramics, for which Teruel has been renowned since the 13C. The upper floors contain prehistoric (an Iron Age sword from Alcorisa), Iberian, Roman (a catapult) and Arab (an 11C censer) objects.

Catedral de Santa María de Mediavilla

Pl. de la Catedral. ◔*Open Jun–Oct Mon–Sat 11am–2pm, 4–8pm, Sun 4.30–8pm; Nov–May Mon–Sat 11am–2pm, 4–7pm, Sun 4–7pm.* ⬤*3€.* ℘978 61 80 16.
The cathedral, originating in the 13C (tower), was enlarged in the 16C and again in the 17C. The late 13C **artesonado ceiling**★, once hidden beneath star vaulting, is a precious example of Mudéjar art. Its beams and consoles are painted with decorative motifs, people at court and hunting scenes.
In the north transept is a 15C **altarpiece** of the Coronation of the Virgin. Scenes shown in perspective along the second band suggest Flemish influence. The 16C **high altar retable** is by **Gabriel Joli**, known for powerful portraits and skill in illustrating movement by a marked turn of the body.

Iglesia de San Pedro

Matías Abad. ◔ *Open daily Sept–Jul 10am–2pm, 4–8pm; Aug 10am–8pm.* ⬤*4€.* ℘978 62 41 05.
In spite of 18C alterations, the church retains a Mudéjar tower and east end.
The adjoining **Mausoleo de los Amantes de Teruel** (The Mausoleum of the Teruel Lovers) shows the deceased in an alabaster relief by Juan de Ávalos (20C). Glass panes reveal their remains.

EXCURSIONS

Albarracín★

38km/23.6mi W along the N 234 and A 1512.
Hidden in the Sierra de Albarracín, this medieval city tinged with pinkish hues stands in an exceptional **site**★, on a cliff above the Guadalaviar river. The ramparts rising behind the town were built by the Moors in the 10C and restored by the Christians in the 14C. Caves in the surrounding sierra contain **rock engravings** from the Upper Palaeolithic era, such as the sites at Callejón del Plou and Cueva del Navaza *(5km/3mi SE towards Bezas and Valdecuenca).*

Zaragoza★★

The domes of the Basílica del Pilar dominate Zaragoza, on the right bank of the River Ebro. The city, rebuilt after the 19C War of Independence, combines historic monuments with bustling modern boulevards. Zaragoza is a university and religious centre. The Virgen del Pilar (Virgin of the Pillar) makes it the leading Marian shrine in Spain. Expo 2008 brought a facelift to Zaragoza.

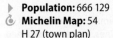

▶ **Population:** 666 129
⏱ **Michelin Map:** 54
 H 27 (town plan)
🛈 **Info:** Calle Eduardo Ibarra 3. ☎976 72 13 33. www.zaragoza.es.
◐ **Location:** Zaragoza is in NE Spain in a fertile pocket watered by the Aragón canal and the Ebro, Gállego, Jalón and Huerva rivers. 🚉Zaragoza-Delicias, Rioja 33

THE CITY TODAY

There has probably not been a better time to visit Zaragoza than now, following the successful Expo 2008 (*see sidebar*). The city has become much more visitor-friendly than ever before with new hotels, new visitor attractions, better communications (within the city and with the rest of Spain) and improvements in its eating and drinking places. The only downside, of course, is an inevitable hike in prices.

A BIT OF HISTORY

Caesaraugusta-Sarakusta – Salduba, at the confluence of the Ebro and its tributaries, became Roman Caesaraugusta in 25 BC. On 2 January in AD 40, according to tradition, the Virgin appeared to St James, leaving the pillar around which the **Basílica de Nuestra Señora del Pilar** was later built. The Uncounted Martyrs of the 3C, persecuted by Diocletian, are interred in the crypt of **Santa Engracia**.

Water, Water...

The theme of **Expo 2008** was Water and Sustainable Development. The most iconic structures from the Expo are located in Avenida de Ranillas: the **Water Tower**, a 76m/249ft high skyscraper in the shape of a water droplet, and the **Bridge Pavilion**, a 270m/295yd long bridge shaped in a curving line over the River Ebro.

To learn more of the Roman city, visit the **Caesaraugusta theatre museum** (*San Jorge 12;* ⏱*open Tue–Sat 10am–9pm, Sun and public holidays 10am–2pm;* ✆*3.50€;* ☎*976 20 50 88*); the **Caesaraugusta public baths museum** (*San Juan y San Pedro 3–7;* ⏱*open Tue–Sat 10am–2pm, 5–8pm, Sun and public holidays 10am–2pm;* ✆*2.50€;* ☎*976 29 72 79*); the **Caesaraugusta Forum Museum** (*pl. la Seo 2;* ⏱*open Tue–Sat 10am–2pm, 5–9pm, Sun and public holidays 10am–2pm;* ✆*2.50€;* ☎*976 39 97 52*) and the **Caesaraugusta River Port Museum** (*pl. San Bruno 8;* ⏱*open same hours as Forum Museum;* ✆*2.50€;* ☎*976 39 31 57*).

Muslim occupation of the city renamed Sarakusta lasted four centuries. The **Aljafería** (*see Sights*), a palace built by the first Benihud monarch of an 11C taifa kingdom, is a unique example of Hispano-Muslim art.

Capital of Aragón – The Aragón kings freed Zaragoza from the Moors and proclaimed it capital. The city retained its autonomy and prospered. It protected its Muslim masons, who embellish the apse of **La Seo** (*Cathedral,* *see Sights*), and the **San Pablo** (*San Pablo 42*) and **Magdalena** (*pl. Magdalena*) church in Mudéjar style. Houses with elegant patios and *artesonado* ceilings reflect prosperity in the 16C.

Two heroic sieges – Zaragoza resisted a siege by Napoleon's army from June to 14 August, 1808. Exultant Zaragozans sang "The Virgin of Pilar will never be

French." Alas! General Lannes laid siege from 21 December until 20 February, 1809. By its end, 54 000, half of the city, had died. The shrapnel-pitted **Puerta del Carmen** (Carmen Gate; *av. César Augusto*) still bears witness.

SIGHTS
La Seo★★
Pl. de la Seo. ⏱ *Open summer Tue–Fri 10am–6pm, Sat 10am–12.30pm, 3–6pm, Sun 10am–11.30am, 2–6pm; winter Tue–Fri 10am–2pm, 4–6pm, Sat 10am–1pm, 4–6pm, Sun 10am–noon, 4–6pm.* ✆3€; *Tapestry Museum 2€.* ✆*976 29 12 31. www.cabildo dezaragoza.org.*

The Cathedral of Zaragoza, La Seo, of remarkable size, includes all styles from Mudéjar to Churrigueresque, although it is basically Gothic. The tall belfry was added in the 17C, the Baroque façade in the 18C. View the Mudéjar **east end** from calle del Sepulcro.

The interior has five aisles of equal height. Above the high altar is a Gothic **retable**★ with a predella carved by the Catalan Pere Johan, and three central panels of the Ascension, Epiphany and the Transfiguration sculpted by Hans of Swabia (the stance and modelling of the faces and robes strike a German note).

The **surrounding wall of the chancel** (*trascoro*) and some of the side chapels were adorned in the 16C with carved figures, evidence of the vitality of Renaissance Spanish sculpture. Other chapels, ornamented in the 18C, show Churrigueresque exuberance. One exception is the **Parroquieta**, a Gothic chapel with a Burgundian-influenced 14C tomb and a Moorish **cupola**★ in polychrome wood with stalactites and strapwork (15C).

Museo Capitular★
In the sacristy. Exhibited are paintings, an enamel triptych, and church plate including silver reliquaries, chalices and an enormous processional monstrance made of 24 000 pieces.

Museo de Tapices★★
An outstanding collection of Gothic hangings, woven in Arras and Brussels.

Basílica de Nuestra Señora del Pilar by the Ebro
J. Balanya/ MICHELIN

La Lonja★
Pl. del Pilar. ⏱ *Open during exhibitions Tue–Sat 10am–2pm, 5–9pm, Sun and public holidays 10am–2pm.* ✆*976 39 72 39.*

Zaragoza, like other trading towns, founded a commercial exchange as early as the 16C. These buildings, in a style between Gothic and Plateresque, include some of the finest civil architecture in Spain. The vast hall is divided in three by tall columns, their shafts ornamented with a band of grotesques. Coats of arms supported by cherubim mark the start of the ribs which open into star **vaulting**.

The **ayuntamiento** (town hall; *pl. del Pilar 18*) has been rebuilt in traditional Aragón style with ornate eaves. Two modern bronzes stand at the entrance.

Basílica de Nuestra Señora del Pilar★
⏱*Open daily 5.45am–8.30pm (9.30pm in summer and on public holidays).* ✆*No charge.* ✆*976 29 95 64.*

Successive sanctuaries on this site have enshrined the miraculous pillar (*pilar*) above which the Virgin appeared. The present building, Zaragoza's second cathedral, was designed by Francisco Herrera the Younger in about 1677.

A buttressed quadrilateral, it is lit by a central dome. The cupolas, with small lantern towers, whose ornamental tiles

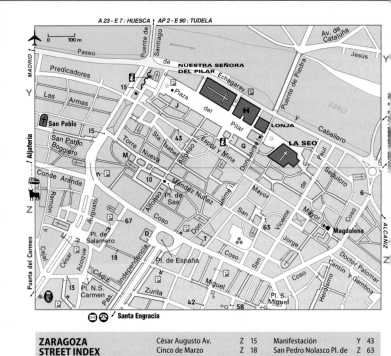

reflect in the Ebro, were added by Ventura Rodríguez in the 18C.

Inside, some of the frescoes decorating the cupolas were painted by Goya as a young man.

The **Capilla de la Virgen** (Lady Chapel) by Ventura Rodríguez is virtually a miniature church. It contains, in a niche on the right, the pillar and a Gothic wood statue of the Virgin. The Virgin's mantle is changed every day except on the 2nd of the month (the Apparition was on 2 January), and the 12th of the month (for the celebration of the Hispanidad, 12 October). Pilgrims kiss the pillar through an opening at the rear.

The **high altar** is surmounted by a **retable**★ by Damián Forment of which the predella is outstanding. The **coro** is closed by a high grille and adorned with Plateresque stalls.

Museo Pilarista★

Inside the Basilica. ⏰*Open Tue–Sun and public holidays 9am–2pm, 4–6pm.* ⊘*2€.* ☎*976 39 74 97.*

Displayed are sketches made by Goya, González, Velázquez and Bayeu for the cupolas of Our Lady of the Pillar, a model by Ventura Rodríguez, and some of the jewels which adorn the Virgin during the Pilar festivals. Among old ivory pieces are an 11C hunting horn and a Moorish jewellery box.

Aljafería★

Av. de Madrid. Access by Conde de Aranda. ⏰*Open Apr–Oct daily 10am–2pm, 4.30–8pm; Nov–Mar Fri–Wed 10am–2pm, 4–6.30pm. Last admission 30min before closing.* ⏰*Closed Fri mornings Nov–Mar.* ⊘*3 €; no charge Sun.* ☎*976 28 95 28. www.corte saragon.es.*

It is unusual to find such magnificent Moorish architecture in this part of

Spain. Built in the 11C by the Benihud family, it was modified by the Aragonese kings (14C) and Catholic Monarchs (15C) before being taken over by the Inquisition and later converted into a barracks.

The Moorish palace centres on a rectangular patio bordered by porticoes with delicate tracery and carved capitals. The **musallah**, the mosque of the emirs, is restored with *mihrab* and multifoil arches and floral decoration.

The first floor and the staircase are in theFlamboyant Gothic of the Catholic Monarchs. Only the ornate **ceiling**★, its cells divided by geometric interlacing and decorated with fir cones, remains of the throne room.

EXCURSION
Fuendetodos

▶ *45km/28mi SW along the N 330; after 21km/13mi bear left onto the Z 100.* ✆ *976 14 38 67. www.fuendetodos.org.*

It was in a modest house, now the **Casa Natal de Goya y Museo del Grabado** (🕐 *open Tue–Sun and public holidays 11am–2pm, 4–7pm;* 🕐 *closed 1 Jan, 24, 25, 31 Dec;* 🎫 *3€;* ✆ *976 14 38 30)* in this village that the great painter Francisco Goya y Lucientes was born in 1746. There is a display of his etchings next door.

ADDRESSES

🛏 STAY

⊜🛢 **Hotel Las Torres** – *Pl. del Pilar 11.* ✆ *976 39 42 50. www.hotellastorres. com. 54 rooms.* ⊡ *6€.* An agreeable hotel, lacking great charm, but with a magnificent location in front of the Basilica in Plaza del Pilar. The rooms are carefully maintained if basic.

⊜⊜🛢🛢 **Hotel Sauce** – *Espoz y Mina 33.* ✆ *976 20 50 50. www. hotelsauce.com. 40 rooms.* ⊡ *7.49€.* This friendly, family-run hotel enjoys a good position in the centre of the city, a few metres from Zaragoza's two main squares. The rooms are all different and are perfectly adequate despite being on the small side.

🍴 EAT

⊜ **Casa Portolés** – *Santa Cruz 21.* ✆ *976 39 06 65. Closed Mon.* This tavern-style restaurant has a bar at the entrance where you can enjoy a range of tapas and *raciones*. The restaurant itself, a pleasant mix of arches and exposed brick, serves fine food and market-based cuisine. A good location close to the Plaza del Pilar in a small square by Calle Espoz y Mina.

⊜⊜🛢 **Antonio** – *Pl. San Pedro Nolasco 5.* ✆ *976 39 74 74. Closed Sun and Mon eves, Sun in Jul–Aug.* A good restaurant that compensates for its modest size with attentive service. Have a drink at the bar while waiting for a table. Often filled up with regulars.

TAPAS

Bodeguilla de la Santa Cruz – *Santa Cruz 3.* ✆ *976 20 00 18. www.larepublic ana.net. Closed Sun.* The décor in this pleasant, centrally located bar is a throw-back to wine cellars of years gone by. Small, but full of atmosphere, with tapas served at the bar and outside.

Los Victorinos – *José de la Hera 6.* ✆ *976 39 42 13. Closed for lunch.* This small, lively bar adorned with bullfighting memorabilia is located in a narrow street near the Plaza del Pilar and Plaza de la Seo. The great selection of delicious, beautifully presented tapas on the bar is not to be missed.

PILAR FESTIVALS

Beginning on 12 October every year, Zaragozans extol their Virgin with incredible pomp and fervour. The 12th brings a **floral offering** to the Virgin del Pilar in the Basilica. On the 13th at about 7pm the **Rosario de Cristal** procession journeys by the light of 350 carriage-borne lanterns. Other festivals include the **Gigantes y Cabezudos** procession (cardboard giants and dwarfs with massive heads) and bullfights.

ASTURIAS AND CANTABRIA

Asturias, to the east, and Cantabria, to the west, make up the central part of Spain's northern Atlantic coastline. The countryside, watered and made verdant by the highest rainfall in the country, rises sharply inland, and the region is frequently compared to more northern climes; perhaps a scaled-down maritime Switzerland, or a version of misty Ireland.

Whichever, it is a far cry from the classic sun-baked Spanish images of the south. Roads wind along valley floors hemmed in by lush meadows with cider apple orchards and grazing dairy cows. Olive oil may be king elsewhere in Spain but here butter is the norm. Maize is an important crop, evident in the large number of distinctive *hórreos* (squat drying sheds), so typical of Asturian villages. The coast is indented by deep inlets (*rías*) and lined by low cliffs, and boasts many beautiful beaches.

Highlights

The Picos de Europa

The "Peaks of Europe" mountain range, which straddle both Asturias and Cantabria, rise to 2 648m/8 688ft.

This is modest by Alpine standards but their proximity to the sea adds drama and they provide some of the best walking terrain in Spain. The area is particularly popular in August, both with foreign and Spanish visitors (the latter fleeing the heat of the interior and south) though large enough so that it rarely feels busy.

One of the few pinchpoints is Fuente Dé (in Cantabria) where a cable car makes a spectacular ascent up the face of the central massif; from here walkers and climbers can penetrate further and higher into the mountains; the views from the top are scintillating.

 Picos de Europa

Asturias

Asturias is the only part of Spain never to have been conquered by the Moors. Aside from the bragging rights that this gives its independently minded natives – who have their own Romance language as well as many indigenous customs– it also influenced the development, or rather non-development, of the region as it became a backwater for several centuries. One of the consequences of this isolation was the development of a unique art and architectural form known as Asturian Pre-Romanesque art which can still be seen in 14 buildings, mostly churches, built between the 8C and 10C which also symbolise the birth and development of the Asturian Monarchy and of the first Christian kingdom on the Iberian Peninsula.

Other idiosyncratic Asturian features include bagpipes – keep an ear open for students practising in city squares – emphasising the region's historic Gallic influences, and cider (*sidra*) thanks to the large amount of orchards. This is drunk in *sidrerías* (cider bars), where there is always a protocol: a small amount of cider is theatrically poured from a height of around 30cm/1ft in order to aerate it; this is known as "throwing the cider" to produce an *estrella*, or star. The ideal temperature is cool but not, (like lager-style beer) chilled. Asturias is also renowned for its cheeses, particularly the blue-veined *cabrales*. It goes particularly well with a glass of *sidra*.

The capital of Asturias is Oviedo, a modern city rebuilt around its fine

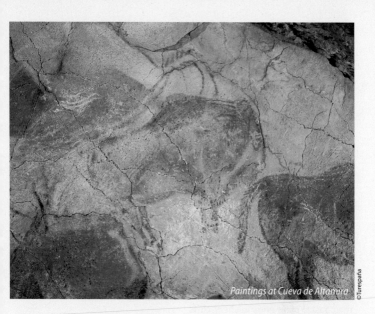
Paintings at Cueva de Altamira ©Turespaña

casco antiguo (old town). Some of the region's Pre-Romanesque churches (and a palace) can be found in and around town. The region's second city is Gijón, a more down-to-earth place, albeit with its share of historical sites. Gijón gets very lively in summer.

The Costa Verde is a magnificent stretch of varied uncommercialised coastline, taking in fishing villages, flooded inlets (*rías*), sheer cliffs and lovely beaches.

- Costa Verde
- Oviedo

Cantabria

Cantabria is the stretch of land sandwiched between the Bay of Biscay and the mountains of the Cantabrian Cordillera; in fact the mountains are so dominant that elsewhere in Spain Cantabria is known as La Montaña.

It is too cool and wet for most northern Europeans to holiday here (it receives less than 60 per cent of the sunshine hours of the south) but for that very reason it has long been popular with the Spanish, as a respite from the summer heat.

Santillana del Mar, labelled "the prettiest village in Spain" by Jean-Paul Sartre, is the jewel of the Cantabrian coast.

The medieval centre is a preserved national-historic monument, showcasing architectural styles from the 14C to the 18C. Nearby is the world-famous Altamira Cave, "the Sistine Chapel of Prehistoric Art" with its amazing drawings of animals.

Beautifully located on a sandy bay, Santander is the regional capital and main port of arrival for both Cantabria and Asturias.

Near by the resort of El Sardinero is a favourite for beach lovers. Santander also makes a good base for touring both Cantabria and Asturias.

- Costa de Cantabria
- Santander
- Santillana del Mar

Costa
Verde★★★

Asturias

The Green Coast of Asturias is named for the colour of the sea, pine and eucalyptus trees along the shore, and wooded pastures inland. Towns and villages are nestled in picturesque coves, where fishing is the main activity. On a clear day the Picos de Europa and Cordillera Cantábrica are a stunning backdrop.

- ▶ **Population:** 65 136
- ◔ **Michelin Map:** 571 and 572 (town plan of Gijón) B8-15
- ▣ **Info:** Gijón: Rodriguez Sampedro. ℘985 34 17 71; Llanes: Alfonso IX (La Torre building). ℘985 40 01 64; Luarca: Los Caleros 11. ℘985 64 00 83. www.infoasturias.com.
- ◖ **Location:** The N 634 runs along the northern coast of Asturias, affording sea and mountain views.
- ♣ **Kids:** MUJA, the Jurassic Museum is unmissable.

🚗 DRIVING TOURS

Along the rocky coast, low cliffs are interrupted by sandy inlets; the estuaries are narrow and deep. West of Cudillero, the coastal plain ends in sheer cliffs overlooking small beaches.

① FROM LLANES TO GIJÓN
145km/90mi W.

Llanes
The clifftop promenade affords a good view of the once fortified port, the rampart ruins and castle and the squat Iglesia de Santa María. In mid-August, see the St Roch festival dances (the *Pericote* and the children's *Prima* dance;

www.san-roque.com) in brilliant local costume.

Ribadesella
31km/19.2mi W of Llanes.
The town and port of Ribadesella are on the right side of the estuary opposite a holiday resort.

Cuevas de Tito Bustillo★
🕑 *Guided tours (1hr) Apr–8 Sept Wed–Sun 10am–4.30pm. ◎3€; no charge Wed (reservations required). ℘985 86 11 20.*

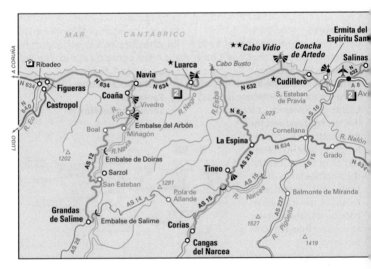

These caves are famous for their **wall of paintings**★ by Palaeolithic inhabitants (20 000 BC) of horses, stags and a doe.

La Isla
26km/16mi W of Ribadesella.
Squat drying sheds or *hórreos*, typical of Asturias, stand beside the houses in the small, attractive village.

MUJA (Museo del Jurásico de Asturias – Jurassic Museum)
Open 2 Jan–20 Jun and 22 Sept–Dec Wed–Sun 10.30am–2.30pm, 4–7pm; 21 Jun–21 Sept daily 10.30am–2.30pm, 4–8pm. Closed 1 Jan, 24, 25, 31 Dec. 6€; child 4€. Final admission 1hr before closing. 902 30 66 00. www.museojurasico.com.
Between Colunga and Lastres is this dinosaur footprint of a building dedicated to these creatures. Dinosaur prints are found in the area.

Mirador del Fito★★★
12km/7.4mi SE of La Isla on AS 260.
This viewpoint has a spectacular panorama of the Picos de Europa and the coast.

Priesca
17km/10.5mi W of Fito.
The capitals in the chancel in the **Iglesia de San Salvador** (*985 89 32 02*) resemble those at Valdediós (*see entry*).

Villaviciosa
11km/6.8mi W of Priesca along N 632.
Emperor Charles V arrived here in 1517 to take possession of Spain. The **Iglesia de Santa María** (*open Tue–Sun 11am–1pm, 5–7pm*) is decorated with a Gothic rose window.

Amandi
3km/1.8mi S of Villaviciosa.
The bell gable of the **Iglesia de San Juan** (*closed to the public; 985 89 00 73*) stands on high ground. The remodelled church retains a 13C portal with sophisticated **decoration**★. Inside the **apse**★, the frieze from the façade reappears to form a winding ribbon that follows the curves of the intercolumniation.

Valdediós★
7km/4.3mi S of Villaviciosa.
The **Iglesia de San Salvador** (*open May–Oct daily 11.15am–1pm, 4.30–6pm; Nov–Apr Mon–Fri 11.15am–1pm, Sat–Sun 4–5.30pm; 1€; 985 89 23 24*), consecrated in 893 and known as *El Conventín*, dates from the end of the Asturian period of architecture (8C–10C).

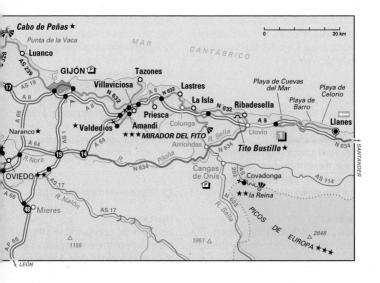

The **Monasterio de Santa María** (monastery) consists of a 13C Cistercian church and cloisters dating from the 15C, 17C and 18C (◷*open Apr–Sept Tue–Sun 11am–1pm, 4.30–6pm; Oct–Mar Tue–Fri 11.15am–1pm, Sat–Sun 11.15am–1pm, 4–5.30pm;* ◷*closed 1 Jan, Easter Sun and 25 Dec;* ◉*1€;* ✆*985 89 23 24; www.valdedios.org).*

Gijón
36km/22mi NW of Valdediós.
🚉*Avenida Juan Carlos I.*
Gijón is a lively city with a population of over 275 000. On **Plaza del Marqués** is the late 17C **Palacio de Revillagigedo** (◷*open Jul–Sept Tue–Sat 11am–1.30pm, 4–9pm, Sun and hols noon–2.30pm; Oct–Jun daily 10.30am–1.30pm, 4–8pm;* ◷*closed 1 Jan, Wed of Carnival, 29 Jun, 25 Dec;* ◉*no charge;* ✆*985 34 69 21),* with an elegant façade. Nearby is the fishermen's quarter, Cimadevilla.
Vestiges of a Roman past, include the **Termas Romanas del Campo Valdés** (Roman baths) in the old quarter *(Campo Valdés;* ◷*open Jul–Aug Tue–Sat 11am–1.30pm, 5–9pm (8pm Sun and hols); Sept–Jun Tue–Sat 10am–1pm, 5–8pm, Sun and hols 11am–2pm, 5–7pm;* ◷*closed 16 Jan, 1 May, 15 Aug, 24, 25, 31 Dec;* ◉*2.40€;* ✆*985 18 51 51).* The **Torre del Reloj** *(Recoletas 5;* ◷*open Sat–Sun 11am–2pm; Tue–Fri Jul–Aug 11am–2pm, 5–9pm, Jan–mid-Jun Oct–Dec 10am–2pm; Easter Week late Jun and Sept 10am–2pm, 5–8pm;* ◉*no charge;* ✆*985 18 13 29)* is also well worth a visit, for its history displays and splendid views.

② FROM GIJÓN TO CASTROPOL
179km/118mi to the W.

Cabo de Peñas★
The road runs through moorland to this cape, the northernmost point in Asturias. From the cliff near the lighthouse, there are fine **views** of the coast.

Salinas
This is a rapidly expanding resort. The rock islet of La Peñona (footbridge) affords a **view**★ of the beach, one of the longest on the Costa Verde.

Ermita del Espíritu Santo
Muros de Nalón. 19km/11.8mi W of Salinas.
The hermitage commands an extensive **view**★ west along the coastal cliffs.

Cudillero★
9km/6mi W of la Ermita.
The fishing village makes an attractive **picture**★: tall hillside houses in pastel shades and white cottages with brown-tiled roofs lead down to the harbour full of fishing boats.
Continue west for some of the area's best beaches: Playa Concha de Artedo (4km/2.5mi), Playa de San Pedro (10km/6.2mi) and, best of all, Playa del Silencio (15km/9.3mi).

Cabo Vidio★★
14km/8.7mi NW of Cudillero.
Catch the coastal **views**★★ from near the lighthouse on this headland.

Excursion to the Narcea River
91km/57mi to Cangas del Narcea along the N 634 and AS 216, branching S at the Cabo Busto.

Tineo
50km/31mi SW of Cabo Vidio.
Perched 673m/2 208ft up the mountainside, the town of Tineo commands an immense mountain **panorama**★★.

Monasterio de Corias
28km/17mi SW of Tineo. 🚶*Guided tours Jun–Sept Mon–Sat 11am–7pm, Sun 11am–noon.* ◉*No charge.* ✆*985 81 01 50.*
The 11C monastery, rebuilt after a 19C fire, was occupied for 800 years by Benedictines. .

▷ *Return to the coast road (N 632).*

Luarca★
Luarca is in a remarkable **site**★ at the mouth of the winding río Negro, spanned by seven bridges. A lighthouse,

church and cemetery stand on the headland once occupied by a fort. For an interesting **view**★, take the lighthouse road left, then circle the church to the right and return to the harbour.

Excursion along the Navia Valley

82km/51mi along the AS 12 (2hr30min each way).

The River Navia flows along an enclosed wild valley below several high peaks.

After Coaña, turn right at a sign marked "castro".

Circular foundations and paving remain from a **Celtic village** on a mound. For a striking **panorama**★★ of the **Arbón dam**, pause at the viewpoint. Past Vivedro, there is another fine **panorama**★★, and as the road climbs, the **confluence**★★ of the Navia and the Frío is impressive from a giddy height. Beyond Boal, the valley is blocked by the high **Doiras dam**.

Grandas de Salime

The **Museo Etnográfico** (*av. del Ferreriro; open Jul–Aug Tue–Sun 11.30am–2pm, 4–7.30pm; Sept–Jun Tue–Sat 11.30am–2pm, 4–6.30pm, Sun and public holidays 11.30am–2.30pm; 1.50€, no charge on Tue; 985 62 73 31; www.museodegrandas.com)* traces Asturian life through re-created rooms and artefacts.

4km/2.5mi away is the **embalse de Salime**. with viewpoints.

Return to Navia, then continue W along the N 634.

From Figueras on the ría Ribadeo you can view **Castropol**, which resembles an Austrian village, with its whitewashed main square. Opposite stands Ribadeo, its Galician counterpart (*see RÍAS ALTAS*).

ADDRESSES

STAY

Hotel Carlos I – *Pl. Carlos I 1–4, Villaviciosa. 985 89 01 21. www.vivirasturias.com. 16 rooms. 4€. Closed Jan–2nd week in Mar.* This family-run hotel was formerly an 18C nobleman's house. The rooms are spacious and attractively furnished and offer excellent value.

Hotel Rural Casa Manoli – *Carretera de Paredes, Almuña. 2km/1.2mi SE of Luarca along the Paredes road, then bear left. 985 47 00 40. www.hotelluarcarural.com. 16 rooms. 3€.* This small family hotel enjoys a peaceful rural setting on the outskirts of Luarca. Pleasant small garden and inexpensive, comfortable rooms.

Hotel Rural Camangu – *Camangu. 4.5km/3mi E of Camangu. 985 85 76 46. www.camangu.com. 10 rooms. Closed 2nd fortnight in Dec, Feb.* This small family-run country hotel in a small village near Ribadesella is an excellent base for excursions into the local countryside. Pleasant décor, good value and a friendly welcome.

EAT

El Álamo – *Rapalcuarto. 10km/6.2mi E of Figueras along the N 634. 985 62 86 49. www.restauranteelalamo.com. Closed Tue for dinner.* This roadside restaurant is renowned for its traditional cuisine and its generous, reasonably priced lunchtime menu.

Casa Tista – *Toriello 47, Toriello. 5km/3mi E of Ribadesella along the AS 263. 985 86 09 54. Closed Nov, Tue in Sept–Jul.* This long-standing family-owned restaurant is famous for its excellent fish and seafood.

Sport – *Rivero 9, Luarca. 985 64 10 78. Closed 6 Jan–6 Feb, Wed for dinner.* This popular bar has a dining area with a regional flavour, and a more formal area upstairs with views onto the estuary. The location near the fish market guarantees the freshness and quality of the fare.

Oviedo★★

Asturias

The capital of Asturias has a long and eventful history. Its old quarter is sprinkled with enchanting plazas and streets lined with sculptures. Strolling about this World Heritage Site is a delight.

THE CITY TODAY

Oviedo is excellent for shopping and is particularly well known for its leather goods. Despite its World Heritage status it is not afraid to keep its public monuments up to date, dedicating a prominent statue to Woody Allen *(calle de Milicias Nacionales)*, who won the Prince of Asturias Arts prize in 2002. Allen visited the city to collect his award and said of it, "Oviedo is a delicious city, exotic, beautiful: it´s as if it didn´t belong to this world, as if it didn´t exist at all... Oviedo is a fairytale."

A BIT OF HISTORY

The capital of the Kingdom of Asturias (9C–10C) – Alfonso II, the Chaste (791–842), moved his court to Oviedo and rebuilt the former Muslim town. The heir to the throne of Spain is still called the Prince of Asturias.

Two Battles of Oviedo – In 1934, Oviedo was heavily damaged in fighting between miners and right-wing government forces. In 1936, Oviedo was the scene of a three-month siege when the garrison rose in revolt against the Republican government during the Spanish Civil War.

Prince of Asturias Awards – have been presented from here since 1981, for achievements in sciences, humanities or public affairs.

SIGHTS

OUTSIDE THE OLD QUARTER

Antiguo Hospital del Principado
(Former Principality Hospital)

▶ *Leave Oviedo on Conde de Toreno (marked on the plan).*

▶ **Population:** 220 644
Michelin Map: 572 B 12 (town plan)
Info: Calle Marqués de Santa Cruz 1. ℘985 22 75 86. http://turismo. ayto-oviedo.es.
Location: The A 66 links Oviedo to the north coast at Gijón (29km/18mi) and to León (121km/75mi S). Calle Uría
Parking: Avoid looking for a space in the old quarter.
Timing: Stroll the old town first.

The façade of the 18C hospital, now the Hotel Reconquista, bears a fine Baroque **coat of arms★**.

Iglesia de San Julián de los Prados★

Selgas 1. Open May–Sept Mon–Fri 10am–1pm, Sat 9.30am–12.30pm, 3.30–5.30pm, public holidays 4–7pm; Oct–Apr Tue–Sat 9.30am–11.30am, Mon 10am–12.30pm, public holidays 4–5.30pm. Guided tours (30min). 1.20 €. ℘607 35 39 99.

This outstanding early 9C work has a characteristic porch, twin aisles, wide transept and, at the east end, three chapels with barrel vaults. The walls are covered in **frescoes★** of Roman influence. A fine transitional Romanesque **Christ in Glory★** is in the central apse.

Santuarios del Monte Naranco★ (Mount Naranco Church and Chapel)

4km/2.5mi along Av. de los Monumentos to the NW.

The former audience chamber (now a church) and part of the chapel remain of the 9C summer palace of Ramiro I.

Centro de Recepción e Interpretación del Prerrománico Asturiano

Just above the parking area, to the left.

🕐Open Mon, Wed–Fri 11am–1.30pm,
4–6pm (7.30pm Jun–Sept), Sat–Sun and
public holidays 11am–2pm, 4–6.30pm
(10am–2pm, 4–8pm Jun–Sept). ✆No
charge. 🕿985 11 49 01.
Panels explain Asturian art (in Spanish
only); a video is narrated in English,
Spanish, French and German.

Iglesia de Santa María del Naranco★★

Monte del Naranco. 🕐*Open Apr–Sept
Tue–Sat 9.30am–1pm, 3.30–7pm,
Sun–Mon 9.30am–1pm; Oct–Mar
Tue–Sat 10am–12.30pm, 3–4.30pm,
Sun–Mon 10am–12.30pm.* ✆*3€;
no charge Mon morning.* 🕿*985 29
56 85. www.santamariadelnaranco.
blogspot.com.*

This harmonious church is supported
by grooved buttresses and lit by vast
bays. The lower floor is a vaulted crypt.
On the upper floor (a former reception
hall), two loggias open off the great
chamber. Decoration is delicate and
unified. From outside, there is a fine
view of Mount Aramo, with Oviedo in
the foreground.

Iglesia de San Miguel de Lillo★

Monte del Naranco. 15min on foot.
🕐*Open same hours as Iglesia de Santa
María.* 🕿*985 29 56 85.*
What remains is probably only a third
of the original church, which probably
collapsed in the 13C.
The aisles are narrow. Several claustral-
type windows remain. The delicate
carving is a delight: on the door
jambs★★ are identical scenes in relief of
arena contests. An Asturian cord motif is
repeated on the capitals and on vaulting
in the nave and gallery.

👣 WALKING TOUR
OLD TOWN

*Allow 1hr30min. Follow the route
on the town plan.*

▷ *Enter by San Francisco, and proceed
along the right side of the street.*

Antigua Universidad

The austere 17C stone-fronted university
was restored after the Civil War. Opposite
the façade is *Mujer Sentada (Seated
Woman)* by Manolo Hugué, one of many
sculptures set in the old town.

Plaza de Porlier

View the cathedral in the next plaza. The
Palace of the Count of Toreno (right)
dates from 1673; the **Camposagrado**
(opposite), an 18C edifice, houses the
Law Courts (note spread eaves).

Plaza de de Alfonso II el Casto (Plaza de la Catedral)

Note the coat of arms on the façade of
the 17C **Palacio de Valdecarzana**. The
majestic Cathedral rises at the far end of
the square. The **Palacio de la Rúa** was
built at the end of the 15C.

Catedral★

Pl. Alfonso II. 🕐*Open Jul–Sept
Mon–Sat 10am–7pm; Oct–Jun Mon–Fri
10am–1pm, 4–7pm, Sat 10am–1pm,
4–6pm.* 🕐*Closed public holidays.* 🕿*985
22 10 33.*
The main work was carried out between
1412 and 1565 in Flamboyant Gothic
style. The south tower tapers into a
delicate openwork spire. Three 17C
Gothic portals pierce the asymmetrical
façade; figures of the Transfiguration are
above the central portal. On the walnut-
panelled doors (also 17C) are figures of
Christ and St Eulalia.
Interior – The Cathedral has three
aisles, the triforium surmounted by
tall stained-glass windows, and an
ambulatory. A splendid 16C polychrome
high altarpiece★★ shows scenes from
the Life of Christ. On either end of the
transepts are 18C Baroque panels, and
in the south transept, next to the main
chapel, the 17C polychromed stone
image of The Saviour.
The **Capilla de Alfonso II El Casto**
(Alfonso II The Chaste), on the site of
the original church, is the pantheon of
Asturian kings. The decoration inside
the gate (end of north transept) is Late
Gothic. In the embrasures are figures of
the Pilgrim St James, St Peter, St Paul and

St Andrew, and on a mullion, a Virgin of Milk. Renaissance and Baroque elements intermingle.

Cámara Santa

Access by the south transept of the Cathedral. ◷ *Open daily 10am–1pm and 4–6pm (7pm Mar–15 May; 4pm 14 Sept–Oct; 8pm 16 May–13 Sept).* ◷ *Closed public holidays.* ⊸*1.50€ (3€ with museum and cloisters); no charge Thu evening.*

The Cámara Santa was built by Alfonso II early in the 9C and reconstructed in the Romanesque period.

These 12 **statue columns**★★ representing the Apostles are among the most masterly sculptures of 12C Spain. The artist was obviously influenced by the Pórtico de la Gloria (Doorway of Glory) in Santiago Cathedral. Capitals illustrate the marriage of Joseph and Mary, the Holy Women at the Tomb and lion and wild boar hunts.

The **tesoro**★★ (treasury) in the apse includes outstanding ancient gold and silver plate: the **Cruz de los Ángeles** (Cross of the Angels), a gift from Alfonso II in 808, studded with precious gems, Roman cabochons and cameos; and the **Cruz de Victoria** (908), faced with chased gold, precious stones, and enamel, supposedly carried by Pelayo at Covadonga.

Claustro

◷*Open same hours as Cámara Santa.*
The Gothic cloisters (14C–15C) have intersecting pointed arches and delicate tracery in the bays. The **Capilla de Santa Leocadia** *(to the left on entering)* contains an altar, tombs from the time of Alfonso II and an unusually small stone altar. The **sala capitular** (chapter house) contains fine 15C stalls.

▷ *Return to Pl. de Alfonso II El Casto.*

To the right of the Cathedral (*leaving*), low reliefs and busts compose an homage to the kings of Asturias.
To the left, at calle Santa Ana, note the unexpected Moorish *alfiz* window enclosure in the remaining east wall

of the 9C **Iglesia de San Tirso** (⊸*no charge;* ✆*985 22 07 02).*

▷ *Turn left onto Tránsito de la Virgen alongside the Cathedral.*

Beyond the arch that connects the Cathedral to the Palacio Arzobispal (archbishop's palace, *left*) is the Romanesque former cathedral. Just ahead in Plaza de la Corrada del Obispo are the rather loud façade of the **Palacio Arzobispal** (late 16C) and the imposing 18C **Puerta de la Limosna** (alms gate).

▷ *Continue along San Vicente.*

Museo Arqueológico

San Vicente 5. ◷*Open Tue–Sat 10am–1.30pm, 4–6pm, Sun and public holidays 11am–1pm.* ✆*985 21 54 05.*
This archaeological museum is in the former Convento de San Vicente (16C–18C). Two galleries off the 15C Plateresque cloisters display pre-Romanesque art. Fragments and reproductions evidence the sophistication of Asturian art. Among exhibits are the Naranco altar; low reliefs showing Byzantine influence, and column bases from San Miguel de Lillo.

After the museum, go under the arch and cross the Plaza de Feijoo, past the **Iglesia de Santa María la Real de la Corte** and the palace-like façade of the 18C **Monasterio de San Pelayo**.

▷ *Turn right onto Jovellanos and look back at the city wall. Return to Santa Ana.*

Museo de Bellas Artes de Asturias (Fine Arts Museum)

Santa Ana 1–3. ◷ *Open Sept–Jun Mon–Fri 10.30am–2pm, 4.30–8.30pm, Sat 11.30am–2pm, 5–8pm, Sun and public holidays 11.30am–2.30pm; Jul–Aug Tue–Sat 10.30am–2pm, 4–8pm, Sun and public holidays 10.30am–2.30pm.* ⊸*No charge.* ✆*985 20 42 32. www. museobbaa.com.*

The museum is in three buildings. The core collection of Spanish painting is

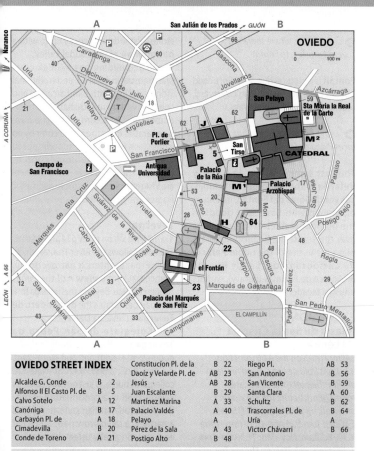

enriched by Italian and Flemish works. There is also a sculpture collection. Among the works in the 18C **Palacio de Velarde** are a complete **Apostolado** by **El Greco** (ground floor); the Gothic panels of the *Santa Marina Retable* (on the stairway); the *Triptych of Don Alvaro de Carreño* by the master of the *Legend of Mary Magdalene*; a *Burial of Christ* and a magnificent *Apostle* by **Ribera**; a *Crucifixion* by **Zurbarán**; a *San Pedro* by Murillo; the portrait of *Charles II at Ten Years* by Carreño de Miranda, and two portraits by **Goya** (*Jovellanos* and *Charles IV*) on the first floor. The second floor is devoted to Asturian and Spanish art of the 19C and early 20C.

A passageway leads to the second floor of the 17C **Casa Oviedo-Portal**. Worth seeing are a gallery dedicated to **J Sorolla**; a *Musketeer with Sword and Cupid* by **Picasso**; and paintings by Gutiérrez-Solana, Regoyos and Nonell. *As you leave,* take a look at the enchanting Plaza de Trascorrales, with its brightly coloured houses and its sculpture of *The Milkmaid*.

▶ *Take Cimadevilla to reach Plaza de la Constitución.*

Along **Plaza de la Constitución** are the **ayuntamiento** (City Hall), with 17C and 18C porticoes, and the Iglesia de San Isidoro, from the same era.

▸ *Take Fierro, where there is a covered market, to Fontán.*

Fontán is a picturesque area. Porticoed houses have an enchanting courtyard, reached by multiple archways.

▸ *Leave by the archway that faces Plaza de Daoíz y Velarde.*

The first sight in **Plaza de Daoíz y Velarde** is the sculpture ensemble, **Las vendedoras del Fontán**, in honour of women who have sold goods in the outdoor market of these streets over the years. The beautiful tree-set plaza is the site of the noble **Palacio de Camposagrado**. Beside it is the Biblioteca de Asturias (library), with its unusual façade.

EXCURSIONS
Iglesia de Santa Cristina de Lena★

34km/21mi S on the A 66 (junction 92). ▸*At Pola de Lena, head for Vega del Rey then take the signposted road.* ▯*Park before the rail viaduct and walk up the steep path (15min).* ◷*Open Tue–Sun Apr–Oct 11am–1pm, 4.30–6.30pm; Nov–Mar 11.30am–1pm, 4.30–6pm.* ◌*1.21€; no charge Tue.* ✆ *985 49 05 25.*

Santa Cristina de Lena (9C) is a well-proportioned church built of golden stone. It stands on a rocky crag, with a **panorama**★ of the Caudal Valley.

The little building has a Greek cross plan unusual in Asturias, and traditional stone vaulting, with blind arcades, and columns with pyramid-shaped capitals emphasised by a cord motif. The nave is separated from the raised choir by an iconostasis in which the superimposed arches increase the impression of balance. The low reliefs in the chancel are Visigothic sculptures (note geometric figures and plant motifs).

Teverga

43km/27mi SW on the N 634 and AS 228. The road follows the River Trubia, which, after Proaza, enters a narrow gorge. Glance back for a **view**★ of the Peñas Juntas cliff face. Beyond the Teverga fork the road penetrates the **desfiladero de Teverga**★ (Teverga Defile).

The **Colegiata de San Pedro de Teverga** (*La Plaza;* ◷*open Mon–Fri noon–2pm, 4–6pm, Sat–Sun 11am–2pm, 4–7pm;* ◌*2€.* ✆*985 76 42 75*), a late 12C collegiate church, is just outside La Plaza village. Built in a continuation of pre-Romanesque Asturian style, it includes a narthex, a tall narrow nave and a flat east end, originally three chapels. The narthex capitals are carved with stylised animal and plant motifs.

ADDRESSES

⌂ STAY

🛏🛏 **Carreño** – *Monte Gamonal 4.* ✆*985 11 86 22. www.hotelcarreno.com. 42 rooms.* ⊡*6€.* Convenient location between the rail and bus stations with comfortable good value rooms.

🛏🛏 **Hotel Casa Camila** – *Fitoria de Arriba 28.* ✆*985 11 48 22. www.casacamila.com. 7 rooms.* ⊡*8.50€. Restaurant*🛏🛏. This charming, well-maintained hotel on Monte Naranco is the perfect hideaway if you're looking for peace and quiet away from the city.

⏦ EAT

🍽🍽🍽 **Las Campanas de San Bernabé** – *San Bernabé 7.* ✆*985 22 49 31. www. fade.es/lascampanas. Closed Sun, Aug.* A pleasant décor of brick walls and oak beams, and good, reasonably priced regional cuisine in the centre of town.

🍽🍽🍽 **El Raitán y El Chigre** – *Pl. Trascorrales 6.* ✆*985 21 42 18. www. elraitan.com. Closed Tue, Wed for dinner.* This rustic-style restaurant at the heart of the historic quarter serves delicious set-price Asturian dishes. .

Picos de Europa★★★

The Picos de Europa, highest range in the Cordillera Cantábrica and just 30km/18.6mi from the sea, include deep gorges cut by gushing mountain rivers and snow-capped peaks jagged with erosion.

The south face is less steep than the north, where the higher peaks are concentrated, and looks out over a harsh terrain of outstanding beauty. **Parque Nacional de los Picos de Europa**, covering 64 660ha/159 775 acres, protects the region's flora and fauna.

Michelin Map:
572 C 14-15-16

Info: Cangas de Onís: *Avenida de Covadonga.* *℘985 84 86 14;* Covadonga: *El Repelao.* *℘985 84 61 35.* www.cangasdeonis.com.

Location: The Picos de Europa rise along the northern coast, between Gijón and Santander.

Don't Miss: A hike to any of several spectacular mountain viewpoints.

 DRIVING TOURS

⑴ DESFILADERO DE LA HERMIDA (LA HERMIDA DEFILE)

From Panes to Potes
27km/16.7mi – allow about 1hr.
A **ravine**★★, 20km/12.4mi long, extends to either side of a basin containing the hamlet of La Hermida. The narrow gorge is bare and lacking in sunlight.

Iglesia de Nuestra Señora de Lebeña
Lebeña. Open Tue–Sun 10am–1.30pm, 4.30–7.30pm. ◉1€. *℘942 84 03 17.*
The small 10C Mozarabic church stands amid poplars at the foot of tall cliffs. The belfry and porch are later additions. The church houses a venerated 15C sculpture of the Virgin Mary.

Potes
9km/5.6mi S of Lebeña along N 621.
Potes is a delightful village in a pleasing **site**★ in a fertile basin set against jagged crests. From the bridge, view old stone houses and the 15C **Torre del Infantado** (tower), now the town hall.

⑵ THE CLIMB TO FUENTE DÉ★★
30km/19mi on the N 621 – allow about 3hr.

Monasterio de Santo Toribio de Liébana
Approach along a signposted road on the left. Open Tue–Sat 10am–1.30pm, 4–7.30pm. ◉No charge. *℘942 73 05 50.*
The monastery was founded in the 7C and grew to considerable importance when a fragment of the True Cross was placed in its safekeeping. A *camarín (access through the north aisle of the church)* contains the largest known piece of the True Cross in the *lignum crucis* reliquary, a silver gilt Crucifix. The transitional Romanesque church is restored to its original harmonious proportions. The monastery was the house of **Beatus**, the 8C monk famous for his **Commentary on the Apocalypse**, copied in the form of illuminated manuscripts.
There is a **view**★ of Potes and the central range from the lookout point at the end of the road.

Fuente Dé★★
21km/13mi W of Liébana.
The parador is at 1 000m/3 300ft. Nearby, the cableway **(teleférico)** rises 800m/2 625ft to the top of the sheer rock face (◉*only weather permitting, Oct–Jun 10am–6pm; Jul–Sept 9am–*

8pm; ⊚14€; ℰ942 73 66 10). During the **ascent** you may see wild chamois. The **Mirador del Cable**★★ commands a splendid panorama of the upper valley of the Deva and Potes. A path leads to the Aliva refuge. Erosion of the karst limestone produces stony plateaus and huge sink-holes known as **hoyos**.

③ PUERTO DE SAN GLORIO (SAN GLORIO PASS)

From Potes to Oseja de Sajambre
83km/52mi – allow about 3hr.
The road crosses the Quiviesa Valley, then climbs through pastures.

Puerto de San Glorio★
Alt 1 609m/5 279ft. A track leads north from the pass *(1hr there and back)* to near the Peña de Llesba and the **Mirador de Llesba**, a magnificent **viewpoint**★★.
To the right is the east range; to the left, the steep south face of the central massif. In the left foreground is Coriscao peak (2 234m/7 330ft).

◗ *At Portilla de la Reina, bear right onto LE 243.*

Puerto de Pandetrave★★
19km/11.8mi NW of Puerto de San Glorio.
This pass (1 562m/5 125ft) affords a **panorama** of the three ranges: in the right foreground, the Cabén de Remoña and Torre de Salinas, both in the central massif. In the distance, in a hollow, is the village of Santa Marina de Valdeón.
⊘ *The road between Santa Marina de Valdeón and Posada de Valdeón is narrow but passable.*

Puerto de Panderruedas★
21km/13 mi NW Puerto de Pandetrave.
The road climbs to pastures at 1 450m/4 757ft. ⛷Walk up the path to the left *(15min there and back)* to the **Mirador de Piedrahitas**★★ *(viewing table)* for an impressive view of the immense cirque which closes the Valdeón Valley. To the northeast is the Torre Cerredo peak (2 648m/8 688ft), highest in the range.

Puerto del Pontón★
8km/5mi SW of Puerto de Panderruedas.
Alt 1 280m/4 200ft. From the pass, get a fine **view**★★ of the Sajambre Valley. The descent to Oseja de Sajambre begins with hairpin bends in below the western range; it continues as a spectacular road tunnelled into the mountainside.

④ DESFILADERO DE LOS BEYOS★★★ (LOS BEYOS DEFILE)

From Oseja de Sajambre to Cangas de Onís
38km/23.6mi – allow about 1hr along N 625.

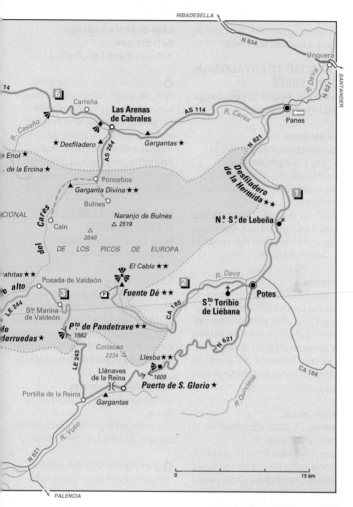

Mirador de Oseja de Sajambre★★

There is an awe-inspiring **view**★★ of the Oseja de Sajambre Basin: the sharp Niaja peak at its centre rises to 1 732m/5 682ft, and of the Los Beyos defile opens between walls of broken rock strata.

Desfiladero de Los Beyos★★★

4km/2.5mi NW of the Mirador de Oseja de Sajambre.

This is one of the most beautiful gorges in Europe, 10km/6.2mi long, cut by the Sella. The limestone is exceptionally thick here; an occasional tree clings to its sides.

Desfiladero de Los Beyos

223

which there remain the apse and an elegantly decorated side portal.

5 THE ROAD TO COVADONGA AND THE LAKES
From Cangas de Onís to Covadonga
35km/22mi – allow about 3hr.

Cueva del Buxu
Guided tours (30min) Wed–Sun 9am–1pm, 3–5.30pm. Restricted to 25 visitors per day; reservations recommended. 3€; no charge Wed. 608 17 54 67.
The cave in the cliff face contains charcoal drawings and rock engravings from around 14 000 years ago: including a stag, horse and bison.

Covadonga
16km/10mi SE of the Cueva del Buxu.
This famous shrine, a landmark in Spanish history, is nestled in a magnificent **setting**★★ at the bottom of a narrow valley surrounded by impressive peaks. **Don Pelayo** defeated the Moors at Covadonga (722), marking the beginning of the Spanish Reconquest.

La Santa Cueva
Open daily 8.30am–7pm (8pm in summer). 985 84 61 15.
The cave, dedicated to the Virgin of the Battlefield, holds the deeply venerated 18C wooden statue of the Virgin, patron of Asturias, **La Santina**.

Basílica
Explanada Basílica, Cangas de Onís. Open daily 9am–6.30pm. No charge. 985 84 60 16. www. santuariodecovadonga.com.
Before the neo-Romanesque Basilica built between 1886 and 1901 stands a statue of Pelayo. The **museo** (*open daily 10.30am–2pm, 4–7.30pm; 3€; 985 84 60 96*) contains gifts to the Virgin including a magnificent **crown**★ with more than 1 000 diamonds.

Lago de Enol★ and Lago de la Ercina★
(Lake Enol and Lake Ercina)

Continue to the lakes along the CO 4. The road is steep; look back to an extensive panorama. After 8km/5mi, you reach the Mirador de la Reinaaa with a view of the rock pyramids which make up the Sierra de Covalierda. Beyond the pass, two rock cirques are the settings of Lago de Enola and Lago de la Ercinaa (lakes, alt 1 232m/4 042ft).

6 GARGANTAS DEL CARES (CARES GORGES)
From Covadonga to Panes
90km/56mi – allow one day.

Just out of Portillo la Estazadas village there is a splendid **panorama**★★ of the rock wall, which closes off the Río Casaño Valley. From a viewpoint on the right, shortly after Carreña de Cabrales, there is a glimpse of the fang-like crest of **Naranjo de Bulnes** (2 519m/8 264ft).

Las Arenas de Cabrales
10km/6.2mi E of Las Estazadas along AS 114.
This is the main production centre for *cabrales*, a blue ewes' milk cheese.

Bear right onto AS 264, which runs through the Upper Cares Valley.

Upper Cares Valley
The Poncebos road leads south, through a pleasant **ravine**★. After the embalse de Poncebos (reservoir) a track (*3hr there and back on foot*) leads up to the village of Bulnes. From Poncebos to Caín (*3hr30min one way*) a path follows the Cares and plunges into the **gorge**★★ to the foot of the central massif (*here you can take a taxi back to Poncebos*).

Return to Arenas de Cabrales.

Beyond Arenas the **gorges**★ are green with moss and the occasional tree. Humpbacked bridges and fragile footbridges span the emerald waters.

ADDRESSES

🏨 STAY

🛏🛏🛏 **La Estrada** – *Inocencio del Valle 1, Arriondas.* *985 84 07 67. www.laestradahotel.com. 21 rooms. Closed Nov–Mar.* A small yet inviting family-run hotel, with wooden floors and comfortable furniture, located in the centre of Arriondas.

🛏🛏🛏 **Hotel del Oso** – *Cosgaya, 9km/5.6mi SE of Fuente Dé along the Potes road.* *942 73 30 18. www. hoteldeloso.com. 50 rooms. ⊇10€. Restaurant🛏🛏🛏. Closed Jan–early Feb.* This hotel is at the very heart of the Picos de Europa on the banks of the River Deva, amid spectacular high peaks. Behind the sober brick façade, rooms are large and comfortable, particularly in the annexe. The restaurant specialises in regional cuisine.

🛏🛏🛏🛏 **Parador de Cangas de Onís** – *Villanueva, 3km/1.8mi NW of Cangas de Onís along the Arriondas road.* *985 84 94 02. www.parador.es. 64 rooms. ⊇17€. Restaurant🛏🛏🛏.* Benedictine monks chose to settle on this very spot next to the River Sella in their search for tranquillity and beauty.

🍴 EAT

🛏🛏 **El Bodegón** – *San Roque, Potes.* *942 73 02 47. Closed fortnight in May, Wed.* El Bodegón is a converted old stone-fronted house in the town centre. The rustic, wood-adorned interior is pleasant, although tables are somewhat close. A good, traditional menu.

🛏🛏🛏🛏 **Casa Marcial** – *La Salgar 10. 4km/2.5mi N of Arriondas.* *985 84 09 91. www.casamarcial.com. Closed 7–31 Jan, Sun for dinner, Mon, 15 Oct–15 May Sun–Thu for dinner.* A modest facade contrasts with the rock and timber interior with modern decorations. Creative menu.

Costa de Cantabria★

Cantabria

The Cantabrian coast is a succession of gulfs, capes, peninsulas, *rías*, splendid bays, most notably at Santander and Santoña, traditional summer beach resorts, and delightful towns dotted with impressive mansions. This area is also rich in caves bearing traces of human habitation in the Palaeolithic Age.

🚗 **DRIVING TOUR**

From East to West

Castro Urdiales
The medieval heart of this attractive town cum-resort, set above a vast bay, clusters round its mighty Gothic church **Iglesia de Santa María de la Asunción** (🕐 *open Tue–Sat 10am–1pm, 4–7.30pm;*

- **Michelin Map:** 572 B 16-20
- **Info:** Comillas: Bajos del Joaquín del Ayuntamiento Piélago 1. *942 72 25 91;* San Vicente de la Barquera: Avenida Generalísimo 20. *942 71 07 97. www. turismodecantabria.com.*
- **Location:** Explore this part of Spain's northern coast via the fast inland road or the slower, winding coastal route through charming villages with spectacular views.

no charge; *942 86 15 86),* plus a ruined castle and lighthouse. Beaches lie to east and west.

Laredo
25km/15.5mi W of Castro Urdiales off N 634.

The **old town** adjoins a long beach lined by modern buildings.

Limpias
8km/5mi S of Laredo.
The fishing village on the banks of the ría Asón is known for a miracle which occurred in 1919, when a deeply venerated Baroque Crucifix attributed to Juan de Mena shed tears of blood.

Santuario de Nuestra Señora de la Bien Aparecida
12km/7.4mi SW of Limpias.
A road winds up to the Baroque shrine. offering a splendid **panorama**★.

Santoña
17km/10.5mi NW of Laredo.
This fishing port facing Laredo was a French headquarters in the Peninsular War. The **Iglesia de Nuestra Señora del Puerto** (*Alfonso XII 11; open daily 9am–1pm, 3–8.30pm; 942 66 01 55*), remodelled in the 18C, has, in addition to Gothic aisles, Romanesque features including carved capitals and an old font.

Bareyo
14km/8.7mi W of Santoña off CA 141.
The tiny **Iglesia de Santa María**, overlooks the ría de Ajo. It retains original Romanesque moulded arches and historiated capitals. The **font** is probably Visigothic.

Peña Cabarga
35km/22mi SW of Bareyo off E 70.
A steep road rises to the summit (568m/1 863ft) and a monument to the Conquistadores and the Seamen Adventurers of Castilla. From the top there is a splendid **panorama**★★.

Santander★ *See SANTANDER*

Santillana del Mar★★
See SANTILLANA DEL MAR

Museo de Altamira★★
See SANTILLANA DEL MAR

Comillas★
54km/33.5mi W of Santander off E 70.
Comillas is a pleasant seaside resort with a delightful plaza, a beach and easy access to the extensive sands at Oyambre – 5km/3mi west. It was a royal residence at the time of Alfonso XII. In its large park is the neo-Gothic **Palacio de Sobrellano**, the **Capilla Panteón de los Marqueses de Comillas** (*both open daily 15 Jun–14 Sept 9.30am–2.30pm, 4–8pm; 15 Sept–14 Jun 9.30am–2.30pm, 3.30–6pm; 3€ each; 942 72 03 39; www.comillas.es*) and Gaudí's outlandish **El Capricho**, now a restaurant.

San Vicente de la Barquera★
11km/6.8mi W of Comillas along N 634.
This resort attracts visitors to its vast **beach**★, across the inlet. The hilltop **Iglesia de Nuestra Señora de los Ángeles** has two Romanesque portals, Gothic aisles and tombs from the 15C and 16C. On the Unquera road is a fine **view**★ of San Vicente.

Cueva el Soplao★
Near Rábago, 20km/12.4mi S of San Vicente de la Barquera. Open Apr–Sept daily from 10am (Oct–Mar Tue–Sun). Reservations advised. 10€. 902 82 02 82. www.elsoplao.es.
Visit this impressive cave as a regular tourist, or in adventure mode with boots, helmet and the rest. Entry is through mining tunnels. Notable are oddly shaped stalactites and salagmites and ghost figures.

ADDRESSES

STAY

⬤⬤ **Pensión La Sota** – *La Correría 1, Castro Urdiales. 942 87 11 88. 19 rooms. 3.50€. Closed 2nd fortnight in Dec.*

This small pensión stands on the main square of Castro Urdiales in the heart of the old quarter. Though small, the guest rooms are well furnished with modern bathrooms.

🛏️🛏️🛏️ **Hotel Gerra Mayor** – *Los Llaos, Gerra. 5km/3mi NE of San Vicente de la Barquera. 942 71 14 01. www. hgerramayor.com. 20 rooms. 4€.* . This simple hotel, formerly a farmhouse, is superbly located between the sea and the mountains. It is perfect for peace and quiet and makes a pleasant base from which to explore the coastline.

¥ EAT

🍽️🍽️🍽️ **Maruja** – *Av. Generalísimo, San Vicente de la Barquera. 942 71 00 77. www.restaurantemaruja.es.*

Closed fortnight in Jun and Nov; Wed and Sun for dinner Sept–Jun. This small restaurant is one of the best-known along the Cantabrian coast, with traditional dishes using local produce.

🍽️🍽️🍽️ **Mesón Marinero** – *La Correría 23, Castro Urdiales. 942 86 00 05. www.mesonmarinero.com* . This famous name in Cantabrian gastronomy specialises in seafood of excellent quality. The choice of tapas at the bar is equally impressive.

Santander★

Cantabria

Santander enjoys a magnificent location★★ on a bay bathed by the azure waters of the Cantabrian Sea. It is best enjoyed on foot, with its long maritime front – one of the finest in Spain – lined by attractive gardens offering incomparable views. Superb beaches draw summer visitors.

▶ **Population:** 182 302
🕐 **Michelin Map:** 572 B 18 (also town plan)
📍 **Info:** Jardines de Pereda. 942 20 30 00. http:// portal.ayto-santander.es.
🔵 **Location:** Santander sprawls to the west of the bay. The A 8 motorway runs SE to Bilbao (116km/72mi). 🚉 Plaza de las Estaciones

THE CITY TODAY

The constant movement of passengers to and from the boat terminal of Santander in summer, and the throng of students at the international university for the rest of the year, means there is generally a buzz in Santander. Most visitors however stay at the nearby resort of **El Sardinero**, simply passing through the town.

SIGHTS

The **paseo de Pereda**★, along the sea-front, is lined by the imposing Banco de Santander building and the Palacete del Embarcadero, an exhibition centre.

Museo de Prehistoria y Arqueología de Cantabria★

⏱️*Open 16 Sept–15 Jun Tue–Sat 9am–1pm, 4–7pm; 16 Jun–15 Sept Tue–Sat 10am–1pm, 4–7pm, Sun and public holidays 11am–2pm.* No charge. 942 20 71 05.

The archaeological museum in the Diputación shows finds from prehistoric caves in Cantabria, and remains of extinct animals from the Quaternary era. The richest period is the Upper Palaeolithic from which there are bones engraved with animal silhouettes and **batons**★ (from El Pendo) made of horn and finely decorated.

Three large circular steles, used for funerary purposes, are representative of the apogee of the Cantabrian culture (Bronze Age). Roman finds are mostly from Julióbriga (*see AGUILAR DE CAMPOO – Driving Tours)* and Castro Urdiales, and include coins, bronzes and pottery figurines. A medieval Mozarabic belt clasp made from bone is dated from the 10C.

Santander disasters

The old port and centre of Santander has been ravaged twice over the last century or so. In 1893 the Cabo Machichaco cargo boat blew up, killing more than 500 people and destroying much of the port area. Less than half a century later, on 15 February 1941, at a time when the city was attempting to recover from the Civil War, a tornado struck Santander: the sea swept over the quays and a fire broke out, almost completely destroying the centre. Reconstruction was undertaken to a street plan of blocks of no more than four or five storeys, and space was allocated to gardens beside the sea, promenades such as the paseo de Pereda which skirts the pleasure boat harbour known as Puerto Chico, and squares such as plaza Porticada.

Catedral de Nuestra Señora de la Asunción

Pl. del Obispo José E Eguino. Entry is through the restored Gothic cloisters. Guided tours (30min) Jul–Aug 10am–1pm, 4–7.30pm. No charge. 942 22 60 24.

The fortress-like cathedral was badly damaged in a 1941 fire, but has been rebuilt in its original Gothic style. A Baroque altarpiece dominates the presbytery; the **font** to the right of the ambulatory was brought here from Sevilla by soldiers of the Reconquest.
Iglesia del Cristo★ – Access to the fine 13C crypt is through the south portal. Excavations in the Evangelist nave have brought to light the remains of a Roman house with the relics of St Emeterio and St Celedonio, patron saints of the city. The Baroque Christ at the high altar is from the Castilian School.

Museo de Bellas Artes (Fine Arts Museum)

Rubio 6. Open 16 Sept–14 Jun Mon–Fri 10.15am–1pm, 5.30–9pm, Sat 10am–1pm; 15 Jun–15 Sept Mon–Fri 11.15am–1pm, 5.30–9pm, Sat 10.30am– 1pm. Closed public holidays. No charge. 942 20 31 20.

Works include a portrait of Ferdinand VII by **Goya**; a series of Goya etchings – *Disasters of War, La Tauromaquia* and *Caprichos* – and several 16C-18C paintings by Flemish and Italian artists.

Museo Marítimo del Cantábrico

San Martín de Bajamar. Open Tue– Sun 15 Sept–Apr 10am–7pm; 2 May–14 Sept 10am–6pm. Closed 1 Jan, Easter Sat, 1 May, 25 Dec. 6 €. 942 274962. www.museosdecantabria.com.

This new museum on the seafront covers all aspects of the region's maritime past and present, including an aquarium and a very impressive blue whale skeleton.

Biblioteca de Menéndez Pelayo

Guided tours (20min) Mon–Fri 9.30am–11.30am. Closed public holidays. 942 23 45 34. www. bibliotecademenendezpelayo.org.

Marcelino Menéndez y Pelayo (1856– 1912), one of Spain's greatest historians, bequeathed this fabulous library of nearly 43 000 books and manuscripts by great Castilian authors.

Península de la Magdalena★★

With its magnificent position and sublime views, this peninsula is one of Santander's major sights. The small **zoo** (seals, penguins, polar bears etc.; No charge) on the El Sardinero side, and the replicas of the galleons in which Francisco de Orellana explored the Amazon are popular with children.

The **Palacio de la Magdalena** was a summer residence for Alfonso XIII. Today, it is occupied by the Menéndez Pelayo International University.

Walk to Cabo Mayor★

Allow 2hr; 4.5km/3mi round trip from the junction of calle García Lago and calle Gregorio Marañón, at the far end of El Sardinero. By car, 7km/4.3mi N.

This attractive walk, adjoining the Mataleñas golf course, runs along the coast, offering magnificent views all the way.

EXCURSIONS
El Sardinero★★
With its three magnificent **beaches**, the residential and resort area of El Sardinero is one of Santander's main attractions.

👫 Parque de la Naturaleza de Cabárceno
Obregón.15km/9.3mi S. Open Jul–Aug daily 9.30am–7pm; Sept–Oct, Mar–Jun daily 9.30am–6pm; Nov–Feb Mon–Fri 10am–5pm, Sat–Sun and public holidays 10am–6pm. 👓 *Mar–Oct 15€, Child 12€; Nov–Feb 12€ (child 8€).* 📞 *942 56 37 36. www.parquedecabarceno.com.*

An old iron mine in the Sierra de Cabarga is part of an environmental rehabilitation project which includes a superb **game park**.

Castañeda
24km/15mi SW via the N 623 and N 634. The **Colegiata** (🕐 *open Tue–Sat 10am–1pm, 4–7.30pm;* 👓 *no charge;* 🔦 *guided tours Jul–Aug;* 📞 *942 84 03 17)*, a former collegiate church from the end of the 12C, stands in a pleasant valley. The unusually deep doorway is simple and elegant.

Puente Viesgo★
26km/16mi SW along the N 623. The caves were inhabited in prehistoric times.

Cueva del Castillo★
🔦 *Guided tours (45min) May–Sept daily 10am–2pm, 4–6.30pm; Oct–Apr Wed–Sun 9.30am–4.55pm.* 👓 *3€.* 📞 *942 59 84 25.*

Cave dwellers began engraving and painting the walls towards the end of the Palaeolithic Age.

ADDRESSES

🛏 STAY
🍽🍽🍽 **Las Brisas** – *La Braña 14, El Sardinero.* 📞 *942 27 50 11. www.hotellasbrisas.net. 13 rooms.* 👓 *5€. Closed Nov–Mar.* An attractive building with a tower, in the El Sardinero district next to the beach. Sitting rooms have lovely details, and the service and attention in this small establishment are personalised.

🍽🍽🍽🍽 **Palacio del Mar** – *Av. de Cantabria 5, El Sardinero.* 📞 *942 39 24 00. 66 rooms.* 🍽 *13€. Restaurante Neptuno*🍽🍽. A modern building with attractive design and comfortable rooms, including some with hydromassage baths. The restaurant has its own distinctive ocean theme.

🍴 EAT
🍽 **Mesón Rampalay** – *Daoíz y Velarde 9.* 📞 *942 31 33 67. Closed 2nd fortnight in Dec, Tue.* This bar-restaurant is located in a street running parallel to paseo Pereda, next to the Iglesia de Santa Lucía. A long bar and a number of tables, where you can enjoy traditional specialities such as red peppers with tuna, seafood salad, and mushrooms with cod.

🍽🍽🍽 **El Serbal** – *Andrés del Rio 7.* 📞 *942 22 25 15. Closed Sun eve, Mon.* Run with professionalism and sporting modern décor, this restaurant and bar is known for its seasonal, creative menus.

FESTIVALS
In addition to the International Music and Dance Festival (*www.festivalsantander.com)* held around the city every year in August, Santander also hosts the fiesta of St James (Santiago) in July, with its bullfights and range of popular concerts and performances.

BOAT TRIPS
Throughout the year, vessels known as *reginas* provide a shuttle service between Santander and Somo and Pedreña (two districts on the other side of the bay). In summer, excursions around the bay and along the Cubas river are also available for visitors, with departures from the Embarcadero del Palacete dock on paseo de Pereda. (📞 *942 216 753; www.losreginas.com).*

Santillana del Mar★★

Cantabria

Santillana del Mar ("of the sea") is in fact located a few kilometres inland. Santillana retains a medieval appearance, its mansions embellished with family coats of arms.

A BIT OF HISTORY

Santillana developed around a monastery which sheltered the relics of St Juliana, who was martyred in Asia Minor – the name Santillana is a contraction of Santa Juliana. Throughout the Middle Ages, the monastery was famous as a place of pilgrimage and was particularly favoured by the Grandees of Castilla. In the 11C it became powerful as a collegiate church; in the 15C, the town, created the seat of a marquisate, was enriched by the fine mansions which still give it so much character.

☞ WALKING TOUR

The **town**★★ has two main streets, both leading to the collegiate church. Start in **calle de Santo Domingo**, with the 17C Casa del Marqués de Benemejís to the left and the Casa de los Villa, with its semicircular balconies, to the right.

▷ *Turn left into Juan Infante.*

Plaza de Ramón Pelayo

Along this vast, pleasing triangular square are the **Parador Gil Blas** and the 14C **Torre de Merino** (Merino Tower, *right*); the **Torre de Don Borja**, with its elegant pointed doorway; and *(left)* the 18C ayuntamiento (town hall), Casa del Águila and Casa de la Parra.

Calle de las Lindas *(end of the square on the right)* runs between massive houses with austere façades to **calle del Cantón** and **calle del Río**, which lead to the collegiate church. On the corner, note the escutcheon of the Casa de Valdivieso (now the Hotel Altamira). Many shops along these streets sell local cheese, chocolates and crafts.

▶ **Population:** 4 049
⚙ **Michelin Map:** 572 B17
▣ **Info:** Calle Jesús Otero. ℘942 81 82 51. www. santillanadelmar.es.
▷ **Location:** Santillana is surrounded by verdant hills, between Santander and Comillas (16km/10mi W).
♟♙ **Kids:** Visit the zoo on the Puente de San Miguel road.

As you approach the church, you will see several noble residences on the right-hand side: the Casa del **Marqués de Santillana**, with its impressive windows; the **Casa de los Hombrones**, named after the two knights supporting the Villa coat of arms; and the **Casa de Quevedo** and the **Casa de Cossío**, both with magnificent coats of arms. On the left, before the Colegiata, the **house of the Archduchess of Austria** is adorned with three coats of arms.

Colegiata★

Pl. del Abad Francisco Navarro.
🕐*Open Tue–Sun 10am–1.30pm, 4–7.30pm.* ⊜*3€ (includes visit to the Claustro).* ℘*942 84 03 17.*
The collegiate church dates from the 12C and 13C. The design of the east end is pure Romanesque.

Claustro★

These cloisters are a fine example of 12C Romanesque style. Each pair of capitals is carved by a master craftsman. The **capitals**★★ in the south gallery, which illustrate a scene, often in allegory, are very expressive: look out for Christ and six of the disciples; and the beheading of John the Baptist and Daniel in the Lion's Den, among other themes.

Interior

The vaulting in the aisles was rebuilt at the end of the 13C with intersecting ribs. The aisles and apses are out of line and the cupola, unusually, is almost elliptical. The chancel contains a 17C Mexican beaten **silver altarfront** and Roman-esque stone figures of **four Apostles**★. The 16C Hispano-Flemish **altarpiece**★ has the original polychrome wood predella showing the Evangelists in profile.

Skirt around the exterior of the east end to appreciate the Romanesque apses and the restored Renaissance **Palacio de los Velarde**.

Convento de Regina Coeli

▶ *Return to your starting-point.*

The restored 16C Convento de Clarisas (Convent of the Poor Clares) is the **Museo Diocesano** (◷*open Tue–Sun (daily in summer) 10am–2pm, 4–7pm; ◉3€; ✆942 84 03 17; www.santillanamuseo diocesano.com)*, a museum with a collection of paintings, sculptures and religious gold and silver. The Baroque carvings and ivory are noteworthy. A large coat of arms adorns the 18C **Casa de Los Tagle** *(end of the street)*.

Children will be interested by the **zoo** (♟♙◷*open daily 9.30am–dusk; ◉16€, child 9€; ✆942 81 81 25; www.zoosantil lanadelmar.com)* along the Puente San Miguel road.

SIGHTS
♟♙ MUSEO DE ALTAMIRA★★

2km/1.2mi SW. ◷*Open May–Oct Tue–Sat 9.30am–8pm, Sun and public holidays 9.30am–3pm; Nov–Apr Tue–Sat 9.30am–6pm, Sun and public holidays 9.30am–3pm.* ◷*Closed 1, 6 Jan, 1 May, 24, 25, 31 Dec. ◉3€; child 1.50€; no charge Sat afternoon, Sun, 18 Apr, 18 May, 12 Oct, 6 Dec. ✆942 81 88 05. http://museodealtamira.mcu.es.* ◉*Purchase tickets in advance at Banco de Santander.*

Cueva de Altamira

○▬*The original cave is not open.*
The Altamira caves consist of galleries with wall paintings and engravings dating back to the Solutrean Age, 20 500 years ago. The most impressive paintings are in the Sala de los Polícro-mos (Polychrome Chamber). Known

Houses in Santillana del Mar ©Turespaña

as the **Sistine Chapel of Prehistoric Art**, it has an outstanding **ceiling**★★★ painted mainly during the Magdalenian period (15000–12000 BC). Numerous polychrome bison are shown asleep, crouched and galloping with extraordinary realism.

Neocueva

A guided tour (30min) using the latest in technology includes replicas of the cave entrance and the Sala de los Polícromos, with extraordinary wall paintings.

Museo

The museum covers the evolution of humans and daily life in the Upper Palaeolithic period. Other caves with wall paintings in Cantabria are also shown.

ADDRESSES

🏨 STAY

⊜⊜ **Hotel Colegiata** – *Carretera Los Hornos. 1km/0.6mi N of Santillana on the S 474, towards Suances. ✆942 84 01 37. www.hotelcolegiata.com. 22 rooms. ⬚7.22€. Restaurant⊜. Closed Jan.* This rural country house in a hilly setting overlooking Santillana has been converted into a delightful hotel with comfortable rooms and a popular restaurant. An excellent alternative for those hoping to escape the hustle and bustle of Santillana.

CASTILLA-LEÓN

Castilla-León occupies the northern part of Spain's great Meseta, a semi-arid plain around 1 000m/3 280ft above sea level. The land is almost empty of trees; wide terraced valleys are dotted with rock pinnacles, narrow defiles and gentle hills. Vast spaces open up with a scale and grandeur unusual in Europe. Some call it eerie and romantic, others label it harsh and monotonous. Its history is certainly romantic; Castilla means land of castles and it was home to the legendary (and very real) El Cid, who fought both with and against the Moors. The weather is less romantic, with sub-zero winters and baking summers.

Highlights

1 Exploring the historic **Old Town** of **Segovia** (p268)
2 People watching in **Plaza Mayor, Salamanca** (p261)
3 Walking the **city walls** by night in **Ávila** (p236)
4 Strolling the gardens of **Granja de San Ildefonso** in **Segovia** (p253)
5 Calm in the cloisters of the **Monasterio de Santa Huerta** in **Soria** (p267)

Southwest

The striking Sierra de Gredos marks the southern border of Castilla y León, peaking at nearly 2 600m/8 530ft with glacial cirques and lakes.

Ávila, 107km/67mi northwest of Madrid, is a remarkable example of a town whose 11C walls and romantic towers have been neither removed nor exceeded. For a period in the 16C Ávila was the heart of Spanish religious life, thanks to its two most famous inhabitants, St Teresa of Ávila and St John of the Cross.

Salamanca is one of Spain's most beautifully preserved and attractive historic cities. Its university is as old as Oxford in England and its lively students make sure that the town buzzes. Just 25km/15.5mi east of the Portuguese border, Ciudad Rodrigo is another splendidly preserved (small) town, where nobles' mansions and palaces bristle with bold carved standards. Declared a national monument, the rural settlement of La Alberca is a far cry from Salamanca – you are more likely to see donkeys than students in its main plaza.

- La Alberca
- Ávila
- Ciudad Rodrigo
- Sierra de Gredos
- Salamanca

Southeast

The mountain resorts of the Sierra de Guadarrama provide oases in this sun-baked land; Pedraza de la Sierra, for example, a lovely village encircled by medieval walls, is popular as a weekend bolt hole. Theis mountain range also includes the Palacio de la Granja de San Ildefonso, home to one of Spain's loveliest formal gardens. Just north, Segovia is famous for its Roman aqueduct – a triumph of both art and engineering, and its fairytale castle (Alcázar), actually a fanciful mid-19C reconstruction of the medieval original. However, the Alcázar is just one component of one of the finest (and most authentic) historic towns in all Spain. By comparison the large city of Valladolid, once capital of Castilla, is prosaic, though its Isabelline-style architecture and National Museum of Sculpture are outstanding.

- Sierra de Guadarrama
- Palencia
- Segovia
- Valladolid
- Zamora

Northwest

León was once the capital of a kingdom that covered nearly a quarter of present-day Iberia. The city grew rich on its location on the medieval pilgrimage route for Santiago de Compostela and its old centre retains splendid monuments from this period. Its Cathedral, with the richest stained glass in Spain, and its Panteón Real, are unmissable.

Roman aqueduct, Sevogia

S. Sergent/MICHELIN

A night in the stunning Parador Hotel San Marcos, formerly the headquarters of the Order of St James/Santiago, is a great experience.

- 🦽 **León**
- 🦽 **Puebla de Sanabria**

East

The ancient capital of Castilla, **Burgos** is a pleasant city known for its daily evening paseo along the topiaried riverside, and famous for its magnificent Cathedral, the third largest in Spain, which contains relics (and the remains) of El Cid. Burgos was also Franco's headquarters during the Civil War and still leans heavily to the right. Aguilar de Campoo marks the northeast border of the region, and from the nearby Pico de Tres Mares there is a wonderful panorama across to the Picos de Europa in Cantabria.

Built on a wind-blown plateau the small town of Soria enjoys a fine setting above the River Duero, and has a number of fine medieval monuments and churches. South of here the Monasterio de Santa María de Huerta contains striking Gothic architecture. Also close to Soria are: the outstanding Monasterio de Santo Domingo de Silos featuring some of the most beautiful cloisters in Spain; the charming little village of Covarrubias; the historic town of El Burgo de Osma.

- 🦽 **Burgos**
- 🦽 **Covarrubias**
- 🦽 **El Burgo de Osma**
- 🦽 **Monasterio de S María de Huerta**
- 🦽 **Soria**

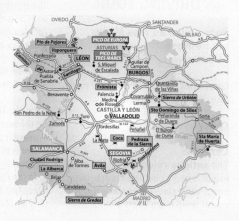

233

Aguilar de Campoo

The Castillo de Aguilar stands on a desolate outcrop typical of this part of the Meseta. Below the castle stretches the medieval old town, with its handsome main square, gateways, walls, and mansions adorned with coats of arms.

> **Population:** 7 196
> **Michelin Map:** 575 D 17
> **Info:** Plaza de España 30. ℘979 12 36 41. www.aguilardcampoo.com.
> **Location:** Aguilar is in northern Spain, inland from the coast and west of the Basque region. Calle Camesa de Valdivia
> **Don't Miss:** A drive to the Pico de Tres Mares.
> **Timing:** Take half a day.

SIGHTS

Colegiata de San Miguel

Pl. de España. Open Holy Week, 15 Jul–14 Sept Tue–Sun 10.30am–1.30pm, 4–7pm. *1.50€.* ℘979 12 26 88.
This Gothic church has Romanesque elements and two fine 16C tombs which bear statues of the Marquesses of Aguilar at prayer. Look for the lifelike sculpted tomb of archpriest García González.

Monasterio de Santa María la Real

Ctra de Cervera. On the edge of town towards Cervera de Pisuerga. Open Jul–Aug daily 10.30am–2pm, 4–8pm. Sept–Jun Tue–Fri 4–7pm, Sat–Sun and public holidays 10.30am–2pm, 4.30–7.30pm. *1.80€ (museum included).* Guided tours 3€. ℘979 12 56 80. www.santamarialareal.org.
This fine, thoroughly restored transitional (12C–13C) monastery houses a Romanesque interpretation centre.

🚗 DRIVING TOUR

To the Pico de Tres Mares via Reinosa

66km/41mi N.

Cross a vast plain and ascend the south face of the Cordillera Cantábrica.

> *Follow the A 67.*

Cervatos

The **antigua colegiata**★, a Romanesque former collegiate church, bears imaginative carved **decoration**★. The portal tympanum bears a meticulous openwork design. There is a frieze of lions while varied figures decorate the modillions. The carving on the capitals and consoles supporting the arch ribs is dense and sophisticated. The 14C nave has intersecting rib vaulting. *key next door;* ℘942 75 50 49.

> *Continue, then turn off to the right.*

Retortillo

Only an oven-vaulted apse and arch with two finely carved capitals illustrating warriors remain of a small Romanesque **church**. Adjacent are the ruins of a villa of the Roman city of **Julióbriga** (open Wed–Sun 10.30am–1.30pm, 4–7pm; *3€;* ℘626 32 59 27).

> *Return to the A 67.*

Reinosa

The nearby Embalse del Ebro (a reservoir) and the Alto Campoo ski resort (℘942 77 92 23; www.altocampoo.com) make this a growing tourist centre.

> *From Reinosa, take the CA 183 to the Pico de Tres Mares (27km/17mi).*

Pico de Tres Mares★★★

On the way, paths from Fontibre lead to a greenish pool, the **source of the Ebro** (Fuente del Ebro), Spain's largest river, at an altitude of 881m/2 890ft.
To the Pico de Tres Mares by chairlift (Dec–Apr). Rivers flow from the peak (2 175m/7 136ft) to three seas (*mares*

in Spanish), hence its name. The Híjar joins the Ebro to reach the Mediterranean; the Pisuerga flows into the Duero to the Atlantic. The Nansa flows north into the Cantabrian sea. At the crest is a splendid **panorama**★★★: to the north, of the Nansa and the Embalse de la Cohilla (Cohilla Dam) below Monte Cueto (1 517m/4 977ft), and circling

right, the Embalse del Ebro, the Sierra de Peña Labra, the Embalse de Cervera de Pisuerga and the Montes de León; due west, the Picos de Europa including 2 618m/8 589ft Peña Vieja, and Peña Sagra (2 042m/6 699ft). In the foreground is the eroded mass of the Peña Labra (2 006m/6 581ft).

La Alberca★★

La Alberca is a delightful village in the Sierra de la Peña de Francia, where stunning scenery joins heritage architecture, rooted traditions and gastronomic treats.

EXCURSIONS
Peña de Francia★★
15km/9.6mi W.
The Peña, a shale crag, at 1 732m/5 682ft is the peak of the Peña de Francia range. The approach affords stunning **panoramas**★★ of the Hurdes mountains, the heights of Portugal and the Sierra de Gredos. A Dominican monastery with a **hostelry** (◉◉◉; 28 rooms; ✆923 16 40 00; open in summer only) is at the top.

Avenida de Las Batuecas★
To the S.
This road climbs gradually to the Portillo Pass (1 240m/4 068ft) then plunges into a deep, green valley where lies the Batuecas Monastery. Beyond Las Mestas is the desolate and isolated **Las Hurdes** region.

⬤ DRIVING TOUR

Tour of The Sierra de Béjar and Sierra de Candelario
76km/47mi to the SE – allow one day.

Meander through the gorges of the Alagón and Cuerpo de Hombre rivers amid walnut and oak forests.

◯ *Head east. After 2km/1.2mi, turn to Cepeda, then Sotoserrano. Head*

▸ **Population:** 1 177
◔ **Michelin Map:** 575 K 11
▤ **Info:** La Puente 9. ✆923 41 50 36. http://laalberca.com.
◗ **Location:** La Alberca is west of Madrid in Salamanca province. La Alberca's haphazard streets lead to the main square (plaza Mayor), irregular and arcaded. Old architecture abounds: houses of stone on the first floor, half-timbered and balconied above.

towards Lagunilla to reach the N 630 at Puerto de Béjar.

Baños de Montemayor, a pleasant spa, and **Hervás**, with its old **judería** (Jewish quarter) are in this area.

◯ *Return to Puerto de Béjar. One road heads towards Candelario.*

Candelario★★
This picturesque village on the flank of the **sierra** retains its traditional stone homes with elegant balconies on steep streets.

Béjar
4km/2.5mi NW.
Béjar, known for its textiles, stretches along a narrow rock platform.

◯ *Leave Béjar along the SA 515.*

Miranda del Castañar
34km/21mi W.

Pass the 15C **castle**, cross the bullring, and penetrate the old quarter through the Puerta de San Ginés.

A little further afield, the charming villages of **Mogarraz** *(10km/6.2mi W)* and **San Martín del Castañar** *(10km/6.2mi N)* are also well worth a visit.

▷ *Continue towards the Peña de Francia; take SA 202 back to La Alberca.*

ADDRESSES

🏠 STAY

CANDELARIO

🍴🍴 **Hotel Artesa** – *Mayor 57.* ☏*923 41 31 11. www.artesa.es. 9 rooms.* 🛏*4.30€. Restaurant*🍴🍴🍴*. Closed 1 week between Jun–Jul.* This simple hotel occupies an old house in the village centre. Rooms are modest but tastefully decorated. The hotel has a pleasant terrace and a shop selling local products.

🍴 EAT

CANDELARIO

🍴🍴 **Mesón La Romana** – *Nuñez Losada 4.* ☏*923 41 32 72. Reservations recommended. Closed Sun eve–Fri lunch.* This delightful restaurant, situated next to the church and behind the town hall, in a restored house in the upper village, is the ideal place to enjoy the renowned grilled meats of the region. Make sure you also try the delicious grilled fresh goat's cheese or a mushroom speciality.

FESTIVALS

On 15 August, the village performs the ancient mystery play, or **Loa**, relating the triumph of the Virgin Mary over the devil.

Ávila★★

Ávila is one of the best-preserved fortified cities in Europe; its numerous convents and churches shelter behind magnificent 11C walls.

THE CITY TODAY

Ávila is mostly a day-tripper's city but a night here is definitely worthwhile, preferably in the 16C parador occupying a former palace. The town is hardly hopping but there are enough tapas bars and drinking holes to make a night of it – try around the Plaza del Mercado Chico.

Wherever you go in town you will be reminded of the town's favourite daughter, Santa Teresa, if only by the *yemas de Santa Teresa*, a tooth-melting egg-yolk-and-sugar confection produced by the local nuns.

SIGHTS

Murallas★★ (City walls)

🕐*Open Apr–16 Oct daily 10am–7.15pm; 17 Oct–30 Mar Tue–Sun 11am–6pm.* 💶*4€.* ☏*920 25 50 88.*

▸ **Population:** 56 144
🕐 **Michelin Map:** 575 or 576 K 15 – Map 121 Alrededores de Madrid
ℹ **Info:** Plaza de Pedro Dávila 4. ☏*920 21 13 87.* www.avilaturismo.com.
▶ **Location:** Sitting at 1 131m/3 710ft, NW of Madrid, Ávila has a harsh and windy winter climate. 🚂Avenida José Antonio
🚫 **Don't Miss:** The city walls.
🕐 **Timing:** Start with the walls and Cathedral.

Europe's most striking medieval fortifications, with 90 bastions and towers and eight gateways, enclose an area 900m/2 953ft by 449m/1 476ft.

Most date from the 11C; and despite 14C modifications, maintain their unity. Walk the sentry path along the top; the best **view** of the walls is from **Cuatro Postes**, on the Salamanca road.

Catedral★★

Pl. de la Catedral. Open Nov–Mar
Mon–Fri 10am–5pm, Sat 10am–6pm,
Sun and public holidays noon–5pm;
Apr–Jun and Oct Mon–Fri 10am–6pm,
Sat 10am–7pm, Sun and public holidays
noon–6pm. Last entry 45min before
closing. 4€. 920 21 16 41.

The fortified **east end** of the Cathedral
is set into the ramparts, crowned with
a double row of battlements. Granite
and defensive design make it austere,
despite window tracery, portal carvings
and decoration along the upper tower,
buttresses and pinnacles. The 14C **north
doorway** with French Gothic decoration, its stone eroded, was removed in
the 15C from the **west front** during a
renovation by Juan Guas. Its current
placement, from the 18C, is more suitable for a palace.

The surprising **interior** has a high Gothic
nave, a chancel with sandstone patches
of red and yellow and many **works of
art★★**. The **trascoro** (1531) holds lovely
Plateresque statues (left to right): the
Presentation of Jesus in the Temple, the
Adoration of the Magi and the Massacre
of the Innocents). The **choir stalls** are
from the same period. There are two
delicate wrought-iron **pulpits** – Renaissance and Gothic.

Construction lasted from 1135 to the
14C; windows in the apse are Romanesque. The large painted **altarpiece**
(c. 1500) by Pedro Berruguete and Juan
de Borgoña has a gilt wood surround
with Isabelline features and Italian Renaissance pilasters. Four carved panels
on the high altar show the Evangelists
and the four Holy Knights. The central
panel is Vasco de la Zarza's masterpiece:
the alabaster **tomb★★** of Don Alonso
de Madrigal, Bishop of Ávila in the 15C,
called El Tostado (Swarthy). He is shown
before a beautiful Epiphany.

Museo de la Catedral

Open Apr–Nov Mon–Sat 10am–6pm;
Dec–Mar Mon–Sat 10am–5pm, Sun
noon–4.30pm. 4€. 920 21 20 14.
Enter the museum via a 13C **sacristy★★**
with notable eight-ribbed vault, mas-

Murallas at dusk
R. Mattes/MICHELIN

sive 16C altarpiece and sculptures of the
Passion in imitation alabaster. View a
head of Christ by Morales painted on a
tabernacle door, a portrait by El Greco, a
huge Isabelline grille, late 15C antiphonaries and a colossal 1571 monstrance
(1.7m/5ft 8in) by Juan de Arfe. The
Gothic **cloisters** are restored.

In plaza de la Catedral, the **Palacio de
Valderrábanos**, now a hotel, has a fine
15C doorway with family crest.

Basílica de San Vicente★★

Pl. San Vicente. Open daily
10am–1.30pm, 4–6.30pm (except dur-
ing religious services). 1.40€. 920
25 52 30.

This vast 12C–14C Romanesque basilica,
with ogive vaulting, is on the reputed
site of the 4C martyrdom of St Vincent of
Zaragoza and his sisters. The ensemble
includes the 14C south gallery with slender columns, a cornice over the length of
the nave, the tall west front porch and
two incomplete towers.

The **west portal★★** is outstanding for
the statue columns below the richly
decorated cornice and lifelike covings.
Beneath the 14C **lantern★** is the **martyrs' tomb★★**, a late 12C masterpiece
under a rare 15C Gothic canopy with
pagoda top. The martyrdom of St Vincent and his sisters is attributed to the
unknown sculptor of the west portal.
The scenes of their capture, flaying and
torture are particularly powerful.

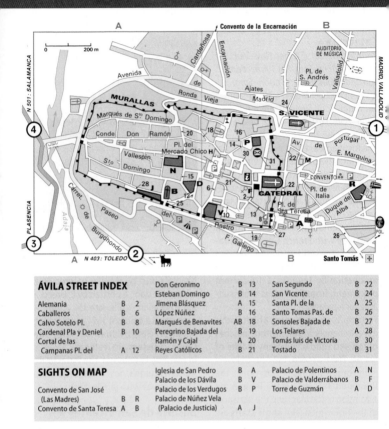

Real Monasterio de Santo Tomás★

Pl. de Granada 1. ⏰Open daily 10am–12.45pm, 4–7.45pm. ⚏3€ (church, oriental museum, cloisters and choir). ☏920 22 04 00.

This late 15C Dominican monastery, at times a summer residence of the Catholic Monarchs, was also the university. The **church** façade includes the common motifs of the monastery: details are emphasised with long lines of balls, and the yoke and fasces emblem of Ferdinand and Isabel. The church has a single aisle, its arches on clusters of slender columns. Two galleries were accessible only from the cloisters by the monks. The fine **mausoleum**★ (1512) is of Prince Juan, only son of the Catholic Monarchs. Its alabaster table with delicate Renaissance sculpting is by Domenico Fancelli, who created the Catholic Monarchs' mausoleum in Granada. In a north chapel is the Renais-

sance tomb of Juan Dávila and his wife, the prince's tutors.

Claustro (Cloisters) – Beyond the plain 15C **Claustro de los Novicios** is the **Claustro del Silencio**★, intimate and generously carved on its upper gallery. The Claustro de los Reyes (Catholic Monarchs' Cloister) is larger and more solemn with spectacularly bare upper arching.

From the Claustro del Silencio, stairs lead to beautiful 15C Gothic **choir stalls** with pierced canopies and arabesques; and from the upper gallery, to the high altar gallery where one can see Berruguete's high relief masterpiece, the **retable of St Thomas Aquinas**★★ (c. 1495).

Iglesia de San Pedro

Pl. de Santa Teresa. ⏰Open daily 10am–12.30pm, 6.30–8pm. ⚏No charge.

This Romanesque church on vast **plaza Santa Teresa** has early Gothic pointed arches and delicate rose window.

Mansión de los Verdugo

Lopez Núñe. Closed to the public.
The façade of this Gothic Renaissance palace, marked with a family crest, is flanked by two stout square towers.

Mansión de los Polentinos

Vallespín. ⚲ *Closed to the public.*
This palace, now a barracks, has a fine Renaissance entrance and patio.

Torreón de los Guzmanes

Pl. Corral de las Campanas.
⚲ *Closed to the public.*
Also called the Oñates Palace, it has a massive square corner tower with battlements, dating from the early 16C.

Palacio de Núñez Vela

Pl. de la Catedral 10. **Patio** *is freely accessible.*
The Renaissance palace of the Viceroy of Peru is now the Law Courts. Windows are framed by slender columns and coats of arms. The patio is lovely.

Palacio de los Dávila

Pl. Pedro Dávila.
⚲ *Closed to the public.*
Two 14C Gothic buildings with coats of arms give onto plaza Pedro Dávila and two others, belonging to the Episcopal Palace, face plaza de Rastro.

ADDRESSES

🛏 STAY

🍽 **Puerta del Alcázar** – *San Segundo 38.* ✆*920 21 10 74. www.puertadelalcazar.com. 27 rooms. Restaurant* 🍽.
A charming hotel right in the centre of Ávila close to the Cathedral. The rooms are well maintained and the restaurant has a modern décor with stone columns.

🍽 **Palacio de los Velada** – *Pl. de la Catedral 10.* ✆*920 25 51 00. www.veladahoteles.com. 144 rooms.* 🍽*13€. Restaurant* 🍽. Enjoy all the comforts in a 16C building redolent of history in Castilian décor. The hotel focuses on its beautiful patio.

🍷 EAT

🍽 **Siglo Doce** – *Pl. de la Catedral 6.* ✆*920 25 28 85. www.siglodoce.com. Reservations recommended.*
A 12C house beside the Cathedral, rustic, unpretentious. The most popular dish is Ávila veal chop.

🍽 **Doña Guiomar** – *Tomás Luis de Victoria 3.* ✆*920 25 37 09. Closed Sun for dinner.* A popular choice with locals, recently renovated with minimalist touches. Good views of the market across the street.

SPECIALITIES

The city is also famous for its candied egg yolks *(yemas de Santa Teresa)*, named for Ávila's patron saint. Give them a try.

El Burgo de Osma★

This attractive Castilian town with porticoed streets and squares, below the ruins of its castle, has long been a bishop's seat. Its notable 18C Baroque buildings include the San Agustín hospital and the imposing Cathedral.

▸ **Population:** 5 158
Ⓒ **Michelin Map:** 575 H 20
🛈 **Info:** Plaza Mayor 9.
✆975 36 01 16.
www.burgosma.es.
◉ **Location:** El Burgo de Osma is NE of Madrid on the N 122, 56km/35mi SW of Soria and 139km/87mi SE of Burgos.

VISIT
Catedral★
Pl. de la Catedral. ⓘ*Open Tue–Fri and Sun 10.30am–1pm, 4–6pm, Sat 10.30am–1pm, 4–7pm.* ✆*No charge.* ✆*975 34 09 62.*

This Gothic sanctuary was built after a Cluniac monk, Don Pedro de Osma, vowed to replace the former Cathedral. The east end, transept and chapter house were built in the 13C; the late Gothic cloisters and chancel received Renaissance embellishments in the 16C. The sacristy, royal chapel and 72m/236ft belfry are from the 18C.

The Gothic decoration on the late 13C **south portal** includes, on the splays, statues of Moses, Gabriel, the Virgin, Judith, Solomon and Esther; on the lintel, a Dormition and on the pier, Christ showing his wounds (late 15C).

The interior is remarkable for the elevation of the nave, the delicate wrought-iron screens (16C) by Juan de Francés, the **high altar retable** by Juan de Juni, and the 16C white marble **pulpit** and **trascoro altarpiece**.

The 13C polychrome limestone **tomb of San Pedro de Osma★** is in the west transept. In the **museum**, among the **archives** and **illuminated manuscripts★** are a richly illustrated 1086 **Beatus** and a 12C manuscript with the signs of the zodiac.

EXCURSIONS
Peñaranda de Duero★
47km/29mi W along the N 122 and BU 924.

The small Castilian town is dominated by the ruins of its castle.

Plaza Mayor★
Around the 15C pillory in the square are half-timbered houses on stone piers.

To one side is the **Palacio de los Condes de Miranda★** (ⓘ*open Tue–Sun Oct–Mar 10am–2pm, 3–6pm; Apr–Sept 10am–2pm, 4–7.30pm;* ✆*guided tours every hour (30min);* ✆*947 55 20 13),* a palace with a Renaissance façade. A patio with a two-tier gallery, a grand staircase and chambers with **artesonado ceilings★**

make this one of the finest Renaissance residences in Spain.

Cañón del Río Lobos
15km/10mi N on the SO 920.

The landscape along this 25km/15.5mi stretch of the Río Lobos is riddled with caves, depressions and chasms. *For further information, contact the Centro de Interpretación del Parque Natural,* ✆*975 36 35 64.*

Calatañazor
25km/15.5mi NE on the N 122.

Along Calatañazor's steep, stone-paved streets, time has stood still. From the castle ruins, view the plain where Almanzor is said to have been defeated by the Christians.

Castillo de Gormaz
14km/8.7mi S on the SO 160. ✆*975 35 05 60.*

These 10C Moorish castle ruins, overlooking the Duero, are the largest in Europe (446m/1 463ft in length, 26 towers).

Berlanga del Duero
28km/17.4mi SE on C 116 and SO 104.

Berlanga, below its massive 15C castle, was a strongpoint along the Duero. In the Gothic **Colegiata** (✆*guided tours available in advance;* ✆*975 34 30 57),* a monumental 16C hall-church, two chapels contain Flamboyant altarpieces and the 16C recumbent alabaster statues of its founders.

Some 8km/5mi southeast in **Casillas de Berlanga** is the **Iglesia de San Baudelio de Berlanga** (ⓘ*open Wed–Sat Nov–Mar 10am–2pm, 3.30–6pm; Apr–May Sept–Oct 10am–2pm, 4–7pm; Jun–Aug 10am–2pm, 5–9pm, Sun and public holidays 10am–2pm.* ✆*0.60€, no charge Sat–Sun, 23 Apr, 18 May, 12 Oct, 6 Dec;* ✆*975 22 13 97),* an unusual 11C Mozarabic chapel, its roof supported by a massive pillar. The gallery rests on a double tier of arches. All was covered with frescoes in the 12C. Hunting scenes and geometric patterns can still be made out.

Burgos★★

Burgos sits on the banks of the River Arlanzón, on a windswept plateau at the heart of the Spanish Meseta. The most famous of its monuments is the magnificent Cathedral, whose lofty Gothic spires dominate the city's skyline.

A BIT OF HISTORY

Founded by Diego Rodríguez in 884, Burgos was capital of Castilla and León from 1037 until the fall of Granada in 1492. Yet commerce and the arts flourished afterwards: the town became a wool centre for the sheep farmers of the Mesta (*see SORIA)*; architects and sculptors from northern Europe transformed monuments. Burgos became Spain's Gothic capital with outstanding works including the Cathedral, the Monasterio de las Huelgas Reales (Royal Convent of Las Huelgas) and the Cartuja de Miraflores (Carthusian monastery). The end of the 16C brought the decline of the Mesta and of the town's prosperity.

Burgos was the seat of Franco's government from 1936 to 1938. **Land of El Cid (c. 1040–99)** – The exploits of Rodrigo Díaz, of Vivar *(9km/5.5mi N of Burgos)* light up the late 11C history of Castilla. The brilliant captain first supported the ambitious King of Castilla, Sancho II, then Alfonso VI, who succeeded his brother in dubious circumstances. Alfonso, jealous of his exploits against the Moors, banished the hero.

Díaz entered service first with the Moorish King of Zaragoza and subsequently fought Christian and Muslim armies with equal fervour. Most famously, he captured Valencia at the head of 7 000 men, chiefly Muslims, after a nine-month siege in 1094. He was finally defeated by the Moors at Cuenca and died soon after (1099). His widow held Valencia against the Muslims until 1102 when she set fire to the city, then fled to Castilla with El Cid's body. The couple were buried in San Pedro de Cardeña *(10km/6.2mi SE of Burgos)*, but their ashes were moved to Burgos Cathedral in 1921.

▶ **Population:** 177 879
⌖ **Michelin Map:** 575 E 18-19 (town plan)
ℹ **Info:** Plaza de Alonso Martínez 7. ℘947 20 31 25. www.turismoburgos.org.
▶ **Location:** Burgos is in the north of Spain, 88km/54.6m from Palencia, 117km/73mi from Vitoria-Gasteiz and 120km/74.5mi from Valladolid, at 856m/2 808ft, exposed to bitter winds in winter. ↠Avenida Principe de Asturias
⊘ **Don't Miss:** The Cathedral and the monasteries.
⊘ **Timing:** Noble Burgos merits at least a day of exploration.

Legend has transformed the stalwart but ruthless 11C warrior, the Campeador (Champion) of Castilla, El Cid (*Seid* in Arabic), into a knight of exceptional valour. The epic poem *El Cantar del Mío Cid* appeared in 1180 and was followed by ballads. In 1618 Guillén de Castro wrote a romanticised version of El Cid, *Las Mocedades del Cid* (Youthful Adventures of El Cid) upon which Corneille, in 1636, based his drama *Le Cid*.

SIGHTS

CATHEDRAL★★★

Pl. de Santa María. ◷*Open daily 19 Mar–Oct 9.30am–7.30pm; Nov–18 Mar 10am–7pm.* ⌾*4€.* ℘*947 27 39 50.*

The third-largest Cathedral of Spain (after Sevilla and Toledo) illustrates the transformation of French and German Flamboyant Gothic into an exuberant Spanish style. It is a showcase of European Gothic sculpture.

Ferdinand III laid the first stone in 1221. At the beginning of the 13C, under Maurice the Englishman, then Bishop of Burgos, who had collected drawings during a journey through France (at that time very much influenced by the Gothic style), the nave, aisles and portals were built by local architects.

The 15C saw the building of the west front spires and the Capilla del Condestable (Constable's Chapel) and the decoration of other chapels. Architects and sculptors from Flanders, the Rhineland and Burgundy were brought by another Burgos prelate, Alonso de Cartagena, on his return from the Council of Basel.

These artists found new inspiration in Mudéjar arabesques and other Hispano-Moorish elements. The most outstanding, the Burgundian **Felipe Vigarny**, the Fleming **Gil de Siloé** and the Rhinelander **Johan of Cologne**, integrated rapidly and with their sons and grandsons – Diego de Siloé, Simon and Francis of Cologne – created what was essentially a Burgos school of sculpture.

The cloisters were built in the 14C, while the magnificent lantern over the transept crossing – the original of which collapsed after some particulary daring design work by Simon of Cologne – was rebuilt by Juan de Vallejo in the mid-16C.

Exterior

A walk round the Cathedral reveals how the architects took ingenious advantage of the sloping ground (the upper gallery of the cloisters is level with the Cathedral pavement) to introduce delightful small precincts and closes.

West front

The ornate upper area, with its frieze of Spanish kings and two openwork spires, is the masterwork of Johan of Cologne.

Interior

The design of the interior is French inspired, while the decoration bears an exuberant Spanish stamp.

Portada de la Coronería (Coronería Doorway) (1)

The statues at the jambs have the grace of their French Flamboyant Gothic originals, though their robes show more movement. The Plateresque **Portada de la Pellejería (2)** (Skinner's Doorway) in

the transept was designed by Francis of Cologne early in the 16C.

Around by the east end it becomes obvious that the Constable's Chapel, with its Isabelline decoration and lantern with pinnacles, is one of the Cathedral's later additions.

Portada del Sarmental (Sarmental Doorway) (3)

The covings are filled with figures from the Celestial Court. The tympanum is a remarkable showing of each Evangelist in a different position as he writes.

Crucero, Coro and Capilla Mayor★★ (Transept crossing, choir stalls and chancel)

The splendid star-ribbed lantern of the transept crossing rises on four massive pillars to 54m/177ft above the funerary stones of El Cid and Ximena, inlaid in the crossing pavement.

The imposing unit of 103 walnut choir stalls, carved by Felipe Vigarny between 1507 and 1512, illustrates biblical stories on the upper, back rows and mythological and burlesque scenes at the front. The handsome recumbent statue of wood, plated with enamelled copper, on the tomb at the centre, from the 13C, is of Bishop Maurice.

The high altar **(4)** retable is a 16C Renaissance work in high relief against an intrinsically Classical background of niches and pediments.

Claustro

The 14C Gothic cloisters present a panorama of Burgos sculpture in stone, terracotta and polychrome wood.

The **Capilla de Santiago** (St James' Chapel) **(5)** contains the Cathedral treasure of plate and liturgical objects. In the **Capilla de Santa Catalina** (St Catherine's Chapel) are manuscripts and documents, including the marriage contract of El Cid. On the 15C carved and painted consoles, Moorish kings pay homage to the King of Castilla.

The **sacristía** (sacristy) **(6)** houses the *Christ at the Column* by Diego de Siloé, a supreme example of Spanish Expressionism in post-16C Iberian

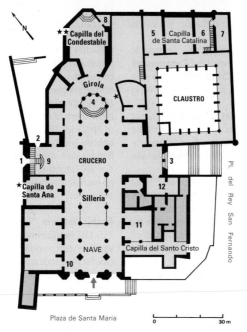

Plaza de Santa María

0   30 m

sculpture. The **sala capitular** (chapter house) **(7)** displays, besides 15C and 16C Brussels tapestries symbolising the theological and cardinal virtues, a Hispano-Flemish diptych, a *Virgin and Child* by Memling and, above, a painted wood Mudéjar *artesonado* ceiling (16C).

Capilla del Condestable★★ (Constable's Chapel)

A magnificent grille closes off the area. The Isabelline chapel, founded by Hernández de Velasco, Constable of Castilla, in 1482 and designed by Simon of Cologne, is lit by a lantern surmounted by an elegant cupola with star-shaped vaulting.

All the great early Renaissance sculptors of Burgos co-operated in the decoration of the walls and altarpiece. The heraldic displays in the chapel are striking. On either side of the altar, the Constable's escutcheon, held by male figures, seems suspended over the balustrades of the tribune.

Statues of the Constable and his wife lie on their tomb, carved in Carrara marble, and beside them is an immense garnet-coloured marble funerary stone for the

names of their descendants. On the right side of the chapel is a Plateresque door to the sacristy (1512) **(8)** where there is a painting of *Mary Magdalene* by Pietro Ricci.

Girola★ (Ambulatory)

The *trasaltar* (at the back of the high altar), carved partly by **Felipe Vigarny**, includes an expressive representation of the Ascent to Calvary.

Escalera Dorada or Escalera de la Coronería (Golden or Coronation Staircase) (9)

The majestically proportioned staircase was designed in pure Renaissance style by Diego de Siloé in the early 16C. Twin pairs of flights are outlined by an ornate, elegant gilded banister by the French master ironsmith, Hilaire.

Capillas

Each of these side chapels is a museum of Gothic and Plateresque art: **Gil de Siloé** and Diego de la Cruz co-operated on the huge Gothic altarpiece in the **Capilla de Santa Ana**★ which illustrates the saint's life. In the centre is a Tree of Jesse with, at its heart, the first meeting of Anne and Joachim and at the top, the Virgin and Child.

At the beginning of the Cathedral nave, near the roof, is the **Papamoscas** or **Flycatcher Clock (10)**, with a jack which opens its mouth on the striking of the hours.

In the **Capilla del Santo Cristo** (Chapel of Holy Christ) is a Crucifixion with the particularly venerated figure complete with hair and covered with buffalo hide to resemble human flesh.

The **Capilla de la Presentación** (Chapel of the Presentation) **(11)** contains the tomb of the Bishop of Lerma, carved by Felipe Vigarny, and the **Capilla de la Visitación** (Chapel of the Visitation) **(12)**, the tomb of Alonso de Cartagena by Gil de Siloé.

Monasterio Santa María Real de las Huelgas★★ (Royal Convent of las Huelgas)

Compases. 1.5km/1mi W of Burgos; take avenida del Monasterio de las Huelgas. ⏰ *Open Tue–Sat 10am–1.15pm, 3.45–5.45pm, Sun and public holidays 10.30am–2.15pm.* ⏰ *Closed 1, 7 Jan, 21 Mar, 1, 30 May, 30 Jun, 25 Dec.* ⤳ *Guided tours (50min) available.* ⤳*5€; free Wed and Thu for EU citizens.* ✆ *947 20 16 30.*

Las Huelgas Reales, the summer palace of the kings of Castilla, was converted in 1180 into a convent by Alfonso VIII and his wife Eleanor, daughter of Henry II of England. The nuns were Cistercians of high lineage, the abbess all-powerful; by the 13C the convent's influence, both spiritual and temporal, extended to more than 50 towns and it had become a place of retreat for members of the house of Castilla and even became the royal pantheon.

Rearrangement over the centuries has resulted in a somewhat divided building featuring the Cistercian style of the 12C and 13C, alongside Romanesque and Mudéjar features (13C–15C) as well as Plateresque furnishings.

Iglesia

The clean lines of of this church are pure Cistercian. The interior is divided by a screen: from the transept, open to all, you can see the revolving pulpit (1560), in gilded ironwork, which enabled the preacher to be heard on either side. Royal and princely tombs, originally coloured, rich in heraldic devices and historical legend, line the aisles, while in the middle of the nave, the nuns' *coro*, is the tomb of Alfonso VIII and Eleanor of England. The rood screen retable, delicately carved and coloured in the Renaissance style, is surmounted by a fine 13C Deposition. The altar is flanked on each side by two handsome 13C and 14C tombs.

Gothic cloisters

13C–15C. Enough fragments of Mudéjar vaulting stucco remain in these Gothic cloisters to suggest the delicacy of the strapwork inspired by Persian ivories and fabrics.

Sala Capitular

The chapter house holds the **pendón**★, a trophy from the Battle of Las Navas de Tolosa, decorated with silk *appliqué.*

Romanesque cloisters

Late 12C. In these Romanesque cloisters, slender paired columns, topped by highly stylised capitals, combine to create an effect of elegance. Several rooms in this part of Alfonso VIII's former palace were decorated by Moors.

The **Capilla de Santiago** (Chapel of St James) retains an *artesonado* ceiling with original colour and stucco frieze. According to legend, the statue of the saint with articulated arms conferred knighthood on princes of royal blood.

Museo de Telas Medievales★★ (Museum of Medieval Fabrics)

The fabrics, court dress and finery displayed in the former loft provide a vivid view of royal wear in 13C Castilla. Of the clothes, (tunics, pelisses and capes) found in the tombs, the most valuable come from that of the Infante Fernando de la Cerda (who died in 1275), son of Alfonso X, the Wise. This tomb, which escaped French desecration in 1809, contained a long tunic, *pellote* (voluminous trousers with braces) and

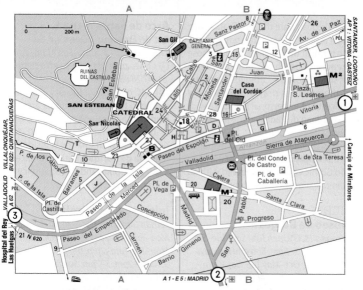

a large mantle, all of the same material
embroidered with silk and silver thread.
There is also a *birrete*, a silk crown adorned
with pearls and precious stones.

Cartuja de Miraflores (Miraflores Carthusian Monastery)

Ctra de la Cartuja. 4km/2.5mi E. ⏰*Open
Mon–Sat 10.15am–3pm, 4–6pm, Sun
and public holidays 11am–3pm, 4–6pm.*
⊜*No charge.*

This former royal foundation, entrusted
to the Carthusians in 1442, was chosen
by Juan II as a pantheon for himself and
his second wife, Isabel of Portugal. The
church was completed in full Isabelline
Gothic style in 1498.

Iglesia★

The sobriety of the façade, relieved only
by the buttress finials and the founders'
escutcheons, gives no indication of the
elegant interior vaulting and gilded
keystones.

Sculpture ensemble in the Capilla Mayor★★★ (apse)

Designed by the Fleming Gil de Siloé at
the end of the 15C, it comprises the high
altarpiece, the royal mausoleum and a
funerary recess.

The polychrome **altarpiece**, the work
of Siloé and Diego de la Cruz, is striking.
The usual rectangular compartments
are replaced by circles crowded with
biblical figures.

The white marble **mausoleo real**
(royal mausoleum) is in the form of
an eight-pointed star in which are
recumbent statues of Juan II and
Queen Isabel, parents of Isabel the
Catholic. Dominating the exuberant
Flamboyant Gothic decoration of
scrolls, canopies, pinnacles, cherubim
and armorial bearings, executed with

rare virtuosity, are the four Evangelists. In an ornate **recess** in the north wall is the tomb of the Infante Alfonso, whose premature death gave the throne to his sister Isabel the Catholic. The statue of the prince at prayer is technically brilliant but impersonal (compare with that of Juan de Padilla in the Museo de Burgos, *see Sights*).

Also in the church are a 15C Hispano-Flemish triptych (to the right of the altar) and Gothic **choir stalls** carved with an infinite variety of arabesques.

SIGHTS

Museo de Burgos★
Miranda 13. Open Jun–Sept Tue–Sat 10am–2pm, 5–8pm, Sun and holidays 10am–2pm; Oct–May Tue–Sat 10am–2pm, 4–7pm, Sun and public holidays 10am–2pm. *1.20€; no charge Sat–Sun, 18 May.* 947 26 58 75.
This excellent museum showcases the ethnography of the region.

Prehistoric and Archaeological Department
In the Casa de Miranda, a Renaissance mansion with an elegant patio, this section holds objects from the Prehistoric to Visigothic periods. Of particular interest are the rooms devoted to Iron Age sites, to the Roman settlement of Clunia and the Roman funerary steles.

Fine Arts Department
The Casa de Ángulo houses art from the region covering the period from the 9C to the 20C. There are several precious items from the Santo Domingo Monastery at Silas: an 11C **Hispano-Moorish casket**★, delicately carved in ivory in Cuenca and highlighted with enamel plaques, the 12C **Frontal** or **Urn of Santo Domingo**★ in beaten and enamelled copper, and a 10C **marble diptych**. On the **tomb**★ of Juan de Padilla, Gil de Siloé beautifully rendered the face and robes of the deceased. The collection of 15C painting includes a *Christ Weeping* by Jan Mostaert.

Arco de Santa María★
Pas. del Espolón. Open Tue–Sat 11am–2pm, 5–8.50pm, Sun 11am–2pm. Closed public holidays. *No charge.* 947 28 88 68.
The 14C gateway in the city walls was modified to form a triumphal arch for Emperor Charles V and embellished with statues of the famous including (top right) El Cid with Charles V. Inside are the **Sala de Poridad**, with magnificent Mudéjar cupola, and the pharmacy of the ex-Hospital de San Juan.

Iglesia de San Nicolás
Fernán González. Open Jul–Sept Mon–Fri 9am–2pm, 4–6pm; Oct–Jun Mon–Fri 11am–2pm, 6–7pm, Sat 9.30am–2pm, 5–7pm, Sun and public holidays only open before or after Mass. *1€.* 947 20 70 95. www.parroqui asanestebansannicolas.com.
The **altarpiece**★ of this Gothic church, carved by Simon of Cologne in 1505, is large and ornate with more than 465 figures. The upper part shows the Virgin crowned at the centre of a circle of angels; St Nicolas is surrounded by scenes from his life – note the voyage by caravel to Alexandria – and below, there is a rear view of the *Last Supper*.

Iglesia de San Esteban: Museo del Retablo
San Esteban. Open Jun–Oct Tue–Sat 10.30am–2pm, 4–7pm, Sun and public holidays 10.30am–2pm; Nov–May Tue–Sat 10.30am–2pm, 4.30–7pm, Sun and public holidays 10.30am–2pm. *1.20€.* 947 27 37 52.
The Retable Museum is in this delightful 14C Gothic **church**★. The interior is a magnificent setting for the 18 retables, exhibited according to their religious significance in the church's three naves. The *coro alto* contains a small collection of gold and silverwork.

Iglesia de San Gil
San Gil 12. Open Tue–Sun Jul–Sept 10am–2pm, 5–8pm; Oct–Jun only open before or after Mass. *No charge.* 947 26 11 49.

One of the city's most beautiful churches. Hidden behind its sober façade is a late Gothic temple. Noteworthy are the Nativity Chapel and Buena Mañana chapels, the latter containing a retable by Gil de Siloé.

Plaza Mayor

This delightful circular main square is typically lined by a portico.

Casa del Cordón

Pl. de la Libertad. ⏱ *Patio: open Mon–Fri 9am–2.30pm.* 👁*No charge.*
The 15C palace of the Constables of Castilla (now housing a bank, the Caja de Ahorros) displays a thick Franciscan cord motif, hence the name. It is where Columbus was received by the Catholic Monarchs on his return from his second voyage to America, and where Philip the Fair died suddenly of a chill.

Museo de Pintura Marceliano Santa María

Pl. de San Juan. ⏱ *Open Tue–Sat 11am–2pm, 5–9pm, Sun 11am–2pm.* ⏱*Closed public holidays.* 👁*No charge.* 📞*947 20 56 87.*
Impressionist canvases by Marceliano Santa María (1866–1952) are shown in the ruins of the former Benedictine monastery of San Juan.

Hospital del Rey

Hospital del Rey. ⏱ *Open same hours as law faculty Mon–Fri and Sat morning.* 📞*947 25 87 77.*

Founded by Alfonso VIII as a hospital for pilgrims, it retains its entrance, the Patio de Romeros, with its fine 16C Plateresque façade. Today, it is the seat of the University of Burgos.

Castillo

⏱ *Open Oct–Jun Mon–Fri 10am–2pm, 4.30–7.30pm, Sat–Sun and public holidays 11am–2pm (and 4–7pm Apr–Jun); Jul–Sept daily 11am–2pm, 5–8.30pm.* 👁*3.50€.* 📞*947 28 88 74.*
This restored hilltop fortress dominates Burgos. Dating from the 9C, it was destroyed by troops of Napoleon. Views are magnificent.

EXCURSION

Archaeological finds in the Sierra de Atapuerca

Take the N 120 towards Logroño.
In Ibeas de Juarros (13km/8mi), head to the Emiliano Aguirre hall (beside the main road). 👁*Guided tours (2hr) of the caves and Museo Emiliano Aguirre by prior arrangement.* 👁*4€.* 📞*902 02 42 46. www.atapuerca.com.*
This is one of the world's most important palaeontological sites. Excavations at **La Dolina** have uncovered remains of hominids who lived around 800 000 years ago. The fossil register at the **Sima de los Huesos** (Chasm of Bones) is the largest in Europe, dating from between 400 000 and 200 000 years ago. Visitors can walk along the trench and visit a small archaeological museum.

ADDRESSES

🛏 STAY

👁🍽 **Hotel Jacobeo** – *San Juan 24.* 📞*947 26 01 02. www.hoteljacobeo. com. 14 rooms.* ☕*4.50€.* This restored mansion is set in the heart of the old quarter. The rooms are pleasant if small.

👁🍽🍽 **Hotel Landa** – *3.5km/2mi S along the A 1.* 📞*947 25 77 77. 39 rooms.* ☕*16€. Restaurant*👁🍽🍽. The Landa occupies part of a restored medieval castle. Especially notable are the majestic lobby, a great dining

hall under stone vaults, individually styled and well-appointed rooms, and a spectacular covered pool.

🍴 EAT

👁🍽 **Ponte Vecchio** – *Vitoria 111 (passaje).* 📞*947 22 56 50.* Italian restaurant with murals inspired by ancient Rome. Good service, and a welcoming environment.

👁🍽🍽 **Rincón de España** – *Nuño Rasura 11.* 📞*947 20 59 55.* Summer terraces with views to the Cathedral; Castilian fare includes house specialities prepared in a wood-fired oven.

Ciudad Rodrigo★

Ciudad Rodrigo appears high on a hilltop, guarded by the square tower of its 14C Alcázar (now a parador) and medieval ramparts. A Roman bridge spans the río Águeda from the Portuguese side. After the Reconquest in the 12C, the town was repopulated by Count Rodrigo González for whom it is named; later it became a border stronghold and was involved in all the conflicts between Castilla and Portugal. Wellington's success against the French in 1812 won him the title of Duke of Ciudad Rodrigo and Grandee of Spain. The area is planted with ilex trees, under which pigs and fighting bulls graze.

▸ **Population:** 13 975
◐ **Michelin Map:** 575 K 10
▤ **Info:** Plaza de las Amayuelas 5. ℘923 46 05 61. www.aytociudadrodrigo.es.
◑ **Location:** Ciudad Rodrigo is west of Madrid along one of the main routes to Portugal.
◉ **Don't Miss:** The city walls and Roman bridge.
◔ **Timing:** Take at least a morning to walk into the past in Ciudad Rodrigo.

◖ WALKING TOUR
THE OLD TOWN

◐ *Start your visit at the plaza de las Amayuelas.*

Catedral★★
Pl. San Salvador. ◔ *Open late Jan–mid-Mar Tue–Sat noon–2pm, 4–6pm, Sun 1–2pm, 4–6pm; mid-Mar–Jun Tue–Sat noon–2pm, 4–7pm, Sun noon–1pm, 4–6pm; Jul–late Jan Mon–Fri noon–2pm, 4–6.30/7pm, Sat noon–2pm, 4–7/8pm, Sun 1–2pm, 4–7pm;* ✦*2.50€.* ℘*923 48 14 24.*

The Cathedral was built in two stages, first from 1170 to 1230 and then in the 14C; in the 16C Rodrigo Gil de Hontañón added the central apse. Note the delicate ornamentation of the blind arcades. The 13C **Portada de la Virgen**★ (Doorway of the Virgin), masked outside by a Classical belfry, has a line of Apostles carved between the columns beneath the splayings and covings.

In the interior, the Isabelline choir stalls in the *coro* were carved by Rodrigo Alemán. The fine Renaissance **altar**★ in the north aisle is adorned with an alabaster masterpiece by Lucas Mitata.

The **cloisters**★ are made up of diverse architectural styles. In the west gallery, the oldest part, Romanesque capitals illustrate man's original sin. Opening off the east gallery is a Plateresque door decorated with medallions.

The **Museo Catedralicio** is worth a visit. Note too the 16C **Palacio de los Miranda** on Plaza de San Salvador.

◐ *Return to the Cathedral; in front is the Capilla de Cerralbo.*

Capilla de Cerralbo
Cardenal Pacheco. ℘*923 49 84 00.*
The chapel, built between 1588 and 1685, is pure and austere but harmonious.

◐ *The arcaded plaza del Buen Alcalde is to the right. Take the street to the left to reach plaza del Conde.*

Palacio de los Castro★ (or Palacio de los Condes de Montarco)
Pl. del Conde.
This late 15C palace, on Plaza del Conde (Count), has a long façade punctuated by delicate windows. The Plateresque doorway is surrounded by an *alfiz* and flanked by two twisted columns showing Portuguese influence

◐ *Head to the plaza Mayor, passing the 16C Palacio de Moctezuma to the right.*

Plaza Mayor★

Two Renaissance palaces stand on the lively main square: the first, now the **ayuntamiento** (town hall; *guided tours Sat–Sun 11am;* 923 49 84 00), has a façade with two storeys of basket arcading forming a **gallery**★ and a loggia, while the second, the **Casa de los Cueto**, has a decorative frieze.

◐ *Continue to Juan Arias, lined by the Casa del Príncipe or Casa de los Águilas, a 16C building in Plateresque style.*

Murallas (Ramparts)

The walls, built on Roman foundations in the 12C, were converted to a full defensive system on the north and west flanks in 1710. There are several stairways up to the 2km/1.2mi-long sentry path.

◐ *The imposing keep of Henry of Trastámara's castle stands on the SW corner of the walls, alongside the Roman bridge spanning the Águeda river. Nowadays, the castle is the town's parador.*

Covarrubias★

This historic Castilian village of half-timbered houses and a Renaissance palace is partly surrounded by medieval ramparts. Covarrubias is the burial place of Fernán González, one of Castilla's great historic figures and the catalyst behind the kingdom's independence.

▸ **Population:** 643
◔ **Michelin Map:** 575 F 19
▤ **Info:** Monseñor Vargas. 947 40 64 61.
◐ **Location:** Covarrubias is 40km/25mi SE of Burgos.
◔ **Timing:** The Monasterio de Santo Domingo deserves a visit of several hours.

SIGHTS

Colegiata★

Pl. Rey Chidasvinto 3. ◔*Open Mon, Wed–Fri 10.30am–2pm, 4–7pm, Sun and public holidays 10.30am–noon, 4–7pm. Organ Mass Sun noon.* ⊚*2€.* 947 40 63 11.

This Gothic collegiate church contains 20 medieval tombs, including those of Fernán González and the Norwegian Princess Cristina who married the Infante Philip of Castilla in 1258.

Museo Parroquial (*pl. Rey Chindasvinto 3;* ◔*open Mon and Wed–Sun 10.30am–2pm, 4–7pm;* ⊚*2€*) – Note paintings by Pedro Berruguete and Van Eyck. A 15C Flemish **triptych**★, with central relief of the Adoration of the Magi, is said to be by Gil de Siloé.

EXCURSIONS

Monasterio de Santo Domingo de Silos★★

Valle de Tabladillo. 18km/11mi SE. ◔*Open Tue–Sat 10am–1pm, 4.30–6pm, Sun–Mon and public holidays 4.30–6pm. Gregorian Mass Mon–Fri 9am, Sat 1pm, Sun and public holidays noon.* ◔*Museum and pharmacy closed 1 Jan, 25 Dec and public holidays.* ⊚*3€.* 947 39 00 68. www.abadiadesilos.es.

This site, originally Visigothic, was occupied by Benedictine monks from France in 1880. The monastery is renowned for its concerts of Gregorian chants.

Claustro★★★

The cloisters are among the most beautiful in Spain. The lower galleries have about 60 rounded arches supported by paired columns and, in the middle of each gallery, by a group of five columns. The eight low reliefs on the corner pillars are masterpieces of Romanesque sculpture. The styles of three different sculptors can be seen. The **capitals**, apart from those which are historiated, illustrate a fantastic bestiary which derives from the Mudéjar use of animal and plant

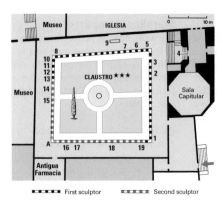

First sculptor   Second sculptor

motifs. *The most interesting have been numbered in the description of the galleries that follows.*

Southeast pillar

The Ascension is represented to the left, and Pentecost to the right.

East gallery

(**1**): strapwork, (**2**): entwined plants, (**3**): harpies defended by dogs.

Northeast pillar

This shows the Descent from the Cross and above, the earth and the moon on the point of being clouded over; on the other side is the Entombment and the Resurrection as one composition. Opposite the pillar is the fine **Puerta de las Vírgenes** (doorway) (**4**) to the former Romanesque abbey church.

North gallery

(**5**): entwined plants, (**6**): the Elders of the Apocalypse, (**7**): harpies attacked by eagles, (**8**): birds. The gallery also contains St Dominic's 13C tomb (**9**): three Romanesque lions bear the saint.

Northwest pillar

This pillar shows Christ on the road to Emmaus and before St Thomas.

West gallery

(**10**): strapwork, (**11**): birds with necks entwined, (**12**): flamingoes, (**13**): birds and lions ensnared by plant tendrils. The capitals that follow are by the second sculptor. (**14**): the birth of Jesus, (**15**):

scenes of the Passion. Note the well-preserved 14C *artesonado* ceiling.

Southwest pillar (A)

By the third artist: an Annunciation (the Virgin Mary is crowned by two angels) and on the right a Tree of Jesse.

South gallery

(**16**) and (**17**): plant tendrils ensnaring birds and stags, (**18**): eagles clutching hares, (**19**): grimacing monsters.

The **museo** (museum) displays an 11C chalice of St Dominic's with filigree decoration, an enamel reliquary, and a 10C–11C manuscript of the Mozarabic rite.

The **Antigua Farmacia** (old pharmacy) contains fine Talavera ceramic jars.

The present **church** (1756–1816) combines the rounded volume of Baroque with Herreran plain grandeur.

Garganta de la Yecla

21km/13mi SE and 3km/1.8mi SW of Santo Domingo de Silos – 🚶 *20min.*

A footpath follows a deep narrow gorge.

Lerma

23km/14.3mi W along the C 110.

Lerma owes its splendour and Classic town plan to the extravagance and corruption of the **Duke of Lerma**, Philip III's early 17C favourite.

The quarter built by the duke retains steep cobbled streets and houses with wood or stone porticoes. The ducal palace, with its austere façade, stands on the spacious **plaza Mayor**★. The **Colegiata** church (*guided tours organized by tourist office;* 🕾 *947 17 70 02; www.citlerma.com*) has a 17C gilded bronze statue by Juan de Arfe of the duke's nephew, Archbishop Cristóbal de Rojas.

Quintanilla de las Viñas

24km/15mi N. *Take the C 110, the N 234 towards Burgos, then bear right onto a signposted road.*

The road follows the Arlanza Valley. Below and to the right, are the ruins of the **Monasterio de San Pedro de Arlanza**.

Iglesia de Quintanilla de las Viñas★

🕐*Open Wed–Sun Oct–Apr 10am–5pm; May–Sept 10am–2pm, 4–7.30pm.* 🚫*No charge.* 📞*947 39 20 49.*

The church – reputedly 7C Visigothic – is of great archaeological interest. Only the apse and transept remain. The frieze depicts bunches of grapes, leaves and birds as well as highly stylised motifs. The foliated scrollwork is repeated inside on the keystones of the triumphal arch.

Sierra de
Gredos★★

The massif of the Sierra de Gredos includes Pico de Almanzor (2 592m/8 504ft), highest peak in the Cordillera Central. The north face of the sierra is marked by glacial cirques and lakes; the south by a steep granite wall and gullies. Fertile valleys produce apples in the north and grapes, olives and tobacco on the sheltered south slope. Wildlife is protected in the Reserva Nacional de Gredos.

- 🔆 **Michelin Map:** 575 or 576 K 14, L 14
- **Info:** Plaza San Pedro, Ávila. 📞 920 37 23 68.
- **Location:** The sierra is almost due west of Madrid (M 501 via San Martín de Valdeiglesias) and south of Ávila (N 502 to Puerto del Pico).
- 🕐 **Timing:** Take a country drive of up to a day, stopping according to your interests.
- 👥 **Kids:** Safari Madrid game park.

SIGHTS
San Martín de Valdeiglesias

This old market town, with 14C castle walls built by the Lord High Constable Álvaro de Luna, is a starting point for explorations.

Toros de Guisando

6km/3.7mi NW.

The *Bulls of Guisando* are four roughly carved granite figures in an open field. Similar ancient figures, possibly Celt-Iberian, are found elsewhere in Ávila province. They are similar to the stone *porcas* (sows) seen in the Trás-os-Montes region of Portugal.

Embalse de Burguillo★ (Burguillo Reservoir)

20km/12.4mi NW.

The man-made lake on the Alberche river is frequented by water sports enthusiasts.

Pantano de San Juan

8km/5mi E.

The road down to this lake affords attractive **views**★ of the Alberche reservoir, its banks covered in pines. The area is popular with Madrid residents in summer for water sports.

👥 Safari Madrid

27km/16.7mi SE at Aldea del Fresno.🕐*Open spring Mon–Fri 10.30am–7.30pm; summer daily 10.30am–8pm; autumn daily 10.30am–5.30pm; winter daily 10.30am–5.30pm;* 🚫*13€; child 9€.* 📞*918 62 23 14. www.safarimadrid.com.*

This is one of Spain's largest game parks, with animals from all over the world.

▶ *From San Martín de Valdeiglesias, take the M 501 (which becomes the C 501), towards Arenas de San Pedro.*

Arenas de San Pedro

The main monument of this attractive town at the foot of the sierra is the Gothic **Iglesia de Nuestra Señora de la Asunción** (*pl. Federico Fernández 8; ℘920 37 00 19*).

Cuevas del Águila★ (Águila Caves)

9km/5.6mi S of Arenas de San Pedro.
▷ *Bear right immediately beyond the village of Reamacastañas and continue for 4km/2.5mi along the unsurfaced road.* ○*Open daily 21 Sept–21 Mar 10.30am–1pm, 3–6pm; 22 Mar–20 Sept 10.30am–1pm, 3–7pm.* ⊙6€. ℘920 37 71 07. www.grutasdelaguila.com.

A single vast chamber is open to the public. Among the many concretions are lovely frozen streams of calcite, ochre crystals coloured by iron oxide and massive pillars still in process of formation.

Puerto del Pico road★

29km/18mi NE of Arenas de San Pedro.
The road through the sierra crosses **Mombeltrán** (15C castle with well-preserved exterior), then winds upwards, parallel to a Roman road, used for years as a stock route. From the pass (1 352m/4 436ft) there is a good **view** of the mountains and, in the foreground (south), of the Tiétar Valley and, beyond, the Tajo. Beyond the pass is an austere boulder-strewn landscape.

The **Parador de Gredos**, first in Spain (1928), stands in a magnificent **setting**★★ with far-reaching views.

Laguna Grande★

12km/7.4mi S of Hoyos del Espino. ⊙ *Park at the end of the road.* ▣A well-marked path leads up to Laguna Grande (*2hr*), a glacial basin fed by mountain torrents. Halfway along is an unforgettable **panorama**★ of the Gredos cirque.

Sierra de
Guadarrama★

The Sierra de Guadarrama is an oasis in the desert of Castilla, its snow-capped peaks visible from Ávila, Segovia and Madrid. Steep granite and gneiss slopes are covered in oaks and pines. Mountain-born streams feed the province's reservoirs. Mountain resorts, such as Navacerrada, Cercedilla, Guadarrama and El Escorial provide refuge for Castilians fleeing torrid summers on the Meseta.

⚙ **Michelin Map:** 575 or 576 J 17-18

▤ **Info:** Puerto de Navacerrada. ℘918 52 00 98. www.puertonavacerrada.com.

▷ **Location:** The mountain range stretches around 100km/62mi SW to NE between Ávila and Madrid.

○ **Timing:** Take a full-day drive, or longer to hike.

🚘 DRIVING TOUR

From Manzanares El Real to Segovia

106km/65.8mi – allow one day excluding visits to Segovia and Riofrío.

Manzanares el Real

The **castillo**★ (○*open Mon–Fri 10am–4pm, Sat–Sun 10am–6pm;* ⊙3€; ℘91 853 00 08; www.manzanareselreal.org) was built by the Duke of Infantado in the 15C. This gem of civil architecture is well proportioned, the austerity of its lines relieved by bead mouldings on the turrets and the Plateresque decoration on the south front, possibly by Juan Guas.

Sierra de la Pedriza

This granite massif of the foothills, in turns rose-coloured rock and eroded screes, is popular with rock climbers, particularly near Peña del Diezmo (1 714m/5 623ft).

> *Continue along the M 608, alongside the Santillana reservoir, to Soto del Real, then follow the M 611.*

Puerto de la Morcuera

As you reach the pass (1 796m/5 892ft), an extensive view opens towards El Vellón reservoir. A descent through moorland brings you to the wooded Lozoya depression. The río Lozoya is a well-known trout stream.

Monasterio de Santa María de El Paular★

2km/1.2mi from Rascafría.

Guided tours (45min) Mon–Sat noon, 1pm, 5pm; Sun 1pm, 4pm, 6pm. No charge. ℘918 69 14 25.

Castilla's earliest Carthusian monastery (1390) stands in the cool Lozoya Valley. The reconstructed complex includes a hotel in a former palace. The **church** has a Flamboyant doorway by Juan Guas. There is a magnificent 15C alabaster **altarpiece**★★ illustrating the Lives of the Virgin and Christ. The Tabernáculo (Tabernacle) is decorated in exuberant Baroque.

Puerto de los Cotos

1 830m/6 004ft. The pass is a base for ski lifts. From the upper terminus at Zabala, hike in summer to the Laguna de Peñalara *(15min)*, a former glacial cirque, the Picos de Dos Hermanas (Summit of the Two Sisters) *(30min)* and Peñalara (2 429m/7 967ft), the highest point in the sierra *(45min)*.

Puerto de Navacerrada★

1 860m/6 102ft. The pass, a ski resort on the borders of the two Castillas, commands a beautiful **view**★ of the Segovian plateau. A train runs to Cercedilla.

> *Take the CL 601 towards Valsaín and La Granja.*

Palacio Real de La Granja de San Ildefonso★★

Pl. de España 17. Open Apr–Sept Tue–Sun 10am–6pm; Oct–Mar 10am–1.30pm, 3–5pm. 5€; no charge Wed for EU citizens, 18 May. ℘921 47 00 19.

La Granja is a little Versailles at 1 192m/3 911ft, built in 1731 by Philip V, in pure nostalgia for the palace of his childhood. Philip V and his second wife, Isabel Farnese, are buried in the collegiate church.

The palace

Galleries and chambers, faced with marble or hung with velvet, are lit by chandeliers.

A **Museo de Tapices**★★ (Tapestry Museum) contains principally 16C Flemish hangings, notably *(3rd gallery)* nine of the *Honours and Virtues* series and a 15C Gothic tapestry of *St Jerome* after a cartoon by Raphael.

Gardens★★

Open daily Oct and Mar 10am–6.30pm; Apr until 7pm; Nov–Feb until 6pm; May–15 Jun and Sept until 8pm; 16 Jun–Aug until 9pm. Fountains Wed, Sat–Sun and public holidays 5.30pm. Illumination of Diana baths Sat 10.30–11.30pm. No charge; fountains 3.40€.

The ground was levelled with explosives before the French landscape gardeners (Carlier, Boutelou) and sculptors (Dumandré, Thierry) started work. The woodland vistas are more natural, however. The chestnut trees, brought from

France at great expense, are magnificent. The **fountains**★★ begin at the Neptune Basin, go on to the New Cascade (Nueva Cascada), a multicoloured marble staircase in front of the palace, and end at the Fuente de la Fama (Fame Fountain), which jets up a full 40m/131ft.

Real Fábrica de Vidrios y Cristales de La Granja (Royal Glass Factory)

🕐 *Open 15 Sept–14 Jun Tue–Sat 10am–6pm, Sun and public holidays 10am–3pm; 15 Jun–14 Sept Tue–Fri 10am–6pm, Sat 10am–7pm, Sun and public holidays 10am–4pm.* 🕐 *Closed 1, 6 Jan, 29 Sept, 25 Dec.* ⬜*4€.* 𝒫*921 01 07 00. www.fcnv.es.*

Although the works date to the reign of Philip V, the present building was erected in 1770, under Charles III. It is a rare example of early industrial architecture and is now the National Glass Centre and museum.

Riofrío★ 👃 *See SEGOVIA*

Segovia★★★ 👃 *See SEGOVIA*

ADDRESSES

🏠 STAY

⬜⬜🍽 **Hotel La Posada de Alameda** – *Grande 34, Alameda del Valle. 6km/3.7mi NE of El Paular along the M 604.* 𝒫*918 69 13 37. 22 rooms. Restaurant*⬜⬜🍽. This attractive rural inn started life as a dairy farm before its conversion to a modern-style hotel adorned with designer furniture. The lounge areas and bedrooms, some with dormer windows, are simple yet cosy, with stone floors and functional bathrooms. The *posada* also has a bright, attractive restaurant.

🍴 EAT

⬜⬜🍽 **Asador Felipe** – *Mayo 2, Navacerrada.* 𝒫*918 53 10 41. Closed Mon–Fri between Oct–Jun.* The popular Asador Felipe is just a few metres from the Restaurante Felipe, owned by the same proprietor and in business for over 20 years. Delicious grilled meats cooked over an open fire, typically Castilian décor, and a pleasant terrace for the summer months.

León★★

León, once the capital of a kingdom, was an important pilgrim stop on the Way of St James and retains fine Romanesque and Gothic monuments.

THE CITY TODAY

León is a lively city, thanks in no small part to its 14 000-strong student population with lots of good places to eat drink and party. The centre of attention by night is the Plaza de San Martin in Barrio Húmedo on the edge of the historic centre. For a more old-fasioned elegant drinking stage try the Plaza Mayor. León is also good for shopping, particularly in its many small arts and crafts and antiques shops.

▸ **Population:** 135 119
👃 **Michelin Map:** 575 E 13 (town plan)The City Today
🔲 **Info:** Plaza de la Regla 3. 𝒫987 23 70 82. www.leon.es.
◯ **Location:** León is on the northern edge of the Meseta. The AP 66 motorway runs north to Oviedo (121km/75mi). Palencia (128km/79.5mi) and Valladolid (139km/86.3mi) are to the southeast. 🚌Calle Astorga
◑ **Don't Miss:** The Cathedral.

A BIT OF HISTORY

The medieval town – In the 10C, the kings of Asturias moved their capital from Oviedo to León, and fortified it. By the 11C and 12C León had become virtually the centre of Christian Spain. Ramparts and peeling stucco over old brick in the east of the city recall the early medieval period.

The most evocative quarter, the Barrio Húmedo (wet quarter, for its many small bars), lies between the **Plaza Mayor** and **Plaza de Santa María del Camino**, an attractive square with wooden porticoes.

The modern city – Modern León is a sprawling industrial city. But its artistic tradition continues in Gaudí's neo-Gothic palace, **Casa de Botines** on plaza de San Marcelo.

CATHEDRAL★★★

Pl. Regla. ⏱ *Open Jul–Sept Mon–Fri 9.30am–2pm, 4–7.30pm, Sat 9.30am–2pm, 4–7pm; Oct–May Mon–Fri 9am–1.30pm, 4–7pm, Sat 9.30am–1.30pm; 1–23 Jun Mon–Fri 9.30am–1.30pm, 4–7pm, Sat 9.30am–1.30pm; 24–30 Jun Mon–Sat 9.30am–1.30pm, 4–7pm.* ⏱ *Closed public holidays.* ⊛*4€; Claustro 1€.* ☏ *987 87 57 70. www.catedraldeleon.org.*

The Cathedral, built mainly between the mid-13C and late 14C, is true Gothic in style even to the very high French-inspired nave with vast windows.

Main façade

The façade is pierced by three deeply recessed and richly carved portals. The gently smiling Santa María Blanca *(a copy: original sculpture in the apsidal chapel)* stands at the pier of the central doorway; on the lintel is a Last Judgement. The left portal tympanum illustrates scenes from the Life of Christ; the right portal includes the Dormition and the Coronation of the Virgin.

South façade

The statues decorating the jambs of the central doorway are extremely fine.

Catedral de León

©Eric Naud/iStockphoto.com

Interior

The outstanding **stained-glass windows**★★★ – 125 windows and 57 oculi with an area of 1 200sq m/12 917sq ft – are unique in Spain; by their sheer number they weaken the walls.

The west front rose and the three central apsidal chapels contain 13C–15C glass; the Capilla de Santiago (St James Chapel) shows Renaissance influence.

The Renaissance **trascoro**★, by Juan de Badajoz, includes four magnificent alabaster high reliefs framing Esteban Jordán's triumphal arch.

The high altar **retable**, painted by Nicolás Francés, is a good example of the 15C international style. To the left is a remarkable **Entombment**★, showing Flemish influence, attributed to the Master of Palanquinos. A silver reliquary contains the remains of San Froilán, the city patron. Several Gothic tombs can be seen in the ambulatory and transept, in particular that of Bishop Don Rodrigo – in the Virgen del Carmen Chapel to the right of the high altar – which is surmounted by a multifoil arch.

Claustro★

The galleries are contemporary with the 13C–14C nave but the vaulting, with ornate keystones, was added at the beginning of the 16C. The galleries are interesting for the frescoes by Nicolás

Francés and for the Romanesque and Gothic tombs.

Museo Catedralicio

Guided tours (1hr) Jun–Sept Mon–Sat 8.30am–1.30pm, 4–8pm, Sun and public holidays 8.30am–2.30pm, 5–8pm; Oct–May Mon–Sat 8.30am–1.30pm, 4–7pm, Sun and public holidays 8.30am–2.30pm, 5–7pm. 3.50€.

Among items in the museum are a French-inspired 15C statue of St Catherine, a Christ carved by Juan de Juni in 1576 (meant to be viewed from below), and a Mozarabic Bible.

SIGHTS
Colegiata Real de San Isidoro de León★★

Pl. de San Isidoro 4. Open Sept–Jun Mon–Sat 10am–1.15pm, 4–6.30pm, Sun and public holidays 10am–1.30pm; Jul–Aug Mon–Sat 9am–8pm, Sun and public holidays 9am–2pm. Closed 1 Jan, 25 Dec. 3€, no charge Thu afternoon. 987 87 50 88. www.sanisidorodeleon.org.

The **basilica**, built into the Roman ramparts, was dedicated in 1063 to Isidore, Archbishop of Sevilla, whose ashes had been brought north for burial in Christian territory. Of the 11C church only the pantheon remains. The apse and transept of the present basilica are Gothic; the balustrade and the pediment on the south front were added during the Renaissance.

Panteón Real★★★

In the Colegiata Real de San Isidoro de León.

The Royal Pantheon is one of the earliest examples of Romanesque architecture in Castilla. The **capitals**★ on the short, thick columns bear traces of the Visigothic tradition yet at the same time exhibit notable advances in sculpture, showing scenes for the first time.

The 12C **frescoes**★★★ are outstanding. They illustrate not only New Testament themes but also country life.

The pantheon is the resting place of 23 kings and queens and many children.

Tesoro★★

Colegiata Real de San Isidoro de León.

The 11C reliquary containing the remains of San Isidoro is made of wood, faced with embossed silver and covered in a Mozarabic embroidery. The famous **Cáliz de Doña Urraca**★ (Doña Urraca chalice) comprises two Roman agate cups mounted in the 11C in a gold setting inlaid with precious stones. The plaques of the 11C **Arqueta de los Marfiles**★ (Ivory Reliquary) each represent an Apostle. The library contains over 300 incunabula and a 10C Mozarabic Bible.

Convento de San Marcos★ (Former Monastery of St Mark)

Pl. de San Marcos. 987 23 73 00. www.parador.es.

This former monastery, connected with the Knights of the Order of Santiago (St James) since the 12C, is now a parador. The 100m/328ft long **façade**★★ has a remarkable unity of style in spite of the addition of an 18C Baroque pediment. It has two storeys of windows, niches friezes and cornices, engaged columns, pilasters and medallions in high relief illustrating biblical and Spanish personages. The **church** front (on the extreme right), emblazoned with scallop shells, symbols of the pilgrimage to Santiago de Compostela, remains incomplete.

MUSAC (Museo de Arte Contemporáneo de Castilla y León)

Av. de los Reyes Leoneses 24. Open Tue–Sun 10am–3pm, 4–9pm. Closed 1 Jan, 25 Dec. No charge. 987 09 00 00. http://musac.es.

This evocative building by Mansilla + Muñón, a centre for modern art, is covered in coloured crystals and focuses on living, working artists.

Museo de León★

Pl. de San Marcos. Open Oct–Jun Tue–Sat 10am–2pm, 4–7pm, Sun and public holidays 10am–2pm; Jul–Sept Tue–Sat 10am–2pm, 5–8pm, Sun and public holidays 10am–2pm. 1.20€.

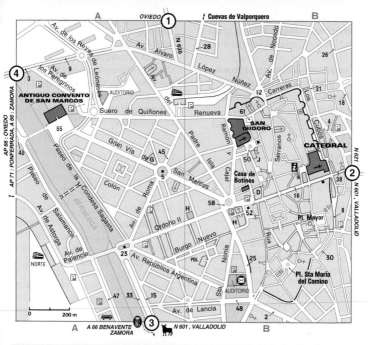

℘987 23 64 05. http://turismo.iranon.org/museodeleon.

This museum displays the 10C Votive Cross of Santiago de Peñalba and an outstanding 11C ivory crucifix, the **Cristo de Carrizo**★★★. Byzantine influence is apparent in the small figure. The **cloister** galleries, built between the 16C and 18C, serve as a lapidary museum. The northeast corner contains a low relief of the Nativity with an interesting architectonic perspective by Juan de Juni. The **sacristy**★ is a sumptuous creation by Juan de Badajoz (1549) with decorated ribbed vaulting.

EXCURSIONS

San Miguel de Escalada★

28km/17.4mi W. Leave León via ③ on the town plan. ◷ *Open year-round Tue–Sat 10.30am–1.15/1.45pm, 4.30–6pm/8pm, Sun and holidays 10.30am–1.15/1.45pm;* ◷ *closed 1, 6 Jan, 2 May, 24, 25, 31 Dec;* ✆*no charge).* In the 11C Alfonso III gave this abandoned **monastery** to refugee monks from Córdoba., today the surviving church is the best-preserved Mozarabic building in Spain. The **outside gallery**★, built in 1050, has horseshoe-shaped arches resting on carved capitals at the top of smoothly polished columns. An earlier church **(iglesia**★**)** from 913 has wooden vaulting, and a balustrade of panels carved with Visigothic (birds, grapes) and Moorish (stylised foliage) motifs.

Cuevas de Valporquero★★ (Valporquero Caves)

47km/29mi N on the LE 311. ⌚*Guided tours (1hr 15min) daily Mar–May and Oct–Dec 10am–5pm; Jun–Sept*

10am–2pm, 3.30–7pm. 🖅*6.10€.* ℘*987 57 64 08.*

Neutral lighting sets off extraordinary shapes – there is a stalactite "star" hanging from the roof of the large chamber – and there are 35 tones of red, grey and black in the mineral oxide-stained stone.

ADDRESSES

🛏 STAY

⊖⊖🍴🍷 **Parador Hotel San Marcos** – *Pl. San Marcos 7.* ℘*987 23 73 00. www.parador.es. 209 rooms.* 🍽*20€. Restaurant*⊖🍷🍴. Few hotels can claim to have a façade that is a masterpiece of Plateresque art! The interior continues the visual feast with its magnificent church and impressive Renaissance cloisters. Every corner of this former convent and pilgrims' hostel is a piece of art and history, in what is the most exclusive establishment in the parador chain.

⊖⊖🍷🍴 **La Posada Regia** – *Regidores 11.* ℘*987 21 31 73. www.regialeon.com. 36 rooms. Restaurant*⊖⊖🍷🍴. A small, welcoming hotel in the old quarter of León, just a stone's throw from the Cathedral. The building itself dates

from the 14C and is an attractive mix of open brickwork and stone. Spacious, attractively furnished bedrooms.

🍴 EAT

⊖🍷🍴 **Rancho Chico II** – *Pl. de San Martín 7.* ℘*987 26 04 83. Closed Wed, 2nd fortnight in Sept .* For more than 20 years this restaurant has been earning plaudits from locals for its reasonably priced, simple, traditional fare. Its location on the pleasant and lively plaza de San Martín is an added bonus. Possible to eat on the terrace in fine weather.

⊖🍷🍴 **Amancio** – *Juan Madrazo 15.* ℘*987 27 34 80. Closed Mon, Sun and Wed for dinner and 1st fortnight in Aug.* A family-run establishment combining traditional cooking with moderate prices. Table service is exceptional.

Palencia

Palencia is a tranquil provincial capital situated in the fertile Tierra de Campos region. It was here that Alfonso VIII created the first Spanish university in 1208. Irrigation of the region has opened up an important horticultural industry.

CATHEDRAL★★

Pl. de la Inmaculada.
🕐*Open May–Oct 10am–1.30pm, 4–7pm; Oct–Apr 10am–1.30pm, 4.30–7pm.* 🖅*1.50€, 2€ with museum, 3€ guided tours.* ℘*979 70 13 47.*
Palencia's little-known Cathedral is a 14C–16C Gothic edifice with Renaissance features. The original 7C Visigothic

▶ **Population:** 82 626
⟳ **Michelin Map:** 575 F 16
🛈 **Info:** Mayor 105. ℘979 74 00 68. www. palenciaporsupuesto.com.
◗ **Location:** Palencia is close to the A 62 heading NW to Burgos (88km/55mi) and SE to Valladolid (50km/31mi) and Salamanca (166km/104mi). 🚌Plaza de los Jardinillos
◒ **Don't Miss:** The Cathedral.

chapel lay forgotten during the Moorish occupation, until Sancho III de Navarra came upon it while hunting.

Interior★★

The Cathedral contains an incredible concentration of art in all the styles of the early 16C: Flamboyant Gothic, Isabelline, Plateresque and Renaissance. The monumental high altar **retable** (early 16C) was carved by Felipe Vigarny, painted by Juan of Flanders and is surmounted by a Crucifix by Juan de Valmaseda. The 16C tapestries on the sides were commissioned by Bishop Fonseca. The *coro* grille, with a delicately wrought upper section, is by Gaspar Rodríguez (1563); the choir stalls are Gothic, the organ gallery, above, is dated 1716. The **Capilla del Sagrario** (Chapel of the Holy Sacrament) is exuberantly Gothic with a rich altarpiece by Valmaseda (1529). The central **triptych**★ is a masterpiece, painted in Flanders by Jan Joest de Calcar in 1505 – the donor, Bishop Fonseca, is shown at its centre.

Museo Catedralicio★

To the right of the west door. Open 1 Oct–15 May Mon–Sat 8.45am–1.30pm, 4–6.30pm, Sun 11.15am–1pm; 16 May–30 Sept Mon–Sat 8.45am–1.30pm, 4.30–7.30pm, Sun 11.15am–1pm. *3€; 1€ crypt.* 979 70 13 47.

The collection includes a *St Sebastian* by El Greco and four 15C Flemish **tapestries**★ of the Adoration, the Ascension, Original Sin and the Resurrection of Lazarus.

EXCURSIONS

Iglesia de San Martín de Frómista★★

29km/18mi NE along the N 611. Open daily Apr–Jun and 1–15 Oct 10am–2pm, 4.30–8pm; 16 Oct–31 Mar 10am–2pm, 3.30–6.30pm. *1€; no charge Wed.* 979 81 01 28. www.fromista.com.

Pilgrims on the way to Santiago de Compostela used to stop here. The only vestige of the famous Benedictine **Monasterio de San Martín** is a church, built in 1066, with beautifully matched stone blocks of considerable size. This was a model for many others in the region.

Baños de Cerrato

14km/8.7mi SE.

▷ *Cross the railway at Venta de Baños; turn right towards Cevico de la Torre. Bear left at the first crossroads.*

Iglesia de San Juan Bautista★

Open Winter Tue–Sun 10.30am–1.30pm, 4–6pm; Summer Tue–Sun 10am–1.30pm, 4.50–8pm. *1€; no charge Wed.* 979 77 03 38.

This, the oldest church in Spain, was built by Visigothic King Recceswinth, while he was taking the waters in Baños de Cerrato, in 661.

Pedraza★★

Weekend visitors flock to Pedraza, encircled by medieval walls, to wander its enchanting streets and to eat roast lamb or suckling pig.

SIGHTS

The **Puerta de la Villa**, a fortified gateway, opens into a maze of alleys bordered by country-style houses. The first medieval building of interest is the **Cárcel de la Villa** (open Sat–Sun and public holidays 11.30am–2pm,

▶ **Population:** 848

Michelin Map: 575 or 576 I 18

Info: Real 40. 921 50 86 66. www.pedraza.info.

Location: The village stands north of Madrid on the slopes of the Sierra de Guadarrama.

Don't Miss: A guided tour of the Romanesque Iglesia de San Salvador.

Timing: An afternoon.

Pedraza

©Turespaña

3.30–7pm; 2.50€; ☏921 50 99 60), the former jail.

The splendid **plaza Mayor** is surrounded by ancient porticoes topped by balconies and the slender Romanesque bell tower of San Juan. A 16C **castle** (*guided tours (30min) Wed–Sun; please book in advance; ☏921 50 98 25*) houses works by artist **Ignacio Zuloaga**.

EXCURSION
Sepúlveda
25km/15.5mi N.

Puebla de Sanabria

Puebla de Sanabria is an attractive mountain village near the Portuguese border. The 15C castle of the Count of Benavente overlooks it white houses and late 12C church.

SIGHTS
Valle de Sanabria
19km/11.8mi NW.
Follow the lake road; turn right after 14km/8.7mi; after a further 6km/3.7mi turn left. This valley of glacial origin, now a nature reserve, was hollowed out at the foot of the Sierras de Cabrera Baja and Segundera. It is a delightful area, well known for its hunting and fishing.

Lago de Sanabria
The largest glacial lake in Spain, at 1 028m/3 373ft, is used for water sports, and for salmon-trout fishing.

You'll get a good view of the village's terraced **site**★ on the slopes of a deep gorge.

🅿️ *Park at the town hall square*, overlooked by castle ruins. Walk up to the **Iglesia de San Salvador** (*Subida al Salvador 10; free guided tours available in summer; ☏921 54 02 37*) for a fine view. The church is typical Segovia Romanesque with one of the oldest side doors in Spain, dating from 1093.

Centro de Interpretación del Parque Natural de las Hoces del Duratón (Duratón Gorges)
🕐 *Open Oct–Jun daily 10am–5pm; Jul–Sept Sun–Fri 10am–2pm, 4–7pm; Sat and public holidays 10am–6pm. ☏921 54 05 86.*
This centre provides information about hiking routes and canoe companies.
The **park** runs along the middle stretch of the river, hemmed in by spectacular 70m/230ft walls, under the simple Romanesque hermitage (*ermita*) of San Frutos.

> ▶ **Population:** 1 595
> 🖈 **Michelin Map:** 575 F 10 – Castilla y León (Zamora)
> 🗊 **Info:** Muralla del Mariquillo, Robledo. ☏980 62 07 34. www.pueblasanabria.org.
> 🖝 **Location:** Puebla de Sanabria is along the A 52 motorway, close to the Embalse de Cernadilla (reservoir).

San Martín de Castañeda
There are attractive **views**★ of the rushing Tera and the mountain-encircled lake all the way to this Galician-looking village with an 11C Romanesque **church** (*pl. de la Iglesia; ☏980 62 67 55*).

Salamanca★★★

Salamanca evokes its rich history through its venerable university, narrow streets, and splendid buildings of golden stone. Blessed with what is rwidely regarded as the most magnificent main square in Spain, Salamanca has long been a favoured destination for foreign students and visitors alike.

THE CITY TODAY

The University of Salamanca may no longer be in the same league academically as the Oxfords and Harvards of this world but its 30 000 or so (international and Spanish) students certainly know how to party and bring a real joie de vivre to the city. If you are young, want to study Spanish for a couple of weeks and enjoy a lively typical Spanish social life too, this is the place to be.

A BIT OF HISTORY

A tumultuous past – Salamanca flourished under the Romans who built the **Puente Romano** (Roman bridge). Alfonso VI took the city from the Moors in 1085. In 1218, Alfonso IX established a centre for study, later to become an important university. In 1520, Salamanca rose against the royal authority of Emperor Charles V (*see SEGOVIA*). In the 16C it reached its artistic and intellectual zenith.

Los Bandos – During the 15C, rivalry between noble factions (*bandos*) saw the city's streets bathed in blood. The *bandos* remained active until 1476.

The university was founded in 1218 and grew under the patronage of kings of Castilla and high dignitaries. Its great and famous members include the Infante Don Juan; St John of the Cross and his teacher, the humanist **Fray Luis de León** (1527–91); and **Miguel de Unamuno** (1864–1936), Professor of Greek, rector, and philosopher.

Art in Salamanca – In the late 15C and early 16C, two major painters were working in Salamanca: **Fernando Gallego**, one of the best Hispano-

- ▶ **Population:** 155 740
- **Michelin Map:** 575 and 576 J 12-13
- **Info:** Plaza Mayor 32. ℰ923 21 83 42. www.salamanca.es.
- **Location:** Salamanca is in western Castilla y León region, accessible from Ávila (98km/61mi SE on the N 501), Valladolid (115km/72mi NE on the A 62) and Zamora (62km/39mi N on the N 630). It's an excellent base from which to explore the Sierra de la Peña de Francia. ▬Paseo de la Estación
- **Don't Miss:** The University and main square.

Flemish artists, and **Juan of Flanders** (c. 1465–1519), whose work is outstanding for the subtle delicacy of its colours.

The 15C also saw the evolution of the original Salamanca patio arch, in which the line of the Mudéjar curve is broken by counter-curves and straight lines. The 16C brought Salamancan **Plateresque** art to an ebullient climax.

SIGHTS

MONUMENTAL CENTRE★★★

Allow one day.

▶ *Follow the itinerary on the town plan.*

Plaza Mayor★★★

The Plaza Mayor is the life and soul of Salamanca. All the city's major streets converge on the square, where locals and visitors alike meet. It was built by Philip V between 1729 and 1755 and is among the finest in Spain, designed principally by the Churriguera brothers. Four ground-level arcades with rounded arches, decorated by a series of portrait medallions of Spanish kings and famous men such as Cervantes, El Cid and Columbus, support three storeys rising in perfect formation to an elegant balustrade. On the north and east sides are the pedimented fronts of the **ayuntamiento** (town hall) and the Pabellón Real (Royal Pavilion).

◯ *Take Prior to plaza de Monterrey.*

Casa de las Muertes (House of Death)

⊶ *Closed to the public.*
The early 16C Plateresque façade is attributed to Diego de Siloé. Its name is attributable to the skulls carved on the upper part of the facade.

Convento de las Úrsulas (Ursuline Convent)

Pl. de las Úrsulas 2. ◯ *Open daily 11am–1pm, 4.30–6pm.* ◯*Closed last Sun in month.* ℘*923 21 98 77.*
The 16C church contains the **tomb**★ of Alonso de Fonseca with delicate low reliefs attributed to Diego de Siloé. The **museum**, with its *artesonado* and coffered ceilings, houses panels and fragments of an altarpiece by Juan de Borgoña. There are also works by Morales the Divine, an *Ecce Homo* and a *Pietà*.

Palacio de Monterrey

Pl. Monterrey 2.
Built in 1539, this typical Renaissance palace has an openwork balustrade crowning a long top-floor gallery, between corner towers.

Iglesia de la Purísima (Church of the Immaculate Conception)

Pl. de las Agustinas. ◯*Open Apr–Sept Tue–Sun 11.30am–1.30pm, 4.30–8pm; Oct–Mar open for Mass.* ◌*No charge.* ℘*923 21 27 38.*
The **Immaculate Conception**★ by Ribera hangs above the high altar.

Plaza de San Benito

On this delightful square are the **Iglesia de San Benito**, and mansions of Salamanca's old noble rival families.

Casa de las Conchas★ (House of Shells)

Compañía 2. ◯ *Indoor Pario: open Oct–Mar Mon–Fri 9am–9pm, Sat 9am–2pm, 4–7pm, Sun 10am–2pm, 4–7pm; Apr–Sept Mon–Fri 9am–9pm, Sat 9am–2pm, 5–8pm, Sun 5–8pm.* ◌*No charge.* ℘*923 26 93 17.*
This late 15C house (now a library) is carved with 400 scallop shells in its golden stone wall. It has decorative Isabelline windows and beautiful wrought-iron grilles. The **patio** has delicate mixtilinear arches and openwork balustrades, carved lions' heads and coats of arms.

La Clerecía

Compañía 5. ◯ *Open Mon–Fri 1.15pm, Sat 7.30pm, Sun and public holidays 12.30pm.* ◌*No charge.* ℘*923 26 46 60.*
This Jesuit College was begun in 1617; its Baroque towers were finished by Andrés García de Quiñones in 1755.

Patio de las Escuelas★★★ (Schools' Square)

This small square, off the old calle Libreros, is surrounded by the best examples of Salamanca Plateresque.The former university principals' residence is the **Casa-Museo Unamuno** (◯ *open Tue–Fri 9am–1.30pm, 4–6pm, Sat–Sun and public holidays 10am–1.30pm;* ◌*1.80€;* ℘*923 29 44 00)*, a museum dedicated to the philosopher.

Universidad

Patio de Escuelas. ◯ *Open Mon–Fri 9.30am–1.30pm, 4–7pm, Sat 9.30am–1.30pm, 4–6.30pm, Sun and public holidays 10am–1pm.* ◌*4€; no charge Mon morning, 18 May.* ℘*923 29 44 00.* www.usal.es.
The University's sumptuous 1534 **entrance**★★★ is a brilliant composition. Above the twin doors, covered by basket arches, the carving is in ever greater relief, to compensate for increasing height. A central medallion in the first register shows the Catholic Monarchs who presented the doorway; in the second are portrait heads in scallop-shell niches; in the third, flanking the

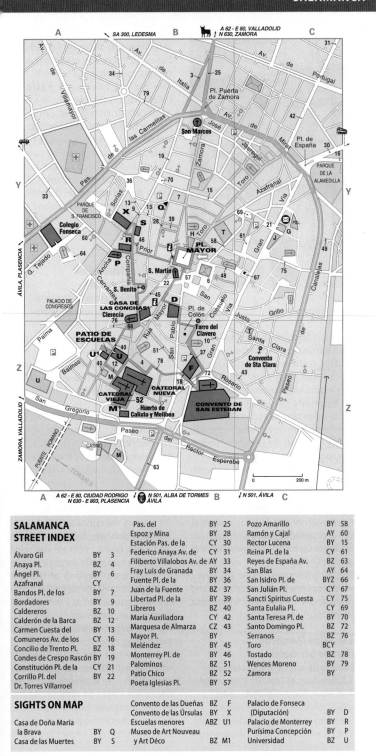

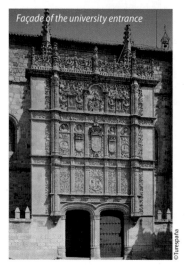

Façade of the university entrance

©Turespaña

pope supported by cardinals, are Venus and Hercules and the Virtues. The most famous motif is the Death's head surmounted by a frog (on the right pilaster, halfway up) symbolising the posthumous punishment of lust.

The lecture halls are around the **patio**: the **Paraninfo** (Great Hall) is hung with 17C Brussels tapestries and a portrait of Charles IV from Goya's studio; the hall where Fray Luis de León lectured in theology is as it was in the 16C.

The grand staircase rises beneath star vaulting, its banister carved with foliated scrollwork and, at the third flight, a mounted bullfight.

A gallery on the first floor has its original, rich **artesonado ceiling** with stalactite ornaments and a delicate low relief frieze along the walls. A Gothic door with a fine 16C grille opens into the 18C library, which contains books, incunabula and manuscripts, some of which date back to the 11C.

Escuelas Menores (Minor Schools)

Patio de Escuelas. Open Mon–Fri 9.30am–1pm, 4–7pm, Sat 9.30am–1pm, 4–6.30pm, Sun 10am–1pm. 4€. 923 29 44 00. http://iuce.usal.es/

Standing to the right of the hospital, and crowned by the same openwork Renaissance frieze, is the entrance to the Minor (preparatory) Schools – a Plateresque portal decorated with coats of arms, roundels and scrollwork.

The typical Salamanca **patio**★★ (1428) has lovely lines. To the right of the entrance is a new exhibition room with a fine Mudéjar ceiling; the **University Museum** opposite exhibits what remains of the ceiling painted by Fernando Gallego for the former university library. This section of the **Cielo de Salamanca**★ (Salamanca Sky) illustrates constellations and signs of the zodiac. Several works by Juan of Flanders and Juan of Burgundy stand out in the museum.

Catedral Nueva★★ (New Cathedral)

Pl. Anaya. Open daily Oct–Mar 9am–1pm, 4–6pm; Apr–Sept 9am–8pm. Closed Sun afternoon Nov–Feb. No charge. 923 21 74 76. www.catedralsalamanca.org.

Construction began in 1513, although additions continued to be made until the 18C – hence the variety of architectural styles.

The **west front**★★★ is divided into four wide bays outlined by pierced stonework, carved as minutely as the keystones in the arches, the friezes and the pinnacled balustrades. The Gothic decoration of the central portal, which includes scenes such as a Crucifixion between St Peter and St Paul, overflows the covings and tympanum.

The **north doorway**, facing the **Colegio de Anaya**, bears a delicate low relief of Christ's entry into Jerusalem. The restored lower section of the last archivolt contains the surprising figure of an astronaut as well as a mythological animal eating ice-cream.

The **interior** is notable for the pattern of the vaulting, the delicacy of the cornices and the sweep of the pillars. The eight windows in the lantern are given added effect by a drum with scenes from the Life of the Virgin painted in the 18C by the Churriguera brothers, who also designed the ornate Baroque stalls in the *coro*, the *trascoro* and the north organ loft.

Catedral Vieja★★★ (Old Cathedral)

Pl. Anaya. ⏱ *Open Oct–Mar Mon–Sat 10am–12.30pm, 4–5.30pm; Apr–Sept daily 10am–7.30pm.*⏱ *Closed Sun afternoon Nov–Feb.* 🎫*4.25€ (incl. museum and cloisters).* ☎*923 21 74 76. www.catedralsalamanca.org.*▶ *Enter by the first bay off the south aisle in the new Cathedral.*

The builders of the new Cathedral respected the fabric of the old which is almost totally masked outside. It was built in the 12C and is a good example of the Romanesque, the pointed arching being a legitimate, if unusual, innovation; the **cimborrio** (lantern), or Torre del Gallo, with two tiers of windows and ribbing, is outstanding. Beneath the vaulting, capitals are carved with scenes of tournaments and imaginary animals.

The **altarpiece**★★ in the central apsidal chapel was painted by Nicholas of Florence in 1445 and comprises 53 compartments decorated in surprisingly fresh colours showing the architecture and dress of the times. The Virgin of the Vega is a 12C wooden statue, plated in gilded and enamelled bronze.

Recesses in the south transept contain French-influenced 13C recumbent figures and frescoes.

Claustro – Capitals from earlier Romanesque galleries destroyed during the 1755 Lisbon earthquake remain in these cloisters. The adjoining **Capilla de Talavera**, with a Mudéjar dome on carved ribs, was where the ancient Mozarabic rite was celebrated. A museum in three rooms and the Capilla de Santa Catalina contains works by Fernando Gallego and his brother Francisco and others by Juan of Flanders (St Michael altarpiece).

The **Capilla Anaya** contains the outstanding 15C alabaster **tomb**★★ of Diego de Anaya, archbishop first of Salamanca and then of Sevilla. Surrounding it is a magnificent Plateresque grille. There are also a 15C **organ**★ and superb 16C recumbent statues.

From the **patio Chico** you can see the old Cathedral apse and the scallop tiling on the **Torre del Gallo** (Cockerel Tower). From here, calle Arcediano leads to the delightful **Huerto de Calixto y Melibea**.

Museo de Art Nouveau y Art Déco

Gibraltar 14. ⏱ *Open Tue–Fri 11am–2pm, 4–7pm, Sat–Sun and public holidays 11am–8pm.* ⏱ *Closed 1, 6 Jan, 24–25, 31 Dec.* 🎫*3€.* ☎*923 12 14 25. www.museocasalis.org.*

This modern art museum is in the Modernist Casa Lis, dating from the beginning of the 20C. Its collection includes works by R Lalique, vases by E Galle and small sculptures by Hagenauer.

Convento de San Esteban★ (St Stephen's Monastery)

⏱ *Open daily Oct–Mar 9am–1pm, 4–6pm; Apr–Sept 9am–1pm, 4–5pm.* 🎫*1.50€; no charge Mon (except holidays) 9am–noon.* ☎*923 21 50 00.*

Gothic pinnacles adorn the side buttresses of this 16C–17C building; the sculpture of the **façade**★★ is quintessentially Plateresque. A low-relief *Martyrdom of St Stephen* is by Juan Antonio Ceroni (1610). In the 17C **cloisters**★, note the prophets' heads in **medallions** and grand staircase (1553).

The large **church** has star vaulting in the gallery and a main altarpiece by José Churriguera. Crowning it is a painting, *The Martyrdom of St Stephen*, by Claudio Coello.

Convento de las Dueñas

Pl. Concilio de Trento. ⏱ *Open Oct–Mar daily 11.30am–12.45pm, 4.30–5.30pm; Apr–Sept Mon–Sat 10.30am–12.45pm, 4.30–6.45pm, Sun and public holidays 11am–12.45pm, 4.30–6.45pm.* 🎫*1.50€.* ☎*923 21 54 42.*

The Renaissance **cloisters**★★ have profusely carved capitals, extraordinarily forceful in spite of their small size.

Torre del Clavero

Consuelo. ⚿ *Closed to the public.*
The octagonal keep is all that remains of a castle built in 1450. Mudéjar trellis-work decorates its turrets.

Colegio Mayor Arzobispo Fonseca

Fonseca 4. 🕐 *Chapel and Cloisters: open daily 10am–2pm, 4–7pm.* ☎*923 29 45 70.*
The **patio**★ of this Renaissance palace combines Salamanca mixtilinear arches at one end with a corbelled gallery – supported by distorted atlantes – on the right and an arcade on the left.

EXCURSION

Alba de Tormes

23km/14mi SE on the N 501 and C 510.
Only the massive keep remains of the **castle of the dukes of Alba** (🕐 *open daily 10.30am–1.30pm, 4.30–7pm; 3€*). The remains of St Teresa of Ávila are in the Carmelite Convent.
The **Iglesia de San Juan** (🕐*open Tue–Fri 10.30am–11am, 11.30am–1.30pm, 4.30–6pm, Sat–Sun 10am–2pm, 4–6pm; ⚿1€*), featuring a Romanesque-Mudéjar east end, contains an outstanding 11C **sculpture ensemble**★ in the apse, showing a noble Christ and the Disciples.

ADDRESSES

🛏 STAY

🍴🍽 **Hostal Catedral** – *Mayor 46 1ºB.* ☎*923 27 06 14. Reservations recommended. 5 rooms.* ⬜*3€.* Because of its location (some windows open directly onto the cathedral), it would have been impossible to give this hostal any other name! Occupying the first floor of an attractive stone building, it is tastefully decorated with spotless bathrooms.

🍴🍽 **Hostal Plaza Mayor** – *Pl. del Corrillo 20.* ☎*923 26 20 20. www.hostalplazamayor.es. 19 rooms.* Ideally situated just behind pl. Mayor, opposite the Romanesque church of San Martín. The hotel's interior design highlights the main features of the house, such as its attractive wooden beams.

🍴🍽🍽 **Hosteria Casa Vallejo** – *San Juan de la Cruz 3.* ☎*923 28 04 21. www.hosteriacasavallejo.com. 13 rooms. Restaurant*🍴🍽🍽. *Closed fortnight in Feb and Jun.* A small hotel located off Plaza Mayor. The refurbished interior is in contrast to the 19C façade. Air-conditioned rooms and an adjacent tapas bar.

🍴🍽🍽🍽 **Hotel Rector** – *Rector Esperabé 10.* ☎*923 21 84 82. www.hotelrector.com. 13 rooms.* ⬜*12€.* A charming small hotel with spectacular views of the Cathedral and elegant, well-appointed rooms.

🍴 EAT

🍽 **El Bardo** – *La Compañía 8.* ☎*923 25 92 65. www.restauranteselbardo.com. Closed 24–25 Dec, 1 Jan.* A typical student haunt with vaulted ceilings and a lively atmosphere. Vegetarian dishes available.

🍽🍽 **La Fonda del Arcediano de Medina** – *Reja 2.* ☎*923 21 57 12. Reservations recommended. Closed Mon.* This restaurant has a solid local reputation, both as a result of its cuisine and good wine list. Meats and *bacalao* (cod) are the specialities. Pleasant décor.

🍽🍽🍽 **El Mesón** – *Pl. Poeta Iglesias 10.* ☎*923 21 72 22. Closed Wed in winter.* A restaurant with a high reputation within the city which has a bar with various tapas and a small dining room with a local carvery menu.

TAPAS

Mesón Cervantes – *Pl. Mayor 15.* ☎*923 21 72 13. www.mesoncervantes.com.* A bar with typical Castilian décor and fine views of plaza Mayor serving modern, innovative cuisine. Popular with Salamanca's young crowd at night. Try the house *sangría.*

Momo – *San Pablo 13.* ☎*923 28 07 98. www.momosalamanca.net. Closed Sun between Jul–Aug.* The contemporary version of a tapas bar. Tapas and skewers come cold and hot, and there's a dining room in the basement.

♈ CAFÉS

Café-Bar Tío Vivo – *Clavel 3–5.* ℘923 25 91 74. www.tiovivosalamanca.com. The name originates from the tío vivo (merry-go-round) on the bar. The cine-camera, spotlights and the decoration lend an American feel.

Capitán Haddock – *Concejo 13.* ℘923 24 75 46. The entrance is through a narrow passageway which gives no hint of the stylish décor and subdued lighting inside.

Café Novelty – *Pl. Mayor 2.* ℘923 21 49 56. www.cafenovelty. com. Famous since 1905, Miguel de Unamuno used to meet here. The wooden chairs and marble tables conjure up images of the philosopher engaged in animated discussion, while its terrace offers a wonderful view of one of Spain's finest squares.

La Regenta – *Espoz y Mina 25.* ℘923 12 32 30. www.cafelaregenta.com. This typical café with a 19C atmosphere has an older feel than those above.

Monasterio de
Santa María de
Huerta★★

In 1144, a Cistercian community came to the Soria region on the border between Castilla and Aragón. Monks settled in Huerta in 1162. The sober Cistercian style was slightly modified by Renaissance innovations.

VISIT

🕐 *Open Mon–Sat 10am–1.30pm, 3.45–6pm, Sun and public holidays 11.30am–12.30pm, 3.45–6pm.* ◈2€. ℘975 32 70 02.
The monastery is entered through a 16C **triumphal arch**.

CLOISTERS AND CLAUSTRO HERRERIANO (HERRERAN CLOISTERS)

16C–17C. The buildings around the cloisters are the monks' living quarters.

Claustro de los Caballeros★ (Knights' Cloisters)

13C-16C. The cloisters owe their name to the many knights buried there. The arches at ground level are elegant, pointed and purely Gothic; above, the 16C gallery has all the exuberance and imagination of the Plateresque (it is a copy of the gallery in the Palacio de Avellaneda in Peñaranda de Duero, near Burgos).

🔹 **Michelin Map:**
Map 575 I 23
🔹 **Location:** The monastery stands close to the A 2 highway linking Madrid and Zaragoza (131km/82mi NE).

The decorative medallions are of Prophets, Apostles and Spanish kings.

Sala de los Conversos (Lay Brothers' Hall)

12C. This is divided by stout pillars, crowned with stylised capitals.

Cocina

The kitchen has a monumental central chimney.

Refectorio★★

The refectory, a masterpiece of 13C Gothic, rises 15m/49ft above the 35m/114.8ft long hall and has a wonderful rose window. A beautiful staircase, its arches on slender columns, leads to the **reader's lectern**.

Iglesia

The church has been restored to its original state although the royal chapel has kept sumptuous Churrigueresque decoration. Between the narthex and the aisles is an intricate 18C wrought-iron screen. The **coro alto** (choir) is beautifully decorated with Renaissance panelling and woodwork. The Talavera *azulejos* on the floor are very old.

Segovia★★★

This austere, imposing city, at 1 000m/3 280ft, rises on a triangular rock like an island in the Castilian plain. Its sturdy walls enclose a complicated maze of narrow streets dotted with Roman monuments and mansions.

A BIT OF HISTORY

Noble Segovia, residence of King Alfonso X, the Wise, and King Henry IV, played a decisive role in the history of Castilla. The 15C marked its golden age, when its population numbered 60 000.

Isabel the Catholic, Queen of Castilla – On the death of Henry IV in 1474 many grandees refused to recognise the legitimacy of his daughter, Doña Juana, known as **La Beltraneja**. In Segovia, the grandees proclaimed Henry's half-sister, Isabel, Queen of Castilla – thus preparing the way for Spain's unification (Isabel was married to Ferdinand, heir apparent of Aragón). La Beltraneja, aided by her husband, Alfonso V of Portugal, pressed her claim, but renounced it in 1479 after defeats at Toro and Albuera.

The "Comuneros" – In 1520, just three years after he had landed in Asturias to take possession of his Spanish dominions, the Habsburg Charles I departed in order to be proclaimed Holy Roman Emperor (as Charles V). An uprising started that was to become known as the revolt of the Comunidades. The catalysts included the absence of Charles V, his Flemish court, which devalued Castilian nobles, and his attempt to impose new taxes.

At the root of the Comuneros movement was the opposition of Castilian towns, the middle classes and merchants to the alliance between Charles V and the landed aristocracy. The Comuneros were finally crushed at Villalar in 1521.

CIUDAD VIEJA★★ (OLD TOWN)
4hr – see town plan

▶ **Population:** 56 858

Michelin Map: 575 or 576 J 17 – map 121 Alrededores de Madrid – local map *Sierra de GUADARRAMA – Castilla-León (Segovia)*

Info: Plaza de Azoguejo 1. ℘921 46 67 20. www.turismodesegovia.com.

Location: Segovia is 92km (57mi) NW of Madrid. Calle Obispo Quesada 1

Don't Miss: The Alcázar, and a meander along streets lined with palaces.

Timing: Allow a full day in town, plus time for excursions.

Acueducto★★★
Pl. del Azogüejo.
This elegant structure was built during the reign of Trajan in the 1C to bring water from the River Acebeda to the upper part of town and remains one of the finest examples of Roman engineering still standing . It is 728m/2 388ft long, rises to 28m/92ft in plaza del Azoguejo where the ground is lowest, and consists of two tiers of arches.

Casa de los Picos
Juan Bravo 33. ⏰*Open Apr–Oct daily noon–2pm, 7–9pm; Nov–Mar Mon–Fri noon–2pm, 6–8pm, Sat–Sun noon–2pm, 7–9pm.* ⬥*No charge.* ℘921 46 26 74.
The house, faced closely with diamond-pointed stones, is the most original of Segovia's 15C mansions.

Casa del Conde de Alpuente
Pl. Conde Alpuente.
The elegant façade of this 15C Gothic house is adorned with *esgrafiado* designs.

Alhóndiga
Pl. de Alhóndiga. ⬥*No charge.*
This old 15C granary is now used as an exhibition room.

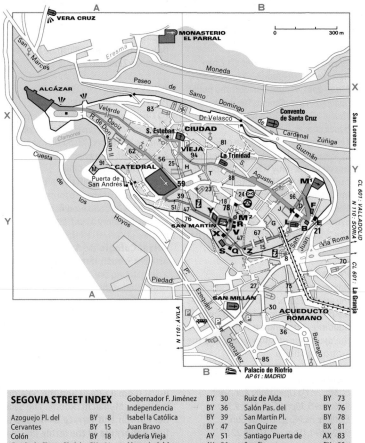

Plaza de San Martín★

This lovely square in the heart of the old aristocratic quarter is the most evocative part of historic Segovia. Around the square stand the **Casa del Siglo XV** (15C House), also known as Juan Bravo's house, with a gallery beneath the eaves, the 16C tower of the **Casa de los Lozoya** the Plateresque façade of the **Casa de Solier** (also known as Casa de Correas) and ornate entrances to other large houses. In the middle of the square is the 12C **Iglesia de San Martín★** (open for Mass; ℘921 46 26 43), a church framed on three sides by a covered gallery on pillars with carved strapwork and animal figures on the capitals.

Museo de Arte Contemporáneo Esteban Vicente

Plazuela de las Bellas Artes. ○ *Open Tue–Wed 11am–2pm, 4–7pm; Thu–Fri 11am–2pm, 4–8pm; Sat–Sun and public holidays 11am–8pm.* ◎*3€; no charge Thu.* ℘*921 46 20 10. www.museoeste banvicente.es.*

The museum is in the palace of Henry IV in the Hospital de Viejos (Old People's Hospital). The only trace of the original building is the fine chapel with a Mudéjar ceiling, now an auditorium. The museum exhibits the work of artist Esteban Vicente (1904–2001).

The 17C **antigua cárcel** (old prison) has a decorative Baroque pediment.

Plaza Mayor

Dominated by the impressive Cathedral, the arcaded square with its terrace cafés is a popular meeting place. Among the buildings surrounding the square are the *ayuntamiento* (town hall) and the Teatro Juan Bravo.

Catedral★★

Pl. Mayor. ○ *Open daily Apr–Sept 9.30am–6.30pm; Oct–Mar 9.30am–5.30pm.* ◎*3€; no charge Sun 9.30am–1.15pm.* ℘*921 46 22 05.*

This was built during the reign of Emperor Charles V to replace a Cathedral destroyed during the Comuneros' Revolt in 1521. It is an example of the survival of the Gothic style in the 16C when Renaissance architecture was at its height. The beautiful golden stone, the stepped east end with pinnacles and delicate balustrades and the tall tower bring considerable grace to the massive building. The width of the aisles combines with the decorative lines of the pillars and ribs in the vaulting to make the interior both light and elegant. The chapels are closed by fine wrought-iron screens. The first off the south aisle contains as altarpiece an *Entombment* by Juan de Juni. The *coro* stalls, in late 15C Flamboyant Gothic style, are from the earlier Cathedral.

Claustro★ – The 15C cloisters from the former Cathedral, near the Alcázar, were rebuilt on the new site. In the Sala Capitular (chapter house) beautiful 17C Brussels **tapestries**★ illustrate the story of Queen Zenobia.

Alcázar★★

Pl. de la Reina Victoria Eugenia. ○ *Open daily Apr–Sept 10am–7pm; Oct–Mar 10am–6pm (Fri–Sat in Oct till 7pm).* ◎*4€; tower 2€; no charge 3rd Tue of month (except holidays) and for EU citizens.* ℘*921 46 07 59.*

The Alcázar, on a cliff overlooking the valley, was built above a former fortress in the early 13C and modified in the 15C and 16C by Henry IV and Philip II. In 1764, Charles III converted the building into a **Real Colegio de Artillería** (Royal Artillery School), but in 1862 it suffered a devastating fire. Reconstruction was completed at the end of the 19C, hence its neo-Gothic look.

The furniture and richly decorated Mudéjar *artesonado* work, mostly from the 15C, are original and were brought from various Castilian towns. Its keep is flanked by corbelled turrets. The main rooms of note are the Chamber Royal (Cámara Real) and the Sala de los Reyes (Monarchs' Room). The Sala del Cordón and terrace command a fine **panorama** of the fertile Eresma Valley, the Monasterio de El Parral, the Capilla de la Vera Cruz and the Meseta. The artillery school houses a museum recalling the chemical laboratory located here in the 18C and the French chemist **Louis Proust**, who formulated his law of constant proportions in Segovia. The **views** from the keep (152 steps) stretch across the city to the Sierra de Guadarrama.

Iglesia de San Esteban (St Stephen's Church)

Pl. de San Esteban. ○━ *Closed to the public.* ℘*921 46 60 70.*

One of the latest (13C) and most beautiful of Segovia's Romanesque churches. The porticoes running along two of its sides have finely carved capitals.

The five-storey **tower**★ has elegant bays and slender columns on the corners. The interior is in Renaissance style. Inside, the altar in the south transept has a 13C polychrome Gothic figure of Christ.

Iglesia de la Santísima Trinidad (Holy Trinity Church)

Pl. de la Trinidad 6. ⏰ *Open during Mass.* 🚫*No charge.*

This austere Romanesque church has a decorated apse with blind arcading and capitals carved with imaginary beasts and plant motifs.

Iglesia de San Juan de los Caballeros

Pl. de Colmenares. ⏰ *Open Jul–Sept Tue–Sat 10am–2pm, 5–8pm, Sun and public holidays 10am–2pm; Oct–Jun Tue–Sat 10am–2pm, 4–7pm, Sun and public holidays 10am–2pm.* 🚫*1.20€; no charge members of the International Council of Museums.* 📞*921 46 33 48.*

This is Segovia's oldest Romanesque church (11C). Its portico (taken from the church of San Nicolás) has carvings of portrait heads, plant motifs and animals. The church, which was almost in ruins at the turn of the 20C, was bought by Daniel Zuloaga, who converted it into his home and workshop. Today it houses the **Museo Zuloaga**, exhibiting drawings by the artist and by his nephew, Ignacio Zuloaga.

Plaza del Conde de Cheste

On the square stand the palaces of the **Marqués de Moya**, the **Marqués de Lozoya**, the **Condes de Cheste** and the **Marqués de Quintanar**.

Iglesia de San Sebastián

Pl. de San Sebastián.

This small Romanesque church stands on one side of a quiet square.

OUTSIDE THE WALLS
Iglesia de San Millán★

Av. Fernández Ladreda. ⏰ *Open for Mass.* 🚫*No charge.* 🚶*Guided tours available in summer and Holy Week, please phone tourist office.* 📞*921 46 09 63.*

The early 12C church stands in the middle of a large square, which allows a full view of its pure, still primitive Romanesque lines and two porticoes with finely carved modillions and capitals. The three aisles have alternating pillars and columns as in Jaca Cathedral. The apse has blind arcading and a decorative frieze. The transept has Moorish ribbed vaulting.

Monasterio El Parral★

Alameda del Eresma. ⏰ *Open Jun–22 Sept Tue–Sat 10am–12.30pm, 4.15–6.30pm, Sun and public holidays 10am–11.30am, 4.15–6.30pm. Mass with Gregorian chants May–Nov Mon–Sat 1pm, Sun and public holidays noon.* 🚫*No charge.* 📞*921 43 12 98.*

The monastery was founded by Henry IV in 1445 and later entrusted to the Hieronymites. The **church**, behind its unfinished façade, has a Gothic nave with beautifully carved doors, a 16C altarpiece by Juan Rodríguez and, on either side of the chancel, the Plateresque tombs of the Marquis and Marchioness of Villena.

Iglesia de la Vera-Cruz★

Ctra de Zamarramala. ⏰ *Open Tue 4–6pm, Wed–Sun 10.30am–1.30pm, 4–6pm (Apr–Oct Sat–Sun 10.30am–1.30pm, 4–7pm).* 🚫*1.75€.* 📞*921 43 14 75.*

The unusual polygonal chapel was erected in the 13C, probably by the Templars; it now belongs to the Order of Malta. A circular corridor surrounds two small chambers, one above the other, where secret ceremonies were conducted. The Capilla del Lignum Crucis holds an ornate Flamboyant Gothic altar. There is a good view of Segovia.

Convento de Santa Cruz

Cardenal Zúñiga. ⏰ *Open Sept–Jun Mon–Fri 9am–8pm, Sat 9am–1pm; Jul–Aug Mon–Fri 9am–8pm.* 📞*921 41 24 10.*

The convent pinnacles, the decorated Isabelline **entrance** with a Calvary, a *Pietà*, and the emblems of the Catholic Monarchs, can be seen from the road.

Iglesia de San Lorenzo

Iglesia.
The Romanesque church with its unusual brick belfry stands in a picturesque square surrounded by corbelled half-timbered houses.

EXCURSIONS

Palacio Real de La Granja De San Ildefonso★★

See Sierra de GUADARRAMA

Palacio Real de Riofrío★

Bosque de Riofrío, Navás de Riofrío.
11km/6.8mi S on the N 603. Open *Apr–Sept Tue–Sun and public holidays 10am–6pm; Oct–Mar Tue–Sat 10am–1.30pm, 3–5pm, Sun and public holidays 10am–2pm.* 5€; no charge *Wed for EU citizens.* 921 478 01 42.
The palace Riofrío was planned by Isabel Farnese as the equal of La Granja, which she had to vacate on the death of her husband, Philip V. Construction began in 1752 but though it was very big – it measures 84m x 84m (276ft x 276ft) – it was never moer than a hunting lodge. This palatine construction was never completed and Isabel never lived in it. It is built around a grand Classical-style courtyard. The green and pink façade reflects Isabel's Italian origins.

Castillo de Coca★★

Camino Antigua Cauca Romana, Coca.
52km/32mi NW along the C 605 and SG 341. Guided tours Nov–Mar Mon–Fri 10.30am–1pm, 4.30–6pm, Sat–Sun *and public holidays 11am–1pm, 4–6pm; Apr–Sept Sat–Sun and public holidays 11am–1pm, 4.30–7pm.* Closed 1st Tue *in month.* 2.50€. 921 57 35 54.
This **castillo** (fortress), on the outskirts of Coca village, is the most outstanding example of Mudéjar military architecture in Spain. It was built in the late 15C by Moorish craftsmen for the archbishop of Sevilla, Fonseca, and consists of three concentric perimeters, flanked by polygonal corner towers and turrets with, at the centre, a massive keep. It is the epitome of all fortresses, but with the sun mellowing the pink brick and the interplay of shadows on battlements and watchtowers, it can be attractive as well as awesome.
The torre del *homenaje* (keep) and *capilla* (chapel), which contains Romanesque wood carvings, are open to the public.

Arévalo

60km/37mi NW along the C 605.
Isabel the Catholic spent her childhood in the 14C **castle** with its massive crenellated keep which dominates the town. Of note also are Romanesque-Mudéjar brick churches, and several old mansions.
Plaza de la Villa★, the former Plaza Mayor, is one of the best-preserved town squares in Castilla with its half-timbered brick houses resting on pillared porticoes. They blend in perfectly with the Mudéjar east end of the Iglesia de Santa María and its blind arcading.

ADDRESSES

🏠 STAY

💬🍽 **Hotel Las Sirenas** – *Juan Bravo 30.* 921 46 26 63. www.hotelsirenas. com. *39 rooms.* Traditional hotel in the old quarter with an elegant stone façade, feature staircase and an old hairdressing salon.
💬🍽🍽 **La Casa Mudéjar** – *Isabel la Católica 8.* 921 46 62 50. www. lacasamudejar.com. *40 rooms.* 7€. Beautifully renovated hotel with a coffered mudéjar-style ceiling delightful

🍽 EAT

decorations. Enjoy Castilian and sephardic cuisine in the patio dining area.

💬🍽🍽 **Narizotas** – *Pl. Medina del Campo 2.* 921 46 26 79. www.narizotas. net. Traditional restaurant serving roast suckling pig and a tasting menu; pleasant street terrace with music.
💬🍽🍽🍽 **Mesón de Cándido** – *Pl. del Azoguejo 5.* 921 42 59 11. www. mesondecandido.es. The most famous restaurant in the province, set in a 15C house beneath the aqueduct, serving rich traditional Castilian cuisine.

Soria★

This tranquil provincial capital stands on the banks of the Duero, the river that relieves the harsh Castilian summer. The desolate scenery and medieval atmosphere have been immortalised by poets such as Antonio Machado.

▸ **Population:** 39 078
⌚ **Michelin Map:** 575 G 22
Info: Medinaceli 2.
℘975 21 20 52.
www.ayto-soria.org.
Location: Soria lies in NE Spain at an altitude of 1 050m/3 445ft on a plateau buffeted by the winds of the Meseta.
🚌Calle Carretera Madrid

SIGHTS

Iglesia de Santo Domingo★

Pl. de los Condes de Lérida 3. ⌚ *Open daily 7am–9pm.* ⊘*No charge.*

The west front of this church has two tiers of blind arcades and a richly carved **portal**★★. The church's founders were Alfonso VIII and his queen, Eleanor Plantagenet (they appear on either side of the portal), hence the French appearance. The figures on the archivolt are shown in great detail. The scenes include the early chapters of Genesis (on the capitals of the jamb shafts), the 24 Elders of the Apocalypse playing stringed instruments, the Massacre of the Innocents, and Christ's childhood, Passion and Death (in ascending registers on the archivolt).

Palacio de los Condes de Gómara (Palace of the Counts of Gómara)

Pl. de Aguirre 3. ⌚ *Patio: open daily 9am–2pm.* ℘975 21 16 78.

The long façade, part Renaissance, part Classical, the bold tower and double patio exemplify late 16C opulence.

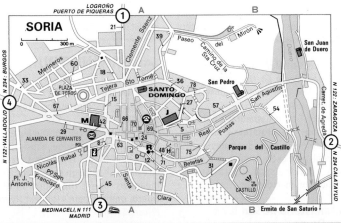

Iglesia de San Juan de Rabanera

Caballeros. ⏱ *Open for Mass 15 Jul–15 Sept Tue–Sun 11am–2pm, 5–7pm.* ✎*No charge.*

The Romanesque portal taken from a ruined church dedicated to St Nicolas recalls the events of the saint's life in the capitals on the slender columns on the right and on the tympanum. The decoration at the east end shows Byzantine and Gothic influences. Crucifixes inside are Romanesque over the altar and Baroque in the north transept.

Museo Numantino (Numancia Museum)

Pas. del Espolón 8. ⏱ *Open Jul–Sept Tue–Sat 10am–2pm, 5–8pm; Oct–Jun Tue–Sat 10am–2pm, 4–7pm, Sun and public holidays 10am–2pm.* ✎*1.20€; no charge Sat–Sun, 23 Apr, 18 May, 12 Oct, 6 Dec.* ✆*975 22 13 97.*

The collections in the recently restored museum illustrate the development of Soria from the Palaeolithic Age to today. Note the artefacts from Celt-Iberian necropolises and the coloured pottery from Numancia (👣*see Excursion*).

Concatedral de San Pedro

Pl. de San Pedro. ⏱ *Open Jul–Aug daily 10am–8pm; Sept–Jun for Mass at 7pm.* ✎*No charge.*

The 16C Gothic Cathedral is light and spacious; the **cloisters**★ are older, with three Romanesque galleries. The capitals have been delicately re-sculpted in a pure Romanesque style that recalls Santo Domingo de Silos.

Monasterio de San Juan de Duero

Pas. de las Ánimas. ⏱ *Open Oct–Jun Tue–Sat 10am–2pm, 4–7pm; Jul–Sept Tue–Sat 10am–2pm, 5–8pm, Sun and public holidays 10am–2pm.* ✎*0.60€; no charge Sat–Sun, 23 Apr, 18 May, 12 Oct.* ✆*975 23 02 18.*

The monastery founded by the Hospitallers of St John of Jerusalem is in a rustic setting along the Duero. Only the graceful gallery arcading, with four different orders, remains of the 12C–13C **cloisters**★. The intersecting, overlapping arches owe much to Moorish art. The church contains a small lapidary museum. Two small chambers with beautiful historiated capitals stand at the entrance to the apse; the ciborium effect is unusual, like one might find in an Orthodox church.

Parque del Castillo (Castle Park)

Lines composed about the Soria countryside by Sevillan poet Antonio Machado (1875–1939) come alive here: "violet mountains, poplars beside green waters".

Ermita de San Saturio (San Saturio Hermitage)

Pas. San Saturio. 1.3km/0.8mi S of N 122. ⏱*Open Tue–Sat 10.30am–2pm, 4.30–6.30pm (7.30pm Jan–Mar Nov–Dec; 8.30pm Jul–Aug), Sun 10.30am–2pm.* ✎*No charge.* ✆*975 18 07 403.*

A shaded path beside the Duero leads to the cave where the holy man sat in meditation. The 18C octagonal chapel is built into the rock.

🚗 DRIVING TOUR

SIERRA DE URBIÓN★★

⚠*Roads are liable to be blocked by snow Nov–May.*

Surprisingly, this part of the Sistema Ibérico mountain range, which rises to 2 228m/7 310ft, is hilly and green. Streams rush through pinewoods and meadows; one is the source of the Duero, one of Spain's longest rivers (910km/565mi).

Laguna Negra de Urbión★★

53km/33mi NW by 🚲 on the plan and the N 234. ⏱*About 1hr.*

▶ *At Cidones bear right towards Vinuesa; after 18km/11mi head for Montenegro de Cameros. After 8km/5mi bear left onto the Laguna road (9km/5.6mi).*

The **road**★★, after skirting the Cuerdo del Pozo reservoir *(embalse)*, continues through pines to **Laguna Negra** (alt 1 700m/5 600ft), a small glacial lake at the foot of a semicircular cliff over which cascade two waterfalls.

Laguna Negra de Neila★★
About 86km/53mi NW by 🚲 on the plan and the N 234.

▶ *At Abejar turn right towards Molinos de Duero; continue to Quintana de la Sierra then turn right for Neila (12km/7mi), then left for Huerta de Arriba; 2km/1mi on the left is the road to Laguna Negra.*

The **road**★★ through picturesque countryside commands changing views of the valley and Sierra de la Demanda. The lake lies at 2 000m/6 561ft.

Valladolid★

The former capital of Castilla and of a great empire stands amid a landscape of vineyards and cereal crops. Today, this important provincial capital preserves architectural vestiges that bear witness to its rich and illustrious past.

A BIT OF HISTORY
From the 12C, Castilla's kings frequently resided at Valladolid. Peter the Cruel married there, as did Ferdinand and Isabel; it was the birthplace of Philip IV and his sister Anne of Austria, mother of Louis XIV.

Castillo de Simancas *(11km/6.8mi SW; 🕐 only open for study; 🕿 983 59 00 03)* – Charles V made this castle a repository for state archives. The collection is a history of Spanish administration from the 15C to the 19C.

SIGHTS
Colegio de San Gregorio
Cadenas de San Gregorio 1–2.
This is Valladolid's most impressive Isabelline building. On the sumptuous **entrance**★★★, attributed to Gil de Siloé and Simon of Cologne, fantasies from savages to interwoven thorn branches create a strongly hierarchical composition rising from the doorway. The college is the seat of the **Museo Nacional de Escultura**★★★.

▶ **Population:** 318 461
🕭 **Michelin Map:** 575 H 15 (town plan)
🏠 **Info:** Acera de Recoletos (Pabellón de Cristal). 🕿983 21 93 10. www.ava.es.
▶ **Location:** The city is at the centre of the northern section of the Spanish Meseta. ▱▱▱Calle Recondo
👪 **Kids:** The interactive Museo de la Ciencia (Science Museum).

Iglesia de San Pablo (St Paul's Church)
Pl. de San Pablo 4. 🕐 Open summer Sun 7.30am–9.30pm; rest of year Mon–Sat 7.30am–10am, 12.30–1.30pm, 7.30am–9.30pm, Sun and public holidays 7.30am–2pm, 6–9.30pm. ⬤No charge. 🕿983 35 17 48.
The **façade**★★★ is outstanding. The lower section, by Simon of Cologne, consists of a portal with an ogee arch all framed in a segmental arch, and above, a large rose window and two coats of arms supported by angels.

IN THE CENTRE
The historical centre of Valladolid is a blend of carefully tended plazas, lively pedestrian ways, and a pleasant park, the Campo Grande. The Plaza Mayor, the lovely and spacious focus of the city, dates from the 16C.

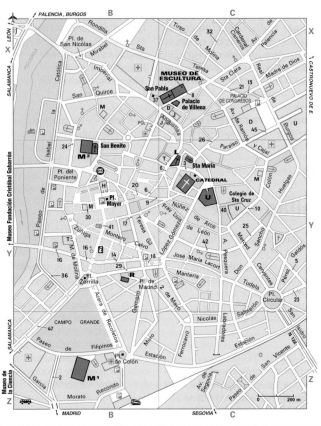

Museo Nacional Colegio de San Gregorio★★★ (National Museum of Sculpture)

Cadenas de San Gregorio 1–2.

🕐 *Open Tue–Sat 10am–2pm, 4–6pm, Sun and public holidays 10am–2pm.*

🕐 *Closed 1, 6 Jan, 1, 13 May, 8 Sept, 24–25, 31 Dec.* 👝*2.40€; no charge Sat afternoon, Sun morning, 18 May, 12 Oct, 6 Dec.* 📞*983 25 40 83. http://museoescultura.mcu.es.*

From the 16C to the 17C Valladolid was a major centre for sculpture, reflected in this museum's wonderful collection of religious statues in polychrome wood, a material well suited to the expression of the dramatic.

On the ground floor of the Palacio de Villena, aside from paintings (including an attractive *Pietà* by Pedro Berruguete) are the magnificent sculptures of two 16C Mannerist masters: **Alonso**

Berruguete (a remarkable altarpiece designed for the San Benito church) and **Juan de Juni** (*The Crucifixion* and the portentous ensemble **Burial of Christ**). Outstanding works by **Gregorio Fernández**, leading 16C exponent of Castilian Baroque, include *Passage to the Sixth Agony* and **Christ Recumbent**. There are also works of the Andalucían School (Martínez Montañés, Pedro de Mena, Alonso Cano).

On the second floor are works from the Renaissance by **Diego de Siloé** (*The Holy Family*) and **Felipe Vigarny** (*Virgin and Child*, a model of grace and elegance). There is also an excellent painting by **Rubens** (*Democritus and Heraclitus*).

On the third floor are Late Baroque (18C) works, such as *St Francis of Assisi* by Salzillo and *Head of St Paul* by Juan Alonso de Villabrille y Ron. On the way down, admire a magnificent **Neapolitan nativity** of more than 180 figures.

Capilla del Colegio de San Gregorio★

Located within the Colegio.

Designed by Juan Guas, this lovely Gothic chapel with elevated choir contains an altarpiece by Berruguete, a tomb by Felipe Vigarny and carved choir stalls.

Catedral★

Arribas 1. ○ *Open Tue–Fri 10am–1.30pm, 4.30–7pm, Sat–Sun and public holidays 10am–2pm.* ∞*2.50€.* ℘*983 30 44 62. www.archivalladolid.org.*

The Cathedral, commissioned in about 1580 by Philip II from Herrera, was distorted by the architect's 17C and 19C successors – in the octagonal tower, and the Baroque upper façade by Alberto Churriguera.

Never completed, the **interior** remains one of Herrera's triumphs. The altarpiece (1551) in the central apsidal chapel, where figures come to life, is by Juan de Juni.

Museo Diocesano y Catedralicio★

In the funerary chapels of the former Gothic Cathedral.

Note the Mudéjar cupolas in the Capilla de San Llorente. There is a **collection**★ of sculptures, paintings, silverware and ornaments. Note two busts by Pedro de Mena (*Ecce Homo* and *Dolorosa*), two 13C tombs, two 13C Christs (one Protogothic with four nails), a dramatic *Ecce Homo* by Gregorio Fernández, the sculpture group *Lament for Christ* (c. 1500) and a 16C silver monstrance by Juan de Arfe. Outside, note, on the Baroque University façade, sculptured and heraldic decoration by Narciso and Antonio Tomé.

Colegio Mayor de Santa Cruz

Cardenal Mendoza 1. ○━*Closed to the public.* ℘*983 42 30 32.*

This lovely late 15C college is one of the first Renaissance buildings in Spain; the carved decoration at the entrance is Plateresque but the rusticated stonework is Classical. The Neoclassic balconies and windows are 18C additions.

Iglesia de Nuestra Señora de las Angustias

Angustías. ℘*983 34 40 13.*

The church, built by one of Herrera's disciples, contains Juan de Juni's masterpiece, the **Virgen de los Siete Cuchillos**★ (Virgin of the Seven Knives).

Patio Herreriano – Museo de Arte Contemporáneo Español (Modern Spanish Art Museum)

Jorge Guillén 6. ○ *Open Tue–Fri 11am–8pm, Sat 10am–8pm, Sun 10am–3pm.* ○*Closed 25 Dec, 1 Jan.* ∞*4€; 1€ on Wed.* ℘*983 36 29 08. www.museo patioherreriano.org.*

The lovely **Herreran patio**★ of the ex-monastery of San Benito and a newer annex house this collection of Spanish art since 1917.

Museo Oriental

Pas. Filipinos 7. ○ *Open Mon–Sat 4–7pm, Sun and public holidays 10am–2pm.* ∞*3€.* ℘*983 30 68 00.*

The museum, in a Neoclassical college (18C) designed by Ventura Rodríguez, houses **Chinese art**★ (bronze, porcelain, lacquerware, coins and silk embroidery) and Philippine art with important **ivory pieces**★.

Casa de Cervantes

Rastro 7. ©*Open Tue–Sat 9.30am–3.30pm; Sun 10am–3pm.* © *Closed 1, 13 May, 8 Sept, 24–25, 31 Dec.* ⊚*2.40€; no charge Sun, 6 Dec.* ℘*983 30 88 10.*
The author of *Don Quixote* lived in this house from 1603 to 1606; some of his simple furnishings remain.

BEYOND THE CENTRE
♟♟ Museo de la Ciencia (Science Museum)

Av. Salamanca s/n. ©*Open Sept–Jun Tue–Sun 10am–7pm; Jul–Aug 11am–9pm.* ⊚*9€; child 6€, no charge for 1 child on Sat; planetarium 4€.* ©*Closed 1, 6 Jan, 24–25, 31 Dec.* ℘*983 14 43 00. www.museocienciavalladolid.es.*
This interactive science museum includes a planetarium.

EXCURSIONS
Peñafiel★

55km/34mi E along the N 122.
Peñafiel was a strongpoint along the Duero during the Reconquest and its massive 14C castle **Castillo**★ *(©open Oct–Mar Tue–Fri 11.30am–2.30pm, 4.30–7.30pm, Sat–Sun and hols 11.30am–2.30pm, 4.30–8.30pm; Apr–Sept Tue–Sun 11.30am–2.30pm, 4.30–8.30pm; ©closed 1, 6 Jan, 24–25, 31 Dec; ⊚6€ museum and castle, 2.50€ castle only; ℘983 88 15 26; www.turismopenafiel.com)* is sited at the meeting point of three valleys. Its imposing keep, reinforced by machicolated turrets houses the **Museo Provincial del Vino de Valladolid**, featuring local wines.
Also notable is the **Convento de San Pablo** *(©open daily 9.30am–2pm, 5–8pm;* ☛*guided tours available,* ℘*983 88 01 28;* ⊚*no charge).* Its church (1324) has a Mudéjar east end, with Renaissance vaulting in the 16C Capilla del Infante (Infante Chapel).

Tordesillas

30km/19mi SW along the A 62.
The kings of Spain and Portugal signed the famous **Treaty of Tordesillas** here

in 1494, dividing up the New World. **Juana the Mad** locked herself away here on the death of her husband Philip the Fair in 1506.

Real Monasterio de Santa Clara★

Alonso del Castillo Solorzano. ©*Open Oct–Mar Tue–Sat 10am–1.30pm, 4–5.45pm; Apr–Sept Tue–Sat 10am–1.30pm, 4–6.30pm, Sun and public holidays 10.30am–1.30pm, 3.30–5.30pm.* ⊚*3.60€; free Wed for EU citizens; 2.25€ Arabic baths.* ℘*983 77 00 71.*
The palace built by Alfonso XI in 1350 was converted to a convent by Peter the Cruel. He installed María de Padilla here, to whom he might have been married. For María, homesick for Sevilla, he commissioned Mudéjar decoration. The **patio**★ has multifoil and horseshoe arches, strapwork decoration and multicoloured ceramic tiles. In the **Capilla Dorada** (Gilded Chapel) are mementoes and works of art.
The choir of the **church** has a particularly intricate **artesonado ceiling**★★.

Medina del Campo

54km/34mi SW along the A 62 and the A 6; 24km/15mi from Tordesillas. 🚆*Avenida de la Estación 27.*
In the Middle Ages Medina was famous for its fairs. A large market is held on Sundays. Isabel the Catholic died here in 1504.

Castillo de la Mota★

Av. del Castillo. ©*Open Apr–Sept Mon–Sat 11am–2pm, 4–7pm, Sun and public holidays 11am–2pm; Oct–Mar daily 11am–2pm, 4–6pm.* ⊚*No charge.* ℘*983 80 10 24.*
Juana the Mad often stayed in this large 13C–15C castle. Cesare Borgia was imprisoned in the keep for two years.

Villa de Almenara-Puras: Museo de las Villas Romanas (Museum of Roman Villas)

51km/31.8mi S by the N 601. Turn at Almenara and continue 3km/1.9mi S. ©*Open Tue–Sun Apr–15 Oct 10.30am–2pm, 4.30–8pm; 16 Oct–30 Dec and Mar 10.30am–2pm, 4–6pm.* ©*Closed*

24–25, 31 Dec. ⊜*3€.* ✆*983 62 60 36.*
www.museodelasvillasromanas.com.
This museum also features the remains
of a sumptuous villa of the 4C and the
underlying 3C structure.

Medina de Rioseco
40km/25mi NW along the N 601.
The picturesque narrow main street,
or **Rúa**, of this agricultural centre is

lined by porticoes on wooden pillars.
The 16C **Iglesia de Santa María** *(pl.
de Santa María;* ○*open Tue–Sun 11am–
2pm, 4–7pm;* ○*closed 1, 6 Jan, 25 Dec;*
⊜*1.80€;* ✆*983 72 03 19)* feature a central
altarpiece carved by Esteban Jordán. The
Capilla de los Benavente★ (Benavente
Chapel, 16C) contains a 16C retable by
Juan de Juni. The treasury holds a 16C
monstrance by Antonio Arfe.

ADDRESSES

🏠 STAY

⊜⊜🍽 **Hotel El Nogal** – *Conde Ansurez
10.* ✆*983 34 03 33. www.hotelelnogal.
com. 26 rooms.* ⊡*4€. Restaurant*⊜⊜*.*
This small hotel lies within the triangle
of the Plaza Mayor, Cathedral and
Museo de Escultura. The international-
style rooms here are bright and airy
and reasonably priced, given the
quality. The hotel restaurant is pleasant with an often lively ambience.

⊜⊜🍽 **Hotel Imperial** – *Pas. 4.* ✆*983
33 03 00. www.himperial.com. 63 rooms.*
⊡*9€. Restaurant*⊜⊜*.* An authentic
Valladolid institution set in a 16C
Gallo mansion, impeccably maintained
with contemporary requirements.

🍽 EAT

⊜⊜ **Covadonga** – *Zapico 1.* ✆*983 33
07 98. Closed 2nd fortnight in Jul.* The
uninspiring modern appearance of this
restaurant is quickly forgotten inside,
with a friendly welcome, excellent service and wholesome, plentiful cuisine.

⊜⊜🍽 **El Figón de Recoletos** – *Acera
de Recoletos 3.* ✆*983 39 60 43. Closed
20 Jul–12 Aug, Sun eve.* This Castilian
restaurant with its dark wood décor and
sturdy chairs is frequented by business
types, families and tourists alike. The
roast peppers *(pimientos asados)*, lamb
brisket *(falda de cordero)* and grilled
chops *(chuletitas)* are popular choices.

Zamora★

**Zamora stands in a plain on the
banks of the River Duero. The 12C
and 13C saw the construction
of the Cathedral and numerous
Romanesque churches.**

A BIT OF HISTORY
Traces remain of the walls which made
Zamora the western bastion along
the Duero in the Reconquest. Zamora
figured in repeated struggles for the
throne of Castilla.

SIGHTS
Catedral★ *Pl. de la Catedral.*
○*Open Tue–Sun Mar–Sept 10am–
2pm, 5–8pm; Oct–Feb 10am–2pm,
4.30–6.30pm.* ⊜*2€.* ✆*980 53 06 44.*

▸ **Population:** 66 672
◔ **Michelin Map:** 575 H 12
🔲 **Info:** Plaza de Arias
   Gonzalo. ✆*980 53 36 94.*
   http://zamoradipu.es/
   patronato.
▶ **Location:** Zamora is NW
   of Madrid. 🚉Carretera
   de la Estación

The Cathedral was built between 1151
and 1174 and subsequently altered. The
north front is Neoclassical in keeping
with the square in front; it contrasts,
however, with the Romanesque bell
tower and the graceful cupola covered
in scallop tiling. The south front, the
only original part, has blind arcades

and a Romanesque portal with unusual covings featuring openwork festoons. The aisles are transitional Romanesque-Gothic, the vaulting ranging from broken barrel to pointed ogive. Slender painted ribs support the luminous **dome**★ on squinches above the transept. Late Gothic master woodcarvers worked here. Notable are fine **grilles** enclosing the presbytery, the *coro* and some chapels, two 15C Mudéjar pulpits, and **choir stalls**★★, decorated with biblical figures or with allegorical and burlesque scenes.

Museo Catedralicio (Cathedral Museum)

🕐*Open same hours as Cathedral but from 11am.* 📞*980 53 22 95.*

The museum, off the Herreran cloisters, displays 15C Flemish and 17C **tapestries**★★. Also note the 16C Renaissance monstrance and a Virgin and Child and Little St John sculpted by Bartolomé Ordóñez. The **Jardín del Castillo** (Castle Garden) to the rear commands fine views.

Romanesque churches★

🕐*Open Tue–Sun 2 Mar–Sept 10am–1pm, 5–8pm; Oct–6 Jan 10am–2pm, 4.30–6.30pm.*

The 12C saw many original Romanesque churches built in Zamora province. Features included portals without tympana, surrounded by multifoil arches and often possessing heavily carved archivolts. Larger churches had domes on squinches over the transept crossing. The best examples in Zamora are the **Magdalena** (los Francos; 📞*980 53 18 02)*, **Santa María la Nueva** (pl. de Santa María la Nueva; 📞*980 53 40 47)*, **San Juan de Puerta Nueva** (pl. Mayor), **Santa María de la Horta** (barrio de la Horta), **Santo Tomé** (pl. Santo Tomé) and **Santiago del Burgo** (Santa Clara; 📞*980 53 40 47)*.

Seigniorial mansions

Palacio del Cordón (Museo Provincial; pl. de Santa Lucía 2; 🕐*open Tue–Sat 10am–2pm, 4–8pm, Sun and public holidays 10am–2pm;* ✆*1.20€;*

📞*980 51 61 50)* and **Palacio de los Momos** (San Torcuato 7) have elegant Isabelline windows.

EXCURSIONS
San Pedro de la Nave★

▶ *19km/11.8mi NW. Leave Zamora on the N 122–E 82. Follow the N 122 for 12km/7.4mi then turn right.*

The late 7C Visigothic **church** (🕐*open Mar–Sept Tue–Sun 10am–1pm, 5–8pm; Oct–6 Jan Fri–Sat 10am–2pm, 4.30–6.30pm, Sun 10am–2pm;* ✆*no charge;* 🔑*ask for the keys at the nearby bar;* 📞*980 56 91 67)*, endangered by the damming of the Esla, was rebuilt at El Campillo. It is remarkable for the Biblical carving on the transept **capitals**. The frieze, halfway up, presents Christian symbols including grapes and doves.

Arcenillas
7km/4.3mi SE on the C 605.

In the village church (Nuestra Señora de la Asunción; *phone for key:* 📞*980 57 14 47)*, 15 **panels**★ depicting the Life, Death and Resurrection of Christ have been reassembled from the late 15C Gothic altarpiece designed for Zamora Cathedral by **Fernando Gallego**, one of the great Castilian painters of the age.

Benavente
66km/41mi N along the N 630.

The Renaissance **Castillo de los Condes de Pimentel** (Castle of the Counts of Pimentel; 📞*980 63 03 00)*, now a parador, retains its 16C Torre del Caracol (snail tower), with fine valley **views**.

The transitional **Iglesia de Santa María del Azogue** (pl. de Santa María; 📞*980 63 42 11)* has five apses and two Romanesque portals. A beautiful 13C *Annunciation* stands at the crossing.

The **Iglesia de San Juan del Mercado** (plazuela de San Juan 4; 📞*980 63 00 80)* has a 12C carving on the south portal illustrating the journey of the Magi.

Toro
33km/21mi E along the N 122–E 82.

This town on the Duero has a number of Romanesque churches, sadly in poor

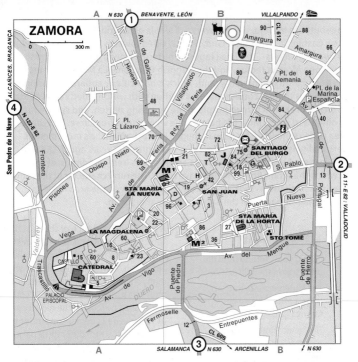

ZAMORA STREET INDEX

Alfonso IX	B	2	Damas	A	20	Riego	B	72
Alfonso XII	B	3	Feria	B	21	Sacramento	B	74
Antonio del Aguila Pl.	A	5	Francos Rúa de los	A	22	San Torcuato	B	78
Arias Gonzalo Pl. de	A	8	Fray Diego de Deza Pl.	A	23	San Torcuato Ronda de	B	80
Cabañales	B	12	Horta	B	27	San Vicente	B	82
Candelaría Pas.	B	13	Ignacio Gazapo	B	36	Santa Clara	B	84
Catedral Pl. de la	A	15	Leopoldo Alas Clarín	B	40	Santa Lucía Pl.	B	86
Ciento Pl. de los	A	16	Mayor Pl.	B	42	Santiago	B	75
Constitución Pl. de	B	18	Morana Cuesta de la	A	48	Tres Cruces Av.	B	88
Corral Pintado	B	19	Notarios Rúa de los	A	60	Víctor Gallego	B	90
			Príncipe de Asturias Av.	B	66	Viriato Pl.	B	96
			Puebla de Sanabria	A	70	Zorilla Pl. de	B	99
			Puentica Pl. de la	A	69			

SIGHTS ON MAP						
	Casa de los Momos	B	J	Museo de la Semana Santa	B	M1
	Casa del Cordón	B	M2			

repair. The **Iglesia de San Lorenzo** (&980 69 47 47) is the best-preserved of these.

Colegiata de Santa María La Mayor★
Pl. de la Colegiata. ◷*Open Tue–Sun Mar–Sept 10.30am–2pm, 5–7.30pm; Oct–6 Jan 10am–2pm, 4.30–6.30pm.* ⊚*2€.* &*980 69 47 47.*
Construction began in 1160 with the elegant transept lantern and ended in 1240 with the west portal. The Romanesque **north portal** illustrates the Old Men of the Apocalypse *(above)* and angels linked by a rope.

The Gothic **west portal**★★, repainted in the 18C, is the church treasure.
Statues on the pier and tympanum jambs have youthful faces. Start beneath the **cupola**★, one of the first of its kind in Spain, with two tiers of windows in the drum. Polychrome wood statues stand against the pillars at the end of the nave on consoles, one carved with an amusing version of the Birth of Eve (below the angel). In the sacristy is the **Virgin and the Fly**★, a magnificent Flemish painting by either Gérard David or Hans Memling.

CASTILLA-LA MANCHA

The southern Meseta, which covers the whole of Madrid-Castilla-La Mancha (New Castile), is a vast tableland, slightly tilted towards the west, watered by two large rivers – the Tajo (Tagus), which cuts a deep gorge through the limestone Alcarria region, and the sluggish Guadiana. La Mancha comes from the Arab *manxa* meaning dry land, which is particularly apparent in summer. Despite this there is considerable cultivation with wind-ruffled cereal fields, stretches of saffron turned purple in the flowering season, and serried ranks of olives and vines. Most of Spain's table wines come from here, and the area is also renowned for its manchego cheese. La Mancha's most famous personality is Don Quixote, created by Cervantes 400 years ago. A Quixote trail leads in his (fictional) footsteps and includes (real) windmills, of the type at which the errant knight would have tilted. The rural character of the region persists; small towns look more like large villages with the arcaded *Plaza Mayor* (main square) still the hub of activity and gossip.

Highlights

1. Gazing upon **Toledo** from the other side of the Tajo *(p302)*.
2. The Museum of Abstract Art, set in a *casas colgada* in **Cuenca** *(p289)*
3. The iconic "Don Quixote windmills" at **Consuegra** *(p287)*
4. The spectacular natural formations of the **Serranía de Cuenca** *(p290)*
5. The sculptures in the cathedral at **Sigüenza** *(p292)*

Toledo and West

Toledo is the jewel of Castilla-La Mancha. It is surrounded, moat-like, on three sides by the Tajo, with parts of its city wall and gateways still intact, little changed in appearance over the centuries. Until 1560, when the capital moved to Madrid (70km/43.5mi north), the city was the nerve centre of not only Spain but of a burgeoning empire. In the following years it declined rapidly and slid into the political backwaters.

A happy circumstance of this was that "progress" bypassed Toledo, and its old town remained largely untouched. Today it is World Heritage-listed with many very tangible reminders of its multi-faith, multifaceted past. If you're not spoiled by Toledo, the old city part of Talavera de la Reina, famous for the ceramic work which decorate its palaces, mansions and chapels, is well worth a visit. Nearby Oropesa is a charming village, home to a fine parador.
- **Talavera de la Reina**
- **Toledo**

South

The flat landscapes of the south conjure up the archetypal Don Quixote images of La Mancha, captured most perfectly at Consuegra where the castle and line of windmills overlooking the town lack only an aged knight on horseback (plus faithful retainer). Belmonte is another classic La Mancha settlement with a fine 15C fortress. Close to the southern tip of the region, where vast areas are devoted to vineyards, the town of Almagro is home to one of Castile's finest main squares; several of its numerous historic buildings, one of which is now a parador,

The Don Quixote Route

To celebrate the 400th anniversary of the publication of Miguel de Cervantes' famous novel an extensive 2 500km/1 553mi *Ruta Don Quijote* – which is in fact a series of routes – have been created in La Mancha. For further details and to see the routes visit www.donquijotedelamancha2005.com and click on The Don Quixote Route.

Windmills at Consuegra

©Turespaña

carry reminders of its former role as headquarters of the Military Order of the Knights of Calatrava.

- **Albacete**
- **Almagro**
- **Belmonte**

Cuenca (city and province)

This World Heritage city is famous for its *casas colgadas* (hanging houses) which perch precariously on the edge of the cliff. Even without the hanging houses however the old town and superb Museum of Abstract Art would place Cuenca high on most visitors' itineraries. Around the town the Serranía de Cuenca, a limestone plateau pitted with swallow-holes *(torcas)* and cut by gorges *(hoces)* makes for a spectacular and curious touring landscape. Also in Cuenca province is the massive 16C castle-monastery of Uclés.

- **Cuenca**
- **Uclés**

Northeast

For a place of fewer than 6 000 people, charming Sigüenza is remarkable for two imposing buildings set amid its medieval streets. The cathedral would be more at home in a major metropolis and features some outstanding sculptures. The mighty fortress was once a Moorish *alcázar*, then a Christian stronghold, home to most of the Castilian monarchs and capable of housing up to 1 000 soldiers; today it is a parador, welcoming visitors who are happy to leave the beaten track.

Guadalajara is a more prosaic town, but still worth a visit for its late 15C Palace of the Duke of Infantado.

- **Guadalajara**
- **Sigüenza**

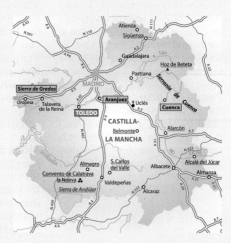

Albacete

Albacete (from *Al Basite*, "plain" in Arabic), capital of Lower La Mancha, stands on a dry plateau that juts into the fertile east. Heritage structures stand alongside modern buildings and residential districts.

SIGHTS
Museo Provincial de Albacete
Parque Abelardo Sánchez. ◔*Open Tue–Sat 9am–2pm, 4.30–7pm, Sun and public holidays 9am–2pm.* ◔*Closed 1 Jan, Maundy Thu, Good Fri, 25 Dec.* ◌*1.20€; no charge Sat–Sun.* ✆*967 22 83 07.*

This modern building is in Abelardo Sánchez Park. Its Fine Arts Museum (Museo de Bellas Artes) collects works of landscape artist Benjamín Palencia (1894–1980). The Joaquín Sánchez Jiménez Archaeology Museum displays Iberian sculptures (Room 6) including the **sphinx of Haches**, the **hind of Caudete**, and the lion from Bienservida, and above all **Roman dolls with movable joints**★ (Room 9).

Catedral de San Juan Bautista
Pl. de la Virgen de los Llanos. ◌*Closed for renovations; call for reopening details.* ✆*967 21 53 42.*

Construction began in the late 16C. The façade and side doorway are additions. Three naves are separated by large Ionic columns. Mannerist paintings decorate the sacristy. The Capilla de la Virgen de los Llanos is a fine chapel dedicated to the Virgin of the Plains, the city's patron. The Renaissance altarpiece is by the Maestro de Albacete.

Pasaje de Lodares
This narrow conservatory passageway, lined by shops and homes, links calle Mayor with calle del Tinte. It is emblematic of Albacete. Decorative columns and allegorical figures proliferate.

▶ **Population:** 166 909
◔ **Michelin Map:** 576 O-P 24 – Castilla-La Mancha (Albacete)
▯ **Info:** Calle Tinte 2, Edificio Posada del Rosario. t967 58 05 22. www.albacete.es.
◑ **Location:** The A 35 and A 30 lead to Valencia (NE) and Murcia (SE); the A 32 runs SW to Andalucía. ▭Calle Ferrocarril
◈ **Don't Miss:** Stroll Pasaje de Lodares for a taste of old Albacete.
◔ **Timing:** Spend a morning, then see caves and castles nearby.

EXCURSIONS
Alarcón★
103km/65mi NW.
◑*Take the A 31 to Honrubia, then turn right onto the A 3. Alarcón, named for Alaric, its Visigothic founder, rises above a loop of the Júcar river.*

The 13C–14C castle is now a parador. The **location**★★★ made the fortress practically impregnable. It follows a triangular plan, with a double protective enclosure. **Don Juan Manuel** (1282–1348) wrote many of his cautionary tales while living there.

Amid the whitewashed façades of Albacete, note the **Iglesia de Santa María** *(Dr Agustín Tortosa)*, a Renaissance church with an elegant Plateresque doorway and a fine sculpted 16C altarpiece. On **Plaza de Don Juan Manuel** are the *ayuntamiento* (town hall), with its porticoed façade, the Iglesia de San Juan Bautista, a Herreran church, and the Casa-Palacio, adorned with attractive grilles.

Alcalá del Júcar★
60km/37.3mi NE along the CM 3218.
The road winds through steep **gorges**. The Júcar river encircles the magnificent **site**★ of the village, between its castle and church overlooking a fertile plain unusual for arid La Mancha. A walk

through Alcalá's maze of steep alleyways reveals attractive views at every turn. Dwellings hollowed out of rock have long corridors leading to cliffside balconies; some can be visited.

Cueva de la Vieja

70km/43.5mi E along the A 35, via Alpera. ⏰*Open Mon–Fri 10am–2pm.* ⬅*2.50€.*

This easily accessible cave retains clearly visible prehistoric paintings. Stylised human silhouettes are shown hunting stags with bows and arrows. Note females in robes and a figure with a plumed headdress.

Almansa

74km/46mi E along the A 35. ▭*Plaza 1º de Mayo.*

Almansa's maze of streets and lanes spreads around a limestone crag crowned by a medieval castle.

Iglesia de la Asunción – *Below the castle.* The church owes its mix of styles to a remodelling. The Renaissance portal is attributed to Vandelvira.

Palacio de los Condes de Cirat *(pl. de Santa María)* – The fine Mannerist-style doorway of this mansion, the **Casa Grande**, bears an escutcheon flanked by crude figures.

Castle *(Castillo;* ⏰*open daily 10am–2pm, 6–8pm (summer), 5–7pm (spring and autumn), 4–6pm (winter);* ⏰*closed public holidays;* ⬅*3€;* ✆*967 31 12 59)* – Stroll

restored 15C ramparts, perched along the rock ridge, commanding a view of the plain. Keystones in the keep *(torre de homenaje)* bear the coat of arms of the Marqués de Villena.

Alcaraz

79km/49mi SW along the A 32.

Alcaraz stands isolated on a red clay rise. The town grew rich manufacturing carpets and retains its Renaissance character in buildings influenced by the great **Andrés de Vandelvira**, born here in 1509.

Plaza Mayor – On the main square are: the 15C Pósito, once a granary; the 16C **ayuntamiento** (town hall) with emblazoned façade; the 17C **Lonja** del Corregidor, standing against the **Torre del Tardón** (clock tower; ✆*967 38 08 27; www.alcutur.org)*; and the 15C **Iglesia de la Trinidad**.

Old houses front the **calle Mayor**. Note a façade with the two warriors and the Plateresque **Puerta de la Aduana** (Customs Doorway) of the Casa Consistorial. Stepped alleys head from the right-hand side of the square.

The path to the cemetery passes under two arches to attractive views of brown rooftops and the countryside.

From Alcaraz you can make a picturesque **excursion** 46km/28.5mi south to the **source of the River Mundo** where there are wooded valleys, springs, caves and falls.

Almagro★

Set in the red earth of La Mancha, Almagro's stone-paved streets and façades with coats of arms recall the Military Order of the Knights of Calatrava. The 16C Convento de San Francisco is now a parador.

A BIT OF HISTORY

The impressive architecture of this charming town, the birthplace of the explorer Diego de Almagro (1475–1538), can be explained by its eventful history. From the 13C until the end of

▶ **Population:** 18 581

⛛ **Michelin Map:** 576 P 18 – Castilla-La Mancha (Ciudad Real)

▯ **Info:** Plaza Mayor 1. ✆926 86 07 17. www.ciudad-almagro.com.

▷ **Location:** Almagro is on the plain south of Madrid. ▭Paseo de la Estación

⊚ **Don't Miss:** A walk through streets frozen in time.

the 15C, Almagro was the stronghold of the Military Order of the Knights of Calatrava and the base from which they administered their possessions. Between 1750 and 1761, the town became the capital of the province as a result of the favours of the Count of Valparaíso, the then Minister of Finance under Ferdinand VI. From the 16C to the 19C, a number of religious orders established convents and monasteries here.

SIGHTS

You will walk along cobbled streets past whitewashed houses and convents and monasteries with fine stone doorways.

Plaza Mayor★★

This long square, one of the most beautiful in Castile, was the scene of bullfights and tournaments. A stone colonnade frames two sides, under two rows of windows with green surrounds.

The 17C **Corral de Comedias★** (pl. Mayor 18; ◷ open daily 27 Oct–Mar 10am–2pm, 4–7pm; Apr–Jun Sept–26 Oct 10am–2pm, 5–8pm; Jul 10am–2pm, 6–9pm; ⊙2.50€, performances 3.50€; ℘926 86 15 39) is the only intact original theatre in Europe. Wooden porticoes, oil lamps, stone well and scenery wall combine in a superb example of popular architecture. Summer performances are part of the annual International Festival of Classical Drama (www. festivaldealmagro.com).

From near the statue of Diego de Almagro, take calle de Nuestra Señora de las Nieves (note fine doorways) to the left, to the triangular plaza Santo Domingo, surrounded by mansions. Turn left into calle de Bernardas, to face the spectacular Baroque doorway of the **Palacio de los Condes de Valparaíso**. Follow calle de Don Federico Relimpio; go left on calle de Don Diego de Almagro, dominated by the 16C **Convento de la Asunción de Calatrava** (◷ open daily 10am–2pm, 4–7pm (winter noon–2pm, 4–6pm); ⊙1.50€; ℘926 86 03 50), with its fine Renaissance staircase.

At the Plaza Mayor, turn right at the end onto calle Gran Maestre and the

Museo Nacional del Teatro

(◷ open Aug–Jun Tue–Fri 10am–2pm, 4–7pm, Sat 11am–2pm, 4–6pm; Jul Tue–Fri 10am–2pm, 6–8pm, Sat 11am–2pm, 6–8pm, Sun and public holidays 11am–2pm; ⊙2.40€; ℘926 26 10 14; http://museoteatro.mcu.es), in an 18C palace, showing old documents, costumes, and models of theatre sets.

EXCURSIONS

Parque Nacional de las Tablas de Daimiel

31km/19mi N by the CM 4107 and N 420. From Daimiel, take a tarmac road to the right (7km/4.5mi).

These wetlands cover 1 928ha/4 764 acres in the heart of dry La Mancha. The tablas are floodplains, where marshes of the Guadiana and Cigüela rivers are a habitat for a huge variety of birds in winter and dry out in summer.

Parque Natural Lagunas de Ruidera

67km/42mi NE.

This park, covering 3 772ha/9 320 acres, comprises 15 lagoons linked by streams, gullies and waterfalls.

San Carlos del Valle★

46km/29mi E.

The 18C **Plaza Mayor★** is charming, with a Baroque church with four lantern turrets. The house at no. 5, a former hospice, retains a stone doorway and typical patio.

Valdepeñas

34km/21mi SE along the CM 412.
🚄 Paseo de la Estación.

This wine centre is at the southern tip of the vast grape-growing area of La Mancha. Blue- and white-coloured houses rise above shady porticoes on plaza de España.

The late Gothic **Iglesia de la Asunción** (Church of the Assumption), has a Plateresque upper gallery. The Ermita de la Veracruz (hermitage; ℘926 33 82 35) is locally venerated.

Visit the cellars of the **Cooperativa La Invencible** (Torrecilla 102; ◷ open Mon–Fri 9am–1pm, 3–7pm by reservation *only; (☏926 32 27 77)*, the largest bodega in the town.

Sacro Castillo y Convento de Calatrava la Nueva★

32km/19.8mi SW. 7km/4.3mi SW of Calzada de Calatrava, turn right onto a paved road (2.5km/1.5mi). ○*Open Oct–Mar Tue–Fri 11am–2pm, 4–6pm, Sat 10am–2pm, 4–6pm, Sun 10am–6pm; Apr–Sept Tue–Fri 11am–2pm, 5.30–8pm, Sat–Sun 10am–2pm,* 5.30–8.30pm. ∞*No charge.* ☏*926 69 31 19.*

This semi-ruined citadel occupies a magnificent **hilltop site** which dominates the route to Andalucía.
The gateway leads into vaulted stables. The second perimeter, built into rock, houses religious buildings, including the impressive **church**, lit by an immense rose window, and brick swallow's nest vaulting, probably the work of Moorish prisoners. Views from the towers include the ruined **Castillo de Salvatierra** .

Belmonte★

Belmonte is classic La Mancha: its whitewashed houses overlooked by an imposing church and castle. It's easy to imagine Don Quixote astride his trusty steed entering the town.

VISIT
Iglesia Colegial de San Bartolomé★

Iglesia. ○ *Open Tue–Sun 11am–2pm, 4–6.30pm (8pm Apr–Sept).* ∞*2€.* ☏*967 17 02 08.*
This 15C collegiate church holds 15C–17C **altarpieces**. **Choir stalls**★ from the cathedral in Cuenca starkly illustrate scenes from Genesis and the Passion.

Castillo★

○┅*Closed for renovation.* ☏*967 17 00 08.*
This 15C fortress with six circular towers was built by the Marqués de Villena, and long abandoned. In 1870 the new owner, Eugenia de Montijo, installed an ugly brick facing in the patio.
The empty rooms hold beautiful Mudéjar **artesonado**★ ceilings – the audience chamber is outstanding – and delicately carved stone window surrounds. Follow the curtain walls to the stepped merlons for views of the village and countryside.

▶ **Population:** 2 274
⚲ **Michelin Map:** 576 N 21 – Castilla-La Mancha (Cuenca)
▯ **Info:** Castillo de Belmonte. ☏967 17 07 41. http://perso.wanadoo.es/belmonte/ofitur.htm.
◕ **Location:** Belmonte is SE of Madrid (157km/98mi NW) in the heart of La Mancha.

EXCURSION
Villaescusa de Haro

6km/3.7mi NE along the N 420.
The magnificent 1507 **Capilla de la Asunción**★ (Chapel of the Assumption) of the parish church boasts, a Gothic-Renaissance altarpiece and a wrought-iron screen with florid Gothic arches.

Consuegra

90km/56mi NE along the N 420.
A row of 11 *molino de vientos* (windmills) stands alongside the 13C castle on a hill overlooking the town, making up the classic picture-postcard image of Don Quixote's La Mancha.
The castle (○*open daily 9am–2pm, 3.30–6pm (4.30–7pm May–Sept);* ∞*4€;* ☏*925 47 57 31)* once belonged to the Knights of St John and some of the rooms have been interpreted according to the time of their tenure.

Cuenca★★

Cuenca's spectacular **setting**★★ is a rocky platform hemmed in by the Júcar and Huécar ravines *(hoces)* in defiance of the laws of gravity. The magnificently preserved old city is on UNESCO's World Heritage List.

⤫ WALKING TOUR
CIUDAD ANTIGUA★★ (OLD TOWN)
2hr30min.

▷ *From the car park, pass through the 16C Renaissance-style Arco del Bezudo, follow San Pedro to the San Pedro church, then turn left onto ronda de Julián Romero.*

Ronda Julián Romero
This delightful stepped alley runs above the Huécar gorge to the cathedral.

Convento de las Carmelitas
This ex-Carmelite convent houses the **Fundación Antonio Pérez** (*see entry*) and Museo Internacional de Electrografía *(camino del Pozuelo;* ⏱*open Mon–Sat 11am–9pm, Sun and public holidays 11am–2pm;* ⊛*No charge;* ☏*969 17 91 15).*

▶ **Population:** 54 600
⚙ **Michelin Map:** 576 L 23 – Castilla-La Mancha (Cuenca)
🅸 **Info:** Alfonso VIII 2. ☏969 24 10 51; Avenida Cruz Roja 1. ☏969 24 10 50. www.cuenca.org.
▷ **Location:** Cuenca lies 164km/102mi E of Madrid in the Montes Universales, on the edge of the central Meseta. 🚍Calle Mariano Catalina
🅿 **Parking:** Follow signs for the *casco antiguo.* Cross plaza Mayor and leave your car in the free car park.
🕭 **Don't Miss:** Hanging houses and vertiginous canyon views.

Catedral de Nuestra Señora de Gracia★
Pl. Mayor. ⏱*Open May–Jun Sat 10.30am–2pm, 4–7pm, Sun 10.30am–2pm, 4–6.30pm; Jul–Sept Mon–Fri 10am–2pm, 4–7pm, Sat 10am–7pm; Oct–Apr daily 10.30am–2pm, 4–6.30pm.*

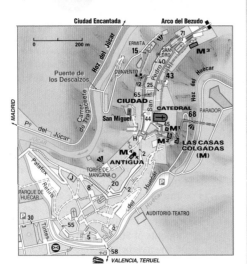

🕐 *Closed 1 Jan, 25 Dec.* 💰*2.80€.*
📞*969 22 46 26.*
The Cathedral was started in the 13C
in Norman-Gothic style. One of two
towers collapsed after an early 20C fire.
The interior, a mix of Gothic architecture
and Renaissance decoration, has superb
wrought-iron chapel **grilles**★, a twin
ambulatory, a **triforium** and an elegant
Plateresque **door**★ into the chapter
house with carved walnut panels by
Alonso Berruguete.

▶ *Walk along the right-hand side of
the Cathedral and take Canónigos.*

This street is lined by the Palacio Episcopal, housing the **Museo Diocesano**★, and the **Museo de Cuenca** (🔆*see
entry*).

Casas Colgadas★ (Hanging Houses)
These restored 14C houses contain
the **Museo de Arte Abstracto** (🔆*see
entry*) and a restaurant. The best **view**★
of these gravity-defying buildings can
be enjoyed from across the **Puente de
San Pablo**, an iron bridge that leads to
the Convento de San Pablo, the city's
parador. This panorama is enchanting
when illuminated.

▶ *Return to the Cathedral and
head along José T Mena.*

Iglesia de San Miguel
Bajada de San Miguel.
🕐 *Open during Holy Week for
performances.* 📞*969 23 21 19.*
This Gothic-style former church is one of
the main venues for Cuenca's Religious
Music Week.

▶ *Return to the Plaza Mayor. Follow
calles Severo Catalina and Pilares.*

Plaza de las Angustias★
An 18C Franciscan monastery and
a Baroque hermitage, the Virgin in
Anguish, stand in this quiet square
between the town and the ravine.

Museo de Arte Abstracto Español
©Turespaña

▶ *Return to San Pedro and continue to
the San Pedro church. Bear left into an
alley which ends at the edge of the Júcar
ravine, for a good view.*

SIGHTS
Museo de Arte Abstracto Español★★
Canónigos s/n. 🕐*Open Tue–Fri and
public holidays 11am–2pm, 4–6pm, Sat
11am–2pm, 4–8pm, Sun 11am–2.30pm.*
🕐*Closed 1 Jan, Maundy Thursday
(afternoon), Good Friday, 18, 21 Sept, 24,
25, 31 Dec.* 💰*3€.* 📞*969 21 29 83.
www.march.es.*
The views from the Museum of Abstract
Spanish Art are veritable works of art
in themselves. The collection includes
works by Chillida, Tàpies, Saura, Zóbel,
Cuixart, Sempere, Rivera and Millares.

Museo de Cuenca★
Obispo Valero 6. 🕐*Open Apr–Oct
Tue–Sat 10am–2pm, 5–7pm, Sun and
public holidays 11am–2pm; Nov–Mar
Tue–Sat 10am–2pm, 4–7pm, Sun and
public holidays 11am–2pm.* 💰*1.20€.
No charge Sat–Sun.* 📞*969 21 30 69.*
This museum displays prehistoric
objects, sculpture, coins and ceramics
found in Roman excavations. Note the
top of a **Roman altar**★ found at Ercávica
illustrating ritual items.

Museo de las Ciencias de Castilla-La Mancha

Pl. de la Merced 1. ⏰*Open year-round Tue–Sat 10am–2pm, 4–8pm (mid-Sept–mid-May 7pm), Sun 10am–2pm; , Sun 10am–2pm.* ⏰*Closed 1 Jan, Maundy Thu, Good Fri, 25 Dec.* 🎫*1.20 €; no charge Sat–Sun, 18, 31 May, 12 Oct.* ☎*969 24 03 20. www.jccm. es/museociencias.*

This lively modern science museum also has a planetarium.

EXCURSIONS
Las Hoces (Ravines)

Roads parallel to the river circling Cuenca's rock spur afford amazing views of the hanging houses. The **Hoz del Júcar** is the shorter, more enclosed ravine. *Round tour of 15km/9.6mi.*

The **Hoz del Huécar** course swings from side to side between gentler slopes given over to market gardening.

▷ *Turn left at the end of the ravine for Buenache de la Sierra and left again for the Convento de San Jerónimo.*

In a right bend, there's a **view**★ of grey rock columns and, in the distance, of Cuenca. Enter through the gateway.

Las Torcas★

▷ *Take the N 420 then bear left after 11km/6.5mi.*

The road crosses a conifer wood where the *torcas*, odd and occasionally spectacular depressions, can be seen.

SERRANÍA DE CUENCA★

270km/168mi – allow 1 day.

Wind and water have formed whimsical landscapes in limestone, amid pines and numerous streams.

Ventano del Diablo

▷ *25.5km/15.8mi from Cuenca along the CM 2105.*

The Devil's Window, an opening in rock, overlooks the depths of the **Garganta del Júcara** (Júcar Gorges).

Ciudad Encantada★

▷ *Follow the road signposted to the right of the CM 2105.*

🚶 A circuit directs visitors through this Enchanted Forest, to the Tobogán (Toboggan Slope) and the Mar de Piedras (Sea of Stones). To reach the **Mirador de Uña** (2km/1mi),

▷ *Take the road from the car park.*

Enjoy the **view** of the Júcar Valley dominated by towering cliffs.

Los Callejones

3km/1.8mi from Las Majadas.
🚗*Leave your car on the esplanade.*

This isolated spot is a maze of eroded blocks, arches and the narrow alleyways which lend their name to the area: The Alleyways.

Nacimiento del río Cuervo★ (Source of the Cuervo)

30km/18.6mi N of Las Majadas towards Alto de la Vega.
🚗*Leave the car after the bridge and walk up 500m/547yd.*

A footpath leads to **waterfalls**★ at the beginnings of the Cuervo river.

Hoz de Beteta★ (Beteta Ravine)

30km/18.6mi NW along the CM 2106 and CM 2201 towards Beteta.

This impressive ravine was cut by the River Guadiela. From Vadillos, a road to the left leads to the spa of Solán de Cabras. The road (CM 210) continues through the **River Escabas valley**. Before reaching Priego *(3km/1.8mi)*, a branch to the right leads to the **Convento de San Miguel de las Victorias**, in an impressive **setting**★.

ADDRESSES

🏠STAY

🛏🛏**Posada Huécar** – *Pas. del Huécar 3.* ☎*969 21 42 01. www.posadahuecar. com. 22 rooms.* 🍴*3€.* Behind the sober, salmon-coloured façade is a pleasant hotel with simply furnished but perfectly adequate rooms, all with TV, and a delightful garden. A good location in the old part of Cuenca.

ℐ/ EAT

⊜⊜ **Mesón Mangana** – *Pl. Mayor 3. ℘969 22 94 51. Closed 15 Oct–15 Nov, Thu.* The perfect spot for a meal when visiting the old quarter. Good home cooking and local specialities, excellent sausages, mature Manchego cheese and grilled meats.

⊜⊜⊜ **Mesón Casas Colgadas** – *Canónigos. ℘969 22 35 09. www.meson-casascolgadas.com. Closed Mon eve, Tue.* A well-known local landmark housed in one of the city's famous hanging houses *(casas colgadas)*, with a stupendous view of the Huécar Ravine. The cuisine fuses modern and traditional.

Guadalajara

Guadalajara ("river of stones" in Arabic) in the 14C became the fief of the **Mendozas**, an illustrious family in Spanish history. It includes the poet Íñigo López de Mendoza, first **Marquis of Santillana** (1398–1458); his son, **Cardinal Pedro González de Mendoza** (1428–95); and the second Duke of Infantado, who built the palace at the north entrance to the town in the 15C.

SIGHTS
Palacio del Infantado★ (Palace of the Duke of Infantado)
Pl. de los Caídos. ◐Open Tue–Sat 10am–2pm, 4–7pm, Sun and public holidays 10am–2pm. ◐Closed 1, 6 Jan, Good Fri, 1 May, 24, 25, 31 Dec. ⊜1.20€. ℘949 21 33 01.

The late 15C palace, by Juan Guas, is a masterpiece of Isabelline civil architecture fusing Gothic and Mudéjar styles. The **façade**★ is adorned with diamond stonework and the Mendoza coat of arms. The upper gallery is a series of paired ogee windows interposed between corbelled loggias.
The effect is splendid in spite of windows added in the 17C.
The two-storey **patio**★ is just as remarkable with multifoil arches on turned columns and extremely delicate Mudéjar ornamentation. The once-sumptuous interior was damaged during the Spanish Civil War.

▶ **Population:** 81 221
◔ **Michelin Map:** 576 K 20 – map 121 Alrededores de Madrid – Castilla-La Mancha (Guadalajara)
▯ **Info:** Plaza de los Caídos 6. ℘949 21 16 26. www.guadalajara.es.
◑ **Location:** Guadalajara is NE of Madrid along the A 2 motorway. ▭Calle Francisco Aritio
◉ **Don't Miss:** The Palacio del Infantado.

Francis I of France, captured at Pavia in 1525, was received here with pomp on his way to imprisonment in Madrid.
The palace houses the **Museo Provincial de Guadalajara** *(◐open Oct–Apr Tue–Sat 10.30am–2pm, 4.15–7pm, Sun and public holidays 10.30am–2pm; May–Sept Tue–Sat 10.30am–2pm; ⊜1.20€, no charge Sat–Sun; ℘949 21 27 73).*

EXCURSION
Pastrana
42km/26mi SE on the N 320.
This picturesque town was the seat of the **Princess of Eboli**, involved in intrigues in the time of Philip II.
The **Palacio Ducal** *(not open to the public)* stands on Plaza de la Hora (Hour Square), so named because a princess confined to the palace was allowed an hour at the window every day.

The 16C **Colegiata** *(Melchor Cano 1;* ⏲ *open Mon–Sat 11.30am–2pm, 4.30–6.30pm, Sun and public holidays 12.45pm–2.30pm, 4.30–6.30pm;* ⊛ *no charge for church; 2.50€ for entry to crypt, church and museum;* ✆ *949 37 00 27),* a collegiate church, contains, in the sacristy, four Gothic **tapestries**★ woven in Tournai after cartoons by Nuno Gonçalves which illustrate the capture of Arzila and Tangier by Alfonso V of Portugal in 1471. They reveal a mastery of composition, love of detail (armour and costume) and talent for portraiture.

Sigüenza★

Sigüenza descends in pink and ochre tiers below a cathedral fortress and castle. The old quarter is a maze of narrow streets lined by Romanesque mansions.

SIGHT
Catedral★★

Serrano Sanz. 🔍 *Guided tours mid-May–mid-Nov Tue–Sun 11am, noon, 1pm, 5pm, 6pm; 16 Nov–14 May Tue–Sun 11am, noon, 4.30pm, 5.30pm.* ⊛ *4€.* ✆ *619 36 27 15.*

The nave, begun in the 12C, was completed in 1495. In the **north aisle**, the **doorway**★ into the Capilla de la Anunciación is decorated with Renaissance pilasters, Mudéjar arabesques and Gothic cusping.

In the **north transept** is a fine **sculptured unit**★★: a 16C **porphyry doorway** opens onto cloisters of marble. The

▶ **Population:** 5 013
🗺 **Michelin Map:** 576 I 22 – Castilla-La Mancha (Guadalajara)
ℹ **Info:** Serrano Sanz 9. ✆ 949 34 70 07. www.siguenza.es.
▶ **Location:** Sigüenza is 128km/75mi NE of Madrid, 22km/14mi from the A 2 road to Zaragoza. 🚆 Calle Alfonso VI

sacristy ceiling★ by Covarrubias is a profusion of heads and roses between which peer thousands of cherubim.

The **chancel** *(presbiterio)* has a beautiful 17C wrought-iron grille framed by alabaster **pulpits**★. The **Doncel tomb**★★, in the south transept features a realistic figure of a youth which is a major work of sepulchral art.

Talavera de la Reina

Talavera is synonymous with the *azulejos* (ceramic tiles) which brought it fame and prosperity. On the right bank of the Tajo, spanned by a 15C bridge, it retains part of its medieval walls and Mudéjar churches.

SIGHT
Basílica de Nuestra Señora del Prado (Basilica of the Prado Virgin)

Jardines del Prado 6. ⏲ *Open daily 7am–2pm, 5–10pm (4–9pm during summer).*

▶ **Population:** 87 763
🗺 **Michelin Map:** 576 M 15 – Castilla-La Mancha (Toledo)
ℹ **Info:** Calle Palenque 2. ✆ 925 82 63 22. www.talavera.org.
▶ **Location:** Talavera is on the A 5 highway linking Madrid (120km/74mi NE) and Badajoz. 🚆 Paseo de la Estación

The church, virtually an *azulejos* museum, gives a good idea of the evolution of the local style.

Talavera Ceramics

Since the 15C, the name Talavera has been associated with **ceramic tiles** with blue and yellow designs used to decorate the palaces, mansions and chapels. Visit the **Museo de Cerámica Ruiz de Luna** (pl. de San Agustín; ℘925 80 01 49) to see ceramics dating from the 15C to modern times. Talavera now manufactures decorative crockery and green items are made in **El Puente del Arzobispo**, a village (34km/21mi SW) specialising in pottery drinking jars.

EXCURSION
Oropesa
32km/20mi W.
This delightful hilltop village is crowned by its **castle**★ originally built in 1366 but rebuilt in 1402. Part of it is open as a visitor attraction (pl. del Palacio 1; open Fri–Sat 10am–2pm, 4–6pm, Sun and public holidays 11am–2pm, 4–6pm; ✎2€; ℘925 45 00 06) while most of it now serves as a parador. It enjoys far-reaching views across to the Sierra de Gredos.

Toledo★★★

Golden Toledo rises dramatically on a granite eminence encircled by a steep ravine of the Tajo (Tagus). It is as spectacular in setting as it is rich in history, buildings and art. Every corner has a tale to tell, every aspect reflects a brilliant fusion of east and west, of Christian, Jewish and Moorish cultures during the Middle Ages.

THE CITY TODAY
In peak visitor season Toledo can resemble something of a medieval theme park with large groups of visitors on day trips from Madrid clogging up its narrow streets. In shop windows in the main streets are garish displays of Toledan steel, once the deadliest weaponry in the world, wielded by Spanish heroes from El Cid to the Conquistadores. Nowadays it is marketed as the "official" arms of *Lord of the Rings* or *Conan the Barbarian*.

If you are visiting in peak season try to stay the night and do your exploration early (before the groups arrive) and late (after they have gone). Don't expect much nightlife as Toledo after dark is a fairly staid place.

▶ **Population:** 80 810
⬡ **Michelin Map:** 576 M 17 (town plan) – map 121 Alrededores de Madrid – Castilla-La Mancha (Toledo)
▤ **Info:** Puerta de Bisagra. ℘925 22 08 43; Plaza del Ayuntamiento 1, ℘925 25 40 30. www.toledo-turismo.com.
▷ **Location:** Toledo is 71km/44mi SW of Madrid.
▣ **Parking:** Try to park below the centre of the city, and walk or take a taxi up.
⬤ **Don't Miss:** El Greco's masterpiece, *The Burial of the Count of Orgaz.*
◔ **Timing:** Monumental Toledo is compact. Walk around for an overview, then return for a visit to the sites of most interest.

A BIT OF HISTORY
Roman town to Holy Roman city – The Romans fortified the strategic settlement into a town they named Toletum. It passed into the hands of the barbarians, and in the 6C to the Visigoths, who made it a royal seat until they were defeated

by the Moors at Guadelete in 711. After the revolt of the taifas in 1012, Toledo was capital of an independent kingdom. In 1085 it was conquered by Alfonso VI, who soon moved his capital from León. Alfonso VII was crowned emperor in Toledo, hence the title of imperial city. The city of Moors, Jews and Christians began to prosper.

The Catholic Monarchs gave it the Monastery of St John but lost interest after they reconquered Granada in 1492. Emperor Charles V had the Alcázar rebuilt. In his reign the city took part in the Comuneros' Revolt led by **Juan de Padilla**, a Toledan.

After 1561 when Philip II named Madrid as Spain's capital, Toledo was relegated to the role of spiritual centre.

Toledo and the Visigoths – By 554 the Visigoths had made Toledo their capital. Christianity was adopted in 589. Toledo was abandoned to the Moors amid internal strife in 711.

Toledo and the Jews – In the 12C the Jewish community numbered 12 000.**Saint Ferdinand III** (1217–1252) encouraged diversity which brought about a cultural flowering, and the city developed into a great intellectual forum. **Alfonso X the Wise** (1252–1284) gathered a court of learned Jews and established the *School of Translation*. In 1355 a pogrom was instigated by supporters of Henry IV of Trastamara. After repeated attacks, the Jews were expelled in 1492.

Mudéjar art in Toledo – The Mudéjar style established itself in Toledo after the Reconquest of the city, in palaces (Taller del Moro), synagogues (El Tránsito, Santa María la Blanca) and churches. Brick was widely used. Moorish stuccowork, *artesonado* and *azulejos* became commonplace. In the 13C and 14C, most Toledan churches were given Romanesque semicircular **east ends**, blind arcades took on variations unknown elsewhere, and **belfries** were built square and decorated until they resembled minarets. The edifices often have a nave and two aisles – a Visigothic influence – Roman tripartite apses and Moorish wood vaulting.

SIGHTS
Catedral★★★

Pl. del Ayuntamiento. ⏰*Open Tue–Sat 10am–6.30pm, Sun and public holidays 2–6pm.* ✎*7€.* ✆ *925 22 22 41. www. architoledo.org/catedral.*

The Cathedral dominates the **Plaza del Ayuntamiento**. Construction began in the reign of Ferdinand III (St Ferdinand) in 1227. Unusually, the design was French Gothic, but as building continued until the end of the 15C, its architecture came to reflect Spanish Gothic. Despite additions, the church is outstanding for its sculptured decoration and works of religious art.

Exterior

The **Puerta del Reloj** (Clock Doorway), in the north wall, from the 13C, was modified in the 19C.

The **main façade** is pierced by three tall 15C portals; the upper registers were completed in the 16C and 17C. The central **Puerta del Perdón** (Pardon Doorway) is crowded with statues and crowned with a tympanum illustrating the Virgin Mary presenting the 7C bishop of Toledo with a chasuble.

The harmonious tower is 15C; the dome was designed by El Greco's son in the 17C. In the south wall is the 15C **Puerta de los Leones** (Lion Doorway) designed by Master Hanequin of Brussels and decorated by Juan Alemán. The neo-Classical portal is from 1800.

▷ *Enter through the Puerta del Mollete, left of the west front.*

Interior

The size and sturdy character of the cathedral, with five unequal aisles and great pillars, are striking. Wonderful stained glass (1418–1561) colours the windows; magnificent wrought-iron grilles enclose the chancel, *coro* and chapels.

Capilla Mayor

The chancel, the most sumptuous section, was enlarged in the 16C.

The immense polychrome **retable**★★, carved in detail in Flamboyant style with

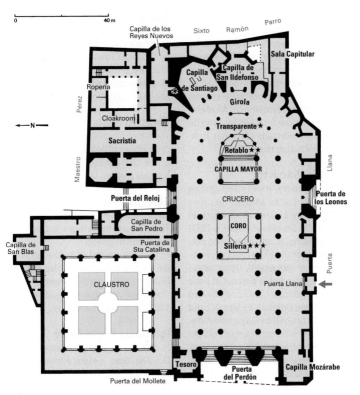

0   40 m

Capilla de los Reyes Nuevos — Sixto — Ramón — Parro

Pérez

Roperia

Cloakroom

Maestro

Sacristía

Puerta del Reloj

Capilla de San Pedro

Capilla de San Blas

Puerta de Sta Catalina

CLAUSTRO

Puerta del Mollete

Tesoro

Puerta del Perdón

Plaza del Ayuntamiento

Capilla de Santiago

Capilla de San Ildefonso

Sala Capitular

Girola

Transparente ★

Retablo ★★

CAPILLA MAYOR

CRUCERO

Puerta de los Leones

Llana

CORO

Silleria ★★★

Puerta Llana

Puerta

Capilla Mozárabe

← N →

the Life of Christ, is awe-inspiring. The silver statue of the Virgin at the predella dates from 1418. The Plateresque marble tomb of Cardinal Mendoza on the left is by Covarrubias.

Coro

14C high reliefs and wrought-iron enclosed chapels form the perimeter of the choir, itself closed by an elegant iron screen (1547). The lower parts of the 15C and 16C **choir stalls**★★★ were carved by Rodrigo Alemán to recall the conquest of Granada; the alabaster 16C upper parts, by Berruguete *(left)* and Felipe Vigarny *(right)* portray Old Testament figures. The central low relief, the Transfiguration, is also by Berruguete. The style of his work creates the impression of movement. Two organs and a Gothic eagle lectern complete the set. The 14C marble *White Virgin* is French.

Girola

The double ambulatory, surmounted by an elegant triforium with multifoil arches, is bordered by seven apsidal chapels separated by small square chapels. The vaulting is a geometrical wonder.

There is little room to step back for a good look at the **Transparente**★, the contentious but famous work by Narciso Tomé which forms a Baroque island in the Gothic church.

Illuminated through an opening in the ambulatory roof (made to allow light to fall on the tabernacle), the *Transparente* appears as an ornamental framework of angels and swirling clouds and rays surrounding the Virgin and the Last Supper. In the **Capilla de San Ildefonso** (Chapel of San Ildefonso), the central tomb of Cardinal Gil de Albornoz (14C) is the most notable.

Sala Capitular (Chapter House)

The antechamber has an impressive Mudéjar ceiling and two Plateresque carved walnut wardrobes. Remarkable Mudéjar stucco doorways and carved Plateresque panels precede the chapter house with its multicoloured **Mudéjar ceiling**★. Below frescoes by Juan de Borgoña are portraits of former archbishops including two by Goya.

Sacristía (Sacristy)

The first gallery, its vaulted ceiling painted by Lucas Jordán, includes **paintings by El Greco**★ of which **El Expolio** (*The Disrobing of Christ*, c. 1577) is outstanding. It sets an exalted personality against swirling robes to establish Baroque movement. Other works include a remarkable portrait of *Pope Paul III* by Titian, a *Holy Family* by Van Dyck, a *Mater Dolorosa* by Morales and the *Taking of Christ* by Goya, which displays his skill in composition, use of light and in portraying individuals in a crowd. Pedro de Mena's (17C) famous sculpture, *St Francis of Assisi*, is in a glass case. In the vestry are portraits by Velázquez *(Cardinal Borja)*, Van Dyck *(Pope Innocent XI)* and Ribera.

The old laundry *(ropería)* contains liturgical objects dating back to the 15C. The **Nuevas Salas del Museo Catedralicio** (Cathedral Museum's New Galleries; *c/ Cardenal Cisneros;* ⏲ *open Mon–Sat 10.30am–6.30pm, Sun and public holidays 2–6.30pm;* ⏲ *closed 1 Jan, Corpus Christi, 15 Aug, 25 Dec;* ◉*4.95€*) displays works by Caravaggio, El Greco, Bellini and Morales.

Tesoro (Treasury)

A Plateresque doorway by Covarrubias opens into the chapel under the tower. Beneath a Mudéjar ceiling note the splendid 16C silver-gilt **monstrance**★★ by Enrique de Arfe, weighing 180kg/392lb and 3m/10ft high, paraded at Corpus Christi. The pyx at its centre is fashioned from gold brought by Christopher Columbus.

Capilla Mozárabe (Mozarabic Chapel)

The chapel beneath the dome was built by Cardinal Cisneros (16C) to celebrate Mass according to the Visigothic or Mozarabic ritual which had been threatened with abolition in the 11C.

Claustro (Cloisters)

The simplicity of the 14C lower gallery contrasts with the bold murals by Bayeu of the Lives of Toledan Saints (Santa Eugenia and San Ildefonso).

CENTRE OF OLD TOLEDO★★★

Allow 1 day – see town plan.

There is something to see and enjoy at every step in Toledo.

Ringing the square before the Cathedral are the 18C **Palacio Arzobispal** (Archbishop's Palace), the 17C **Ayuntamiento** (Town Hall) with classical façade and the 14C **Audiencia** (Law Courts).

Iglesia de Santo Tomé

Pl. del Conde. ⏲ *Open daily mid-Oct–Feb 10am–5.45pm; Mar–mid-Oct 10am–6.45pm.* ◉*1.90€; no charge Wed from 4pm.* ☎*925 25 60 98.* *www.santotome.org.*

The church, like that of San Román, has a distinctive 14C Mudéjar tower. Inside is El Greco's famous painting **The Burial of the Count of Orgaz**★★★ executed in about 1586. The interment is transformed by the miraculous appearance of St Augustine and St Stephen. Figures in the lower register are portraits of acquaintances of the painter; the sixth from the left is said to be El Greco. Above, Christ prepares to receive the soul of the count.

Casa-Museo de El Greco★ (El Greco Museum)

Samuel Leví.

⊶ *Closed for renovations.* ☎*925 22 40 46. www.toledo-turismo.com.*

In 1585, El Greco moved into a house similar to this one. In what would have been the artist's workroom is a signed *St Francis and Brother León.*

On the first floor are an interesting *View and Plan of Toledo* and the complete

Old Toledo and the Alcázar ©Turespaña

series of individual portraits of the Apostles and Christ (later and more mature than those in the cathedral).

The **capilla** on the ground floor, with a multicoloured Mudéjar ceiling, has a picture in the altarpiece of *St Bernardino of Siena* by El Greco.

Sinagoga del Tránsito★★

Samuel Leví. ◑ *Open Tue–Sat 10am–2pm, 4–9pm, Sun and public holidays 10am–2pm.* ◑ *Closed 1 Jan, 24, 25, 31 Dec.* ◉*2.40€.* ℘*925 22 36 65.*

Of the ten synagogues that once stood in the Jewish quarter (Judería), only this and Santa María la Blanca remain. It was financed in the 14C by Samuel Ha-Levi, treasurer to King Peter the Cruel. In 1492 it was converted into a church.

Unpretentious outside, it is covered inside with amazing **Mudéjar decoration★★**.

Above the rectangular hall is an *artesonado* ceiling of cedarwood; just below are 54 multifoil arches, some blind, others pierced with delicate stone tracery. Below again runs a frieze, decorated at the east end with *mocárabes* and on the walls with inscriptions in Hebrew to the glory of Peter the Cruel, Samuel Ha-Levi and the God of Israel. In the east wall, inscriptions describe the synagogue's foundation. The women's balcony opens from the south wall.

The adjoining rooms, once a Calatrava monastery, are the **Museo Sefardí** (*Sephardic Museum;* ◑*open Mar–Nov Tue–Sat 10am–2pm, 4–9pm; Dec–Feb*

Tue–Sat 10am–2pm, 4–6pm, Sun and public holidays 10am–2pm; ◑*closed 1 Jan, 1 May, Corpus Christi, 24, 25, 31 Dec;* ◉*2.40€, no charge Sat afternoons, Sun mornings, 18 May, 12 Oct, 6 Dec*) displaying tombs, robes, costumes and books. Several are gifts from descendants of Jews expelled in 1492.

Sinagoga de Santa María La Blanca★

Reyes Católicos 4. ◑ *Open daily 10am–6pm.* ◑ *Closed 1 Jan, 25 Dec.* ◉*1.90€.* ℘*925 22 72 57.*

This was the principal synagogue in Toledo in the late 12C. In 1405 it was given to the Knights of Calatrava as a church. Subsequent modifications incredibly left the Almohad-style nave untouched with five tiered aisles separated by octagonal pillars supporting horseshoe-shaped arches. The whitewashed pillars set off intricately carved **capitals★** adorned with pine cones and strapwork. The polychrome wood altarpiece is 16C.

Monasterio de San Juan de los Reyes★ (St John of the Kings Monastery)

Reyes Católicos 17. ◑ *Open daily Apr–Oct 10am–7pm; Nov–Mar 10am–6pm.* ◉*1.90€; free for EU citizens, and Wed 3.30–5.45pm.* ℘*925 22 38 02.*

The Franciscan monastery commemorates the victory over the Portuguese at Toro in 1476. The overall style is Isabelline, which fuses Flamboyant Gothic

TOLEDO STREET INDEX

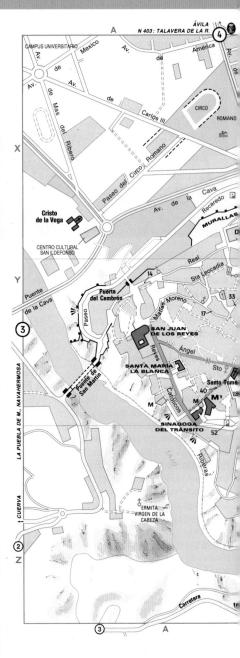

SIGHTS ON MAP

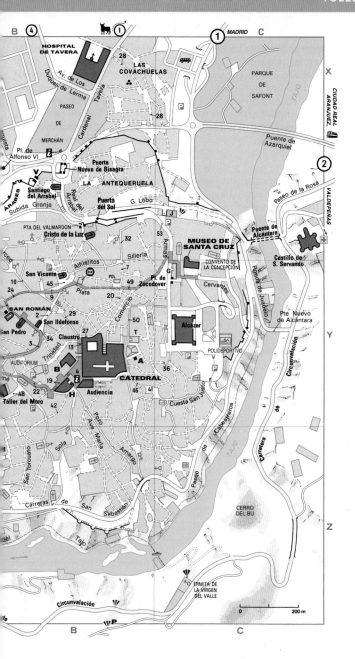

Iglesia de San Román	BY	Murallas Árabes	ABX	Puerta del Cambrón	AY
Iglesia de San Vicente	BY	Museo de Santa Cruz	CXY	Puerta del Sol	BX
Iglesia de Santiago		Palacio Arzobispal	BY	B	Puerta Nueva de Bisagra	BX
del Arrabal	BX	Parador	BZ	P	Santa María la Blanca	AY
Iglesia de Santo Tomé	AY	Portada de S. Clemente	BY	K	Sinagoga del Tránsito	AYZ
Monasterio de San		Posada de la Hermandad	BY	A	Taller del Moro	BY
Juan de los Reyes	AY	Puerta Antigua de Bisagra	BX	V		

with Mudéjar and Renaissance art. The exterior is somewhat austere, relieved by pinnacles and a stone balustrade. Covarrubias designed the north portal, including in the decoration the figure of John the Baptist. The fetters depicted were taken from Christian prisoners freed from the Muslims.

Claustro

The cloisters are attractive with Flamboyant bays and the Plateresque upper galleries (1504) crowned with a pinnacled balustrade. The upper gallery has Mudéjar *artesonado* vaulting.

Iglesia

The church, burned by the French in 1808, has a typically Isabelline single wide aisle; at the crossing are a dome and a lantern. The **sculptured decoration**★ by Flemish architect Juan Guas provides a delicate stone tracery *(crestería)* which at the transept forms twin tribunes for Ferdinand and Isabel. The transept walls are faced with a frieze of royal escutcheons, supported by an eagle, symbol of St John.

Not far away are a Visigothic palace and the **Puerta del Cambrón** (hawthorn gateway; *pas. de Recaredo*), once part of the town perimeter, rebuilt in the 16C.

> ◗ *Turn left out of Santo Tomé onto the Travesía de Campana alley.*

Cross the small plaza del Padre Mariana past the monumental Baroque façade of the **Iglesia de San Ildefonso** and that of the **Iglesia de San Pedro**.

Iglesia de San Román: Museo de los Concilios y de la Cultura Visigoda★ (Museum of the Councils of Toledo and Visigothic Culture)

San Román. ◷*Open Tue–Sat 10am–1.45pm, 3.30–6pm, Sun and public holidays 10am–1.45pm.* ◷*Closed 1 Jan, 1 May, 25 Dec.* ◷*0.60€.* ◢*925 22 78 72.*
The 13C Mudéjar church, at the summit of Toledo, has a tower resembling Santo Tomé's. Aisles are divided by horseshoe arches. The walls are covered in 13C

frescoes of the raising of the dead, the Evangelists and, on the far wall, one of the Councils of Toledo. The apse was modified in the 16C with a cupola by Covarrubias. Note the 18C **altarpiece**. The collections include fine bronze jewellery and copies of votive crowns decorated with cabochon stones from Guarrazar (originals in the Museo Arqueológico, Madrid). On the walls are steles, fragments from capitals, balustrades from the choir and pilasters.

In Plaza de San Vicente, note the Mudéjar east end of the **Iglesia de San Vicente**. Continue up calle de la Plata with its houses with carved entrances.

Plaza de Zocodover

This bustling triangular square is the heart of Toledo. It was rebuilt after the Civil War as was the Arco de la Sangre (Arch of Blood), which opens onto calle de Cervantes.

Museo de Santa Cruz★★ (Santa Cruz Museum)

Miguel de Cervantes 3. ◷ *Open Mon 10am–2pm, 4–6.30pm, Tue–Sat 10am–6.30pm, Sun and public holidays 10am–2pm.* ◷*No charge.* ◢*925 22 14 02.*
This fine group of Plateresque hospital buildings was begun by Enrique Egas and completed by Covarrubias, who was responsible for the **façade**★★. On the gateway tympanum Cardinal Mendoza, the hospital's sponsor, kneels before the Cross supported by St Helena, St Peter, St Paul and two pages; on the arches are the cardinal virtues. Above, two windows frame a high relief of St Joachim and St Anne.

The museum is known for its **16C and 17C pictures**★ including 18 paintings by **El Greco**★. The size of the nave and transept – forming a two-tiered Greek cross – and the beautiful coffered ceilings are outstanding.

Ground floor

The first part of the nave contains 16C Flemish tapestries, **primitive paintings**★, and the *Astrolabios* or *Zodiac* tapestry, woven in Flanders in the mid-15C for Toledo cathedral, still strikingly original. Note, in the south transept, the *Ascension* and the *Presentation of Mary in the Temple* by the Maestro de Sijena. In the second part of the nave hangs the immense pennant flown by Don Juan of Austria at the Battle of Lepanto. The north transept contains a *Christ at the Column* by Morales.

First floor
A staircase leads to the upper gallery of the north transept with **paintings by El Greco**★. There are gentle portraits of the Virgin and St Veronica as well as a version of the *Expolio*, later than the original in the cathedral. Most famous is the late **Altarpiece of the Assumption**★, from 1613. The figures are notably elongated, the colours rasping.

The south transept contains a *Holy Family at Nazareth* by Ribera, the specialist in tenebrism who here showed himself a master of light and delicacy.

In the first part of the nave are 16C Brussels tapestries showing the life of Alexander the Great; and 17C statues from the studio of Pascual de Mena.

The **Plateresque patio**★ has bays with elegant lines complemented by the openwork balustrade and enhanced by Mudéjar vaulting and by the magnificent **staircase**★ by Covarrubias. Adjoining rooms house a museum of archaeology and decorative arts.

WITHIN THE CITY WALLS
Alcázar
Cuesta de Carlos V 2.
⊶*Closed for restoration.* ℘*925 22 16 73. www.toledo-turismo.com.*
The Alcázar, destroyed and rebuilt so many times, massively dominates all else. Emperor Charles V converted the 13C fortress, of which El Cid had been the first governor, into an imperial residence. The work was entrusted to Covarrubias (1538–1551) and then Herrera, who designed the austere south front. The siege and shelling for eight weeks in 1936 left the fortress in ruins. The Falangist commander allowed his son to be shot rather than surrender.
The Alcázar is restored to its appearance at the time of Charles V – an innovation

is the *Victory Monument* by Ávalos in the forecourt. Inside are underground galleries where families sheltered in the 1936 siege.

Weapons and uniforms are displayed in museum rooms off the patio.

Posada de la Hermandad (House of the Brotherhood)
Hermandad 6.
This 15C building was once a prison.

Puerta del Sol
Carretas.
The Sun Gate in the second perimeter, rebuilt in the 14C, is a fine Mudéjar construction with two circumscribing horseshoe arches. At the centre a later low relief shows the Virgin presenting San Ildefonso with a chasuble. At the top, the brick decoration of blind arcading incorporates an unusual sculpture of two girls bearing the head of the chief *alguacil* (officer of justice), allegedly a rapist, on a salver.

Cristo de la Luz (Christ of the Light)
Cristo de la Luz. ◐ *Open 15 Aug–31 Jul Sat–Sun 10am–2pm, 3–8pm. Times subject to excavation works.* ⊙*2.30€.* ℘*925 25 41 91.*
This 12C Mudéjar church succeeded a mosque which in turn replaced a Visigothic church. It is named for the miraculous appearance in a mosque of a lamp illuminating a Crucifix when Alfonso VI first entered Toledo. Arches of different periods, intersecting blind arcades, and a line of horizontal brickwork surmounted by Cufic characters make up the façade. Inside, Visigothic pillars support superimposed arches like those in the mosque in Córdoba. Nine domes, each different, rise from square bays.
The gardens lead to the Puerta del Sol. Enjoy the panorama from the top.

Iglesia de Santiago del Arrabal (St James on the Outskirts)
Real del Arrabal. ⊶*Closed to the public.* ℘*925 22 06 36.*

San Vicente Ferrer is said to have preached from the Gothic Mudéjar pulpit of this beautifully restored church.

Puerta Nueva de Bisagra (New Bisagra Gate)

Puerta de Bisagra.
The gate was rebuilt by Covarrubias in 1550 and enlarged under Philip II. Massive round crenellated towers, facing the Madrid road, flank a giant imperial crest.

Puerta Antigua de Bisagra (Old Bisagra Gate)

Pas. Recaredo.
Alfonso VI entered Toledo in triumph through this Moorish gate in 1085.

Museo Taller del Moro

Taller del Moro. ◷ *Open Tue–Sat 10am–2pm, 4–6.30pm, Sun and public holidays 10am–2pm.* ⊗*No charge.* ℘*925 22 71 15.*
This workshop *(taller)*, a building yard for the cathedral, is an old palace. Mudéjar decoration can still be seen in rooms lit by small openwork windows.

BEYOND THE WALLS
Hospital de Tavera★

Duque de Lerma 2. ◷ *Open Mon–Sat 10am–2.30pm, 3–6.30pm, Sun 10am–2.30pm.* ⬙*Guided tours every 45 min from 10.15am.* ⊗*2.50€; 4€ with museum.* ℘*925 22 04 51.*
The hospital was begun by Bustamante in 1541 and completed by González de Lara and the Vergaras in the 17C. After the Civil War, the Duchess of Lerma rearranged her **apartments**★ in 17C style. These hold valuable paintings.
In the vast library, the hospital archives contain volumes bound in leather by Moorish craftsmen. El Greco's *Holy Family* is arresting, the portrait of the Virgin perhaps the most beautiful by the artist. Note also the *Birth of the Messiah* by Tintoretto, the *Philosopher* by Ribera and, in an adjoining room, his strange portrait of the *Bearded Woman*.
On the first floor, in the reception hall, is El Greco's sombre portrait of *Cardinal Tavera*, painted from a death mask.

Beside it are *Samson and Delilah* (Caravaggio) and two portraits of the *Duke and Duchess of Navas* (Antonio Moro).
A gallery leads to the **church** from the twin patio. The Carrara marble portal is by Alonso Berruguete, who also carved the tomb of Cardinal Tavera. The retable at the high altar was designed by El Greco, whose last work, a **Baptism of Christ**★, is displayed. The artist's use of brilliant colours and elongated figures is at its most magnificent.
The hospital pharmacy, facing the patio, has been restored.

Puente de Alcántara

At the ends of the 13C bridge are a Mudéjar tower and a Baroque arch *(east).* Across the Tajo, behind ramparts, is the restored 14C **Castillo de San Servando** (castle*; now a youth hostel;* ℘*925 22 45 54*). A plaque on the town wall by the bridge recalls how **St John of the Cross** (1542–1591) escaped through a window from his monastery prison nearby.

Puente de San Martín

The medieval bridge, rebuilt in the 14C, is marked at its south end by an octagonal tower; the north end is 16C.

Cristo de la Vega

Travesía Cristo de la Vega.
The Church of Christ of the Vega, formerly St Leocadia, stands on the site of a 7C Visigothic temple, the venue of early church councils. Although modified in the 18C, it retains a fine Mudéjar apse. A modern Crucifix replaces one which figures in many legends.

VIEWPOINTS

The city's incomparable **site**★★★ can be appreciated from the *Carretera de Circunvalación*, a ring-road which parallels the loop of the Tajo from the Puente de Alcántara (Alcántara Bridge) to the Puente de San Martín. For truly memorable views, it is worth going to the **viewpoints** among olive groves on the surrounding hills.
The terrace of the parador, above the *carretera de circunvalación*, is a superb vantage point.

ADDRESSES

STAY

⊖⊜ **Hotel La Almazara** – 3.5km/2mi SW along the Cuerva road. ✆925 22 38 66. www.hotelalmazara.com. 28 rooms. ☞5€. Closed 10 Dec–30 Mar. This former cardinal's residence, its walls clad with ivy, is reached via a lane planted with olive trees. Bedrooms are spacious and bright.

⊖⊜⊜⊜ **Hostal del Cardenal** – Pas. Recaredo 24. ✆925 22 49 00. www.hostaldelcardenal.com. 27 rooms. ☞8.42€. This charming hotel, half-hidden in a delightful garden, stands at the foot of the city walls. Behind the splendid stone façade, the rooms are elegantly decorated with wood furnishings and antiques. The restaurant is superb.

EAT

⊖⊜ **La Abadía** – Nuñez de Arce 3 (pl. de San Nicolás). ✆925 25 11 40. www.abadiatoledo.com. Complex lighting and modern furniture in the basement of a 16C palace create a highly original overall effect and a pleasant backdrop to creative cuisine. Not for the claustrophobic.

⊖⊜⊜ **Casón de los López de Toledo** – Sillería 3. ✆925 25 47 74. www.cason toledo.com. Closed Sun evenings. Time has stood still in this stone mansion built around a patio. A delightful setting for highly original cuisine.

SHOPPING

Toledo is renowned for **damascene ware** (black steel inlaid with gold, silver and copper thread) .

FESTIVALS

Toledo's **Corpus Christi** procession is one of the largest in Spain (www. corpuschristitoledo.es).

Uclés

The massive Monasterio d'Uclés was the seat of the Order of Santiago from 1174 to 1499).

SIGHT
Monasterio d'Uclés
◷Open daily 10am–8pm. ◷Closed 1 Jan, 25 Dec. ⊜3€.
This massive castle-like monastery was begun in 1529 in Plateresque style; most of the work was undertaken by Herrera's disciple, **Francisco de Mora** (1553–1610), hence its nickname, the Little Escorial. The entrance is via a beautiful Baroque **portal**★★. Note the Baroque well and the magnificent **artesonado**★ ceiling in the refectory. The ramparts command a fine view.

EXCURSION
Roman Segóbriga
In Saelices, 14km/8.7mi S of Uclés. Leave the A 3 at exit 103/104 and follow signs towards Casas de Luján.

▸ **Population:** 259
Michelin Map: 576 M 21 – Castilla-La Mancha (Cuenca)
Info: Calle Castillo. ✆969 13 50 58. www. monasteriodeucles.com.
Location: Uclés in the province of Cuenca, SE of Madrid.

The **museum** (ctra de Saelices a Villamayor de Santiago; ◷open Tue–Sun Apr–Sept 10am–9pm; Oct–Mar 10am–6pm; ⊜4€, no charge 18, 31 May, 12 Oct, 6 Dec) in **Saelices** provides an overview of the 5C BC Celtiberian site which became an important Roman crossroads town. By the 1C AD, it had a theatre and an imposing **amphitheatre**★, with a capacity for 5 000 spectators. Parts of the baths and walls also remain.

CATALUNYA AND ANDORRA

Geographically Catalunya is a triangle of varied landscapes, from snow-topped peaks to sun-kissed beaches, set between the French border, Aragón and the Mediterranean. Culturally Catalunya is a nation unto itself. It has its own language, its own flag, its own proud history and traditions, and icons in art (Dalí) architecture (Gaudí) and football (FC Barcelona). Catalunya is also an industrial region with manufacturing and processing centred around Barcelona and Tarragona. Barcelona has been the shop window and public face of Catalunya since the hugely successful Olympics of 1992. However as early as the 1950s north European visitors were flocking to the Costa Brava; they still come here in large numbers, as they do further south to the Costa Dorada. The Pyrenees and Andorra welcome mostly domestic and cross-border visitors – skiers and walkers.

Highlights

1 The roof terrace of Gaudí's **La Pedrera/Casa Milà** (p309)
2 Tarragona's atmospheric **Medieval Quarter** and **Cathedral** (p362)
3 Admiring the inimitable artworks at the **Teatre-Museu Dalí** (p337)
4 Walking the hermitage trails in the **Sierra de Montserrat** (p327)
5 Getting away from it all in the **Ebro Delta** wetlands (p364)

The Mountains

The Pyrenees, between Andorra and the Cap de Creus headland, is a green wooded area with peaks over 3 100m/10 170ft high.

This is wonderful walking territory, dotted with delightful villages and Romanesque churches and a smattering of ski resorts and other adventure sports opportunities.

The waymarked walking trails of the Parc d'Aigüestortes i Estany de Sant Maurici are particularly good. Andorra is famous for its duty-free shopping but excels in its skiing and walking opportunities; the spectacular Port d'Envalira pass, the highest in the Pyrenees, is well worth the trip.

- **Andorra**
- **Parc d'Aigüestortes i Estany de Sant Maurici**
- **Pirineos Catalanes**
- **Solsona**

Barcelona and Montserrat

Spain's favourite visitors' city shows no signs of flagging in the popularity stakes. It really is one of the few metropolises in the world that is all things to all people: atmospheric cobbled streets; medieval and Modernist masterpieces; world-class art galleries and museums; colourful street theatre; beaches and buzzing restaurants, bars and nightlife. If it all gets a little too much, the serene atmosphere and breathtaking setting of Montserrat is the antidote.

- **Barcelona**
- **Montserrat**

Costa Brava and Inland

The Costa Brava was "discovered" and made fashionable by artists such as Dalí, Picasso and Marc Chagall, and was in the vanguard of Spain's plunge into mass-market tourism. Fortunately, it has, with a few ugly exceptions (most notably Lloret de Mar), remained true to its name, meaning "wild or rugged coast", and is still the most beautiful of Spain's holiday costas. Beaches range from rocky coves to long soft golden sands and the rugged coastline, softened by greenery, is rarely less than interesting.

The international gateway to the coast is Girona, a typical Catalunyan city with real character and history and many of the features of a "mini-Barcelona". Figueres, the spiritual home of Salvador Dalí, is likely to delight even the most doubtful art sceptics.

- **Costa Brava**
- **Figueres**
- **Girona/Gerona**
- **Vic**

Congost de Collegats, Pirineos Catalanes

B. Brillion/MICHELIN

Costa Dorada and inland

The Costa Dorada takes its name from the long golden *(daurada)* beaches that begin south at the Ebro Delta and stretch almost as far as Sitges.

With the exception of Salou and Sitges, the resorts here are mostly low key and (aside from Salou) geared to Spanish holidaymakers.

Sitges is by far the most attractive and liveliest Costa Dorada resort. It has a beautiful unspoiled old town attracting an arty, gay (in both senses of the word) party crowd who flock here from Barcelona at weekends for its excellent beaches and nightlife.

Tarragona also has good beaches but this fine old historic town is best known for its world-class Roman heritage and a magnificent cathedral. By contrast just 10km/6.2mi away is Spain's best theme park, Port Aventura.

A short hop from the coast the city of Lleida (Lérida)

and the small town of Montblanc boast many surviving medieval features, while Poblet and Santes Creus are two of the finest monasteries in Spain.

Tortosa, on the Ebro, has a fine cathedral and the delta wetlands beyond are a distant cry from the cities and resorts.

- 🚲 **Lleida/Lérida**
- 🚲 **Montblanc**
- 🚲 **Sitges**
- 🚲 **Tarragona**
- 🚲 **Tortosa**

Parc Nacional d'Aigüestortes i Estany de Sant Maurici★★

This national park in the Catalan Pyrenees abounds in falls and rushing streams. Twisting waterways – *aigües tortes* – wind between mossy meadows and wooded slopes. Glaciers created the harsh beauty of U-shaped valleys, high mountain lakes and snow-covered peaks. Vegetation includes firs and Scots pines. Birch and beech trees provide a stunning splash of colour in autumn.

SIGHTS

The park's 14 119ha/34 888 acres, between altitudes of 1 500m/4 921ft and 3 000m/9 842.5ft, are mainly granite and slate.

Both entries (Espot, to the east, and Boí, to the west) have parking areas.

Take an organised excursion by four-wheel drive (private vehicles are prohibited). Paths are well signposted, and there are four mountain refuges.

Head first for the Casa del Parque Nacional L'Estudi in Boí or the Casa del Parque Nacional in Espot. Both open Jun–Sept Mon–Sat 9am–1pm, 3.30–6.45pm, Sun and public holidays 9am–1pm; Oct–May Mon–Sat 9am–2pm, 3.30–5.45pm, Sun and public holidays 9am–2pm. Closed 1, 6 Jan, 25–26 Dec. Tours 6.70€ (half-day); 13.30€ (full-day); 23.20€ (with hikes). ℘973 69 61 89.

Parc Nacional d'Aigüestortes

B. Brillon/MICHELIN

- **Population:** 52 224
- **Michelin Map:** 574 E 32–33. Local map, see PIRINEOS CATALANES – Catalunya (Lleida)
- **Info:** Centro del Parque de Boí: Graieres 2. ℘973 69 61 89; Centro del Parque de Espot: Prat del Guarda 4. ℘973 62 40 36. http://mediambient.gencat.net/eng.
- **Location:** The park is just west of Andorra and south of France.
- **Don't Miss:** A forest walk up to grand panoramas.
- **Timing:** Allow a day for the park, with hikes.

Lago de Sant Maurici

Reached by a tarmac road from Espot.
The lake, surrounded by forest, reflects the peaks of the Sierra dels Encantats.

HIKES

Portarró d'Espot

3hr there and back on foot from the Estany de Sant Maurici.
The path crosses the Sant Nicolau Valley. At Redó lake, admire the splendid **panoramas★★**.

Estany Gran

3hr there and back on foot from Sant Maurici lake.
Beside the lake, mountain streams form impressive waterfalls.

Estany Negre

5hr there and back on foot from Espot; 4hr from Sant Maurici lake.
Cross the stunning Peguera Valley to Estany Negre (Black Lake), hemmed in by awesome summits.

Aigüestortes

Western section. 3hr there and back.
The entry road leads to Aigüestortes where a stream winds through rich pastures. Hike to Estany Llong.

Barcelona★★★

Most cosmopolitan of Spanish cities, capital of Catalunya, Barcelona is open and welcoming, melding tradition and the avant-garde. It is a Mediterranean metropolis, a major port, and a centre of modern art that lives life to the full.

THE CITY TODAY

Barcelona is not only the most popular visitors' city in southern Europe, it is also an industrial centre and busy port, a university town and seat of the Generalitat de Catalunya government. Moreover it has a thriving cultural life for its own citizens with an opera house, theatres and concert halls. In all but name it is a capital city.

The 1992 Olympic Games brought large-scale planning projects that radically changed Barcelona and since then the city regeneration and improvements has continued apace. The Forum of Cultures in 2004 led to the redevelopment of the Sant Adrià del Besòs waterfront.

A BIT OF HISTORY

The growth of the city – Founded by the Phocaeans, the city grew as Roman **Barcino**, within a 3C fortified wall. In the 12C, Barcelona became the capital of Catalunya and seat of the expanding kingdom of Aragón-Catalunya. Catalan Gothic architecture blossomed.

Catalunya sided with the Archduke of Austria in the War of the Spanish Succession (1701–14), and in defeat lost its autonomy. Montjuïc hill was fortified by the victors, and construction was prohibited except in the old city. Building outside the walls began again in the mid-19C. Industrialisation followed, along with two International Exhibitions, in 1888 and 1929. Modernist architecture flowered.

Catalan identity – Catalan, banned under the Franco regime, is the proud language along with Castilian Spanish, used on all street names and with a flourishing literature.

A thriving centre for artists – Barcelona remains a hub for great artists. Painters

▶ **Population:** 1 615 908

🕐 **Michelin Map:** 574 H 36 (town plan) – map 122 Costa Brava. Michelin City Plans Barcelona 40, 41 and 2040 – Catalunya (Barcelona)

ℹ **Info:** Pl. de Catalunya 17; Ciutat 2 (Pl. de Sant Jaume); Pl. dels Països Catalans (Estació de Sants); Rambla dels Estudis 115 (Cabina Rambla); Pl. Portal de la Pau (Mirador de Colom). www.barcelonaturisme.com.

◖ **Location:** Seaside Barcelona is the hub of northeastern Spain. The AP 7 motorway runs from Murcia to Girona and France; the C32 heads to the resorts to the north and south to Tarragona; the C 16 veers inland to Manresa (59km/37mi NE) and the C 17 to Vic. ▬Plaça Canonge Rodó (Clot Aragó); Av. Marquès de l'Argentera (Estació de França); Pas. de Gràcia; Pl. de Catalunya Estació; Pl. Estació (Sant Andreu Comptal); Pl. dels Països Catalans (Sants).

🅿 **Parking:** Don't even think about driving in Barcelona. Use the excellent Bus Turistic to get about (www.tmb.net/en_US/turistes/busturistic/busturistic.jsp).

🎫 **Don't Miss:** Sagrada Família church, and Modernist masterpieces of architecture along Passeig de Gràcia.

🕐 **Timing:** Start from the Gothic Quarter, and see the Ramblas, Passeig de Gràcia and Sagrada Familia before all else.

👪 **Kids:** El Poble Espanyol; Parc Güell; the Aquarium.

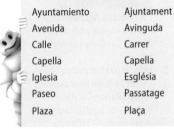

Castilian vs Catalan vs: Common Spelling Differences

Ayuntamiento	Ajuntament
Avenida	Avinguda
Calle	Carrer
Capella	Capella
Iglesia	Església
Paseo	Passatage
Plaza	Plaça

Picasso, Miró, Dalí, Tàpies, sculptor Subirachs and the architects Gaudí, Josep Lluís Sert, Bofill and Bohigas all lived here.

SIGHTS

El Ensanche and Modernist Architecture★★

⚓ *See general plan.*

Barcelona's Eixample (*Ensanche*, or enlargement) grew in the 19C. In Ildefons Cerdà's 1859 grid plan, streets circumscribe blocks of houses (*mançanes* in Catalan or *manzanas* in Castilian) octagonal in shape with trimmed corners. Wide avinguda Diagonal and La Meridiana cross the grid to meet on Plaça de les Glòries Catalanes.

In this ordered new section architects transformed El Ensanche into the centre of Modernism in Barcelona.

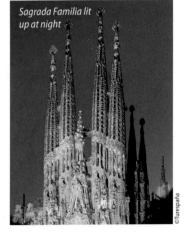

Sagrada Familia lit up at night

©Turespaña

La Sagrada Familia★★★ (Church of the Holy Family)

Mallorca 401. 🕐 *Open daily Oct–Mar 9am–6pm; Apr–Sept 9am–8pm; 25–26 Dec, 1, 6 Jan 9am–2pm.* 🎟11€, 13€ *(combined with Casa-Museu Gaudí).* 👥*Guided tours (1hr15min) daily May–Oct 11am, 1pm, 3pm, 5pm; Nov–Apr 11am, 1pm, 15€ (must be reserved in advance).* 📞 *932 08 04 14. www.sagradafamilia.cat.*

The project, begun in 1882, was taken over by Gaudí in 1883. He planned a Latin Cross church with five aisles and a transept with three aisles. Three façades were each to be dominated by four spires representing the Apostles with a central spire to represent Christ and the Evangelists. The nave was to be a forest of columns. In his lifetime, only the crypt, the apsidal walls, one of the towers and the **Nativity façade**★★ were finished. The Nativity façade comprises three doorways, Faith, Hope and Charity. Work resumed in 1940. The Passion façade was completed in 1981.

The top of the east spire affords a good **view**★★ of the work on the church, and of Barcelona. Domènech i Montaner's **Hospital Sant Pau**★ *(Sant Antoni Maria Claret 167;* 🕐*info office open daily 10am–2pm;* 📞*902 07 66 21)*, with its remarkable glazed tile roofs, may be seen at the end of avinguda de Gaudí.

Passeig de Gràcia★★

Along this boulevard, with elegant wrought-iron **street lamps**★ by Pere Falqués (1900), lies some of Barcelona's finest Modernist architecture, in the **Manzana de la Discordia**★★ (Block of Discord): no. 35 **Casa Lleó Morera**★ (1905) by Domènech i Montaner, no. 41 **Casa Amatller**★ (1900) by Puig i Cadafalch *(now the Instituto Amatller and the Centro del Modernismo, which arranges tours of Modernist Barcelona;* 🕐*open Mon–Sat 10am–8pm, Sun 10am–3pm;* 📞*934 87 72 17; www.amatller.org)*, and no. 43 **Casa Batlló**★★ (1904–06) by Gaudí, with its extraordinary mosaic façade and undulating roof *(*🕐*open daily 9am–8pm;* 🎟*16.50€;* 📞*932 16 03 06; www.casabatllo.es).*

Combined Tickets and Discounts

Three tickets offering discounts are available to tourists in Barcelona:

◆ **Barcelona Card:** (2, 3, 4 or 5 days; 26€/31.50€/36€/42€) gives unlimited transport, discounts from 20% to 50% or free entry for over 80 museums, shows, shops, transportation and restaurants. On sale at the city's tourist offices. For further information: 906 30 12 82 or visit www.barcelonaturisme.com.

◆ **Articket:** Valid six months, cost 20€, for entry to Museu Picasso, La Pedrera Caixa Catalunya, Fundació Antoni Tàpies, MACBA, CCCB, MNAC and the Fundació Joan Miró. 902 10 12 12. www.articketbcn.org.

◆ **Arqueoticket:** Valid one year, cost 18€, for entry to: Museu d'Arqueologia de Catalunya, Museu Barbier-Mueller d'Art Precolombí, Museu Egipci de Barcelona, Museu d'Història de la Ciutat de Barcelona, and Museu Marítim de Barcelona. For information: 906 30 12 82 or visit www.barcelonaturisme.com.

◆ **Ruta del Modernisme:** A Route pack including a guidebook and discount booklet offering discounts of up to 50% to the Modernist buildings in Barcelona, exploring the works of Gaudí, Domènech i Montaner and Puig i Cadafalch. 18€ (available from tourist offices). 933 17 76 52. www.rutadelmodernisme.com.

La Pedrera or Casa Milà★★★

Provença 261–265. Open daily *Nov–Feb 9am–6.30pm (last admission 6pm); Mar–Oct 9am–8pm.* Closed 1, *6 Jan, 25–26 Dec.* 9.50€. 902 40 09 73. www.fundaciocaixacatalunya.org. With its undulating lines, this magnificent Gaudí building resembles a submarine cliff. Visit the **roof and attic**★ and a **residential floor**★. The **Espai Gaudí** exhibits drawings and models by the artist. The roof, with its forest of chimneys, provides fine **views**★. **El Piso**★ is a re-created apartment of an early 20C upper-class family.

▷ *Turn right from Plaça de Joan Carles I into avinguda Diagonal.*

Diagonal

Palau Baró de Quadras (1904; open *Tue–Sat 10am–8pm, Sun and public holidays 10am–2pm; www.casaasia.es*), a Modernist building on the right (no. 373), was designed by Puig i Cadafalch. Along on the left (no. 416), his **Casa de les Punxes (Casa Terrades★)** bears the stamp of Flemish influence.

Parc Güell★★

Olot 1–13. Open daily May–Sept *10am–9pm; Oct–Apr 10am–8pm.* No charge. 934 13 24 00.
Gaudí's imagination shines in the most famous of his commissions by Güell. In this enchanted forest are mushroom-shaped pavilions, a mosaic dragon, the **Chamber of the Columns**, whose undulating mosaic roof covers a forest of sloping columns, and the remarkable **rolling bench**★★. **Casa-Museu Gaudí** *(ctra del Carmel entrance;* open daily *Oct–Mar 10am–6pm; Apr–Sept 10am–8pm; last admission 15min before closing;* closed 1 Jan, 6 Jan (afternoon), 25–26 *Dec (afternoon);* 5.50€; *(13€ combined with Sagrada Família)* 932 19 38 11; www.casamuseugaudi.org) is the architect's house.

Palau de la Música Catalana★★

Palau de la Música 4–6. Guided *tours (50min) daily 10am–3pm; Aug and Holy Week 10am–6pm.* 12€. 902 47 54 85. www.palaumusica.org.
This concert hall (1905–08) is Domènech i Montaner's most famous work. The **exterior**★ displays lavish mosaics. The interior, dominated by an **inverted cupola**★★ of polychrome glass, is

GETTING THERE

Airport – ✆902 40 47 04.
www.aena.es. 18km/11mi from the
city centre. Can be reached by local
train (*Línea 2, Cercanías;* ✆*902 24 02 02*) every 30min from 6am to 11.38pm,
or by the bus service from the plaça
de Catalunya and plaça d'Espanya,
departing every 15min from 5.30am to
12.15am (◉*4.05€;* ✆*934 15 60 20*). By
taxi, the fare from the city centre will
be approximately 20€ (✆*932 23 51 51*).
Taxis – The city's black and yellow
taxis are an efficient, inexpensive
way of getting around the city. Radio
Taxi Barcelona: ✆932 25 00 00;
Radio Taxi 033: ✆933 03 30 33 *(www.
taxibarcelona.cat)*.
Metro – *Metro stations are shown on
the maps in this guide (◉).* For further
information: ✆933 18 70 74 or visit
www.tmb.net. Information on access
for the disabled can be obtained on
✆934 12 44 44.
The network is open Mon–Thu
5am–midnight; Fri–Sat and days
preceding public holidays 5am–2am;
Sun 6am–midnight; and 6am–11pm
on weekday public holidays. A free
metro guide is available. Metro **tickets
and cards** can also be used on buses,
the "Tramvía Blau" (a tourist tram in
the Diagonal section of the city) and
train services operated by Ferrocarriles
de la Generalitat de Catalunya. In
addition to single tickets, multi-
journey cards include the T-1 (valid for
ten trips), T-DIA (unlimited travel for
one day), T50/30 (50 trips in 30 days)
and the T-MES (unlimited travel for
one month).
Streetcars – There are four lines
(T1, T2, T3 and T4).
Regional railway network
– *Ferrocarriles Catalanes train stations
are shown on the maps in this guide
(*✆*932 05 15 15; www.fgc.cat).* Free
connections to the metro system may
be made at these stations: Avinguda
Carrilet /L'Hospitalet, Espanya,
Catalunya and Diagonal/Provença.
Bus Turístic – This excellent service
offers visitors a variety of bus itineraries throughout the city. Daily departures from Plaça de Catalunya starting
at 9am (◉*21€ 1 day; 27€ 2 days)*.
Boat trips – The Las Golondrinas
company organises trips around
the port *(approx 35min)*. Departures
from Portal de la Pau, opposite the
Columbus monument. ✆934 42 31
06. www.lasgolondrinas.com.

SIGHTSEEING

Publications – The **Guía del Ocio**
(www.guiadelociobcn.com) is a weekly
guide on sale at newspaper stands
containing a list of every cultural
event in the city. The city's airport
and tourist offices are also able to
provide visitors with a full range
of booklets and leaflets produced
by the Generalitat de Catalunya's
Department of Industry, Commerce
and Tourism.

DISTRICTS

Barri Gòtic – Following an intense
restoration programme undertaken
during the 1920s, the area containing
the city's major historical buildings
was renamed the Gothic quarter.
Ciutat Vella – The old city includes
districts as diverse as Santa Anna,
La Mercè, Sant Pere and El Raval.
The last, which used to be known
as the Barri Xino (Chinatown), now
contains Barcelona's leading cultural
centres and is a fine example of urban
renovation.
Eixample – Eixample (Ensanche)
developed following the destruction
of the city's medieval walls. The
district personifies the bourgeois,
elegant Barcelona of the end of the
19C, with its prestigious boutiques,
smart avenues and some of the best
examples of Modernist architecture.
Gràcia – This *barrio*, situated at the
end of the Passeig de Gràcia, is one
of the city's most characteristic areas.
Gràcia developed from its early
agricultural origins into an urban area
as a result of the influx of shopkeepers,
artisans and factory workers. During
the 19C, Gràcia was renowned for its

Republican sympathies. Today, it still hosts a number of popular fiestas.

Ribera – With its narrow alleyways and Gothic architecture, this former fishermen's quarter still retains an unquestionable charm. Its main attractions are the Carrer Montcada and the Església de Santa Maria del Mar.

Barceloneta – Barceloneta is famous for its outdoor stalls, restaurants and nautical atmosphere.

Vila Olímpica – The Olympic Village was built to accommodate sportsmen and sportswomen participating in the 1992 games. Nowadays, it is a modern district with wide avenues, landscaped areas and direct access to some of Barcelona's restored beaches.

Les Corts – This district is located at the upper end of Diagonal and includes the **Ciudad Universitaria** and the **Camp Nou**, the home of Barcelona Football Club and

its football-orientated **Museu FC Barcelona** (www.fcbarcelona.com).

Sarrià – Sarrià nestles at the foot of the Serra de Collserola and has managed to retain its traditional, tranquil character. The neighbouring districts of **Pedralbes** and **Sant Gervasi de Cassoles**, at the foot of Tibidabo, have become a favourite hangout for the city's well-heeled inhabitants.

Sants – One of the city's main working class districts close to the railway station of the same name.

Horta-Guinardó – This *barrio* at the foot of Collserola was first populated by peasants and then by factory workers. It is home to the **Laberinto de Horta** (to the north), an 18C property with attractive gardens, and the **Velódromo**, a venue for sporting events and major music events.

---

decorated with sculpted groups and mosaic figurines. A concert in this odd venue is a memorable occasion.

Fundació Antoni Tàpies★★

Aragó 255. Closed for renovation. 934 87 03 15. www.fundaciotapies.org. Tàpies established his foundation in an ex-publishing house designed by Domènech i Montaner. The brick building

is crowned by an aerial sculpture by Tàpies, *Núvol i Cadira* (cloud and chair), the emblem of the museum.

The bare interior, where everything is painted in the brown, beige, grey and ochre favoured by Tàpies, is lit by skylights (a cupola and a pyramid). Paintings and sculptures trace the development of Tàpies' work since 1948.

The Ribera District

During the 13C and the 14C the Catalan fleet exercised unquestionable supremacy over the western basin of the Mediterranean. Important merchant families acquired considerable social status and the Carrer de Montcada became a showcase for their high expectations and new standards of living. This street, named after the Montcada, an influential family of noble descent, is a unique ensemble of merchants' palaces and aristocratic mansions, most of which date back to the late Middle Ages. Behind the austere façades are quaint little patios with galleries and porches typical of Catalan Gothic architecture.

The following is a selection of small palaces: the 15C Palau de Berenguer de Aguilar, now the Museu Picasso, the 14C Palau del Marqués de Lió which houses the Museu Tèxtil i d'Indumentària (Textile and Costume Museum), the 17C Palau Dalmases at no20 with Baroque frieze decorations on the staircase, and the 16C Palau Cervelló-Giudice at no25, now the Maeght Gallery, with a fine flight of steps.

BARRI GÒTIC★★ (GOTHIC QUARTER)

♿*See plan of old city.*

The Gothic quarter, named for the many buildings constructed between the 13C and 15C, holds traces of Roman settlement and massive 4C walls.

Plaça Nova

This is the heart of the quarter, where the Romans built an enclosure with walls 9m/29.5ft high. Two watchtowers that flanked the West Gate (converted to a house in the Middle Ages) remain.

Opposite the Cathedral, the **Collegi d'Arquitectes** (College of Architects; *pl. Nova amb carrer del Bisbe*) is a modern surprise, its decorative band of cement engraved by Picasso.

Catedral★

Pl. de la Seu. ⏱*Open daily 8am–1.15pm, 4.30–7.30pm.* ⊙*4€.* ✆*933 42 82 60. www.catedralbcn.org.*

The cathedral is on **Plaça de la Seu**, marked on one side by the **Casa de l'Ardiaca**★ (12C–15C; *Santa Llúcia 1;* ⏱*open Sept–Jun Mon–Fri 9am–8.45pm, Sat 9am–1pm; Jul–Aug Mon–Fri 9am–7.30pm;* ✆*933 18 11 95*), and on the other by the **Casa de la Canonja** (16C) and **pia Almoina**, which house the **Museu Diocesà de Barcelona** (*av. de la Catedral 4;* ⏱*open Tue–Sat 10am–2pm, 5–8pm, Sun and public holidays 11am–2pm;* ⏱*closed 1 Jan, 25–26 Dec;* ⊙*6€;* ✆*933 15 22 13*).

The cathedral was built on the site of a Romanesque church, from the late 13C to 1450. The façade and spire are 19C, based on old French designs.

The Catalan Gothic **interior**★ has an outstanding elevation with slender pillars. The nave is lit by a fine lantern-tower; the perspective is broken by the **coro**★★, with double rows of beautifully carved **stalls**. Note the humorous scenes adorning the misericords. In the early 16C, the backs were painted with the coats of arms of knights of the Order of the Golden Fleece by Juan de Borgoña, in one of the most impressive achievements of European heraldry.

The side chapels hold exquisite retables and marble tombs. The white marble **choir screen**★ was sculpted in the 16C after drawings by Bartolomé Ordóñez. Statues illustrate the martyrdom of St Eulàlia, patron of Barcelona. Her relics lie in the **crypt**★ in a 14C Pisan-style alabaster sarcophagus.

The Capella del Santísimo (*right of the entry*) contains the 15C *Christ of Lepanto*, said to have been on the prow of the galley of Don Juan of Austria in the Battle of Lepanto (1571). In the next chapel is a Gothic retable by Bernat Martorell, also the artist of the **retable of the Transfiguration**★ in the ambulatory.

Cathedral roof visit – *by lift from an ambulatory chapel.* Metal walkways under the imposing silhouettes of the cathedral towers and cupola allow exceptional **views**★★ of the city.

Claustro★

The cloisters are an oasis, and are home to a flock of geese. In the chapter house, a museum houses a *Pietà* by Bermejo (1490), altarpiece panels by the 15C artist Jaime Huguet and the missal of St Eulàlia, enhanced by delicate miniatures.

Museu Frederic Marès★

Pl. de Sant Lu 5–6. ⏱*Open Tue–Sat 10am–7pm, Sun 10am–8pm, public holidays 10am–3pm.* ⊙*4.20€; no charge first Sun in month, Wed and Sun (from 3pm).* ✆*923 56 35 00. www.museumares.bcn.cat.*

The entry (in the Palau Reial Major) is on tiny **Plaça de Sant Lu**, always full of mime artists and street musicians. The collections, in the Palau Reial Major (*enter by Pl. de Sant Lu*), were left to the city by sculptor Frederic Marès (1893–1991).

Sculpture Section

The works on two floors and in the crypt are in chronological order from the Iberian period to the 19C. Note the **Christs and Calvaries**★ in polychrome wood (12C–14C), Romanesque and Gothic **Virgins with Child**★; a 16C **Holy Entombment**★ and **The Vocation of**

St Peter★, an expressive 12C relief attributed to the master Cabestany.

Gabinete del Coleccionista
Everyday objects, mainly 19C, include items from recreational rooms, the smoking parlour and the women's boudoir (spectacles, fans, clothes, etc.).

PLAÇA DEL REI★★
On this splendid square stand the Palau Reial Major (at the back), the **Capella de Santa Àgata** (right) and the **Palau del Lloctinent**. In the right corner, the Casa Clariana-Padellàs, housing the **Museu d'Història de la Ciutat**★★, is a 15C Gothic mansion moved stone by stone when the via Laietana was built in 1931.

Capella de Santa Àgata★★
Pl. del Rei. ◷*Open Jun–Sept Tue–Sat 10am–8pm, Sun 10am–3pm; Oct–May Tue–Sat 10am–2pm, 4–8pm, Sun 10am–3pm.* ◉*4€ (for all of the square's sights).* ☏*933 19 02 22.*
This 14C palatine chapel is covered by intricate polychrome woodwork panelling. The **Altarpiece of the Constable**★★ by Jaime Huguet (1465) depicts the life of Jesus and the Virgin Mary. In the centre, the *Adoration of the Three Wise Men* is a Catalan masterpiece.
A staircase leads to the **Mirador del Rei Martí**, a five-storey tower with a lovely **view**★★ of the old city.

Saló del Tinell
This lofty 14C room, 17m/56ft high, is topped with a double-sloped ceiling set on six monumental arches. It is said that the Catholic Monarchs welcomed Columbus here after his first voyage.

Museu d'Història de la Ciutat★★
Pl. del Rei s/n. ◷*Open Jun–Sept Tue–Sat 10am–8pm; Oct–May Tue–Sat 10am–2pm, 4–7pm.* ◷*Closed 1 Jan, 1 May, 24 Jun & 25 Dec.* ◉*5€.* ☏*932 56 21 22. www.museuhistoria.bcn.cat.*

The visit includes Roman remains, and outbuildings of the Palau Reial Major.

Palau del Lloctinent
This 16C late-Gothic palace was the residence of the viceroys of Catalunya.

The Roman city★★★
Under the museum and Plaça del Rei are Roman foundations, drainage, and reservoirs. In adjoining vaulted rooms are sculptures from the 1C–4C (busts of Agrippina, Faustina and Antoninus Pius). Two 13C Gothic frescoes were uncovered in the Sala Jaime I in 1998.

Palau Reial Major
Pl. del Rei. ◷*Open Jun–Sept Tue–Sat 10am–2pm, 4–8pm, Sun 10am–3pm; Oct–May Tue–Sat 10am–8pm, Sun 10am–3pm.* ◉*4€ (for all of the square's sights).* ☏*933 15 11 11.*
Built in the 11C and 12C, the palace acquired its present appearance in the 14C. It was the seat of the counts of Barcelona and the kings of Aragón. Arches link huge buttresses in the façade; the original façade has rose windows.

Plaça de Ramon Berenguer el Gran
From the Plaça, Roman walls are visible, incorporated into the Palau Reial.

Ajuntament (Town Hall)
Pl. de Sant Jaume 1. ◉*Guided tours Sun 10am–1.30pm, Corpus Cristi 10am–8pm, 23 Apr 10am–6.30pm.* ◉*No charge.* ☏*934 02 70 00. www.bcn.cat.*
The town hall façade on Plaça Sant Jaume is Neoclassical; that on Carrer de la Ciutat is an outstanding 14C Gothic construction.

Palau de la Generalitat (Provincial Council)
Pl. de Sant Jaume 4. ◷*Open to the public 23 Apr, 24 Sept, 11 Sept.* ◉*Guided tours (50min) 2nd and 4th Sat–Sun of each month, 10.30am–1.30pm.* ◉*No charge. booking required.*

934 02 46 00. www.gencat.cat/ generalitat/eng/guia/palau/visites.htm. This vast 15C–17C edifice is the seat of the Autonomous Government of Catalunya. It has a Renaissance-style façade on Plaça de Sant Jaume (c. 1600).

Carrer del Bisbe

To the left is the side wall of the Palau de la Generalitat (Provincial Council). Above a door is a fine early 15C medallion of St George by Pere Johan.

On the right side is the **Casa dels Canonges** (Canons' Residence), residence of the President of the Generalitat. A neo-Gothic covered gallery (1929), over a star-vaulted arch, links the two.

Carrer del Paradis

At no. 10 stand four Roman **columns**★, remains of the Temple of Augustus. Carrer Paradis leads into Carrer de la Pietat, bordered on the left by the Gothic façade of the Casa dels Canonges. The Cathedral cloister doorway opposite is adorned with a wooden 16C sculpture of a *Pietà*.

Plaça de Sant Felip Neri

Pl. de Sant Felip Neri 5.

The Renaissance houses on this square were moved here when via Laietana was built. The **Museu del Calçat** (footwear museum) includes Columbus' shoes. (*open Tue–Sun and public holidays 11am–2pm; 2.50€; *933 01 45 33).

Museu d'Art Contemporàni de Barcelona (MACBA)★★

*Pl. dels Àngels 1. Open 25 Sept–23 Jun Mon, Wed–Fri 11am–7.30pm, Sat 10am–8pm, Sun and public holidays 10am–3pm; 24 Jun–24 Sept Mon and Wed 11am–8pm, Thu–Fri 11am– midnight, Sat 10am–8pm, Sun and public holidays 10am–3pm. Closed 1 Jan, 25 Dec. 3€. *934 12 08 10. | www.macba.es.*

The monumental museum **building**★★, designed by American Richard Meyer, fuses the rationalist Mediterranean tradition with contemporary architecture. Two significant works

can are outside: *La Ola* by Jorge Oteiza and Eduardo Chillida's mural, *Barcelona* (*see Sights).

The **standing collections**★ in pristine white halls cover major artistic movements of the past 50 years. Exhibits include works influenced by Constructivism and Abstract art (Klee, Oteiza, Miró, Calder, Fontana), as well as creations by experimental artists (Kiefer, Boltanski, Solano) and names of the 1980s (Hernández, Pijuán, Barceló, Tàpies, Ràfols Casamada, Sicilia).

LA RAMBLA AND AROUND★★

The most famous promenade in Barcelona, La Rambla's five sections follow an old riverbed bordering the Gothic quarter. La Rambla separates the Eixample district from the old quarter, and is alive at all hours with locals, tourists and down-and-outs and vendors.

The upper section, by Plaça de Catalunya, is Rambla de Canaletes, followed by Rambla dels Estudis or Rambla dels Ocells (Avenue of the Birds).

Església de Betlem

La Rambla 107. No charge.

This Baroque church – the interior was razed by a fire in 1936 – has retained its imposing façade, facing Carrer Carme.

Antic Hospital de la Santa Creu

Hospital 56.

These Gothic, Baroque and Neoclassical buildings are a haven in this district. An ex-hospital is the Library of Catalunya. A charming planted **Gothic patio**★ (Jardines de Rubio y Lluch) can be reached through a hall decorated with *azulejos*.

Palau de la Virreina★

*La Rambla 99. *933 16 10 00. www.bcn.cat/virreinacentredelaimatge.* The elegant 1778 palace of the Vicereine of Peru, with Baroque and Rococo decorations, hosts major exhibitions. Alongside is the traditional Mercat (market) de Sant Josep (La Boqueria).

Modernist Architecture

Modernism developed between 1890 and 1920 alongside similar movements in other parts of Europe, such as Art Nouveau in both France and Great Britain and Jugendstil in Germany. Modernist architecture sprang from artistic exploration that combined new industrial materials with modern techniques, using decorative motifs like curve and counter-curve and asymmetrical shapes in stained glass, ceramics and metal. It enjoyed great success in Catalunya at a time when large fortunes were being made as a result of industrialisation. The most representative architects of the style were Antoni Gaudí, Domènech i Montaner, Puig i Cadafalch and Jujol. A parallel movement in Catalan literature known as Renaixença also flourished during this period.

Down La Rambla on the right side stands the city's opera house, the **Gran Teatre del Liceu** (La Rambla 51–59; ☏ 934 85 99 00; www.liceubarcelona.com), rebuilt after a 1994 fire. Opposite lies **Plaça de la Boqueria**, a charming esplanade whose pavement was decorated by the artist Joan Miró.

Església de Santa Maria del Pi★

Pl. del Pi 7. ⏱ Open daily 9.30am–1pm, 5.30–8pm. ☏ 933 18 47 43. www.parroquiadelpi.com.
This 14C Catalan Gothic church on a square is striking for its simplicity and the size of its single nave.

Plaça Reial★★

This vast pedestrian square shaded by palms and lined with cafés is surrounded by Neoclassical buildings. Gaudí designed the lampposts by the fountain. A stamp and coin market is held Sunday mornings.

Palau Güell★★

Nou de la Rambla 3. ⏱ Open Tue–Sat 10am–2.30pm. ⏱ Closed public holidays. ⬤No charge. ☏ 933 17 39 74. www.palauguell.cat.
Gaudí designed the Güell residence (1886–90). Note the parabolic entry arches and the extravagant bars typical of the Modernist movement. The most striking interior features are the **grand hall** and the innovative use of materials and the treatment of light as a design element of each space.
La Rambla meets the sea at **La Rambla de Santa Mònica**. The former **Convent de Santa Mònica** (no. 7; ⏱open winter Mon–Sat 11am–8pm, Sun and public holidays 11am–3pm; ☏ 933 16 28 10; www.artssantamonica.cat) is a modern arts centre that hosts exhibitions. The wax museum **(Museu de Cera)** is here (pas. de la Banca 7; ⏱ open Mon–Fri 10am–1.30pm, 4–7.30pm, Sat–Sun and public holidays 11am–2pm, 4.30–8pm; summer daily 10am–10pm; ⬤10€; ☏ 933 17 26 49; ww.museocerabcn.com)

Monument a Colom

Pl. Portal de la Pau. ⏱ Open daily Nov–Apr 10am–6.30pm; May–Oct 10am–8.30pm. ⏱ Closed 1 Jan, 25 Dec. ⬤2.20€. ☏ 932 85 38 34.
This 1886 monument commemorates the return of the great navigator. A lift to the top gives a fantastic view over the city.

Centre de Cultura Contemporània de Barcelona (CCCB)

Montalegre 5. ⏱ Open Tue–Wed, Fri–Sun 11am–8pm, Thu 11am–10pm. Ticket desks close 30min before museum. ⏱ Closed 1 Jan, 25 Dec. ⬤4.50€ (one exhibition), 6€ (two or more). ☏ 933 06 41 00. www.cccb.org.
This centre of art exhibitions, near MACBA, is in restored premises. Its **patio**★ combines original mosaics and silk-screen floral motifs with modern elements, like the side wall of glass.

CARRER DE MONTCADA★★

1hr30min including a visit to the Museu Picasso – ⬤see plan of old city.

Two Modernist Masters

Josep Puig i Cadafalch (1867–1956) – The mixture of regional and foreign architectural tradition in his work reflects the Plateresque and Flemish styles. His main works are the Casa de les Punxes, the Casa Macaya (1901) and the Palau Baró de Quadras (1904).

Lluís Domènech i Montaner (1850–1923) – He attained his highly decorative style through extensive use of mosaics, stained glass and glazed tiles. His main works include the Palau de la Música Catalana, Castell dels Tres Dragons, Hospital de Sant Pau and Casa Montaner i Simó.

Museu Picasso★

Montcada 15–23. ○ *Open Tue–Sun and public holidays 10am–8pm.* ○ *Closed 1 Jan, 1 May, 24 Jun, 25–26 Dec.* 9€; *free first Sun of month and every Sun from 3pm.* ℘932 56 30 00. *www.museupicasso.bcn.es.*

The Gothic palaces of Berenguer de Aguilar and Baron de Castellet and the Baroque Palau Meca are the setting for the museum. The works here are dedicated, in most cases, to Picasso's friend Sabartès, shown in several portraits.

Picasso's early genius is evident in portraits of his family, *First Communion* and *Science and Charity* (1896). Among examples of his early Paris work are *La Nana* and *La Espera*; *Los Desemparados* (1903) is from his Blue Period, *Señora Casals* from his Rose Period. His **Las Meninas series**★ consists of variations on the famous picture by Velázquez. Picasso's skill as an engraver is seen in his outstanding etchings of bullfighting and his talent as a ceramist in vases, dishes and plates made in the 1950s.

Museu Barbier-Mueller d'Art Precolombí

Montcada 12–14. ○ *Open Tue–Fri 11am–7pm, Sat 10am–7pm, Sun and public holidays 10am–3pm.* ○ *Closed 1 Jan, Good Fri, 1 May, 24 Jun, 25–26 Dec.* 3€; *free first Sun of month (10am–7pm).* ℘933 10 45 16. *www.barbier-mueller.ch.*

The beautifully restored 12C Palau Nadal houses this interesting collection of pre-Columbian art.

Església de Santa Maria del Mar★★

Pl. de Santa Maria 1. ○ *Open daily 9am–1.30pm, 4.30–8pm.* No charge. ℘933 10 23 90.

This church is one of the most beautiful in the Catalan Gothic style, built in the 14C by humble sailors to compete with the cathedral of the wealthy. The result is a graceful church of outstanding simplicity. The west front is adorned only by a portal gable and the buttresses flanking the superb Flamboyant **rose window**★. The **interior**★★★ gives the impression of spaciousness due to the elevation of the nave, and side aisles divided only by slender pillars.

THE SEAFRONT★

Allow half a day. Bus 14 follows the seafront to Vila Olímpica.

The seafront, from Montjuïc to the Besòs river, was completely redesigned for the 1992 Olympic Games, turning Barcelona once again towards the sea.

Drassanes (Shipyards)★★ and Museu Marítim★★

Av. de les Drassanes. ○ *Open daily 10am–8pm, ticket office closes 7.30pm.* ○ *Closed 1, 6 Jan, 25–26 Dec.* 6.50€ *(9.60€ with ride; 7.20€ with Mirador de Colom).* ℘93 342 99 20. *www.museu maritimbarcelona.org.*

The **ropeworks** are among the best examples of civil Gothic architecture in Catalunya. Ten sections remain from the shipyard, under a timber roof supported by sturdy stone arches. This is an ideal setting for a **Maritime Museum** with its interactive displays and priceless artefacts. Among many models is a lifesize replica of the **Royal Galley of Don Juan of Austria**★★, Christian flagship at the Battle of Lepanto (1571). The **Portulan of Gabriel de Vallseca** (1439) belonged to Amerigo Vespucci. The area around the port includes the Moll de Bosch i Alsina (or **Moll de la Fusta**), a palm-lined promenade.

Port Vell★

The old harbour is a lively leisure area featuring bars, the **Maremàgnum** shopping and leisure centre *(www.mare magnum.es)*, an **aquarium** and the **IMAX** cinema *(www.imaxportvell.com)*.

👥 Aquàrium★

Moll d'Espanya del Port Vell. 🕐 *Open daily 9.30am–9pm (9.30pm Jun, Sept, Weekends and public holidays; 11pm Jul–Aug); last admission one hour before closing.* ⬚*17€; child 12€.* ☎*932 21 74 74. www.aquariumbcn.com.*
One of Europe's most impressive sub-aquatic zoos includes a spectacular viewing tunnel, 80m/262ft long.

Basílica de la Mercè★

Pl. de la Mercè 1. 🕐 *Open daily 10am–1pm, 6–8pm.* ⬚*No charge.* ☎*933 15 27 56.*
The entry of this 1760 church has the only curved Baroque façade in Barcelona. The façade on Carrer Ample is Renaissance and was moved from elsewhere. A Gothic statue in the interior, the **Mare de Déu de la Mercè**★, is by Pere Moragues (1361).

La Llotja★

Pas. Isabel II 1. ☎*933 19 24 12. www.casallotja.com.*
The building housing the Chamber of Commerce and Industry was completely rebuilt in the 18C. The **Gothic hall**★★, a lofty chamber with three naves separated by triple round arches, remains from the medieval building.

Estació de França★

Avinguda del Marquès de l'Argentera 6. This huge iron structure with glass roof is the terminal for trains to France.

Parc de la Ciutadella★

🕐 *Open daily 10am–dusk.* ☎*934 13 25 00.*
Built by Philip V to control rebellious Barcelona, the citadel was demolished in 1868 and replaced by gardens. It hosted the 1888 World Fair.

Castell dels Tres Dragons★★

Parc de la Ciutadella. 🕐 *Open Tue–Sat 10am–6.30pm, Sun 10am–2.30pm.* 🕐 *Closed 1 Jan, 25 Dec.* ⬚*5.30€*

Gaudí (1852–1926)

Antoni Gaudí, born in Reus, studied architecture in Barcelona. His style was influenced first by Catalan Gothic architecture with its emphasis on large areas of space (wide naves, the effect of airy spaciousness) and subsequently by the Islamic and Mudéjar styles. He also studied nature, observing plants and animals, which inspired his shapes, colours and textures. He gave full rein to these images – liana-like curves, the rising and breaking of waves, rugged rocks and the serrations on leaves and flowers – when designing his fabulous buildings. Part of his great originality lay in his use of parabolic arches and spirals (as can be seen in the chimneys of Casa Milà). An intensely religious man, Gaudí drew upon a great many religious symbols for his buildings, especially for the Sagrada Família (Church of the Holy Family) on which he worked for over 40 years. He spent his last years here, hidden away in a small room in the middle of the site, until his tragic death when he was run over by a tram.

Gaudí worked a great deal for the banker **Eusebi Güell**, his patron and admirer, who asked him to design his private houses.

Gaudí's main works are the Sagrada Família, Casa Batlló, La Pedrera, Casa Vicens, Palau Güell, Pavellons Güell and the Parc Güell.

(includes Natural History Museum and Botanical Garden); no charge first Sun of the month. ✆932 56 22 00. www.bcn.cat/museuciencies.

Domènech i Montaner built this pavilion for the World Fair in neo-Gothic style, using unadorned brick and iron. It houses the **Museu de Zoologia**★, with a collection of all zoological species.

Waterfall

Gaudí collaborated on the design of this waterfall while still a student.

👥 Parc Zoològic★

Parc de la Ciutadella. 🕐 Open Jan–early Mar and late Oct–Dec 10am–5.30pm; late Mar–May and early Oct 10am–7pm; Jun–Sept 10am–8pm; ticket office closes 1hr before zoo. 🕐 Closed 25 Dec. ✎16€; child 9.60€. ✆902 45 75 45. www.zoobarcelona.com.

This zoo covers much of Parc de la Ciutadella. Animals from all over the world are kept in a natural setting. A dolphin show is held in the Aquarama.

LA BARCELONETA★

The "Iberian Naples" has quaint narrow streets, and restaurants and stalls offering seafood dishes.

Museu d'Història de Catalunya★

Palau de Mar, Pl. de Pau Vila 3. 🕐 Open Tue, Thu–Sat 10am–7pm, Wed 10am–8pm, Sun and public holidays 10am–2.30pm. 🕐 Closed 1, 6 Jan, 25–26 Dec. ✎4€; no charge 23 Apr, 18 May, 11, 24 Sept, first Sun of month. ✆932 25 47 00. www.mhcat.net.

This museum in an ex-warehouse details Catalunya from prehistory to now.

▶ At the end of the passeig Nacional, continue into the passeig Marítim.

Vila Olímpica★

Built for the 1992 Olympics, this is one of Barcelona's most modern areas. Gardens and avenues of the Olympic Village are dotted with sculptures. The **marina**★★ designed by JR de Clascà has bars, restaurants and pavement cafés. Most striking are two 153m/502ft **towers** (Hotel Arts and the Torre Mapfre). The **view**★★★ from the top takes in Mallorca on a clear day.

MONTJUÏC★

1 day, including museum visits – ♿see general plan.

The fort built on this 173m/568ft mountain during the 1640 rebellion is now a military museum (🕐open Apr–Oct Tue–Sun 9.30am–8pm; Nov and Mar Sat–Sun and public holidays 9.30am–8pm; Dec–Feb Tue–Fri 9.30am–5pm, Sat–Sun and public holidays 9.30am–7pm; ✆933 29 86 13; www.museomilitarmontjuic.es). The castle commands city and harbour **views**★. The **Plaça d'Espanya** remains from the 1929 exhibition, along with the illuminated **fountain** (Font Magica) by Carles Buïgas, the **reception pavilion**★★ by Mies van der Rohe, of outstanding simplicity, and the Spanish Village (Poble Espanyol, or Pueblo Español in Castilian).

CaixaForum

Av. Marqués de Comillas 6–8. 🕐 Open Mon–Fri and Sun 10am–8pm, Sat 10am–10pm. 🕐 Closed 1, 6 Jan, 25 Dec. ✎No charge. ✆934 76 86 00. http://obrasocial.lacaixa.es.

A magnificent Modernist early 20C textile factory, built by Puig i Cadafalch, now houses a cultural centre with exhibits from a splendid modern art collection of more than 800 works. The entry is a tree of steel and glass.

Museu Nacional d'Art de Catalunya (MNAC)★★★

Palau Nacional, Parc de Montjuïc. 🕐 Open Tue–Sat 10am–7pm; Sun and public holidays 10am–2.30pm. 🕐 Closed 1 Jan, 1 May, 25 Dec. ✎8.50€; no charge 18 May, 11, 24 Sept and first Sun of month. ✆936 22 03 76. www.mnac.cat.

This museum of Catalan art in the Palau Nacional built for the 1929 fair includes remarkable **Romanesque and Gothic collections**★★★.

Romanesque art

The display evokes contemporary churches. Note 12C frescoes by Sant Joan de Boí *(Room 2)*, the late 11C lateral apses by Sant Quirze de Pedret *(Room 3)*, the Santa Maria de Taüll ensemble (12C), dominated by a fine *Epiphany* and Sant Climent de Taüll *(Room 5)* with the remarkable *Christ in Majesty:* the apse is a Renaissance masterpiece. Note the anti-naturalism and geometry.

Altar frontals are painted on a panel or carved. In the magnificent sculpture galleries is the polychrome *Majestad de Batlló* (13C). The museum also presents superb **capitals**★ *(Room 6)*, silverware and enamels. Paintings from the chapter house of **Sigena** (1200) evidence a great stylistic shift.

Gothic art

Exhibits of 13C–14C Catalan Gothic art include stone retables attributed to **Jaime Cascalls** *(Rooms 15 and 16)*; the collection of Catalan Gothic art *(Room 30)*, with works by **Guerau Gener, Juan Mates, Ramon de Mur**, **Juan Antigó**, **Bernardo Despuig** and **Jaime Cirera**; a room dedicated to **Bernardo Martorell** *(Room 32)*, for whom detail and shading were paramount; the famous *Virgin of the Councillors* by **Luis Dalmau**; works by the **Master of La Seu d´Urgell** *(Room 34)* and, lastly, 14C–15C funerary sculpture *(Room 50)*.

Other Collections

The **Cambó Collection** includes painters of the rank of Zurbarán, Tintoretto, El Greco, Rubens, Cranach the Elder and Goya. The **Thyssen-Bornemisza Collection** selected from the Museu Thyssen comprises works from the Middle Ages to the 18C, notably paintings of the Virgin and Child. Portraits represent several schools of the 15C–18C.

In the **Renaissance and Baroque** section are Flemish and Italian masters along with works of Ayne Bru, Pere Nunyes and Pedro Berruguete. Other **19C–20C** artworks here include paintings by Fortuny, Modernist furniture, sculpture, and posters by Gaudí, Doménech i Montaner, Casas, Rusiñol and others.

⚎ Poble Espanyol★ (Spanish Village)

▶*Av. Marqués de Comillas.* ⏰*Open Mon 9am–8pm, Tue–Thu 9am–2am, Fri 9am–4am, Sat 9am–5am, Sun 9am–midnight, 24 Dec 9am–8pm, 25 Dec 9pm–2am, 1 Jan 1am–8pm.* ⬚*8.50€; child 5.50€.* ☏*935 08 63 30. www.poble-espanyol.com.*

This "village", reflecting life in various parts of Spain, was built for the 1929 exhibition. Walk through a small Castilian square, a street in an Andalucían village with white houses set off by flowering geraniums, or by a Mudéjar tower from Aragón. There are restaurants, bars and shops, and craftsmen making traditional Spanish wares. The **Collection of Contemporary Art** has works of Picasso, Miró, Dalí and Spanish artists from the 1950s to the present.

Anella Olímpica★

This complex high on the mountain consists of the **Olympic Stadium**★, with its 1929 façade *(now a football venue; www.rcdespanyol.cat)*, and the nearby **Palau Sant Jordi**★★, a sports centre designed by Arata Isozaki. The **telecommunications tower** is the work of Santiago Calatrava.

Fundació Joan Miró★★★

Parc de Montjuïc. ⏰*Open Tue–Wed, Fri–Sat 10am–7pm (8pm Jul–Sept), Thu 10am–9.30pm, Sun and public holidays 10am–2.30pm; last entry 15min before closing.* ⬚*8€.* ☏*934 43 94 70. www.fundaciomiro-bcn.org.*

Joan Miró (1893–1983), a leading figure in Avant-Garde art, is linked to Barcelona: a mural at the airport, pavement mosaics on La Rambla, the famous logo of the savings bank La Caixa. Born in Barcelona, Miró spent 1921 and 1922 in Paris, where he painted **La Masía**, signalling his departure from figurative art. Between 1939 and 1941 he executed **Constellations**, 23 panels expressing the horror of the Second World War.

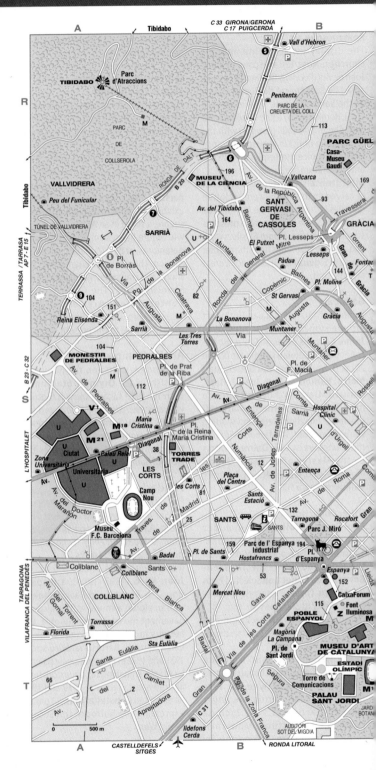

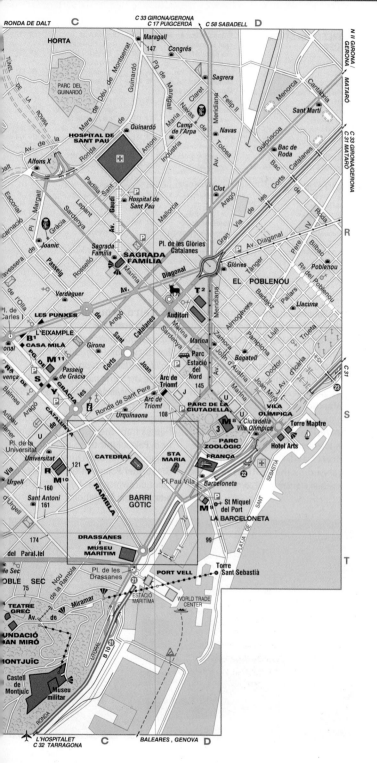

Miró's Foundation is housed in a modern building of harmonious proportions designed by Josep Lluís Sert, a close friend. The 10 000 items were largely executed during the last 20 years of his life. A small exhibition of contemporary art includes Alexander Calder's **Fountain of Mercury**.

Teatre Grec★

This 1929 open-air theatre hosts dance, concerts and stage performances organised by the **Festival del Grec** (www.barcelonafestival.com).

Museu d'Arqueologia de Catalunya★

Pg. de Santa Madrona 39–41. 🕐 *Open Tue–Sat 9.30am–7pm, Sun and public holidays 10am–2.30pm.* 🎟*3€; no charge last Sun in month, 23 Apr, 18 May, 11 Sept and public holidays.* 📞*934 23 21 49. www.mac.es.*

Household effects, ceramics and votive figures trace the history of Catalunya from Palaeolithic times through to the Visigothic. The collection is housed in the former Palace of Graphic Arts on Montjuïc, which was built for the 1929 International Exhibition.

Fundació Joan Miró

THE CIUTAT UNIVERSITÀRIA DISTRICT
Monestir de Santa Maria de Pedralbes★★

Bajada Monestir 9. ⏰ *Open Apr–Sept Tue–Sat 10am–5pm, Sun and public holidays 10am–3pm; Oct–Mar Tue–Sat 10am–2pm, Sun and public holidays 10am–3pm.* ⏰ *Closed 1 Jan, 1 May, Good Fri, 24 Jun, 25 Dec.* ⊚6€. ☎932 03 92 82.

Founded in the 14C by King James II of Aragón and his fourth wife, the monastery has a fine Catalan Gothic **church**★ with the tomb of the foundress. The three-storey **cloisters**★ surrounded by cells and oratories are sober and elegant. The Sant Miquel Chapel is adorned with beautiful **frescoes**★★★ by Ferrer Bassá (1346), whose works combine the attention to detail of the Siena School with the acute sense of volume and perspective of Tuscan masters.

Palau de Pedralbes (Pedralbes Palace)

Av. Diagonal 686. ⏰*Open Tue–Sun 10am–6pm, public holidays 10am–3pm.* ⏰*Closed 1 Jan, 1 May, 24 Jun, 25–26 Dec.* ⊚4.20€ *(includes Decorative Arts Museum and Textile and Costume Museum); no charge first Sun in month.* ☎932 56 34 65. www.museuceramica. bcn.es.

This residence for King Alfonso XIII (1919–1929) was influenced by palaces of the Italian Renaissance. It houses the **Museu de les Artes Decoratives**★, with household items from the Middle Ages to the industrial design era; and the **Museu de Ceràmica**, showing evolutions in ceramics from the 13C.

ADDITIONAL SIGHTS

CosmoCaixa *(Isaac Newton 26)*
Església de Sant Pau del Camp (cloisters★*) (Sant Pau 99)*
Teatre Nacional de Catalunya *(Pl. de les Arts 1)*
Auditorio *(Lepant 150)*
Torre Agbar *(Av. Diagonal 211)*

EXCURSIONS
Monestir de Sant Cugat del Vallès★★

20km/12.4mi W by BP 1417. ⏰ *Open Jun–Sept Tue–Sat 10am–1.30pm, 3–8pm, Sun and public holidays 10am–2.30pm; Oct–May Tue–Sat 10am–1.30pm, 3–7pm, Sun and public holidays 10am–2.30pm.* ⏰ *Closed 1, 6 Jan, 25–26 Dec.* ⊚3€. ☎935 89 63 66.

A Benedictine **monastery** was built in the Middle Ages where an earlier chapel held the relics of St Cucufas (murdered here around AD 304).

The oldest part of the **Església**★ (church) is the 11C belfry. Note the 14C **All Saints Altarpiece**★ by Pere Serra.

The **Claustro**★, among the largest Romanesque cloisters in Catalunya, is a museum. During the 11C–12C a double row of columns (144 in all) was built around a close; in the 16C an upper gallery was added above a blind arcade. Skilfully carved **Romanesque capitals**★ are Corinthian, ornamental, figurative and historiated (biblical scenes). The sculptor, Arnaud Cadell, portrayed himself at work on a northeast corner column, and inscribed his name.

Terrassa/Tarrasa

31km/19mi NW along the C 58.

This industrial town retains some remarkable pre-Romanesque churches showing Pyrenean influence and Roman and Visigothic features.

Conjunto Monumental de Esglésias de Sant Pere★★

⏰ *Open Tue–Sat 10am–1.30pm, 4–7pm, Sun 11am–2pm.* ⏰ *Closed public holidays.* ☎937 83 37 02.

The **Antiguo baptisterio de Sant Miquel**★ was built in the 9C using late Roman remains. The dome rests on eight pillars; four have Roman capitals, four are Visigothic. Alabaster windows in the apse filter light onto 9C-10C pre-Romanesque wall paintings. The crypt's three apses have horseshoe arches.

The magnificent Romanesque Lombard church of **Santa Maria**★ has an octagonal cupola and a *cimborrio* (lantern); a 5C mosaic survives in front. A 13C wall fresco in the south transept, of the martyrdom of Thomas à Becket, retains bright colours. Note the 15C north transept altarpiece by Jaime Huguet, **St Abdon and St Sennen**★★. **Sant Pere** is a rustic church begun in the 6C on a trapezoid plan with a Romanesque transept crossing. In the apse is a curious **stone altarpiece**★.

Masía Freixa★

Plaça de Josep Freixa i Artem.
This bizarre mansion (1907) with its accentuated parabolic arches is one of Catalonia's most striking Modernist works.

Museu de la Ciència y la Tècnica de Catalunya★

Rambla d'Ègara 270. ○Open Sept–Jun Tue–Fri 10am–7pm, Sat–Sun 10am–2.30pm; Jul–Aug Tue–Sun 10am–2.30pm. ○ Closed 1, 6 Jan, 25–26 Dec. ⊕3.50€; no charge first Sun of the month. ℘937 36 89 66. www.mnactec.cat.
This excellent modern National Museum of Science and Technology museum is housed in a 1909 woollen mill.

Serra de Montserrat★★

49km/31mi NW along the C 58.
The grand **site**★★★ of the Macizo de Montserrat (Montserrat Massif) was the setting for Wagner's Parsifal. Hard Eocene conglomerates rise above eroded formations. It is the main site of devotion to the Virgin in Catalunya. **Views**★★ from the road are impressive.
The Montserrat cable car runs from near Monistrol de Montserrat.

Monastery and Basilica

○ Open daily 7.30am–8pm. ⊕5€ (museum). ℘938 77 77 66. www.abadiamontserrat.net.
The Benedictines arrived in the 9C and every century since then has seen

additions to the monastery. In 1812, it was sacked by the French.
The present buildings are 19C and 20C. At the end of the dark, ornate **basilica** (15C) is **La Moreneta** ★★, the shrine of the Black Madonna. By legend this 12C polychrome statue of the Black Madonna, now above the high altar, was discovered in a cave by shepherds.

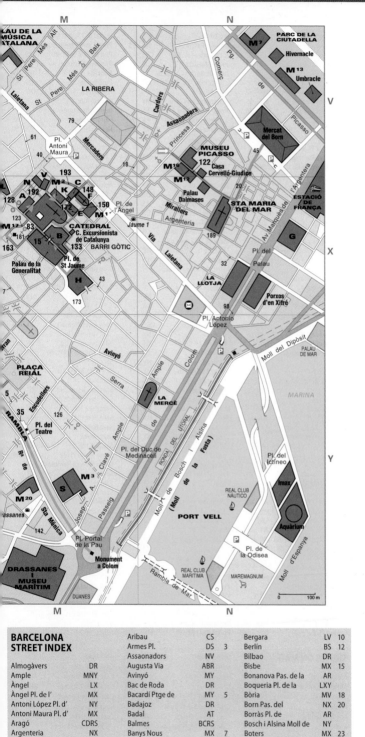

SIGHTS ON MAP

The Basilica is famous for its **Gregorian chant**, particularly during Mass at 11am and Vespers at 6.45pm.

The **Escolanía**, (*Mon–Thu 1pm and 6.45pm, Fri 1pm, Sun and festivals noon and 6.45pm. ℘938 77 77 67. www.escolania.cat*) one of the world's oldest boys' choirs, is another great aural experience.

HERMITAGES AND VIEWPOINTS

Tourist office. ℘938 77 77 01. www. montserratvisita.com. Access via the mountain trails, cable cars or funiculars. Sant Joan: Jan–Mar and Nov–Dec Mon–Fri 11am–4pm; Sat–Sun and public holidays 10am–4pm; Apr–Jun and Sept–Oct daily 10am–5.40pm; Jul–Aug daily 10am–7pm. 6.30€ round-trip (every 20min). ℘93 205 15 15. Santa Cova: daily 10am–1pm, 2–5pm (4pm Nov–Feb). 2.50€ (every 20min).
The 13 hermitages, abandoned since the arrival of Napoleon's troops, offer historical interest and fine views.

Ermita de la Trinitat (*45min on foot),* charmingly nestled in a bucolic plain, is sheltered by three mountains: El Elefante (The Elephant), La Preñada (Pregnant Woman) and La Momia (The Mummy). On a clear day, **Sant Jeroni**★ (*1hr30min on foot or by car*) at 1 238m/4 062ft, offers a **panorama** from the Pyrenees to the Balearic Islands. **Ermita de Santa Cecilia** features an attractive 11C **Romanesque church**★. Its east end is circled by Lombard bands. The statue of the Virgin was found in **Santa Cova** (holy cave), *1hr walk*, which has views of the Llobregat Valley. **Sant Miquel**★ (*30min from the monastery; 1hr from the upper terminal of the Sant Miquel funicular*) has a general view of the monastery. **Sant Joan** (*30min from upper terminal of the Sant Joan funicular*) offers a beautiful panorama; the Ermita de San Onofre may be seen clinging to the rock face.

ADDRESSES

🏠STAY

⊝🛏 **Hotel Condal** – *Boquería 23 (Barri Gótic).* 🚇*Liceu.* ☎*933 18 18 82. www. hotelcondal.es. 53 rooms.* Steps from La Rambla, this hotel is a fine base for visiting the old city. Personnel are attentive, and the rooms are adequate.

⊝🛏🛏 **Best Western Hotel Medicis** – *Castillejos 340 (Eixample).* 🚇*Hospital Sant Pau.* ☎*934 50 00 53. www.best westernhotelmedicis.com. 29 rooms.* This modern hotel, near the Sagrada Família, has functional but comfortable rooms, a good value for those who prefer to stay along the "Modernist Route".

⊝🛏🛏 **Hotel Gaudí** – *Nou de la Rambla 12 (Ciutat Vella).* 🚇*Liceu.* ☎*933 17 90 32. www.hotelgaudi.es. 73 rooms.* 🍽*10€.* Its location opposite the Palau Güell and Modernist décor evoke the namesake artist. Try for a room with balcony on an upper floor for superb views of the city and the Palau Güell.

⊝🛏🛏 **Hotel Granvía** – *Gran Via de les Corts Catalanes 642 (Eixample).* 🚇*Cataluyna.* ☎*933 18 19 00. www. nnhotels.es. 53 rooms.* 🍽*23€.* This impressive banker's residence from the late 19C was converted into a hotel in 1936. The room rates here are very reasonable given the charming setting.

⊝🛏🛏 **Hotel Hesperia Metropol** – *Ample 31 (Ribera).* 🚇*Jaume I.* ☎*933 10 51 00. www.hesperia-metropol.com. 71 rooms.* 🍽*11€.* This pleasant hotel close to the waterfront is situated in a narrow street in the old quarter, between the post office and the Basílica de La Mercè. An attractive feature here is the lobby in a covered patio. The guest rooms are comfortable, with the usual creature comforts.

⊝🛏🛏🛏 **Hotel Arts Barcelona** – *Marina 19.* 🚇*Ciutadella-Vila Olímpica.* ☎*932 21 10 00. 483 rooms.* 🍽*30€. Restaurant*⊝🛏🛏🛏. Barcelona's most luxurious hotel, with an emphasis on modern art and design, is in the Vila Olímpica. Every room enjoys impressive views of the city and Mediterranean.

⊝🛏🛏🛏 **Regencia Colón** – *Sagristans 13–17 (Barri Gótic).* 🚇*Jaume I.* ☎*933 18 98 58. www.hotelregenciacolon.com. 50 rooms.* 🍽*10€. Restaurant*⊝🛏🛏. Renovated in 1999, this hotel is located next to the city Cathedral and the Barcelona Ramblas in the Gothic Quarter, with a wonderful view over the Plaça de Catedral. Functional rooms with floor tiling and well-maintained bathrooms. The restaurant offers creative Mediterranean cuisine.

🍴 EAT

⊝🛏 **Senyor Parellada** – *Hotel Banys Orientals, L'Argentaria 37 (Ciutat Vella).* 🚇*Jaume I.* ☎*933 10 50 94. www.senyor parellada.com.* Located in a 19C building, this restaurant has various dining rooms adorned with chandeliers and wooden furniture along with a delightful patio, topped with a glass roof. Regional cuisine with good value prices.

⊝🛏 **La Taula** – *Sant Màrius 8.* 🚇*Lesseps.* ☎*934 17 28 48. www.lataula.com. Closed Aug, Sat for lunch, Sun, public holidays.* A small restaurant with beautifully detailed décor. A lively atmosphere where they concentrate on continental cuisine with a creative 'surprise menu' and La Taula menu.

⊝🛏🛏 **Can Majó** – *Almirall Aixada 23 (Ciutat Vella).* 🚇*Barceloneta.* ☎*932 21 54 55. www.canmajo.es. Closed Sun for dinner, Mon.* A famous family-run restaurant overlooking the port where they serve an exquisite menu of seafood dishes on an attractive terrace.

⊝🛏🛏 **Elx** – *Moll d'Espanya-Mare magnum, Local 9 (Ciutat Vella).* 🚇*Barceloneta.* ☎*932 25 81 17. www. restaurantelche.com.* A restaurant with lovely views over the fishing harbour, with modern décor and a menu that specialises in seafood and rice dishes.

⊝🛏🛏 **Los Caracoles** – *Escudellers 14 (Ciutat Vella).* 🚇*Liceu.* ☎*933 01 20 41. www.loscaracoles.es.* Founded in 1835, this famous restaurant, one of the gastronomic emblems of Barcelona, is located on the corner of carrers Escudellers and Nou de Sant Franc. The décor here consists of tiled floors, wine barrels, murals and photos. Regional and traditional cuisine.

La Provença – *Provença 242 (Eixample). Diagonal. 933 23 23 67. www.laprovenza.com.* In the Eixample district, just a stone's throw from the Passeig de Gràcia, pleasant and with cheerful, tasteful, décor, serving a range of regional cuisine. Good for the price.

El Tragaluz – *Pas. de la Concepció 5 (Eixample). Diagonal. 934 87 01 96. www.grupotragaluz. com/tragaluz.* One of Barcelona's most charismatic and dynamic restaurants takes up three storeys with unique sliding greenhouse roof. It serves Mediterranean and avant-garde fare.

Casa Calvet – *Casp 48 (Eixample). Urquinaona. 934 12 40 12. www.casacalvet.es. Closed Sun and public holidays.* The former offices of a textile company, in a magnificent Modernist building designed by Gaudí, are dominated by iron beams and wood floors. Traditional Mediterranean dishes show creative touches.

Casa Leopoldo – *Sant Rafael 24 (Ciutat Vella). Liceu. 934 41 30 14. www.casaleopoldo.com. Closed Sun and public holidays for dinner, Mon, Holy Week, a week in Jan, Aug.* This classic Barcelona restaurant is decorated with bullfighting mementos, signed photos of famous customers and a superb bottle collection.

Quatre Gats – *Montsió 3 bis (Ciutat Vella). Catalunya. 933 02 41 40. www.4gats.com.* The symbol of Modernist and bohemian Barcelona. This landmark café was a meeting place for artists such as Picasso, Casas and Utrillo. Reasonable lunchtime menu.

Xiringuito Escribà – *Ronda Litoral 42 (Vila Olímpica-Poble Nou). Ciutadella-Vila Olímpica. 932 21 07 29. www.escriba.es.* Open along the sea since 1906, this is a Barcelona summer institution, a good place to enjoy paella and music in a genuine setting.

La Boqueria market
R. Mattes/MICHELIN

TAPAS

Euskal Etxea – *Placeta Montcada 1–3 (Ribera). Jaume I. 933 10 21 85. http:// euskaletxeak.org. Closed Christmas week and a fortnight in Aug.* By the church of Santa Maria del Mar, a bar and cosy dining room, the perfect setting for a glass of *txacolí* (a Basque white wine) and Basque pork chops and fried fish.

Irati Taverna Basca – *Cardenal Casañas 17 (Barri Gòtic). Liceu. 933 02 30 84. www.sagardi.com.* Near the Plaça de la Boqueria, in one of the busiest districts, a typical tapas bar with a counter full of Basque skewers along with a grill room with a limited menu.

El Xampanyet – *Montcada 22 (Ribera). Jaume I. 933 19 70 03. Closed Sun, Holy Week and Aug.* In an alleyway close to the Picasso Museum, this bar is famous for anchovies and sparkling wine.

CAFÉS

Café de la Opera – *Rambla dels Caputxins 74 (Ciutat Vella). Liceu. 933 17 75 85. www.cafeoperabcn.com.* Because of its history, Modernist façade and 19C atmosphere, this café is one of the most famous in the city. Not to be missed!

El Paraigua – *Pas. de l'Enseyança 2 (Horta). Jaime I. 933 02 11 31.* This unusual café, in an ex-umbrella factory, is decorated with mirrors and Modernist furnishings. Its cocktail bar is in a vaulted 1650 cellar; the music is classical.

🍷 BARS AND 🍸/CAFÉS

Bar Pastís – *Santa Mònica 4 (Ciutat Vella).* 🚇*Drassanes.* 📞*933 18 79 80. www. barpastis.com.* Enjoy a pastís in this bar with 40 years of tradition as you listen to Jacques Brel, Moustaki and Edith Piaf; or dance a tango until dawn on Tuesday or enjoy French chansons late Saturday.

La Fira – *Provença 171 (Eixample).* 🚇*Diagonal.* 📞*933 23 72 71.* An attractive bar decorated with robots and fairground amusements.

Jamboree – *Pl. Reial 17 (Ciutat Vella).* 🚇*Liceu.* 📞*933 01 75 64. www.masimas. com.* The meeting point in Barcelona for jazz musicians and aficionados.

London Bar – *La Rambla 34 (Ciutat Vella).* 🚇*Liceu.* 📞*933 18 52 81.* A favourite with circus performers when it first opened in 1909. Hemingway, Miró and others also came here to enjoy its lively atmosphere.

Luz de Gas-Port Vell – *Moll del Dipósit (Port Vell in front of Palau de Mar).* 🚇*Barceloneta.* 📞*932 09 77 11. www. luzdegas.com.* One of the busiest and most unusual summer drinking spots, at the port, it is partly on the pier as an open-air bar, and partly an enclosed wooden bar with a small dance floor.

Margarita Blue – *Josep Anselm Clavé 6 (Ciutat Vella).* 🚇*Drassanes.* 📞*934 12 54 89. margaritablue.com.* Unusual decoration (mirrors of all shapes and sizes, weird objects and antique lamps) helps make this one of the city's most popular bars, hosting weekly shows and concerts. The cuisine is Tex-Mex.

Marina Port Olympic – *Pas. Maritim Port Olympic.* 🚇*Ciutadella Vila Olímpica.* One of the lieveliest spots has something for every taste, from restaurants to fast food, bars like the Gran Casino, and discos, including the popular Luna Mora.

La Paloma – *Tigre 27 (Sant Antoni).* 🚇*Universitat.* 📞*933 01 68 97.* One of the most packed of the city's clubs since 1903, with live music and a guest DJs from all over.

Torres de Ávila – *Av. del Marquès de Comillas 25 (Sants/Montjuïc).* 🚇*Espanya.* 📞*934 24 93 09.* This popular venue, refurbished by designers Mariscal and Arribas, attracts large crowds in summer.

🎭 ENTERTAINMENT

The **Palau de la Música Catalana** *(Sant Pere Més Alt;* 📞*902 44 28 82; www. palaumusica.org).* **Gran Teatre del Liceu** *(La Rambla 51–59;* 📞*934 85 99 00; www. liceubarcelona.com)* and the **Auditorio** *(Lepant 150;* 📞*932 47 93 00; www.audi tori.com)* are the biggest concert halls. Major pop and rock concerts are held in the **Palau Sant Jordi**, **Velódromo de Horta**, **Plaça de Toros Monumental** *(Marina 749; www.torosbarcelona.com)* and **Sot del Migdia** *(Foc 154).* The **Festival del Grec** *(end Jun–early Aug;* 📞*933 16 10 00; www.barcelona festival.com)* is held at several venues, including the **Teatre Grec de Montjuïc**.

🛒 SHOPPING

ANTIQUES

Bulevard dels Antiquaris – *Pas. de Gràcia 55 (Eixample).* 🚇*Diagonal.* 📞*932 15 44 99. www.bulevarddelsantiquaris.com.* An area containing over 70 shops selling a range of artwork and antiques.

Plaça de la Catedra – *Ciutat Vella.* 🚇*Jaume I.* A small market with stalls selling antiques is held here on public holidays.

Plaça Sant Josep Oriol – *Ciutat Vella.* 🚇*Liceu.* Mirrors, furniture, and paintings are sold at this popular weekend market.

La Palla and Banys Nous – *Ciutat Vella.* 🚇*Liceu.* These two streets are well known for their reputable antique shops.

ART GALLERIES

Barcelona's most prestigious galleries can mainly be found in Carrer Consell de Cent **(Carles Tatché**, **René Metras**, **Sala Gaudí)**, along the Rambla de Catalunya **(Joan Prats**; *www. galeriajoanprats.com)*, on the periphery of the Born market and around the MACBA. The **Galeria Maeght** *(www. maeght.com)* and the **Sala Montcada** are both located in carrer Montcada.

Costa Brava★★★

Spain's Costa Brava (literally "Wild Coast") is a twisted, rocky shoreline where the Catalan mountains fall away into the sea. Beautiful inlets, clear waters, picturesque harbours, and leisure and sporting activities draw tourists to these shores. Inland there are delightful medieval towns and villages.

🚗 DRIVING TOURS

1 ALBERES COASTLINE★★

Portbou. Roses 65km/40mi – half a day.
The foothills of the Serra de l'Albera form huge, enclosed bays, like those of Portbou and El Port de la Selva. The clifftop **road section**★★ from Portbou to Colera offers fine views of one of the most craggy coastlines in Catalunya.

El Port de Llançà

🚃 *Plaça de la Estación.*
A pleasant tourist resort sited on a bay sheltered from winds like the *tramontana* and sudden Mediterranean storms. The shallow waters are ideal for a swim.

▶ *Take the GI 612 for 8km/5mi.*

El Port de la Selva★

This bay is bathed in golden sunlight at dusk. Traditional white houses stand beside numerous flats and hotels. Fishing is still one of the main activities.

Monestir de Sant Pere de Rodes★★★

7km/4.3mi from El Port de la Selva.
🅿 *Leave your car in the car park and proceed on foot for 10min.* 🕐 *Open Tue–Sun Oct–May 10am–5.30pm; Jun–Sept 10am–8pm.* 🕐 *Closed 1 Jan, 25 Dec.* 💰*3.60€; no charge Tue.*
📞 *972 28 75 59.*
This imposing Benedictine monastery stands in a beautiful **setting**★★ that dominates the Gulf of León and the Cap de Creus peninsula. Begun in the 10C, it was pillaged, and abandoned in

Michelin Map: 574 E 39, F 39, G 38-39 – Catalunya (Girona)

Info: Girona: Rambla de la Llibertat 1. 📞972 22 65 75; Blanes: Plaça Catalunya 21. 📞972 33 03 48; Cadaqués: Des Cotxe 2 A. 📞972 25 83 15. www.costabrava.org.

Location: The Costa Brava is the coastline from Blanes up to Portbou on the border with France. Lloret de Mar, Tossa de Mar and Platja d'Aro are major tourist centres; towns to the north are more low key.

Kids: Beaches are the main attractions for younger tourists.

the 18C. The remarkable **church**★★★, showing pre-Romanesque influence, is an unusual example of architectural harmony. The central nave has barrel vaulting, the two lateral ones have surbased vaulting. They are separated by huge pillars, reinforced with columns on raised bases. Splendid **capitals**★, intricate tracery and acanthus leaves evoke the tradition of Córdoba and Byzantium. The left arm of the transept leads to an upper ambulatory offering a sweeping view of the central nave. The 12C **bell tower**★★ is a magnificent example of Lombardy Gothic.

The coast between El Port de la Selva and Cadaqués features many irregular creeks with crystal-clear waters, accessible only by sea. The road inland offers lovely views of the region.

▶ *Return to El Port de la Selva and turn right on the GI 613.*

Cadaqués★★

Cadaqués lies south of the Cap de Creus in a delightful **setting**★ enclosed by mountains. It was a humble fishing village until modern artists (Dalí, Picasso, García Lorca, Buñuel, André Breton, Paul Éluard etc) made it fashionable.

White houses with picturesque porticoes cluster around the **Església de Santa Maria** *(pl. Dr Callis 15;* ⏰ *open daily 11am–8pm;* ☎*972 25 85 00)*, whose sober exterior contrasts with its interior: note the lovely **Baroque altarpiece**★★ in gilded wood. The town hosts an annual international music festival *(early Aug; www.festivalcadaques.cat)*.

▶ *Head N for 2km/1.2mi.*

Portlligat★

The **Casa-Museu Salvador Dalí**★ *(*⏰*open 15 Jun–15 Sept daily 9.30am–9pm; 16 Sept–6 Jan, 15 Mar–14 Jun Tue–Sun 10.30am–6pm.* ⏰*Closed 1 Jan, 24–25 Dec.* ⬡*10€.* ☎*972 25 10 15; www.salvador-dali.org)* is a cluster of fishermen's houses. Dalí's workshop, library, rooms and garden are all open to the public.

▶ *Continue 4km/2.5mi N*

Parque Natural de Cap de Creus★★

Steep roads and paths wind between cliffs and hidden bays. Enjoy a spectacular **view**★★★ from the **lighthouse** at the highest point.

▶ *Return to Cadaqués, then head SW on the Gl 614 and E on the C 260.*

Roses★

Sailors of Rhodes founded a colony in a splendid natural harbour overlooking the Golfo de Roses. Its 16C Renaissance **citadel**★ *(av. de Roses;* ⏰*open Tue–Sun Apr–Sept 10am–8pm; Oct–Mar 10am–6pm;* ⏰*closed 1, 6 Jan, 25 Dec;* ⬡*3€;* ☎*972 15 14 66; www.rosesfhn.org)*, a pentagon with many bastions, was commissioned by Charles V. The Benedictine monastery inside was destroyed by the French during the War of Independence. The town is both resort and fishing port.

②THE EMPORDÀ PLAIN★

Roses to Begur 75km/46.5mi – 1 day
The fertile plain lies along the coast.

▶ *Leave Roses on the C 260 towards Castelló d'Empúries.*

Empuriabrava★

The luxury marina-residential development allows backyard docking.

Castelló d'Empúries★

The former capital of the principality of Empúries (11C–14C) is on a promontory near the coast. The 14C–15C **Basílica de Santa Maria**★ is flanked by a typical Catalan belfry. The **portal**★★ is a unique example of Gothic art in Catalunya: the tympanum illustrates the Adoration of the Magi while the Apostles are shown on the jambs. The large central nave is lined by fine cylindrical pillars. The alabaster **retable**★ in the high altar (15C), with conical pinnacles, depicts the Passion. *(*⏰*open Jun–Sept 10am–1pm, 4–8pm, Sun and public holidays 11am–12.30pm, 4–8pm; Oct–May Sat–Sun 11am–12.30pm, 4–8pm.* ☎*972 25 05 19)*.

The village retains buildings from its golden age: the **Ajuntament** (Maritime Commodities Exchange), combining Romanesque and Gothic elements, and the **Casa Gran**, of Gothic inspiration.

▶ *Leave Castelló d'Empúries towards Sant Pere Pescador. From here, continue S until you reach the Gl 623.*

L'Escala★

This resort has sandy beaches and a long fishing tradition (anchovies are salted). Two inlets protect its harbour.
The Empúries ruins are located to the N.

Empúries/Ampurias★★

Puig i Cadafalch. ⏰*Open daily Oct–May 10am–6pm; Jun–Sept 10am–8pm.* ⏰*Closed 1 Jan & 25 Dec.* ⬡*3€; no charge last Sun in month, 23 Apr, 18 May and 11 Sept.* ☎*972 77 02 08. www.mac.cat.*

Greco-Roman Ampurias (*Emporion* to the Greeks, meaning market) was built on a striking seaside **site**★★. It is still possible to make out the old town, or **Paliápolis**, the new town or **Neápolis**, and the Roman town.

In the mid-6C BC, the Phoenicians founded Paliápolis, on an offshore island, now joined to the mainland

and occupied by the village of Sant Martí d'Empúries. A town began to develop on the shore opposite: Neápolis. As a Roman ally during the Punic Wars, it saw the arrival of an expedition led by Scipio Africanus Major in 218 BC. In 100 BC the Roman town was established to the west. The two centres coexisted until Augustus bestowed Roman citizenship upon the Greeks. The colony suffered from barbarian invasions in the 3C AD. At one time it was a bishopric, as basilica ruins show.

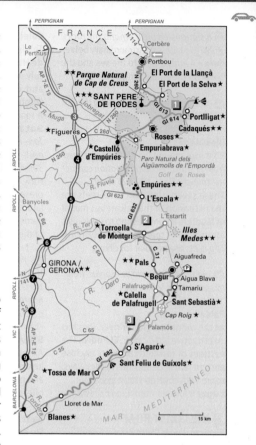

Neápolis

The **Templo de Asclepio** (Aesculapius – god of healing) and a sacred precinct contained altars and statues of the gods. Nearby stood a **watchtower** and drinking water cisterns. The **Templo de Zeus Serapis** (a god associated with the weather and with healing) was surrounded by a colonnade. The **Agora** was the centre of town life; three statues remain. A street from the agora to the sea was bordered on one side by the **stoa** or covered market. Behind it are the ruins of a 6C **palaeo-Christian basilica** with a rounded apse.

Museu Arqueológic d'Empúries

A section of Neápolis is displayed along with models of temples and finds from the excavations.

The Roman Town

Unlike Neápolis, this is a vast, geometrically laid out town, partially excavated, with some restored walls. **House no. 1** (entrance at the back) has an atrium (inner courtyard) with six columns. Around this are residential apartments, the peristyle, or colonnaded court, and the impluvium, or rainwater catchment. The reception rooms are paved in geometric, black-and-white mosaic.

House no. 2B has rooms paved with their original mosaic. One has been reconstituted in clay with its walls resting on stone foundations.

The **forum**, a large square lined by porticoes and, to north and south respectively, by temples and shops, was the centre of civic life. A porticoed street led through the city gate to the oval **amphitheatre** which is still visible.

▷ *Take the GI 632 to Bellcaire d'Empordà, then turn left onto the GI 640.*

Torroella del Montgrí★

Despite a Baroque front, the 14C **Església de Sant Genís** (pas. de l'Església) is a fine example of Gothic Catalan art. The **castle** on Montaña de Montgrì (🚶1hr *on a signposted path among the rocks; ℘972 75 51 80)* is an extraordinary **belvedere**★★ with a view to the sea and the Gavarres mountain range.

Continue for 5km/3mi along the GI 641 to L'Estartit.

Illes Medes★★

Boat trips around the islands are offered from l'Estartit. For information contact the tourist office. ℘972 75 19 10.

These seven islets and coral reefs are the extension of the calcareous massif of Montgrí. It is interesting to ecologists for its marine species and ecosystems. The islets are popular for diving.

Return to Torroella de Montgrí from L'Estartit, then follow the C 31.

Pals★★

At the mouth of the Ter river, Pals has an attractive old quarter, **El Pedró**. The vestiges of fortified ramparts enclose ancient houses and winding alleyways, some with covered stairways.

Begur *is located 7km/4.3mi E of Pals.*

3 THE COAST ROAD★★

Begur to Blanes 98km/61mi – 1 day

Plains and mountains that extend down to the sea alternate with long beaches and **coves** of astounding beauty: **Aiguafreda**, **Aigua Blava**, **Tamariu**, sheltered by pine trees and dotted with luxury villas and exclusive hotels.

Begur★

The town overlooks pretty creeks from an altitude of 200m/656ft above the sea. The castle ruins (16C–17C) offer a nice view of Begur.

Leave Begur and head for Llafranc.

Far de Sant Sebastià★

2km/1.2mi from Llafranc.

Built in 1857, the lighthouse stands on a tiny isthmus surrounded by steep cliffs. The nearby hermitage commands a lovely **view**★.

Calella de Palafrugell★

This fishing port is known for its **Festival de Habaneras** on the first Saturday in July. Visitors enjoy Afro-Cuban songs and dances while sipping *cremat*, flambéed coffee with rum.

A road southward leads to the **Jardin Botánic del Cap Roiga** *(open Jan–Feb Sat–Sun 9am–8pm; Mar–Dec daily 9am–6pm; 3€; ℘972 61 55 30)*. A terraced park carved out of the rock, overlooking the Mediterranean, presents more than 1 200 plant species laid out along shaded avenues. These gardens offer some wonderful **views**★★ of the coast.

Follow directions to Palafrugell, then take the C 31 to Palamós. Beyond, the C 253 skirts the coast; beaches alternating with rocky inlets. The C 31 is quicker though less scenic.

S'Agaro★

An elegant resort with chalets and luxury villas surrounded by tidy gardens and pine forests. The camino de Ronda offers fine views★ of the sheer cliffs.

Sant Feliu de Guíxols★

Sheltered from the last spurs of the Serra de les Gavarres, this is one of the most popular locations of this coast. Its seaside boulevard, passeig de la Mar, is lined with pavement cafés. The **Església-Monastir de Sant Feliu**★ *(open for Mass; ℘972 82 15 75)* is part of a former Benedictine monastery. Its remains tower over the small municipality. It has retained its Romanesque façade, known as the **Porta Ferrada**★★, with horseshoe arches dating to pre-Romanesque times. The interior (14C) is Gothic in style.

The lookout by the chapel of Sant Elm commands beautiful **views**★★.

Follow the GI 682, enjoying spectacular views of the coast.

Tossa de Mar★

This sandy beach curves around to Punta del Faro, the promontory on which stand the lighthouse and the 13C walls of the

Vila Vella★ (old town). The **Museu Municipal**★ *(Roig i Soler;* 🕐 *open Tue–Sat 10am–noon, 4–6pm, Sun 10am–2pm;* 🎫*3€;* 📞*972 34 07 09)* contains artefacts from an ancient Roman villa nearby, and works by artists who stayed in the 1930s including Chagall, Masson and Benet. Between Tossa and **Lloret de Mar** (the most commercialised tourist resort of the Costa Brava), the road follows a spectacular **clifftop route**★★.

▶ *Continue along the GI 682.*

Blanes★

The **Passeig Marítim**★ offers a lovely panorama of Blanes and its beach. The remains of the Castillo de Sant Joan are to the east, above the 14C Gothic Església de Santa Maria. To the southeast is the **Jardí Botànic de Marimurtra**★ *(pas. Karl Faust;* 🕐 *open daily Apr–May and Oct 9am–6pm; Jun–Sept 9am–8pm; Nov–Mar 10am–5pm;* 🎫*5.50€;* 📞*972 33 08 26)*, a botanical park with 5 000 plant species including many rare exotic varieties. At each bend the twisting paths reveal wonderful **views**★ of Cala Forcadera and the coast.

ADDRESSES

🏨 STAY

🛏 **Hotel Ubaldo** – *Unió 13, Cadaqués.* 📞*972 25 81 25. www.hotelubaldo.com. 26 rooms.* The hotel's simple façade masks a pleasant interior of white walls, curving furniture and soft lighting. Comfortable rooms overlook the alleyways of the old quarter.

🛏 **Hotel La Goleta** – *Pintor Terruella 22, El Port de LLança.* 📞*972 38 01 25. www.hotellagoleta.com. 28 rooms. Restaurant* 🛏. Close to the port, the La Goleta offers comfort and an interesting décor of paintings and other furnishings. A friendly atmosphere and good value for money.

🛏 **Hotel Rosa** – *Pi i Rallo 19, Begur.* 📞*972 62 30 15. www.hotel-rosa.com. 21 rooms. Restaurant* 🛏. *Closed Nov–Feb.* This small hotel in a restored stone house by the church is popular with a younger set for its modern décor, functional furniture and well-planned lighting. The restaurant serves traditional cuisine.

🛏 **Almadraba Park Hotel** – *Platja Almadraba, 4km/2.5mi SE of Roses.* 📞*972 25 65 50. www.almadrabapark. com. 60 rooms. Restaurant* 🛏. *Closed Nov–Feb.* A hotel offering impeccable service in a delightful natural setting amid lovely gardens. The building itself, modern in design and south facing, looks onto manicured gardens that descend to the sea in terraces. All the guest rooms enjoy wonderful views.

🛏 **Hotel Diana** – *Plaça de Espanya 6, Tossa de Mar.* 📞*972 34 18 86. www.hotelesdante.com. 21 rooms. Closed 16 Nov–3 Apr.* The interior of this splendid Modernist building by the sea is exquisite, with an high ceilings, cool rooms and a patio adorned with a marble fountain. The rooms are comfortable and furnished in style.

🛏 **Hotel Plaça** – *Pl. Mercat 22, Sant Feliu de Guíxols.* 📞*972 32 51 55. www.hotelplaza.org. 19 rooms.* 🍽*7€.* A practical choice for location and functional character. Pleasant, bright rooms – some overlook a square that's lively on market days. Outdoor jacuzzi and solarium on the top floor.

🛏 **Hotel Port Lligat** – *Avenida Salvador Dalí 1, Port Lligat.* 📞*972 25 81 62. www.port-lligat.net/hotel. 30 rooms.* 🍽*8€.* The creature comforts in this attractive blue and white building in a cove full of fishing boats near Dalí's house are particularly popular with guests. Every room is different, and if you don't mind paying a bit extra, ask for one with a sea view.

🛏 **Hotel Sant Roc** – *Pl. Atlàntic 2 (Sant Roc district), Calella de Palafrugell.* 📞*972 61 42 50. www.santroc.com. 47 rooms.* 🍽*11.50€. Restaurant. Closed mid-Nov–late Mar.* This charming building crowned by a small tower enjoys a peaceful, relaxing setting amid pine groves overlooking the Mediterranean. The rooms are spacious and elegant, while the restaurant terrace enjoys fine views of neighbouring coves. Half-board compulsory in summer.

⏲ EAT

Can Rafa – *Pas. 7, Cadaqués. Exit 4 from AP 7 towards Cadaqués* 📞*972 15 94 01.* Good local cuisine in a dining room covered with photos from the 1970s. Great bay views from the terrace.

Casa Buxó – *Major 18, Sant Feliu de Guíxols.* 📞*972 32 01 87. Closed mid-Dec–mid Mar.* An elegant restaurant with regional décor and large mirrors in the windows. A very good menu of local dishes complements the service.

La Brasa – *Pl. Catalunya 6, El Port de la Llançà.* 📞*972 38 02 02. www.restaurantlabrasa.com. Closed Mon for dinner, Tue (Sept–Jun).* The low-key atmosphere invites visitors in to enjoy grilled fish and meat. There's also a pleasant shady terrace.

Ca la Maria – *Unió 5, Mollet de Peralada. 4km/2.5mi N of Peralada.* 📞*972 56 33 82. www.restaurantcalamaria.net. Closed Sun for dinner, Tue and a fortnight in Feb.* A large restaurant in quiet Mollet, 16km/10mi inland. An unpretentious setting for real Catalan cuisine. Always busy at weekends.

Victoria – *Passeig del Mar 23, Tossa de Mar.* 📞*972 34 01 66. www.hrvictoriatossa.com. Closed 15 Nov–31 Jan, Tue (Sept–Jun).* A pleasant restaurant specialising in seafood and fish dishes, with a terrace overlooking the beach. There are also hotel rooms available with sea views.

El Bulli – *Cala Montjoi Ap. 30, Roses. 13km/8mi SE of Roses.* 📞*972 15 04 57. www.elbulli.com. Closed Oct–Holy Week. Reservations required.* A unique culinary experience by Ferran Adrià, with a tasting menu blended with technique and imagination. A holiday in the wonders of molecular gastronomy.

🍸 NIGHTLIFE

Avinguda Just Marlès Vilarrodona – *Av. Just Marlès Vilarrodona, Lloret de Mar.* At nightfall, this wide throroughfare sees a mix of beautiful girls, hunky men, and flower vendors at the doors to bars. At least ten discos: Londeners, Flamingo, Moef Gaga and Tropics, one of the largest and most modern on the Costa Brava; not to forget St Trop (one street over), the only one that can face up to Tropics, with 3 floors, 7 bars, and 200 000 watts of light.

Mojito Bar – *Codolar 2, Tossa de Mar.* A small cocktail bar with a relaxed air in the pedestrianised section of the resort. The Mojito mainly concentrates on salsa, flamenco and Sevillanas.

Moxo – *Empuriabrava.* The Moxo is the focal point for nightlife in this modern tourist resort, which has about 20 bars, nightclubs and restaurants. The Saloon specialises in country music and the Glass in techno.

Passarel-la – *Passeig maritim Apt. Correus 116, Empuriabrava. by the C-260 to Roses.* 📞*972 45 20 97. www.passarel-la.com.* Dance by moonlight at this beachside disco, or inside in two spaces with different music. There's also a large swimming pool here.

Rachdingue – *Roses road, Vilajuïga.* 📞*972 53 00 23. www.rachdingue.com.* This disco, started up by Dalí, is in a stone barn on a promontory, with a pool and garden bar.

🎭 ENTERTAINMENT

Water World – *Vidreres Road, Lloret de Mar.* 📞*972 36 86 13. www.waterworld.es.* 🎟*25€; child 15€. Closed 3 Oct–17 May.* The region's best water park.

🛍 SHOPPING

Carrer de l'Aigüeta – *La Bisbal d'Empordà.* Ceramics are a centuries-old tradition, with all sorts of objects in the shops on this street. Try El Risser.

Figueres★

Figueres, capital of Alt Empordà, the birthplace of Surrealist artist **Salvador Dalí** (1904–89), is one of Catalunya's premier destinations. Dalí spent his last years here, building his extravagant museum.

A BIT OF HISTORY

The end of the Spanish Civil War – The last meeting of the Republican Cortes was held here on 1 February 1939. Three days later, Girona fell to the Nationalists. Two days after, the Republican leaders crossed into France.

SIGHTS

The Dalian World

Salvador Dalí and Surrealism – Born in 1904, Dalí was to become one of most famous Surrealist artists. His "paranoid-critical" method, based on an ironic vision of reality, resulted in his expulsion from the Surrealist ranks by its founder, André Breton. In his most famous paintings, *The Great Masturbator, The Persistence of Memory, Atomic Leda and Premonition of the Civil War*, Dalí expresses his personal world through bland forms loaded with sensuality and sexual connotations.

The Dalian attractions in Figueres are both located around the lively Plaça de Dalí i Gala.

Teatre-Museu Dalí★★

Pl. de Dalí i Gala. ⏰*Open Mar–May and Oct Tue–Sun 9.30am–6pm; Jun daily 9.30am–6pm; Jul–Sept daily 9am–8pm; Nov–Feb Tue–Sun 10.30am–6pm; last entry 45min before closing.* ⏰*Closed 1 Jan, 25 Dec.* ⬡*11€.* ☎*972 67 75 00. www.salvador-dali.org.*

▶ **Population:** 42 809
◔ **Michelin Map:** 574 F 38 – map 122 Costa Brava. See local map under Costa Brava – Catalunya (Girona).
🗎 **Info:** Plaça del Sol. ☎972 50 31 55.
◗ **Location:** Figueres is located 20km/12.4mi inland, at the heart of the area known as the Ampurdán, at the crossroads of routes leading to the Costa Brava and the French city of Perpignan, 58km/36mi N. 🚌Plaça de La Estació.
🐾 **Don't Miss:** Everything Dalí: the Museum and Tower.
◕ **Timing:** Take a half-day at least, or longer if your world is Dalí's.

The theatre-museum, a world of folly and caprice, may charm or exasperate but never fails to impress. The artist himself said: "The museum cannot be considered as such; it is a gigantic surrealist object, where everything is coherent, where nothing has eluded my design." To a restored 1850 theatre Dalí added an immense glass dome (beneath which he is buried) and patio, and decorated everything with fantasy objects: giant eggs, bread rolls, basins and gilt dummies. He gave his eccentricity full rein in the squares around the museum where figures perch on columns of tyres, as well as inside. Some of his canvases are exhibited as well as works by Pitxot and Duchamp.

Dalí in the Area Around Figueres

Further examples of Dalí's creativity can be seen in two museums within a short distance of Figueres: the first, the **Casa-Museu Salvador Dalí▲**, is situated in the charming fishing village of **Cadaqués**★★ (⬡*see COSTA BRAVA*), 31km/19.2mi E of Figueres on the C 260 and GI 614; the second, the **Casa-Museu Castell Gala Dalí** (⬡*see GIRONA/GERONA*), in Púbol, 16km/10mi E of Girona on the C 66, is housed in the castle that Dalí gave to his wife, Gala, as a gift in 1970.

Torre Galatea★

The decoration of this tower by Dalí used vivid colours and fantasy objects.

FORÇA VELLA (OLD TOWN)

Figueres also has a pleasant historical centre with attractive squares and alleys. The Rambla is a pleasant street full of outdoor bars and restaurants,

Museu de Joguets★

Hotel París, Sant Pere 1. ◐ *Open Jun–Sept Mon–Sat 10am–7pm, Sun and public holidays 11am–6pm; Oct–May Tue–Sat 10am–6pm, Sun and public holidays 11am–2pm.* ◐ *Closed 1 Jan, 25 Dec.* ◔*5€.* ✆*972 50 45 85. www.mjc.cat.*

The museum displays toys and stuffed animals from different countries.

Museu de l'Empordà

Rambla 2. ◐ *Open Tue–Sat 11am–7pm, Sun and public holidays 11am–2pm.* ◐ *Closed 1 Jan, 1 Jun and 25–26 Dec.* ◔*2€; no charge with Museu Dalí ticket.* ✆*972 50 23 05. www.museu emporda.org.*

This building houses collections devoted to the art, history and archaeology of the region. Of note is the exhibition of works by 19C and 20C painters (Nonell, Sorolla, Dalí and Tàpies).

Església de Sant Pere

Pl. de l'Església. ◐ *Open Tue–Fri 9am–1pm, 4.30–8pm (9pm Sat); Sun 8.30am–1pm, 6–9pm.* ◐ *Closed 1, 6 Jan, 25–26 Dec.* ◔*2€; no charge 18 May.* ✆*972 50 03 25.*

Built in the late 13C, this church has a single nave of Gothic influence. Most of the church was rebuilt after the Spanish Civil War.

EXCURSION

Castell de Sant Ferran★

◔◔*Guided tours (2hr) daily Jul–Sept and Holy Week 10.30am–8pm; Oct–Jun 10.30am–3pm.* ◐ *Closed 1 Jan 25 Dec.* ◔*3€.* ✆*972 50 60 94. www.castillosanfernando.org.*

This mid-18C fortress, with star-shaped perimeter, defended the border with France. The castle was the second largest of its kind in Europe, with a parade ground alone that covered 12 000sq m/ 14 340sq yd. The **stables**★ are worthy of particular note. The **views**★ from the walls take in the Empordà plain.

ADDRESSES

🏠 STAY

◔◔◔◔◔ **Hotel Duràn** – *Lasauca 5.* ✆*972 50 12 50. www.hotelduran.com. 65 rooms.* ⛉*9.50€. Restaurant*◔◔◔◔ This hotel is in the town centre near the Dalí Museum, with large, comfortable rooms. The restaurant, specialising in Catalan dishes, is where Dalí himself used to dine.

◔◔◔◔◔ **Hotel Mas Falgarona** – *Avinyonet de Puigventós. 5.4km/3.3mi SW of Figueres on the N 260.* ✆*972 54 66 28. www.masfalgarona.com. 11 rooms. Restaurant*◔◔◔◔. This luxury hotel is housed in an old farmhouse. The minimalist décor, enhanced by various works of modern art, brings out the natural beauty of the stone, brick and wood. Delightful garden with pool.

🍴 EAT

◔◔◔◔◔ **Mas Pau** – *Avinyonet de Puigventós. 5km/3mi SW of Figueres on the N 260.* ✆*972 54 61 54. www.maspau. com. Closed 6 Jan–15 Mar, Sun evenings, Mon, Tue lunchtime.* This 16C farmstead has been sympathetically restored and decorated in exquisite taste with numerous antiques and beautiful bedrooms. Another feature is its cosy garden terraces. If you are a gourmet this is the perfect place to stay (or just visit for a meal ; ◔◔◔◔) as the maître d' and head chef respectively spent over 10 years at El Bulli restaurant, frequently ranked number one in the world.

Girona/ Gerona★★

Girona, with its heritage quarter, stands on a strategic site that has made it the target of repeated sieges. Its ramparts were built and rebuilt by Iberians, Romans and Catalans. Charlemagne's troops assaulted the city, and in 1809, Girona resisted Napoleon's troops for more than seven months.

THE CITY TODAY

Once seen as merely the international gateway to the region, Girona is now welcoming curious foreign visitors who have "done" Barcelona and are seeking similarly historic characterful Catalunyan cities to explore. With a mix of atmospheric streets and historic sights which reflect the city's rich multicultural heritage, all in a compact centre with a river running through its heart, Girona makes for a very satisfying day away from the coast.

SIGHTS
FORÇA VELLA (OLD TOWN)
Allow 3hr

Narrow alleys lead up to the Cathedral, with its monumental stairway, the **Escaleras de la Pera**. The 14C **Pia Almoina** building (*right*) is a fine example of Gothic architecture.

Catedral★

Pl. de la Catedral. ⏰*Open daily Apr–Oct 10am–8pm; Nov–Mar 10am–7pm.* 🎟*5€ (incl. nave, colisters and museum); no charge Sun.* 📞*972 21 58 14. www.catedraldegirona.org.*

▶ **Population:** 94 484
🅖 **Michelin Map:** 574 G 38 (town plan) – map 122 Costa Brava – Catalunya (Girona)
🅘 **Info:** Rambla de la Llibertat 1. 📞972 22 65 75. www.ajuntament.gi/turisme.
🅛 **Location:** Girona connects with Barcelona (97km/60.2mi SW) and France via the N II and AP 7. The C 255 leads to Palafrugell (39km/24mi SW) and the C 250 to Sant Feliu de Guíxols (36km/22mi SW), both on the coast. 🚉Plaça de Espanya
🅟 **Parking:** Park along one of the wider streets and walk into the old city.
🅓 **Don't Miss:** A walk through the old Jewish quarter is essential.
🕓 **Timing:** Walk around the old town, to the main sites, and also just to wander among the orange-and-ochre heritage buildings.

The Baroque façade is like an altarpiece with a single huge oculus. The rest of the building is Gothic: the chancel (1312) is surrounded by chapels; the single Gothic **nave**★★ is the largest in the world, and largely unadorned. A silver-gilt embossed 14C **altarpiece**★ traces the Life of Christ. The Sant Honorat chapel has the outstanding tomb, in a Gothic niche, of Bishop Bernard de Pau.

Girona and Judaism

Girona's Jewish community, which settled on both sides of **Carrer de la Força** in the city's old quarter, was the second largest in Catalunya after Barcelona, and became famous in the Middle Ages for its prestigious Kabbalistic School, which existed for over 600 years from the 9C until the expulsions of 1492. This past can be felt in atmospheric narrow alleyways such as Carrer Cúndaro and Carrer Sant Llorenç, the latter home to the **Centro Bonastruc ça Porta**, dedicated to the town's Jewish history.

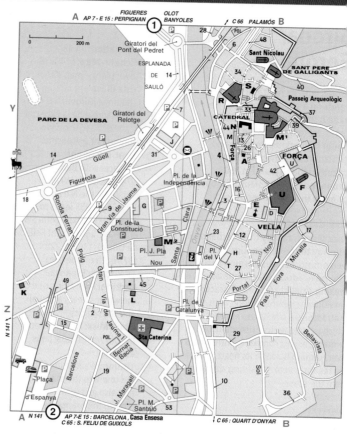

Museu-Tresor de la Catedral★★

The treasury houses one of the most beautiful copies of the **Beatus**★★, or *St John's Commentary on the Apocalypse* (8C). The 10C embossed silver **Hixem Casket** is a fine example of Caliphate art, and there is Gothic silver and plate of the 14C and 15C. The end room contains the **Tapís de la Creació**★★★ (Tapestry of Creation), dating from about 1100, showing Christ in Majesty surrounded by the stages of creation.

The 12C–13C **cloisters**★, remain – like the 11C Torre de Carlomagno (Charlemagne Tower) – from an earlier Romanesque cathedral.

Museu d'Art de Girona★★

Pujada de la Catedral 12. ○*Open Mar–Sept Tue–Sat 10am–7pm, Sun 10am–2pm; Oct–Feb Tue–Sat 10am–6pm, Sun 10am–2pm.* ○*Closed 1, 6 Jan, 25–26 Dec.* ⊙*2€.* ℘*972 20 38 34. www.museuart.com.*

The museum, in the Palau Episcopal, exhibits art from the Romanesque to the present. Holdings include a 10C portable altar from Sant Pere de Rodes of embossed silver, the 12C–13C **beam from Cruïlles**★, and apse paintings from Pyrenean churches. Among altarpieces in the Throne Room is one from **Sant Miquel de Cruïlles**★★ by Luis Borrassá (15C), Catalunya's greatest Gothic artist. Note the splendid **Púbol altarpiece**★, by Bernat Martorell (1437). The panels of the **Sant Feliu altarpiece** by Juan de Borgoña mark the transition from Gothic to Renaissance style.

Colegiata de Sant Feliu★

Pujada Sant Feliu 29. ○ *Open Mon–Sat 10am–1pm, 4–6pm, Sun 4–6pm.* ⊙*No charge.* ℘*972 20 14 07.*

This church outside the walls must originally have been a martyry over the tombs of St Narcissus, Bishop of Girona, and St Felix. The later Gothic church holds eight **early Christian sarcophagi**★, two with outstanding carvings, including a spirited **lion hunt**★.

Banys àrabs★ (Arab Baths)

Ferran el Católic. ○ *Open Apr–Sept Mon–Sat 10am–7pm, Sun and public holidays 10am–2pm; Oct–Mar Mon–Sat 10am–2pm.* ○*Closed 1, 6 Jan, 25–26 Dec.* ⊙*2€.* ℘*972 21 32 62. www. banysarabs.org.*

These late-12C baths were built in accordance with Muslim tradition. They consist of four rooms in a row. Steps opposite lead to the **Passeig Arqueològic (Archaeological Promenade)** from which you can view the Ter Valley.

Monestir de Sant Pere de Galligants★

Pl. Santa Lucía. ○*Open Oct–May Tue–Sat 10am–2pm, 4–6pm, Sun and public holidays 10am–2pm; Jun–Sept Tue–Sat 10.30am–1.30pm, 4–7pm, Sun and public holidays 10am–2pm.* ○*Closed 1, 6 Jan, 25–26 Dec;* ⊙*2.30€.* ℘*972 20 26 32. www.mac.cat.*

Not far from Sant Nicolau stands the fortified Romanesque church of Sant Pere, set into the town walls, housing the **Museu Arqueològic.** Shown are Medieval memorial plaques and the magnificent 4C Roman **tomb of Las Estaciones**★.

Parc de la Devesa★

This park contains the largest grove of plane trees in Catalunya.

EXCURSION

Casa-Museu Castell Gala Dalí★

In Púbol. 16km/10mi E along the C 66 towards La Bisbal d'Empordà. ○ *Open 15 Mar–14 Jun and 16 Sept–1 Nov Tue–Sun 10am–6pm; 15 Jun–15 Sept daily 10am–8pm; 2 Nov–31 Dec Tue–Sun Dec 10am–5pm.* ○ *Closed 1 Jan, 25 Dec.* ⊙*7€.* ℘*972 48 86 55.*

In 1970, Salvador Dalí gave this 14C castle to his wife Gala. It now displays objects in a Surrealist atmosphere.

🚗 DRIVING TOUR

FROM GIRONA TO SANTA PAU

64.5km/40mi – allow one day.

▶ *Head N from Girona along the C 66.*

Banyoles

20km/12.4mi NW of Girona.

Banyoles is set by a **lake**★. The **Museu Arqueològic Comarcal**★ in a Gothic building shows the Palaeolithic Jaw of Banyoles *(placeta de la Font 11;* ○*open Sept–Jun Tue–Sat 10.30am–1.30pm, 4–6.30pm, Sun 10.30am–2pm; Jul–Aug Tue–Sat 10.30am–1.30pm, 4–7.30pm, Sun 10.30am–2pm;* ⊙*3€;* ℘*972 57 23 61).*

A road 8km/5mi road around the lake passes the 13C **Església de Santa Maria de Porqueres**★, its columns sculpted with odd figures *(crta de circumval.lació de l'estany; ⊙ open by arrangement, Sat 4.30–7pm, Sun 10am–1pm; ℘972 57 04 95).*

▷ *Drive 13km/8mi NW along C 150 then take C 66 just after Melianta.*

Besalù★★

The first view of Besalú, across the river, with its Roman **fortified bridge**★, rebuilt in the medieval period, is extremely picturesque. The **ancient city**★★ retains ramparts and many medieval buildings, including the Romanesque **Església de Sant Pere**★ with unusual lion-flanked window *(pl. de Sant Pere; ⌁ guided tour by arrangement; ⊜2.40€; ℘972 59 12 40).* and traditional **ritual baths** (12C) in the Jewish quarter *(⌁ guided tour daily 10.30 a.m, noon, 1.30pm, 4.30pm & 6pm; Sun and public holidays 1.30pm, 6pm; ⊜1.20€; ℘972 59 12 40).*

▷ *Head 14km/8.7mi Walong the N 260.*

Castellfollit de la Roca★

The village, in **Parc Natural de la Garrotxa**★, includes a medieval centre around the church of Sant Salvador.

▷ *Continue 8km/5mi along the N 260.*

Olot★

The 18C Neoclassical and Baroque **Església de Sant Estève**★, houses an unusual painting by El Greco – **Christ Bearing the Cross**★ *(℘972 26 04 74).* The **Museu Comarcal de la Garrotxa**★ displays a fine **collection of paintings and drawings**★★ by 19C and 20C Catalan artists *(Hospici 8; ⊙ open Oct–Jun Tue–Fri 10am–1pm, 3–6pm, Sat 11am–2pm, 4–7pm, Sun and public holidays 11am–2pm; Jul–Sept Tue–Sat 11am–2pm, 4–7pm, Sun and public holidays 11am–2pm; ⊜3€; no charge first Sun of month; ℘972 27 11 66; www.mnac.cat).*

Note also the splendid **Modernist façade**★ of the **Casa Solà-Morales**★, by Domènech i Montaner.

▷ *Take the GI 524 east 9.5km/6mi.*

Santa Pau★

The Castillo de Santa Pau and the 15C–16C parish church both stand on the arcaded square of this village.

ADDRESSES

⌂ STAY

⊝⊝ **Hotel Condal** – *Joan Maragall 10. ℘972 20 44 62. www.hotelcondalgirona. com. 28 rooms.* Bourgeois mansion in the city centre with rooms that are simple, clean and bright.

⊝⊝ **Hotel Ultonia** – *Av. de Jaume I 22. ℘972 20 38 50. www.hotelhusaultonia. com. 45 rooms. �6€.* A hotel in classic style on one of the main streets. Public areas are rather reduced, but this is balanced by large, functionally comfortable rooms.

⊘ EAT

⊝⊝⊝⊝ **El Celler de Can Roca** – *Can Sunyer 48, Ctra de Taialà 40. ℘972 22 21 57. www.cellercanrocacom. Closed Sun, Mon.* Bold combinations, of creative cuisine and an extensive wine list.

TAPAS

Boira – *Pl. de la Independència 17–18.* Modern bar under the arcades popular with Girona's young crowd. Great view of river refelctions from the first floor.

⊽ BARS AND ⊘CAFÉS

Cu-Cut – *Plaça de la Independència 10. ℘972 22 85 25.* Attractive, welcoming bar which often hosts concerts and poetry readings.

La Terra – *Ballesteries 23. ℘972 21 92 54.* A pleasant bar overlooking the Onyar River.

Lleida/Lérida★

Lleida, an ancient citadel, was stormed by the legions of Caesar, and occupied by the Moors from the 8C to the 12C. The Arab fortress, the Zuda, sited like an acropolis, was savaged by artillery fire in 1812 and 1936. The glacis has been converted into gardens. Lleida is an important fruit-growing centre.

SEU VELLA★★★ (OLD CATHEDRAL)

To reach the Cathedral, take the lift from Plaça de Sant Joan. Turó la Seu Vella. ◷*Open Tue–Sun Oct–May 10am–1.30pm, 3–5.30pm; Jun–Sept 10am–1.30pm, 6–7.30pm.* ◈*2.40€; no charge 23 Apr, 11, 18 May, 11, 29 Sept; 0.40€ (lift access to Cathedral).* ℘*973 23 06 53.*

The Cathedral **site**★ dominates the city from inside the walls. It was built between 1203 and 1278 over a mosque; the octagonal belfry was added in the 14C. Philip V converted it into a garrison fortress in 1707.

Església★★

The **capitals**★ of this transitional-style church are outstanding for their variety and detail. Those in the apses and transept illustrate the Old Testament, those in the nave and aisles, the New Testament.

Moorish influences show in the exterior decoration, particularly the Puerta de Els Fillols (Godchildren's Doorway) and Puerta de la Anunciata (Annunciation Doorway). The extremely delicate carving, reminiscent of Moorish stuccowork, has come to be known as the Romanesque School of Lleida. It is seen throughout the region, in particular on the superb **portal**★★ of the Església de **Agramunt** *(52km/32.3mi NE).*

Claustro★★

The cloisters have an unusual position in front of the church. Their 14C galleries are remarkable for the size of the bays and the beautiful stone tracery. The Gothic style shows Moorish influence in

▶ **Population:** 131 731
⚙ **Michelin Map:** 574 H 31 – Catalunya (Lleida)
🖹 **Info:** Major 31 bis. ℘902 25 00 50. www.turismedelleida.com.
◉ **Location:** Lleida is linked to Barcelona by the AP 2 motorway, the Pyrenees by the C 1313 and N 240, and Huesca via the N 240. 🚊Plaça Berenguer IV
🅿 **Parking:** Space is limited in the old quarter.
◈ **Don't Miss:** A walk up to the Zuda for commanding views of city and plain.

the plant motifs on the **capitals**★. There is a fine view from the south gallery.

In the southwest corner stands the Gothic **bell tower**★★, 60m/197ft high. Along Carrer Major are the 13C **Palau de la Paeria**, now the town hall *(ajuntament)*, with its fine **façade**★; the **Hospital de Santa Maria**, with a **patio**★ showing Renaissance influence; and the 18C **Seu Nova** (New Cathedral; ◷*open daily 9.30am–1pm, 5.30–8.15pm;* ℘*973 26 94 70).*

◐ *Exit through the Puerta del Lleó towards Carrer Sant Martí*

Església de Sant Martí★

Jaume I el Conqueridor 1. ◷ *Open Oct–May Tue–Sat 10am–2pm, 4–7pm, Sun and public holidays 10am–2pm; Jun–Sept Tue–Sat 10am–2pm, 4–8pm, Sun and public holidays 10am–2pm.* ◷ *Closed 1, 6 Jan, Good Fri, Easter Mon, and 25–26 Dec.* ◈*4€; no charge first Sun in month, 11, 18 May, 11, 29 Sept.* ℘*973 28 30 75. www.museudelleida.cat.*

This 12C church was substantially remodelled three centuries after, and was later used as a barracks and a prison. **Sacred art**★ from the Museu Diocesá is on display in the nave.

Església de Sant Llorenç

Pl. de Sant Josep 6. ◷ *Open Mon–Fri 9.30am–12.30pm, 5–7pm. Sat–Sun and public holidays 11am–12.30pm, 5–8pm.* ℘*973 26 79 94.*

This late Romanesque church (13C) shows Gothic influence in its belfry pointed arches and fine retable.

Hospital de Santa Maria

Pl. de la Catedral. ◷ *Open summer Tue–Fri 10am–2pm, 6–9pm, Sat 11am–2pm, 7–9pm, Sun 11am–2pm; winter Tue–Fri 10am–2pm, 5.30–8.30pm, Sat noon–2pm, 5.30–8.30pm, Sun noon–2pm.* ◷ *Closed 1 Jan, Easter Mon, 1 May, 26 Dec.* ℘*973 27 15 00. www.fpiei.es.*

This former hospital, from the 15C, has a fine **patio**★, showing clear Renaissance influence. It is now used by the Institute of Lleida Studies).

Palau de la Paeria

C.Major. ◷ *Open Mon–Sat 11am–2pm, 5–8pm, Sun 11am–2pm.* ◿*No charge.* ℘*973 70 03 00.* ℘*973 70 03 94.*

This 13C building in with a lovely **façade**★, serves as the town hall, and houses an **archaeology museum**.

ADDRESSES

🛏 STAY

◿◍ **Hotel Real** – *Av. Blondel 22.* ℘*973 23 94 05. www.hotelrealllleida.com. 57 rooms.* ◿*8.50€. Restaurant*◿◍. A centrally located hotel, with recently renovated rooms at a very reasonable price. Its restaurant serves traditional cuisine.

🍴 EAT

◿◍◍ **El Celler del Roser** – *Cavallers 24.* ℘*973 23 90 70. www.cellerdelroser. com. Closed Sun evening.* A rustic bodega in the old quarter specialising in Traditional Catalan cooking; their speciality, *bacalao* (salt cod), is highly recommended.

Montblanc★★

Montblanc lies in an impressive **setting**★ amid vineyards and almond orchards. Within its ancient walls lie narrow, cobbled streets, stone buildings, and legends and deep secrets from a golden age in the 14C.

SIGHTS

The Ramparts★★

The ramparts were commissioned by Peter IV of Aragón in the mid-14C. Two thirds of the original walls (1 500m/5 000ft) remain, along with 32 square towers and two of four gates: that of Sant Jordi (S) and Bover (NE).

Església de Santa Maria★★

Pl. de l'Església. ◷ *Open daily 11am–1pm, 4–6pm.* ℘*977 86 17 33 (tourist office).*

- ▸ **Population:** 7 069
- ◔ **Michelin Map:** 574 H 33 – Catalunya (Tarragona)
- 🛈 **Info:** Antigua Església de Sant Francesc. ℘977 86 17 33. www. montblancmedieval.org.
- ◑ **Location:** Montblanc is in Catalunya at the crossroads of the N 240 (Tarragona-Lleida) and the C 240 from Reus (29km/18mi S). 🚌Roberto Aguilo 12

This beautiful Gothic church overlooking the city has a single nave and radiating chapel. The unfinished façade is Baroque. The interior features a sumptuous 17C **organ**★★, a Gothic altarpiece in polychrome stone (14C) and an elegant silver monstrance.

Museu d'Art Frederic Marès

Pedrera 2. ◷ *Open Tue–Sat 10am–2pm, 4–7pm, Sun 10am–2pm.* ◷ *Closed 1, 6 Jan, 8 Sept, 25 Dec.* ⊚*2.90€.* ✆*977 86 03 49. www.mccb.cat.*

This museum in a late-19C former prison contains religious paintings and sculptures from the 14C to the 19C, in particular fine 14C wooden statues. The Plaça de Santa Bárbara, a little higher up, offers fine views.

Museu Comarcal de la Conca de Barberà★

Pedrera 2. ◷ *Open Tue–Sat 10am–2pm, 4–7pm, Sun 10am–2pm.* ◷ *Closed 1 Jan, 25–26 Dec.* ⊚*2.90€.* ✆*977 86 03 49. www.mccb.cat.*

A 17C house holds archaeological and ethnographical artefacts from the area as well as 18C ceramic flasks belonging to an apothecary.

Plaça Mayor

Among the arcades of shops and cafés around the main square, note the town hall *(ayuntamiento)* and the Gothic-style Casa dels Desclergue.

Església de Sant Miquel★

Pl. de Sant Miquel. ◗◌*Guided tours by prior arrangement.* ✆*977 86 17 33 (tourist office).*

Fronted by a Romanesque façade, this small 13C Gothic church has pure, sober lines. It hosted the Estates General of Catalunya several times in the 14C and15C. Next to the church stands the **Palau del Castlà**, formerly the residence of the king's representative. A 15C prison is on its ground floor.

Call Judío (Jewish Quarter)

Only the Carrer dels Jueus (Street of Jews) and part of a Gothic house in Plaça dels Àngels remain of the former Jewish district. Another interesting building is the 14C **Casa Alenyà**, a Gothic house of slender proportions.

OUTSIDE THE WALLS
Convent i Santuari de la Serra★

◷ *Open 11am–1pm, 4–6pm.* ⊚*4€.* ✆*977 86 17 33 (tourist office).*

This ex-convent of the Order of St Clare stands on a small hill. It houses the venerated **Mare de Déu de la Serra**, an alabaster statue made in the 14C.

Hospital de Santa Magdalena★

◷ *Open daily 10am–7pm.*

The remarkable though small 15C **cloisters** illustrate the transition between Gothic and Renaissance. The vertical perspective on the ground floor, featuring fluted columns and pointed arches, is broken in the upper section.

Museu Molins de la Vila

1km/0.6mi towards Prenafeta. ◗◌*Guided tours (1hr) by prior arrangement.* ⊚*3.20€.* ✆*977 86 03 49.* These are two medieval flour mills.

DRIVING TOUR

THE CISTERCIAN ROUTE
90km/56mi – allow one day.

Along this route, visit the most important Cistercian monasteries in Catalunya, founded in the 12C after the reconquest of Catalunya by Ramon Berenguer IV.

▷ *Exit Montblanc on the N 240 to l'Espluga de Francolí. From here, follow the T 700 for 4km/2.5mi.*

Monestir de Poblet★★★
Zona del Monasterio, Vimbodí. ◗◌*Guided tours (45min) Mon–Sat 10am–12.45pm, 3–6pm (5.30pm 13 Oct–15 Mar), Sun and public holidays 10am–12.30pm, 3–5.30pm (6pm 15 Jun–14 Sept).* ◷ *Closed 1 Jan, 25–26 Dec.* ⊚*6€ (9€ with Santes Creus and Vallbona).* ✆*977 87 02 54. www.poblet.cat.*

The splendid **site**★ of one of the largest and best-preserved Cistercian

Montblanc in the Middle Ages

Until 1489, Montblanc was a thriving town with a prosperous Jewish community *(Jueus)*. Its golden age was the 14C, when its economic supremacy was reflected in the political arena with several Estates General being held in the town at the instigation of Catalan-Aragonese monarchs.

monasteries is sheltered by the Prades mountains. Founded in the 12C, it enjoyed the protection of the crown of Aragón.

A 2km/1.2mi-perimeter protected the monastery and its vegetable gardens.

Capella de Sant Jordi★★

The Late Gothic interior of this tiny 15C chapel features splendid broken barrel vaulting. An inner wall with polygonal towers enclosed annexes where visitors were received. The 15C **Porta Daurada** (Golden Door), named after the gilded bronze sheets that form its covering, was commissioned by Philip II.

Plaça Major★

On this irregular main square stand the 12C **Capella de Santa Caterina**, shops, a hospital for pilgrims and a carpentry workshop. On the right are the ruins of the 16C Abbatial Palace and the **stone cross** erected by Abbey Guimerà, also 16C. A third wall (608m/1 995ft long, 11m/36ft high and 2m/6.5ft thick), built by Peter the Ceremonious, surrounds the monastery proper, fortified by 13 towers. On the right stands the **Baroque façade of the church**, built around 1670 and flanked, 50 years later, by heavily ornate windows. Pleasing in itself, it breaks with the overall austerity.

Porta Reial★

This is the gateway to the conventual buildings, appearing somewhat like the entrance to a fortress.

Palau del Rei Martí★

Beyond the door, to the right, a narrow staircase rises to this 14C Gothic palace. Its splendid rooms are wonderfully light thanks to pointed bay windows.

Locutorio

Originally a dormitory for converts, this room became a wine press. The 14C vaulting rests directly on the walls.

Cellar

This magnificent Gothic cellar *(celler)* below the monks' sleeping quarters is used as a concert hall.

Claustro★★

The size of these cloisters (40 x 35m/131 x 115ft) and their sober lines indicate the monastery's importance. The south gallery (c. 1200) and huge lavabo or **templete**★ with its marble fountain and 30 taps are in pure Romanesque style; the other galleries, built a century later, have floral motif tracery; beautiful scrollwork adorns the **capitals**★.

The **kitchen** *(cocina)* and the huge **monk's refectory** *(refectorio de los monjes)*, both built around 1200 and still in use, open onto the cloisters. The **library** *(biblioteca)* – the former scriptorium – is crowned by ogival vaulting on 13C columns. The 13C **chapter house**★★ *(sala capitular)*, through a Romanesque doorway, has four slender octagonal columns and palm-shaped vaulting.

Església★★

The light, spacious church is typically Cistercian. It has pure lines, broken barrel vaulting, and unadorned capitals. The windows and wide arches dividing the nave join in a large eave. The church incorporated numerous altars for its growing community; the apse was ringed by an ambulatory and radiating chapels, a feature more commonly found in Benedictine churches.

The **royal pantheon**★★ *(panteó reial)*, the church's most original feature, has immense shallow arches spanning the transepts, surmounted by the royal

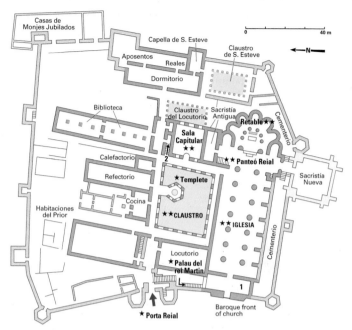

SANTA MARIA DE POBLET: THIRD PERIMETER WALL

Periods of contruction ▇ 12C-13C ▇ 14C ▇ 16C ☐ 17C-18C

tombs. These were constructed of alabaster in about 1350.

The **retable**★★ *(retablo)* at the **high altar** *(altar mayor)* is a monumental marble Renaissance altarpiece carved by Damián Forment in 1527. Figures in four superimposed registers can be seen glorifying Christ and the Virgin.

In the narthex, an opening to the outside world added in 1275, is the Renaissance **altar of the Holy Sepulchre (1)**.

A wide flight of stairs leads from the north transept to the monks' dormitory.

Dormitorio

Massive central arches support the ridge roof above the vast, 87m/285ft long gallery.

▷ *Leave Poblet on the T 232 towards Maldà. From here, take the road to Vallbona.*

Monestir de Vallbona de les Monges★★

Mayor. 🚶 *Guided tours (45min), Tue–Sat 10.30am–1.30pm, 4.30–6.45pm, Sun and public holidays noon–1.30pm, 4.30–6.45pm (6pm in winter).* 🕐*Closed 1 Jan, 25 Dec.* ⊜*3€ (9€ with Poblet and Santes Creus Monasteries).* ℘*973 33 02 66. www.vallbona.com.*

The Cistercian **Monestir de Santa Maria** completes the Cistercian Trinity. The convent was founded in 1157 by the hermit Ramon de Vallbona and became a Cistercian community for women.

Església★★

Built chiefly in the 13C and the 14C, this church is a fine example of transitional Gothic. The interior is simple and surprisingly light thanks to two octagonal lantern towers: one (13C) lies above the transept crossing while the other (14C) overlooks the centre of the nave. The church contains the beautiful tombs of Queen Violante of

Hungary, wife of James I the Conqueror of Aragón, and her daughter, as well as a huge polychrome Virgin from the 15C.

Cloisters★

The east and west galleries are Romanesque (12C–13C). The 14C Gothic north wing features attractive capitals with plant motifs. In the south gallery (15C) note the 12C statue of Nuestra Señora del Claustro (of the Cloisters).

 Head towards Rocallaura then towards Montblanc along the C 240 to link up with the AP 2. Turn off onto the TP 2002 at exit 11.

Monestir de Santes Creus★★★

Pl. Jaume el Just, Aiguamurcia. 46km/29mi SE of Vallbona. Guided tours (2hr). Open Tue–Sun 16 Mar–15 Sept 10am–1pm, 3–6.30pm; 16 Sept–15 Jan 10am–1pm, 3–5pm; 16 Jan–15 Mar 10am–1pm, 3–5.30pm.. 3.60€; no charge Tue. 977 63 83 29.

The monastery was founded in the 12C by monks from Toulouse and its plan is similar to that of Poblet, with three perimeter walls. A Baroque gateway leads to the courtyard where the monastic buildings, enhanced with fine *sgraffiti*, now serve as shops and private residences. To the right is the abbatial palace, with its attractive patio, now the town hall; at the end stands the 12C–13C church.

Gran Claustro★★★ (Great Cloisters)

Construction began in 1313 on the site of earlier cloisters. The ornamentation on capitals and bands illustrates Gothic motifs: plants and flowers, animals, biblical, mythological and satirical themes. The Puerta Real or Royal Gate on the south side opens onto cloisters with Gothic bays with lively carvings – note Eve shown emerging out of Adam's rib, and the fine tracery of the arches (1350-1430). In contrast, the transitional style of the **lavabo** appears almost clumsy. Carved noble tombs fill the niches.

The chapter house★★ (*sala capitular*) is an elegant hall with arches on four pillars.

Stairs next to the chapter house lead to the 12C **dormitory** (*dormitorio*), a gallery divided by diaphragm arches supporting a timber roof, now used as a concert hall.

Església★★

The church, begun in 1174, closely follows the Cistercian pattern of a flat east end and overall austerity. The lantern (14C), stained glass, and the superb apsidal **rose window** relieve the bareness. Ribbed vaults rest on pillars which extend back along the walls and end in unusual consoles. Gothic canopies at the transept openings shelter the **royal tombs**★★: on the north side (c. 1295) that of **Pere the Great** (III of Aragón, II of Barcelona) and on the south (14C), that of his son, **Jaime II**, the Just, and his queen, **Blanche d'Anjou**. The Plateresque decoration below the crowned recumbent figures in Cistercian habits, was added in the 16C.

Claustro Viejo (Old Cloisters)

Although they were built during the 17C, these "old cloisters" occupy the site of former cloisters dating back to the 12C. The design is simple with a small central fountain and eight cypresses in the close. Leading off are the kitchens, refectory and the **royal palace** (note a splendid 14C **patio**★).

ADDRESSES

⍟ EAT

Fonda dels Àngels – *Plaça dels Àngels 1. 977 86 01 73. Closed Sept. 9 rooms. 4.50€. Restaurant.* This small, family-run inn at the heart of the former Jewish quarter has been converted from a Gothic-style house, of which an original ogival window has been preserved. Simple but pleasant rooms, plus a popular restaurant serving interesting local cuisine.

Pirineos Catalanes★★★

These mountains are deeply cut by isolated valley, with their own personality and traditions, especially in art developed during the Romanesque period. All offer delicious regional cuisine and opportunities for skiing, hunting, fishing, mountain climbing and adventure sports. The area is great for driving around and the following tours can be followed on the map in this section.

DRIVING TOURS

1 UPPER VALLEY OF THE TER★

Vall de Camprodón to Vall de Ribes to Vall de Núria
87km/54mi – allow 1 day.

Two large valleys lie in the Ripollès area under mountains towering to 3 000m/10 000ft.

Vall de Camprodón
Molló
The 12C Romanesque church has a lovely Catalan belfry.

◐ *Take the C 38 then turn left and stay on this road as it climbs gradually NE and then dips SE to Beget. 28km/17.4mi SW total.*

Beget★★
This attractive mountain village with stone houses enjoys a pleasant **setting**★ deep in a peaceful valley.
The **San Cristòfol church**★★ (10C–12C) with Lombard arcatures and slender lantern-tower, houses the **Majestad de Beget**★, a magnificent figure of Christ carved in the 12C (◐*open daily 9am–7pm; ask for the keys from Joan Coma, Carrer Bellaire;* ⌀*1€;* ℘*972 74 01 36).*

◐ *Return to the left turn and continue SW along C 38 for 19km/11.8mi.*

◐ **Michelin Map:** 574 D 32, E 32–37 and F 32–37 – Catalunya (Girona, Lleida)

🛈 **Info:** Camprodon: Plaça d'Espanya 1. ℘972 74 00 10; Carretera Comarcal 151, km 23,5. ℘972 74 09 36. www.valldecamprodon. org; Puigcerdà: Querol 1. ℘972 88 05 42; La Seu d'Urgell: Avinguda Valls d'Andorra 33. ℘973 35 15 11, www.laseu.org; Pas. Joan Brudieu 15. ℘973 35 31 12; Tremp: Plaça de la Creu 1. ℘973 65 00 09, www.ayuntamentdetremp. com; Vielha: Sarriulera 10. ℘973 64 01 10. www.turisme.aran.org. www.visitpirineos.com.

◐ **Location:** The Pyrenees extend almost unbroken for 230km/143mi from the Mediterranean to the high Arán Valley (2 500m/8 202ft). The last range, the Montes Alberes, plunges into the Mediterranean from 700m/2 297ft.

◐ **Timing:** Geography will oblige you to select one or two valleys to explore from the south access.

Camprodón★
Camprodón is at the confluence of the Ritort and Ter rivers, crossed by a 12C humpbacked bridge, **Pont Nou**★. The community developed around the **Monestirio de Sant Pere**. Only the 12C **Romanesque church**★ remains.

Monasterio de Sant Pere de Camprodón★
Pl. de Santa Maria. ℘*972 74 09 36.* ⌀*No charge.*
These cloisters are simple and elegant, with sweeping arches and slender columns with capitals, decorated with plant motifs. The **museum** houses a collection of embroidered fabric.

Palacio de l'Abadia

Opposite the church on the square stands the 14C former Abbatial Palace. The **medieval bridge**★ spans the Ter river on the way towards Ripoll.

 Travel SW through the Vall Alto del Ter along C 26 for 11km/6.8mi.

Monasterio de Sant Joan de les Abadesses★★

Open Mar–Apr and 16 Sept–Oct daily 10am–2pm, 4–6pm; May–15 Sept daily 10am–2pm, 4–7pm; Nov–Feb Mon–Fri 10am–2pm, Sat–Sun 10am–2pm, 4–6pm. ∞2€. ℘972 72 23 53. www.santjoandelesabadesses.cat.

The monastery was founded in the 9C under the rule of a Benedictine abbess, though it soon shut out women.

With its arches and columns with carved capitals the church recalls those of southwest France. A magnificent 1251 **Descent from the Cross**★★ in polychrome wood is in the central apse. In 1426 an unbroken host was discovered on the Christ figure's head; it is venerated to this day.

 About 8km/5mi further SW along the same road is Ripoli in Vall de Ribes.

Vall de Ribes
Ripoll★
℘972 70 23 51. www.ripoli.cat.

Monasterio de Santa Maria★

Pl. de l'Abat Oliba. Open daily Nov–Mar 9am–1pm, 3–7pm; Apr–Oct 9am–1pm, 3–6pm. ∞3€. ℘972 70 02 43.

All that remains of the original monastery are the church portal and the cloisters. In 1032, Abbot Oliba consecrated an enlarged **church**★, a jewel of early Romanesque art that was damaged over the years. It was rebuilt at the end of the 19C to the original plan.

The **portada**★★★, or portal design, is composed of a series of horizontal registers illustrating the glory of God victorious over His enemies (Passage of the Red Sea). The **Claustro**★ **(cloisters)** abutting the church dates to the 12C; others were added in the 14C.

 Head N along the N 152 for 17km/10.5mi

Ribes de Freser

www.vallderibes.cat.

This famous spa stands at the confluence of three rivers and is known for the healing properties of its waters. A rack railway runs to the Vall de Núria.

 Continue 7km/4.3mi N along N 152 to the Vall de Núria.

Vall de Núria★

The valley is surrounded by a rocky amphitheatre stretching from Puigmal to the Sierra de Torreneules. The Virgin of Núria, the patron saint of Pyrenean shepherds, is venerated in a sanctuary located in the upper part of the valley.

2 LA CERDANYA★★

From Vall de Núria to La Seu d'Urgell

104km/64.6mi – about 3hr.

The fertile Cerdanya Basin, watered by the River Segre, was formed by subsidence. The northern section, La Cerdagne, was ceded to France under the Treaty of the Pyrenees in 1659.

The **Túnel del Cadí**, opened in 1984, facilitates access from Manresa.

From Ribes de Freser to Puigcerdà, the road cut into the cliff face up to the Collado de Toses commands impressive **views**★ of the Segre and its slopes.

 From Ribes de Freser, head NW to Molina for 29km/18mi.

La Molina

www.lamolina.com.

This is one of Catalunya's most important ski resorts. The village of Alp is popular in winter and in summer.

 The N 152 joins with the E 9, which rises and offers a sweeping view of the vast Cerdanya plain. After 15km/9.3mi you reach Puigcerdà.

Puigcerdà

The capital of Cerdanya, which developed on a terrace overlooking the River Segre, is one of the most popular holiday resorts of the Pyrenees, with old-fashioned shops, ancient streets and balconied buildings.

▶ *Continue NE along the N 152 for 6km/3.7mi.*

Llívia

This 12sq km/5sq mi Spanish enclave in France, 6km/3.7mi from Puigcerdà, results from an administrative subtlety. Under the Treaty of the Pyrenees, France was to be granted the Roussillon area as well as 33 villages from Cerdanya. But, since Llívia was considered to be a town, it remained part of Spain.

Llívia features Europe's oldest chemist's shop, the **Farmacia de Llívia**★ *(Forns 10;* ⏰*open Tue–Sun Apr–Jun 10am–6pm; Jul–Sept 10am–7pm; Oct–Mar 10am–4.30pm;* ⏰*closed 1, 6 Jan, 24–26, 31 Dec;* ✆*972 89 60 11).*

▶ *Return to Puigcerdà and take the N 260 SW to Bellver de Cerdanya. About 23km/14.2mi.*

Bellver de Cerdanya★

Poised on a rocky crag dominating the Vall del Segre, Bellver de Cerdanya has a fine main square with beautiful balconied stone houses and wooden porches.

▶ *31km/19.2mi further W is La Seu d'Urgell.*

La Seu d'Urgell/Seo de Urgell★

This city of prince-archbishops stands where the Valira, which rises in Andorra, joins the Segre river.

Catedral de Santa Maria★★

Santa Maria. ⏰*Open Oct–May Mon–Sat 10am–1pm, 4–7pm; Jun–Sept Mon–Sat 10am–1pm, 4–8pm; Sun and public holidays 10am–1pm.* ⏰*3€ (with museum).* ✆*973 35 32 42.*
The cathedral, started in the 12C, shows strong Lombard influence. The central section of the west face, crowned by a small campanile, is typically Italian.

Inside, the nave rises on cruciform pillars, surrounded in French style by engaged columns. A most effective twin-arched gallery on the east transept wall reappears outside.

The **cloisters**★ are 13C; the east gallery was rebuilt in 1603 and features granite capitals illustrating humans and animals carved by masons from the Roussillon. The Santa Maria door (southeast corner) opens into the 11C **Església de Sant Miquel**★, the only remaining building of those constructed by St Ermangol.

The cathedral houses the **Museu Diocesano**★, which has works of art dating from the 10C to the 18C. The most precious is a beautifully illuminated 11C **Beatus**★★, one of the best-preserved copies of St John's Commentary on the Apocalypse written in the 8C by the priest Beatus of Liébana.

Of note also is an interesting **papyrus**★ belonging to Pope Sylvester II. The crypt contains the 18C funerary urn of St Ermangol.

③ VALL DEL SEGRE★

From La Seu d'Urgell to Tremp
73km/45mi – allow 3hr.

The River Segre forms a huge basin where it flows into the Valira.

Congost de Tresponts★★

The Segre winds through dark rocks (puzolana) and pastures. Downstream, the limestone of Ares and Montsec de Tost offers a typically Pyrenean landscape dropping to a cultivated basin, where the river disappears.

Coll de Nargó

http://collnargo.ddl.net.
This hamlet has one of the most splendid Romanesque churches in Catalunya, dating back to the 11C: **Sant Climent**★ has a single nave and a pretty apse adorned with Lombard bands. Its sober **bell tower**★ is pre-Romanesque.

Pantà d'Oliana★
The dam is surrounded by grey rocks with lively waterfalls in spring. From the road the sight is quite spectacular.

Collado de Bòixols Road★★
Between the Coll de Nargó and Tremp, the L 511 follows canyons on slopes clad in pine and holm oak, or barren hillsides. Further on, the road proceeds up the slope, under yellow and pink crests, offering lovely **landscapes**, especially from the Collado de Bòixols.
Then the road enters a wide U-shaped valley, where terraced cultivation extends to the foot of the glacial ridge of Bòixols, to which cling the church and nearby houses. The road descends the valley until it eventually merges into the Conca de Tremp.

4 VALL DEL NOGUERA PALLARESA

From Tremp to Llavorsí
143km/89mi – allow 1 day.

Pallars
Pallars is in the uppermost region of the Catalan Pyrenees. The highest summit is Pica d'Estats (3 145m/10 318ft). To the north is **Pallars Sobirà**, at the heart of the Pyrenees; to the south, **Pallars Jussà** incorporates the vast pre-Pyrenean zone formed by Conca de Tremp. The road follows the bed of the Noguera Pallaresa, and after La Pobla de Segur, cuts across a limestone landscape of remarkable uniformity.

Tremp
In the centre of the Conca de Tremp – a huge basin with lush crops – the village retains its old quarter and three towers from its walls. The **Església de Santa María**★ houses an astonishing 2m/6.5ft high Gothic statue in polychrome wood: **Santa Maria de Valldeflors**★ (14C). The municipality has a reservoir, the **pantano de Sant Antoni**★.

▷ *The C 13 follows the river course and spans the pantano de Sant Antoni.*

La Pobla de Segur
℘973 68 02 57. www.pobladesegur.cat.
This popular resort is the only means of access to the Valle de Arán, Alta Ribagorça and Pallars Sobirà.

Vall Fosca★
Hemmed in by peaks, this valley is dotted with delightful hamlets, each with its Romanesque church: **Torre de Capdella** *(www.torredecapdella.org)*, **Espui** and **Capdella**. In the upper valley, in a large lake area, the main attraction is **Lago Gento**.

▷ *Return to La Pobla de Segur and proceed upwards along the N 260.*

Congost de Collegats★★
Eroded by torrents, the red, grey and ochre limestone rocks take on the appearance of spectacular cliffs. Note the **Roca de l'Argenteria**★, stalactite-shaped rocks near the Gerri de la Sal.

Sort
℘973 62 10 02.
The resort is famous throughout Europe because of its wild waters and canoeing events held on the Noguera Pallaresa.

▷ *At Rialp, turn left towards Llessui.*

Vall de Llessui★★
The road winds way up to the northwest, through a steep granite landscape featuring a great many ravines.

5 UPPER VALLEY OF THE NOGUERA PALLARESA★

From Llavorsí to Port de la Bonaigua
105km/65mi – allow half a day.

Mountains dominate a wild landscape.

Llavorsí
http://llavorsi.ddl.net.
The village is at the confluence of the Aneu, Cardós and Ferrera basins.

▷ *Take the L 504 and proceed N.*

Vall de Cardós★

The Noguera de Cardós is the axis of this valley.

▶ *Return to Llavorsí and take the C 13 towards Baqueira.*

Vall d'Aneu★★

Below is the valley of **Espot**, a picturesque village beside a mountain stream, gateway to the Pallars section of a **national park**★★ (*see Parc Nacional d'AIGÜESTORTES I ESTANY DE SANT MAURICI*).

Beyond Esterri d'Aneu the road crosses a breathtaking landscape, dotted with Romanesque churches such as the **Església de Sant Joan d'Isil**★, glimpsed between summits, and twists up to **Port de la Bonaigua** (2 072m/6 799ft), circled by many peaks.

⑥ LA VALL D'ARÁN★★

From Port de la Bonaigua to Bossòst
45km/28mi – allow half a day.

The **Arán Valley**, in the northwest tip of the Catalan Pyrenees, occupies the upper valley of the Garonne river. Its isolation has helped it to preserve its local traditions and language (*aranes* is a variation of the *langue d'oc* of southern France). The Vielha Tunnel ended the valley's seclusion in 1948. In recent years the region has seen the creation of several ski resorts.

Baqueira Beret

℘973 63 90 10. www.baqueira.es.
This ski resort, rising from 1 500m/4 900ft to 2 510m/8 230ft, offers excellent lodging and services.

▶ *Travel along the C 28, 4.3km/2.6mi NW of Baqueira.*

Salardú★

973 64 51 97. www.torismearan.org.
Salardú is a charming village with granite and slate houses gathered around the **Església de Sant Andreu**★ (12C–13C), whose interior contains some

interesting 16C **Gothic paintings**★★ and a fine 12C **Christ in Majesty**★★, a stylised 65cm/25in wooden statue of remarkable anatomical precision. Note the slender octagonal belfry (15C).

▶ *Continue on the C 28, 2.8km/1.7mi slightly SW of Salardú.*

Arties★

The Romanesque church has an apse decorated with scenes illustrating the Last Judgement, Heaven and Hell.

▶ *Head along the C 28, 4.5km/2.8mi W of Arties.*

Escunhau

The **Església de San Pedro**★ has a fine 12C **portal**★★ bearing an expressive Christ and unusual capitals decorated with human faces.

▶ *Continue on the C 28. Betren is 1.6km/1mi W of Escunhau.*

Betren

The **Església de San Esteve**★, built during the transition from Romanesque to Gothic, boasts archivolts on the **portal**★★, decorated with human faces, alluding to the Last Judgement and the Resurrection.

▶ *1.4km/0.8mi NW further is Vielha.*

Vielha

At an altitude of 971m/3 186ft, the capital of the Arán Valley is a holiday resort. Don't miss the 16C and 17C homes in the old town as well as the **Església Parroquial de Sant Miquèu**★with its 14C octagonal tower and 13C Gothic doorway. Inside lies the **Cristo de Mijaran**★, a fragment dating from a 12C Descent from the Cross.

▶ *Another 16km/10mi NW of Vielha is Bossòst.*

Bossòst

The **Església de la Purificació de Maria**★★ is the area's best example of Romanesque architecture (12C). Its

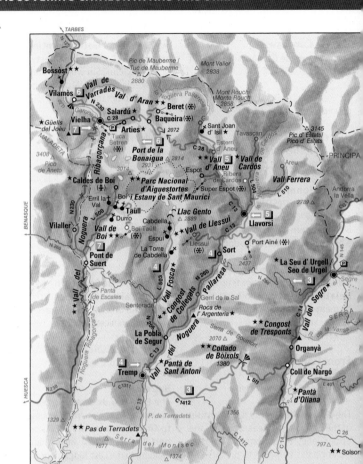

three naves are separated by sturdy columns. Its three apses are adorned with Lombard bands and the pretty, colourful north **doorway** features archaic relief work in its tympanum, depicting the Creator surrounded by the Sun, the Moon and symbols of the Evangelists.

7 VALL DEL NOGUERA RIBAGORÇANA★★

From Vielha to Caldes de Boí
54km/34mi – about 3hr.
The Upper Ribagorça has summits over 3 000m/9 842.5ft, vast glacial cirques, pretty lake areas and steep valleys.The Vielha tunnel was constructed through the Maladeta massif in 1948.

Vilaller
http://vilaller.ddl.net.
Poised on an outcrop, the village is dominated by the octagonal belfry of its 18C Baroque church, Sant Climent.

El Pont de Suert
9km/6mi S of Vilaller
The area, dotted with attractive hamlets – **Castelló de Tor, Casòs, Malpàs** – retains its rusticity and charm.

○ *Take the road up to Caldes de Boí.*

Vall de Boí★★
22km/14mi NE of Pont de Suert.
Watered by the Noguera de Tor and the Sant Nicolau, this valley is renowned for its cluster of Lombard **Romanesque**

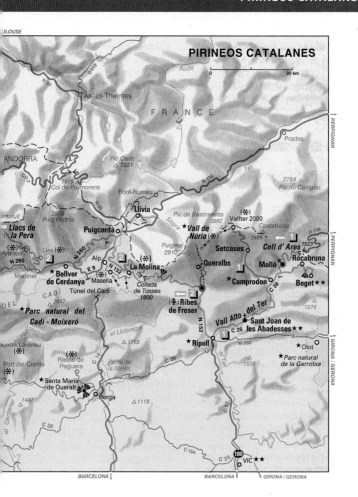

PIRINEOS CATALANES

churches (11C–12C), the finest in the Pyrenees. With slate roofs and irregular masonry, they stand out for their pure, sober lines and for the wall frescoes *(several reproductions remain)* now in the **Museu d'Art de Catalunya** *(see BARCELONA)*. Note the distinctive high silhouette of the belfries, separate but resting against the nave, and ornamentation of Lombard bands.

▷ *Beyond Erill la Vall turn right onto a narrow road leading to Boí.*

Taüll★

Taüll is famous for the frescoes of its two early 12C churches. Considered to be masterpieces of Romanesque art, they are exhibited in Barcelona's Museu d'Art de Catalunya. The village of labyrinthine streets, stone houses and wooden balconies clusters around the **Església de Santa Maria**★ *(open daily 10am–8pm; 1.20€; 973 69 40 00)*, a Romanesque church with three naves separated by cylindrical pillars. Just outside the village is the **Església de Sant Climent**★★ *(open mid–late Mar late Jun–late Sept 10am–2pm, 4–8pm; late Mar–late Jun, late Sept–mid Mar 10am–2pm, 4–7pm; 1.20€; 973 69 40 00)* with its slender six-storey belfry. A replica of the famous Pantocrator of Taüll is in the apse.

▷ *Return to the road to Caldes de Boí.*

Parc Nacional d'Aigüestortes i Estany de Sant Maurici★★

Access by the road from Boí to Caldes de Boí (*Parc Nacional d'AIGÜESTORTES I ESTANY DE SANT MAURICI*).

Caldes de Boí★

9km/6mi N of Taüll. 📞 *973 69 62 10. www.caldesdeboi.com.*

At an altitude of 1 550m/5 084ft, Caldes de Boí is a thermal spa with 37 springs at temperatures between 240ºC and 560ºC (750ºF to 1330ºF). Nearby is the ski resort of **Boí-Taüll**.

ADDRESSES

🏠 STAY

Hotel Casa Peyró – *La Plaça 7, Coll. 13km/8mi S of Caldes de Boí on the L 500.* 📞 *973 29 70 02. 9 rooms. Restaurant. Closed Nov and 1 week in Jun.* A pretty stone-built house that is A good choice for its location between Parque Nacional d'Aiguestortes, the Caldes de Boí spa and the ski slopes of Boí-Taüll.

El Pont 9 – *Camí Cerdanya 1, Camprodón.* 📞 *972 74 05 21. www. elripolles.com/riga. Closed 2nd week in Jan, fortnight in late Jun–early Jul, fortnight in mid-Oct.* A small restaurant located on the middle of Camprodon, with excellent table service and modern décor, serving traditional Catalan cuisine.

Maristany – *Av. Maristany 20, Camprodón.* 📞 *972 13 00 78. www. hotelmaristany.com. Closed 10 Dec–1 Feb. 10 rooms. Restaurant.* On the outskirts of town, in a quiet and well-kept area. Rooms are modern and comfortable. The cosy restaurant is in an annex.

Parador de Arties – *Ctra de Baqueira, Arties.* 📞 *973 64 08 01. www.parador.es. 57 rooms.* 🍽*17€. Restaurant.* This handsome building includes parts of the architectural legacy of the Portalà family, including a 16C tower and chapel. Its exterior combines wood, stone and slate, in perfect harmony with the Pyrenees all around.

🍴 EAT

Casa Perú – *Sant Antoni 6 – Bagergue, 2km/1.2mi N of Salardú.* 📞 *973 64 54 37. www.casaperu.es. Closed 1–15 Jul and weekdays in winter.* For many, the Casa Perú is the perfect mountain restaurant; with its excellent location in a small village of stone houses, low ceilings, rustic tableware and deliciously flavoured cuisine. Make sure you try the *olla aranesa*, a local stew, as well as the wide selection of game dishes.

El Grau de l'Ós – *Jaume II de Mallorca 5, Bellver de Cerdana.* 📞 *973 51 00 46. Closed fortnight in May and in Nov, Mon & Tue.* This village home has been carefully restored without losing its rustic feel. Despite its traditional bent, the menu occasionally comes up with original combinations such as liver with mango, or canneloni with mushrooms.

🏃 SPORT

Skiing is the most popular sport in the Pirineos Catalanes. The region has numerous ski resorts, some with large hotels. The best known include **La Molina** (📞 *972 89 20 31; www.lamolina. com*), in Girona province, and **Baqueira-Beret** (📞 *973 63 90 10; www.baqueira. es*)popular with the Spanish royal family, in the Val d'Aran (Lleida).

For general information also visit *www. acem-cat.com.*

Sitges★★

Sitges is a resort famous for its two lovely beaches. Its 2km/1.2mi-long Passeig Marítim is dotted with hotels and luxury residences. Sitges was an important Modernist centre, which is evident from many of its buildings.

SIGHTS
OLD TOWN★★
1hr30min

The parish church dominates the breakwater of La Punta. Balconies of white houses are brilliant with flowers. Museums in neo-Gothic mansions display canvases from the late 19C, when Rusiñol and Miguel Utrillo (father of the French painter) painted here.

Museu Cau Ferrat★★

Fonollar. ◷ Open 15 Jun–30 Sept Tue–Sat 9.30am–2pm, 4–7pm, Sun and public holidays 10am–3pm; 1 Oct–14 Jun Tue–Sat 9.30am–2pm, 3.30–6.30pm, Sun and public holidays 10am–3pm. ◷ Closed 1 Jan, 24 Aug, 23 Sept, 25–26 Dec. ◉3.50€ (6.40€, with Museu Maricel & Museu Romàntic); no charge first Wed of month. ☏938 94 03 64.

Santiago Rusiñol (1861–1931) added Gothic features to two 16C fishermen's houses, which he left to the town, with ceramics, paintings and sculptures. Among the **paintings**, note two remarkable works by El Greco: *Penitent Mary Magdalene* and *The Repentance of St Peter*. The gallery also contains canvases by Picasso, Casas and Rusiñol himself *(Poetry, Music and Painting).*

The museum takes its name from the **wrought-iron** collection *(cau ferrat).* Among the objects on display are a set of 16C braziers. There is also a **ceramics** section.

Museu Maricel★

Fonollar. ◷ Open 15 Jun–30 Sept Tue–Sat 9.30am–2pm, 4–7pm, Sun and public holidays 10am–3pm; Oct–14 Jun Tue–Sat 9.30am–2pm, 3.30–6.30pm, Sun and public holidays 10am–3pm.

▸ **Population:** 27 070
◔ **Michelin Map:** 574 I 35 – Catalunya (Barcelona)
▯ **Info:** Sinia Morera 1. ☏938 94 50 04. www.sitgestour.com.
▸ **Location:** Sitges is a coastal resort between Barcelona and Tarragona. ▭Plaça Eduard Maristany.
▯ **Kids:** The Museu del Ferrocarril is the place to admire steam engines.

◷ Closed 1 Jan, 24 Aug, 23 Sept, 25–26 Dec. ◉3.50€ (6.40€ with Museu Cau Ferrat and Museu Romàntic); no charge first Wed of month. ☏938 94 03 64.

This museum in a 14C hospital displays medieval and Baroque art. A footbridge links it to an adjacent mansion.

Casa Llopis-Museu Romàntic★

Sant Gaudenci 1. ◷ Open 15 Jun–30 Sept Tue–Sat 9.30am–2pm, 4–7pm, Sun and public holidays 10am–3pm; 1 Oct–14 Jun Tue–Sat 9.30am–2pm, 3.30–6.30pm, Sun and public holidays 10am–3pm. ◷ Closed 1 Jan, 24 Aug, 23 Sept, 25–26 Dec. ◉3.50€ (6.40€, with Museu Maricel & Museu Cau Ferrat); no charge first Wed of month. ☏938 94 29 69.

This late-18C bourgeois house gives a good idea of middle- and upper-class life during the Romantic period with frescoes on the walls, English furniture, mechanical devices and musical boxes. Dioramas show scenes of daily life.

The **Lola Anglada collection** is an outstanding display of 17C, 18C and 19C dolls from all over Europe.

SIGHTSEEING

A combined ticket *(◉6.30€)* provides access to the following museums: Cau Ferrat, Maricel del Mar and the Casa Llopis-Museu Romàntic.

EXCURSIONS

Vilanova i la Geltrú★

7km/4.3mi SW. ▭Pl. d'Eduard Maristany.

Situated in a small bay, this is an important fishing harbour and a holiday resort.

Museu Romàntic Can Papiol★

Major 32. ▭Closed for restoration till late 2010. ℰ938 93 03 82.

This mansion, built 1780–1801 by the Papiol family, evokes the life of the devout, well-to-do industrial middle class. Austerity reigns in the library with its 5 000 or so volumes, in the chapel with its strange relic of St Constance and in the reception rooms with its biblical scenes in grey monochrome. However, the opulence of the house is evident in the furnishings, the ballroom and the Louis XVI apartment where the French General, Suchet, once stayed.

Biblioteca-Museu Balaguer★

Av. Víctor Balaguer. ◷Open Jun–Sept Tue–Wed Fri–Sat 10am–2pm, 4–7pm, Thu 10am–2pm, 6–9pm, Sun 10am–2pm; Oct–May Tue–Wed Fri–Sat 10am–2pm, 4.30–7.30pm, Thu 10am–2pm, 6–9pm, Sun 10am–2pm. ⊚3€; no charge Thu afternoon and first Sun of month. ℰ938 15 42 02. www.victorbalaguer.cat.

This library-museum in a curious Egyptian-Greek building was an initiative of poet-historian-politician **Víctor Balaguer** (1824–1901). The **contemporary art collection** includes Catalan works from the 1950s and 1960s (Legado 56). Small works outline the evolution of painting since the end of the 14C. There are also **16C and 17C paintings** (El Greco, Murillo, Carducho, Maino, Carreño, etc.) and Egyptian and Asian art.

▪▪ Museu del Ferrocarril★

Pl. d'Eduard Maristany. ◷ Open Aug daily 11am–2pm, 5–8pm; Sept–Jul Sun–Fri 10.30am–2.30pm, Sat 10.30am–2.30pm, 4–6.30pm. ⊚5€; child 4€. ℰ938 15 84 91. www.museudelferrocarril.org.

This is one of the most impressive collections of railway engines in Spain.

ADDRESSES

▨ STAY

⊝⊜⊜ **Hotel Romàntic y la Renaixença** – *Sant Isidre 33. ℰ938 94 83 75. www.hotelromantic.com. 69 rooms. Closed Nov–Feb.* This establishment takes up two 19C buildings, each with period décor and a certain decadent charm. Rooms are sombre but cosy, with somewhat antiquated bathrooms. Lovely interior courtyard with trees.

ⴵ EAT

⊝ **La Oca** – *Parellades 41. ℰ938 94 79 36. Closed Nov.* This inexpensive, modern restaurant, well located in the centre of Sitges, is known for its grilled meats, roast chicken and fast service. A cheap menu is also available at lunchtime.

⊝⊜⊜⊜ **Maricel** – *Pas. de la Ribera 6. ℰ938 94 20 54. www.maricel.es. Closed second fortnight in Nov, Tue for dinner (Jul–Aug all day), Wed for lunch.* The seafront Maricel specialises in elaborate and innovative Mediterranean cuisine. The speciality is seafood, accompanied by good soups.

FIESTAS

Sitges is known for its Corpus Christi flowers, for the Catalunya International Cinema Festival *(early October; www.cinemasitges.com)*, vintage car rally *(Mar)* and international theatre festival *(Jun)* Its major fiesta, is on 24 August, the feast day of Sant Bartomeu, celebrated with a huge firework display and a traditional parade of giant figures. The town is also famous for its exuberant Carnival.

Solsona★★

Solsona is a tranquil town with a
noble air and attractive squares.
Elegant medieval residences line its
gently sloping streets.

SIGHTS

Museu Diocesà i Comarcal★★ (Diocesan and Regional Museum)

Pl. del Palau 1. ⏲ *Open Oct–Apr
Tue–Sun 10am–1pm, 4–6pm, public
holidays 10am–2pm; May–Sept
Tue–Sun 10am–1pm, 4.30–7pm, public
holidays 10am–2pm.* ⊚*2€.* ℘*973 48
21 01. http://museu.bisbatsolsona.cat.*
Romanesque and Gothic **paintings**★★
in the Palau Episcopal (Episcopal Palace,
an 18C Baroque building), are excellent
examples of Catalan art.
The frescoes include a painting from
the **Sant Quirze de Pedret church**★★,
discovered beneath an overpainting.
Executed in an archaic style, it shows
God, with arms outstretched, in a circle
which represents Heaven, surmounted
by a phoenix symbolising immortality.
Totally different are the thinly outlined
13C paintings from **Sant Pau de
Caserres**★ – in particular, wonderful
angels★★ of the Last Judgement.
Known for its **altar fronts**, another
highlight of the museum is **La Cena
de Santa Constanza**★, a realistic Last
Supper, by Jaime Ferrer (15C).
In the **Museu de la Sal** (Salt Museum),
everything is carved out of rock salt
from Cardona.

Catedral★

Pl. de la Catedral. ⏲ *Open Mon–Fri
10am–1pm, 4–7.30pm, Sat 10am–1pm,
4–7pm, Sun 10am–1pm, 4–6pm.* ⊚*No
charge.* ℘*973 48 23 10.*
Only the belfry and the apse remain
of the Romanesque church; the rest is
Gothic with Baroque additions such
as the portals and the sumptuous 18C
Capella de la Virgen (Lady Chapel) off
the south transept. This chapel houses
the **Mare de Déu del Claustro**★, a
beautifully carved Romanesque figure
of the Virgin Mary in black stone.

▶ **Population:** 9 166
⦿ **Michelin Map:** 574 G 3 –
Catalunya (Lleida)
🛈 **Info:** Carretera Bassella 1.
℘973 48 23 10.
www.elsolsonesinvita.com
◉ **Location:** The capital of the
Solsonès region is on the C
1410 road linking Manresa
with the C 1313 heading
into the Pyrenees.

ADDITIONAL SIGHTS

Museu del Ganivet i Eines de Tall
(Travessia Sant Josep 9)
Ayuntamiento (town hall – 16C; Sant
Pau 23)

EXCURSION

Cardona★

20km/12.4mi SE along the C 55.
Cardona sits at the foot of an imposing
castle.

Castillo de Cardona★

This spectacular hilltop fortress, at
589m/1 933ft, dates back to the 8C.
Of the 11C buildings there remain only
a truncated tower, the **Torre de la
Minyona**, and the collegiate church,
surrounded by Vauban-style walls
and bulwarks built in the 17C and 18C.
The castle is a parador, commanding
a marvellous **view**★of the **muntanya
de sal**★★ (⏲guided tours (1hr) Tue–Fri
10am–3pm (descent to mine 11.30am and
1.30pm), Sat–Sun every 30 min 10am–
6pm; ⊚10€; ℘938 69 24 75; www.
salcardona.com), a salt mine worked
since Roman times.

Colegiata de Sant Vicenç★★

⏲ Open Tue–Sun Oct–May
10am–1.30pm, 3–5.30pm; Jun–Sept
10am–1.30pm, 3–6.30pm. ⏲ Closed
1 Jan, 25–26 Dec. ⊚3€; no charge Tue.
℘938 69 24 75. http://www.mhcat.net.
The collegiate church built in 1040 has
Lombard features. The groined vaulting
in the **crypt**★ rests on six graceful
columns. The Gothic cloisters date from
the 15C.

Tarragona★★

Tarragona, with its ancient and medieval heritage, is also a modern town with wide avenues and a lively commercial centre. Its gardened seafront promenade skirts the cliffside and surrounds the old city and Palace of Augustus, following the city walls in the shadow of the Cathedral. Long a major port, Tarragona also has 15km/9.3mi of beaches that attract summer visitors.

▶ **Population:** 137 536
⚑ **Michelin Map:** 574 I 33 – Catalunya (Tarragona)
▯ **Info:** Major 39. ℘977 25 07 95. www.tarragona turisme.cat.
▷ **Location:** Tarragona is in Cataluña in NE Spain, SW along the coast from Barcelona. ▭Passeig de Espanya
▲▲ **Kids:** Port Aventura theme park; Costa Caribe water park.

SIGHTS
ROMAN TARRAGONA★★
Passeig Arqueològic★
(Archaeological Promenade)

Av. Catalunya. ◷ *Open Oct–before Holy Week Tue–Sat 9am–5pm, Sun and public holidays 10am–3pm; Holy Week–Sept Tue–Sat 9am–9pm, Sun and public holidays 9am–3pm.* ◷ *Closed 1, 6 Jan, 1 May and 25–26 Dec.* ◌*3€ (10€ combined with other Museu d'Història sites).* ℘*977 24 57 96. www.museutgn.com.*

Scipios built Tarragona's walls in the 3C BC on existing Cyclopean bases. They were so massive that they were long thought to have been barbarian or pre-Roman. Medieval inhabitants rebuilt the ramparts; 18C citizens remodelled them but still left us with walls bearing the marks of 2 000 years of history. A garden walk follows the walls.

Museu Nacional Arqueològic de Tarragona★★
(Archaeological Museum)

Pl. del Rey 5. ◷ *Open Jun–Sept Tue–Sun 9.30am–8.30pm; Oct–May Tue–Sat 9.30am–1.30pm, 3.30–7pm; Sun and public holidays 10am–7pm.* ◌*2.40€ (includes entry to Necrópolis).* ℘*977 23 62 09. www.mnat.es.*

The exhibits, mostly from Roman times, are from Tarragona or its environs.

The **Roman architecture** *(Room II, ground floor)* section gathers vestiges of the most imposing buildings in Tarraconensis. The **Roman mosaics★★** collection is the finest in Catalunya. Exhibits in Rooms III *(first floor)* and VIII *(second floor)* testify to the high craftsmanship of the Romans. The most extraordinary piece is the **Mosaic**

Capital of Tarraconensis

The history of Tarragona dates back many centuries. The imposing ramparts built of enormous Cyclopean blocks of stone indicate that it was founded by peoples from the eastern Mediterranean early in the first millennium BC. In due course it suffered occupation by the Iberians. The Romans, who by 218 BC had control of the larger part of the peninsula, developed Tarraconensis into a major city and overseas capital. Although it could never equal Rome, it enjoyed many of the same privileges as the imperial capital and Augustus, Galba and Hadrian did not disdain to live in it.

Conversion to Christianity, often attributed to the work of St Paul, brought it appointment as a metropolitan seat, and its dignitaries the primacy of Spain. This honour was retained throughout the barbarian invasions of the 5C and the destruction of the Moors in the 8C but lost finally to the ambition of Toledo in the 11C. The city was then abandoned until the 12C, when it reverted to the Christians.

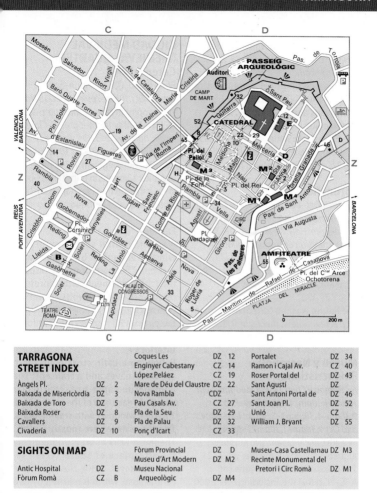

of the Medusa★★ (late 2C), with its penetrating gaze. **Roman sculpture**★ *(Rooms VI to X, second floor)* is exemplified by superb **funerary sculptures** *(Room IX)*. Note *(Room VI)* the bust of Lucius Verusa, executed in the 2C, a perfect example of the art, and the small **votive sculpture of Venus**★.

Recinte Monumental del Pretori i del Circ Romà★ (Praetorium and Roman Circus)

Pl. del Rey 5. Open Jun–Sept Tue–Sat 9am–9pm, Sun 9am–3pm; Oct–May Tue–Sat 9am–7pm, Sun 10am–3pm. Closed 1, 6 Jan, 1 May, 25–26 Dec. 3€ (10€ combined with other Museu d'Història sites). 977 24 19 52. www.museutgn.com.

Visit the **vaulted underground galleries**★ of a restored 1C BC square tower, or enjoy the sweeping **view**★★ from the top. **Hippolyte's sarcophagus**★★, found virtually intact on the bed of the Mediterranean, bears fine and lively sculptured ornamentation.

The vast **Roman Circus** (325m x 115m/1066ft x 378ft) was designed for chariot races. Only a few terraces, vaults and sections of the façade remain.

Amfiteatre★★

Parque del Miracle. Open Oct–before Holy Week Tue–Sat 9am–5pm, Sun and public holidays 10am–3pm; Holy Week–Sept Tue–Sat 9am–9pm, Sun and public holidays 9am–3pm. Closed 1, 6 Jan, 1 May, 25–26 Dec.

⌖3€ (10€ combined with other Museu d'Història sites). ✆977 24 25 79. www.museutgn.com.

The seaside elliptical amphitheatre is in a naturally sloped **site**★. Bishop Fructuosus and his deacons, Augurius and Eulogius, were martyred here in 259. The Església de Santa Maria del Miracle (church) replaced a Visigothic basilica in the 12C and is itself now in ruins.

Forum Romà

🕐 Open Oct–before Holy Week Tue–Sat 9am–7pm, Sun and public holidays 10am–3pm; Holy Week–Sept Tue–Sat 9am–9pm, Sun and public holidays 9am–3pm. 🕐 Closed 1, 6 Jan, 1 May, 25–26 Dec. ⌖3€ (10€ combined with other Museu d'Història sites). ✆977 24 25 01.

The Forum was the core of the Roman city. A few reliefs, pieces of frieze and sections of a street remain.

Museu y Necrópolis Paleocristianas

Av. Ramon y Cajal 78. 🕐Open Jun–Sept 10am–1.30pm, 4–8pm; Nov–Feb 9.30am–1.30pm, 3–5.30pm; Mar–May and Oct 9.30am–1.30pm, 3–6pm. ⌖2.40€ (includes entry to Museu Arqueològic); no charge Tue. ✆977 25 22 86. www.tarragonaturisme.cat.

A 3C–7C burial site, including over 2 000 tombs, were uncovered at this location in 1923. A section has been restored for viewing, with many of the remains now in the Archaeological Museum.

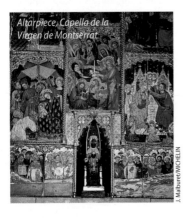
Altarpiece, Capella de la Virgen de Montserrat

J. Malburet/MICHELIN

CIUDAD MEDIEVAL (MEDIEVAL QUARTER)
Catedral★★

Pl. de la Seu. 🕐 Open Mon–Sat 1 Jun–15 Oct 10am–7pm; 16 Oct–15 Nov 10am–5pm; 16 Nov–15 Mar 10am–2pm; 16 Mar–31 May 10am–6pm. 🕐 Closed public holidays. ⌖3.80€ (includes Museu Diocesá). ✆977 21 10 80.

Construction began in 1174 on the site of Jupiter's Temple, in transitional Gothic style, although the side chapels are both Plateresque and Baroque.

Façade★

A Gothic central section with rose window is flanked by Romanesque sections. The **main doorway** displays the Last Judgement, with expressive relief work. The archivolts are carved with Apostles and Prophets. On the pier, the Virgin (13C) receives the Faithful.

Interior★★

Following a Latin cross plan, there are three naves and a transept. The Romanesque apse has semicircular arches. At each end of the transept are 14C rose windows with stained glass. The three naves are mostly Gothic. The finest work of art is undoubtedly the **altarpiece of Santa Tecla**★★★ (Capella Mayor, 1430), closing off the central apse, which is reached by two Gothic doorways. Santa Tecla (St Thecla) is the city's patron saint.

This work by Pere Joan shows a talent for detail, ornamentation and the picturesque. To the right of the altar lies the 14C **Tomb of the Infante Don Juan de Aragón**★★, attributed to an Italian master.

The **Capella de la Virgen de Montserrat** (second chapel, left) houses a **retable**★ by Luis Borrassà (15C). **Reliefs**★ in the Capella de Santa Tecla (third chapel in the right-hand aisle) recount the saint's life. The **Capella de los Sastres**★★ (to the left of the Capella Major) features intricate ribbed vaulting, a lovely altarpiece and paintings. Sumptuous tapestries are decorated with allegorical motifs.

Claustro★★

The 12C–13C cloisters are unusually large – each gallery is 45m/148ft long. The arches and geometric decoration are Romanesque, but the vaulting is Gothic, as are the supporting arches.

Moorish influence is evident in the *claustra* of geometrically patterned and pierced panels filling the oculi below the arches, the line of multifoil arches at the base of the Cathedral roof and the belfry in one corner, rising 70m/230ft. Inlaid in the west gallery is a mihrab-like stone niche, dated 960.

A remarkable **Romanesque doorway**★, with a Christ in Majesty, links the cathedral to the cloisters.

Museu Diocesá★★

Pl. de la Seu. ◷ *Open same hours as Cathedral.*

The capitular outbuildings contain religious vestments, paintings, altarpieces and reliefs. Tapestries in Room III include the 15C Flemish **La Buena Vida**★. In the Capella del Corpus Christi are a richly ornate **monstrance**★ (n°105) and a polychrome alabaster relief work depicting St Jerome (16C).

Antiguo Hospital★

Coques.

This 12C–14C hospital, now used by the local council, is a surprising mix of styles, including the original Romanesque façade and doorway.

Museu-Casa Castellarnau★

Cavallers. ◷ *Open Oct–before Holy Week Tue–Sat 9am–7pm, Sun and public holidays 10am–3pm; Holy Week–Sept Tue–Sat 9am–9pm, Sun and public holidays 9am–3pm.* ◷ *Closed 1, 6 Jan, 1 May , 25–26 Dec.* ⊚*3€ (10€ combined with other Museu d'Història sites).* ✆ *977 24 22 20. www.museutgn.com.*

The Emperor Charles V is said to have stayed in this wealthy 14C–15C residence. It features a pretty Gothic patio and fine 18C furniture.

EXCURSIONS

Acueducto de Les Ferreres★★

Leave the city along rambla Nova.

4km/2.5mi from Tarragona you will see the well-preserved two-tier Roman aqueduct on your right, 217m/712ft long. ▮*You can walk (30min) through the pines to the base.*

Mausoleo de Centcelles★★

4km/2.5mi NW. Exit the city along avinguda Ramon i Cajal. Take the Reus road; bear right after crossing the Francolí. Turn right in Constantí into Centcelles; continue 450m/492yd on an unsurfaced road; turn left just before the village. ◷ *Open Jun–Sept Tue–Sat 10am–1.30pm, 4–7.30pm, Sun and public holidays 10am–1.30pm; Oct–May Tue–Sat 10am–1.30pm, 3–5.30pm, Sun and public holidays 10am–1.30pm.* ◷ *Closed 1, 6 Jan, 25–26 Dec.* ⊚*1.80€.* ✆ *977 52 33 74. www.mnat.es.*

Two monumental buildings in a vineyard are faced with pink tiles. They were built in the 4C by a wealthy Roman near his vast summer residence. The first chamber is covered by an immense cupola (diameter: 11m/36ft), decorated with **mosaics**★★ on themes such as hunting, Daniel in the lion's den, etc. The adjoining chamber has an apse on either side.

Torre de los Escipiones★

Leave Tarragona along via Augusta. After 5km/3mi turn left.

The upper and central parts of this square funerary tower (1C) bear reliefs portraying Atis, a Phrygian divinity associated with death rituals (not the Escipion brothers as once thought).

Villa Romana de Els Munts★

12km/7.4mi E along the N 340. Leave Tarragona along via Augusta.
◷ *Open Jun–Sept Tue–Sat 10am–1.30pm, 4–7.30pm, Sun and public holidays 10am–1.30pm; Oct–May Tue–Sat 10am–1.30pm, 3–5.30pm, Sun and public holidays 10am–1.30pm.* ◷ *Closed 1, 6 Jan, 25–26 Dec.* ⊚*1.80€.* ✆ *977 23 62 09. www.mnat.es.*

This Roman villa nestles in Altafulla, in a privileged **site**★★ gently sloping towards the sea. The L-shaped arcaded passage was flanked by gardens and **baths**★ with a complex plan.

Arco de Berà★

Follow the via Augusta. The arch is situated in the locality of Roda de Berà, 20km/12.4mi along the N 340.
The Vía Augusta once passed under this imposing, well-proportioned arch (1C). Its eight grooved pilasters are crowned by Corinthian capitals.

🧍👥 Port Aventura★★

10km/6.2mi SW towards Salou.
🕐 *Open daily from 10am, please phone for closing times. ☞44€; child 35€ (76€/63€ for three days including Costa Caribe). ✆902 20 22 20. www. portaventura.co.uk. Tickets can be purchased 24hr in advance through the services of Servi-Caixa or at the park ticket offices.* 🅿 *7€ per day.*
The huge Universal Studios Port Aventura amusement park is divided into five geographical zones, each with its characteristic rides, performances, shops and eateries.
Mediterrània at the park entrance is a coastal town. In **Polynesia**★, a path winds through tropical vegetation.
China★★ is the heart of the park, symbolising the magic and mystery of a millenary civilisation. The star attraction is **Dragon Khan**★★★, one of the world's most spectacular roller coasters, with eight gigantic loops. **Mexico**★★ spans Mayan ruins, colonial Mexico, Mariachi music and traditional Mexican cuisine. In the **Far West**★★ town of **Penitence**, visitors play the lead in a western or dance in the saloon.Adjacent is the **Caribe Aquatic Park** *(☞24€; child 19€)*, with a Caribbean island theme.

Salou

10km/6.2mi SW. 🚌Carles Roig.
This is the principal resort on the Costa Dorada, very popular with British and German tourists. Aside from Port Aventura *(👆see above)* the most popular day off the beach is at 🙂**Aquopolis** a very popular water park and dolphinarium *(La Pineda;* 🕐*open 14 May–30 Jun, 1–20 Sept 11am–6pm; Jul–Aug 10am–7pm; 21 Sept–9 Oct 11am–5pm; ☞23.95€; child 17.95€;* ✆*902 34 50 11; www.aquopolis.es/costa-daurada).*
Salou merges into the attractive little fishing port of **Cambrils** *(8km/5mi W;* 🚌 *Avinguda Virgen de Montserrat).* renowned for the quality of its fish restaurants.

Parque Natural del Delta del Ebro★★ (Ebro Delta Nature Reserve)

25km/15.5mi E. www.deltebre.net.
This vast delta, is a swampy stretch of alluvium deposits collected by the Ebro and now acts as a bird reserve. There are boat trips between Deltebre and the river mouth *(*✆*977 480 128; www. creuers-delta-ebre.com).*

ADDRESSES

🏠 STAY

🛏🍴 **Hotel Urbis Centre** – *Pl. Corsini 10.* ✆*977 24 01 16. www.hotelurbiscentre. com. 44 rooms.* 🍽*7.50€. Restaurant*🛏🍴*.* Situated near the convention centre and the old city, this modest family hotel offers functional rooms with updated bathrooms.

🛏🍴🍴 **Hotel Imperial Tarraco** – *Pas. Palmeres.* ✆*977 23 30 40. www.hotel husaimperialtarraco.com. 170 rooms.* 🍽*13€. Restaurant* 🛏🍴*.* Despite its luxury tag, the rates here are not extortionate. The hotel is housed in a half-moon-shaped modern building near the city's Roman ruins, overlooking the amphitheatre. Many of the international-style rooms enjoy views of the Mediterranean.

🍴 EAT

🛏🍴🍴🍴 **Merlot** – *Caballers 6.* ✆*977 22 06 52. Closed Sun, Mon lunchtime, first fortnight in Feb, last week in Dec.* The vaulted ceiling, subtle lighting and high-quality rustic furniture create a refined, intimate ambience. The menu covers a range of Catalan dishes (rice dishes in particular) as well as an excellent selection of home-made desserts.

♀ CAFÉS

Pla de la Seu – *Pl. de la Seu 5–7.* ℘*977 23 04 07.* The best feature of this establishment is its terrace facing the cathedral. Perfect for a refreshment before or after your visit. Live music on weekends.

Rest. Rovira – Vinatería – *Av. Prat de la Riba 34.* ℘*977 22 61 58.* The impressive choice at this prestigious wine bar includes a huge selection of sparkling wines from Catalunya. The Sumpta also has its own restaurant.

Tortosa★

Tortosa, for centuries the last town before the sea, once guarded the region's only bridge. From the Castillo de la Suda, a castle (now a parador), enjoy a fine view of the Ebro and the valley. Tortosa's artistic endowment ranges from Gothic monuments to fine examples of Modernism.

SIGHTS
CIUDAD ANTIGUA★ (OLD TOWN)
Catedral★★

Croera. ○ *Open Tue–Sat 10am–1pm, 4–6pm, Sun 12.30–2pm.* ⊚*3€.* ℘*977 44 17 52.*
The Cathedral was built in pure Gothic style even though construction, begun in 1347, continued for 200 years.
The 18C Baroque **façade★** is lavishly decorated: capitals with plant motifs, curved columns and outstanding reliefs.
In Catalan tradition the lines of the **interior★★** are plain, the high arches divided into two tiers only in the nave. The retable at the high altar has a large 14C wood **polyptych★** illustrating the Life of Christ and the Virgin Mary. Another interesting work is the 15C **altarpiece of the Transfiguration★**. Two stone 15C **pulpits★** in the nave are carved with low reliefs: those on the left illustrate the Evangelists, those on the right, Saints Gregory, Jerome, Ambrose and Augustine.

- ▶ **Population:** 35 734
- ⏱ **Michelin Map:** 574 J 31 – 65km/40.4mi from Peñíscola – Catalunya (Tarragona)
- ▯ **Info:** Plaça del Carrilet 1. ℘977 44 96 48. www. turismetortosa.com.
- ▶ **Location:** Tortosa is 14km/8.7mi off the coastal motorway in Catalunya. ▭Carrer Poeta Vicente García 6 y 12

Capella de Nuestra Señora de la Cinta★ (Chapel of Our Lady of the Sash)

Second chapel off the south aisle.
Built in Baroque style between 1642 and 1725, it is decorated with paintings and local jasper and marble; at its centre is the sash of Our Lady *(services of special veneration: first week in September).* The stone **font** is said to have stood in the garden of the antipope Benedict XIII, Pedro de Luna, and bears his arms.

Palau Episcopal★ (Bishop's Palace)

Croera 9. ○ *Open Mon–Fri 10am–2pm.* ○*Closed public holidays.* ⊚*No charge.* ℘*977 44 07 00.*
The 14C Catalan patio of this palace, built in the 13C–14C, is known for its straight flight of steps which occupies one side, and the arcaded gallery. On the upper floor, the **Gothic chapel★**, has ogive vaulting in which the ribs descend to figured bosses.

Reials Col·legis de Tortosa★

Sant Doménec. ⏱ *Open Mon–Fri 9am–1.30pm, 4–7pm, Sat 9am–2pm.* ✆*977 44 15 25.*

In 1564 Emperor Charles V sponsored this lovely Renaissance ensemble. The **Colegio de Sant Lluís**★ at one time educated newly converted Muslims. The fine oblong **patio**★★ is curiously decorated with characters in a wide range of expressions and attitudes. The Renaissance façade of the **Colegio de Sant Jordi y de Sant Domingo** bears a Latin inscription (*Domus Sapientiae,* House of Knowledge).

Església de Sant Domènec

Sant Doménec.
Built in the 16C, this church was once part of the Reales Colegios.

Llotja de Mar

Canonge Macip.
The maritime exchange is a fine example of Gothic architecture (16C).

Vic★★

This important commercial centre and thriving industrial town (leather goods, food processing and textiles) lies in the foothills of the Pyrenees. Monumental buildings testify to its history as a Roman centre. Vic makes a good base for exploring the mountains while also being within striking distance of Barcelona.

THE CITY TODAY

Vic sees few overnighting north European visitors. It is known locally for its wide choice of good quality restaurants so if you wish to escape fellow tourists and fill up on authentic Catalunyan cooking, before walking it off in the mountains, this is the place to come.

SIGHTS

OLD QUARTER★

Wide avenues (*ramblas*) follow the old walls, of which a few remnants remain.

Museu Episcopal★★★

Pl. Bisbe Oliba 3. ⏱*Open Apr–Sept Tue–Sat 10am–7pm, Sun and public holidays 10am–2pm; Oct–Mar Tue–Fri 10am–1pm, 3–6pm, Sat 10am–7pm, Sun and public holidays 10am–2pm.* ⏱*Closed 1, 6 Jan, Easter Sunday, 25–26 Dec.* ✆*5€; no charge first Thu of every month, 18 May, 5 Jul.* ✆*938 86 93 60.* *www.museuepiscopalvic.com.*

- ▸ **Population:** 38 946
- ⊙ **Michelin Map:** 574 G 36 – Catalunya (Barcelona)
- ℹ **Info:** Ciutat 4. ✆938 86 20 91. www.victurisme.cat.
- ◑ **Location:** Vic is in NE Spain, north of Barcelona.

This magnificent museum displays Romanesque and Gothic works, along with fabrics and costumes, jewellery, ceramics and other arts.

Sala del Románico★★★ (Romanesque Gallery)

On exhibit are the *Descent of Erill la Vall,* a sculptural ensemble; the painting *Canopy of Ribes de Freser;* and outstanding **altar fronts**. The *Lluça Altar* marks the transition to the Gothic style.

Salas del Gótico★★★ (Gothic Galleries)

Among items from the early Gothic period (after 1275) are a magnificent marble altarpiece by **Bernat Saulet**, a *Virgin of Boixadors*, the altar front of Bellver de Cerdanya and parts of an altarpiece by **Pere Serra**. The impressive collection of international Gothic altarpieces (15C) includes the **Santa Clara** and *Sant Antoni i Santa Margarida* altars, both by Borrasà, the *de Guimerà* altar, the work of Ramon de Mur, and the *Verdú* altarpiece of Jaume Ferrer II.

The paintings of Jaume Huguet mark the transition to the Renaissance.

Tejido e Indumentaria★★ (Textiles and Costumes)

A magnificent display of 13C–18C textiles and liturgical wear (14C–19C).

Catedral★

Pl. de la Catedral. ⏰ *Open daily 10am–1pm, 4–7pm.* 🎟2€. 📞938 86 44 49.

An elegant 11C Romanesque belfry and crypt remain from earlier churches.

The Neoclassical Cathedral was built between 1781 and 1803. In 1930 the famous Catalan artist **Josep Maria Sert** decorated the **interior**★ with wall paintings. These were burned during the Civil War, and repainted by Sert before his death in 1945.

The **paintings**★★ have a power reminiscent of Michelangelo. They evoke the mystery of the Redemption *(chancel)* from the time of Adam's original sin *(transept)* to the Passion *(apse)*, the Evangelists and the Martyrs *(nave)*. Scenes on the back of the west door illustrate the triumph of human injustice in the Life of Christ and in the history of Catalunya: Jesus chasing the moneylenders *(right)*; Jesus condemned *(centre)* and the road to Calvary *(left)*. The monochrome golds and browns in the murals lend the effect of a relief.

The former high altar **retable**★★ *(end of the ambulatory)* is a 15C alabaster work in 12 panels. The Gothic tomb is of the canon who commissioned the retable, by the same sculptor.

Claustro★ (Cloister)

Tracery-filled 14C arches surround the small close. In a cloister gallery is the tomb of the painter JM Sert, surmounted by his unfinished *Crucifixion*.

Palau Episcopal

Santa Maria. 📞938 86 15 55.

The 12C episcopal palace has been modified significantly. The **Sala dels Sínodes**, decorated in 1845, and the patio are the main features.

Plaça Major★

Note façades with Modernist, Gothic and Baroque details on this busy arcaded square. A popular market is held in the square every Saturday.

EXCURSIONS

Monestir de Sant Pere de Casserres★

19km/11.8mi NE of Vic. ⏰ *Open Tue–Sun Nov–Feb and 16 Sept–Oct 11am–5.30pm; Mar–14 Jun 10am–5.30pm; 15 Jun–15 Sept 10am–7pm; ticket office closes 30min before monastery.* ⏰*Closed Tue if Mon is bank holiday, 25 Dec.* 🎟3€. 📞937 44 71 18. www.santperedecasserres.com.

▷ *17km/11.6mi NE of Vic. Take the C 153 NE from Vic, then turn right towards Tavernoles and Parador. At Parador take a paved lane to the left (3.5km/2.2mi).*

Stop just before Parador for a fine **view**★★ *(right)* of the marsh of Sau, between high banks. The small Romanesque monastery enjoys a privileged **location**★★ at the end of a long and narrow peninsula in the marsh.

Monestir de Santa Maria de L'Estany★

Pl. del Monestir, L'Estany. ⏰*Open Tue–Sat 9am–1pm, 4–7pm, Sun and public holidays 10am–2pm.* ⏰*Closed 1 Jan, 25–26 Dec.* 🎟2€. 📞938 30 08 01.

▷ *24km/15mi SW of Vic. Leave Vic along the C 25 towards Manresa. Turn right at Exit 164 and follow the BP 4313.*

The village of **L'Estany**★ grew up around this medieval Augustinian monastery. The bell tower of the 12C Romanesque church was rebuilt in the 15C. The arcades of the beautiful **cloisters**★ are supported by matching columns and decorated with 72 remarkable **capitals**★★. The north gallery is Romanesque and narrative; the west, decorative with palm fronds and gaunt griffons; the south, geometrical and interlaced; the east features wedding scenes and musicians.

Through the Serra de Montseny★

The Serra de Montseny, an extension of the Pyrenees, is a granite massif covered in beeches and cork oaks. To the southeast, the **Parque Natural de Montseny** covers 17 372ha/42 925 acres; its highest peaks are Matagalls (1 695m/5 560ft) and **Turó de l'Home** (1 707m/5 601ft).

From Vic to Sant Celoni via the Northern Road

> 60km/37.3mi. Leave Vic to the S; turn left after 6km/3.7mi.

The road goes through pine and beechwoods past delightful **Viladrau**.

After **Arbúcies**, it runs beside the river then turns for **Breda**, with the Romanesque tower of the **Monestir de Sant Salvador★**, and Sant Celoni (Plaça de l´Estació).

From Sant Celoni to la Ermita de Sant Marçal★★

Beyond Campins, the road rises with **views**, to the lake (embalse) of Santa Fè (1 130m/3 707ft). The hermitage is 7km/4.3mi ahead on Matagalls ridge.

From Sant Celoni to Tona via Montseny★
43km/27mi.

There are good **views** of the serra along here. Beyond Montseny, the road rises to a wild area, then descends to Tona past the Romanesque church in **El Brull** and the tower of **Santa Maria de Seva**.

Principat d'Andorra★★
Principality of Andorra

The seven parishes that make up the principality of Andorra occupy high plateaux and valleys cut by charming mountain roads. In recent years Andorra has seen urbanisation, hydroelectric schemes and a tourism boom. But tradition remains in the terraced slopes planted with tobacco and in religious pilgrimages (the famous Catalan *aplec*).

ANDORRA TODAY
Andorra is well known for the duty-free shopping opportunities it offers, primarily in the tiny capital of Andorra la Vella. In fact an astonishing 10 million visitors a year descend upon the principality, many clutching their credit card. The main skiing valleys are also very busy in season, with some 50 million euros recently invested in their infrastructure. By contrast the outlying villages remain largely uncommercialised.

- ▶ **Population:** 71 822
- **Michelin Map:** 574 E 34-35
- **Info:** Andorra la Vella: Plaça de la Rotonda. ☏00 376 82 71 17. Barcelona: Pau Claris. ☏932 15 91 04. www.tourisme-andorre.net.
- ◉ **Location:** Andorra is tucked between Spain and France. Andorra La Vella is located 20km/12.4mi from La Seu d'Urgell.
- **Parking:** Forget about parking on the crowded streets of Andorra la Vella.

A BIT OF HISTORY
Until 1993 Andorra was a co-principality subject to an unusual political regime dating back to the days of feudalism. The neighbouring rulers, the Bishop of Urgell and the President of the French Republic, enjoyed rights and exercised powers over this small territory, which was jointly governed by them. At present

Andorra is a sovereign state – a full member of the United Nations.

SIGHTS

Andorra la Vella

Houses in the capital cluster onto a terrace overlooking the Gran Valira. Streets in the old quarter remain almost intact, as has the **Casa de la Vall** (Parliament House; *Vall; guided tours (30min, must be booked one month in advance) Mon–Sat 9.30am–1.30pm, 3–6.30pm; 00 376 82 91 29*). This ancient stone building houses the Consell General de les Valls, both Parliament and courthouse to the small nation.

To the east, Andorra la Vella joins the lively municipality of Les Escaldes, dominated by **Caldaea** *(www.caldea.com)*, a thermal spa with futuristic lines featuring Turkish baths, jacuzzis, bubble beds, hot marble slabs, etc.

Estany d'Engolasters (Engolasters Lake)

The Engolasters plateau is a pastured extension of Andorra la Vella used for sports and recreation. The fine Romanesque tower of the church of Sant Miquel rises above the rolling plains. Climb over the crest among the pine trees at the end of the road and descend on foot to an impressive hydroelectric dam, surrounded by trees, which has raised the waters of the lake (alt 1 616m/5 301ft) by a total of 10m/33ft.

Santuari de Meritxell

Beyond Los Bons pass lies a lovely **site**★ of houses gathered under a ruined castle and the Capella de Sant Romà. Nearby stands the church of Nuestra Señora de Meritxell (*open Sept–Jun Wed–Mon 9.15am–1pm, 3–6pm; Jul–Aug daily 9.15am–1pm, 3–7pm; no charge*), national sanctuary of the principality since 1976.

Canillo

The bell tower of the church set against rocks is the highest in Andorra. At its side is an ossuary, characteristic of early Iberian occupation.

Església de Sant Joan de Caselles

Av. Sant Joan de Caselles, Canillo. Open Jul–Aug daily 10am–1pm, 3–7pm; otherwise prior booking required. *No charge. 00 376 84 41 41.*

Below an openwork tower and rows of ornamental windows, this church is one of the best examples of Romanesque architecture in Andorra. Behind the wrought-iron grid of the presbytery stands a painted altarpiece by the master **Canillo** (1525), representing the life and visions of the Apostle St John. The Romanesque **Crucifixion**★ was restored in 1963: a Christ in stucco was placed atop a fresco illustrating the Calvary.

Port d'Envalira★★

Roads may be snow-blocked but usually reopen within 24hr.

Alt 2 407m/7 897ft. Envalira boasts the highest altitude of major Pyrenean passes. On the Atlantic-Mediterranean divide, it commands a lovely mountain panorama.

Pas de la Casa★

Alt 2 091m/6 861ft. Once only a frontier post, the highest village in Andorra is the main ski resort of the region.

Ordino

Park by the church in the upper town. Ordino is a quaint village with a maze of charming alleyways. Admire the wrought-iron grilles of the church, and nearby, the 18m/60ft balcony adorning the Casa de Don Guillem, built for a master blacksmith.

EXTREMADURA

Extremadura – it means "beyond the River Douro" – forms much of the boundary between Spain and Portugal. In Roman times, it was at one with present-day Portugal, making up the Roman territory known as Lusitania. This was the heyday of the region, when Mérida, the home of Emperor Augustus, was its capital. Some 1 500 years later a very different (Holy) Roman Emperor, Charles V, also chose to retire here, far from the cares of the world. Like La Mancha, Extremadura is dominated by the harsh unforgiving arid plain known as La Meseta. Add to this barren terrain its isolation from the rest of Spain (even today it is known as the back of beyond), an unrewarding system of absentee landlord farming, and it is no wonder that over the centuries so many Extremadurans have chosen to make their fortune elsewhere.

The region's most famous sons were its Conquistadores: Cortés, conqueror of Mexico; Pizarro, conqueror of Peru; Hernando de Soto, first European discoverer of the Mississippi; Francisco de Orellana, first European discoverer of the Amazon; Vasco Núñez de Balboa, who crossed Panama and discovered the Pacific, and many more ... The legacy of their (often ill-gotten) riches can be still seen in Extremadura's larger towns and cities, most notably in Cáceres and Trujillo. Extremadura is Spain's least densely populated region; in many areas sheep outnumber humans (lamb is not surprisingly a speciality), while storks wheel majestically overhead and nest on tall buildings and towers. Summers are punishingly hot, so visit in spring or autumn.

Highlights

1. Sitting in **Mérida**'s Teatro Romano, imagining the past (*p379*)
2. Wandering the time-capsule streets of Old **Cáceres** (*p373*)
3. Taking a coffee in the Plaza Mayor in charming **Trujillo** (*p381*)
4. Paying homage to the Virgin in the Monasterio de **Guadalupe** (*p376*)
5. Crossing the Puente Romano bridge near **Alcántara** (*p376*)

North

The north, Upper Extremadura, is the most fertile land in the region, especially the verdant Valle de la Vera, where crops include cotton, wheat, market-garden produce and around 80 per cent of all Spain's tobacco.

The hilltop town of **Plasencia**, an important agricultural centre which comes alive on market day, is a highlight. Built mostly between the 12C and 14C, its old mansions and churches retain their atmosphere and the cathedral is one of Extremadura's finest. Close by is the monastery of Yuste, the retirement home of Charles V whose realm once spanned almost 4 million sq km/1 544.4sq mi across Europe and the Americas.

🔵 **Plasencia**

Central

The ancient walled city of Cáceres, designated a World Heritage site, is the jewel of Extremadura. Time seems to have stood still here since the 16C/17C, leaving a feast of medieval architecture, including the finest assembly of Gothic and Renaissance mansions in Spain.

Guadalupe is famous for its splendid Mudéjar monastery, the second most important Marian shrine in the country (after Montserrat), home to the venerated and miraculous effigy of the Virgin of Guadalupe. The cult of the Virgin was exported by the Conquistadores and is still widespread throughout Latin America.

Trujillo is a charming small town, redolent of Conquistador wealth with mansions built on the exploits of Pizarro (his four half brothers, also from Trujillo), de Orellana and other adventurers.

🔵 **Cáceres**
🔵 **Guadalupe**
🔵 **Trujillo**

Teatro Romano, Mérida
©Turespaña

South

By controlling the flow of the Guadiana by means of a series of dams a large area of the south around Badajoz has been reafforested and devoted to develop high-yield crops such as maize, sunflowers, market-garden produce and above all animal fodder. Badajoz is the area's main city, crowning a hill overlooking the Río Guadiana which forms the border between Spain and Portugal.

Mérida was the headquarters of Western Roman Iberia and retains many important monuments including the splendid Roman Theatre, where plays are still staged in July and August.

Given its proximity to Andalucia, it is perhaps no surprise that Zafra, Extremadura's southernmost town of any size, has a Moorish feel with its little white houses. Its 15C castle is now a sumptuous parador. Stay the night here and you will be following in the footsteps of Hernán Cortés, who lodged in the castle before setting off for the New World.

- Badajoz
- Mérida
- Zafra

Paradores in Extremadura

Although the provision of reasonable accommodation has improved in recent years, Extremadura still lacks the choice of hotels that most other regions in Spain offer. This is all the more reason to stay in the historic paradores at Plasencia, Trujillo, In Cáceres, Mérida and Zafra you can really feel part of the region's rich history.

Badajoz

Once an Arab fortress, Badjoz crowns a hill along the Guadiana river and the border with Portugal. Original walls, a fortress and ramparts, its 16C Puente Royal bridge and a fine gateway are reminders of the past.

A BIT OF HISTORY

in the 11C Badajoz became capital of a Moorish kingdom. Because of Its frontier location however it was besieged and pillaged in the 16C Wars of Succession between Spain and Portugal.

SIGHTS

Catedral de San Juan Bautista

Pl. de España. ⓄOpen daily. No charge. ☎924 22 39 99.

The 13C Gothic cathedral was considerably remodelled during the Renaissance. Its fortress tower boasts delicate Plateresque friezes and window surrounds. The impressive *coro* has 16C stalls and the sacristy l holds six fine 17C Flemish tapestries.

Museo Arqueológico Provincial

Pl. de José Álvarez y Sáenz de Buruaga. ⓄOpen Tue–Sun 10am–3pm. ⓄClosed 1 Jan, 24, 25, 31 Dec. No charge. ☎924 22 23 14.

This modern museum in the 16C Palacio de la Roca in the *alcazaba* displays prehistoric and protohistoric steles and figurines; Roman mosaics and bronze tools; Visigothic **pilasters** carved with plant and geometric motifs; medieval artefacts; and Islamic pieces.

- **Population:** 146 832
- **Michelin Map:** 576 P 9 (town plan) – Extremadura (Badajoz)
- **Info:** Pasaje de San Juan. ☎924 22 49 81. www.aytobadajoz.es.
- **Location:** The A 5 links with Mérida (62km/39mi W), the EX 100 connects the town with Cáceres (91km/57mi NE). Avenida Carolina Coronado

Museo de Bellas Artes

Duque de San Germán 13. ⓄOpen Tue–Sat 10am–2pm, 4–8pm, Sat–Sun 10am–2pm. ⓄClosed public holidays. No charge. ☎924 21 24 69.

This fine arts museum in two elegant 19C mansions holds a collection of paintings, sculpture and sketches, particularly from the 19C and 20C.

Museo Extremeño e Iberoamericano de Arte Contemporáneo

ⓄOpen Tue–Sat 10.30am–1.30pm, 5–8pm, Sun 10am–1.30pm. ⓄClosed public holidays. No charge. ☎924 01 30 60. www.meiac.org.

The town's contemporary art museum displays cutting-edge exhibits.

EXCURSIONS

Olivenza

25km/15.5mi SW.

Portuguese influence shows in this white-walled town set in olive groves.

The Rise and Fall of Don Manuel

Manuel Godoy Álvarez de Faria (1767–1851), the son of a modest provincial *hidalgo* in Badajoz, left his family at 17 for the Court where he enlisted in the Guards. Favours from Queen María Luisa assisted him in a meteoric career in politics; by the age of 25 he had been appointed prime minister. His rapid success earned him little sympathy from the Court, or from the common people, who, outraged, accused him of being in Napoleon's pay. They insisted on his leaving the country. After the Aranjuez uprising, he followed the royal family into exile at Bayonne where he drew up Charles IV's act of abdication which was to deliver Spain to Napoleon. He died, unknown, in Paris.

The War of the Oranges

At the end of the 13C, Olivenza was given in dowry to King Denis of Portugal. In 1801, it was ceded to Spain to prevent the Alentejo invasion – begun by Godoy's troops – becoming a major conflict between the two nations. The skirmish, however, left no other souvenir than the story of Godoy's futile gesture of sending oranges to Queen María Luisa from trees at the foot of the Elvas ramparts.

not least in its early 16C Manueline style of architecture, late Gothic, with Renaissance, Moorish elements and maritime motifs

Iglesia de Santa María Magdalen★★ *(pl. Santa María)* – Diego and Francisco de Arruda, architects of the famous Torre de Belém in Lisbon, are believed to have designed the church's nave. Note the sumptuous altarpieces and *azulejos* in the Baroque sanctuary.

Museo Etnográfico González Santana *(pl. de Santa María; open Tue–Fri 11am–2pm, 4–7pm, Sat 10am–2pm, 4–7pm, Sun 10am–2pm; closed 1, 6 Jan, 1, 15 May, 24, 25, 31 Dec; 1€.; 924 49 02 22)* – This ethnographic museum is in the 18C Panadería del Rey (King's Bakery) within a medieval castle. The keep, built by João III of Portugal in 1488, offers fine views. Re-created workshops include a tailor's and a blacksmith's.

Ayuntamiento (Town Hall; *pl. de la Constitución; www.ayuntamientodeolivenza.com*) – The **doorway**, is built in graceful Manueline style adorned with two armillary spheres, symbols of 15C–16C Portuguese discoveries.

Cáceres★★★

The Almohad walls and towers of this World Heritage Site, a provincial capital, enclose a rare ensemble of intact Gothic and Renaissance noble houses.

- **Population:** 92 187
- **Michelin Map:** 576 N 10 (town plan) – Extremadura (Cáceres)
- **Info:** Plaza Mayor. 927 01 08 34. http://turismo.caceres.es.
- **Location:** Cáceres is strategically situated at the heart of Extremadura in west-central Spain. Avenida Juan Pablo II nº 6
- **Don't Miss:** The city walls and mansions redolent of the past.
- **Timing:** Allow a half-day in Cáceres, then explore the region.

THE CITY TODAY

Cáceres was a thriving commercial site as far back as 25 BC under Roman rule and contains a heady mix of Roman, Moorish, Sephardic and Renaissance architecture still enclosed by its medieval walls, The old town is one of only six towns in Spain to be declared a UNESCO World Heritage Site.

WALKING TOUR

CÁCERES VIEJO★★★ (OLD CÁCERES)

1hr30min.

Within Moorish walls lies a group of Gothic and Renaissance mansions beyond compare in Spain. The unadorned, ochre façades of the 15C and 16C reflect their owners, the Ulloas, the Ovandos and the Saavedras, who in battles against infidels and heathens won prestige, not wealth. The fortified towers of Cáceres were demolished on the command of Queen Isabel in 1477.

▶ *Follow the route on the plan.*

Pass beneath the **Arco de la Estrella** (Star Arch; *Pl. Mayor*), which was built into the wall by Manuel Churriguera in the 18C.

Plaza de Santa María★

On all sides are golden ochre façades. The front of the **Palacio Mayoralgo** (Mayoralgo Palace; *☛ closed to the public*) has elegant paired windows while the **Palacio Episcopal** (Bishop's Palace; *free access is available to the patio portico*) has a 16C bossed doorway with medallions of the Old and New Worlds on either side.

Iglesia de Santa María

Pl. Santa María. ⏰*Open Mon–Sat 10am–2pm, 5–8pm, Sun and public holidays 9.30am–2pm, 5–7.30pm.* ✆*1€.* 🖉*927 21 53 13.*
This 16C church has three Gothic aisles of almost equal height, with lierne and tierceron vaulting from which ribs descend into slender columns engaged in the main pillars. The fine carved high altar retable (16C) is difficult to see.
Continue to the top of Calle de las Tiendas to the **Casa de los Carvajal** (*Amargura 1;* ⏰*open Mon–Fri 10am–2pm, 5–7pm, Sat–Sun and public holidays 10am–2pm, 5–8pm;* ✆*no charge;* 🖉*927 25 55 97*) flanked by a 15C tower. Visit chambers, patio and chapel.

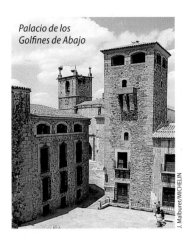
Palacio de los Golfines de Abajo

J. Malburet/MICHELIN

Palacio de los Golfines de Abajo★ (Lower Golfines Palace)

Pl. de Santa María.
☛*Closed to the public.*
This splendid late 15C Gothic-Plateresque mansion is of stone. The paired window derives from the Moorish *ajimez;* the fillet, delicately framing the windows and door, recalls the *alfiz.* A Plateresque frieze with winged griffons was added in the 16C.

Plaza San Jorge

Note the austere 18C façade of the Jesuit church of **San Francisco Javier.**

Iglesia de San Mateo

Plaza de San Mateo. ⏰*Open for Mass.*
The church's high Gothic nave, begun in the 14C, abuts a 16C *coro alto* set on a vaulted arcade. Inside are a Baroque altarpiece and side chapels with tombs with decorative heraldic motifs.
Past the church, in the calle Orellana the 15C **Torre de la Plata** (Silver Tower) and **Casa del Sol** (Sun House, for the Solís family crest over the arch) have unusual parapets.

Casa de las Cigüeñas

Plaza de San Mateo. ⏰*Open daily 11am–1pm, 5–8pm.* ✆*No charge.*
The Stork House retains the only 15C battlemented tower.

Casa de las Veletas (Weather Vane House)

Pl. de las Veletas. ⏰*Open Jun–Sept Tue–Sat 9.30am–2.30pm, 5–8.30pm, Sun and public holidays 10am–2pm; Oct–May Tue–Sun 9.30am–2.30pm, 4–7.15pm.* ✆*1.50€; free for EU citizens.* 🖉*927 01 08 77.*
This 18C mansion houses the **Museo de Cáceres.** Collections include Bronze Age steles, Celt-Iberian statues of wild boar (*verracos*) and local dress and crafts. The 11C **aljibe** (cistern) is still fed from the roof and sloping square. It is covered by five rows of horseshoe-shaped arches supported by granite capitals.

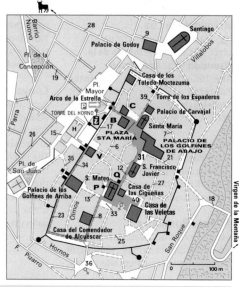

SIGHTS ON MAP			
Casa de la Generala	V	Palacio Episcopal	C
Casa del Sol	Q	Torre de los Plata	P
Palacio Mayoralgo	B		

Casa del Comendador de Alcuéscar

Ancha 6.

This palace, also called the **Palacio de Torreorgaz**, with fine Gothic tower, delicate window surrounds and an unusual corner balcony, is a parador. Down the alley is the **Palacio de los Golfines de Arriba** (*see entry*) with plain façade and attractive patio. Further on, the **Casa de la Generala** is the law school.

▷ *Go through the ramparts opposite.*

The steps to Plaza Mayor del General Mola afford an interesting view of the walls.

EXTRAMUROS
Iglesia de Santiago (St James' Church)

Pl. de Santiago. ⌑No charge.

The Romanesque church is the birthplace of the Military Order of the Knights of Cáceres who in turn founded the Order of the Knights of St James.

The altarpiece by Berruguete (1557) bears scenes from the Life of Christ.

These surround a vigorous, finely portrayed St James the Moorslayer.

The **Palacio de Godoy** opposite has an impressive coat of arms on the corner and a fine inner patio.

EXCURSIONS
Santuario de la Virgen de la Montaña

Sierra de la Mosca. 3km/1.8mi E.
🕐*Open daily 9am–1pm, 4–8pm.*
🕐*Closed 22 Apr–1st Sun in May.*
✆*927 22 00 49.*

In this 17C Baroque shrine is a statuette of the Virgin (*romería*, or pilgrimage, the first Sunday in May). The esplanade offers a **view**★ of the plateau.

Museo Vostell-Malpartida

▷ *15.2km/9.3mi E along the N 521 to Malpartida de Cáceres; the museum is 3km/1.8mi beyond (follow signposts).*
🕐*Open Tue–Sun 10am–1.30pm, 4–6pm.* ⌑*2€; no charge Wed.* ✆*927 01 08 12. www.museovostell.org.*

The museum in an 18C wool-washing plant was created by Hispano-German artist Wolf Vostell. It includes works by Canogar, the Crónica team, Saura, Maciunas, Brecht and Higgins.

Arroyo de la Luz

20km/12.4mi W along the N 521 and C 523. To find the **Iglesia de la Asunción**, *head for the tower.*

The 16C altarpiece has 16 **painted tablets**★ and four medallions by **Morales the Divine**, a rare assemblage of his works in one place.

Alcántara

65km/40mi NW via the N 521 and C 523. Alcántara is famed for its Roman bridge from which it took its ancient name (*Al Kantara* in Arabic).

Puente Romano★

2km/1.2mi NW on the road to Portugal. This magnificent bridge (106 AD), of massive unmortared granite blocks, has withstood the test of time including formidable floodwaters. Note the small temple at one end and the central triumphal arch.

Convento de San Benito

Regimiento de Argel. Guided tours (45min) daily Apr–Sept 10am–2pm, 5–8pm; Oct–Mar 10am–2pm, 4–6.30pm. No charge. 927 39 00 80.

The old headquarters of the Military Order of Alcántara stands high above the Tajo. The 16C monastery has a Plateresque church with star vaulting, a Gothic patio and a graceful Renaissance gallery used as the backdrop for plays.

ADDRESSES

STAY

Hotel Iberia Plaza Mayor – *Pintores 2. 927 24 76 34. www.iberiahotel.com. 38 rooms. 4€. Closed late Dec.* This pleasant central hotel is housed in a 17C building. Cosy rooms, excellent value.

Parador de Cáceres – *Ancha 6. 927 21 17 59. www.parador. es. 33 rooms. 15€. Restaurant.* The 14C Torreorgaz Palace has been transformed into the city's delightful parador. Tasteful furnishings, comfortable rooms and well worth the expense.

EAT

El Figón de Eustaquio – *Pl. de San Juan 12. 927 24 81 94. http://elfigondeeustaquio.com.* Most traditional restaurant in the city, superbly located on the fringes of Plaza Mayor.

El Puchero – *Pl. Mayor 9. 92 724 54 97. www.restauranteelpuchero.com.* Enjoy regional specialities in this fine traditional establishment.

Guadalupe★★

Guadalupe's monastery bristles with battlements and turrets above a picturesque village with brown tile roofs. The road above the **old village**★ commands a good **view**★ of the magical setting.

SIGHTS

Monasterio★★

Guided tours (1hr) daily 30 Mar–26 Oct 8.30am–8pm; 27 Oct–29 Mar 8.30am–9pm. 4€. 927 36 70 00. The monastery, abandoned in 1835, was restored by Franciscans after 1908. The

- **Population:** 2 114
- **Michelin Map:** 576 N 14 – Extremadura (Cáceres)
- **Info:** Plaza Santa María de Guadalupe. 927 15 41 28. www.puebladeguadalupe.net.
- **Location:** Guadalupe is SW of Madrid, on the slopes of the Guadalupe range.
- **Don't Miss:** The monastery.

complex dates from the late 14C–early 15C, but the numerous additions result in

Reina de las Españas (Patron of Hispanicity)

The first shrine is believed to have been built following the discovery of a miraculous Virgin by a shepherd in 1300. Alfonso XI, having invoked the Virgin of Guadalupe, as she was known, shortly before his victory over the Moors at the **Battle of Río Salado** (30 October 1340) had a grandiose monastery built in gratitude and entrusted it to the Hieronymites. The pilgrimage centre, richly endowed by rulers and deeply venerated by the people, exercised a great influence in the 16C and 17C when it became famous for craftsmanship – embroidery, gold and silversmithing, illumination – and more importantly, situated as it was at the heart of the kingdom of the Conquistadores, a symbol of the **Hispanidad** – that community of language and civilisation which links the Spanish of the Old and New Worlds. Christopher Columbus named a West Indian island after the shrine; the first American Indians converted to Christianity were brought to the church for baptism and Christians freed from slavery came in pilgrimage to leave their chains as votive offerings.

Solemn processions on 12 October celebrate the Day of the Hispanidad.

a confused crowding of buildings within the fortified perimeter. The monastery contains artistic treasures.

Façade

15C. The façade, golden in colour, exuberant in its Flamboyant Gothic decoration, overlooks a picturesque square. Moorish influence can be seen in the sinuous decoration. Bronze reliefs on the 15C doors illustrate the Lives of the Virgin and Christ.

Iglesia (Church)

14C. One of the first buildings, the church received 18C additions, such as gilt Baroque decoration on the vaulting and the pierced balustrade above the nave. An intricate 16C grille by Valladolid ironsmiths closes the sanctuary, which has a large classically ordered 17C retable by Giraldo de Merlo and Jorge Manuel Theotocopuli, son of El Greco. The Virgin of Guadalupe in the altarpiece **(1)** can be seen more clearly from the **camarín**★.

Camarín★

18C. A chapel-like room where the Virgin of Guadalupe rests.
Riches of every description abound: jasper, gilded stucco and marble and precious wood marquetry frames for nine canvases by Luca Giordano. The Virgin sits on an enamelwork throne (1953), a small 12C figure carved in darkened oak, obscured beneath embroidered veil and mantle.

Sala Capitular (Chapter house)

The chapter house contains a remarkable collection of 87 **antiphonaries and books of hours with miniatures**★ by the monks of Guadalupe.

Claustro Mudéjar

The 14C–15C cloisters are remarkable for their size and the two storeys of horseshoe arches. Note a small Mudéjar Gothic temple and, in a corner, a lavabo faced with multicoloured tiles.

Camarín, Monasterio de Guadalupe

©Turespaña

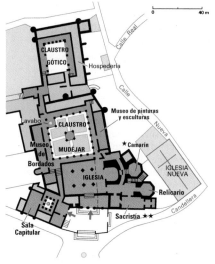

Sacristía★★ (Sacristy)

17C. Canvases by Carreño de Miranda hang in the antechamber. The sacristy combines Classical architecture and ornate Baroque decoration. The unexpected harmony and rich colouring set off **paintings by Zurbarán★★** to perfection. The 11 canvases, painted in a serene yet forceful style between 1638 and 1647, are of Hieronymite monks and scenes from the Life of St Jerome including *The Temptation*.

Relicario (Reliquary Cabinet)

This contains a collection of the Virgin of Guadalupe's mantles and the crown, worn only in solemn processions.

Claustro Gótico (Gothic Cloisters)

In the *hospedería* (hostelry). The cloisters were built in the 16C in Flamboyant Gothic style to serve as a dispensary for the monastery's four hospitals.

Museo de Bordados (Embroidery Museum)

🕐*Open daily 9.30am–1pm, 3.30–6.30pm.* ⊚*4€ (with Painting and Sculpture Museum).*

The museum, in the former refectory, displays a fine collection of **copes and altarfronts★★**, embroidered by the monks between the 15C and the 19C.

Museo de Pinturas y Esculturas (Painting and Sculpture Museum)

Works include a 16C triptych of the *Adoration of the Magi* by Isembrandt, an ivory Christ attributed to Michelangelo, an *Ecce Homo* by Pedro de Mena, eight small canvases of the monks by Zurbarán, and Goya's *Prison Confession*.

EXCURSION
Puerto de San Vicente (San Vicente Pass)

40km/25mi E on the C 401.

The **road★** to the pass crosses the Las Villuercas range. The climb *(8km/5mi)* beyond the Guadarranque Valley affords wonderful **views★** of jagged green mountain ranges above the wild moorland.

ADDRESS

🏨**STAY**

⊜⊜⊜ **Hospedería del Real Monasterio** – Pl. Juan Carlos I. ☎*927 36 70 00. www.monasterio guadalupe.com. 47 rooms.* ⊒*6.50 €. Restaurant*⊜⊜*. Closed 15 Jan–15 Feb.* The hotel's superb setting, around the monastery's Gothic cloisters, and its comfortable, quiet rooms ensure a memorable stay. Excellent value for money plus a good restaurant. Highly recommended.

Mérida★

This historic town in Extremadura, capital of Roman Lusitania, retains monuments from this illustrious era.

SIGHTS
ROMAN MÉRIDA★★

In 25 BC, the Romans founded *Emerita Augusta* on the River Guadiana and at the junction of major Roman roads. They lavished upon it temples, a theatre, an amphitheatre and even a 400m/437yd circus.

Museo Nacional de Arte Romano★★ (National Museum of Roman Art)

José Ramón Mélida. ⏲*Open Mar–Nov Tue–Sat 10am–2pm, 4–9pm, Sun 10am–2pm; Dec–Feb Tue–Sat 10am–2pm, 4–6pm, Sun 10am–2pm.* 3€. ☎*924 31 19 12. www.museoromano.com.*

An imposing brick **building**★ by Rafael Moneo Vallés, reminiscent of a Roman amphitheatre, displays Mérida's rich archaeological collections.
Sculptures include the head of Augustus *(at the end of the second bay)*. In the last bay are statues, caryatids and giant medallions (Medusa and Jupiter) which made up the frieze of Mérida's forum. Wonderful **mosaics**★ may be viewed up close.
In the basement are remains of Roman villas and tombs.

Teatro Romano★★ (Roman Theatre)

Av. de los Estudiantes. ⏲*Open daily Jun–Sept 9.30am–1.45pm, 5–7.15pm; Oct–May 9.30am–1.45pm, 4–6.15pm.* 7€. ☎*924 31 20 24.*

The theatre, built by Agrippa in 24 BC, seated 6 000. A high stage wall was decorated in Hadrian's reign (2C AD) with colonnade and statues. Great granite blocks over the passages are skilfully secured without mortar.

- **Population:** 55 568
- **Michelin Map:** 576 P 10 – Extremadura (Badajoz)
- **Info:** Paseo José Álvarez Saénz de Buruaga. ☎924 00 97 30. www.merida.es.
- **Location:** Mérida is close to the A 5 highway to Portugal. Calle Cardero
- **Don't Miss:** Roman sites.

Anfiteatro★ (Amphitheatre)

Av. de los Estudiantes. ⏲*Open same hours as Roman Theatre.* 4€.

The 1C BC arena held 14 000 spectators. It staged chariot races and was flooded for mock sea battles. Original steps remain; a few tiers are reconstructed. A wall crowned by a cornice protected noble spectators from beasts during gladiatorial combats.

Casa Romana del Anfiteatro (Roman Villa)

Av. de los Estudiantes. ⏲*Open same hours as Roman Theatre.* 4€. ☎*924 31 20 24.*

Water channels, pavements foundations and mosaics remain.

Casa del Mitreo

Oviedo. ⏲*Open same hours as Roman Theatre.* 4€.

The patios of this 1C villa served to distribute light and collect rainwater. Visible remains include the **Cosmological Mosaic**★.

Templo de Diana

Santa Catalina. *No charge.*

Corinthian columns and fluted shafts of this temple are visible. Its stones were

---

Combined Entrance Ticket

This ticket (10€), on sale at all the city's major monuments, allows entry to the theatre, amphitheatre, Roman houses, Alcazaba and the Iglesia de Santa Eulalia.

used in the 16C to build the palace of the Count of Corbos.
Two Roman **bridges** still span the Albarregas and Guadiana. Polychrome arches remain from two **aqueducts**.

Alcazaba

Graciano. ◯*Open same hours as Roman Theatre.* ⌖*4€.* ☏*924 31 20 24.*
The Moors built this fortress in the 9C to defend the 792m/866yd **Puente Romano**★ (Roman Bridge) across the Guadiana. Inside the walls is a **cistern**.

Basílica de Santa Eulalia★

Av. de Extremadura 15. ◯*Open Mon–Sat Jun–Sept 9.30am–1.45pm, 5–7.15pm; Oct–May 9.30am–1.45pm, 4–6.15pm.* ◯*Closed religious holidays.* ⌖*4€.* ☏*924 31 20 24.*
Excavations show that the site was occupied in turn by a palaeo-Christian necropolis, a 5C basilica and this 13C Romanesque church.

Plasencia★

In this tranquil provincial town are interesting Renaissance buildings such as the New Cathedral. Between February and July migrating storks decorate rooftops and towers.

SIGHTS
BARRIO VIEJO (OLD QUARTER)

Houses with wrought-iron balconies make up the neighbourhood.

Catedral★

Pl. de la Catedral. ◯*Open Mon–Sat Apr–Oct 9am–1pm, 5–7pm; Nov–Mar 9am–1pm, 4–6pm.* ◯*Closed public holidays in the afternoon.* ⌖*3€.* ☏*927 41 48 52.*
The cathedral is in fact two buildings from different periods. A Romanesque-Gothic edifice was built in the 13C and 14C. At the end of the 15C, its east end was demolished for a new cathedral with a bolder design.
Only the chancel and transept were completed. Enter by the north door which has rich Plateresque decoration. A door left of the *coro* opens into the **old cathedral** (parish church of Santa María). The cloisters have pointed arches

- ▶ **Population:** 40 105
- ☍ **Michelin Map:** 576 L 11 – Extremadura (Cáceres)
- ▤ **Info:** Plaza de la Torre de Lucía. ☏927 01 78 40. www.aytoplasencia.es.
- ◖ **Location:** Plasencia stands where the Sierra de Gredos meets the Extremadura plain.
  🚌 Calle Alfonso Camargo

and Romanesque capitals while the chapter house is covered by a fine dome. In the shortened nave is a museum of religious art.
Inside the **Catedral Nueva** (New Cathedral), the tall pillars and slender ribs illustrate the mastery of the famous architects: Juan de Java, Diego de Siloé and Alonso de Covarrubias.
The **altarpiece**★ is decorated with statues by the 17C sculptor Gregorio Fernández; the **choir stalls**★ were carved in 1520 by Rodrigo Alemán.
Start from plaza de la Catedral and leaving on your right the **Casa del Deán** (Deanery) with its unusual corner window, and the **Casa del Dr Trujillo**, now the Law Courts (Palacio de

Justicia), make for the Gothic **Iglesia de San Nicolás**, a church which faces the beautiful façade of the **Casa de las Dos Torres** (House with Two Towers).

Continue to the **Palacio Mirabel**. This palace, flanked by a massive tower, contains a two-tiered patio and the Museo de Caza (Hunting Museum). A passage beneath the palace *(door on right-hand side)* leads to **calle Sancho Polo** and a quarter near the ramparts of stepped alleys, white-walled houses and washing hanging from the windows. Turn right for **plaza Mayor**, an asymmetrical square surrounded by porticoes and full of busy cafés.

EXCURSIONS
Monasterio de Yuste★
1.8km/1mi from Cuacos de Yuste.
Open Tue–Sun Apr–Sept 10am–6pm; Oct–Mar 10.30am–1.30pm, 3–5.15pm. 2.50€. 927 17 21 30. www.yustedigital.com.
In 1556, a weary Emperor **Charles V** retired to this modest Hieronymite monastery in a serene setting.
The monastery, devastated during the War of Independence, is partially restored. Of Charles V's small palace one sees the dining hall, the royal bedroom adjoining the chapel, the Gothic church and, lastly, the two fine cloisters, one Gothic, the other Plateresque.

Coria
42km/26mi W. Take the N 630 S. After 7km/4.3mi turn right onto the EX 108.
This town overlooking the Alagón Valley retains Roman walls and gateways, rebuilt in the Middle Ages.

Catedral de la Asunción de Nuestra Señora★
Plaza de la Catedral. Open daily 15 May–31 Oct 10am–2pm, 4.30–8pm; 1 Nov–14 May 10am–1pm, 4–7pm. 2€. 924 50 39 60.
The Gothic cathedral, embellished with elegant Plateresque decoration in the 16C, is crowned with a Baroque tower and has a sculptured frieze.
The tall, single aisle has vaulting adorned with lierne and tierceron ribs typical of the region. Note the 18C altarpiece and, in the *coro*, the wrought-iron grilles and the Gothic choir stalls.

Trujillo★★

Modern Trujillo conceals the charm of the old town, on a granite ledge above. It was hastily fortified by the Moors in the 13C, and embellished over centuries with mansions built by those who had made their fortunes in the Americas.

A BIT OF HISTORY
Cradle of the Conquistadores – "Twenty American nations", it is said, "were conceived in Trujillo". **Francisco de Orellana** left in 1542 to explore the country of the Amazons. Native son **Francisco Pizarro** (c. 1475–1541) plundered the riches of the Inca Emperor Atahualpa and was murdered amid untold riches in his own palace.

- **Population:** 9 860
- **Michelin Map:** 576 N 12 – Extremadura (Cáceres)
- **Info:** Plaza Mayor. 927 32 26 77. www.trujillo.es.
- **Location:** Trujillo is situated on the A 5 linking Madrid and Badajoz.
- **Don't Miss:** The old town and its mansions.

SIGHTS
OLD QUARTER
Trujillo's old quarter is less austere than that of Cáceres. Mansions were built later in the 16C and 17C, decorated with arcades, loggias and corner windows, and whitewashed. They form changing compositions along steep alleys.

Plaza Mayor★★

One of the most beautiful squares in Spain is irregular, lined by mansions, its levels linked by wide flights of steps. By night, it is positively theatrical.

Equestrian statue of Pizarro

Pl. Mayor.

This 1927 bronze is by American sculptors Charles Rumsey and Mary Harriman.

Iglesia de San Martín

Pl. Mayor. ○ *Open daily 10am–2pm, 4–7pm.* ⊗*1.40€.*

16C. The rubble and freestone walls of the church enclose a vast nave chequered with funerary paving stones.

Palacio de los Duques de San Carlos★ (Palace of the Dukes of Saint Charles)

Pl. Mayor. ○ *Open daily 10am–1pm, 4–6pm.*

17C. Now a convent. The granite façade, decorated in Classical Baroque style, has a corner window topped by a crest with a double-headed eagle. View the **patio** with two tiers of rounded arches and a fine staircase of four flights.

Palacio de los Marqueses de Piedras Albas (Palace of the Marquises of Piedras Albas)

Calle Sillería.

A Renaissance loggia has been accommodated into the original Gothic wall.

Palacio de los Marqueses de la Conquista (Palace of the Marquises of the Conquest)

Pl. Mayor. ○ *Open daily 10am–2pm, 4.30–7pm.*

The palace of Hernando Pizarro, the conquistador's brother, has an exceptional number of windows with iron grilles. To the left of a Plateresque corner **window**★, added in the 17C, are busts of Francisco Pizarro and his wife; on the right are Hernando and his niece, whom he married.

Ayuntamiento Viejo (Former Town Hall)

16C. Three tiers of Renaissance arcades from a palace in ruins form the façade of the Palacio de Justicia (Law Courts).

Casa de las Cadenas (House of Chains)/ Torre del Alfiler (Alfiler Tower)

Pl. Mayor.

This is where Christians freed from the Moors traditionally left their chains. Its "needle tower", including a Mudéjar belfry, is a favourite spot for storks.

Palacio de Orellana-Pizarro

This 16C palace has a beautiful Plateresque upper gallery.

Iglesia de Santiago

○ *Open daily 10am–2pm, 4–7pm.* ⊗*1.40€.*

The church's 13C Romanesque belfry and the tower of the Palacio de los Chaves frame the Arco de Santiago (St James Arch), one of seven gateways.

Iglesia de Santa María★

Pl. de Santa María. ○ *Open daily Apr–Sept 10am–2pm, 5–9pm; Oct–Mar 10am–2pm, 4–7pm.* ⊗*1.25€.* ✆*927 32 30 05.*

This 13C Gothic church is Trujillo's pantheon. The panels of the Gothic **retable**★ are by Fernando Gallego. From the top of the belfry there is a delightful **view** of brown tile roofs, the Plaza Mayor arcades and the castle.

Castillo

Cerro Cabeza de Zorro. ○ *Open daily Jun–Sept 10am–2pm, 5–8.30pm; Oct–May 10am–2pm, 4–8pm.* ○ *Closed 1 Jan, Easter Monday, 29–31 Aug in afternoon, 25 Dec.* ⊗*1.30€.* ✆*651 86 96 51.*

The castle stands out on a granite ledge, its massive crenellated wall reinforced by heavy towers. Above the keep is the patron of Trujillo, Our Lady of Victory. View Trujillo from these walls.

Zafra

A 15C *alcázar* (now a parador) guards this white-walled town, one of the oldest in Extremadura. It was built by the Dukes of Feria with nine round towers, white marble Renaissance patio and delightful gilded salon.

- ▶ **Population:** 16 218
- ⚸ **Michelin Map:** 576 Q 10 – Extremadura (Badajoz)
- ▣ **Info:** Plaza de España 8. ℘924 55 10 36. http://zafra.dip-badajoz.es.
- ◐ **Location:** SW of Madrid in Extremadura, 7km/4.3mi W of the N 630.
  🚉Avenida de la Estación

SIGHTS

Squares★

The large 18C **plaza Grande** and the adjoining smaller 16C **plaza Chica** are lined by fine arcaded houses.

Iglesia de la Candelaria

Rotonda de la Candelaria.
℘924 55 01 28.

The 16C transitional Gothic-Renaissance church has a massive red-brick belfry. In the south transept is an **altarpiece** by Zurbarán painted in 1644.

EXCURSIONS

Llerena

42km/26mi SE along the N 432.

The **plaza Mayor** of this country town is one of the most monumental in Extremadura. The composite façade of the **Iglesia de Nuestra Señora de la Granada** (Church of Our Lady of Granada; *pl. San Juan;* ℘924 87 23 25) is harmonised by the interplay of white limestone and brick; the delicacy of superimposed arcades contrasts with the mass of a great Baroque belfry.

Jerez de los Caballeros

42km/26mi SW along the EX 101 and EX 112.

Jerez de los Caballeros is the birthplace of **Vasco Núñez de Balboa** (1475–1519), who crossed Panama and in 1513 discovered the Pacific Ocean. The town's name, tradition and atmosphere stem from the Knights Templar – Caballeros del Temple – to whom the town was given in 1230 by Alfonso IX of León on its recapture from the Moors.

Jerez stands on a hillside and its steep lanes lined by white-walled houses are a foretaste of Andalucía. On the summit is the ornate San Bartolomé *(pl. de San Bartolomé).*

Plaza Grande
©Turespaña

This remote region, around the size of Belgium, or Maryland, fronts the Atlantic on Spain's northern and western borders. In appearance and culture it is akin to the Celtic regions of Ireland, Wales and Brittany; far removed from the archetypal images of southern Spain. Geologically speaking, Galicia is an ancient eroded granite massif. Its highest peaks rise to just over 2 000m/6 600ft but the average altitude is less than 500m/1 600ft. None the less, the overall impression is that of a hilly and mountainous region.

The climate is influenced by the sea: temperatures are mild and vary little (the annual average is 13°C/55°F). Rainfall is abundant, providing the verdant landscapes which give the whole of Spain's northern coast its nickname "Green Spain". Galicia is Spain's chief fishing region and is renowned for its delicious seafood even though most of the catch is canned.

The Galician natives are a fiercely independent people – even by Spanish standards – with their own culture, folklore and Galician language, *gallego*, not unlike Portuguese.

Highlights

1 Standing in front of the Cathedral at **Santiago de Compostela** (p401)

2 Walking atop the Roman city walls at **Lugo** (p388)

3 Strolling through the delightful Old Quarter at **Pontevedra** (p392)

4 Touring the **Ría de Vigo** and taking in the wonderful views (p398)

5 Relaxing in a wonderful setting on the beach at **A Toxa/LaToja** (p397)

North Coast

Capital of Galicia until 1982, La Coruña is Spain's sixth-largest port and a bustling centre of industry. For visitors it offers a charming cobbled old town with narrow alleyways and pretty plazas. La Coruña has two distinctive landmarks, both visible from sea: its ancient lighthouse, the oldest working example in the world, built on Roman foundations, and its *solanas/miradores* – balconies that are totally glassed in, glimmering and reflecting from tall buildings.

The Rías Altas, deep inlets backed by verdant pine and eucalyptus, stretching eastwards from La Coruña and Asturias shelter some fine beaches and low-key resorts. By contrast, the Costa de la Muerte (Coast of Death), west of La Coruña to Cabo Finisterre (Cape Finisterre), has been the graveyard of many a ship, dashed against its rocks, but is worth a visit for both its drama and (when the wind isn't howling) calm beauty.

- **La Coruña/A Coruña**
- **Rías Altas**

West Coast

The Rías Bajas, its inlets , creeks and coastline more spectacular than its counterpart north, is Galicia's most attractive and most important holiday area. There are several good resorts, even though these are mostly unknown outside Spain. Chief among these is A Toxa/La Toja, which enjoys a beautiful setting. The best beaches are to be found offshore on the Ilas Cíes, reached by boat from Vigo.

Vigo is Spain's leading fishing port and enjoys a picturesque natural harbour location. The area's other city, Pontevedra, boasts a charming old quarter with much historic interest.

- **Pontevedra**
- **Rías Bajas**

The Pilgrim's Route

The end of a long and arduous route for hundreds of thousands each year, both the city and the cathedral of Santiago de Compostela rank towards the top of Spain's highlights. The cathedral in particular is a wonder, a magnificent mix of medieval Gothic and Baroque. The

Catedral de Santiago de Compostela

C. Labonne/MICHELIN

old part of town has all the hallmarks of Spain's finest cities: narrow atmospheric historic streets with good places to eat and drink, frequented year-round by a lively Spanish and cosmopolitan crowd of all ages enhanced by its high university population.

There is no official starting point for The Way of St James (El Camino de Santiago) though the Spanish leg begins just across the French border (at two points) just across the Pyrenees, then heads east through Navarra, Rioja, Castile and Galicia, via country lanes, secondary roads, tracks and paths, all conveniently waymarked by the pilgrim's symbol of a scallop shell. Along the route a hospitailty "industry" has developed since the Middle Ages, with numerous inns providing refreshments and shelter, albeit often of a rudimentary nature. By contrast travellers seeking a reward for their endeavours might like to consider a night in the luxurious Parador at Santiago de Compostela. It is one of the oldest hotels in the world and also one of the finest in all Spain.

The Way measures around 750km/465mi from Ronces-valles to Santiago, or nearer 800km/500mi if you begin the journey further south at Puerto de Somport.

♨ **Santiago de Compostela**
♨ **The Way of St James**

Inland

The interior is primarily an agricultural region where mixed farming is the norm: maize, potatoes, grapes and rye, and renowned beef herds in Orense province. The latter features some beautiful countryside and the Gargantas de Sil (Sil river canyon) is well worth the trip. Press on through the dull suburbs of Orense to discover a fine bustling old quarter and a splendid late medieval cathedral.

Lugo is the jewel of the Galician interior, with a characterful old town enclosed by the best preserved Roman walls in Spain.

♨ **Lugo**
♨ **Ourense/Orense**

La Coruña/
A Coruña★

This pleasant Galician city is set on a rocky islet, linked to the mainland by a strip of sand. At the northern end of the harbour, the charming Ciudad old quarter of small squares and Romanesque churches is in contrast to the wide streets of the business centre on the isthmus. The warehouses and industry of the **Ensanche** district are a reminder that La Coruña is Spain's sixth largest port.

▸ **Population:** 245 164

Michelin Map: 571 B 4 (town plan) – Galicia (La Coruña)

Info: Edificio Sol – Rúa Sol s/n. ℘981 18 43 44. www.coruna.es.

Location: La Coruña, on the north coast, links to Santiago de Compostela by the AP 9 motorway. The A 6 heads SE past Lugo (97km/60mi SE) and on to Madrid. Calle Joaquín Planelles Riera

Kids: Acquarium Finisterrae.

A BIT OF HISTORY

Spanish Armada – Philip II's ill-fated "Invincible Armada" set out for England from La Coruña in 1588. A year later, Elizabeth I sent Drake to burn La Coruña but the town was saved by **María Pita**, who gave the alarm.

The 19C – During the Peninsular War, Marshal Soult of France defeated the English in the Battle of Elviña in 1809. In the late 19C, La Coruña consistently supported liberal insurgents and suffered severe reprisals.

SIGHTS

Colegiata de Santa María del Campo

Pl. Santa María 1. ◷ *Open Tue–Fri 10am–1pm, 5–7pm, Sat 10am–1pm.* ◷ *Closed public holidays.* ✆*No charge.* ℘*981 20 31 86.*
This Romanesque church has a triple barrel-vaulted nave strengthened by arches with plaster borders. Note the fine 13C–14C portal, Gothic rose window and tower. A **Museum of Sacred Art** (Arte Sacro) is on one side of the church. In the square stands a 15C Calvary.

Iglesia de Santiago

Parrote 1. ◷ *Open Mon–Fri 8am–1pm, 5.30–7pm, Sat–Sun 10am–1pm, 4.30–7pm.* ✆*No charge.* ℘*981 20 56 96.*
The church is a mix of Romanesque and Gothic.. The stone pulpit is beautifully carved.

EL CENTRO (CENTRAL DISTRICT)
Avenida de la Marina★

The avenue, facing the harbour, is lined by tall houses with glassed balconies. Along one side is the paseo de la Dársena and on the other the **Jardines de Méndez Núñez**, gardens with a variety of flowering trees.

Plaza de María Pita

The vast café-lined square honours a local 16C heroine. It has a great many terrace cafés.

Castillo de San Antón: Museo Arqueológico e Histórico

Pas. del Parrote. ◷ *Open Jul–Aug Tue–Sat 10am–9pm, Sun and public holidays 10am–3pm; Sept–Jun Tue–Sat 10am–7.30pm, Sun and public holidays 10am–2.30pm.* ✆*2€.* ℘*981 18 98 50.* www.ctv.es/USERS/sananton.
This fortress dates from the period of Philip II and now houses an archaeological museum, including exhibits on prehistoric gold and silver.

Museo de Bellas Artes

Avenida Zalaeta. ◷ *Open Mon–Fri 10am–8pm, Sat 10am–2pm, 4.30–8pm, Sun 10am–2pm.* ◷ *Closed hols.* ✆*2.40€; no charge Sat afternoon and*

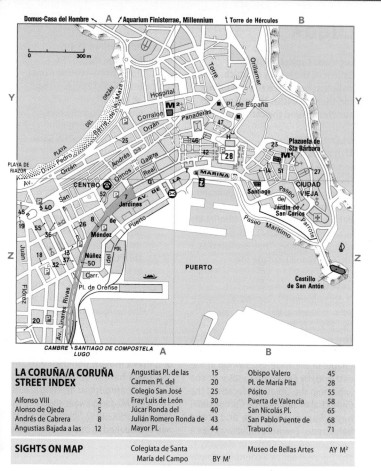

Domus-Casa del Hombre ／ A ／ Aquarium Finisterrae, Millennium ＼ Torre de Hércules B

Sun. ☎981 22 37 23. http://museobela-sartescoruna.xunta.es.
Light and spacious exhibition rooms are dedicated to art from the 16C to the 20C, including sketches by Goya.

Domus-Casa del Hombre

Santa Teresa 1. ⏰ Open daily Jul–Aug 11am–9pm; Sept–Jun 10am–7pm. . ☜2€, no charge 5 Feb, 10, 18 May, 7 Oct, 10, 16 Nov. ☎981 18 98 40. www.casaciencias.org.

This museum **building**★ designed by **Arata Isozaki**, is emblematic of the city. The façade is a double curve shaped like a sail, covered in slate. The other wall uses an old quarry to create a screen of large stone blocks. Displays deals with the human species and genetics through texts and interactive displays.

Acquarium Finisterrae

Pas. Marítimo. ⏰ Open Jul–Aug daily 11am–9pm; Sept–Jun Mon–Fri 10am–7pm, Sat–Sun and hols 10am–8pm. . ☜10€; child 4€. ☎981 18 98 42. www.casaciencias.org/en/aquarium.

This excellent aquarium highlights local marine ecosystems.

Torre de Hércules (Hercules Tower or Lighthouse)

Avenida de Navarra. ⏰ Open daily year-round 10am–5.45pm, later in summer. ☜2€. ☎981 22 37 30.

This is the oldest functioning lighthouse in the world, dating from the 2C AD. The original outer ramp was enclosed in 1790. From the top (104m/341ft), there is a good **view** of the town and the coast.

Lugo★

Lugo was capital of Roman Gallaecia, the legacy of which includes the town walls, old bridge and thermal baths. The old quarter huddles around the cathedral.

OLD TOWN
Murallas★★
Ronda de la Muralla.
The Roman walls were built in the 3C, although they have been significantly modified. They are made of schist slabs levelled at a uniform 10m/32.8ft in a continuous 2km/1.2mi perimeter with 10 gateways. They are listed as a UNESCO World Heritage site.

Catedral★
Pl. Santa María. ◷ *Open daily 8am–8.30pm.* ⌨*No charge; museum 1€.* ℘*982 23 10 38.*
The Romanesque church (1129) has Gothic and Baroque additions. The Chapel of the Wide-Eyed Virgin at the east end, by Fernando Casas y Novoa (who built the Obradoiro façade of the Cathedral in Santiago de Compostela) has a Baroque rotunda and stone balustrade. The north doorway has a fine Romanesque **Christ in Majesty**★. The figure is above a capital curiously suspended, carved with the Last Supper. The nave is roofed with barrel vaulting and lined with galleries, a feature common in pilgrimage churches. There are two immense wooden Renaissance altarpieces at the ends of the transept – the south one is signed by Cornelis de Holanda (1531). A door in the west wall of the south transept leads to the small but elegant **cloisters**.

City squares
The 18C **Palacio Episcopal**, facing the north door of the cathedral on **Plaza de Santa María**, is a typical *pazo*, one storey high with smooth stone walls, advanced square wings framing the central façade and decoration confined to the Gil Taboada coat of arms on the main doorway. **Plaza del Campo**, behind the palace, is lined by old houses. Calle

▸ **Population:** 95 416
⚙ **Michelin Map:** 571 C 7 (town plan) – Galicia (Lugo)
▯ **Info:** Calle Miño, 8–10 Bajo. ℘982 23 13 61. www.lugoturismo.com.
◗ **Location:** Lugo is in central Galicia in NW Spain, 96km/59.6mi SE of La Coruña/A Coruña along the A 6, 94km/58.4mi NE of Ourense/Orense on the N 540, and 135km/83.8mi SW Santiago de Compostela on the A 6 and A P9.
🚌Plaza de Conde Fontao
◉ **Don't Miss:** The sundials at Museo Provincial.
◷ **Timing:** See the Cathedral and walls first, then explore the surrounding area

de la Cruz with its bars and restaurants, and **Plaza Mayor**, dominated by the 18C **town hall**, with its gardens and esplanade, are popular meeting places. The Alejo Madarro sweet shop (*rúa da Reina 13;* ℘*982 22 97 14; www.madarro. net*) first opened its doors in the middle of the 19C.

Museo Provincial
◷*Open Jul–Aug Mon–Fri 11am–2pm, 5–8pm, Sat 10am–2pm; Sept–Jun Mon–Fri 10.30am–2pm, 4.30–8.30pm, Sat 10.30am–2pm, 4.30–8pm, Sun and public holidays 11am–2pm.* ◷*Closed 1 Jan, 22 May, 24, 25, 31 Dec, Tue of Carnival week and public holidays Jul–Aug.* ⌨*No charge.* ℘*982 24 21 12. www.museolugo.org.*
This museum of regional art, is housed in the former Monasterio de San Francisco. A room is devoted to ceramics from Sargadelos, and there are sundials and other objects from the Roman period. The former cloister of San Francisco contains an interesting collection of sundials, as well as several altars and sarcophagi. The connecting **Museo Nelson Zúmel** is dedicated to Spanish paintings from the 19C and 20C.

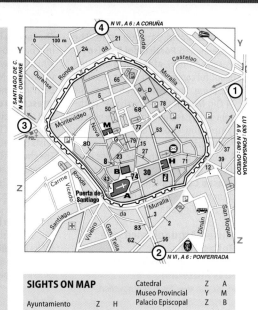

SIGHTS ON MAP

			Catedral	Z	A
			Museo Provincial	Y	M
Ayuntamiento	Z	H	Palacio Episcopal	Z	B

Ourense/ Orense

Since Antiquity, Orense (Ourense in Galician, from a legendary gold mine) has been famous for its hot springs.Its Roman bridge is a crossing for pilgrims to Santiago de Compostela.

SIGHTS

Catedral★

Pl. del Trigo 1. ◐ *Cathedral: open 8.30am–1.30pm, 4.30–8.30pm; Museum: open daily noon–1pm, 4.30–6.30pm.* ◉*No charge.* ℘*988 22 09 92.*

The 12C–13C cathedral has been repeatedly modified. The **Portada Sur** (South Door), in the Compostelan style, lacks a tympanum, but is profusely decorated with carvings. The **Portada Norte** (North Door) has two statue columns and, beneath a great ornamental arch, a 15C Deposition framed by a Flight into Egypt and statues of the Holy Women.

▸ **Population:** 107 057

◔ **Michelin Map:** 571 E 6, F 6 (town plan) – Galicia (Orense)

▯ **Info:** Lugar Ourense, Calle Burgas, 12 Bajo. ℘988 36 60 64. www. turismodeourense.com.

◐ **Location:** Orense is 101km/62.7mi E of Vigo along the A 52 motorway; 100km/62mi SE of Pontevedra via the N 541; 105km/65mi SE of Santiago de Compostela on the N 525 and the AP 53. ▱Calle Eulogio Gómez Franqueira

The interior is noteworthy for its pure lines. At the end of the 15C, a Gothic-Renaissance transitional-style **lantern**★ was built above the transept. The ornate Gothic high altar retable is by Cornelius de Holanda. The 16C and 17C **Capilla del Santísimo Cristo** (Chapel of the Holy Sacrament), off the north transept, is decorated with exuberant sculpture in the Galician Baroque style. The triple-arched **Pórtico del Paraíso**★★ (Paradise Door), at the west end, has beautiful carvings and bright medieval colouring. The central arch shows the 24 Old Men of the Apocalypse; to the right is the Last Judgement. The pierced tympanum above, like the narthex vaulting, is 16C.

A door in the south aisle opens onto the 13C chapter house, now a **museum (Museo Catedralicio)** which includes church plate, statues, chasubles and a 12C travelling altar.

Museo Arqueológico y de Bellas Artes (Archaeological and Fine Arts Museum)

Pl. Mayor. ⚬═ *Closed for renovation.* ✆ *988 22 38 84.*

Collections in the former bishop's palace on Plaza Mayor include prehistoric specimens, cultural objects (mainly statues of warriors) and an early 18C woodcarving of the **Camino del Calvario**★ (Stations of the Cross).

Claustro de San Francisco★

Lorenzo Fernández "Xocas". 🕐 *Church is open for Mass only.* ✆ *988 24 03 77.*

The elegant 14C cloisters consist of horseshoe-shaped Gothic arches resting on slender, paired columns. Diamond and leaf decoration adds simple sophistication. Some of the **capitals** illustrate the hunt or historic figures.

EXCURSIONS
Monasterio de Osera★

34km/21mi NW. Leave Orense on the N 525. After 23km/14mi turn right towards Cotelas. ⚬═ *Guided tours (45min), Mon–Sat 10am, 11am, noon, 3.30pm, 4.30pm, 5.30pm (and 6.30pm Apr–Sept), Sun 12.30pm, 3.30pm, 4.30pm, 5.30pm (and 6.30pm Apr–Sept) .* ⚬═ *2€.* ✆ *988 28 20 04.*

The grandiose 12C Cistercian monastery, called the Escorial of Galicia, was founded by Alfonso VII. It stands isolated in the Arenteiro Valley, a region that once abounded in bears *(osos)* as the name suggests.

The **façade** (1708) is in three sections. In a niche below the statue of Hope, which crowns the doorway, is the figure of a Nursing Madonna with St Bernard at her feet. Of note inside are an **escalera de honor** (grand staircase) and the **Claustro de los Medallones** (Medallion Cloisters) decorated with 40 busts of historic personages.

The **church** (12C–13C), hidden behind the Baroque façade of 1637, has retained the customary Cistercian simplicity modified only by frescoes in the transept, painted in 1694.

The **chapter house**★ dates from the late 15C and early 16C and is outstanding for its beautiful vaulting of crossed ribs descending like the fronds of a palm tree onto four spiral columns.

Verín

69km/43mi SE along the A 52.

Verín is a lively, picturesque town with narrow paved streets, houses with glassed-in balconies, arcades and carved coats of arms. Its thermal springs, already famous during the Middle Ages, are reputed for their treatment of rheumatic and kidney disorders.

Castillo de Monterrei

6km/3.7mi W. 🕐 *Open Wed–Sun Sept–Jun 10.30am–1.30pm, 4–7pm; Jul–Aug 10.30am–1.30pm, 5–8pm.* ⚬═ *No charge.* ✆ *988 41 80 02.*

There is a parador next to the castle, a frontier redoubt throughout the Portuguese-Spanish wars. It was more than a castle, with a monastery, hospital and a town which was abandoned in the 19C. The approach is up an avenue of lime trees which commands a full **panorama**★ of the valley below. To enter the castle pass through three walls, the outermost dating from the 17C. At the centre stand the square 15C Torre del Homenaje (Keep) and the 14C Torre de las Damas (Lady's Tower); the courtyard is lined by a three-storey arcade and is less austere. The 13C church has a **portal**★ delicately carved with a notched design and a tympanum showing Christ in Majesty between the symbols of the Evangelists.

Celanova

26km/16mi S on the N 540.

The large, imposing **monastery** on Plaza Mayor was founded in 936 by San Rosendo, Bishop of San Martín de Mondoñedo.

The **church** (*guided tours (50min) at 11am, noon, 1pm, 3pm, 4pm (and 6pm Apr–Oct); 1.20€; ℘988 43 22 01)* is a monumental late 17C edifice built in Baroque style. The coffered vaulting is decorated with geometrical designs, the cupola with volutes. An immense altarpiece (1697) occupies the back of the apse. Note the choir stalls, Baroque in the lower part and Gothic in the upper, as well as the fine organ.

The **cloisters**★★, among the most beautiful in the region, took from 1550 until the 18C to complete. The majestic staircases here are particularly worthy of note.

The **Capilla de San Miguel** *(pl. Mayor; guided tours Mon–Sat 11am, noon, 1pm, 4pm, 5pm (and 6pm Apr–Oct), Sun and public holidays 11.30am, 1pm, 4pm, 5pm (6pm Apr–Oct); no charge; ℘988 43 22 01)*, a chapel behind the church, is one of the monastery's earliest buildings (937) and one of the rare Mozarabic monuments still in good condition.

Santa Comba de Bande

52km/32.5mi S along the N 540 (26km/16mi S of Celanova). 10km/6.2mi beyond Bande, head along a road to the right for 400m/440yd.

The small 7C Visigothic **iglesia**★ *(call to arrange a visit; ℘988 44 30 01)* overlooks the lake. The plan is that of a Greek cross, lit by a lantern turret. The apse is square and is preceded by a horseshoe-shaped triumphal arch resting on four pillars with Corinthian capitals.

TOUR ALONG THE RÍO SIL★

65km/40.3mi E.

▷ *Head along the C 536; after 6km/3.7mi, turn left towards Luintra; continue for a further 18km/11mi. The parador is signposted.*

Parador de Santo Estevo

The ex-Benedictine monastery appears suddenly in a majestic **setting**★, spread over a great spur, against a background of granite mountains deeply cut by the Sil. It retains the church's Romanesque east end and cloisters, built to grandiose proportions largely in the 16C.

Gargantas del Sil★ (Gorges of the Sil River)

▷ *Return downhill on the road on the left towards the Sil (not the signposted turning to the embalse de San Estevo).*

Two dams control the waters of the Sil, which flow through deep gorges. The sides of the valley are dotted with vineyards and small villages.

▷ *Continue along the left bank of the river until you reach the N 120. Turn left towards Orense.*

ADDRESSES

🛏 STAY

🛏 **Hotel Altiana** – *Ervedelo 14. ℘988 37 09 52. 32 rooms. ⊇4€.* Located near the Cathedral and Calle Progreso, the Altiana is a simple but friendly place to stay for those on a budget. Although far from luxurious, the bedrooms all have TVs and en-suite bathrooms and are very reasonably priced.

� EAT

⊖⊝ **Hotel-Restaurante Zarampallo** – *San Miguel 9. ℘988 23 00 08. www. zarampallo.com. Restaurant closed Sun for dinner.* Recommended for its location in the old part of the city and first and foremost for its high-quality menu. If you're planning on staying here, the rooms are basic but comfortable.

Pontevedra★

Quiet Pontevedra has a pleasant mix of fine buildings, plain arcades, cobbled streets, and attractive parks and gardens. Terrace cafés teem in summer, bars are a cosy retreat in winter.

CASCO ANTIGUO★ (OLD QUARTER)

Allow 1hr30min

The old quarter is tucked between calles Michelena, del Arzobispo Malvar and Cobián, and the river. Glass-covered passages and picturesque squares **(Plaza da la Leña; del Teucro, de la Pedreira)** are enchanting. There are endless places to stop for a drink and busy shopping streets such as **Sarmiento**.

Plaza de la Leña★

This is a delightful asymmetrical square surrounded by beautiful façades. Two 18C mansions on the square have been converted into a museum.

Museo Provincial

Pasantería 2. ○ *Open Jun–Sept Tue–Sat 10am–2pm, 4.30–8.30pm, Sun and public holidays 11am–2pm; Oct–May Tue–Sat 10am–2pm, 4–7pm, Sun and public holidays 11am–2pm.* ○ *Closed 1 Jan, 25 Dec.* ∞*No charge.* ℘*986 85 14 55. www.museo.depontevedra.es.*

Plaza de la Leña

J. Malburet/MICHELIN

▸ **Population:** 80 749

◉ **Michelin Map:** 571 E 4 – local map, ○*see RÍAS BAJAS*

▤ **Info:** Lugar Pontevedra, General Gutiérrez Mellado, 1 Bajo. ℘986 85 08 14. www.riasbaixas.depo.es

◐ **Location:** Pontevedra, near the northern coast, is linked by motorway with Vigo (27km/17mi S) and Santiago de Compostela (57km/35mi N). ▭Plaza Calvo Sotelo

The ground floor of the museum holds Bronze Age **Celtic treasures★** from A Golada and Caldas de Reis, and that of Foxados (2C and 1C BC), and a pre-1900 silverware collection with pieces from a number of countries.

The first floor, which is dedicated to paintings, has several 15C Aragonese Primitives.

The second mansion includes a reconstruction of a stateroom from a 19C Spanish frigate, the *Numancia*. On the upper floor are an interesting antique kitchen and 19C Sargadelos ceramics. The museum encompasses the ruins of Santo Domingo and the Sarmiento building (ex-collegiate church of la Compañía de Jesús), beside the Iglesia de San Bartolomé.

Basílica de Santa María la Mayor★

Av. de Santa María 24. ○*Open Mon–Fri 10am–1pm, 6–9pm, Sat 10am–1pm, Sun 10am–2pm, 7–9pm.* ∞*No charge.* ℘*986 86 99 02. www3.planalfa. es/santamarialamayor.*

Old alleyways and gardens surround this delightful 15C-16C Plateresque church. The **west front★** is carved like an altarpiece, divided into separate superimposed registers on which are reliefs of the Dormition and Assumption of the Virgin and the Trinity.

At the summit is the Crucifixion at the centre of an openwork coping finely carved with oarsmen and fishermen.

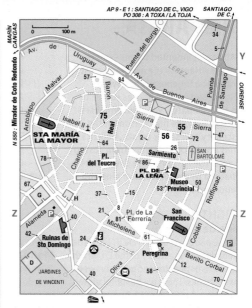

The **interior** mingles Gothic (notched arches), Isabelline (slender cabled columns) and Renaissance (ribbed vaulting) styles.

San Bartolomé

Sarmiento 51.
www.archicompostela.org/ psanbartolome.
This 18C Baroque church has fine scuptures, some by Pedro de Mena.

San Francisco

Jardines de Castro San Pedro. ⏰ *Open Mon–Sat 7.30am–12.45pm, 5.30–9pm, Sun and public holidays 8.30am–1.45pm, 5.30–8.30pm.* ✆*No charge.* ℰ*986 85 11 13.*
The church's simple Gothic façade looks onto the gardens of Plaza da Ferrería. The interior features timber vaulting.

Capilla de la Peregrina (Pilgrim's Chapel)

Pl. de la Peregrina. ⏰ *Open daily 9am–2pm, 4–7pm.* ℰ*986 85 13 75.*
This small 18C church, with scallop-shaped floor plan and convex façade, contains a venerated statue of the patron saint of Pontevedra.

Ruinas de Santo Domingo (Santo Domingo Ruins)

Pas. de Montero Ríos. ⏰ *Open Jun–Sept Tue–Sun 10am–2pm, 5–8.30pm.* ⏰ *Closed 31 May, 1 Oct.* ✆*No charge.* ℰ*986 84 32 38.*
These ruins are a perfect example of medieval romanticism. The Gothic east end is overgrown with ivy. Arranged inside, from the Museo de Pontevedra, are Roman steles, Galician coats of arms and tombs, in particular, tombs of craftsmen showing the tools they used, and tombs of noblemen.

EXCURSION

Mirador Coto Redondo★★

14km/8.7mi S on the N 550.
Take the Vigo road; after 6km/3.7mi, turn right towards Lago Castiñeiras, climbing through pine and eucalyptus woods. The **panorama**★★ from this viewpoint extends over the Pontevedra and Vigo *rías*.

Rías Altas★

Although indented by *rías* – inlets of the Atlantic – the northern coast of Galicia is generally low-lying. Rocks and granite houses suggest a grim climate – yet holidaymakers arrive with the fine season for the scenery and sandy creeks. Galicia's *rías* are described below from east to west. The Rías Altas are deep inlets backed by thick forests of pine and eucalyptus.

SIGHTS

Ría de Ribadeo

See also under COSTA VERDE. The ría de Ribadeo is the estuary of the Eo, which slackens its pace to wind gently between wide banks. There is a beautiful **view**★ up the estuary from the bridge across the mouth of the river.

The old port of **Ribadeo** is an important regional centre and summer resort.

Ría de Foz

Foz, at the mouth of its *ría*, is a small port with a fishing fleet. Its two good beaches are popular in summer.

Iglesia de San Martín de Mondoñedo

Barrio Caritel, Foz. 5km/3mi W.
Take the Mondoñedo road, then immediately turn right. Open daily Oct–May 11am–1pm, 4–6pm; Jun–Sept 11am–1pm, 5–8pm. No charge.
℘982 13 26 07.

Standing almost alone on a height, this archaic church was once part of a monastery and an episcopal seat until 1112. Unusually in this region, it shows no sign of Compostelan influence. The east end, with Lombard bands, is supported by massive buttresses; The transept **capitals**★ are naively carved and rich in anecdotal detail: one shows a table overflowing with food while a dog licks the feet of a suffering Lazarus. The capitals, believed to date from the 10C, show Visigothic plant motifs.

Michelin Map: 571 A 5-7, B4-8, C 2-5, D 2 – Galicia (Lugo, La Coruña/A Coruña)

Info: Ferrol: Edificio Administrativo, Plaza C.J. Cela. ℘981 31 11 79; Foz: Rúa de Lugo 1. ℘982 13 24 26; Viveiró: Avenida de Ramón Canosa, ℘982 56 08 79. www.turgalicia.es.

Location: This series of inlets is in the far northwest corner of the Iberian Peninsula.

Mondoñedo

23km/14mi SW along the N 634.
Mondoñedo rises out of the hollow of a lush valley. Streets are lined with balconied white houses bearing coats of arms. The cathedral square is delightful with its arcades and *solanas* (glassed-in galleries).

The immense façade of the **cathedral**★ *(pl. Catedral;* open daily 9am–1pm, 4.30–8pm; 2€ museum; ℘982 52 10 00) combines the Gothic grace of the three large portal arches and the rose window, all dating from the 13C, with the grandiose Baroque style of towers added in the 18C.

Late 14C frescoes decorate the interior, one above the other (below the extraordinary 1710 organ) illustrating the Massacre of the Innocents and the Life of St Peter. There are a Rococo retable at the high altar; and a polychrome wood statue of the Virgin in the south ambulatory, known as the English Virgin, as the statue was brought from St Paul's, London, in the 16C.

The classical **cloisters** were added in the 17C.

Ría de Viveiro

All **Viveiro** retains of its town walls is the Puerta de Carlos V (Charles V Gateway), emblazoned with the emperor's arms. In summer, the port is a holiday resort. On the fourth Sunday in August, visitors from all over Galicia come for the local Romería do Naseiro festival.

Ría de Santa María de Ortigueira

The *ría* is deep and surrounded by green hills while **Ortigueira** port has quays bordered by well-kept gardens.

Ría de Cedeira

A small, deeply enclosed *ría* with beautiful beaches. The road gives good **views** of **Cedeira** (summer resort).

Ría de Ferrol

The *ría* forms a magnificent harbour entered by a channel guarded by two forts. In the 18C, **Ferrol** (🚇 *Avenida de Compostela)* became (and remains) a naval base. The symmetry of the old quarter dates from the same period.

Betanzos★

Betanzos, a one-time port which has now silted up, stands on a hill at the end of a *ría*. Its old quarter retains three richly ornamented Gothic churches and old houses with glassed-in balconies.

Iglesia de Santa María del Azogue★
Pl. de Fernán Pérez de Andrade.
🕐 Open Mon–Fri 9.30am–1pm, 5–7pm, Sat 9.30am–1pm, Sun and public holidays 11am–1pm. 🎟No charge.
🔊Guided tours available by phoning ☎981 77 36 93.
The name of the 14C–15C church comes from *suk* (marketplace in Arabic). The asymmetrical façade is given character by a projecting central bay pierced by a rose window and a portal with sculptured covings. Niches on either side contain archaic statues of the Virgin and the Archangel Gabriel. Three aisles of equal height, beneath a timber roof, create an effect of spaciousness.

Iglesia de San Francisco★
Pl. de Fernán Pérez Andrade.
♿🕐 Open daily 15 Jun–15 Sept 10am–2pm, 4.30–7pm; 16 Sept–14 Jun 10.30am–1pm, 4.30–6.30pm.
🔊Guided tours; call ☎981 77 36 93.
This Franciscan monastery church, in the shape of a Latin Cross, with a graceful Gothic east end, was built in 1387 by the powerful Count Fernán Pérez de Andrade, Lord of Betanzos and Puentedeume. It is remarkable for the many tombs along its walls, the carved decoration on its ogives and chancel arches and the wild boar sculpted in the most unexpected places. Beneath the gallery to the left of the west door is the **monumental sepulchre★** of the founder, supported by a wild boar and a bear, his heraldic beasts. Scenes of the hunt adorn the sides of the tomb.

Iglesia de Santiago
Pl. de Lanzós. 🕐 Open mid-Jun–mid Sept Mon–Fri 9.30am–1pm, 5–7pm, Sat 9.30am–1pm, Sun and hols noon–2pm; mid-Sept–mid-Jun daily 9.30am–1pm. 🎟No charge. 🔊Guided tours; call ☎981 77 36 93.
The church, built in the 15C by the tailors' guild, stands on higher ground. Above the main door is a carving of St James Matamoros (Moorslayer) on horseback. The arcaded 16C **ayuntamiento** (town hall) is alongside.

Ría de La Coruña
🕐See La CORUÑA/A CORUÑA

Costa de la Muerte (Coast of Death)

The coast between La Coruña and Cabo Finisterre is wild, harsh and majestic, whipped by storms, the graveyard of many a ship smashed against its rocks. Tucked in its more sheltered coves are fishing villages like **Malpica de Bergantiños**, protected by the Cabo de San Adrián (opposite the Islas Sisargas, with a bird sanctuary) or **Camariñas**, famous for its bobbin-lace.

Cabo Finisterre or Fisterra★ (Cape Finisterre)

Corcubión★, near Cabo Finisterre, is an old harbour town of emblazoned houses with glassed-in balconies. The coast **road★** to the cape looks down over the Bahía de Cabo Finisterre, a bay enclosed by three successive mountain chains. The lighthouse on the headland commands a fine **panorama★** of the Atlantic and the bay.

ADDRESSES

⌂ STAY

Pazo da Trave – *Galdo. 3.5km/ 2mi S of Viveiro along the C 640.* ☏*982 59 81 63. www.pazodatrave.com. 18 rooms.* ☐*9€. Restaurant* . A stylish, tastefully furnished hotel in an old stone house with a garden dating back to the 15C. Inside, wood is the predominant theme, as witnessed in the flooring, exposed beams and furniture. Comfortable bedrooms and a good restaurant.

⟡/EAT

O'Centolo – *Av. del Puerto, Fisterra.* ☏*981 74 04 52. www. centolo.com. Closed 22 Dec–15 Feb.* This restaurant is justly popular for its excellent seafood. Choose the modern downstairs bar (with greenhouse) or upstairs dining area with fine views of the fishing port.

Hostal-Restaurante As Garzas – *Porto Barizo 40, Malpica de Bergantiños. 7km/4.5mi SW, towards Barizo.* ☏*981 72 17 65. Closed Mon during Oct–Jun, 2nd fortnight in Oct.* As you would expect, the menu here is strongly influenced by the sea. The building, whitewashed and slate roofed, has a glass-fronted dining room offering good views overlooking the sea. The rooms in the hotel are both pleasant and comfortable.

Rías Bajas★★

The Rías Bajas, a coastline with deep inlets affording safe anchorages, is Galicia's most attractive region for holidaymakers, who enjoy beaches and resorts like those of A Toxa/ LaToja.

🚗 DRIVING TOURS

1 RÍA DE MUROS Y NOIA★★
From Muros to Ribeira
71km/44mi – about 1hr15min.

The *ría* is delightfully wild, its low coastline strewn with rocks. The northern bank is wooded.
Muros is a seaside town with a harbour and local-style houses. **Noia** is notable for its square looking out to sea, upon which stands the Gothic **Iglesia de San Martín**★ *(pl. Suárez Oviedo;* ☏*981 82 01 31)* with a magnificent carved portal and rose window.

2 RÍA DE AROUSA
From Ribeira to A Toxa/La Toja
115km/71mi – about 3hr
Ría de Arousa, at the mouth of the Ulla, is the largest and most indented inlet.

- **Michelin Map:** 571 D 2-3, E 2-3, F 3-4 (town plan of Vigo) – Galicia (La Coruña/A Coruña, Pontevedra)
- **Info:** Baiona: Paseo da Ribeira. ☏986 68 70 67; Vigo: Teófilo Llorente 5. ☏986 22 47 57; Tui: Colón 2. ☏986 60 17 89. www.riasbaixas.depo.es.
- **Location:** The Rías Bajas are four inlets: the Ría de Muros y Noia; the Ría de Arousa; the Ría de Pontevedra; and the Ría de Vigo, all along the northern coast.
- **Kids:** Acquarium Galicia welcomes small marine explorers

Ribeira
A large fishing port with vast warehouses.

Mirador de la Curota★★
9km/5.6.mi NE of Ribeira.
▶ *Take the LC 302 W towards Oleiros and after about 4km/2.5mi turn right onto a narrow road up to the viewpoint.*

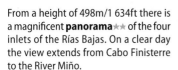

From a height of 498m/1 634ft there is a magnificent **panorama**★★ of the four inlets of the Rías Bajas. On a clear day the view extends from Cabo Finisterre to the River Miño.

Padrón
41km/25.5mi NE of Ribeira.
The legendary boat brought St James to this village. Its mooring stone *(pedrón)* can be seen beneath the altar in the **iglesia parroquial** (parish church) near the bridge. The town, renowned for its green peppers, was home to poet **Rosalía de Castro** (1837–85). Her house is a **museum** (🕐 *open Tue–Fri 10am–1.30pm (2pm in summer), 4–7pm (8pm in summer); Sun and public holidays, 10am–1.30pm; ✆1.50€; 𝒫981 81 12 04; www.rosalia decastro.org).*

Vilagarcía de Arousa
32km/19.8mi SW of Padrón off AP 9.
A garden-bordered promenade overlooks the sea. The **Convento de Vista Alegre**, founded in 1648, on the outskirts, is an old *pazo* with square towers, coats of arms and pointed merlons.

Mirador de Lobeira★
4km/2.5mi S. 🚗 *Take a signposted forest track at Cornazo.*
The view from the lookout takes in the whole *ría* and the hills inland.

Cambados★
12km/7.4mi SW of Vilagarcía de Arousa along PO 549.
The alleys of the old quarter are bordered by beautiful houses. At the northern entrance is the magnificent **plaza de Fefiñanes**★, lined on two sides by the emblazoned Fefiñanes *pazo*, on the third by a 17C church with lines harmonising with the *pazo*, and on the fourth by a row of arcaded houses. On the other side of the village are the romantic ruins of **Santa Mariña de Dozo**, a 12C parish church which is now a cemetery. Try the local white Albariño wine, which has a light fruity flavour.

Isla de la Toja★
20km/12.4mi SW of Cambados off PO 550.
A sick donkey abandoned on the island was the first creature to discover the health-giving properties of the spring in la Toja. The stream has run dry but the pine-covered island in a wonderful **setting**★★ remains the most elegant resort on the Galician coast, with luxury villas and an early 20C palace. A small church is covered in scallop shells.
The seaside resort and fishing harbour of **O Grove** on the other side of the causeway is renowned for its seafood.

🚣 **Acquarium Galicia**
Punta Moreiras, Reboredo. From O Grove head towards San Vicente and turn off at Reboredo. 🕐 *Open 15 Oct–May Fri–Sun and public holidays 10am–8pm, Mon–Thu phone to check; Jun–14 Oct daily 10am–9pm.* ✆*10€; child 7.50€. 𝒫986 73 15 15. www.acquariumgalicia.com.*
The only aquarium in Galicia, has over 150 species on display in 18 tanks. The complex also includes a marine farm where turbot and gilthead are raised.
The **road**★ from A Toxa/La Toja to Canelas affords views of sand dunes and rock-enclosed beaches like that of **La Lanzada**.

③ RÍA DE PONTEVEDRA★
From A Toxa/La Toja to Hío
62km/39mi – about 3hr.

Sanxenxo
A lively summer resort with one of the best climates in Galicia.

Monasterio de Santa María de Armenteira
🕐*Open daily 10am–9pm.* ✆*No charge. 𝒫986 71 83 00.*
In Samieira a small road leads to this Cistercian monastery, where a 12C church and 17C classical-style cloister can be visited.

Combarro★
12km/7.4mi E of Sanxenxo along PO 308.

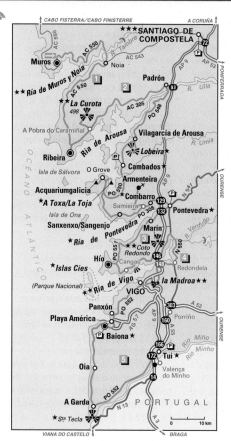

Map labels:
CABO FISTERRA/CABO FINISTERRE — A CORUÑA
★★★ SANTIAGO DE COMPOSTELA
Muros
Noia
Padrón
★★ Ría de Muros y Noia
La Curota 498
A Pobra do Caramiñal
Ría de Arousa
Vilagarcía de Arousa
Lobeira★
Ribeira
Isla de Sálvora
O Grove
Cambados
Armenteira
Acquariumgalicia
Combarro
★A Toxa/La Toja
Samieira
Isla de Ons
Sanxenxo/Sangenjo
Pontevedra★
Marín
★ Ría de Pontevedra
★Coto Redondo
Hío
Cangas
★Islas Cíes
(Parque Nacional)
★ Ría de Vigo
la Madroa ★★
VIGO
Panxón
Redondela
Playa América
Porriño
Baiona ★
Oia
Tui ★
Valença do Minho
A Garda
★Sta Tecla
PORTUGAL
Río Miño
VIANA DO CASTELO — BRAGA
0   10 km

This fishing village with winding alleyways has a good many Calvaries and is famed for its **hórreos**★ (drying sheds).

Pontevedra★
See PONTEVEDRA

Marín
8km/5mi SW of Pontevedra along PO 11. Headquarters of the Escuela Naval Militar (naval academy).

Hío
19km/11.8mi SW of Marín along the AP 9.
The village at the tip of the Morrazo headland has a famous and intricately carved **Calvary**★.

4 RÍA DE VIGO★★
From Hío to Baiona
70km/43mi –about 3hr.
The Vigo inlet is deep and remarkably sheltered inland by hills and out to sea by islands, the Islas Cíes. By Domaio, where the steep, wooded banks draw together and the narrow channel is covered in mussel beds, it becomes really beautiful. From Cangas and Moaña you can see the white town of Vigo covering the entire hillside across the inlet.

Vigo
38km/23.6mi SE of Hío.
Vigo is Spain's principal transatlantic port and leading fishing port. . Vigo's **setting**★ is outstanding: an amphitheatre on the south bank of the ría surrounded by parks and pinewoods. There are magnificent **views**★★ from El Castro hill. Berbés is the picturesque fishermen and sailors' quarter. Adjacent is the A Pedra market where fishwives sell oysters; try them in the local bars.
At Punta de Muiño, are splendid **views** of the *ría* and the **Museo del Mar** *(av. Atlántida 160; open Jun–Sept Tue–Thu 10am–2pm, 5–10pm, Fri–Sat 10am–2pm, 5–8.30pm, Sun and hols 10am–10pm; Oct–May Tue–Thu 10am–2pm, 4–8pm, Fri–Sat 10am–8.30pm, Sun and hols 10am–9pm; no charge; 986 24 77 50; www.museodomar.com)*, where the history of Vigo and the sea is explored.

Islas Cíes★
By boat from Vigo or Cangas (30min). 986 22 52 72. www.mardeons.com.
The beautiful archipelago of crystalline water and white sand guards the entrance to the ría de Vigo. The archipelago is a part of **Parque Nacional de las Islas**

Atlánticas de Galicia (national park). including three islands and Playa de Rodas beach.

Mirador la Madroa★★

6km/3.7mi. ▶ *Exit Vigo along the airport road. After 3.5km/2mi turn left, following signposts to the "parque zoológico" (zoo). The esplanade commands a fine* **view**★★ *of Vigo and the ría.*

The Alcabre, Samil and Canido beaches stretch down the coast south of Vigo.

Panxón

14km/9mi SW along the C 550. A seaside resort at the foot of Monte Ferro.

Playa América

2km/1.2mi S of Panxón.
A very popular, elegant resort in the curve of a bay.

Baiona/Bayona★

5km/3mi SW of Playa América.
It was here, on 10 March 1493, that the caravel *Pinta* – one of the three vessels in Christopher Columbus's fleet – captained by **Martín Alonso Pinzón,** gave the first reports of the New World.

Today, Baiona is a lively summer resort with a harbour for fishing boats and pleasure craft fronted by a promenade of terrace cafés. In the old quarter houses may still be seen with coats of arms and glassed-in balconies. The **ex-colegiata**, former collegiate church *(pl. de Santa Liberata 1;* ◷ *open 11am–12.30pm, 4.30–6.30pm;* ✆*986 68 70 67)* at the top of the town was built in a transitional Romanesque-Gothic style.

Monterreal

◷*Open daily 10am–dusk.*✇*0.60€; 3€ vehicles.* ✆ *986 35 50 00.*
The Catholic Monarchs had a wall built around Monterreal promontory at the beginning of the 16C. The fort within has been converted into a parador, surrounded by a pleasant pinewood. A **walk round the battlements**★ *(about 30min),* rising sheer above the

rocks, affords splendid **views**★★ of the bay, Monte Ferro, the Estela islands and the coast stretching south to the cabo Silleiro headland.

THE ROAD FROM BAIONA

⑤ TO TUI★

58km/36mi
The coast between Baiona and La Guarda is flat and semi-deserted.

Oia

Houses in the fishing village cluster around the former Cistercian abbey of **Santa María la Real** *(www. monasteriodeoia.com)* with its Baroque façade.

La Guarda/A Guarda

13km/8mi S of Oia along PO 552.
This fishing village stands at the southern end of the Galician coastline. To the south, **Monte Santa Tecla**★ (341m/1 119ft) rises above the mouth of the Miño, affording fine **views**★★. ▶ *Follow signs for Citania de Santa Trega.* On the slopes are the extensive remains of a **Celtic city,** inhabited from the Bronze Age to the 3C AD.

▶ *From La Guarda, the PO 552 heads inland parallel to the Miño river.*

Tui/Tuy★

27km/17mi NE of La Guarda along PO 552.
Tui stands just across the border from Portugal in a striking **setting**★. Its old quarter, facing the Portuguese fortress of Valença, stretches down the rocky hillside. The **Parque de Santo Domingo**, including a Gothic church of the same name, commands a good view of Tui and the Portuguese coast.
Since 1884, when a bridge was built by Gustave Eiffel across the Miño, Tui has served as a gateway to Portugal. The historic town is one of the oldest in Galicia; its emblazoned houses and narrow stepped alleys climbing towards the Cathedral testify to its rich past.

ADDRESSES

STAY

Canaima – *Av. de García Barbón 42. ℘986 43 09 34. www.hotelcanaima.es. 50 rooms. ☕4€. Restaurant*. Situated in the centre of Vigo, this well priced hotel has rooms fitted with Castilian furniture; some with balcony views.

Tres Carabelas – *Ventura Misa 61, Baiona. ℘986 35 51 33. www.hoteltrescarabelas.com. 12 rooms. ☕5€.* Family-run hotel in the centre of town. The rooms are equipped with traditional décor and have been recently refurbished.

Pazo de Hermida – *Trasmuro 21, Lestrove. 1km/0.6mi SW of Padrón. ℘981 81 71 10. www.pazodehermida.com. 6 rooms.* This 17C Galician manor hous enjoys a tranquil setting.

EAT

Anduriña – *R. do Porto 58, La Guarda. ℘986 61 11 08. www.restauranteandurinha.com.* This unpretentious and well-known local restaurant has an excellent menu with creative touches, including reasonably priced fish.

La Oca – *Purificación Saavedra 8 (opposite Teis market), Vigo. ℘986 37 12 55. Closed Holy Week, late Jul–early Aug, and for dinner Mon–Fri.* Don't be put off by the slightly out-of-the-way location or the neglected façade of this small family-run restaurant, as the food here is innovative and creative with notable French influences.

Posta do Sol – *Ribeira de Fefiñáns 22, Cambados. ℘986 54 22 85. www.postadosol.com. Closed Wed Oct–Jun.* An attractive little restaurant, decorated in regional style. The speciality is seafood. Also try the *empanadas* and house desserts.

O Fogón da Ría – *Fontecarmoa 3, Vilagarcia De Arousa. ℘986 50 79 62. www.ofogondaria.com. – Closed Mon for dinner, Tue.* Located on the outskirts of the town, this lovely establishment has two dining rooms with rustic décor with a varied menu and good wine list.

TAPAS

Tasca Típica – *R. do Cantón 15, Noia. ℘981 82 12 70.* This old stone building in the centre of Noia has been converted into a typical bar serving tapas and a good-value daily menu. In fine weather, customers can also eat on the terrace.

Santiago de Compostela★★★

In the Middle Ages Santiago de Compostela attracted pilgrims from all of Europe in search of eternal salvations. Today around 100 000 pilgrims make a similar trek to the city, declared a UNESCO World Heritage Site, each year. Whatever the spiritual benefits gained en route, the sightseeing highlight is fittingly, and literally, the final step of the journey; the wondrous Cathedral, which is the focal point of a city that celebrates life and piety in equal measures.

- **Population:** 94 339
- **Michelin Map:** 571 D 4 (town plan) – Galicia (La Coruña/A Coruña)
- **Info:** Rúa do Vilar 63. ℘981 55 51 29. www.santiagoturismo.com.
- **Location:** This pilgrimage city in NW Spain is connected by the AP 9 to Vigo (84km/52mi S) and La Coruña/A Coruña (72km/45mi N) and by the N 547 with Lugo (107km/67mi E). The AP 53 runs SE to Ourense/Orense (111km/69mi). Calle Hórreo 75 A
- **Don't Miss:** The Cathedral.

THE CITY TODAY

Despite its large number of visitors, Santiago de Compostela remains one of Spain's most enchanting cities with its old quarters and maze of narrow streets containing numerous bars and restaurants. The city's 40 000 or so university students mix with the hundreds of thousands of annual visitors from all over the world and ensure a lively cosmopolitan atmosphere.

A BIT OF HISTORY

History, tradition and legends – The Apostle **James the Greater** crossed the seas to convert Spain to Christianity. He returned to Judaea where he fell victim to Herod Agrippa. His disciples fled to Spain with his body. A star is believed to have pointed out the grave to shepherds early in the 9C.

In 844 during an attack against the Moors at **Clavijo**, a knight on a charger, bearing a white standard with a red cross, appeared on the battlefield and brought victory. The Christians recognised St James, naming him *Matamoros* or Moorslayer. The Reconquest and Spain had found a patron saint.

In the 11C devotion spread until a journey to St James' shrine ranked with one to Rome or Jerusalem.

SIGHTS

Plaza del Obradoiro

The majesty of the square makes it a fitting setting for the Cathedral.

Catedral★★★

Pl. del Obradoiro. ⏱*Open daily 7.30am–9pm.* ⊘*No charge.* ☏*981 55 47 48.*
The present cathedral dates mostly from the 11C to the 13C, although from the outside it appears Baroque.

Fachada do Obradoiro★★★ **(Obradoiro façade)** – This Baroque masterpiece by **Fernando Casas y Novoa** was completed in 1750. The central area, given true Baroque movement by the interplay of straight and curved lines, rises to what appears to be a long tongue of flame.

Pórtico de la Gloria★★★ **(Doorway of Glory)** – Behind the façade stands the narthex and the Pórtico de la Gloria, a late 12C wonder by **Maestro Mateo**. The statues of the triple doorway are exceptional both as a composition and in detail.

The doorway is slightly more recent than the rest of the Cathedral and shows Gothic features. Mateo, who also built bridges, had the crypt reinforced to bear the weight of the portico. The central portal is dedicated to the Christian Church, the one on the left to the Jews, that on the right to the Gentiles. The central portal tympanum shows the Saviour surrounded by the Evangelists while on the archivolt are the 24 Elders of the Apocalypse. The engaged pillars are covered in statues of Apostles and Prophets. Note the figure of Daniel with the hint of a smile, a precursor to the famous Smiling Angel in Reims Cathedral in France. The pillar beneath the seated St James bears finger marks; traditionally, on entering the Cathedral, exhausted pilgrims placed their hands here in token of safe arrival. On the other side of the pillar, the statue known as the saint of bumps is believed to impart memory and wisdom.

Interior – The immense Romanesque cathedral displays all the characteristics of medieval pilgrim churches: a Latin Cross plan, vast proportions, an ambulatory and a triforium. The side aisles are covered with 13C groin vaults. At major festivals a huge incense burner, the **botafumeiro** *(displayed in the library)*, is swung from the transept dome keystone by eight men.

The **altar mayor** or high altar, surmounted by a sumptuously apparelled 13C statue of St James, is covered by a gigantic baldaquin. Beneath the altar is the **cripta**, a crypt built into the 9C church. It enshrines the relics of the saint and his disciples, St Theodore and St Athanasius.

The Gothic vaulting of the Capilla Mondragón (1521), and the 9C Capilla de la Corticela, formerly separate, are beautiful. The Renaissance doors to the **sacristía** (sacristy) **(1)** and *claustro*

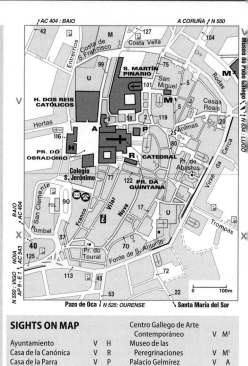

SIGHTS ON MAP

Ayuntamiento	V	H
Casa de la Canónica	V	R
Casa de la Parra	V	P
Centro Gallego de Arte Contemporáneo	V	M²
Museo de las Peregrinaciones	V	M¹
Palacio Gelmírez	V	A

(cloisters) (**2**) on the right arm of the transept are noteworthy.

Museo – 🕐 *Open Jun–Sept Mon–Sat 10am–2pm, 4–8pm, Sun and public holidays 10am–2pm; Oct–May Mon–Sat 10am–1.30pm, 4–6.30pm, Sun and public holidays 10am–1.30pm.* 🕐 *Closed 1, 6 Jan, 25 Jul, 15 Aug, 25 Dec.* ⊛5€. ℘981 56 05 27.
Enter the **tesoro** (treasury), in a Gothic chapel to the right of the nave, from inside of the cathedral.
Exhibits include a gold and silver monstrance by Antonio de Arfe (1539–66). To visit the 11C **cripta**★ (crypt), exit to Plaza del Obradoiro. This is in fact a small Romanesque church with a Latin cross plan. Use the side entry for the rooms devoted to archaeological excavations, the **biblioteca** (library), the **sala capitular** (chapter house) with its granite vault and walls hung with 16C Flemish tapestries, and the rooms with **tapestries**★★ by Goya, Bayeu, Rubens and Teniers.

Claustro★ – *Access via the museum.* This Renaissance cloister was designed by Juan de Álava, who combined a Gothic structure with Plateresque decoration.

Puerta de las Platerías★★ **(Silversmiths' Doorway)** – This is the only intact 12C Romanesque doorway. Not all of the entrance is original. The most impressive figure is David playing the viola on the left door. Adam and Eve can be seen being driven out of the Garden of Eden; the Pardoning of the Adulterous Woman is on the right-hand corner of the left tympanum. The **Torre del Reloj** (Clock Tower) was added at the end of the 17C. To the left stands the **Torre del Tesoro** (Treasury Tower). The 18C Baroque façade of the **Casa del Cabildo** is opposite the *fuente de los caballos,* or horse trough.

Visit the Cathedral roof

Enter by Palacio Gelmírez. 👥 *Guided tours (1hr) Tue–Sun 10am–2pm, 4–8pm.* ⊛10€. ℘981 55 29 85 *(reservations recommended).*
A visit to the roof offers a surprising view of the Cathedral and affords unforgettable views of the city.

Palacio Gelmírez

Pl. del Obradoiro. 🕐 *Open Jun–Sept Mon–Sat 10am–2pm, 4–8pm, Sun and public holidays 10am–2pm; Oct–May Mon–Sat 10am–1.30pm, 4–6.30pm, Sun and public holidays 10am–1.30pm.* 🕐 *Closed 25 Jul, 15 Aug and 25 Dec.* 👁5€. 📞981 57 23 00.

This is the *bishops' palace (left of the cathedral)*. The **Salón Sinodal**★ (Synod Hall) is more than 30m/98ft long and has sculptured ogive vaulting.

Hostal de los Reyes Católicos★ (Hostelry of the Catholic Monarchs)

Pl. del Obradoiro. www.parador.es.

This former pilgrim inn and hospital, now a parador, has an impressive **façade**★ with a splendid Plateresque doorway and four elegant *patios*.

Casco Antiguo★★ (Old town)

The old part of the city is a maze of delightful narrow streets which open out onto lively squares.

Rúa do Franco

This street is lined by old colleges, such as Renaissance-style Colegio de Fonseca, and shops and bars. The Porta de la Faxeiras leads to paseo de la Herradura, the hill that is the setting for fairs. The excellent **view**★ includes the cathedral and the rooftops of Santiago.

Pazo de Bendaña

Pl. del Toral. 🕐*Open Oct–May Tue–Sat 11am–2pm, 4–9pm, Sun 11am–2pm; Jun–Sept Tue–Sat 11am–9pm, Sun 11am–2pm.* 🕐*Closed public holidays.* 👁2€; no charge Sun. 📞981 57 63 94. *www.fundacion-granell.org.*

Inside this 18C noble building, the Fundación Eugenio Granell (1912–2001) displays surrealist art.

Rúa do Vilar

The street leading to the cathedral is bordered by arcaded and ancient houses, as is the parallel **rúa Nova**.

Plaza de la Quintana★★

Along the square at the east end of the Cathedral, bustling with students, are the former **Casa de la Canónica** (Canon's Residence) and the 17C Monasterio de San Paio de Antealtares. Inside is the **Museo de Arte Sacro** (Sacred Art Museum; 🕐*open Apr–Dec Mon–Sat 10.30am–1.30pm, 4–7pm.* 👁1.50€. 📞981 56 06 23).

Opposite, the doorway in the Cathedral's east end, known as the **Puerta del Perdón**★ (Door of Pardon), designed by Fernández Lechuga in 1611 and opened only in Holy Years (when the feast day of St James, 25 July, falls on a Sunday, next occurring in 2010), incorporates all the statues of the Prophets and Patriarchs carved by Maestro Mateo for the original Romanesque *coro*. At the top of a large flight of stairs is the **Casa de la Parra,** House of the Bunch of Grapes, a fine late 17C Baroque mansion.

Monasterio de San Martín Pinario★

Pl. de la Inmaculada 5. 🕐 *Open Tue–Sun 10am–2pm, 4–6pm.* 📞981 58 30 08.

The monastery church has an ornate Plateresque front. The interior, with coffered barrel vaulting, is lit by a Byzantine-style lantern without a drum. The Churrigueresque high altar **retable**★ is by the great architect Casa y Novoa (1730). A grand staircase beneath a cupola leads to 16C–18C cloisters.

The façade overlooking Plaza de la Inmaculada is colossal with massive Doric columns. Plaza de la Azabachería opposite is named for the jet ornament craftsmen *(azabacheros)* who had workshops in this square.

Museo do Pobo Galego (Museum of the Galician People)

🕐 *Open Tue–Sat 10am–2pm, 4–8pm, Sun and public holidays 11am–2pm.* 🕐 *Closed 1 Jan, 25 Dec.*👁No charge. 📞981 58 36 20. *www.museodopobo.es.*

This regional museum, in the former Convento de Santo Domingo de Bonaval (17C–18C), provides an introduction to Galician culture. Rooms are devoted to

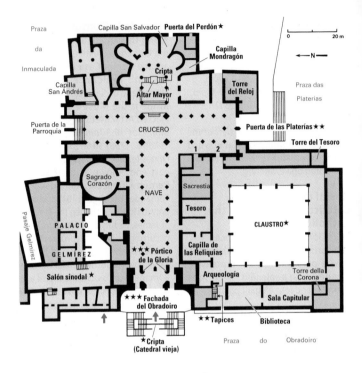

the sea, crafts, painting and sculpture. The building has an impressive triple **spiral staircase**★. The **Centro Gallego de Arte Contemporáneo** (Galician Contemporary Art Centre; ◷open Tue–Sun 11am–8pm; ✆no charge; ✆981 54 66 19; www.cgac.org), designed by the Portuguese architect Álvaro Siza, is situated opposite.

Museo de las Peregrinaciones (Pilgrimage Museum)

San Miguel 4. ◷ *Open Tue–Fri 10am–8pm, Sat 10.30am–1.30pm, 5–8pm, Sun and public holidays 10.30am–1.30pm.* ◷*Closed 1, 6 Jan, 1 May, 25 Jul, 1 Nov, 24–25, 31 Dec.* ✆*2.40€.* ✆*981 58 15 58. www.mdperegrinacions.com.*
This small museum is devoted to the pilgrimages to Santiago. Hardly any of its original medieval features remain.

Colegiata de Santa María la Real del Sar★

Pl. de la Colegiata de Sar. ◷ *Open Mon–Sat 10am–1pm, 4–7pm, Sun and public holidays 10am–1pm.* ✆*981 56 28 91.*

The 12C Romanesque collegiate church has 18C buttresses – a glance inside at the astonishing slant of the pillars will explain why. The only cloister gallery to remain is elegant, with paired **arches**★ decorated with floral and leaf motifs. A museum displays gold and silverwork.

EXCURSIONS
Pazo de Oca★

25km/15.5mi S on the N 525.
◷*Gardens: open daily Nov–Mar 9am–6.30pm; Apr–Oct 9am–8.30pm.* ✆*4€.* ✆*986 58 74 35. www. fundacionmedinaceli.org.*
This austere Galician **manor**, or *pazo*, with a crenellated tower, lines two sides of a vast square. The romantic **park**★★ behind comes as a complete surprise (*see INTRODUCTION – Spanish Gardens*). There are shady arbours, terraces covered with rust-coloured lichen, pools, and a silent lake with a stone boat.

Monasterio de Santa María de Sobrado

56km/35mi W. 🕐 *Open Mon–Sat 10am–1pm, 4.30–7pm, Sun 12.15pm–1pm, 4.30–7pm.* ∞*0.60€.* 🖉*981 78 75 09.*

Sobrado is a vast weatherworn **monastery**, built between the Renaissance and Baroque periods. Despite the severe church façade the interior displays fertile imagination in the design of the **cupolas** in the transept, the sacristy and the Rosary Chapel. Medieval parts of the monastery include the kitchen, chapter house and Mary Magdalene Chapel.

ADDRESSES

🛏STAY

🍽 **Hostal Mapoula** – *Entremurallas 10, 3º.* 🖉*981 58 01 24. www.mapoula. com. 11 rooms.* A small, family-run hostal in the old quarter. Good service and clean rooms with en-suite bathrooms.

🍽 **Hotel San Clemente** – *San Clemente 28.* 🖉*981 56 93 50. www. pousadasdecompostela.com. 10 rooms.* ⌷*6€.* An enviable central location a couple of minutes' walk from the Plaza del Obradoiro; rooms are decorated in brick and wood. Highly recommended.

🍽 **Casa Grande de Cornide** – *Cornide, Teo-Casalonga. 11.5km/7mi SW of Santiago.* 🖉*981 80 55 99. www. casagrandedecornide.com. 10 rooms.* ⌷*7€.* This large, traditional-style Galician house offers peace and quiet. Decor and furnishings are a fusion of the classic and the modern, and offer a cosy atmosphere. in the lovely garden surrounding the house is a swimming pool.

🍽 **Parador Hotel Reyes Católicos** – *Pl. del Obradoiro 1.* 🖉*981 58 22 00. www.parador.es. 137 rooms.* ⌷*20€. Two restaurants* 🍽🍽. The former Royal Hospital founded by the Catholic Monarchs in 1499 has now been converted into a luxury parador. Particularly worthy of note are its inner patios, which trace the typology of such hospitals in the 16C. Elegant rooms, some with four-poster beds.

🍴EAT

🍽 **O Dezaseis** – *R. de San Pedro 16.* 🖉*981 57 76 33. www.dezaseis.com. Reservations recommended. Closed Sun.* Impressive local gastronomy with delicious tapas and excellent wines, beneath the vines on the terrace or in a décor of wood and local stone.

🍽 **Calderón** – *Car. del Conde 8.* 🖉*981 55 43 56. www.calderonrest aurante.com. Closed Aug 3 wks, Sun.* Garden terrace, cosy dining rooms and tapas bar with modern décor.

🍽 **Don Quijote** – *Galeras 20.* 🖉*981 58 68 59. www.quijoterestaurante. com.* A stronghold of traditional Galician cuisine with a popular bar.

🍽 **Casa Marcelo** – *R. Hortas 1.* 🖉*981 55 85 80. www.casamarcelo. net. Closed Feb, Sun, Mon.* This charming restaurant serving innovative cuisine on a well-balanced and varied fixed tasting menu

TAPAS

Bierzo Enxebre – *Troia 10.* 🖉*981 58 19 09. www.bierzoenxebre.com.* Fine tapas bar with three rustic dining rooms including stone columns and timber rafters.

La Bodeguilla de San Roque – *San Roque 13.* 🖉*981 56 43 79. www. labodeguilladesanroque.com.* This bodega has a good reputation for its *revuelta* dishes, chorizos and wines. Pleasant restaurant on the first floor.

Caney – *Hotel Meliá Araguaney, Alfredo Brañas 5.* 🖉*981 59 02 87.* An elegant tapas bar alongside the adjoining Meliá Hotel.

🍷 CAFÉS

Café Derby Bar – *R. das Orfas 29.* 🖉*981 58 65 71.* A classic timeless bar popular with Galician writers.

Cafetería Paradiso – *R. do Vilar 29.* 🖉*981 58 33 94.* A café with a 19C atmosphere.

The Way of St James★★

The discovery of the body of the Apostle James transformed Santiago de Compostela into the most important pilgrimage centre in Europe in the Middle Ages. From the 11C, the veneration of saintly relics gave rise to the Way of St James to this Galician city and today thousands of pilgrims (and curious visitors) walk the same path, called El Camino de Santiago in Spanish.

- **Michelin Map:** 571, 573 and 575 D-E-F 4-26 – Navarra; La Rioja; Castilla y León; Galicia
- **Info:** Astorga: Plaza Eduardo de Castro 5. ℘987 61 82 22; Puente de la Reina: Calle Mayor 105. ℘948 34 08 45. www.xacobeo.es. www. santiago-compostela.net.
- **Location:** The Way of St James runs east to west from the Pyrenees to Santiago de Compostela across northern Spain.

A BIT OF HISTORY

The relics of St James (Santiago) discovered early in the 9C soon became a goal of pilgrimage. In the 11C devotion spread until a journey to St James' shrine ranked with one to Rome or Jerusalem. St James had a particular appeal for the French, united with the Spanish against the Moors, but others made the long pilgrimage along routes organised by the Benedictines, Cistercians and the Knights Templars. Hospitals and hospices received the sick, the weary and the stalwart alike who travelled almost all in the uniform of heavy cape, 2.4m/8ft stave with a gourd attached to carry water, stout sandals and broad-brimmed felt hat marked with three or four scallop shells. A Pilgrim Guide of 1130, the first tourist guide ever written, describes the inhabitants, climate, customs and sights on the way. Churches and towns benefited from the passage of from 500 000 to two million pilgrims a year.

Those from England who "took the cockleshell" often sailed from Parson's Quay in the Plymouth estuary to Soulac and followed the French Atlantic coast, or landed at La Coruña or in Portugal. Routes through France from Chartres, St-Denis and Paris joined at Tours.

Villages along the main route (calle Mayor) grew into towns and some were settled by foreigners or minorities, often French or Jewish.

With time, the faith that impelled pilgrimages began to diminish; trickery and robbery increased; the Wars of Religion among Christians reduced the faithful. In 1589, Drake attacked La Coruña and the bishop of Compostela removed the relics from the cathedral. They were lost and for 300 years the pilgrimage was virtually abandoned. In 1879 they were recovered, recognised by the pope and the pilgrimage recommenced. In Holy Years, on 25 July, when the feast day of St James falls on a Sunday (next in 2010), jubilee indulgences attract yet more pilgrims.

THE WAY IN SPAIN – MAIN HALTS

The ways through France met at Roncesvalles, Behobia and Somport to cross the Pyrenees and continued as the Asturian route from Roncesvalles. A more secure southerly route from Somport, the **Camino Francés,** (via via **Jaca**, **Santa Cruz de la Serós**, **San Juan de la Peña**, the **Monasterio de Leyre** and **Sangüesa** is marked by churches and monasteries in which French architectural influence is obvious. The routes converged at Puente la Reina.

The route from **Roncesvalles** to Puente la Reina was shorter with only one main stop at **Pamplona**.

Puente la Reina★

The 11C humpbacked bridge was built for pilgrims. A bronze pilgrim marks where routes converged.

The wide N 111 circles the old town outside whose walls stands the **Iglesia del Crucifijo** (Church of the Crucifix; ○ *open daily 9am–8.30pm; ∞no charge*). A second nave was added to the 12C main aisle in the 14C and now contains the famous Y-shaped Cross with a profoundly Expressionist **Christ**★ carved in wood, said to have been brought from Germany in the 14C.

Walk along the narrow, elegant main street, calle Mayor, fronted by houses of golden brick with carved wood eaves, to the bridge. You will see the **Iglesia de Santiago** (Church of St James; ○ *open Mon–Fri 10am–2pm, 5–8pm, Sat–Sun 10am–1pm; ∞no charge*), its **doorway**★ crowded with carvings now almost effaced. The nave, remodelled in the 16C, was adorned with altarpieces. Note two statues facing the entrance: St James the Pilgrim in gilded wood, and St Bartholomew.

Iglesia de Santa María de Eunate★★

Muruzábal. 5km/3mi E of Puente la Reina. ○*Open Jan–Nov daily 9am–8.30pm.* ∞*No charge.* ℘*948 34 08 45.* Human bones indicate that this delightful, isolated 12C **Romanesque** building might have been a funerary chapel like that of Torres del Río (*see entry*). The plan is octagonal, with a pentagonal apse outside and a semicircular one inside.

Cirauqui★

Steep, winding alleyways are crowded by houses with rounded doorways, their upper fronts adorned with iron balconies, coats of arms and carved cornices. At the top of the village (*difficult climb*) stands the **Iglesia de San Román** with a multifoil 13C **portal**★.

Estella★ and Monasterio de Irache★ ○See ESTELLA

Los Arcos

The **Iglesia de Santa María de los Arcos** (Church of St Mary of the Arches; *pl. de Santa María;* ⌖guided tours: ℘*948 64 00 21*), with its high tower, is Spanish Baroque inside, with overpowering stucco, sculpture and painting covering every available space. The transept, with its imitation Córdoba leather decoration, is noteworthy. Above the high altar rises the 13C polychrome wood statue of the Black Virgin of Santa María de los Arcos. The cloisters illustrate the elegance and lightness of 15C Gothic.

Torres del Río

The **Iglesia del Santo Sepulcro**★ (Church of the Holy Sepulchre; *Mayor;* ℘*948 64 00 21*) is a tall, octagonal Romanesque building, which might be a funerary chapel, dating from about 1200. The Mudéjar-inspired, star-shaped **cupola** is geometrical perfection. Note also the fine 13C crucifix.

Nájera and Santo Domingo de la Calzada★ ○See La RIOJA

Burgos★★★ ○See BURGOS

Iglesia de Frómista★★
○See PALENCIA

Villalcázar de Sirga

The vast Gothic **Iglesia de Santa María la Blanca** (○*open 15 Oct–20 Apr Sat–Sun noon–2pm, 4–6pm; 1 May–14 Oct daily 10.30am–2pm, 5–8pm;* ∞*1€;* ℘*979 88 80 41*) has a fine carved **portal**★ and two outstanding Gothic **tombs**★. The recumbent statues of the brother of Alfonso X (who had the king murdered in 1271), and his wife Eleanor, are carved in great detail.

Carrión de los Condes

The 11C **Monasterio de San Zoilo**, rebuilt during the Renaissance, has **cloisters**★ (*San Zoilo 23;* ○*open 1 Apr–13 Oct daily 10.30am–2pm, 4–8pm; 14 Oct–31 Mar Tue–Sun 1–2pm, 4–6.30pm;* ∞*1.50€;* ℘*979 88 09 02*) designed by Juan de Badajoz with distinctive vaulting.

The keystones and bosses are adorned with figurines and medallions.

The **Iglesia de Santiago** *(Rúa;* ○*open Jul–Aug daily 11am–1.30pm, 5–7.30pm;* ☞*1€;* ✆*979 88 00 72)* has beautiful 12C carvings on the façade including, on the central coving, an architect with his compass, a barber with his scissors, and other tradesmen. High reliefs above show Gothic influence.

León★★ ○*See LEÓN*

Astorga
☞*Plaza Estación.*

Astorga is renowned for its delicious *mantecadas,* a type of light bread roll.

Catedral de Santa María★
Pl. de la Catedral. ○ *Open daily 9.30am –noon, 5–6.30pm.* ☞*2€.* ✆*987 61 58 20.* Building, begun with the east end in Flamboyant Gothic style in the late 15C, was not completed until the 18C, which explains the rich Renaissance and Baroque façade and towers. The front **porch**★ low reliefs illustrate the Expulsion of the Moneylenders and the Pardoning of the Adulterous Woman, among other events. Above the door is a beautiful Deposition.

The **interior** is surprisingly large, with an upsweeping effect created by innumerable slender columns. Behind the high altar is a 16C **retable**★. Gaspar de Hoyos and Gaspar de Palencia were responsible for the painted, gilt decoration, and **Gaspar Becerra** (1520– 70), an Andalucían who after study in Italy developed a style of humanist sensitivity far removed from the Expressionism of his contemporaries. The **Museo de la Catedral** contains a 13C gold filigree Holy Cross reliquary and a 10C reliquary of Alfonso III, the Great *(*☞*2.50 €; combined entrance with the Museo de los Caminos* ☞*4€).*

Palacio Episcopal
Pl. de Eduardo de Castro.

This fantastic pastiche of a medieval palace was dreamed up by **Gaudí** in 1889. The original, brilliant interior decoration, especially in the neo-Gothic chapel on the first floor, is a profusion of mosaics, stained glass and intersecting ribbed vaults. In the **Museo de los Caminos** (Museum of the Way of St James; ○ *open Oct–Mar Tue–Sun 11am– 2pm, 3–8pm; Apr–Sept daily 11am–2pm, 3.30–6.30pm;* ○ *closed Sun afternoon in Aug;* ☞*2.50€, combined with Museo de la Catedral 4€;* ✆*987 61 68 82)*, medieval art reflects the theme of pilgrimage.

Ponferrada
☞*Avenida del Ferrocarril 9.*

The centre of a mining area, Ponferrada owes its name to an 11C iron bridge built across the Sil for pilgrims. Above the town are the ruins of the **Castillo de los Templarios** (Templars' Castle; ○*open Oct–Apr Tue–Sat 10.30am–2pm, 4–6pm; May–Sept Tue–Sat 10.30am– 2pm, 5–9pm, Sun and public holidays 11am–2pm;* ☞*2.50€;* ✆*987 41 41 41).*

Peñalba de Santiago★
21km/13mi SE.

Peñalba stands in the heart of the so-called Valle del Silencio (Valley of Silence). Its houses are schist-walled with wooden balconies and slate roofs. The Mozarabic **Iglesia de Santiago** *(*○ *open Oct–Mar Tue–Sat 10.30am– 1.15pm, 4.30–6pm, Sun and public holi- days 10.30am–1.15pm; Apr–Sept Tue–Sat 10.30am–1.45pm, 4.30–8pm, Sun and public holiday 10am–1.45pm;* ○*closed 1, 6 Jan, 2 May, 24–25, 31 Dec;* ☞*no charge)*, is all that remains of a 10C monastery. The paired horseshoe portal arch is set off by an *alfiz.*

Las Médulas★
22km/14mi SW. World Heritage Site.

Debris from a Roman gold mine has transformed slopes of the Aquilianos mountains into a magical landscape of rocky crags and strangely shaped hillocks of pink and ochre, covered over the ages by gnarled chestnut trees.

Cebreiro
Cebreiro, not far from the Puerto de Pie- drafita (Piedrafita pass, 1 109m/3 638ft), reflects the hardship of the pilgrim jour- ney. Drystone and thatched houses *(pal-*

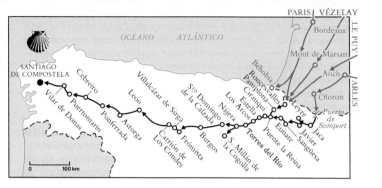

lozas) descend from ancient Celtic huts; in one is an **Ethnographic Museum** (Museo Etnográfico; ⏱*open Wed–Sun 11am–2pm, 3–6pm; ⊜no charge*). A pilgrim inn remains beside the small 9C mountain church where pilgrims venerated the relics of the miracle of the Holy Eucharist (c. 1300), when bread was turned to flesh and wine to blood. Relics in silver caskets presented by Isabel may be seen with the miraculous chalice and paten.

Portomarín

Before centuries-old Portomarín was drowned by a dam, the **church**★ (⏱*open Tue–Sun 10.30am–1pm, 4.30–7pm; ⊜no charge*) of the Knights of St John of Jerusalem was moved stone by stone. It is square, fortified and ornamented with massive arches and Romanesque doors with delicately carved covings. The west door depicts Christ in Majesty with the 24 Old Musicians of the Apocalypse.

Vilar de Donas
6.5km/4mi E of Palas de Rei.
Enter the **church** (⏱*open Tue–Sun 11am–2pm, 3–6pm; ⊜ no charge*), slightly off the main road, through a Romanesque doorway. Lining the walls are tombs of the Knights of the Order of St James, slain in battle. 15C **frescoes**★ decorate the apse, illustrating Christ in Majesty with St Paul and St Luke on his left and St Peter and St Mark on his right and, on the chancel walls, the faces of the elegant young women who gave the church its name (*donas* in Galician).

Santiago de Compostela★★★
⌖*See SANTIAGO DE COMPOSTELA*

ADDRESSES

⌂STAY

⊜⊜**Hotel Madrid** – *Av. de La Puebla 44, Ponferrada. ℘987 41 15 50. www.hotelmadridponferrada.com. 45 rooms.* ⊡*4.50€. Restaurant⊜.* A good central location, friendly staff and clean, comfortable rooms.

⊜⊜**Hotel Real Monasterio San Zoilo** – *Obispo Souto, Carrión de los Condes. ℘979 88 00 49. www.sanzoilo.com. 49 rooms.* ⊡*7€. Restaurant⊜⊜⊜.* This former Benedictine monastery is now a delightful welcoming hotel with elegant architecture. Great value.

⌘/EAT

⊜⊜**La Peseta** – *Pl. San Bartolomé 3, Astorga. ℘987 61 72 75.* This popular, family-run restaurant has a simple dining room, where the cuisine is traditional and reasonably priced.

⊜⊜⊜**Mesón del Peregrino** – *Irunbidea 10, Puente la Reina. 1km/0/6mi NE of Puente la Reina on the Pamplona/Iruña road. ℘948 34 00 75. Closed Sun for dinner, Mon.*
A charming restaurant housed in a magnificent stone mansion with dining rooms overlooking the garden and swimming pool. Creative cuisine is served in tasteful rustic surrounds.

MADRID AND SURROUNDS

Madrid stands at km 0, at the geographical heart of Spain on the flat arid tableland known as the Southern Meseta. In fact it became capital for little more than its conveniently central location, but if Madrid began life as a compromise, these days it is a city of some extremes.

It is probably the noisiest city in Europe; it is the latest and arguably the most buzzing late-night European metropolis, with traffic jams well into the small hours; it is the richest city, alongside London, for art galleries; and, despite the fact that it is the highest European capital, at over 640m/2 100ft above sea level (and enjoys cooling breezes), it is also the hottest capital with the mercury touching 40°C (10°F) in August, when around one third of all Madrileños ("Madridians") flee the city. In terms of general tourism Madrid will never be as popular as its Catalan rival, Barcelona (some would say "arch-enemy", particularly when it comes to football), lacking both proximity to the sea and old-world charm. But it does have bags of historical and architectural interest, great little bars and restaurants and scores highly with city slickers, gourmets and clubbers as well as culture vultures.

Highlights

1 Promenade alongside the locals in the **Parque del Buen Retiro** (p432)

2 Puzzling over *Guernica* in **Museo de Arte Reina Sofía** (p425)

3 Shopping and snacking around **Plaza Mayor** (p425)

4 Taking an "art lesson" at the **Spanish School** in the **Prado** (p413)

5 Strolling in the gardens of the Palacio Real in **Aranjuez** (p432)

Bourbon Madrid

Named after the monarchs who built this area in the 18C, Bourbon Madrid (taking in Salamanca and El Retiro) is an affluent zone of broad avenues, lined with opulent architecture including grand mansions and palaces, some now converted into galleries. Most famous of all is the Prado, but its neighbour, the Museo Thyssen-Bornemisza is arguably its equal and, for many visitors, Madrid's favourite gallery. The third gallery in this "golden triangle of art" is the Museo Nacional Centro de Arte Reina Sofía famous as the home of Picasso's *Guernica*. Whatever your preferences do not rush them, take a break in the beautiful leafy Parque del Buen Retiro, admire the grandiose architecture of set pieces such as the Puerta de Alcalá and enjoy the cafes and people watching in the squares of Plaza de Cibeles and Plaza de Colón. The shopping in Salamanca is the most exclusive in the city.

- **Bourbon Madrid**
- **Salamanca – Retiro**

Old Madrid and Centro

Centring on the Puerta del Sol and Plaza Mayor this is the heart of town for most visitors, combining old and new, narrow alleyways with grand squares, traditional and modern shops, busy markets and a whole host of places to eat and drink. Aside from museums and monuments, the grandiose gargantuan 2 800-room Royal Palace will occupy half a day of your time alone and there are also two splendid monasteries to visit.

- **Old Madrid**
- **Around the Royal Palace**

Moncloa: Casa de Campo District

When the city centre hustle and bustle starts to pall, just west of the Palacio Real is the Parque del Oeste and the less manicured Casa de Campo park, separated by the Manzanares river but connected by a cable car. With a zoo and amusement park the latter is an ideal family jaunt. The area is also home to some fine museums. Immediately west of here is the Ciudad Universitaria ("University City"), Madrid's largest university campus.

- **Moncloa – Casa de Campo**

Museo Nacional Centro de Arte Reina Sofía

©Turespaña

Madrid Excursions

A short trip out of Madrid are two of the country's most famous sights. El Escorial is the 16C royal palatial complex built by Philip II. It is palace, church, monastery, mausoleum and museum all under one massive roof.

Romantics and music lovers will surely want to beat a path to the glorious palace and gardens of Aranjuez to see for themselves what inspired Rodrigo's haunting guitar concerto. If you have time, continue on to the delightful small town of Chinchón. Alcalá de Henares, today a UNESCO World Heritage site, was once a major university and intellectual centre, birthplace of Miguel de Cervantes. At the other end of the cultural spectrum is Parque Warner Madrid, a full-on theme park with thrill rides based on Warner Brothers films and characters.

And finally, if you just cannot get enough of Imperial Spain, there is another fine royal palace to visit at El Pardo.
- **Alcalá de Henares**
- **Aranjuez**
- **El Escorial**

Madrid★★★

Madrid is one of Europe's most cosmopolitan and lively cities, with wide avenues, attractive parks and a general joie de vivre. It became capital of Spain in the 16C when Spain ruled a vast empire and its many monuments and great buildings span the 17C, 18C and 19C. The city is world-famous for its exceptional wealth of paintings.

THE CITY TODAY

Madrid today – Madrid is not only the court and political capital but also its business, administrative, and university centre, with tens of thousands students contributing to the frenetic round-the-clock nightlife for which the city is famous.

The city's most modern edifices are in the **AZCA** area, the result of one of Madrid's most revolutionary projects. Among its noteworthy buildings are the Avant-Garde **Banco de Bilbao-Vizcaya** and the **Torre Picasso**.

A BIT OF HISTORY

Madrid owes its name to the 9C fortress (*alcázar*) of Majerit. In 1085 it was captured by Alfonso VI, who discovered a statue of the Virgin by a granary (*almudín*). He converted the mosque into a church dedicated to the Virgin of the Almudena who was declared the city patron. Emperor Charles V rebuilt the Muslim *alcázar* and in 1561 Philip II moved the court from Toledo to Madrid.

The town really began to develop in Spain's Golden Age (16C). A town plan drawn up in 1656 by Pedro Texeira. King Philip IV gave his patronage to many artists including Velázquez and Murillo, as well as men of letters such as Lope de Vega, Quevedo, and Calderón.

From a town to a city – Madrid underwent its greatest transformations in the18C under the Bourbons. Philip V built a royal palace. Charles III provided Madrid with a splendour hitherto unknown in the Prado and the Puerta de Alcalá, magnificent examples of

▶ **Population:** 3 213 271

🕙 **Michelin Map:** 575 or 576 K 18-19 (town plan)

ℹ **Info:** Plaza Mayor 27. ☎915 88 16 36; Ronda de Toledo 1. ☎913 64 18 76; Plaza de Colón. ☎915 88 16 36; Duque de Medinaceli 2. ☎914 29 49 51; Agustín de Foxá (Estación de Chamartín. ☎913 15 99 76; Estación de Atocha. ☎915 28 46 30. Aeropuerto de Barajas (T4 and T1). ☎913 33 82 48. www.esmadrid.com. www.turismomadrid.es.

◐ **Location:** Europe's highest capital (646m/2 119ft), at the centre of the Iberian Peninsula, with a dry climate: hot summers and cold, sunny winters.

🅿 **Parking:** It's best to park for the duration and use the excellent Metro.

◑ **Don't Miss:** The Prado, the Reina Sofía art collection, crowds in Plaza Mayor.

🕐 **Timing:** Start with the incomparable art museums, and be sure to nap in order to enjoy Madrid's late-hours dining and bars.

👪 **Kids:** Warner Bros Park, Faunia, Faro de la Moncloa, Museo del Ferrocarril and Casa del Campo will keep smaller visitors amused.

Neoclassical town planning. The nobility began building **palaces**, such as **Liria** and **Buenavista**.

The 19C began with occupation by the French and the Madrid rebellion of May 1808 and brutal reprisals. In 1857 the remaining ramparts were demolished and a vast expansion plan (*ensanche*) gave rise to the districts of Chamberí, Salamanca and Argüelles. At the end of the century, **Arturo Soria's** revolutionary *Ciudad Linea* provided for a residential quarter for 30 000 around today's avenida de Arturo Soria.

At the beginning of the 20C, architecture was French-inspired, as in the Ritz and Palace hotels; the neo-Mudéjar style was also popular and brick façades went up all over **(plaza de Toros de las Ventas)**. The **Gran Vía** linked Madrid's new districts in 1910.

MUSEUMS
MUSEO DEL PRADO★★★
Allow 3hr.
Puerta de Velázquez, Pas. del Prado.
Banco de España or Atocha.
 Open Tue–Sun and public holidays 9am–8pm. 24, 31 Dec, 6 Jan 9am–2pm. Last admission 30min before closing.
 Closed 1 Jan, Good Fri, 1 May and 25 Dec. 6€; no charge 2 and 18 May, 12 Oct, 19 Nov, 6 Dec. 913 30 28 00. www.museodelprado.es.

The Prado is the greatest gallery of Classical paintings in the world. The Neoclassical building was designed by Juan de Villanueva under Charles III for a science museum. After the Peninsular War, Ferdinand VII instead installed the Habsburg and Bourbon collections of Spanish painting, expanded over the years.

Spanish School★★★ (15C–18C)
Bartolomé Bermejo *(Santo Domingo de Silos)* and **Yáñez de la Almedina** cultivated an international style. Vicente Masip and his son **Juan de Juanes** *(The Last Supper)* are associated with Raphael. Morales' favourite subject, a *Virgin and Child*, is also outstanding.

In those rooms devoted to the **Golden Age**, two painters stand out: **Sánchez Coello**, and his pupil **Pantoja de la Cruz**, a portraitist at the court of Philip II. **El Greco** stands apart within the Spanish School. Works here date from his early Spanish period *(The Trinity)* to his maturity *(Adoration of the Shepherds)*. Other works are proof that he was a great portraitist, such as **The Nobleman with his Hand on his Chest**. **Ribalta** introduced tenebrism to Spain. **José (Jusepe) de Ribera (Lo Spagnoletto)** is represented by The

Martyrdom of Saint Philip in which the vigorous use of chiaroscuro emphasises the horror of the scene. The portraits and still lifes of **Zurbarán** are peaceful compositions in which chiaroscuro and realism triumph. **Murillo** mainly painted the Virgin but also plain folk *(The Holy Family with a Little Bird* and *The Holy Children with a Shell)*.Works from Spanish historical painting include *The Last Will and Testament of Isabel the Catholic* by Rosales, *Juana the Mad* by F Pradilla and *The Execution of Torrijos and his Colleagues on the Beach at Málaga* by A Gisbert.

Diego Velázquez (1599–1660)
The Prado possesses the greatest paintings of Velázquez. He spent time in Italy (1629–31) where he painted **Vulcan's Forge**. He began to use richer, more subtle colours and developed his figure compositions as in his magnificent **Christ on the Cross**. On his return he painted **The Surrender of Breda** in which his originality emerges. The use of light in his pictures is crucial. He strove towards naturalism in his royal hunting portraits of **Philip IV** and **Prince Baltasar Carlos as a Hunter** (1635, a wonderful rendering of a child) and his equestrian portraits of the royal family, in particular **Prince Baltasar Carlos on Horseback** with the sierra in the background. In 1650 he returned to Italy where he painted landscapes, **The Medici Gardens in Rome**. In his later masterpiece, **Las Meninas** (c. 1656), the Infanta Margarita is shown in the artist's studio in a magnificent display of light and colour. In **The Tapestry Weavers** (c. 1657), Velázquez combined myth and reality.

Goya (1746–1828)
Goya's portraits of the royal and famous, his war scenes, his depictions of everyday life, and finally his **Majas**, all illustrate his extraordinary Realism and enthusiasm for colour. The museum contains 40 cartoons painted in oil between 1775 and 1791 for the Real Fábrica (Royal Tapestry Works), together a delightful picture of 18C Madrid life. **The 3rd of**

GETTING ABOUT

Airport – Madrid-Barajas airport is located northeast of the city, 13km/8mi from downtown. **Bus 200** operates to the airport from the Avenida de América interchange from 5.20am to 1.30am, departing every 10min between 7am and 10pm. Line 204 goes to Terminal 4 from Avenida de América.

Metro line no 8 connects the airport with the city. Airport information (☎902 40 47 04; www.aena.es). Info-Iberia ☎902 40 05 00.

RENFE (Spanish State Railways) – The city's main railway stations are Atocha *(pl. del Emperador Carlos V and Glorieta Carlos V)* and Chamartín *(Agustín de Foxa)*. For information and reservations, call ☎902 24 02 02 (24-hr information; reservations 5.30am–11.50pm); or log on to www.renfe.es. AVE high-speed trains depart from Atocha, taking just 2hr35min to reach Sevilla via Córdoba (1hr50min); Lleida (2hr30min) and Huesca (2hr25min) via Zaragoza (1hr40min); and Toledo (30min). Madrid also has a comprehensive suburban train network *(Cercanías)* which can be used to get to El Escorial, the Sierra de Guadarrama, Alcalá de Henares and Aranjuez.

Inter-city buses – Most buses to other cities depart from the Estación Sur *(Méndez Álvaro 83; ☎914 68 42 00; www.estacionautobusesmadrid.com)*.

Taxis – Madrid has a huge number of registered taxis with distinctive white paintwork with a red diagonal stripe on the rear doors. At night, the green light indicates that the taxi is for hire.

Local buses – For information, call ☎902 50 78 50. A good way of getting to know the city, although traffic jams are a major problem. Passengers should also beware of pickpockets. Times vary from line to line, but generally buses operate between 6am and 11.30pm. Night buses operate from 11.30pm onwards, with most departing from plaza de Cibeles. In addition to single tickets, passengers can also purchase a ten-trip **metro-bus** ticket *(un bono de 10 viajes; 14.50€)* valid on both the bus and metro network, as well as a zone-based monthly ticket *(abono mensual)* which is valid for an unlimited number of bus and metro journeys for one month.

Metro – *Metro stations are shown on the maps in this guide (☎902 44 44 03; www.ctm-madrid.es).* The metro system is the fastest way to get around the city and consists of 13 lines. It operates from 6am to 1.30am. Passengers should beware of pickpockets.

SIGHTSEEING

The Guía del Ocio *(www.guiadelocio.com/madrid)* is a weekly guide containing a list of every cultural event and show in the city. It can be purchased at newspaper stands.

Bus turístico Madrid Visión – This tourist bus offers three different routes around the city (historic Madrid, modern Madrid and monumental Madrid). Tickets, which can be purchased on board, in hotels via a travel agent, or at www.madridvision.es, are valid for 1 or 2 consecutive days. During the period of validity, passengers can hop on and off as much as they like as well as change their route. Services operate 10am–7pm in winter, 10am–9pm in spring and autumn, and 9.30am–midnight in summer. Stops include the Puerta del Sol, plaza de Cibeles, paseo del Prado and Puerta de Alcalá. For information and prices, call ☎917 79 18 88.

DISTRICTS

Madrid is a city full of charm, with its own magnificent parks and impressive buildings. It is a city best explored by strolling through its streets and squares, discovering the delights of its many districts and getting to know its inhabitants.

Centro – This district is made up of several areas, each with their own individual character. It has a reputation for being noisy, chaotic and full of people, although visitors are often surprised by its narrow alleyways and small squares. **Sol-Callao** is the shopping area par excellence, packed with locals and visitors out for a stroll, heading for the main pedestrianised precinct (Preciados district) or for a drink or dinner in one of the many local cafés and restaurants. A number of cinemas are also located in this area. Visitors should take particular care in the evening, especially in streets such as Valverde and Barco.

Barrio de los Austrias – Madrid's oldest district is wedged between calles Mayor, Bailén, Las Cavas and the plaza de la Cebada. Its origins are medieval and it still retains its evocatively named streets and Mudéjar towers. An excellent area for tapas, dinner or a drink. On Sundays, the famous **Rastro** flea market (ꗷsee Rastro) is held nearby.

Lavapiés – This district is located around the square of the same name with many houses dating from the 17C. It is considered to be Madrid's most colourful district with a mix of locals, students and a large immigrant population.

Huertas – Huertas was home to the literary community in the 17C and the Movida movement in the 1980s. Nowadays, it is packed with bars and restaurants and is particularly lively at night, attracting an interesting mixture of late-night revellers.

Malasaña – This part of Madrid, which used to be known as Maravillas, is situated between Las glorietas de Bilbao y Ruiz Jiménez and around plaza del Dos de Mayo. In the mornings, this 19C *barrio* is quiet and provincial, but it is transformed at night by the legions of young people heading towards Malasaña's many bars. For those in search of a quieter night out, the district also has a number of more tranquil cafés.

Alonso Martínez – The average age and financial standing of this district's inhabitants is somewhat higher than in neighbouring Bilbao and Malasaña, as shown by the myriad upmarket bars and restaurants frequented by the city's rich and famous.

Chueca – This district covers an area around the plaza de Chueca; its approximate outer limits are the paseo de Recoletos, calle Hortaleza, Gran Vía and calle Fernando VI. At the end of the last century it was one of Madrid's most elegant districts. Today it is the city's gay area with a multitude of small and sophisticated boutiques.

Salamanca – In the 19C, Salamanca was Madrid's principal bourgeois district designed by the Marquis of Salamanca in the shape of a draughts board with wide streets at right angles. Nowadays, the district is one of the capital's most expensive areas and is home to some of Spain's leading designer boutiques (Serrano and Ortega y Gasset) and an impressive collection of stores selling luxury goods.

The Paseo del Arte

This poetic name refers to the imaginary axis linking Madrid's three greatest museums (the Prado, Thyssen-Bornemisza and the Reina Sofía), which form a close triangle in the same part of the city. The **Paseo del Arte Card**, a combined ticket on sale in each of the museums, entitles the holder to admission to all three of these magnificent art galleries. Cost: ꗷ14.40€.

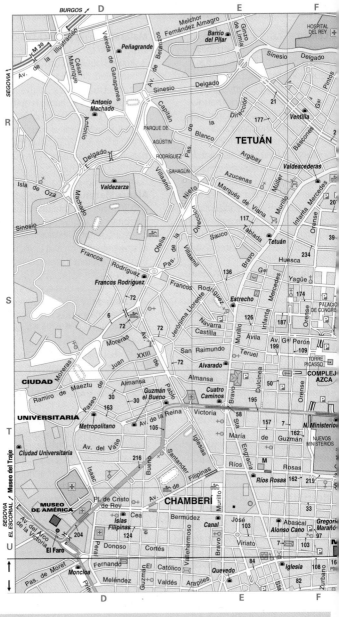

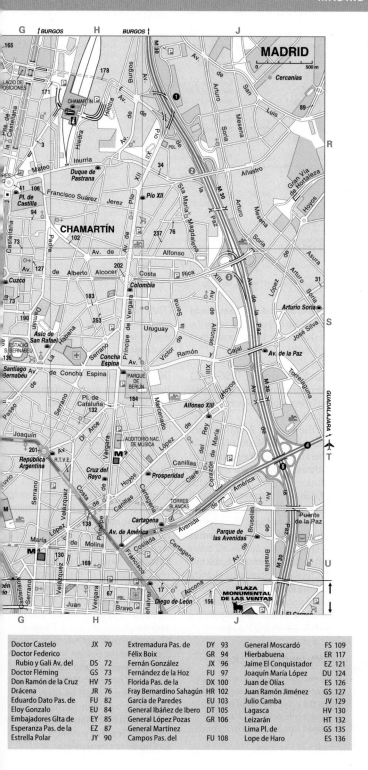

May 1808 in Madrid: the Executions on Principe Pio Hill was inspired by the rebellion against the French occupation (see ARANJUEZ).

Flemish School★★★ (15C–17C)

The exceptional collection of Flemish painting reflects Spain's history with the Low Countries.

Among the Flemish Primitives are Robert Campen, the Mester of Flemalle (*St Barbara*). **Van der Weyden** added great richness of colour, and a sense of composition (*Descent from the Cross*, *Pietà*). Drama is interpreted through melancholy by his successor, **Memling** (*Adoration of the Magi*). There follow the weird imaginings of **Hieronymus Bosch**, El Bosco (*The Garden of Earthly Delights*), which influenced his disciple Patinir (*Crossing the Stygian Lake*), and a **Bruegel the Elder** (*Triumph of Death*). The most Baroque of painters, **Rubens**, breathed new life into Flemish painting (*The Three Graces*). There is a rich collection of his work completed by that of his disciples: **Van Dyck** and **Jordaens**.

Dutch School (17C)

Two interesting works by **Rembrandt** are a *Self-Portrait* and *Artemis*.

Italian School★★ (15C–17C)

The collection is especially rich in works by Venetian painters.

The Italian Renaissance brought with it elegance and ideal beauty as in paintings by **Raphael** (*The Holy Family*, *Portrait of a Cardinal*), Roman nobility and monumental bearing in the work of **Mantegna** (*Dormition of the Virgin*) and melancholic dreaminess in **Botticelli** (*Story of Nastagio degli Onesti*). The spirituality of the magnificent *Annunciation* by **Fra Angelico** belongs to the Gothic tradition.

Colour and sumptuousness triumph with the Venetian school: **Titian** with his exceptional mythological scenes (*Danae and the Golden Shower*, *Venus with the Organist*) and his portrait of *Emperor Charles V*; **Veronese** with compositions set off by silver tones; Tintoretto's golden-fleshed figures springing from shadow (*Washing of the Feet*) and **Tiepolo**'s paintings intended for Charles III's royal palace.

Museum Collections

El Museo del Prado is currently completing a significant expansion. Given the large number of works in stock, some paintings are only displayed in temporary exhibitions.

French School (17C–18C)

The French are represented by **Poussin** landscapes and by **Lorrain** (17C).

German School

A selection includes **Dürer**'s figure and portrait paintings (*Self-Portrait*, *Adam and Eve*) and works by Cranach.

Casón del Buen Retiro★

Alfonso XII 28. ⊜*Banco de España.*
🕐 *Open Mon–Fri 9am–2pm.*
📞*913 30 28 28.*
This annexe focuses on the museum's archive with an extensive art library. The **Gran Salón** has a beautiful roof decoration by Lucas Jordán.

MUSEO THYSSEN-BORNEMISZA★★★

Pas. del Prado 8. ⊜*Banco de España.*
🕐 *Open Tue–Sun 10am–7pm; 24, 31 Dec 10am–3pm; last admission 30min before closing.* 🕐 *Closed 1 Jan, 1 May, 25 Dec.* ⊜6€. 📞*913 69 01 51.*
www.museothyssen.org.
The Neoclassical Palacio de Villahermosa houses an outstanding collection acquired by the Spanish State from **Baron Hans Heinrich Thyssen-Bornemisza**. The museum displays approximately 800 works from the late 13C to the present day, exhibited in chronological order on three floors

Second floor

The visit begins with the Italian Primitives *(Gallery 1)*: **Duccio di Buoninsegna**'s *Christ and the Samaritan Woman*, with its concern for scenic realism. **Gallery 3** displays splendid examples of 15C Dutch religious painting such as **Jan van Eyck**'s *The Annunciation Diptych*. Next to it is the small *Our Lady of the Dry Tree* by **Petrus Christus**; Virgin and Child symbolise the flowering of the dry tree.

The museum possesses a magnificent **portrait collection**. **Gallery 5** contains superb examples of the Early Renaissance and its values of identity and autonomy. These come to the fore in the *Portrait of Giovanna Tornuaboni* by the Italian painter **D Ghirlandaio**.

Raphael's *Portrait of an Adolescent* can be seen in the Villahermosa Gallery *(Gallery 6)* while **Gallery 7** (16C) reveals **Vittore Carpaccio**'s *Young Knight in a Landscape* in which the protagonist's elegance stands out from a background heavy with symbolism. The *Portrait of Doge Francesco Vernier* by **Titian** should not be missed, with its sober, yet diverse tones. After admiring **Dürer's** surprising *Jesus Among the Doctors* (1506, *Gallery 8*), move on to **Gallery 9**, with portraits from the 16C German School including **The Nymph from the Fountain**, one of several paintings by **Lucas Cranach the Elder**, and the *Portrait of a Woman* by **Hans Baldung Grien**. The 16C Dutch paintings in **Gallery 10** include **Patinir**'s *Landscape with the Rest on the Flight into Egypt*. **Gallery 11** exhibits several works by **El Greco** as well as **Titian**'s *St Jerome in the Wilderness* (1575), with its characteristic use of flowing brush-strokes. One of the splendid early works of **Caravaggio**, the creator of tenebrism, *St Catherine of Alexandria*, hangs in **Gallery 12**. In the same gallery is a splendid sculpture (St Sebastian) by Baroque artist **Bernini**. Also here is the *Lamentation over the Body of Christ* (1633) by **Ribera**. The 18C Italian Painting section *(galleries 16–18)* shows Venetian scenes by **Canaletto** and **Guardi**. Also on this floor *(galleries 19–21)* are 17C Dutch and Flemish works. **Van Dyck**'s magnificent *Portrait of Jacques le Roy*, **De Vos**' *Antonia Canis*, and two memorable **Rubens**, *The Toilet of Venus* and *Portrait of a Young Woman with a Rosary*, all hang from the walls of **Gallery 19**.

First floor

Galleries 22–26 represent 17C Dutch painting with scenes of daily life and landscapes. Note **Frans Hals'** *Family Group in a Landscape*, a fine example of a collective portrait.

Interesting portraits stand out from the 18C French and British schools, such as **Gainsborough**'s *Portrait of Miss Sarah Buxton* in **Gallery 28**. 19C North American painting, virtually unknown in Europe, is in the next two rooms *(29 and 30)* with works by the Romantic

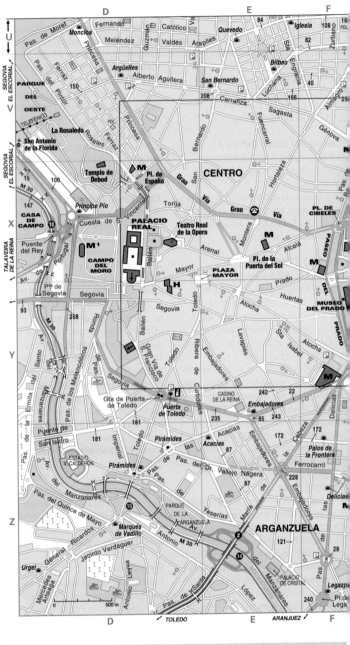

SIGHTS ON MAP

Arco de Cuchilleros	BY, KY	
Ayuntamiento	BY, KY	H
Bolsa de Madrid	NY	
Campo del Moro	DX	
Capilla del Obispo	AZ, KZ	
Capitanía General	AY	
Casa de Campo	DX	
Casa de Cisneros	BZ	
Casa de Pedro		
Calderón de la Barca	BY	D
Casa de la Panadería	BY	
Casón del Buen Retiro	NY	
Catedral N. S.		
de la Almuneda	AY, KY	
Ciudad Universitaria	DT	
El Rastro	BZ	
Faro de La Moncloa	DU	
Hotel Ritz	NY	
Iglesia		
Arzobispal Castrense	AY	F
Iglesia Pontificia		
de San Miguel	BY	
Iglesia de San Andrés	AZ	
Iglesia de San		
Francisco el Grande	AZ, KZ	
Iglesia de San Isidro	BZ, KZ	
Iglesia de San Pedro	BZ, KY	
Instituto Italiano de Cultura	AY	
Jardines de Sabatini	KX	
Jardines de las Vistilla	AZ, KYZ	
Jardín Botánico	NZ	
La Rosaleda	DV	
Mercado de San Miguel	BY	
Monasterio de		
las Descalzas Reales	KLX	
Monumento a Alfonso XII	HX	
Museo		
Arqueológico Nacional	NV	
Museo Cerralbo	KV	
Museo Lázaro Galdiano	GU	M⁴
Museo Municipal	LV	M¹⁰
Museo Nacional Centro		
de Arte Reina Sofía	MZ	
Museo Nacional de		
Artes Decorativas	NX	M⁸
Museo Nacional de		
Ciencia y Tecnología	FZ	M¹²
Museo Naval	NX	M³
Museo Románico	LV	M¹¹
Museo Sorolla	FU	M⁵
Museo Thyssen-Bornemisza	MY	M⁶
Museo de América	DU	
Museo de Carruajes Reales	DX	M¹
Museo de Cera	NV	
Museo de San Isidro	BZ	
Museo de la Ciudad	HT	M⁷
Museo del Ferrocarril	FZ	M⁹
Museo del Prado	MNY	
Museo del Traje	DTU	
Palacio Real	AY	KX
Palacio Vargas	AZ	
Palacio de Buenavista	MX	
Palacio de		
Comunicaciones	NX	
Palacio de Cristal	HY	
Palacio de Linares	NX	
Palacio de Liria	KV	
Palacio de Santa Cruz	CZ, LY	E
Parque de la Quinta		
Fuente del Berro	JVX	
Parque del		
Buen Retiro	NXYZ, GHY	
Parque del Oeste	DV	
Plaza Monumental		
de las Ventas	JU	
Puerta de Alcalá	NX	
Real Academia de Bellas		
Artes de San Fernando	LX	M²
Real Monasterio		
de la Encarnación	KX	
San Antonio de la Florida	DV	
Teatro Real de la Opera	KX	
Teatro de la Zarzuela	MY	
Templo de Debod	DX	
Torre de los Lujanes	BY, KY	B
Warner Bros Park	HZ	

landscape artists Cole, Church, Bierstadt and the Realist Homer.

The European Romanticism and Realism of the 19C is expressed by **Constable**'s *The Lock*, **Courbet**'s *The Water Stream* and **Friedrich**'s *Easter Morning*, together with the three works by **Goya** (*Gallery 31*).

Galleries 32 and **33** are dedicated to Impressionism and Post-Impressionism: magnificent works by Monet, Manet, Renoir, Sisley, Degas, Pissarro, Gauguin, Van Gogh, Toulouse-Lautrec and Cézanne. *At the Milliner* by **Degas** is one of his major canvases. Other works which equally stand out include **Van Gogh's** *"Les Vessenots" in Auvers*, which displays the explosion of brush-strokes synonymous with some of his later works, *Mata Mua* by **Gauguin**, from his Polynesian period, and **Cézanne's** *Portrait of a Farmer*, in which his particular use of colour is used to build volumes, a forerunner of Cubism.

Expressionism is represented in **Galleries 35–40**, following a small display of paintings from the Fauve movement in **Gallery 34**. The Expressionist movement, a highlight of this museum, supposes the supremacy of the artist's interior vision and colour over draughtsmanship. Two highly emblematic paintings by **Grosz**, *Metropolis* and *Street Scene*, hang in **Gallery 40**.

Ground floor

The first few galleries (*41–44*) contain exceptional Experimental Avant-Garde works (1907–24) from European movements: Futurism, Orphism, Suprematism, Constructivism, Cubism and Dadaism. **Room 41** displays Cubist works by **Picasso** (*Man with a Clarinet*), **Braque** (*Woman with a Mandolin*) and **Juan Gris** (*Woman Sitting*), while *Proun 1C* by **Lissitzky** and *New York City, New York* by **Mondrian** are in Room 43.

Gallery 45 shows post-First World War European works by **Picasso** (*Harlequin with a Mirror*) and **Joan Miró** (*Catalan Peasant with a Guitar*), and a 1914 abstract composition by **Kandinsky** (*Picture with Three Spots*). In the next gallery, mainly dedicated to North American painting, are *Brown and Silver I* by **Jackson Pollock** and *Green on Maroon* by **Mark Rothko**, two examples of American Abstract Expressionism. The last two galleries (*47 and 48*) are given over to Surrealism, Figurative Tradition and Pop Art.

Carmen Thyssen-Bornemisza Collection

The more than 250 works on exhibit build on those in the original wing of the museum. Notable are 17C Dutch painting, Impressionism and Post-Impressionism, North American painting, and early Avant-Garde works, especially German.

MUSEO NACIONAL CENTRO DE ARTE REINA SOFÍA (QUEEN SOFÍA ART CENTRE)

Santa Isabel 52. ⊜Atocha. ⊙ Open Mon and Wed–Sat 10am–9pm, Sun 10am–2.30pm. ⊙ Closed 1, 6 Jan, 1, 15 May, 9 Nov, 24–25, 31 Dec. ⊚6€; 14.40€ for Paseo del Arte Card (including Museo del Prado and Museo Thyssen); no charge Sat 2.30–9pm, Sun, 18 May, 12 Oct, 6 Dec. ℘917 74 10 00. www.museoreinasofia.es.

The former Hospital de San Carlos was refurbished to house this outstanding museum of contemporary art. The extension is the work of Jean Nouvel.

Permanent collection★
Avant-Garde movements

Second floor. The 17 rooms exhibit canvases from Avant-Garde movements in Spanish painting from the late 19C to the years following the Second World War. Some rooms cover the work of a single artist: Cubist works by **Juan Gris** in Room 4, Room 6 devoted to **Picasso**. His **Guernica**★★★, commissioned for the Spanish Pavilion at the 1937 World Fair, inspired by the Fascist terror-bombing of Gernika, is renowned for its expressiveness and powerful symbolism, a stark denunciation of the atrocities of war. Room 7 shows a retrospective of **Joan Miró**, with *Snail, Woman, Flower, Star* (1934) and *Woman, Bird and Star (Tribute to Picasso)* (1970); his sculptures are in Room 16. **Dalí** is represented in Room 10, with early works (*Little Girl at the Window* – 1925), together with examples from his Surrealist period (*The Great Masturbator*).

Post-Civil War movements

Fourth floor (Rooms 18–45). Works reflect trends from the late 1940s to the present. Room 19 displays works by artists belonging to **Dau al Set** and **Pórtico**, which emerged in the wake of the Civil War. Rooms 20 to 23 cover the Abstract movement of the 1950s and the early 1960s, illustrated by Guerrero, Ràfols Casamada, Hernández Mompó and members of the **Equipo Crónica**. Informalism is represented in Rooms 27 to 29 with paintings associated with **El Paso** (Millares, Saura, Rivera, Canogar, Feito and Viola) and the **Cuenca Group**. Works by **Tàpies** are in Rooms 34 and 35. The collage series *Gravitaciones* by **Eduardo Chillida** in Rooms 42 and 43 is shown with his sculptures.

Works of the sixties by important U.S. artists (D Judd, B Nauman, B Newman, E Kelly) are in Room 41. Room 44 is dedicated to video.

✎◠ WALKING TOUR
OLD MADRID (CENTRO)★

Steep, narrow streets, small squares, 17C palaces and mansions, houses with wrought-iron balconies dating from the 19C and early 20C characterise Old Madrid, the very heart of the city. ⊙*Try to visit early, or late in the afternoon when the churches are open.*

Plaza Mayor★★

⊜*Ópera.*

The square built by Juan Gómez de Mora in 1619 is the centre of **Habsburg Madrid**. On the north side, the **Casa de la Panadería** (a former bakery, now a tourism centre) was reconstructed by Donoso in 1672. The plaza was the setting for *autos de fé*, mounted bullfights, and the proclamations of kings.

A stamp and coin market is held on Sunday mornings while at Christmas, stalls sell decorations. Shops around the square retain a yesteryear look.

Pass through the **Arco de Cuchilleros** *(pl. Mayor 9)* into the street fronted by old houses with convex façades. The **Cava de San Miguel** provides a rear view of the houses on the square. This area is crowded with small restaurants (mesones) and bars (tavernas). The **Mercado de San Miguel**, an indoor early 20C market, has an elegant iron structure.

▶ *Take Conde de Miranda. Cross plaza del Conde de Barajas and Gómez de Mora to plaza de San Justo or Puerta Cerrada, a city gate. Continue right on San Justo.*

Basílica Pontificia de San Miguel★

San Justo 4. ⊚Tirso de Molina or Ópera. ◷ Open 1 Jul–17 Sept Mon–Sat 10am–1pm, 6–9pm, public holidays 10am–1pm, 6.30–9pm; 18 Sept–30 Jun Mon–Sat 10am–2.15pm, public holidays 10am–2.15pm, 6–9.15pm. ℘915 48 40 11. www.bsmiguel.es.

The basilica by Bonavia is a rare Spanish church inspired by 18C Italian Baroque. Its convex façade, designed as an interplay of inward and outward curves, is adorned with fine statues. The interior is graceful and elegant with an oval cupola, intersecting vaulting, flowing cornices and abundant stuccowork.

▶ *Follow Puñonrostro and del Codo to plaza de la Villa.*

Plaza de la Villa★

⊚Ópera. ☞Guided tours Mon except public holidays 5pm. ⊜No charge. ℘915 88 16 36.

Buildings around the square include the **Ayuntamiento** (town hall), built by Gómez de Mora in 1617, the **Torre de los Lujanes** (Luján Tower), a rare example of 15C civil architecture, and the 16C **Casa de Cisneros**, connected to the Ayuntamiento by an arch.

Calle Mayor

⊚Ópera.

The name, literally Main Street, gives an indication of its importance. At n° 61 is the narrow house of 17C playwright **Pedro Calderón de la Barca**. The Antigua Farmacia de la Reina Madre (Queen Mother's Pharmacy) keeps a collection of chemist's jars and pots. The **Instituto Italiano de Cultura** (n°86; *www.iicmadrid.esteri.it*) occupies a 17C palace.

The Palacio Uceda opposite, from the same period, is now the military headquarters of the **Capitanía General** (Captaincy General). In front of the **Iglesia Arzobispal Castrense** (17C–18C; *℘915 47 35 24*), a monument commemorates an attack on Alfonso XIII and Victoria Eugenia in 1906. In the nearby calle de San Nicolás is the Mudéjar tower of San Nicolás de los Servita.

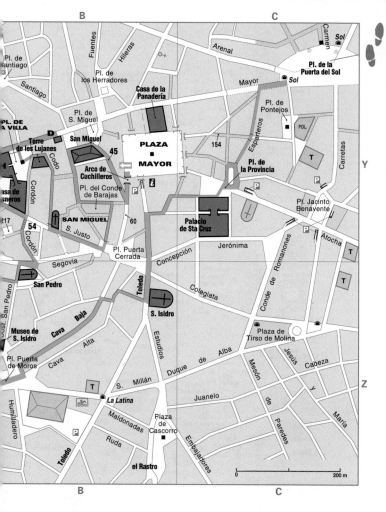

⊙ *Take del Sacramento to plazuela del Cordón; return to del Cordón; continue to Segovia.*

Across the street rises the 14C **Mudéjar tower** of the **Iglesia de San Pedro el Viejo** (Church of St Peter), a rare example of the Mudéjar style in Madrid.

⊙ *Go along del Príncipe Anglona.*

Plaza de la Paja

This was a commercial centre in the Middle Ages. The Palacio Vargas obscures the Gothic **Capilla del Obispo**, a 16C chapel. In plaza de los Carros, the Capilla de San Isidro (chapel) is part of the 17C Iglesia de San Andrés built in honour of Madrid's patron saint. The **Museo de los Orígenes** *(pl. San Andrés 2; ⊙Latina; ⊙ open Sept–Jul Tue–Fri 9.30am–8pm, Sat–Sun 10am–2pm; Aug Tue–Fri 9.30am–2.30pm, Sat–Sun 10am–2pm; ⊙closed*

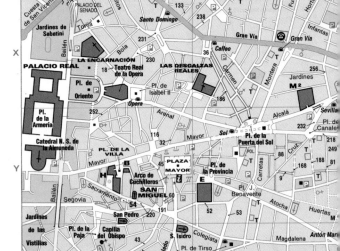

public holidays; ⊜no charge; 🖉913 66 74 15), a museum containing a miracle well and a fine Renaissance patio, is next to this complex of religious buildings. There is also an exhibit on Madrid from prehistory to the installation of the royal court in the 16C.

▸ *Cross Bailén and take the first street on the right.*

Jardines de las Vistillas (Vistillas Gardens)

🚇*La Latina.*

There is a splendid **panorama**★, especially at sundown, of the Sierra de Guadarrama, Casa de Campo, the Catedral de la Almudena and the viaduct.

SIGHTS ON MAP

MADRID STREET INDEX

Basílica de San Francisco el Grande

San Buenaventura 1. ⬡La Latina.
⏱*Open Tue–Fri 11am–12.30pm,*
4–6.30pm. ✏*3€.* ☎*913 65 38 00.*
The church's vast Neoclassical façade is by Sabatini; the circular edifice itself with six radial chapels and a large dome is by Francisco Cabezas. Walls and ceilings have 19C frescoes and paintings (except 18C in the chapels of St Anthony and St Bernardino).

The Capilla de San Bernardino holds an early Goya of St Bernardino of Siena preaching before the King of Aragón (1781). Plateresque **stalls**★ from the Monasterio de El Parral outside Segovia are in the chancel.

16C **stalls**★ in the sacristy and chapter house are from the Cartuja de El Paular, a Carthusian monastery near Segovia.

▷ *Walk along carrera de San Francisco and Cava Alta to Toledo.*

Calle de Toledo

⬡La Latina or Tirso de Molina.
This is one of the old town's liveliest streets. The **El Rastro** flea market is held here (⏱*open Sun and public holidays 9am–2pm;* ⬡*Beware pickpockets*).

▷ *Continue up Toledo for about 200m/656ft.*

Real Colegiata de San Isidro

Toledo 37. ⬡La Latina or Tirso de Molina.
⏱ *Open daily 7.30am–1.30pm, 6–9pm.*
✏*No charge.* ☎*914 20 17 82.*
Formerly the church of the Imperial College of the Company of Jesus (1622), it was the cathedral of Madrid from 1885 until 1993. It contains the relics of Madrid's patron saint, San Isidro.

▷ *Head N on Toledo then continue NE and along Esparteros. Turn right at Mayor then left.*

Plaza de la Puerta del Sol

⬡Gran Vía or Callao.
On the best-known square in Madrid, a small monument displays Madrid's coat of arms, next to an equestrian statue

of Charles III. The clock on the former post office (now the Madrid regional administration) chimes at New Year's. In nearby traditional shops with their colourful wood fronts customers can find fans and mantillas and delicacies.

▷ *Walk E through Plaza de la Puerta del Sol, then onto Alcalá.*

Real Academia de Bellas Artes de San Fernando★ (San Fernando Royal Fine Arts Academy)

Alcalá 13. ⬡Sevilla. ⏱ *Open Tue–Fri 9am–7pm, Sat 9am–2.30pm, 4–7pm, Sun–Mon and public holidays 9am–2.30pm.* ⏱ *Closed 1, 6 Jan, 1, 30 May, 24–25, 31 Dec.* ✏*3€, no charge Wed, 18 May, 12 Oct, 6 Dec.* ☎*915 24 08 64.*
The gallery has a valuable collection of 16C–20C paintings. Spanish paintings from the Golden Age include works by Ribera, Zurbarán, Murillo, Alonso Cano *(Christ Crucified)* and Velázquez. The 18C is also present with works by artists with Bourbon connections (Van Loo, Mengs, Giaquinto, Tiepolo and Bayeu) and above all Goya, including his *Self-Portrait* and studio paintings.

Museo Municipal

Fuencarral 78. ⬡Tribunal.
⏱ *Open Sept–Jul Tue–Fri 9.30am–8pm, Sat–Sun 10am–2pm; Aug Tue–Sun 9.30am–2.30pm.* ⏱ *Closed public holidays.* ✏*No charge.* ☎*917 01 18 63.*
This museum in the former city hospice, an 18C building with superb **portal**★★, retraces the history of the city (⬡*the museum is undergoing a major restoration and only a small section is viewable till the work is complete*).

BOURBON MADRID★★
Plaza de Cibeles★

⬡Banco de España.
In the square is the 18C fountain of Cybele, goddess of fertility, emblematic of Madrid. Many an artist has been inspired to paint the perspectives opening from the square and the impressive buildings around, such as the **Banco de España** (1891), the

Plaza de Cibeles and Palacio de Communicaciones at night

F. Vidal/MICHELIN

18C **Palacio de Buenavista** (Ministry of Defence), the late-19C **Palacio de Linares**, now the home of the Casa de América *(pas. de Recoletos 2; guided tours Sept–Jul Sat–Sun 11am, noon, 1pm; closed 10–11 Oct; 7€; 915 95 48 00; www.casamerica.es)*, and the **Palacio de Comunicaciones** (Post and Telegraph Office, 1919).

Paseo del Prado★

This tree-lined avenue runs from plaza de Cibeles to plaza del Emperador Carlos V, past the Ministerio de la Marina and Museo Naval *(see Sights – Museo Naval)*, the **plaza de la Lealtad** with an obelisk dedicated to the heroes of the 2 May, the Neoclassical **Bolsa** (Stock Exchange) and the emblematic **Hotel Ritz** *(www.ritzmadrid.com)*.

Plaza de Canóvas del Castillo
Banco de España.

This square, with its splendid Fuente de Neptuno (Neptune Fountain), is overlooked by the Neoclassical **Palacio de Villahermosa** housing the **Museo Thyssen-Bornemisza**★★★ *(see Museo Thyssen-Bornemisza)* and the Hotel Palace.

Continuing south, along the left-hand side of the Paseo del Prado are the Prado Museum and the **Real Jardín Botánico** *(Royal Botanical Gardens; open daily Nov–Feb 10am–6pm; Mar and Oct until 7pm; Apr and Jun–Sept until 8pm; May until 9pm; closed 1 Jan, 25 Dec; 2€; 914 20 30 17; www.rjb.csic.es)*, both the work of Juan de Villanueva.

Paseo del Prado

With the 18C drawing to a close, Charles III wanted to develop a public area which would be worthy of Madrid's position as capital of Spain and called upon the court's best architects for his project. In an area outside of the city at the time, Hermosilla, Ventura Rodríguez, Sabatini and Villanueva designed, drained, embellished and built a curved avenue with two large fountains, Cybele and Neptune, at each end, and a third, Apollo, in the centre. To complete the project, the **Botanical Gardens**, **Natural History Museum** (now the Museo del Prado) and the **Observatory**, were also built. The result was a perfect combination of the functional and the ornate dedicated to science and the arts. Since the 16C, the paseo del Prado has been a favourite place for Madrileños to meet and to relax. Today, the avenue retains its dignified air, and provides locals and visitors alike with an opportunity to pass judgement on the vision and imagination of Charles III.

Museo del Prado★★★
♿See Museums .
The Neoclassical building of one of the world's great art museums was built in the reign of Charles III, originally intended for the Institute of Natural Sciences.

Plaza del Emperador Carlos V
⊛Atocha Renfe.
The glass and wrought-iron façade of **Atocha railway station** dominates this square. Enter to view the tropical patio garden, and to glimpse the AVE high-speed train.
The former **Hospital de San Carlos**, opposite, houses the **Museo Nacional Centro de Arte Reina Sofía★** (*♿see Museums*).

▷ *Return towards the Jardín Botánico; walk up cuesta de Claudio Moyano with its second-hand booksellers.*

SIGHTS
Parque del Buen Retiro★★ (Retiro Park)
🕐Open daily Oct–Apr 7am–10pm; May–Sept 7am–midnight. ☏915 58 87 90.
The Retiro is close to the heart of every Madrileño, 130ha/321 acres of greenery with dense clumps of trees, formal flowerbeds and fountains, temples, colonnades and statues.
Beside the lake (Estanque), where boats may be hired, is the imposing **Monumento a Alfonso XII**. Near the graceful **Palacio de Cristal★** (*⊛Ibiza; 🕐open May–Sept Mon–Sat 11am–8pm, Sun and public holidays 11am–6pm; Oct–Apr Mon–Sat 10am–6pm, Sun and public holidays 10am–4pm; 🕐closed 1, 6 Jan, 1, 15 May, 24–25, 31 Dec; ☏915 74 66 14*), in which exhibitions are held, are a pool and a grotto.

Puerta de Alcalá★ (Alcalá Arch)
Pl. de la Independencia. ⊛Retiro.
The arch at the centre of plaza de la Independencia was built by Sabatini between 1769 and 1778 to celebrate the triumphant entry of Charles III into Madrid. The perspective is particularly grand at night, taking in plaza de Cibeles, calle de Alcalá and the Gran Vía.

👥 Museo del Ferrocarril (Railway Museum)
Pas. de las Delicias 61. ⊛Delicias. 🕐Open Sept–Jul Tue–Sun 10am–3pm. 🕐Closed 1, 6 Jan, 1 May, 25 Dec. ⊛4.50€; child 3€. ☏902 22 88 22. www.museodelferrocarril.org.
Not far from Atcocha railway station, the wrought-iron and glass Delicias station, built in 1880, has a collection of steam engines and a delightful restaurant car for snacks.

AROUND THE ROYAL PALACE★★
Plaza de la Armería
Along the vast arcaded square (south side) is the incomplete **Catedral de la Almudena** (*⊛Ópera; 🕐 open daily 9am–8.30pm; ⊛no charge; ☏915 42 22 00*), a cathedral begun in 1879. The neo-Baroque façade harmonises with the palace. The view toward the west extends over the Casa de Campo and the Campo del Moro gardens sloping down to the Manzanares river.

Palacio Real★★ (Royal Palace)
Bailén. ⊛Ópera. 🕐 Open Oct–Mar Mon–Sat 9.30am–5pm, Sun and public holidays 9am–2pm; Apr–Sept Mon–Sat 9am–6pm, Sun and public holidays 9am–3pm; changing of the guard Wed 11am–2pm. 🕐 Closed 1, 6 Jan, 1, 15 May, 12 Oct, 9 Nov, 24–25, 31 Dec and during State receptions. ⊛10€ (11€ with art gallery; 2€ art gallery; 3.40€ armoury); no charge Wed (for EU citizens) and 18 May. ☏914 54 88 00. www.patrimonionacional.es.
The best view of the palace is from Paseo de Extremadura and from the gardens of the **Campo del Moro★** (*🕐open Oct–Mar Mon–Sat 10am–6pm, Sun and public holidays 9am–6pm; Apr–Sept Mon–Sat 10am–8pm, Sun and public holidays 9am–8pm*). This imposing edific,e built by the Bourbons following a fire

at the Habsburg Alcázar, was the royal residence until 1931.

The palace is a quadrilateral made of Guadarrama granite and white stone, 140m/459ft on the sides, on a high bossaged base. The upper register, in which Ionic columns and Doric pilasters alternate, is crowned by a white limestone balustrade.

The north front gives onto the **Jardines de Sabatini**, the west the **Campo del Moro**. **Plaza de la Armería** stands to the south between the west and east wings of the palace. The east façade gives onto **plaza de Oriente**.

Palacio★ (Palace)

A monumental staircase with a ceiling painted by Giaquinto leads to the Salón de Alabarderos (Halberdier Room), with a ceiling painted by Tiepolo.

This leads to the **Salón de Columnas** (Column Room) where royal celebrations and banquets are held. The **Salón del Trono**★ (Throne Room) retains decoration from the period of Charles III and is resplendent with crimson velvet hangings and a magnificent ceiling by Tiepolo (1764) symbolising *The Greatness of the Spanish Monarchy*.

The consoles, mirrors and gilded bronze lions are of Italian design. The following three rooms were the king's quarters, occupied by Charles III in 1764. The Saleta Gasparini, the king's dining room, retains a ceiling painted by Mengs.

The Gasparini antechamber also has a ceiling by Mengs, and Goya portraits of Charles IV and María Luisa of Parma. The **Cámara Gasparini** is covered in pure Rococo decoration.

The Salón de Carlos III was the king's bedroom. The décor is from the period of Ferdinand VII. The **Sala de Porcelana** is, along with its namesake in Aranjuez Palace, the masterpiece of the Buen Retiro Porcelain Factory. Official banquets are held in the Alfonso XII **Comedor de Gala** or Banqueting Hall (for 145 guests), adorned with 16C Brussels tapestries. The two music rooms contain instruments including several made by **Stradivarius**★. In the chapel are frescoes by Corrado Giaquinto and

paintings by Mengs *(Annunciation)* and Bayeu *(St Michael the Archangel)*.

Real Farmacia (Royal Pharmacy)

Several rooms display 18C–20C jars, including a fine 18C Talavera glass jar.

Real Armería★★ (Royal Armoury)

The collection of arms and armour is outstanding. Key pieces include Charles V's suit of armour and armour belonging to Philip II and Philip III. A vaulted hall in the basement contains an excellent collection of Bourbon shotguns.

Plaza de Oriente

This attractive square between the east façade of the Palacio Real and the Teatro Real is pleasant for a stroll. The magnificent equestrian statue of Philip IV is the work of Pietro Tacca (17C).

Teatro Real

Pl. de Oriente. 🚇*Ópera.* 🎧*Guided tours Mon–Fri 10.30am–1pm, Sat–Sun and public holidays 11am–1.30pm.* 🕐 *Closed 1 Jan, 24–25, 31 Dec.* 🎫*4€.* 🖉*915 16 06 96. www.teatro-real.com.* This hexagonal Neoclassical building was created as an opera house in 1850 for Isabel II. It has two façades.

Monasterio de las Descalzas Reales★★

Pl. de las Descalzas. 🚇*Ópera.* 🎧*Guided tours (45min) Tue–Thu and Sat 10.30am–12.45pm, 4–5.45pm, Fri 10.30am–12.45pm, Sun 11am–1.45pm.* 🕐 *Closed 1, 6 Jan, Wed–Sat during Holy Week, 1, 15 May, 9 Nov, 24–25, 31 Dec.* 🎫*5€ (combined with Monasterio de la Encarnación: 6€); no charge Wed (for EU citizens) and 18 May.* 🖉*914 54 88 00. www.patrimonionacional.es.* Joanna of Austria, daughter of Emperor Charles V, founded the convent of Poor Clares in the palace where she was born. It served as a retreat for nobles.

The magnificent grand **staircase**★ is totally decorated with frescoes. In a former dormitory is an extraordinary collection of **tapestries**★★ depicting the Triumph of the Church, woven in Brussels in the 17C to cartoons by Rubens. The **33 small chapels** are sumptuously decorated; outstanding is that of the Virgin of Guadalupe. Convent treasures include portraits of the royal family by Rubens, Sánchez Coello and others.

Real Monasterio de la Encarnación★ (Royal Convent of the Incarnation)

Pl. de la Encarnación 1. ⓜÓpera. *Guided tours (45min) Tue–Thu and Sat 10.30am–12.45pm, 4–5.45pm, Fri 10.30am–12.45pm, Sun 11am–1.45pm.* *🕐 Closed 1, 6 Jan, Wed–Sat during Holy Week, 1, 15 May, 27 Jul, 9 Nov, 24–25, 31 Dec. ⓢ3.60€ (combined with Monasterio de las Descalzas: 6€); no charge Wed (for EU citizens) and 18 May. 𝄞914 54 88 00. www. patrimonionacional.es.*

The convent, on a delightful square near the former Alcázar, was founded in 1611 by Margaret of Austria. The collection of paintings from the 17C Madrid School is particularly rich and includes the interesting *Exchange of Princesses on Pheasant Island* in 1615 by Van der Meulen. There is a polychrome sculpture of *Christ at the Column* by Gregorio Hernández on the first floor.

The **Relicario**★, with ceiling painted by Vicencio Carducci, holds 1 500 relics. The church with quasi-Herreran portal was reconstructed in the 18C after the Alcázar fire.

Plaza de España

ⓜPlaza de España.

The monument to Cervantes in the middle of the city's central esplanade is overwhelmed by 1950s skyscrapers. Starting from the square is the wide **Gran Vía**, lined by shops, cinemas and hotels. Calle Princesa, popular with students, leads towards the **Ciudad Universitaria**★ (University City).

MONCLOA – CASA DE CAMPO DISTRICT
Museo Cerralbo★

Ventura Rodríguez 17. ⓜVentura Rodríguez. 🕐 Call or see website for opening hours. 𝄞915 47 36 46. http:// museocerralbo.mcu.es.

Housed in a late-19C mansion, the Museo Cerralbo displays the collection of the Marquis of Cerralbo, a patron of the arts, including Spanish paintings, furniture, fans, clocks, armour and weaponry, porcelain, and archaeological finds.

Parque del Oeste★ (Park of the West)

This delightful garden, overlooking the Manzanares, was designed at the beginning of the 20C. In the southern part stands the small 4C BC Egyptian **Temple of Debod** (*pas. del Pintor Rosales; ⓜArgüelles; 🕐 open Apr–Sept Tue–Fri 10am–2pm, 6–8pm, Sat–Sun 10am–2pm; Oct–Mar Tue–Fri 9.45am–1.45pm, 4.15–6.15pm, Sat–Sun 10am–2pm; 🕐 closed public holidays; ⓢno charge; 𝄞913 66 74 15)*, rescued from Nubia when the Aswan Dam was being built.

The **paseo del Pintor Rosales** nearby offers pavement cafés and views of Velázquez-like sunsets.

Ermita de San Antonio de la Florida★

Glorieta de la Florida 5. On the edge of the Parque del Oeste. ⓜPríncipe Pío. 🕐 Open daily Oct–May and Jul 8.30am–1pm, 5–8.30pm; Aug–Sept and Jun 8.30am–1pm, 5–6pm. 𝄞915 47 79 37.

This chapel, built in 1798 under Charles IV, and painted by Goya, contains the remains of the artist. The **frescoes**★★ on the cupola illustrate the miracle of St Anthony of Padua – but Goya used the beautiful women of 18C Madrid as models.

Casa de Campo★

This extensive park is popular with Madrileños. Attractions include a lake, a swimming pool and an ⓜ**amusement park**★. (*ctra de Extremadura; ⓜBatán;*

open from noon, call for specific hours; ⬭28.60€, child 21€; ℘902 34 50 09; www.parquedeatracciones.es).

A **teleférico** (cableway) connects to Parque del Oeste. *(pas. del Pintor Rosales–Cerro Garabita; ⬭Argüelles; ⬤open from noon, call for specific hours; ⬭5.10€ round-trip; ℘915 41 11 18; www.teleferico.com)*

The ⬭**zoo-aquarium**★★ here houses one of the largest assortments of animals anywhere in Europe *(Casa de Campo; ⬭Casa de Campo; ⬤open daily, call for specific hours; ⬭18.50€, child 15€; ℘902 34 50 14; www.zoomadrid.com).*

Museo de América★
(Museum of the Americas)

Av. Reyes Católicos 6. ⬭Moncloa.
⬤ *Open Tue–Sat 9.30am–3pm, Sun and public holidays 10am–3pm.*
⬤ *Closed 1 Jan, 1 May, 24–25, 31 Dec.*
⬭*3€; no charge Sun, 18 Apr, 18 May, 12 Oct, 6 Dec. ℘915 49 26 41. http:// museodeamerica.mcu.es.*

This archaeological and ethnological museum focuses on ties between Europe and the Americas. Over 2 500 objects are accompanied by explanations, maps, models, reconstructions of dwellings, etc. Outstanding items are the Stele of Madrid (Mayan), the powerful **Treasure of Los Quimbayas**★ (Colombian), the *Tudela Manuscript* (1553) and the prized Mayan **Tro Cortesiano Manuscript**★★★, one of only four remaining.

Faro de Moncloa
(Moncloa Beacon)

Av. de los Reyes Católicos. ⬭Moncloa.
⊶ *Closed for renovation until early 2010. ℘915 44 81 04.*
From its 76m/250ft high **observatory**★★, there is a wonderful view of Madrid and its surrounding area.

Museo Sorolla★

General Martínez Campos 37.
⬭*Gregorio Marañón or Iglesia.*
⬤ *Open Tue–Sat 9.30am–8pm, Sun and public holidays 10am–3pm.*
⬤ *Closed 1 Jan, 1 May, 24–25, 31*
Dec. ⬭3€. ℘913 10 15 84. http:// museosorolla.mcu.es.

The Madrid home of Joaquín Sorolla (1863–1923), the great Valencian Luminista painter, includes his studio and some of his works.

Museo del Traje
(Costume Museum)

Av. Juan Herrera 2. ⬭Moncloa. ♿
⬤ *Open Tue–Sat 9.30am–7pm, Sun and public holidays 10am–3pm.* ⬤ *Closed 1, 6 Jan, 1 May, 9 Sept, 24–25, 31 Dec.*
⬭*3€, no charge Sat from 2.30pm, Sun, 18 Apr, 18 May, 12 Oct, 6 Dec. ℘915 50 47 00. http://museodeltraje.mcu.es.*

This interesting museum covers clothing from before the 18C through the 20C, and ends with a re-creation of the world of the fashion runway. The designs of couturiers Mariano Fortuny and Balenciaga are featured along with everyday wear.

SALAMANCA – RETIRO
Museo Arqueológico Nacional★★
(Archaeological Museum)

Serrano 13. ⬭Serrano. ⬤ *Open Tue–Sat 9.30am–8pm, Sun and public holidays 9.30am–3pm.* ⬤ *Closed 1, 6 Jan, 1 May, 12 Oct, 9 Nov, 24–25, 31 Dec.*
⬭*No charge. ℘915 77 79 12. http:// man.mcu.es.*

Sharing a building with the **Biblioteca Nacional** *(National Library; pas. de Recoletos 20–22; ⬭Serrano; ⬤open Tue–Sat 10am–9pm, Sun and public holidays 10am–2pm; ⬭no charge; ℘915 80 78 00; www.bne.es)*, this is the best of its type in Spain *(⬤please be advised that it is undergoing renovation and works and a limited number of rooms will be open).*

Prehistoric, Egyptian and Greek Art★

Galleries 1–18.
In the garden is a reproduction of the **Cuevas de Altamira** and their paintings of bison. Galleries are devoted to the Bronze Age and Iron Age (warlike cultures of the northeast with outstanding gold- and silversmithing). Note the splendid bronze Costix **bulls**★

of the Megalithic culture (Talayots) of the Balearic Islands. The gallery dedicated to **Ancient Egypt** displays funerary objects. Classical Athens is also represented by magnificent **Greek vases**★.

Iberian and Roman Antiquities★★
Galleries 19–26.
Exhibits in the Iberian galleries illustrate the origin of local techniques and the influence of the Phoenicians, Greeks and Carthaginians. The second gallery shows sculpture at a peak of artistic expression: the **Dama de Elche**★★★ (Lady of Elche) is an outstanding stone bust, with a sumptuous headdress and corsage. In the same gallery is the **Dama de Baza**★★, a realistic goddess figure of the 4C BC. Other galleries illustrate Spain's adoption of Roman techniques in sculpture, mosaics and ceramics and the incorporation of ideas from Byzantium.

Medieval Decorative Art★
Galleries 27–35.
In this section are the magnificent **votive crowns of Guarrazar**★★ dating from the Visigothic period, made of embossed gold plaques, mixing Germanic and Byzantine techniques.
This section is also devoted to Muslim Spain. Gallery 31 shows the Romanesque portal from the Monasterio de San Pedro de Arlanza (12C) and treasures from San Isidoro de León, notably the magnificent 11C ivory **processional cross**★★ of Don Fernando and Doña Sancha. Rooms 32 and 33 display Romanesque and Gothic art, including engravings, grilles and capitals. Romanesque tombs and capitals, and Gothic sculpture in subsequent galleries, continue to show deep Moorish influence.
Gallery 35 is a reconstruction of a Mudéjar interior, with a magnificent **artesonado**★★ ceiling.

16–19C Art
Galleries 37–38.
Porcelain, furniture, jewels and arms are on display from the Kingdom of the

Austrias (1516–1700). North of the Museo Arqueológico are the **Jardines del Descubrimiento** (Discovery Gardens), with monuments to the discovery of the New World. Directly below is Madrid's **Centro Cultural** (cultural centre).

Museo Lázaro Galdiano★★
Serrano 122. ⓜRepública Argentina.
🕐 *Open Wed–Mon 10am–4.30pm.*
🕐 *Closed public holidays.* ⊚*4€.*
☎*915 61 60 84. www.flg.es.*
This mansion houses **collections**★★ of editor and art lover José Lázaro Galdiano (1862-1947). On the **lower level**, are samples of outstanding paintings by the Master of Perea, Mengs, Zurbarán and Sánchez Coello.
The **main floor** – which retains ceilings painted by Villamil and some lovely items of furniture – is entirely devoted to 15C–19C Spanish Art with magnificent Gothic and Renaissance panels. On the **second floor** are works of the **Flemish School** and Italian works.
The **third floor** houses decorative arts (some 4 000 items): **ivories and enamel**★★★, ceramics, numismatics, arms and fabric.

Museo Nacional de Artes Decorativas
Moltabán 12. ⓜRetiro. 🕐 *Open Tue–Sat 9.30am–3pm, Sun and public holidays 10am–3pm.* 🕐 *Closed 1 Jan, 1 May, 24–25, 31 Dec.* ⊚*3€, no charge Sun, Thu afternoon, 18 Apr, 18 May, 12 Oct, 6 Dec.* ☎*915 32 64 99. http://mnartesdecorativas.mcu.es.*
This museum in a 19C mansion contains a splendid collection of furniture and decorative objects.

Museo Naval
Pas. del Prado 5. ⓜBanco de España.
🕐 *Open Sept–Jul Tue–Sun 10am–2pm.*
🕐 *Closed public holidays.* ⊚*No charge.*
☎*915 23 87 89. www.armada.mde.es.*
On display are ship **models**★, nautical instruments, weapons, and paintings of naval battles. The **map of Juan de la Cosa**★★ (1500) is the first to show the American continent.

Plaza Monumental de las Ventas★ (Bullring)

Alcalá 237. ⊕*Ventas.* ☞*Guided tours (40min) Tue–Sun 10am–2pm.* ℘*915 56 92 37.* ✆*7€. www.las-ventas.com.*
Just to the east of Salamanca is Spain's largest bullring (built 1931), with a capacity of 22 300 spectators. Its **Museo Taurino** (Bullfighting Museum) honours great bullfighters.

Museo de la Ciudad (City Museum)

Príncipe de Vergara 140. ⊕*Cruz del Rayo.* ◷ *Open Tue–Fri 10am–2pm, 4–7pm, Sat–Sun 10am–2pm.* ✆*No charge.* ℘*915 88 65 99.*
Just north of Salamanca, this museum covers Madrid's history from before recorded time. It includes superb **models**★ of neighbourhoods and emblematic buildings.

Faunia★

Av. de las Comunidades 28. 5km/3mi E of Parque El Retiro. ⊕*Sierra de Guadalupe.* ◷ *Open from 10am, call to check specific hours.* ✆*24.70€; child 19.10€.* ℘*913 01 62 35. www.faunia.es.*
This nature-themed park re-creates the planet's ecosystems on a large site of 140 000sq m/167 300sq yd, including some 3 500 small- and medium-sized animals and birds, and over 70 000 trees and plants.

PARQUE WARNER MADRID★

San Martín de la Vega. 25km/15.5mi SE of Madrid. ◷ *Check seasonal schedule.* ✆*35€; child 26.50€; parking 7€ per day.* ℘*902 02 41 00. www.parquewarner.com.*
This park is a great culture-free family-oriented getaway, with assorted bars, restaurants and shops. Area include Hollywood Boulevard, Movie World Studios, DC Super Heroes World, Old West Territory and Cartoon Village, each with appropriately themed rides and activities.

PALACIO REAL DE EL PARDO★

Manuel Alonso, El Pardo. 17km/10.5mi NW of Madrid. ☞*Guided tours (35min) Oct–Mar Tue–Sat 10.30am–4.45pm, Sun and public holidays 10am–1.30pm; Apr–Sept Tue–Sat 10.30am–5.45pm, Sun and public holidays 9.30am– 1.30pm.* ◷ *Closed 1, 6 Jan, 1, 15 May, 9 Nov, 24–25, 31 Dec and for State receptions.* ✆*4€; no charge Wed (for EU citizens) and 18 May.* ℘*913 76 15 00. www.patrimonionacional.es.*
The palace was built by Philip III (1598– 1621) on the site of Philip II's (1556–98) palace which had been destroyed in a fire in 1604. Franco lived here for 35 years; today, it is used by Heads of State on official visits. Decorations include more than 200 **tapestries**★; the majority are 18C from the Real Fábrica de Tápices (Royal Tapestry Factory) in Madrid based on cartoons by Goya, Bayeu, González Ruiz and Van Loo.

ADDRESSES

⌂ STAY

⊖ **Hostal Gonzalo** – *Cervantes 34 (Centro).* ⊕*Antón Martín.* ℘*914 29 27 14. www.hostalgonzalo.com. 15 rooms.*
Located next to the triangle of the Prado, Reina Sofía and Thyssen-Bornemisza museums, this excellent hostel has good soundproofed rooms for a night's rest before exploring the city.

⊖ **Hotel Centro Sol** – *San Jerónimo 5 (Centro).* ⊕*Sol.* ℘*915 22 15 82. www.hostalcentrosol.com. 35 rooms.*
A hotel very close to the Puerta del Sol occupying the second and fourth floors of a building somewhat lacking in charm. However, its rooms, all with TVs and good bathrooms, are very reasonably priced and have been recently refurbished.

⊖⊖ **Hotel Adriano** – *Cruz 26 (Centro).* ⊕*Sol.* ℘*915 21 13 39. www.hostaladriano. com. 22 rooms.* A good central choice in this price range, notable for its well-equipped rooms and original décor, with personalised rooms, especially no. 114, dedicated to soprano Maria Callas.

⊜⊜ **Hotel Mora** – *Pas. del Prado 32 (Retiro).* ⊕*Atocha.* ☏*914 20 15 69. www.hotelmora.com. 62 rooms.* The Mora enjoys a superb location in an impressive building opposite the botanical gardens on paseo del Prado. Comfortable, recently renovated rooms and reasonable rates.

⊜⊜ **Hotel Plaza Mayor** – *Atocha 2 (Centro).* ⊕*Sol.* ☏*913 60 06 06. www.h-plazamayor.com. 34 rooms.* ⊡*7.50€.* An unpretentious hotel, but with a great location right by the city's main square. Behind the modern brick façade, the rooms are small, functional but attractively decorated.

⊜⊜⊟ **Hotel Carlos V** – *Maestro Vitoria 5 (Centro).* ⊕*Callao.* ☏*915 31 41 00. www.hotelcarlosv.com. 67 rooms.* A good central option in a pedestrianised street away from the noise of the city. Although small, the English-style rooms are pleasant and well appointed. An eclectic cafeteria on the first floor.

⊜⊜⊟ **Hotel Inglés** – *Echegaray 8 (Chueca).* ⊕*Sevilla.* ☏*914 29 65 51. www.hotel-ingles.net. 58 rooms.* ⊡*5.35€.* There's no doubting the character of this hotel built in 1853. A good central and moderately priced option in the Chueca district, an area renowned for its lively nightlife. Clean, comfortable rooms.

⊜⊜⊟⊟ **Hotel Casón del Tormes** – *Río 7 (Centro).* ⊕*Plaza de España.* ☏*915 41 97 46. www.hotelcasondeltormes.com. 63 rooms.* ⊡*9€.* Located in a small, quiet street in the centre of the city, just behind the Senate building. Built in the middle of the 1960s, the hotel has large, comfortable rooms which have been recently renovated.

⊜⊜⊟⊟ **Hotel Ritz** – *Pl. de la Lealtad 5 (Retiro).* ⊕*Banco de España.* ☏*917 01 67 67. www.ritz.es. 137 rooms.* ⊡*30€. Restaurant* ⊜⊜⊟⊟. A magnificent early 20C building superbly located near paseo del Prado. The hotel has all the elegance, tradition and comfort you would expect from such a famous

name, plus prices to match. The terrace-garden here is an additional delight.

⊌ EAT

⊜⊜ **La Finca de Susana** – *Arlaban 4 (Huertas).* ⊕*Sevilla.* ☏*913 69 35 57. www.lafinca-restaurant.com. Closed 24–25, 31 Dec, 1 Jan.* Centrally located with food that's good for the price, so it's always full with a with-it young crowd that doesn't mind waiting. Food is traditional, with some *nouvelle* touches. Go early, you can't reserve.

⊜⊜⊟ **La Bola** – *Bola 5 (Centro).* ⊕*Santo Domingo.* ☏*915 47 69 30. www.labola.es. Closed Sun, 24 Dec for dinner.* If you're hoping to try a traditional *cocido madrileño*, look no further than this famous tavern, which has been serving up this traditional dish in earthenware pots for over a century.

⊜⊜⊟ **Casa Lucio** – *Cava Baja 35 (La Latina).* ⊕*La Latina.* ☏*913 65 82 17. www.casalucio.es. Closed Sat lunchtime and Aug.* One of Madrid's best-known addresses frequented by politicians, actors and visitors alike. Typical Castilian décor. Famous for its *huevos estrellados* (fried eggs).

⊜⊜⊟ **La Vaca Verónica** – *Moratín 38.* ⊕*Antón Martín.* ☏*914 29 78 27. www.lavacaveronica.es. Closed Sun for dinner.* The outstanding décor re-creates a cosy, intimate space, with spider lamps, ceiling mirrors, candles and soft lighting. Posters recall Pop Art and Art Nouveau. Specialities include grilled meats and the delicious *pasta con carabineros.*

⊜⊜⊟ **Zerain** – *Quevedo 3 (Huertas).* ⊕*Antón Martín.* ☏*914 29 79 09. www.restaurante-vasco-zerain-sidreria.es. Closed Aug, Sun, Holy Week, 24–25, 31 Dec, 1 Jan.* One of the typical menus at this Basque cider bar near plaza de Santa Ana includes *tortilla de bacalao* (cod omelette) and *chuletón* (meat cutlets). Rustic, but pleasant décor. The cider here is served directly from the barrel.

⊜⊜⊟ **Teatriz** – *Hermosilla 15 (Salamanca).* ⊕*Serrano.* ☏*915 77 53 79.* Designed by Philippe Starck, this former theatre has been converted into an impressive-looking restaurant where you can choose beteween eating in the orchestra or enjoying a drink at the stage bar. The good, reasonably priced menu is based on Mediterranean dishes and Italian specialities.

⊜⊜⊜⊜ **El Amparo** – *Cjón de Puigcerdá 8 (Salamanca).* ⊕*Serrano.* ✆*914 31 64 56. www.arturocantoblanco. com. Closed Sat lunch, Sun.* Top-class restaurant with an original design including split-level dining rooms and roof skylights. Very pleasant atmosphere. Fine cuisine and polished service with prices to match.

TAPAS

Casa Labra – *Tetuán 12 (Centro).* ⊕*Sol.* ✆*915 31 00 81. www.casalabra.es.* This old tavern dating back to the middle of the 19C is a Madrid institution. It was here that Pablo Iglesias founded the Spanish Socialist Party (PSOE) in 1879. Its house speciality is fried cod *(bacalao frito)*, which you can enjoy standing up on the street or at the marble tables inside. Also a restaurant with menu.

José Luis – *Serrano 89 (Salamanca).* ⊕*Ruben Darío.* ✆*915 63 09 58. www. joseluis.es.* A Salamanca institution. In two parts, each with its distinct style, but sharing the same bar. A wide choice of superb tapas; its Spanish omelette is the most famous in the city. Tables outside in summer.

Prada a Tope – *Príncipe 11 (Huertas).* ⊕*Sevilla.* ✆*914 29 59 21. www. pradaatope.es. Closed Sun evening, Mon and fortnight in Aug.* A warm locale in the spirit of El Bierzo, a traditional part of León. Outstanding rustic décor of wood and slate, with long bar, large tables, and walls covered with photos. Great variety of local products on sale.

Taberna de Dolores – *Pl. de Jesús 4 (Huertas).* ⊕*Antón Martín.* ✆*914 33 29 43.* Tiles on the façade, a long bar and a crowd mark this as a place of character, with good draught beer, pickled anchovies and more.

Taberna de la Daniela – *General Pardiñas 21 (Salamanca).* ⊕*Goya.* ✆*915 75 23 29.* A bar with traditional decoration. *Azulejos* on the outside with vermouth on tap and a wide selection of canapés and *raciones*

inside. Specialities here include *cocido madrileño.*

Tasca la Farmacia – *Capitán Haya 19 (Tetuán).* ⊕*Cuzco. Closed Sun, 3 weeks in Aug.* ✆*915 55 81 46.* A delightful local establishment with stone arches and glassware. It is renowned for its cod *(bacalao) raciones.*

☕ CAFÉS

Café de Oriente – *Pl. de Oriente 2.* ⊕*Ópera.* ✆*915 47 15 64. www. cafedeoriente.es.* This classic institution, located in the Plaza de Oriente opposite the Royal Palace, is a delightful place for a drink at any time of day. Pleasant terrace.

Café del Círculo de Bellas Artes – *Alcalá 42.* ⊕*Banco de España or Sevilla.* ✆*913 60 54 00.* The marked 19C atmosphere of this great café with its enormous columns and large windows is in sharp contrast to its young, intellectual clientele. Outdoor terrace in summer. Highly recommended.

Café Gijón – *Pas. de Recoletos 21.* ⊕*Colón or Banco de España.* ✆*915 22 37 37. www. cafegijon.com.* This café, which has long been famous as a meeting point for writers and artists, continues the tradition to this day. Outdoor terrace in summer.

El Espejo – *Pas. de Recoletos 31.* ⊕*Colón.* ✆*913 08 23 47. www.restauranteelespejo. com.* An attractive, Modernist-style café close to the Café Gijón *(see above)*, with a charming wrought-iron and glass canopy.

🎷 NIGHTLIFE

Café Central – *Pl. del Ángel 10.* ⊕*Tirso de Molina.* ✆*913 69 41 43. www. cafecentralmadrid.com.* One of the city's main haunts for jazz lovers since the early 1980s.

Del Diego – *Reina 12.* ⊕*Gran Vía.* ✆*915 23 31 06. Closed Aug, Sun, Holy Week.* A pleasant bar serving some of the city's best cocktails.

Los Gabrieles – *Echegaray 17.* ⊕*Antón Martín.* ✆*913 69 07 57. Closed Sun evening.* Tapas by day and a bar by night. A favourite haunt for foreign students in Madrid, attracted, no doubt, by the historical chronicles on its *azulejo*-decorated panelling.

The Irish Rover – *Av. del Brasil 7.* ⊜*Santiago Bernabéu.* ℘*915 97 48 11.* *http://theirishrover.com. Closed Sun.* A pub within a pub. A section which looks as though it has come straight out of one of Joyce's novels and a tiny lounge are just two of the features of this Irish home-from-home. Daily performances and a small market on Sundays. Young clientele.

Joy Eslava – *Arenal 11.* ⊜*Sol.* ℘*913 66 37 33. www.joy-eslava.com.* This well-known club, occupying a former 19C theatre, has been attracting a colourful crowd of club-goers and famous faces for several decades. On your way home, why not pay a visit to the famous Chocolatería de San Ginés, in the street of the same name.

Libertad 8 – *Libertad 8.* ⊜*Chueca.* ℘*915 32 11 50. www.libertad8cafe.es.* A building over a century old is the setting for this atmospheric café, renowned for its poetry readings and storytellers, attracting young, bohemian audiences.

Palacio de Gaviria – *Arenal 9.* ⊜*Sol.* ℘*915 26 60 69. www.palaciogaviria. com. Open daily from 11pm.* A fascinating club which has been converted from one of Madrid's old palaces. Also famous for its ballroom dancing. Its Thursday-night *fiesta internacional* is very popular with foreigners.

🎭 ENTERTAINMENT

Madrid has over 100 cinemas, including one **Imax** cinema *(www.imaxmadrid. com)*, 20 or so theatres, numerous concert halls and one casino. The **Auditorio Nacional** (opened in 1988; *www.auditorionacional.mcu.es*) has a varied programme of classical music, the **Teatro de la Zarzuela** *(http:// teatrodelazarzuela.mcu.es)* hosts a wide range of shows including Spanish operettas *(zarzuelas)* and ballets, while the **Teatro Real** *(www.teatro-real.es)* offers a season of opera. The **Veranos de la Villa** *(Jul–Aug)* and the **Festival de Otoño** *(Oct–Nov; www.madrid.org/fo)* are two events held in the summer and autumn respectively with an interesting mix of cultural performances.

The **Festival Internacional de Jazz** is another event also held during Oct–Nov.

Berlín Cabaret – *Costanilla de San Pedro 11.* ℘*913 66 20 34.* ⊜*La Latina. www.berlincabaret.com.* One of Madrid's famous venues. Live acts (magicians, drag queens, etc.) and a fun atmosphere.

Café de Chinitas – *Torija 7.* ⊜*Santo Domingo.* ℘*915 47 15 01. www.chinitas. com. Closed Sun.* Very popular with tourists. Dinner shows also available.

Casa Patas – *Cañizares 10.* ⊜*Antón Martín.* ℘*913 69 04 96. www.casapatas. com. Closed Sun.* One of the best venues in which to enjoy a night of flamenco.

🛒 SHOPPING

Capas Seseña – *Cruz 23 (Huertas).* ⊜*Sevilla.* ℘*915 31 68 40. www.sesena. com.* A family firm that dates from 1901, where traditional and contemporary **capes** are crafted by hand from fine fabric. Photos show such clients as Hemingway, Picasso, Catherine Deneuve, Rudolph Valentino and Marcelo Mastroianni.

Casa Mira – *San Jerónimo 30.* ⊜*Sevilla.* ℘*914 29 67 96.* The best *turrones*, *mazapanes* (marzipan) and homemade sweets in Madrid. A family firm since 1842, its wares are of the highest quality, without preservatives or additives, cut and weighed at time of sale.

La Violeta – *Pl. de Canalejas 6.* ⊜*Sevilla.* ℘*915 22 55 22. Closed Aug, Sun, public holidays.* This establishment has served such luminaries as King Alfonso XIII and writers Jacinto Benavente y Valle Inclán since 1915. The bonbons and caramels are popular but the *marron glacé* and glazed violets take the cake.

Art Galleries – Look in and around Atocha, close to the Centro de Arte Reina Sofía, in the Salamanca district (near the Puerta de Alcalá) and on paseo de la Castellana, close to calle Génova.

FIESTAS

On 15 May the feast day of city patron **San Isidro**, is celebrated with, impromptu dancing, rock concerts and its famous bullfighting festival, which lasts for some six weeks.

Alcalá de Henares★

Alcalá has a historic centre★ of 16C–17C colleges and convents and spacious squares. Medieval calle Mayor is adorned with impressive gateways. The university and historic centre are a UNESCO World Heritage site.

A BIT OF HISTORY

Under the Romans the city was an important centre known as **Complutum** but the history of Alcalá is mainly linked to that of its university, founded by Cardinal Cisneros in 1498. It became famous for its language teaching and in 1517, Europe's first Polyglot Bible was published with parallel texts in Latin, Greek, Hebrew and Chaldean. The university was moved to Madrid in 1836.

Alcalá's famous citizens include **Catherine of Aragon**, daughter of the Catholic Monarchs and first wife of Henry VIII, the Renaissance architect **Bustamante**, who designed the Hospital de Tavera in Toledo, and **Miguel de Cervantes**, whose **birthplace** is open to the public (⊙ *open Tue–Sun 10.15am–1.30pm, 4–6.15pm;* ⊜ *no charge;* ℘*918 89 96 54*).

SIGHTS

Antigua Universidad or Colegio de San Ildefonso★

💬 *Guided tours (45min) 11am, noon, 1pm, 5pm, 6pm (and 4pm Oct–Apr); Sat–Sun and public holidays, every 30min 11am–2pm, 5–6.30pm (7.30pm May–Sept).* ⊙ *Closed 1 Jan, 25 Dec.* ⊜*3€ (includes Capilla de San Ildefonso).* ℘*918 85 64 87.*

The original university, on plaza de San Diego, has a beautiful **Plateresque façade**★ (1543) by Rodrigo Gil de Hontañón crowned by a balustrade. The imperial escutcheon of Charles V decorates the pediment of the central section. The majestic 17C **Patio Mayor** was designed by Juan Gómez de Mora, pupil of Herrera and architect of the Plaza Mayor and ayuntamiento (town

hall) in Madrid; at the centre is a well-head with a swan motif, emblem of Cardinal Cisneros. Across the 16C Renaissance Patio de los Filósofos stands the delightful **Patio Trilingüe** (1557) where Latin, Greek and Hebrew were taught. The **Paraninfoa** (1520), formerly used for examinations and degree ceremonies, now sees the solemn opening of the university year and the awarding of the Cervantes literary prize. A gallery is in the Plateresque style, with superb Mudéjar **artesonado**★★ work.

Capilla de San Ildefonso★

Next to the university.

The nave and presbytery of this early 16C chapel are crowned with magnificent **Mudéjar artesonado** ceilings. The delicate **stucco** on the Epistle side of the church is Late Gothic, while the Evangelist side opposite is Plateresque. In the presbytery is the Carrara marble **mausoleum**★★ of Cardinal Cisneros, by Domenico Fancelli and Bartolomé Ordóñez, one of the finest examples of 16C Spanish sculpture.

Catedral Magistral

Pl. de los Santos Niños.

Built between 1497 and 1515, the Cathedral has been remodelled several times. The central portal mixes Gothic, Plateresque and Mudéjar features. The Late Gothic interior contains attractive

---

▶ **Population:** 203 645

⌖ **Michelin Map:** Michelin maps 575 and 576 K 19 – Madrid

ℹ **Info:** Plaza de los Santos Niños. ℘918 81 06 34.

◖ **Location:** Alcalá is on the edge of metropolitan Madrid. 🚃Plaza de la Estación.

🅿 **Parking:** Spots are tight in the old quarter.

👁 **Don't Miss:** The old university

🕐 **Timing:** Take half a day to see Alcalá from Madrid.

wrought-iron **grilles**. The cloisters *(calle Tercia)* house the **Museo de la Catedral** (🕐 *open Tue–Sat 9am–11.30am, 6.30–8.30pm, Sun and hols 9am–12.45pm, 6.30–9pm; ⊙1.80€; ℘918 88 09 30).*

Palacio Arzobispal
Pl. de Palacio.
In the 13C, the bishops of Toledo, lords of Alcalá, erected a palace-fortress here. The Renaissance **façade**, by Alonso de Covarrubias, once fronted a courtyard. The Baroque coat of arms was added later.
On adjoining plaza de San Bernardo, the 17C church of the **Convento de San Bernardo** is crowned by an elliptical dome. The **Museo Arqueológico de la Comunidad de Madrid** (archaeological museum) is in the 17C former **Convento de la Madre de Dios** (🕐*open Tue–Sat 11am–7pm (3pm Sun and hols); ℘91 879 66 66.*

ADDRESSES

🍴 **EAT**

⊜⊜⊜⊜ **Miguel de Cervantes** – *Imagen 12. ℘918 83 12 77. www.hostal mcervantes.com. Closed Sun for dinner.* This restaurant, behind Cervantes' birthplace in a restored town house, serves traditional cuisine in a Castilian setting. A few reasonably priced rooms are also available (⊜⊜⊜).

Aranjuez★★

Aranjuez, on the banks of the Tagus (Tajo), is an oasis in the Castilian plain, renowned for its greenery, particularly around the royal palace. The shaded walks immortalised by composers (the most famous being Joaquín Rodrigo's haunting guitar piece *Concierto de Aranjuez*) and painted by artists are popular with Madrileños at weekends.

A BIT OF HISTORY
The Aranjuez Revolt *(El motín de Aranjuez)* – In March 1808, Charles IV, his queen and the prime minister, Godoy, were at Aranjuez. They were preparing to flee (on 18 March) first to Andalucía, then to America, in the face of popular opposition to the passage transit privileges granted to Napoleon's armies.
On the night of 17 March, Godoy's mansion was attacked by followers of the heir apparent, Prince Ferdinand; Charles IV then abdicated in favour of his son, but Napoleon soon forced both royals to abdicate in his own favour (5 May). These intrigues and the presence of a French garrison in Madrid stirred the revolt of May 1808, the beginning of the War of Independence.

▶ **Population:** 52 224
⚙ **Michelin Map:** 575 and 576 L 19 – Madrid
🗒 **Info:** Plaza de San Antonio 9. ℘918 91 04 27. www.aranjuez.es.
◗ **Location:** Aranjuez is off the A 4 highway linking Madrid with Andalucía, 47km/29.2mi from both the capital and Toledo. 🚉Plaza de la Estación
◉ **Don't Miss:** The Palace and Prince's Garden.

SIGHTS
ROYAL PALACE AND GARDENS★★
The Catholic Monarchs enjoyed the original 14C palace, enlarged by Emperor Charles V. The present palace is mainly the result of an initiative by Philip II who called on the future architects of the Escorial to erect a new palace amid gardens.
In the 18C, the town became a principal royal residence and was considerably embellished. It was, however, ravaged by fire in 1727 and again in 1748, after which the present façade was built.

Ferdinand VI built the town to a grid plan; Charles III added two palace wings and Charles IV erected the delightful Labourer's Cottage.

Palacio Real

Palacio Real★

Pl. de Parejas. Guided tours, Tue–Sun Oct–Mar 10am–5.15pm; Apr–Sept 10am–6.15pm. Closed 1, 6 Jan, 1, 30 May, 5 Sept, 24–25, 31 Dec and during official ceremonies. 5€ (7€ with tour of private chambers); no charge Wed (for EU citizens) and 18 May. 918 91 07 40. www.patrimonionacional.es.

This Classical-style royal palace of brick and stone was built in the 16C and restored in the 18C. In spite of many modifications it retains considerable unity of style. The entry and façades of the wings are marked by archways and domed pavilions mark the angles. The apartments have been left as they were at the end of the 19C.

The **Salón del Trono** (Throne Room), with crimson velvet hangings and Rococo furnishings, has a ceiling painted with an allegory of monarchy – ironically it was in this room that Charles IV abdicated in 1808.

The **Salón de Porcelana**★★ (Porcelain Room) is the palace's most notable room, covered in white garlanded porcelain tiles, illustrating in relief scenes of Chinese life, exotica and children's games, all made in the Buen Retiro factory in Madrid in 1763.

In the king's apartments a music room precedes the Smoking or Arabian Room – a reproduction of the Hall of the Two Sisters in the Alhambra. A fine Mengs *Crucifixion* hangs in the bedroom, and the walls of another room are decorated with **203 small pictures** on rice paper with Oriental-style motifs. A museum of palace life in the days of Alfonso XIII includes a gymnasium, and items such as a tricycle.

Parterre and Jardín de la Isla★ (Parterre and Island Garden)

Open daily Nov–Feb 8am–6.30pm; Mar 8am–7pm; Apr–15 Jun and 16 Aug–Sept 8am–8.30pm; 16 Jun–15 Aug 8am–9.30pm; Oct 8am–7.30pm.

The **Parterre** is a formal garden laid out before the east front by the Frenchman Boutelou in 1746. The fountain of Hercules brings a mythological touch to the balanced display.

The **Jardín de la Isla** was laid out on an island in the Tajo river in the 16C. Cross the canal to reach the park and its fountains hidden among chestnut, ash and poplar trees and boxwood hedges.

Jardín del Príncipe★★ (The Prince's Garden)

Entrance in calle de la Reina.

This vast garden beside the Tajo (150ha/371 acres) has four monumental gateways by Juan de Villanueva. In 1763, Boutelou landscaped the park for the future Charles IV according to the romantic vision then in fashion. A farm, greenhouses with tropical plants and stables for exotic animals were added.

Casa del Labrador★★ (the Labourer's Cottage) – *Guided tours by prior arrangement Tue–Sun and public holidays Oct–Mar 10am–5.15pm; Apr–Sept 10am–6.15pm; closed 1, 6 Jan, 24–25, 31 Dec; 5€, no charge Wed for EU citizens; 918 91 03 05).*

The so-called cottage at the eastern end of the Jardín del Príncipe, named after the humble cottages originally on the site, was built on the whim of Charles IV in Neoclassical style with sumptuous decoration. The iron railing is topped by 20 Carrara marble busts of figures from Antiquity.

The interior is a reflection of Spanish Bourbon taste.

Casa de Marinos (the Sailors' House) – *Reina.* ⏱*Open Tue–Sun and public holidays Apr–Sept 10am–6.15pm; Oct–Mar 10am–5.15pm.* ⏱*Closed 1, 6 Jan, 2, 3 May, 24–25, 31 Dec.* ≈*3.40€; no charge Wed for EU citizens;* ✆*918 91 03 05.*

A museum beside the former landing stage exhibits **falúas reales**★★ (royal vessels) that ferried the royals and guests to the Labourer's Cottage. One, a gift to Philip V from a Venetian count, is remarkable for its ornate decoration in gilded, finely carved wood.

EXCURSION
Chinchón★

21km/13mi NE along the M 305.

Chinchón is famous for its aniseed spirit and, more importantly, the Countess of Chinchón, wife of a 17C viceroy of Peru, to whom the West owes quinine, extracted from the bark of a Peruvian tree (named chinchona in the countess' honour).

Plaza Mayor★★ – The picturesque arcaded square, dominated by its church, is surrounded by houses with wooden balconies. Bullfights are held in summer. The brick former monastery beside the square now houses a parador.

Monasterio de
El Escorial★★★

This symbolic building on the slopes of the Sierra de Guadarrama, commissioned by **Philip II** and designed by Juan de Herrera, heralded a style that combined the grandeur of a palace with the austerity of a committed monastery.

A BIT OF HISTORY

In memory of San Lorenzo – On 10 August 1557, St Lawrence's Day, Philip II defeated the French at St-Quentin. The king decided to dedicate a monastery to the saint, to serve as royal palace and pantheon.

The stupendous project – nearly 1 200 doors and 2 600 windows, 1 500 workmen – was completed in only 21 years (1563–84), which explains the exceptional unity of style.

The general designs of Juan de Toledo were followed after his death in 1567 by **Juan de Herrera**.

Fiestas

The feast day of San Lorenzo (St Lawrence), the patron saint of the village and monastery, is celebrated on 10 August every year.

- ♿ **Michelin Map:** 575 or 576 K 17 – Madrid
- 🛈 **Info:** Grimaldi 4, San Lorenzo de El Escorial. ✆918 90 53 13. 🚌Calle Santa Rosa. www.san lorenzoturismo.org.
- ▶ **Location:** El Escorial is 56km/40mi NW of Madrid, at 1 065m/3 494ft.
- 🔍 **Don't Miss:** The sumptuous royal apartments.
- 🕐 **Timing:** El Escorial is a day trip from Madrid, often paired with El Valle de los Caídos (Valley of the Fallen).

In reaction to the excess ornamentation of Charles V's reign, the architects produce a sober monument with clean, majestic lines.

There is a good **view**★ of the monastery and countryside from **Silla de Felipe II** (Philip II's Seat), from where the king oversaw construction (▶*turn left after the monastery into the road marked Entrada Herrería-Golf).*

SIGHTS
Real Monasterio

Allow half a day.

Juan de Borbón y Battemberg. ⏱ *Open Tue–Sun and public holidays Oct–Mar*

Monasterio de El Escorial

©Turespaña

10am–5pm; Apr–Sept 10am–6pm.
🕐 *Closed 1, 6 Jan, 1 May, 10 Aug, 13 Sept, 24–25, 31 Dec.* 🎫*10€; no charge Wed (for EU citizens) and 18 May.* 🖉*918 90 59 02. www.patrimonionacional.es.*
It is said that the monastery's gridiron plan recalls St Lawrence's martyrdom. It measures 206m x 161m (676ft x 528ft). The austerity of its grey granite emphasises the severity of the architecture. When the king commanded an increase in height, Herrera positioned windows asymmetrically to lessen monotony.

Palacios★★
(Royal Apartments)
Juan de Borbón y Battemberg.
🔊*Guided tours with prior booking Oct–Mar Tue–Fri 4–5pm, Sat 10am–noon, 4–5pm; Apr–Sept Tue–Thu 4–5pm, Fri 4–6pm, Sat 10am–noon, 5–6pm.* 🕐 *Closed 1, 6 Jan, 1 May, 10 Aug, 13 Sept, 24–25, 31 Dec.* 🎫*3.60€; no charge Wed (for EU citizens) and 18 May.* 🖉*918 90 59 02.*
While the Habsburgs remained on the Spanish throne, El Escorial was a place of splendour: the king resided in apartments encircling the church apse. The Bourbons preferred other palaces but when in residence, occupied suites on the north side of the church. The palace took on renewed glory in the 18C in the reigns of Charles III and IV.
A staircase built in the time of Charles IV goes up *(3rd floor)* to the **Palacio de los Borbones** (Bourbon Apartments), sumptuous with Pompeian ceilings and fine **tapestries**★, many from the Real Fábrica (Royal Tapestry Works) in Madrid based on cartoons by Spanish artists, notably Goya. Elsewhere are Flemish tapestries.
The large **Sala de las Batallas** (Battle Gallery) contains frescoes (1587): the Victory at Higueruela in the 15C against the Moors and on the north wall, the Victory at St-Quentin.
The restraint of the **habitaciones de Felipe II** (Philip II's apartments, *second floor*) is striking in comparison with the Bourbon rooms. Those of the Infanta Isabel Clara Eugenia comprise a suite of small rooms with dados of Talavera ceramic tiles. The king's bedroom is off the church. When he was dying of gangrene in 1598, he could contemplate the high altar from his bed.
The paintings in the apartments include a *St Christopher* by Patinir and a portrait of the king in old age by Pantoja de la Cruz. Facing the gardens and the plain, the Salón del Trono (Throne Room) is hung with 16C Brussels tapestries. The Sala de los Retratos (Portrait Gallery), which follows, holds royal portraits.

Panteones★★
(Pantheons)
Access through the Patio de los Evangelistas (Evangelists' Courtyard), with frescoes by Tibaldi and his followers.

445

A marble and jasper staircase leads down to the **Panteón de los Reyes**★★★ (Royal Pantheon) and the remains of monarchs from the time of Charles V, with the exception of Philip V, Ferdinand VI and Amadeus of Savoy.

The octagonal chapel was begun in 1617 under Philip III and completed in 1654. Facing the door is the jasper altar; on either side stand 26 marble and bronze sarcophagi in wall niches. The kings are on the left and the queens whose sons succeeded to the throne, on the right. The ornate chandelier is the work of an Italian artist.

The 19C **Panteón de los Infantes**★ (Infantes' Pantheon) includes princes and princesses and queens whose children did not rule. The sculptures are delicately carved. Conditions are such that the room is well preserved.

Salas Capitulares★ (Chapter Houses)

Two fine rooms, with ceilings painted by Italian artists with grotesques and frescoes, form a museum of 16C–17C Spanish and Italian religious painting. The first room contains canvases by El Greco and Ribera, a *St Jerome* by Titian, and *Joseph's Tunic* by Velázquez. The second room has works from the 16C Venetian School, including paintings by Tintoretto, Veronese and Titian (*Ecce Homo*). A room at the back contains works by Bosch and his followers: the imaginative *Haywain* and the satirical *Crown of Thorns (Los Improperios)*.

Basílica★★

Herrera based his final plan on Italian drawings. He introduced the **flat vault**, in the atrium. The interior owes much to St Peter's in Rome with a Greek Cross plan, a 92m/302ft high cupola above the transept crossing supported by four colossal pillars, and transept barrel vaulting. The frescoes in the nave vaulting were painted by Luca Giordano in Charles II's reign. Red marble steps lead to the sanctuary which has paintings on the vaulting of the lives of Christ and the Virgin by Cambiasso. The massive **retable**, designed by Herrera,

is 30m/98ft tall and is composed of four registers of jasper, onyx and red marble columns between which stand 15 bronze sculptures by Leone and Pompeo Leoni. The tabernacle is also by Herrera. On either side of the chancel are the royal mausoleums with funerary figures at prayer by Pompeo Leoni.

In the first chapel off the north aisle is the *Martyrdom of St Maurice* by Rómulo Cincinato, which Philip II preferred to that of El Greco (see *Nuevos Museos, below*). In the adjoining chapel is a magnificent sculpture of Christ by Benvenuto Cellini.

Patio de los Reyes (Kings' Courtyard)

One of the three Classical gateways opens onto this courtyard, named for the statues of the Kings of Judea on the west front of the church.

Biblioteca★★ (Library)

2nd floor.

The shelving, designed by Herrera, is of exotic woods; the ceiling, sumptuously painted by Tibaldi, represents the liberal arts with Philosophy and Theology at each end. There are also magnificent portraits of Charles V, Philip II and Philip III by Pantoja de la Cruz, and one of Charles II by Carreño.

Philip II furnished the library with over 10 000 books, many of them lost in a 1671 fire. It is now a public library with over 40 000 books and historic manuscripts. The spines face inward for preservation purposes.

Nuevos Museos★★ (New Museums)

Paintings in the **Museo de Pintura** are on religious themes.

First room: canvases from the 16C Venetian School (Titian, Veronese and Tintoretto). Second room: two works by Van Dyck and a small painting by Rubens. Third room: works by Miguel de Coxcie, Philip II's Court Painter. Fourth room: Rogier Van der Weyden's sober and expressive *Calvary*, flanked by an *Annunciation* by Veronese and a *Nativity* by Tintoretto. Fifth room: canvases by Ribera including *St Jerome Penitent*, the *Chrysippus* and *Aesop*, with vividly portrayed faces, and Zurbarán's *St Peter of Alcántara* and the *Presentation of the Virgin*. Last room: paintings by Alonso Cano and Luca Giordano.

On the ground floor, paintings include El Greco's **Martyrdom of St Maurice and the Theban Legionary**★, commissioned by Philip II but rejected by him. Nevertheless, it is now considered one of El Greco's greater works.

OTHER ROYAL BUILDINGS
Casita del Príncipe★
(Prince's or Lower Pavilion)

Jardín de los Moes. SE along the station road. Open Apr–Sept Sat–Sun and public holidays 10am–1pm, 4–6.30pm. Closed 1, 6 Jan, 1 May, 10 Aug, 13 Sept, 24–25, 31 Dec. 3.60€; no charge Wed (for EU citizens) and 18 May. 918 90 59 03.

Charles III commissioned Juan de Villanueva to build a lodge for the future Charles IV. Its exquisite decoration makes it a jewel of a palace in miniature. There are painted **Pompeian-style ceilings**★ by Maella and Vicente Gómez, silk hangings, canvases by Luca Giordano, chandeliers, and a beautiful mahogany and marble dining room.

Casita del Infante
(Infante's or Upper Pavilion)

Ctra de Ávila. 3km/1.8mi SW beyond the golf course. Open Apr–Sept Sat–Sun and public holidays 10am–1pm, 4–6.30pm. Closed 1, 6 Jan, 1 May, 10 Aug,13 Sept, 24–25, 31 Dec. 3.40€; no charge Wed (for EU citizens) and 18 May. 918 90 59 03.

This lodge was designed by Villanueva for the Infante Gabriel, Charles IV's younger brother. The interior is furnished in period style; the first floor was used by Prince Juan Carlos before his accession to the throne.

EXCURSIONS
Valle de los Caídos★★

16km/10mi NW on the M 600 and M 527. Open Tue–Sun Oct–Mar 10am–5.30pm; Apr–Sept 10am–6.30pm; last admission 30min before closing. Closed 1, 6 Jan, 1 May, 17 Jul, 10 Aug, 24–25, 31 Dec. 5€ (11€ combined with El Escorial); no charge Wed (for EU citizens) and 18 May. 918 90 56 11. www.patrimonionacional.es.

The Valley of the Fallen is a striking monument to the dead of both sides of the Spanish Civil War (1936–39), built as a 'national act of atonement' by Republican prisoners on the orders of Francisco Franco.

Basílica★★

The Basilica is hollowed out of the rock face and dominated by a monumental Cross. Its west door is a bronze work crowned by a *Pietà* by Juan de Ávalos. At the entrance to the vast interior is a fine wrought-iron screen with 40 statues of Spanish saints and soldiers. The 262m/859.5ft nave is lined with chapels between which are hung eight copies of 16C Brussels tapestries of the Apocalypse. Above the chapel entrances are alabaster copies of the most famous statues of the Virgin Mary in Spain. A **cupola**★, 42m/137.8ft in diameter, above the crossing, shows in mosaic the heroes, martyrs and saints of Spain approaching both Christ in Majesty and the Virgin Mary. On the altar stands a painted figure of Christ Crucified, the work of Beovides. At the foot of the altar are the remains of Falangist Party founder José Antonio Primo de Rivera and Francisco Franco. Ossuaries hold remains of 40 000 soldiers and civilians from both sides.

La Cruz★

The Cross is 125m/410ft high (150m/492ft including the base), the width 46m/151ft. The immense statues of the Evangelists around the plinth and the four cardinal virtues above are by Juan de Ávalos. There is a good **view** from the base *(access by funicular).*

447

Navarra (Navarre) and the Basque Country (País Vasco) form Spain's northeastern frontier. The latter faces the Atlantic while the former looks across the Pyrenees to France. The region of La Rioja borders the southern edge of both regions. In the Middle Ages the towns and villages of Navarra and Rioja found fame and wealth as staging points on the Camino de Santiago, leaving a rich legacy of religious buildings. Today, with the exceptions of the capitals of Pamplona and Bilbao, few people outside Spain are aware of what lies within these regions. Like the rest of northern Spain, the Basque Country and Navarra are mostly rural with none of the sun-blessed imagery or icons of the south. This is a land where isolated farms and small villages nestle in verdant valleys. Rioja is synonymous with high-quality Spanish wine; the Basque Country is famous for its food.

Highlights

1   Gazing on and visiting Bilbao's **Museo Guggenheim** (p463)

2   Eating and drinking your way around **San Sebastián** (p470)

3   Discovering the rich royal and pilgrimage legacies of **Estella** (p451)

4   Staying at the parador **Castillo de los Reyes de Navarra**, Olite (p450)

5   Watching the bull running at **Pamplona** from a safe distance! (p457)

Navarra: Pamplona and the Pyrenees

Navarra boasts nine border crossings, the most famous of which is Roncesvalles, one of the two starting points for the Spanish leg of the Camino de Santiago, and the site of a legendary 8C battle between the Basques and Charlemagne's Franks. Most visitors who choose Navarra (as opposed to those who are simply passing through) come for its capital Pamplona (Iruña).

Although it is best known for its *encierro* (Running of the Bulls), Pamplona is a rewarding visit year round, with a characterful medieval old town and fine Cathedral.

⚜ **Pamplona (Iruña)**

Navarra: around Pamplona

East of Pamplona, Estella (Lizarra) was not only a medieval royal capital but one of the main halts on the Camino de Santiago – it still is today – and it retains a rich medieval legacy. There are two fine monasteries close by (Irache and Iranzu), but it's worth journeying a little further to the Monasterio de Leyre, which not only occupies a magnificent position but possesses a very atmospheric church and crypt.

Like Estella Sangüesa (Zangoza) was once an important pilgrim's pit-stop and has all the historic religious trimmings to prove it including some remarkable church stone carvings. South of Pamplona Olite and Tudela are two more charming medieval towns. Olite castle was once the fortress of the kings of Navarra; today it is a magnificent parador. Stay here, then continue to Tudela to see its superb Cathedral.

⚜ **Estella (Lizarra)**
⚜ **Monasterio de San Salvador de Leyre**
⚜ **Olite**
⚜ **Sangüesa (Zangoza)**
⚜ **Tudela**

Costa Vasca

The Basque coastal region is known as Vizcaya (Biscay) and is famous for its capital, Bilbo, better known as Bilbao. Just as the 1992 Olympics led to the reinvention of Barcelona, in 1997 Frank Gehry's stunning Guggenheim Museum was the launch pad for the renaissance of Bilbao.

The city's splendid fine arts museum and characterful old quarter were here long before then. Queen of the Costa Vasca is Donostia, better known as San Sebastián. It boasts one of Spain's finest natural settings on a glorious sandy bay,

Museo Guggenheim

attracting Spanish holidaymakers, a fashionable international set and particularly gourmets; it is often referred to as Spain's food capital with more Michelin stars than Madrid or Barcelona, and an atmospheric old quarter chock-a-block with eating and drinking options.

- **Bilbao (Bilbo)**
- **Costa Vasca**
- **Donostia San Sebastián**
- **Fuenterrabía (Hondarribia)**

País Vasco interior

The inland Basque regions of Guizpucoa and Álava are overshadowed by the delights of the coast and overlooked by most visitors.

Those who do make the effort to seek out Vitoria (Gasteiz), the sophisticated Basque capital, are rewarded with a splendid old walled town boasting some fine museums and galleries.

North east of here the old university town of Oñati (Oñate) and nearby Santuario de Arantzazu are worth the trip for the scenic countryside settings alone.

- **Oñate (Oñati)**
- **Vitori-Gasteiz**

La Rioja

Irrigated by the Ebro river a good proportion of Rioja's 5 034sq km (1 944sq mi) is devoted to producing some of Spain's finest wines.

Many of its towns and villages were (and still are) on the Camino de Santiago and there are many tangible reminders of a rich past. The capital, Logroño, has an atmospheric old town; Haro is the place to learn more about Rioja wine

- **La Rioja**

Estella/ Lizarra★★

Navarra

The brick and rough stone façades remind us that Estella (Lizarra in Basque) was the 12C capital of the kings of Navarra and the 19C base of the Carlists. It is also an important staging post on the Way of St James.

SIGHTS

Plaza de San Martín

The once-bustling small square was originally the heart of the freemen's parish. On one side is the **former ayuntamiento** (town hall) dating from the 16C.

Palacio de los Reyes de Navarra★ (Palace of the Kings of Navarre)

San Nicolás 1. ⊙ *Open Tue–Sat 11am–1pm, 5–7pm, Sun and public holidays 11am–1.30pm.* ⊙ *Closed 1 Jan, 25 Dec.* ⊗*No charge.* ℘*948 54 60 37. www. museogustavodemaeztu.com.*

This rare 12C Romanesque civil building is punctuated by arcades and twin bays with remarkable capitals. The palace now houses a contemporary art museum.

Iglesia de San Pedro de la Rúa

San Nicolás 2. ☞*Guided tours (30min) with prior booking Jun–Sept Mon–Fri 5.30pm, Sat 7.30pm; Oct–May Mon–Fri 6.30pm, Sat 7.30pm.* ⊗*No charge for entry.* ℘*948 55 00 70.*

Estella

©Turespaña

▶ **Population:** 14 049
⚙ **Michelin Map:** 573D 23
ℹ **Info:** San Nicolás 3. ℘948 55 63 01. www. estella-lizarra.com.
◑ **Location:** Estella lies in NE Spain near the Pyrenees on the slopes of the Sierra de Andía, along the N 111 linking Pamplona and Logroño (48km/30mi SW).
◔ **Timing:** See the palace and churches, but allow time for aimless wandering in this old town.

The church stands facing the royal palace on a cliff spur formerly crowned by the city castle. It retains outstanding 12C and 13C features.

The unusual **doorway**★ at the top of a steep stairway in the north wall has an equilateral scalloped arch, Caliphate influenced. Similar portals can be seen in Navarra and in the Saintonge and Poitou regions of France. Inside note the transitional Romanesque Virgin and Child, a Gothic Christ and an unusual column of intertwined serpents in the central apse, and a Romanesque Crucified Christ in the apse on the left. The Romanesque **cloisters** lost two galleries when the nearby castle was blown up in the 16C. The skill and invention of the masons are evident in the remaining **capitals**★★; the north gallery series illustrates scenes from the lives of Christ, St Lawrence, St Andrew and St Peter, while plant and animal themes enliven the west gallery.

Calle de la Rúa (The Pilgrim Road)

Note the emblazoned Plateresque façade of the **Casa de Cultura Fray Diego de Estella** (℘ 948 55 17 47), built in 1565, at no. 7.

Iglesia del Santo Sepulcro (Church of the Holy Sepulchre)

Curtidores. Guided tours available with prior booking. 948 55 00 70.
The portal is purely Gothic. Superimposed above are the Last Supper, the three Marys at the Holy Sepulchre and Hell, and Calvary. The niches contain somewhat mannered figures of saints.

Iglesia de San Miguel

Mayor 46. Guided tours (30min) with prior booking Mon–Sat Jun–Sept 6.30pm; Oct–May 5.30pm. No charge for entry. 948 55 04 31 .
The church dominates a quarter that retains narrow streets and a medieval atmosphere. On the tympanum of the north **portal**★ is a figure of Christ surrounded by the Evangelists and mysterious personages. The covings are full of sculptures. The capitals illustrate the childhood of Christ. On the upper register of the walls are eight Statue columns of the Apostles; on the lower register, two **high reliefs**★★, accomplished and expressive, show St Michael slaying the dragon (left) and the three Marys coming from the Sepulchre. The noble bearing, the elegant drapery and the facial expressions make the carving a Romanesque masterpiece.

EXCURSIONS
Monasterio de Irache★

Irache. 3km/1.8mi SW of Estella. Open Nov–mid-Dec Feb–Mar Tue–Sun 10am–1.30pm, 4.30–6pm (Wed–Sun); Apr–Oct Tue–Fri 9am–1.30pm, 5–7pm (Wed–Fri), Sat–Sun 9am–1.30pm, 4–7pm. No charge. 948 55 44 64.
A Benedictine abbey occupied the site in the 10C. Later, this was a major pilgrimage halt and a Cistercian community before becoming a university under the Benedictines, in the 16C.

Iglesia★

This 12C–13C church's apse is purely Romanesque with rib-vaulted nave. The dome on squinches and the *coro alto* are Renaissance; the façade and most of the structures were rebuilt in the 17C.

Claustro

Brackets and capitals illustrate the lives of Christ and St Benedict.

DRIVING TOUR

TOUR THROUGH THE SIERRA DE ANDÍA AND SIERRA DE URBASA★
94km/58mi – about 3hr.

▶ *Leave Estella on NA 120 north towards the Puerto (pass) de Lizarraga. The road crosses beechwoods and rises to a pass that affords extensive views.*

Monasterio de Iranzu

9km/5.6mi N of Estella. Signposted from NA 120. Open daily May–Sept 10am–2pm, 4–8pm; Oct–Dec and Apr 10am–2pm, 4–6pm. 2.40€. 948 52 00 47. www.monasterio-iranzu.com.
The 12C Cistercian monastery, isolated in a wild **gorge**★, is now a college. It is a good example of the Cistercian transitional style from Romanesque to Gothic combining robustness and elegance.
The cloister bays, where not been given a later florid Gothic fenestration, have Romanesque blind arcades, oculi and wide relieving arches. The church, with primitive vaulting, has a flat east end decorated with three windows, symbolising the Trinity, a common Cistercian feature.

Puerto de Lizarraga Road★★

Once out of the tunnel (alt 1 090m/3 576ft) pause at the **viewpoint**★ overlooking the Ergoyena Valley before the descent through woods and pastures.

▶ *Continue to Etxarri-Aranatz; take N 240 W to Olatzi; turn left to Estella.*

Puerto de Urbasa road★★

The road climbs steeply between great boulders and clumps of trees. Beyond the pass (alt 927m/3 041ft) tall limestone cliffs add character to the landscape before the road enters the gorges of the sparkling river Urenderra.

Monasterio de San Salvador de Leyre★

Navarra

At the end of a winding road, a splendid **panorama**★★ opens up: limestone crests form majestic ramparts on whose slopes appear the ochre walls of the monastery.

A BIT OF HISTORY

By the early 11C, the Abbey of San Salvador de Leyre was the spiritual centre of Navarra, and the final resting place of kings.

In the 12C, after union with Aragón, Leyre was neglected. By the 19C it had been abandoned. In 1954, however, a Benedictine community from Silos took over. They restored the 17C and 18C conventual buildings which have now been converted into a hostelry.

IGLESIA★★

30min.

◷ *Open 1 Mar–2 Nov Mon–Fri 10.15am–2pm, 3.30–7pm, Sat–Sun 10.15am–2pm, 4–7pm; 3 Nov–28 Feb Mon–Fri 10.15am–2pm, 3.30–6pm, Sat–Sun 10.15am–2pm, 4–6.30pm.* ⌾*1.95€.*

East End

Built in the 11C. Three apses of equal height, together with the nave wall surmounted by a turret and a square tower make a delightful group. The absence of decoration, apart from several modillions, suggests the building's age.

Crypt★★

The robust 11C crypt, built to support the Romanesque church above, looks even older. The vaulting is relatively high but divided by arches with enormous voussoirs curving down onto massive plain capitals.

▶ **Population:** 573 or 576 E 26
🛈 **Info:** ℘948 88 41 50. www.monasteriodeleyre.com.
◐ **Location:** The monastery is in NE Spain near the Yesa reservoir; 50km/31mi NW of Pamplona and 16km/10mi NE of Sangüesa.

Interior★

In the 13C the Cistercians rebuilt the central aisle with a bold Gothic vault, while retaining earlier Romanesque bays with barrel vaulting, engaged pillars, and perfectly hewn stone. In the north bay a wooden chest contains the remains of the first kings of Navarra.

West Portal★

12C. The portal is called the Porta Speciosa for its decorative richness. Carvings cover every available space. On the tympanum are archaic statues – Christ (centre), the Virgin Mary and St Peter *(on His right)* and St John *(on His left)*; the covings are alive with monsters and fantastic beasts.

EXCURSIONS

Hoz de Lumbier★

14km/8.7mi W.

The Irati gorge between Lumbier and Liédana is barely 5km/3mi long and so narrow that it appears at either end as a crack in the cliff face. There is a good **view** of the gorge from a lookout point on the road (N 240).

Hoz de Arbayún★

31km/19.2mi N along the N 240 and NA 211.

The River Salazar is steeply enclosed within limestone walls. From a point north of Iso there a splendid **view**★★ to the end of the canyon where the cliff walls are clad in lush vegetation.

Olite★

Navarra

Olite, the favourite residence of the kings of Navarra in the 15C, possesses a restored fairytale castle the size of a city in itself. Olite's activities and setting attract numbers of summer visitors.

▶ **Population:** 3 607
◉ **Michelin Map:** 573 E 25
▪ **Info:** Plaza de los Teobaldos 10. ℘948 74 17 03. www.olite.es.
◐ **Location:** Olite stands at the heart of the Navarran plain, 4km/2.5mi from the A 15 motorway linking Zaragoza and Pamplona/Iruña.

SIGHTS

Castillo de los Reyes de Navarra★★ (Fortress of the Kings of Navarra)

Pl. Carlos III El Noble. ◐ *Open daily Jul–Aug and Holy Week 10am–8pm; Oct–Mar 10am–6pm; Apr–Jun and Sept 10am–7pm.* ◐ *Closed 1, 6 Jan, 25 Dec.* ◉2.80€. ℘948 74 00 35. http://guiartenavarra.com/es.

The Palacio Viejo (Old Palace) is Olite's parador. The Palacio Nuevo (New Palace) was ordered built by Charles III, the Noble, in 1406. The French origins of the prince – Count of Evreux and native of Mantes – explain the fortifications, a transition between the massive stone constructions of the 13C and the royal Gothic residences of the late 15C with galleries and courtyards. During the Peninsular War, a fire almost completely destroyed the building. Behind the 15 or so towers marking the perimeter were hanging gardens, along with inner halls and chambers decorated with *azulejos*, painted stuccowork and coloured marquetry ceilings. The most impressive rooms are the Guardarropa (Wardrobe), now housing an exhibition, the Sala de la Reina (Queen's Room) and the Galería del Rey (King's Gallery).

Iglesia de Santa María la Real

Pl. de los Teobaldos. ◐*Open Mon–Sat 9.30am–10am, 6.30–7pm, Sun and public holidays 10.30am–11am, 6–6.30pm.* ◐*Guided tours available with booking.* ℘948 74 12 73.

The church is the former chapel royal. An atrium of slender multifoil arches precedes the 14C **façade★**, a fine example of Navarra Gothic sculpture. The only figurative carving illustrates the lives of the Virgin and Christ. A painted 16C retable frames a Gothic statue of Our Lady.

Iglesia de San Pedro

El Fosal 2. ℘948 74 00 56.

The church façade below the tapering octagonal spire is somewhat disparate. The portal covings are set off by tori (large convex mouldings). Eagles on either side symbolise Gentleness and Violence.

EXCURSIONS

Ujué★

19km/11.8mi NE of Olite, along NA 5 300 (Ctra de San Martin de Unx) to San Martín de Unx, then follow the NA 5310. Ujué, overlooking the Ribera region, remains, with its winding streets, much as it was in the Middle Ages.

Iglesia de Santa María

◐*Open daily 9am–7pm.* ◐*Guided tours of church and fortress available with prior booking.* ℘948 73 92 57.

A Romanesque church was built at the end of the 11C. In the 14C, Charles II, the Bad, began a Gothic church, but the Romanesque chancel remains to this day. The central chapel contains the venerated **Santa María la Blanca**, a plated Romanesque statue honoured with a **romería** (pilgrimage) the Sunday after St Mark's Day (25 April).

Fortaleza (Fortress)

The church towers command a view which extends to Olite, the Montejurra and the Pyrenees. Of the medieval palace there remain lofty walls and a covered watch path circling the church.

Monasterio de La Oliva★

Ctra de Lerida, Carcastillo, 27km/ 16.7mi S of Ujué. ⏲ *Open Mon–Sat 9am–12.30pm, 3.30–6pm, Sun and public holidays 9am–11am, 4–6pm.* 📷*1.80€.* 📞*948 72 50 06. www.monasteriodelaoliva.eu.*
La Oliva was one of the first Cistercian monasteries built outside France.
The buildings, stripped of treasure and trappings, retain a pure Cistercian beauty.

Iglesia★★

The façade of this late 12C church is mostly unadorned, a perfect setting for the interplay of lines of the portal and two rose windows. The interior is surprisingly deep with pillars and pointed arches lined with thick polygonal ribs in austere Cistercian style.

Claustro★

The bays in these late 15C cloisters appear exceptionally light. Gothic elements were grafted onto an older construction: Ogival vaults rise from Romanesque capitals at the entry to the 13C **Sala Capitular** (chapter house).

Pamplona/ Iruña★

Navarra

The old quarter of Pamplona (Iruña in Basque) keeps its narrow medieval streets and arcaded squares. Streets around the plaza del Castillo are named for trades: Zapatería (shoemaker) and Tejería (tilemaker).

A BIT OF HISTORY

Pamplona is said to have been founded by Pompey, who gave his name to the town. The Moors briefly took over in the 8C but were repelled by Charlemagne, who demolished the walls. The townspeople in turn massacred Charlemagne's rearguard.
In the 10C Pamplona became the capital of Navarra, though it was torn for a time between proponents of Castilla and of French rule.

SIGHTS
Catedral★★

Pl. de la Catedral. ⏲*Open Mon–Fri 10am–2pm, 4–7pm, Sat 10am–2pm.* 📷*4.40€.* 📞*948 21 25 94. www.iglesianavarra.org.*
The Gothic Cathedral was built in the 14C and 15C. At the end of the 18C, Ventura Rodríguez rebuilt the west front.

▷ **Population:** 197 275
◔ **Michelin Map:** 573 D 25 (town plan)
ℹ **Info:** Eslava 1 (corner with Plaza San Francisco). 📞 848 42 04 20. www.pamplona.es.
◖ **Location:** Modern Pamplona extends south from the riverside old town. Roads lead to Roncesvalles in the Pyrenees and to Hendaye, both in France. 🚃Plaza Estación
🅿 **Parking:** Don't even try to park in the old city.

Interior★

The nave has wide arches and windows and great bare walls, typical of Navarra Gothic. In front of the finely wrought grille closing the sanctuary stands the alabaster **tomb**★★, commissioned in 1416 by Charles III, the Noble. The reclining figures and **mourners** were carved by Janin Lomme. Note the late 15C Hispano-Flemish altarpiece (south ambulatory chapel).

Epic Poems

According to legend, Roncesvalles was the site where the Basques of Navarra massacred the rearguard of Charlemagne's army in 778 as Roland was leading it back through the Pyrenees to France. The late 12C to early 13C poem of **Bernardo del Carpio** describes Bernardo as a national hero who fought alongside his Basque, Navarran and Asturian companions in arms to avenge the Frankish invasion of Spain; the 12C **Song of Roland**, the first French epic poem, on the other hand, glorifies the heroic but ultimately despairing resistance of a handful of valiant Christian knights against hordes of Saracen fanatics.

Claustro★

The 14C–15C cloisters appear delicate, with elegant Gothic arches surmounted, in some cases, by gables. Sculptured tombs and doors add interest. Off the east gallery is the Capilla Barbazán with beautiful 14C star vaulting. On the south side, the doorway of the Sala Preciosa is a masterwork of the period, its tympanum beautifully carved with scenes from the Life of the Virgin and two statues forming a fine Annunciation. In the southeast corner, a lavabo is turned into a shrine commemorating the Battle of Las Navas de Tolosa.

Museo Diocesano★

Dormitalería 3–5. ◑*Open Mon–Fri 10am–2pm, 4–7pm, Sat 10am–2pm. 4.40€.* ✆*Guided tours available with prior booking.* ✆ ☎*948 21 25 94.*

The Diocesan Museum is in the old refectory and kitchen, which date from 1330. The refectory, a lofty hall with six pointed arches, contains a rostrum decorated with an enchanting scene of a unicorn hunt. The square kitchen has a central lantern rising to 24m/79ft. Displays include a 13C *Reliquary of the Holy Sepulchre* donated by St Louis (Louis IX of France) and polychrome wood statues of the Virgin and Christ. *Follow the narrow, picturesque del Redín to the ramparts.*

Murallas (Ramparts)

La Cuenca de Pamplona zone.

A bastion, now a garden, commands a view of the Puerta de Zumalacárregui (a gate below and to the left), and a stretch of the old walls and a bend in the rivers Arga and Monte Cristóbal.

Museo de Navarra★

Santo Domingo 47. ◑ *Open Tue–Fri 10am–2pm, 5–7pm, Sat–Sun and public holidays 11am–2pm.* ◑ *Closed 1 Jan, Good Fri, 7 Jul, 25 Dec.* ☎*2€; free Sat afternoons and Sun.* ☎*948 42 64 93. www.cfnavarra.es/cultura/museo.*

This museum is on the site of the 16C Hospital de Nuestra Señora de la Misericordia. Only a Renaissance gateway and the chapel remain.

The Roman period *(basement and first floor)* is represented by funerary steles, inscriptions and **mosaic**★ pavements from 2C and 4C villas.

The main exhibit in the Hispano-Moorish section *(Room 1.8)* is an 11C ivory **casket**★ from San Salvador de Leyre sculpted in Córdoba. Romanesque **capitals**★ are from the former 12C cathedral of Pamplona, brilliantly carved with the Passion, the Resurrection and the Story of Job.

The museum also contains **Gothic wall paintings**★ from Artaíz (13C), Artajona (14C), Pamplona (14C), and elsewhere in the province. They share an unobtrusive emphasis on faces and features reminiscent of French miniaturists.

The reconstruction of the interior of the **Palacio de Oriz** is decorated with 16C monochrome panels depicting Adam and Eve and the wars of Charles V.

On the third floor are 17C–18C paintings by Luis Paret and Francisco de Goya (portrait of the *Marqués de San Adrián*).

Iglesia de San Saturnino★

Ansoleaga 21. ◑ *Open Mon–Sat 9am–12.30pm, 6–8pm, Sun and public holidays 10.15am–1.30pm, 5.45–8pm.* ☎*No charge.* ☎*948 22 11 94.*

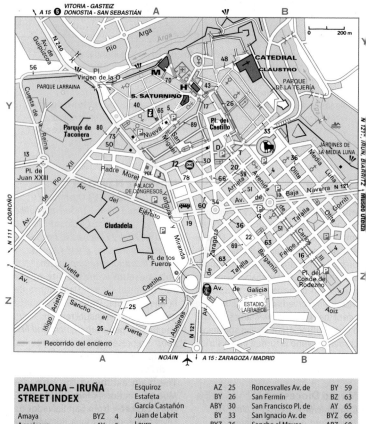

This church in a tangle of narrow streets in the old quarter mingles Romanesque brick towers, 13C Gothic **portals**★ and vaulting and later additions.

Ayuntamiento (Town Hall)

Pl. Consistorial. Open Mon–Fri 8.30am–2.30pm. No charge. 948 42 01 00.

This has a reconstructed **Baroque façade**★ (originally late 17C) with statues, balustrades and pediments.

EXCURSIONS

Museo Oteiza

Cuesta 7, Alzuza. 7 km/4.3mi E. Take the NA 150, then immediately turn left. Open Tue–Fri 10am–3pm, Sat 11am–7pm, Sun 11am–3pm. Ticket office closes 30 min before museum. 4€. 948 33 20 74. www.museooteiza.org.

Jorge Oteiza (1908–2003) was a key figures of modern Spanish abstract sculpture. The museum is beside his house.

The "Sanfermines"

The *feria* of San Fermín is celebrated with joyous ardour from 6 to 14 July each year. Visitors pour in, doubling the town's population, to see the great evening bullfights and enjoy the carefree atmosphere (described by Hemingway in *The Sun Also Rises*). The most spectacular event, and the one most prized by "Pamploneses", however, is the **encierro** or early morning *(around 8am)* running of the bulls. The beasts selected to fight in the evening are let loose with a number of steers to rush through the streets along a set route leading to the bullring (🔥 *see route on town plan).*

Santuario de San Miguel de Aralar★

45km/28mi NW. Follow the A 15, then shortly before Lecumberri, turn onto the NA 751. The NA 751 crosses the Sierra de Aralar through beech woods to this sanctuary (🕐 *open daily 10am–2pm, 4–7pm; ⇌no charge; 🖉948 37 30 13).*

The sanctuary consists of a Romanesque **church**, dated 8C, which encloses a totally independent chapel. The gilt and enamel **altar front**★★ is one of the major works of European Romanesque gold- and silverwork, attributed by some to a late 12C Limoges workshop. It consists of gilded bronze plaques adorned with enamel and mounted precious stones, arranged as an altarpiece. The outstanding multicoloured honeycomb enamelwork is adorned with arabesques and plant motifs.

Roncesvalles/Orreaga★

47km/29mi NE along the N 135.

This 12C mass of buildings served as an important hostelry for pilgrims to Santiago de Compostela. Its square funerary chapel is now the Capilla del Sancti Spiritus (Chapel of the Holy Spirit). A collegiate church is rich in relics.

Iglesia de la Real Colegiata

Única. 🕐Open daily 10am–2pm, 3.30–7pm. ⇌3.90€. ⇌Guided tours available. 🖉948 79 04 80. www.roncesvalles.es.

This Gothic collegiate church, inspired by those of the Paris region, was consecrated in 1219. Beneath the high altar canopy is the silver-plated statue of **Nuestra Señora de Roncesvalles**, created in France in the late 13C.

Sala Capitular (Chapter house)

The beautiful Gothic chamber contains the tombs of the founder, Sancho VII, the Strong (1154–1234), King of Navarra and his queen.

Museo★

Única. 🕐 Open Thu–Tue Jan 10.30am–2.30pm; Apr–Oct 10am–2pm, 3.30–7pm; Nov–Dec and Feb–Mar 10am–2pm, 3.30–5.30pm. 🕐 Closed 1, 6 Jan, 25 Dec. ⇌2.10€. 🖉948 79 04 80.

The museum contains fine pieces of ancient plate: a Mudéjar casket, a Romanesque book of the Gospel, a 14C enamelled reliquary known as "Charlemagne's chessboard", a 16C Flemish triptych, an emerald, said to have been worn by Sultan Miramamolín el Verde in his turban on the day of the Battle of Las Navas de Tolosa in 1212, and a lovely *Holy Family* by Morales.

🚗 DRIVING TOUR

TOUR THROUGH THE VALLE DEL BIDASOA★

100km/62mi N – allow one day.

The Bidasoa cuts through the lower foothills of the western Pyrenees, where villages of typical Basque houses lie amid lush meadows. The Bidasoa river is renowned for its salmon and trout.

▷ *Exit Pamplona along avenida de la Baja Navarra to the N 121A and over the Velate Pass. Follow the NA 2540.*

Elizondo, the capital of the **Valle del Baztán**, has numerous houses decorated with armorial bearings.

▸ *Return to Irutia and follow the N 121B to rejoin the N 121A, heading N towards Berrizaun.*

ADDRESSES

🏨 STAY

🍽🍽🍽🍽 **Hotel Yoldi** – *Av. de San Ignacio 11.* ☎*948 22 48 00. www. hotelyoldi.com. 50 rooms.* ⬜*10.65€.* This renovated hotel is a good choice in the centre of Pamplona. Comfortable and functional rooms and a good location near the bullring. As with everywhere in the city at fiesta time, not easy to get a room here.

🍴 EAT

🍽🍽🍽🍽 **Rodero** – *Emilio Arrieta 3.* ☎*948 22 80 35. www.restauranterodero. com. Closed Sun, Mon evening and Holy Week.* This luxury restaurant behind the

This road heads into the ancient confederation of the **Cinco Villas**, comprising **Etxalar**, **Arantza**, **Igantzi**, **Lesaka** and **Bera**, where many houses bear coats of arms. The typically Basque façades have deep eaves over balconies with delicate balustrades.

bullring is one of the best in the whole province. Family-run with high-quality service and creative, innovative cuisine with prices to match.

TAPAS

Baserri – *San Nicolás 32.* ☎*948 22 20 21. www.restaurantebaserri. com.* The Baserri is widely recognised as being one of the best place for tapas in Pamplona, as witnessed by its numerous prizes and the huge number of locals who come here. Make sure you try the sirloin with roquefort *(solomillos al roquefort).*

Sangüesa/ Zangoza★

Navarra

Situated on the Río Aragón, Sangüesa (Zangoza in Basque) still stands guard over the bridge which in the Middle Ages brought the region and the city so much prosperity. Its monumental and artistic heritage stems from its location on the Way of St James.

SIGHTS
Iglesia de Santa María la Real★
Mayor. 🕐 *Open daily mid-Mar–May and mid-Oct–early Dec 10.30am– 1.30pm; Jun–mid-Oct 10.30am– 1.30pm, 4.30–6.30pm.* 🎫*1.80€.* ☎*948 87 14 11.*
Portada Sur★★ (South Portal) – Late 12C to 13C. The portal is amazingly

▸ **Population:** 5 130
⌚ **Michelin Map:** 573 E 26
ℹ **Info:** Mayor 2. ☎*948 87 14 11. www.sanguesa.org.*
▸ **Location:** Sangüesa is situated 5km/3mi from the N 240, linking Jaca with Pamplona.

crowded with sculpture. The Master of San Juan de la Peña worked on this masterpiece.
The **statue columns**, already Gothic, derive from those at Chartres and Autun. On the **tympanum**, God the Father at the centre of a group of angel musicians receives the chosen at His right, but with his down-pointing left arm reproves sinners. The **covings** swarm with motifs; the second innermost shows the humbler trades: clog-maker, lute-maker and butcher.

Sangüesa and the Way of St James

Fear of the Moors compelled Sangüesans to live until the 10C on the Rocaforte hillside; by the 11C, however, the citizens had moved down to defend the bridge and clear a safe passage for pilgrims. Sangüesa reached its zenith at the end of the Middle Ages when prosperous citizens began to build elegant residential mansions. These contrasted with the austere Palacio del Príncipe de Viana (Palace of the Prince of Viana), residence of the kings of Navarra, now the ayuntamiento (town hall), with its façade (seen through the gateway) flanked by two imposing battlemented towers.

The main street, the former Calle Mayor which was once part of the pilgrim road, is lined with comfortable brick houses with the Classical carved wood eaves and windows with rich Gothic or Plateresque surrounds. In the second street on the right coming from the bridge can be seen the Baroque front of the Palacio de Vallesantoro, a palace protected by monumental overhangs carved with imaginary animals.

The older **upper arches**, marked by an Aragonese severity of style, show God surrounded by the symbols of the Evangelists, two angels and the disciples.

EXCURSIONS
Castillo de Javier★
Javier. 7km/4.3mi NE on the NA 541.
🕐 *Open daily Nov–Feb 10am–2pm, 3.30–6pm; Mar–Oct 10am–2pm, 3.30–7pm.* 🕐 *Closed 1 Jan, 24–25, 31 Dec.* ☞*2€.* ✆*948 88 40 00.*
St Francis Xavier, the patron saint of Navarra, born in this picturesque fortress in 1506. He founded the Society of Jesus,(with Ignatius Loyola), died in 1552 and was canonised in 1622.
The castle was in part destroyed by Cardinal Cisneros in 1516. Its **oratorio**★ (oratory) contains a 13C Christ in walnut and an unusual 15C fresco of the Dance of Death.

Sos del Rey Católico★
13km/8mi SE along the A 127.
It was here, in the **Palacio de Sada** (Sada Palace; *pl. Hispanidad; location of tourist office;* ✆*948 88 85 24*), that Ferdinand the Catholic, who was to unite Spain, was born in 1452. The town still has a medieval air.
On the **plaza Mayor** stand the imposing 16C ayuntamiento (town hall), with large carved wood overhangs, and the Lonja (Exchange) with wide arches.

Iglesia de San Esteban★
(pl. de la Iglesia; 🕐*open mid-Jun–mid-Sept Mon–Sat 10am–1pm, 3.30–6pm, Sun 10am–noon, 3.30–6pm; mid-Sept–mid–Jun Mon–Sat 10am–1pm, 3.30–5.30pm, Sun 10am–noon, 3.30–5.30pm;* ☞*no charge, 1€ crypt;* ✆*948 88 82 03).*
The Church of St Stephen is reached through a vaulted passageway. The 11C **crypt**★ is dedicated to Our Lady of Forgiveness (Virgen del Perdón). Two of the three apses are decorated with fine 14C **frescoes**. The central apse contains outstanding capitals carved with women and birds. The statue columns at the **main door** have the stiff and noble bearing of those at Sangüesa. The church, in transitional style, has a beautiful Renaissance **gallery**★. A chapel contains a 12C Romanesque Christ with eyes open.

Uncastillo
34km/21mi SE; 21km/13mi from Sos del Rey Católico.
The Romanesque **Iglesia de Santa María** *(pl. de la Villa)* has an unusual 14C tower adorned with machicolations and pinnacle turrets. The delicate carving on the **south portal**★ makes it one of the most beautiful doorways of the late Romanesque period. The church gallery with Renaissance **stalls**★ and the **cloisters**★ are 16C Plateresque.

Tudela★

Navarra

Tudela was once part of the Córdoba Caliphate, which is evident from its large Moorish quarter, the Morería. Interesting churches were built following the 12C Reconquest. Irrigation has made the surrounding Ribera region a market-gardening centre.

▸ **Population:** 33 910
🜚 **Michelin Map:** 573 F 25
▤ **Info:** Juicio 4. ℘948 84 80 58. www.tudela.es.
◐ **Location:** Tudela is on the right bank of the River Ebro in NE Spain.
🚉 Plaza Estación

SIGHTS

Catedral★

Pl. Vieja. ◐ *Open Tue–Sat 10.30am– 1.30pm, 4–7pm, Sun 10am–1.30pm.* ▧*3€ museum and cloisters.* ℘*948 40 21 61.*

The 12C–13C cathedral exemplifies the transitional Romanesque-Gothic style. The **Last Judgement Doorway**★ (Portada del Juicio Final), difficult to see, is incredibly carved with nearly 120 groups of figures.

The **interior** is Romanesque in the elevation of the nave, Gothic in its vaulting and clerestory. Gothic works include early 16C choir stalls, the high altar retable and the Byzantine-looking 13C stone reliquary statue of the White Virgin. In the **Capilla de Nuestra Señora de la Esperanza**★ (Chapel of our Lady of Hope), 15C masterpieces include the tomb of a chancellor of Navarra and the main altarpiece.

The 12C–13C **cloisters**★★ *(claustro)* are harmonious. Romanesque arches rest alternately on columns with historiated capitals with scenes from the New Testament and the lives of the saints in a style inspired by the carvings of Aragón. A door of an earlier mosque remains.

St Anne's Feast Day (26 July) is celebrated annually, as at Pamplona/Iruña, with several days of great rejoicing including *encierros* and bullfights. During Holy Week, an event known as the Descent of the Angel takes place on the picturesque **Plaza de los Fueros**, which served as a bullring in the 18C.

Iglesia de San Nicolás de Bari

La Rúa.

In the 18C façade of this church in calle Rúa is a 12C Romanesque tympanum showing God the Father holding his Son, amid symbols of the Evangelists.

EXCURSIONS

Tarazona

21km/13mi SW on the N 121.

Tarazona was once the residence of the kings of Aragón. The royal mansion, now the **Palacio Episcopal** (Episcopal Palace; *Rúa Alta de Bécquer;* ◐*open Sat–Sun and public holidays 11am–2pm, 5–8pm;* ℘*976 64 28 61*), is in a quarter with narrow streets overlooking the quays of the River Queiles.

Catedral

Juicio. ◐ *Open Mon–Sat 10am– 1.30pm, 4–7pm, Sun 10am–1.30pm.* ▧*3€.* ℘*948 40 21 61.*

The Cathedral was largely rebuilt in the 15C and 16C. Its mix of styles includes Aragón Mudéjar in the belfry tower and lantern, Renaissance in the portal and, in the **second chapel**★ as you walk left round the ambulatory, delicately carved Gothic **tombs** of the two Calvillos cardinals from Avignon.

The **Mudéjar cloisters** have bays filled with 16C Moorish plasterwork tracery.

Monasterio de Veruela★★

◐*39km/24mi S from Tudela. From Tarazona (17km/10.5mi), take the N 122 towards Zaragoza then bear right onto the Z 373.*

◐ *Open Wed–Mon Apr–Sept 10.30am– 8.30pm; Oct–Mar 10.30am–6.30pm.* ℘*976 64 90 25.*

Cistercian monks from France founded a fortified monastery in the mid-12C. The 19C Sevillian poet **Bécquer** stayed here while writing *Letters from My Cell*, in which he described the Aragón countryside much in the manner of later guidebooks!

Iglesia★★
The church, built in the transitional period between Romanesque and Gothic, has a sober façade with a single oculus, a band of blind arcades lacking a baseline, and a doorway decorated with friezes, billets and capitals.

Claustro★
The cloisters are ornate Gothic. At ground level the brackets are carved with the heads of men and beasts; above are three Plateresque galleries. In the **Sala Capitular**★ (chapter house), in pure Cistercian style, are the tombs of the first 15 abbots.

In the large interior, the vault groins are pointed over the nave, and horseshoe-shaped elsewhere. A 16C Plateresque chapel is built onto the north transept. The sacristy door opposite is in a surprising Rococo style.

Bilbao★

País Vasco

Bilbao has renewed itself with a new metro system, with distinctive glazed station entrances by Sir Norman Foster; a new footbridge and airport terminal, both by Santiago Calatrava; and a riverside development by Cesar Pelli (of London's Canary Wharf tower). But Bilbao's jewel is the Guggenheim, its spectacular modern art museum designed by Frank Gehry. Bilbao was the birthplace of writer and humanist Miguel de Unamuno (1864–1936).

A BIT OF HISTORY
The city – Founded in the early 14C, old Bilbao is on the right bank of the Nervión, under the Santuario de Begoña (Begoña Sanctuary). It was originally named *las siete calles*, or seven streets, for its layout. The modern *El Ensanche* business district (*ensanche* means "enlargement"), across the river, developed in the 19C. The wealthy residential quarter spreads around Doña Casilda Iturriza park and along Gran Vía de Don Diego López de Haro.

Industry – Industry developed in the middle of the 19C when iron mined nearby was shipped to England. Iron and steelworks were subsequently established.

- ▶ **Population:** 353 340
- ⚭ **Michelin Map:** 573 C 21 (town plan) – País Vasco (Vizcaya) – local map, see COSTA VASCA
- **Info:** Plaza del Ensanche 11. ℘944 79 57 60. www.bilbao.net.
- **Location:** Bilbao is in northeastern Spain's Basque Country. The capital of Vizcaya province is an excellent base from which to explore the Basque Country, with Vitoria-Gasteiz 69km/43mi to the S, Donostia-San Sebastián 102km/63mi to the E, and Santander 103km/64mi to the W. ▭Plaza Circular 2
- **Parking:** It can be difficult to find a space in this industrial city.
- **Don't Miss:** The Guggenheim is a must-see for Spain, not just Bilbao.
- **Timing:** Spend a few hours at the Guggenheim for starters, try out the metro and stroll the riverside.

Greater Bilbao and the ría – Since 1945 Greater Bilbao has included the towns from Bilbao itself to Getxo on

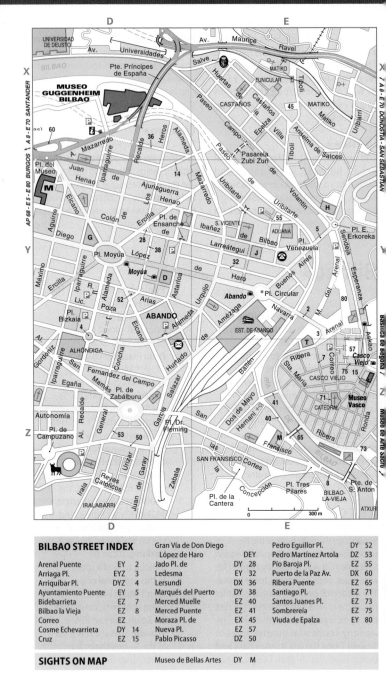

the sea. Industry is concentrated along the left bank in **Baracaldo**, **Sestao**, **Portugalete** with its **transporter bridge** built in 1893, and in Somorrostro where there is an oil refinery.

Santurtzi, a fishing port, is known for its sardines.

Algorta, a residential town on the right bank, is a contrast to heavy industry; **Deusto** is famous for its university.

MUSEO GUGGENHEIM★★★

Av. Abandoibarra 2. ◷ *Open Jul–Aug daily 10am–8pm; Sept–Jun Tue–Sun 10am–8pm.* ◷ *Closed 1 Jan, 24 (5pm), 25, 31 (5pm) Dec. Ticket office closes 30min before museum.* ☞*10.50€ (12.50€ special exhibitions), Bono Artean ticket (Guggenheim and Bellas Artes) 14€.* ℘*944 35 90 80. www.guggenheim-bilbao.es.*

This is the European showcase for the collection founded in New York by art patron Solomon R. Guggenheim (1861–1949), the youngest of the prestigious museums managed by the Guggenheim Foundation. With this stunning museum complex, inaugurated in 1997, acclaimed architect **Frank Gehry** created one of the great buildings of the late 20C, a counterpart to Frank Lloyd Wright's famous 1950 spiral housing the Guggenheim's Fifth Avenue Museum.

Emblem of the City

The museum rises from the banks of the Nervión like a complex ship with billowing sails. Formal geometry and symmetry are abandoned to free forms, creating harmony and lines flowing gracefully out of potential chaos. The composition, shimmering in titanium, demands to be seen from all angles and alters with every change of light. The south entrance, of golden limestone, opens to a soaring **central atrium** (50m/164ft high) which echoes Wright's great spiral, transformed here into a whirl of smoothly moulded shapes and natural light.

Access to the galleries is by glass-fronted lifts or vertiginous suspended walkways and staircases. The largest measures 130m/426.5ft long and 25m/82ft wide, running the length of the riverside site, culminating in a V-shaped metal and stone tower.

Collections

Drawing on the vast Guggenheim collections (more than 6 000 paintings, sculptures and works on paper), the latest Guggenheim Museum focuses on art from the 1950s to the present. Well represented are Modern masters (Picasso, Mondrian, Kandinsky) and major movements such as Abstract Expressionism (Rothko, De Kooning, Pollock), Pop art (Oldenburg, Rosenquist, Warhol), and Conceptual and Minimalist art (Carl André, Donald Judd). Contemporary artists likely to be on view include Anselm Kiefer, Francesco Clemente and Damien Hirst. The museum's own acquisitions include a vast mural by Sol LeWitt and Richard Serra's Snake, three gigantic sheets of undulating steel. Notable Spanish works are by Antoni Tàpies, Eduardo Chillida, Francesc Torres, Cristina Iglesias and Susana Solano. Space is reserved for **Picasso**'s *Guernica*, now in Madrid's Reina Sofía museum.

SIGHTS

Museo de Bellas Artes★

Pl. del Museo 2. ◷ *Open Tue–Sun 10am–8pm.* ◷ *Closed 1 Jan, 25 Dec.* ☞*5.50€; free Wed, Bono Artean ticket (Guggenheim and Bellas Artes) 14€.* ℘*944 39 60 60. www.museobilbao.com.*

The fine arts museum is in two buildings in Doña Casilda Iturriza park.

The **ancient art section**★★ *(old building, ground floor)* exhibits 12–17C Spanish paintings. Romanesque works include a 12C Crucifixion from the Catalan School. The 16C–17C Spanish Classical section has works by Morales, El Greco, Valdés Leal, Zurbarán, Ribera and Goya.

Dutch and Flemish canvases (15C–17C) include *The Usurers* by Quentin Metsys, a *Pietà* by Ambrosius Benson and a *Holy Family* by Gossaert.

The **Basque art section** *(first floor)* holds works by the great Basque painters: Regoyos, Zuloaga, Iturrino etc.

The **contemporary art section** *(new building)* displays works by artists both Spanish – Solana, Vázquez Díaz, Gargallo, Blanchard, Luis Fernández Otieza, Chillida and Tàpies – and foreign – Delaunay, Léger, Kokoschka and Bacon.

Museo Vasco (Basque Museum)

Pl. Miguel de Unamuno 4.
🕐 *Open Tue–Sat 11am–5pm, Sun 11am–2pm.* 🕐 *Closed public holidays.*
⊕*3€; free Thu.* ✆*944 15 54 23.*
www.euskal-museoa.org.
The museum, in the ex-**Colegio de San Andrés** in the old town, provides insight into traditional Basque activities (linen weaving, arts and crafts, fishing). In the centre of the Classicist cloisters stands the primitive, animal-like **idol of Mikeldi**.

Museo Diocesano de Arte Sacro (Sacred Art Museum)

Pl. de la Encarnación 9. 🕐 *Open Tue–Sat 10.30am–1.30pm, 4–7pm, Sun 10.30am–1.30pm.* 🕐 *Closed public holidays.* ⊕*2€; free Thu.* ✆*944 32 01 25. www.eleizmuseoa.com.*

This museum, in the former Convento de la Encarnación (16C), contains a Basque silverware collection and 12C–15C sculptures of the Virgin and Child.

Basílica de Begoña

Virgen de Begoña 38. 🚗*You can drive up but it's easier to take the lift from Esperanza Ascao.*
There is a fine **view of Bilbao** *from the upper terminus footbridge. From Mallona park, take the main street on the right to the sanctuary.* 🕐 *Open daily 9.30am–1.30pm, 4.30–8.30pm.* ✆*944 12 70 91.*
The church contains the venerated figure of Nuestra Señora de Begoña, patron of the province.

ADDRESSES

🛏 STAY

🍴 **Hotel Iturrienea** – *Santa María 14.* ✆*944 16 15 00. www.iturrieneaostatua. com. 21 rooms.* ⊡*5€.* This charming hotel at the heart of the old quarter is housed in a tastefully refurbished old building filled with antiques, and works by local artists. Although the rooms are generally on the small side, the wooden floors add to the homely feel.

🍴 **Hotel Sirimiri** – *Pl. de la Encarnación 3.* ✆*944 33 07 59. www. hotelsirimiri.es. 28 rooms.* ⊡*3€.* Nestled in the old quarter, on the river bank, bedrooms are modern and spacious with large fully equipped bathrooms.

🍴 EAT

🍴 **Goizeko Kabi** – *Particular de Estraunza 4 and 6.* ✆*944 42 11 29. http:// goizekogaztelupe.com. Closed Sun, and 31 Jul–15 Aug.* This regional gastronomic institution, near the Museo de Bellas Artes, is renowned for its high-quality cuisine offering a balanced combination of the traditional and innovative, with outstanding seafood dishes.

TAPAS

El Viandar de Sota – *Gran Vía de Don Diego López de Haro 45.* ✆*944 15 25 00.* This complex of tapas bar, sidrería, and vinoteca is a famous landmark in the modern section of the city.

🍴 CAFÉS

Café Iruña – *Berástegui 4.* ✆*944 23 70 21.* Founded in 1903, this is a city institution, situated in a pleasant square and featuring attractive Mudéjar-inspired ceilings and decoration.

Café La Granja – *Pl. Circular 3.* ✆*944 23 08 13.* This famous café dates from 1926 although its style is more in keeping with the 19C with its marble tables, wooden chairs and decadent air. On evenings during the weekend the quiet, contemplative mood is replaced by a more lively atmosphere and loud music.

FESTIVALS

Bilbao's main annual festival takes place during **Semana Grande** *(www. astenagusia.com)* in mid-August with bullfights, Basque pelota championships and other events.

Costa Vasca★★

País Vasco

The Basque Coast (Costa Vasca) stretches from the Golfo de Vizcaya (Bay of Biscay) to the headland of the Cabo de Machichaco. The steep shoreline, lined by cliffs and indented by estuaries, is a line of fishing villages nestling in inlets.

🚗 DRIVING TOUR

FROM HONDARRIBIA TO BILBAO

247km/154mi – allow 2 days and see map.

Hondarribia/Fuenterrabía★

Fuenterrabía (Hondarribia in Basque) is a resort. **La Marina** is the fishermen's quarter with characteristic wood balconies and bars and cafés. On 8 September, a parade and festival honour the Virgen de Guadalupe, who is said to have delivered the town from a two-month siege by the French in 1638. Overlooking the River Bidasoa, the **Old Town**, an old fortified town, with steep streets, retains its 15C walls. These are punctuated by the **Puerta de Santa María**, a gateway surmounted by the town's coat of arms and twin angels venerating the Virgen de Guadalupe. Picturesque **calle Mayor** is lined with houses with wrought-iron balconies. The **Iglesia de Santa María** (*Mayor; 𝄞943 64 54 58*), a Gothic church with massive buttresses, was remodelled in the 17C and given a Baroque tower. It was the site of a proxy wedding in 1660 between Louis XIV and the Infanta María before the real marriage in France. The **Castillo de Carlos V**, a fortress (*pl. de Armas 14; now a parador*) was constructed in the 10C by Sancho Abarca, King of Navarra, and restored by Charles V in the 16C.

▷ *Leave Fuenterrabía on the harbour road.*

🦻 **Michelin Map:** 574 B-C 21 to 24 – País Vasco (Guipúzcoa, Vizcaya)

🛈 **Info:** Bermeo: Lamera. 𝄞946 17 91 54; Getaria: Parque Aldamar 2. 𝄞943 14 09 57; Hondarribia: Javier Ugarte 6. 𝄞943 64 54 58; Lekeitio: Plaza Independencia. 𝄞946 84 40 17; Zarautz:, Nafarroa Kalea. 𝄞943 83 09 90. www. bizkaiacostavasca.com.

▷ **Location:** The Basque Coast runs from the French border to Bilbao.

Cabo Higuer★

4km/2.5mi N.

Turn left; as the road climbs, you get a **view**★ of the beach, the town and the quayside and from the end of the headland, the French coast and the town of Hendaye.

▷ *Leave Fuenterrabía on the Behobia road; take the first right after the Palmera factory; bear left at the first crossroads.*

Ermita de San Marcial

9km/5.6mi SE.

A narrow road leads up to the wooded hilltop (225m/738ft). The **panorama**★★ from the hermitage includes Fuenterrabía, **Irún** and **Isla de los Faisanes** (Pheasant Island) in the mouth of the River Bidasoa on the border. In the distance are Donostia-San Sebastián and Hendaye beach.

Jaizkibel Road★★

The **drive**★★ along this road (*GI 3440*) is impressive at sunset. After 5km/3mi you reach the Capilla de Nuestra Señora de Guadalupe (Chapel of our Lady of Guadalupe) where there is a lovely **view**★ of the French coast. Past pines and gorse is the Hostal de Jaizkibel (*www.hoteljaizkibel.com*) at the foot of a 584m/1 916ft peak and a lookout

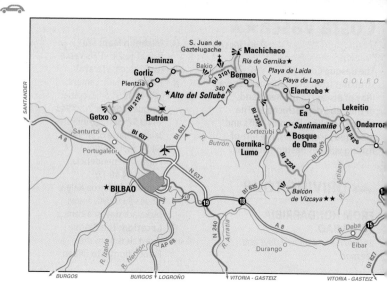

with a superb **view**★★. The road down affords **glimpses**★ of the indented coast, the Cordillera Cantábrica range and the mountains above Donostia-San Sebastián.

▶ *Travel 17km/10.5mi W along the Jaizkibel road.*

Pasaia/Pasajes

Pasaia comprises three villages around a sheltered bay. **Pasai Antxo** is a trading port, **Pasai Donibane**★ and **Pasai San Pedro** are both deep-sea fishing ports, processing cod. To get to **Pasai Donibane**★, either park at the village entrance or take a motorboat from San Pedro. The **view** from the water is picturesque – tall houses with brightly painted wooden balconies, boats and docks, and a single street. A path runs to the lighthouse ([ ] 45min).

Donostia-San Sebastián★★
See DONOSTIA-SAN SEBASTIÁN

▶ *Take the N 1; 7km/4.3mi S of Donostia-San Sebastián take the N 634 towards Bilbao.*

Zarautz

Queen Isabel II made this her summer residence in the 19C. Two **palaces** stand in the old quarter: the 16C property of the Marqués de Narros (*Elizaurre Kalea 2; ☎943 13 09 60*), and the Luzea tower, on Plaza Mayor, with mullioned windows and a machicolated corner balcony. The tower of the church of Santa María (*Guipúzcoa 51; ☎943 83 13 27*) can be seen to one side.

Beyond Zarautz, the road rises to a picturesque **corniche section**★★.

Getaria

Getaria is known for its *chipirones*, or squid, and its rock – *el ratón*, or Monte de San Antón – linked by a causeway. Native son **Juan Sebastián Elcano** set out with Magellan and was the first sailor to circumnavigate the world (1522). A narrow street, lined with picturesque houses, leads to the 13C–15C **Iglesia de San Salvador** (Church of our Saviour; *Nagusia;* ◷*open Mon–Sat 10am–7.30pm (8pm in summer), Sun 10am–12.30pm; ☎943 89 60 24*); its chancel rests on an arch above an alleyway. The gallery is Flamboyant Gothic.

Zumaia

Zumaia has two fine beaches: Itzurun, between cliffs, and Santiago. Near the latter is the house of painter **Ignacio Zuloaga** (1870–1945), converted into a **casa-museo** (◷*open Holy Week–mid-*

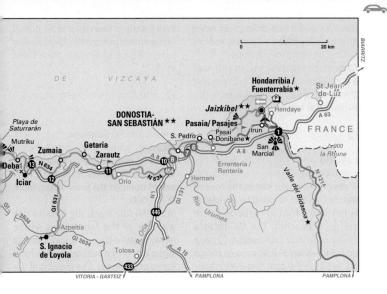

Sept Wed–Sun 4pm–8pm; rest of the

Sept Wed–Sun 4pm–8pm; rest of the year by appointment; ⊗8€ (Oct–Mar), 6€ (Apr–Sept). ℘943 86 23 41; www.ignaciozuloaga.com) showing his works – realistic and popular themes with brilliant colours and strong lines – and his collection of paintings by El Greco, Goya, Zurbarán and Morales.

The 15C **Iglesia de San Pedro** (Church of St Peter) contains a 16C altarpiece by Juan de Anchieta.

▷ *Past Zumaia, go left onto the GI 631.*

Santuario de San Ignacio de Loyola

Zumaia. ⏲*Open daily 10am–1pm, 3–7pm.* ⊗*No charge.* ℘*943 02 50 00. www.santuariodeloyola.org.*

This **sanctuary** was built by the Jesuits to plans by Italian architect Carlo Fontana around the Loyola family manor near Azpeitia at the end of the 17C. It is an important place of pilgrimage especially on St Ignatius' day (31 July).

The basement casemates of the 15C tower are vestiges of the original Loyola manor house, the **Santa Casa**. The rooms in which Ignatius was born, convalesced and converted have been transformed into profusely decorated chapels. The Baroque **basilica** is more Italian than Spanish in style, circular

with a vast cupola (65m/213ft high) attributed to Churriguera.

▷ *Return to the coast.*

The journey by road to Deba is one of the most beautiful in the Basque Country.

Deba

The **Iglesia de Santa María la Real** (*pl. Zaharra 7;* ⏲*open daily 9am–1pm;* ⊗*no charge;* ℘*943 12 24 52*) in this fishing port conceals, beneath the porch in its fortified front, a superb Gothic portal decorated with extremely lifelike statues. The cloister galleries have intricate tracery. There is a splendid **view**⋆ of the coast from the **cliff road**⋆ between Deba and Lekeitio.

Mutriku has one of the region's most delightful beaches, **Saturraran**.

Iciar/Itziar

Pl. Herriko, Deba. ℘*943 19 24 52.*
The fortress-like church contains a Plateresque altarpiece in dark wood.

▷ *Contine W along GI 638.*

Ondarroa

10km/6.2mi W of Deba along GI 638.
The church, standing like a ship's prow, tall Basque houses with washing at the

windows, and the encircling river, make an attractive **picture**★. Canning and fish salting are the main industries.

Onward, on rounding a point you have a good **view**★ of Lekeitio, its beach and the island of San Nicolás, joined to the mainland at low tide.

◗ *Continue W along BI 3438.*

Lekeitio
12km/7.4mi W.
A deeply indented bay at the foot of Monte Calvario, divided by an island, is Lekeitio's fishing harbour. There are good beaches. The 15C **iglesia** (*Independentzia Enparantza;* ◷*open daily 8am–noon, 5–7.30pm;* ⊛*no charge* ; *946 84 09 54*) guarding the harbour has three tiers of flying buttresses and a tall Baroque belfry.

◗ *Continue NW BI 3438.*

Ea
11km/6.8mi NW of Lekeitio
This miniature harbour stands between two hills at the end of a quiet creek.

◗ *Continue NE along BI 3438.*

Elantxobe★
7km/4.3mi NW of Ea.
Fishermen have long used the bay as a natural harbour and built their houses overlooking the water, against steep-sided Cabo Ogoño (300m/1 000ft).

Beyond rose-coloured **Playa de Laga**, a beach circling Cabo Ogoño, you can see **Gernika ría**★ (Estuary), Izaro island, the white outline of the town of Sukarrieta on the far bank, and Chacharramendi island. The resort of **Playa de Laida**, on the *ría*, is popular with Gernika residents.

◗ *Go SW and bear left at Kortezubi.*

Cuevas de Santimamiñe
Barrio Basondo, Kortezubi. ◔☞*Guided virtual tours in the Interpretation Centre Tue–Sun 10am–12.30pm, 3–5.30pm.* ⊛*3€.* *944 65 16 57.*

Wall paintings (◔☞ *closed to the public*) and engravings from the Magdalenian period were discovered in these caves in 1917.

◗ *Return to th main road and bear S.*

Gernika
14km/8.7mi S of Elantxobe.
Picasso's painting, *Guernica* (◷ *see MADRID*), immortalised a Spanish Civil War atrocity: on 26 April 1937, Nazi planes bombed the town, killing more than 1 000.

In the Middle Ages, the Gernika oak was one of the four places where newly created lords of Biscay came to swear that they would respect the local *fueros* or privileges. The remains of the 1 000-year-old tree are in the small temple behind the **Casa de Juntas** (*Allendesalazar;* ◷*open daily 10am–2pm, 4–6pm (7pm Jun and Oct);* ◷*closed 1, 6 Jan, 16 Aug, 24–25, 31 Dec;* ⊛*no charge;* *946 25 11 38*).

18km/11mi south (*via the BI 2224 and BI 3231*), the **Balcón de Vizcaya**★★ (Balcony of Biscay) viewpoint overlooks a chequerboard of meadows and forests.

◗ *Return to Gernika.*

Two viewpoints before Mundaka enable you to take a last look back over still waters. As the road drops downhill, you get a magnificent **view**★ of Bermeo.

Bermeo
15km/9mi NW of Gernika along BI 2235.
The fishermen's quarter, still crowded onto the Atalaya promontory overlooking the old harbour, was protected by ramparts (traces remain), and the grim granite Torre de Ercilla, now the **Museo del Pescador** (*pl. Torrontero;* ◷*open 15 Jun–15 Oct Tue–Sat 10am–1.30pm, 4–7.30pm, Sun 10am–2pm; 16 Oct–16 May Tue–Sat 10am–2pm, 4–7pm, Sun 10am–2pm;* ◷*closed public holidays;* ⊛*no charge;* *946 88 11 71*). dedicated to local fishermen.

◗ *Turn left towards Mungía.*

Alto del Sollube★ (Sollube Pass)
The road up to the low pass (340m/1 115ft) affords a good view of Bermeo.

▶ *Return to Bermeo, follow the coast road left for 3km/1.8mi then turn right.*

Faro (Lighthouse) de Machichaco
From just left of here there is a good view west. The road winds to a **viewpoint★** over the **San Juan de Gaztelugache** headland and its hermitage (🏃*access via a pathway*), the goal of a *romería (pilgrimage)* on Midsummer's Day *(23 Jun)*; there are extensive views from the **corniche road★** between Bakio and Arminza. A belvedere commands an interesting **view★** of the coast, Bakio, valley farms and wooded hinterland.

Arminza
Arminza is the only harbour along a section of wild coast.

▶ *Continue SW.*

Gorliz
7km/4.3mi SW of Arminza.
Gorliz is an attractive beach resort at the mouth of the River Butrón. **Plentzia** nearby *(2km/1.2mi)* is an oyster farming centre and resort.

Castillo de Butrón
⚷ *Closed for restoration.*
This fantasy castle, built on the remains of a 14C–15C construction, is a good example of eclectic, picturesque 19C architecture, and provides insight into medieval castle life.

Getxo
13km/8mi SW of Gorliz.
A **paseo marítimo** (sea promenade) overlooks the coast. From the road up to Getxo's well-known golf course there is a view of the Bilbao inlet and on the far bank, Santurtzi and Portugalete.

Bilbao★ 🕮*See BILBAO*

ADDRESSES

🛏 STAY

🛏 **Pensión Itsasmin** – *Nagusia 32, Elantxobe.* ☎*946 27 61 74. www.itsasmin. com. 12 rooms.* ⊒*5€.* This small hotel in a pedestrian street in the upper part of town has 18 pleasant rooms with parquet flooring and exposed beams. Four of the rooms have port views.

🛏🍴 **Hotel Zubieta** – *Portal de Atea, Lekeitio.* ☎*946 84 30 30. www. hotelzubieta.com. 20 rooms.* ⊒*9.50€.* Between 1922 and 1931, this palatial building by the sea was occupied by the last empress of the Austro-Hungarian Empire. Rooms are larges, comfortable and pleasantly decorated. The hotel also has its own thalasso-therapy centre.

🛏🍴🍴 **Hotel Obispo** – *Pl. del Obispo, Hondarribia.* ☎*943 64 54 00. www. hotelobispo.com. 17 rooms.* Charming hotel housed in a 14C–15C palace located in the upper section of the old quarter. All the rooms are different, with a pleasant mix of exposed beams, stone walls, old furniture and fabrics creating a warm, cosy atmosphere.

🍴 EAT

🍴🍴 **Asador Almiketxu** – *Barrio Almike Auzoa 8, Bermeo. 1.5km/1mi S of Bermeo.* ☎*946 88 09 25. www.almiketxu. com. Closed Nov, Mon.* A varied menu of traditional Basque cuisine, on the outskirts of Bermeo, from where there are fine views of the town and the sea.

🍴🍴 **Iribar** – *Nagusia 34, Getaria.* ☎*943 14 04 06. Closed a fortnight in Apr and Oct.* Traditional restaurant serving reasonably priced grilled fish in the centre of this fishing village.

🍴🍴 **Txiki Polit** – *Pl. de la Musika, Zarautz.* ☎*943 83 53 57. www.txikipolit. com.* This simple tavern with paper tablecloths has an extensive, good-quality menu with specialities that include beef cutlets and a good choice of fish. Several guest rooms on the first floor.

Donostia-San Sebastián★★

País Vasco

San Sebastián (Donostia in Basque) is in a glorious setting on a scallop-shaped bay framed by two hills and the Isle of Santa Clara. Two vast sand beaches follow the curve of the bay: La Concha and fashionable Ondarreta. Gardens and promenades and statuary decorate the town, most notable of which is *El Peine del Viento XV* (**Windcomb 15**), Eduardo Chillida.

A BIT OF HISTORY

The pioneer of tourism – Queen María Cristina of Habsburg chose Donostia-San Sebastián as her summer residence in the 19C, establishing it as a leading resort.

A gastronomic capital – The all-male members of 30 gourmet clubs prepare excellent meals which they consume with cider or *txacolí* wine. Specialities include hake, cod, bream and sardines and squid *(chipirones)*.

SIGHTS
Old Town

The narrow streets of the old town (rebuilt after an 1813 fire) contrast the wide avenues of modern Donostia. The area comes alive at the apéritif hour when locals and tourists (especially the French) crowd the bars and small restaurants in the *calles* Portu, Muñoa, 31 de Agosto and Fermín Calbetón to enjoy tapas and the excellent seafood.

Iglesia de Santa María

Mayor. ◷ *Open Jun–Sept 8am–2pm, 4–8pm; Oct–May 8.30am–2pm, 5–8pm.* ☜*No charge.* ℘*943 42 31 24.* The church has an exuberant late 18C portal and Baroque altars.

Museo de San Telmo

Pl. Zuloaga 1. ◷ *Open Jul–Aug Tue–Sat 9.30am–8.30pm, Sun and public holidays 10.30am–2pm; Sept–Jun Tue–Sat 10.30am–1.30pm, 4–7.30pm,*

Sun and public holidays 10.30am–2pm. ☜*No charge.* ℘*943 48 15 80. www.museosantelmo.com.*

The museum is in a 16C monastery. The Renaissance cloisters hold Basque stone funerary crosses from the 15C–17C carved in traditional Iberian style. The upper gallery is the ethnographic section, with a reconstructed Basque interior.

Paintings include a Ribera, an El Greco, and 19C artists. The chapel was decorated by **José María Sert** with scenes from the city's history.

Paseo Nuevo (Pasealekua Berria)

This promenade almost circles Monte Urgull and affords good **views**.

👪 Aquarium San Sebastián★

Pl. Carlos Biasca de Imaz 1. ◷ *Open Jul–Aug daily 10am–9pm; Oct–Holy Week Mon–Fri 10am–7pm, Sat–Sun and public holidays 10am–8pm; Holy Week–Jun and Sept Mon–Fri 10am–8pm, Sat–Sun and public holidays*

▸ **Population:** 184 248

⚲ **Michelin Map:** 573 (town plan or 574 C 23-24. see plan of Costa Vasca in COSTA VASCA – País Vasco (Guipúzcoa)

ℹ **Info:** Boulevar 8. ℘943 48 11 66. www.donostia.org.

▷ **Location:** Donostia-San Sebastián is on the Gulf of Vizcaya, 25km/15.5mi W of the French border, 102km/63.3mi E of Bilbao. 🚌Paseo de Francia 22

🅿 **Parking:** Space is limited in the old quarter; walking is preferred.

◉ **Don't Miss:** A walk in the old quarter, and a fine seafood repast.

◷ **Timing:** Take a day for San Sebastián and drives nearby.

👪 **Kids:** The Aquarium.

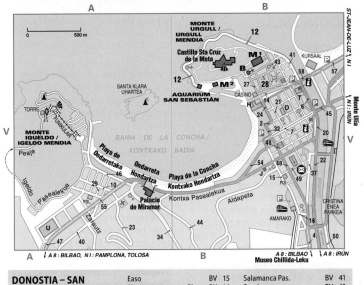

10am–9pm. ⏱ Closed 1 Jan, 25 Dec. 💶12€, child 6€; 📞943 44 00 99. www.aquariumss.com.

This excellent aquarium, one of the best in Europe also includes a natural sciences musem and naval museum. Visitors can cross its **Oceanarium**★– via a tunnel with 360° views.

Museo Naval (Naval Museum)

Pasealekua 24. ⏱ Open Tue–Sat 10am–1.30pm, 4–7.30pm, Sun and public holidays 11am–2pm. 💶1.20€; free Thu. 📞943 43 00 51. http://um.gipuzkoak ultura.net.

Small Basque-oriented museum, showing a traditional way of life at sea.

EXCURSIONS
View from Monte Ulía★

7km/4.3mi E. Follow the N 1 towards Irún and take a right before the summit.

The twisting drive up affords good **views** of the town and its setting.

Museo Chillida-Leku

6km/3.7mi S. Exit the N I, then take the GI 2132 from Rekalde towards Hernani and follow the signposts. ⏱ Open Sept–Jun Wed–Thu 10.30am–3pm; Jul–Aug Mon–Sat 10.30am–8pm, Sun 10.30am–3pm. ⏱ Closed 1 Jan, 25 Dec. 💶8.50€. 📞943 33 53 08. www.eduardo-chillida.com.

By creating this **museum**, Eduardo Chillida (1924–2002), native son and one of the great contemporary sculptors, realised his dream of an open site where visitors could wander among his works. The 12ha/29-acre estate is the setting for 40 large sculptures integrated into the landscape. Smaller sculptures and works on paper are shown in the 16C Zabalaga country house.

ADDRESSES

STAY

⊜⊜ **Pensión Aida** – *Iztueta 9.* ℘*943 32 78 00. www.pensionesconencanto.com.* ⊇*4€.* Just minutes from the old town and Kursaal is this surprisingly comfortable and charming pensión. Most rooms have their own balcony. Free Internet.

⊜⊜ **Pensión Donostiarra** – *San Martín 6, 1º.* ℘*943 42 61 67. www.pensiondonostiarra.com. 15 rooms.* Close to the new cathedral, this is one of the city's classic addresses, recently renovated. Comfortable rooms decorated with parquet flooring, simple furniture and modern bathrooms.

⊜⊜⊜⊜ **Hotel Niza** – *Zubieta 56.* ℘*943 42 66 63. www.hotelniza.com. 40 rooms.* ⊇*11€.* This elegant hotel belonging to the Chillida family opened its doors in the 1920s and has remained a Donostia-San Sebastián institution. An unbeatable location overlooking the bay and beach.

EAT

⊜⊜⊜ **Bodegón Alejandro** – *Fermín Calbetón 4.* ℘*943 42 71 58. www.martinberasategui.com.Closed Sun evening, Mon.* Although owned by a famous chef, the Alejandro serves excellent cuisine at surprisingly reasonable prices.

⊜⊜⊜⊜ **Arzak** – *Av. Alcalde Elosegui 273.* ℘*943 27 84 65. www.arzak.es. Closed second fortnight in Jun, first fortnight in Nov, Sun & Mon.* Renowned for elegant dining rooms with a modern aesthetic, the cooking is exceptional and constantly creative.

TAPAS

Ganbara – *San Jerónimo 21.* ℘*943 42 25 75. Closed Sun evening, Mon, second fortnight in Jun and Nov.* If the famous tapas bar is full the cosy restaurant in the basement is also recommended.

Txepetxa – *Pescadería 5.* ℘*943 42 22 27. Closed Mon, fortnight in Jun and Oct.* This traditional bar in the old town is famous for its delicious anchovies.

FESTIVALS

The main fiesta is the **Semana Grande** *(second week of Aug).* Others include an I **International Film Festival** *(September)* international jazz festival, Basque folklore festivals, plus golf and tennis tournaments.

Oñati/Oñate

País Vasco

Oñati, with its seigniorial residences, monastery and old university, nestles amid the wild beauty of the Udana Valley. It figured prominently in the First Carlist War.

SIGHTS

Antigua Universidad (Old University)

Universitate Etorbidea 8. Open Sept–Jul Mon–Thu 9am–5pm, Fri 9am–2pm; Aug Mon–Fri 9am–2pm; Guided tours Apr–Sept Sat 10am–2pm, 4.30–6.30pm, Sun 10am–2pm; Oct–Mar Sat 11am–2pm, Sun 11am–2pm. ℘943 78 34 53.

▸ **Population:** 10 816
◉ **Michelin Map:** 573 C 22 – País Vasco (Guipúzcoa)
▤ **Info:** San Juan 14. ℘943 78 34 53. www.oinati.org.
◉ **Location:** Oñati stands at the foot of Monte Alona (1 321m/4 333ft), 45km/28mi NE of Vitoria-Gasteiz and 74km/46mi SW of Donostia-San Sebastián.

The university, now administrative headquarters of Guipúzcoa province, was founded in 1542 and functioned until the early 20C. The gateway, by Pierre Picart, is surmounted by pinnacles and crowded with statues.

Ayuntamiento (Town Hall)
Pl. Foruen 1.
This fine 18C Baroque building was designed by Martín de Carrera.

Iglesia de San Miguel
Universitate Etorbidea 1. Guided tours Mon–Fri 9am and 7.15pm, Sat 7pm, Sun 11am and 1pm. 2€. 943 78 34 53.
The Gothic church facing the university was modified in the Baroque period. A Renaissance chapel off the north aisle, closed by beautiful iron grilles, contains an interesting gilded wood altarpiece. The golden stone cloister exterior with is Isabelline Plateresque.

EXCURSIONS
Santuario de Arantzazu★
9km/5.5mi S along the GI 3591. Open daily 8.30am–8pm. 943 78 09 51.
The **scenic cliff road**★ follows the the River Arantzazu, which flows through a narrow gorge. The **shrine** at 800m/2 625ft in a mountain **setting**★ faces the highest peak in the province, Mount Aitzgorri (1 549m/5 082ft). Dominating the church is an immense bell tower 40m/131ft high, with diamond-faceted stone symbolising the hawthorn bush (*arantzazu* in Basque) in which the Virgin appeared to a local shepherd in 1469.

Vitoria-Gasteiz★

País Vasco

Vitoria-Gasteiz is the capital of the largest Basque province and the seat of the Basque government, sited in a cereal-covered plateau. It was founded in the 12C and was surrounded by walls. The old quarter is in the upper section.

CIUDAD VIEJA★★ (OLD TOWN)
1hr30min
Concentric streets – each named after a trade – ring the cathedral. The liveliest streets are to the left of the plaza de la Virgen Blanca.
The **Iglesia de San Pedro** (*Fundadora de las Siervas de Jesús 2*), with its Gothic façade, can also be found in this part of the old town.

Plaza de la Virgen Blanca
The square, dominated by the Iglesia (church) de San Miguel, is surrounded by house fronts with glassed-in balconies, or *miradores*.
The massive monument at the square's centre commemorates Wellington's decisive victory on 21 June 1813, putting

> ▸ **Population:** 232 477
> ⚲ **Michelin Map:** 573
>   D 21-22 (town plan) –
>   País Vasco (Álava)
> ▯ **Info:** Plaza General Loma 1.
>   945 16 15 98. www.
>   alavaturismo.com.
> ▸ **Location:** The city is at
>   524m/1 718ft in NE Spain.
>   A 2h30min walking tour
>   of the historic district
>   departs from the Oficina
>   de Turismo (tourist office).
>   Eduardo Dato 46

to flight King Joseph Bonaparte and his army. It communicates awith the nobly ordered 18C **plaza de España** (or plaza Nueva).

Iglesia de San Miguel
Escaleras de San Miguel 1.
Guided tours available Jul–Sept, organised by the tourist office.
In a jasper niche in the church porch is a polychrome Late Gothic statue of the Virgen Blanca, the city's patron. In the late 14C portal, the tympanum shows the Life of St Michael. In the chancel are an altarpiece by Gregorio Fernández and a Plateresque sepulchral arch.

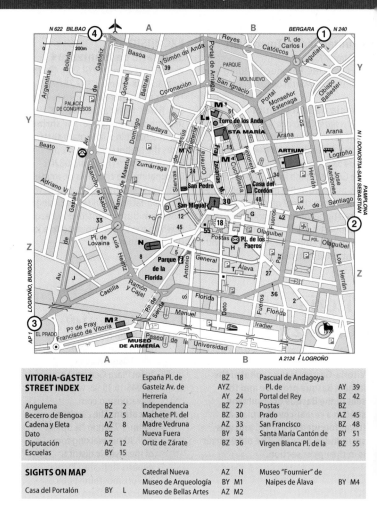

Plaza del Machete

This small, long square lies behind the **Arquillos**, an arcade which links the upper and lower towns. A niche in the east end of San Miguel church contains the *machete* or cutlass, on which the procurator general had to swear to uphold the town's privileges (*fueros*). The 16C **Palacio de Villa Suso** (🕐*open Mon–Fri 8.30am–1.30pm, 9pm in summer*), on the right side, is now a meeting centre.

▶ *Climb the steps adjoining the palace.*

A stroll along **calle Fray Zacarías Martínez**, with wood-framed houses and palaces, is pleasant. The Renaissance north doorway of the Palacio de los Escoriaza-Esquivel (*5–7;* 📞*945 24 76 01*), built on the old town walls, is worthy of special note; if it is open, enter to view the lovely covered courtyard.

Catedral de Santa María

Cuchillería 95–97. 🕐 *Open daily 11am–1pm, 5–7pm.* 🕐 *Closed 1 Jan, 25 Dec.* 🔊 *Guided tour (60min) available with prior booking.* 💶*3€.* 📞*945 25 51 35. www.catedralvitoria.com.*

The construction of the Gothic church-fortress, part of the city's first defensive ring, began at the end of the 13C.

In the 16C wood and brick **Casa Godeo-Guevara-San Juan** is home to a small archaeological museum. The **Casa del**

Portalón, opposite, is a typical late 15C-early 16C shop, now a well-known restaurant. The **Torre de los Anda**, part of the medieval defences, forms a triangle with the two houses.

In calle Cuchillería, in the **Palacio de Bendaña**, a building noted for its corner turret and doorway with *alfiz* surround, is a museum devoted to playing cards. Part of the delightful **Renaissance patio** has been preserved. The **Casa del Cordón** (*Cuchillería 24*), a 16C house, is used for exhibitions.

CIUDAD NUEVA (MODERN TOWN)

As Vitoria-Gasteiz grew in the 18C, neo-Classical constructions began to appear such as the **Arquillos** arcade. In the 19C, the town expanded southwards with the **Parque de la Florida** (Florida Park), the **Catedral Nueva** (New Cathedral, 1907) in neo-Gothic style and two wide avenues: paseo de la Senda and paseo de Fray Francisco, the latter lined by mansions, such as the Palacio de Ajuria Enea, seat of the Lehendakari, or Basque government, and two museums, the Museo de Armería and the Museo de Bellas Artes.

Near Plaza de España is the modern Plaza de los Fueros, the work of architect José Luis Peña Ganchegui and sculptor Eduardo Chillida.

Restoration Work at Catedral de Santa María★★

See Cathedral entry for details.

The diocese has stuggled for centuries to keep this Gothic cathedral from subsiding and tumbling. A programme to realign its walls will run to at least 2010. An innovative hard-hat tour along walkways and passages reveals the secrets of this temple fortress.

Museo Fournier de Naipes★

Cuchillería 54. ⏱ Open Tue–Fri 10am–2pm, 4–6.30pm, Sat 10am–2pm, Sun and public holidays 11am–2pm. ⏱ Closed 1 Jan, Good Fri. ✆No charge. ☎945 18 19 20.

In the playing card factory of Heraclio Fournier is a collection of over 15 000 packs from all over the world, dating from the late 14C to the present. Cards illustrate events, geography, politics and traditional dress and pastimes.

Museo Artium★

Francia 24. ⏱ Open Tue–Thu and Sun 11am–8pm, Fri–Sat 10am–8.30pm. ✆Guided tours available on Wed, Sat & Sun. ✆4.50€. ☎945 20 90 20. www.artium.org.

This museum and cultural centre focuses on the foundations of modern art. A significant selection from its **magnificent collection**★ is shown on a rotating basis. The museum owns more than 1 800 works of Spanish artists, from the Avant Garde of the twenties and thirties (most of the collection) to the most recent. Names are of the stature of Miró, Gargallo, Tàpies, Canogar, Palazuelo, Oteiza and Chillida.

Museo de Armería★ (Museum of Arms and Armour)

Pas. de Fray Francisco 3. ⏱ Open Tue–Fri 10am–2pm, 4–6.30pm, Sat 10am–2pm, Sun and public holidays 11am–2pm. ⏱ Closed 1 Jan & Good Friday. ✆No charge. ☎945 18 19 25.

The well-presented collection housed in a modern building traces the tradition and evolution of weaponry in the Basque Country from prehistoric axes to early 20C pistols. Note the 15C-17C **armour**, including suits of 17C **Japanese armour**.

Museo Diocesano de Arte Sacro (Diocesan Sacred Art Museum)

Catedral María Inmaculada, Pl. de la Magdalena 1. ⏱ Open Tue–Fri 10am–2pm, 4–6pm, Sat 10am–2pm, Sun and public holidays 11am–2pm. ✆No charge. ☎945 16 15 98.

This museum in the ambulatory of the **Catedral Nueva** exhibits Gothic images, Flemish works (*Descent from the Cross* by Van der Goes, *The Crucifixion* by Ambrosius Benson), 16C–18C canvases (*St Francis* by El Greco, several Riberas, *The Immaculate Conception* by Alonso Cano) and silverware.

Museo de Bellas Artes (Fine Arts Museum)

Pas. de Fray Francisco de Vitoria 8.
Open Tue–Fri 10am–2pm,
4–6.30pm, Sat 10am–2pm, 5–8pm, Sun
11am–2pm. Closed 1 Jan & Good
Friday. No charge. 945 18 19 18.
The museum, housed in the early 20C
Historicist Palacio de Agustí, displays
Spanish art of the 18C and 19C and a
comprehensive selection of Basque
costumbrista painting by such artists as
Iturrino, Regoyos and Zuloaga.

Museo de Arqueología (Archaeological Museum)

Correría 116. Open Tue–Fri 10am–
2pm, 4–6.30pm, Sat 10am–2pm, Sun
and public holidays 11am–2pm.
Closed 1 Jan, Good Fri. No charge.
945 18 19 22.
This small museum in the half-timbered
16C Godeo-Guevara-San Juan house
displays finds from excavations in Álava
province. Note the dolmen collections
and Roman monuments, including the
Estela del Jinete (Knight's stele).

EXCURSIONS
Santuario de Estíbaliz

10km/6.2mi E.
Leave Vitoria-Gasteiz by ② on the
*town plan and then take the A 132.
Bear left after about 4km/2.5mi.*

ADDRESSES

STAY

⊝ **Hostal Infanta Doña Leonor** –
*Condes de Toreno 1, Villalcázar
de Sirga.* 979 88 80 48. www.
hostalinfantaleonor.com. 10 rooms.
3.50€. If you're hoping for a good
night's sleep in a peaceful setting, this
modern hostal in the small town of
Villalcázar de Sirga is ideal, with its cosy
rooms, parquet floors and wooden
furniture.

⊝ **Hotel San Martín** – *Pl. San Martín 7,
Frómista.* 979 81 00 00. www.
hotelsanmartin.es. 12 rooms. 6€.
Closed Jan. Despite its simplicity,
this hotel on two floors close to the

Open daily 8am–8pm. No visits
during religious services. No charge.
945 29 30 88.
This Late Romanesque pilgrim shrine
has an attractive wall belfry on the south
front, and a 12C Romanesque statue of
the Virgin.

EAST OF VITORIA-GASTEIZ: MEDIEVAL PAINTINGS

25km/15.5mi.
*Leave Vitoria-Gasteiz by ② on the
town plan and follow the motorway as
far as junction 375.*

Gazeo

Guided tours of Gazeo and Alaiza
Sept–Jun Thu and Fri; Jul–Aug and Holy
Week daily. 945 31 25 35. 2€.
Superb 14C **Gothic frescoes**★★ deco-
rate the chancel of the church **(iglesia)**.
The south wall shows Hell as a whale's
gullet, the north, the Life of the Virgin.
On the roof are scenes from the Life of
Christ.

Alaiza

Follow the A 4111 for 3km/1.8mi,
turn right, then left after a few metres.
Obscure **paintings**★ on the walls
and roof of the church **(iglesia)** apse
probably date from the late 14C. Strange
red outlines represent castles, churches,
soldiers and many other personages.

Romanesque church of San Martín has
12 comfortable, well-equipped rooms,
all with private bathroom and TV. Much
of the cooking in the restaurant is done
in the traditional wood-fired oven.

⊝⊝ **Hotel Dato** – *Dato 28.* 945 14
72 30. www.hoteldato.com. 14 rooms.
The Dato is centrally located with out
of the ordinary décor. The rooms are
impeccably maintained.

⊝⊝ **Hotel Madrid** – *Av. de La Puebla
44, Ponferrada.* 987 41 15 50. www.
hotelmadridponferrada.com. 45 rooms.
4.50€. Restaurant. A good central
location, friendly staff and clean,
comfortable rooms are the main
features of this well-established hotel,
which has been welcoming guests for

more than half a century, and whose longevity is reflected in the overall décor.

⊜⊜⊜ **Hotel Real Monasterio San Zoilo** – *Obispo Souto, Carrión de los Condes.* ☏*979 88 00 49. www.sanzoilo. com. 49 rooms.* ⊐*7€. Restaurant*⊜⊜⊜. This former Benedictine monastery has dispensed with the austerity of former times and is now a delightful hotel where the welcome is both warm and friendly. The architecture – a mix of brick, stone and wood – is soberly elegant, the rooms extremely comfortable and the prices unbeatable.

⊜⊜⊜ **Hotel Palacio de Elorriaga** – *Elorriaga 15, 1.5km/1mi E along Av. de Santiago and the N 104.* ☏*945 26 36 16. www.hotelpalacioelorriaga.com. 21 rooms. Restaurant*⊜⊜⊜. This 16C–17C mansion has been completely restored. Behind the sober walls of stone and brick, the overall effect is delightful with tasteful small touches and an abundance of wood and antique furniture. Guest rooms are cosy with en-suite bathrooms.

⊜⊜⊜ **Pousada de Portomarín** – *Av. de Sarria, Portomarín.* ☏*982 54 52 00. www.pousadadeportomarin. com. 34 rooms.* ⊐*8€. Restaurant*⊜⊜. A peaceful hotel in a modern stone building with fine views of the River Miño. Spacious, comfortable rooms with wood floors and attractive furniture. Some rooms have the added bonus of a terrace. A good restaurant serving traditional cuisine.

⦙/ EAT

⊜⊜⊜ **Arkupe** – *Mateo de Moraza 13.* ☏*945 23 00 80. www.restaurantearkupe. com.* This restaurant is behind the town hall in an 18C national monument with exposed beams. Meats and fish are prepared according to traditional Basque recipes.

⊜⊜⊜ **Gurea** – *Pl. de la Constitución 10.* ☏*945 24 59 33. Closed Mon–Wed for dinner, fortnight in Aug.* The attractive wood façade leads to rustic dining areas where traditional foods are served.

⊜⊜⊜ **La Peseta** – *Pl. San Bartolom 3, Astorga.* ☏*987 61 72 75. Closed second fortnight in Jan, Oct.* This popular, family-run restaurant has a simple, somewhat antiquated dining room, where the cuisine is traditional and reasonably priced. The *cocido maragato* (a stew of assorted animal parts) is popular. There are also 19 modest guest rooms.

⊜⊜⊜ **Mesón del Peregrino** – *Irunbidea 10, Puente la Reina. 1km/0.6mi NE of Puente la Reina on the Pamplona/ Iruña road.* ☏*948 34 00 75. Closed Sun for dinner, Mon.* A charming restaurant housed in a magnificent large stone mansion with dining rooms overlooking the garden and swimming pool. The tasteful décor is rustic in style, creating the perfect atmosphere in which to enjoy the creative cuisine on offer here. The restaurant also has 13 rooms, with prices in the mid- to high price range.

TAPAS

El Rincón de Luis Mari – *Rioja 14.* ☏*945 25 01 27. Closed Sept, Tue .* A simple bar with a large choice of tapas and *raciones*, a fine selection of cured hams, and a good location near the old quarter.

🏃 LEISURE ACTIVITIES

The inhabitants of Vitoria-Gasteiz have the choice of a river beach in Gamarra, to the north, as well as the Urrúnaga and Ullívarri reservoirs offering fishing and water sports. For **adventure activites** (mountain biking, hiking, caving, canyoning, parasailing), contact Tura, ☏945 31 25 35

FESTIVALS

The August Virgen Blanca festival is colourful and perpetuates a strange tradition: everyone lights a cigar as the angel descends from the Torre de San Miguel (St Michael's Belfry). Vitoria's noted **Festival Internacional de Jazz** (*www.jazzvitoria.com*) takes place in mid-July.

La Rioja★

La Rioja

The Ebro Valley in La Rioja is carpeted with vineyards and vegetable fields under the peaks of the Sierra de Cantabria and Sierra de la Demanda. Towns and villages have a rich artistic heritage due to the proximity of the Way of St James.

A BIT OF HISTORY

Rioja Alta (Upper Rioja), to the west around Haro, is devoted to wine-growing while **Rioja Baja** (Lower Rioja), with **Logroño** and Calahorra as its main towns, is given over to the growing of early vegetables. La Rioja flourished thanks to its position on the pilgrim route to Santiago de Compostela, and later became famous for its wine.

SIGHTS

Logroño

Plaza Europa.

The capital of the Rioja region is on the banks of the Ebro. Pilgrims to Santiago de Compostela would have entered this pleasant town through the stone gateway, overlooking the cathedral.

Santa María la Redonda

Portales 14. ◷ *Open Mon–Sat 8am–1pm, 6–8.45pm, Sun 9am–2pm, 6.30–8.45pm.* ◌ *No charge.* ℘ *941 25 11 58.*

Dating from 1435, the church has three naves, three polygonal apses and chapels in its side aisles. These include the Plateresque Chapel of Our Lady of Peace (Nuestra Señora de la Paz), founded in 1541 by Diego Ponce de León.

- **Michelin Map:** 573 E 20-23, F 20-24 – La Rioja, Navarra, País Vasco (Álava)
- **Info:** Logroño: Paseo del Espolón, Principe de Vergara 1. ℘ 941 29 12 60; Nájera: Plaza San Miguel 10. ℘ 941 36 00 41; San Millán de la Cogolla: Monasterio de Yuso, Planta Baja. ℘ 941 37 32 59; Santo Domingo de la Calzada: Mayor 70, bajo. ℘ 941 34 12 30. www.lariojaturismo.com.
- **Location:** La Rioja (from Río Oja, a tributary of the Ebro) covers approximately 5 sq km/1 930sq mi in the provinces of La Rioja, Álava and Navarra.

Museo de la Rioja

Pl. de San Agustín. ◌ *Closed for renovation until 2011.* ℘ *941 29 12 59.*

This regional museum is in a fine 18C Baroque palace.

Laguardia★

Hillside Laguardia is perhaps the most attractive town in Rioja Alavesa, with two imposing towers visible as you approach: San Juan to the south, and the 12C tower of the abbey to the north, once connected to the Gothic Iglesia de Santa María de los Reyes.

Iglesia de Santa María de los Reyes

Mayor. ◌ *Guided tours Tue–Fri 10am–2pm, 4–7pm, Sat 10am–2pm, 5–7pm, Sun 10.45am–2pm.* ◌ *2€.* ℘ *945 60 08 45.*

A superb late 14C **portal★★** retains its 17C polychrome decoration. The tympanum is divided into three scenes relating the life of the Virgin. Note the figure of Christ holding a small child in his hands representing the soul of the Virgin.

TAPAS

The small **calle del Laurel** is without doubt one of the main attractions in Logroño with its huge choice of bars serving delicious local specialities (sweet peppers, mushrooms, etc.).

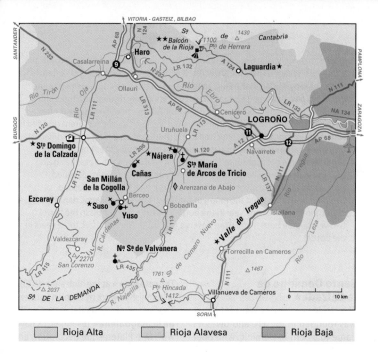

| Rioja Alta | Rioja Alavesa | Rioja Baja |

Centro Temático del vino Villa Lucía (Villa Lucía Wine Centre)

On the way to Logroño.

🕐 Open 2 Jan–24 Dec Tue–Sun 9am–2pm, 4–8pm. ⊕8.50€. ☎945 60 00 32. *www.villa-lucia.com.*

The museum on this lovely estate traces the elaboration of wines.

The **panorama** from the **Balcón de Rioja**★★ or Rioja Balcony 12km/7.4mi northwest of Laguardia near the Puerto de Herrera (Herrera Pass, 1 100m/3 609ft), is extensive.

In Laguardia, Bodegas Ysios are the creation of Santiago Calatrava, who was inspired by the hoops of wine casks (☎guided tours Mon–Fri 11am, 1pm, 4pm, Sat–Sun 11am, 1pm with prior booking; ☎945 60 06 40; www. domecqbodegas.com).

At El Ciego, Frank Gehry, of the Guggenheim, designed the Herederos del Marqués de Riscal cellars, known as la Ciudad del Vino (City of Wine, ☎guided tours (1hr30min) Tue–Sat 10am, noon, 4pm, Sun 11am, 1pm with prior booking; ⊕10€. ☎945 60 60 00; www.marquesderiscal.com).

Haro

This centre is famous for its wines. Elegant 16C and 18C façades recall a prestigious past. In **plaza de la Paz** note the simple lines of the Neoclassical town hall (ayuntamiento), built by Juan de Villanueva in 1769; also note the Baroque tower of the **Iglesia de Santo Tomás** *(pl. de la Iglesia; ☎941 31 16 90).*

Museo del Vino de la Rioja

Bretón de los Herreros 4. 🕐 *Open Tue–Fri 10am–2.30pm, 3.30–7pm, Sat–Sun and public holidays 10am–7pm.* ⊕*2€; no charge Wed.* ☎*941 31 05 47.*

This museum is entirely devoted to wine, from cultivation all the way through to the bottling process.

Museo de la Cultura del Vino – Dinastía Vivanco★

5km/3mi from Haro, in Briones (km 442 on the N 232). ☎*Guided tours by arrangement Tue–Fri 1am, 4pm.* ⊕*7.50€.* ☎*902 32 00 01. www.dinastiavivanco.com.*

This splendid museum covers the history and culture of wine and changing wine technology over 10 000 years.

The Wines of La Rioja

Rioja is the only Spanish appellation with the Denominación de Origen Calificada (DOC) quality label. The wine is the result of over seven centuries of tradition and a superb position in the Ebro Valley between the Sierra de la Demanda and the Sierra de Cantabria. The wine region is traditionally divided into three sub-zones: Rioja Alavesa, Rioja Baja and Rioja Alta. Although seven grape varieties are permitted, the two most commonly used are Tempranillo and Grenache. Red wine accounts for 75% of production and is produced according to two different processes: **carbonic maceration** and **ageing**. The first produces young, fresh wines which are best consumed in the year of production, whereas the ageing process, in Bordeaux oak barrels, results in three different wines, classified according to the time spent in the barrel and the time which has elapsed between the harvest and the moment the wine leaves the cellars: **Crianza** (12 months in the barrel, one year in the bottle), **Reserva** (12 months in the barrel, two years in the bottle) and **Gran Reserva** (24 months in the barrel, three years in the bottle).

Santo Domingo de la Calzada★

This staging post on the Way of St James was founded in the 11C and owes its name to a hermit, Dominic, who built a bridge for pilgrims. Parts of the 14C ramparts can still be seen.

The **old town**★ huddles around the **plaza del Santo**, dominated by the Cathedral and the ex-hospital, now a parador. The streets around the square, particularly the calle Mayor, retain 16C and 17C stone houses with fine doorways. The 18C ayuntamiento (town hall), in nearby plaza de España, is crowned by an impressive escutcheon.

Catedral★

Pl. del Santo. ◷ *Open Mon–Sat 9.30am–1.30pm, 4–6.30pm.* ◷ *Closed public holidays.* ⊜*3.50€.* ℘*941 34 00 33.*

◐ *Entrance via the 14C cloisters, housing the cathedral museum.*

The church is Gothic, apart from the ambulatory and apsidal chapel, which are Romanesque (second half of the 12C). The saint's tomb (13C), beneath a 1513 canopy, is in the south transept, and opposite is a sumptuous **Gothic cage**. This contains a live white cock and hen in memory of a miracle attributed to the saint – a cock about to be eaten sprang up and proclaimed the innocence of a convicted thief.

The **retable**★★ at the high altar (1538) is an unfinished work by Damián Forment. The Cathedral also contains the **Capilla de la Magdalena**★ (Evangelist's nave) with fine Plateresque decoration and magnificent screen.

Abadía de Cañas

Real, Cañas. 13km/8mi SE of Santo Domingo de la Calzada. ◷ *Open Nov–Mar Tue–Sat 10.30am–1.30pm, 4–6pm, Sun 11am–1.30pm, 4–6pm; Apr–Oct Tue–Sat 10am–1.30pm, 4–7pm, Sun 10am–1pm, 4–7pm.* ⊜*3€.* ℘*941 37 90 83. www.abadiadecanas.com.*

This monastery has been inhabited by Cistercian monks since 1170. The 16C church and chapter house are extraordinary examples of the purity and simplicity of Cistercian art.

Ezcaray

This delightful village is a summer resort and ski area. It has houses with stone and wood porticoes, mansions and the church of **Santa María la Mayor** (☛ *guided tours available through tourist office;* ℘*941 35 46 79)* as well as a former tapestry factory founded by Charles III in 1752.

Nájera★

Reconquered by Sancho Garcés I in 920, Nájera was Navarra's capital until 1076.

Monasterio de Santa María la Real★

Pl. de Santa María. ◷ *Open Tue–Sat 10am–1pm, 4–5.30pm, Sun and public holidays 10am–12.30pm, 4–5.30pm.* ☞*3€.* ☞*Guided tours available (3.50€).* ✆*941 36 10 83.*

The monastery was founded by Don García III, King of Navarra, in 1032, where he stumbled upon a statue of the Virgin. The bays in the lower galleries of the **cloisters**★ are filled with Plateresque stone tracery (1520). Beneath the gallery of the **church**★ is the **Panteón Real**★ (Royal Pantheon) of princes of Navarra, León and Castilla of the 11C and 12C.

Basílica de Santa María de Arcos de Tricio

3km/2mi SW of Nájera. ◷ *Open Jul–Sept Tue–Sat 10.30am–1.30pm, 4.30–7.30pm, Sun 10.30am–1.30pm; Oct–Jun Sat Sun and holidays only 10.30am–1.30pm.* ☞*1.50€.* ✆*941 36 16 57.*

This unusual church, with basilical plan, was built in the 5C.

San Millán de la Cogolla

The most attractive approach is via the turn-off from the LR 113 at Bobadilla.

A World Heritage Site, San Millán de la Cogolla was already famous in the 5C when Millán or Emilian de Berceo and his followers settled as hermits. Here the first manuscripts were written in Castilian Spanish.

Monasterio de Suso★

☞*Guided tours daily year-round 9.30am–1.30pm, 3.30–6 /6.30pm.* ☞*3€.* ✆*941 37 30 82. www. monasteriodeyuso.org.*

Housed in a Mozarabic building partly hollowed out of the rock, the monastery overlooks the Cárdenas Valley.

Monasterio de Yuso

◷ *Open Tue–Sun May–Sept 10.30am–1.30pm, 4–6.30pm Oct–Apr 10am–1pm, 4–6pm;.* ☞*4€.* ✆*941 37 30 49. www.monasteriodeyuso.org.*

In the treasury are splendid **ivories**★★ from two 11C reliquaries.

Monasterio de Nuestra Señora de Valvanera

Anguiano. Access via the LR 113. ◷ *Open daily 9am–7pm.* ☞*No charge.* ✆*941 37 70 44.*

This monastery is in a delightful, isolated wooded mountain **setting**★★. The church houses a 12C statue of the patron saint of La Rioja, the Virgen of Valvanera. The complex includes a hostel.

Valle del Iregua★

50km/31mi S of Logroño on the N 111. Near Isallana appear the **rock faces**★ of the Sierra de Cameros, overlooking the Iregua Valley from more than 500m/1 640ft. In the village of **Villanueva de Cameros**, half-timbered houses are roofed with circular tiles.

ADDRESSES

🛏 STAY

⊜⊜⊜ **Hotel Echaurren** – *Padre José García 19, Ezcaray.* ✆*941 35 40 47. www.echaurren.com. 25 rooms.* ⊒*8€. Restaurant*⊜⊜⊜⊜. Standing opposite the church of Santa María la Mayor, this hotel is best known for its cuisine, with traditional and creative menus. Bedrooms are pleasantly comfortable.

⊜⊜⊜⊜ **Parador de Santo Domingo de la Calzada** – *Pl. del Santo 3, Santo Domingo de la Calzada.* ✆*941 34 03 00. www.parador.es. 59 rooms.* ⊒*15€. Restaurant*⊜⊜⊜. Located in front of the cathedral, the parador is housed in a former pilgrims' hospital along the Way of St James. The main lounge, features Gothic-style stone walls and arches.

🍴 EAT

⊜⊜⊜ **Marixa** – *Sancho Abarca 8, Laguardia.* ✆*945 60 01 65. www. restaurantemarisa.com.* Popular and known for traditional cooking. Good views from the dining room, plus comfortable rooms (*10 rooms*⊜⊜⊜).

The eastern coastal strip of Valencia, Alicante and Murcia includes (from north to south) the lesser known Costa del Azahar (Orange Blossom Coast), the hugely popular Costa Blanca (White Coast) and the Costa Calida (Warm Coast). Their beachs and dunes are mostly low-lying with offshore sand bars, pools and lagoons. The climate is Mediterranean but drier than average; little rain falls except during the autumn months when the rivers sometimes flood. The natural vegetation, of olives, almond and carob trees and vines, has gradually been replaced, and the countryside transformed into *huertas* (irrigated areas), lush citrus orchards and market gardens. There are palm groves around Elche and Orihuela in the south and rice is grown in swampy areas. The region's economy is based increasingly around the booming tourist industry.

Highlights

1 Sheltering from the heat in Elche's remarkable **Palm Grove** (p485)

2 The view from the Castillo de Santa Bárbara, **Alicante** (p485)

3 Valencia's stunning **Ciudad de las Artes y las Ciencias** (p500)

4 Enjoying a plate of paella in Valencia's **Old Town** (p499)

5 Exploring the old quarter of picture-postcard **Peñiscola** (p489)

Alicante (Alacant) and Costa Blanca

Alicante province is holiday Spain; around 1 in 5 inhabitants is foreign – mostly British – and the coastal landscape is scarred by huge swathes of building projects. The most famous resort is Benidorm, an evergreen with British and north European package tourists since the 1960s. Its two beautiful (man-made) beaches, excellent theme parks, cheap accommodation amid ugly high-rise hotel canyons and a hedonistic lifestyle, particularly after dark, have come to be a stereotype of tourism on the Costa Blanca in particular and in Spain in general.

Despite the number of English and German voices to be heard, Alicante town remains very Spanish and few foreign tourists stay, or even use the fine beaches here.

The most attractive part of the Costa Blanca is north of Benidorm where, despite being very popular with

holidaymakers, the small towns of Denia (Valencian: Dénia), Jávea (Valencian: Xàbia), Alte and, to an extent, Calpe, have, respectively, each retained their attractive old quarter and a sense of identity.

Exploring the hinterland is often rewarding; a short journey inland from Alicante is Elche, a remarkable oasis of venerable palms amid the sunbaked countryside, while 80km/50mi or so east of Benidorm the Sierra Serella is a particularly beautiful and unspoiled rural area of low mountains, perfect for walkers.

　Alicante (Alacant)

　Costa Blanca

Murcia

Murcia province is a parched, flat and mostly featureless land with a hot and very dry climate. Since the late 1990s its coastline and, increasingly, its hinterland have been built up and paved over with scores of *urbanizaciones* (residential estates, favoured by ex-pats), many built within easy reach of new and very controversial water-thirsty golf courses.

Its coastline is the Costa Cálida ("Warm Coast") with around 250km/155.3mi of long flat beaches, stretching south to the Costa de Almería. The major visitor destination is the Mar Menor, both the largest natural lake in the country and the largest salty lagoon in Mediterranean Europe. Most of it has been converted into a huge holiday area, famous for its internationally acclaimed sporting and leisure village, La Manga. In the midst of the tourist development the city of Murcia remains an unspoiled oasis with a beautiful Cathedral.

　Murcia

Hemisfèric, Ciudad de las Artes y las Ciencias

H. Levy/MICHELIN

Valencia and Costa del Azahar

Frequently called the "New Barcelona", Valencia has always had a fascinating, if somewhat overlooked Old Town, fine beaches and excellent food (it is famous as the home of paella). But the city has only really taken off in visitor terms in the last few years, as a result of two high-profile international projects. The first was the cutting-edge architectural ensemble, La Ciudad de las Artes y las Ciencias (City of Arts and Sciences), by Santiago Calatrava and Sir Norman Foster. This is home to an eclectic range of visitor attractions and performing arts venues. The second project was the America's Cup, the world's biggest and most prestigious yachting event, staged in and around Valencia in 2007. Over 1.5€ billion was invested to convert the port area, including a splendid new state-of-the-art marina, with the aim of establishing Valencia as a world-class yachting centre.

Much less built up than the southern costas, but also with poorer-quality beaches, the Costa del Azahar is a favourite with Spanish and various European holidaymakers, with the notable exception of the British. Resorts tend to be low key and low rise and the hinterland is a broad green carpet of orange trees. The jewel of this coast is Peñíscola, with its Templar's castle rising from a rocky crag almost straight out of the sea (it is often referred to as Spain's Mont St Michel). Inland, amid the mountain region of El Maestrazgo, the small town of Morella boasts an outstanding medieval fortress on a very picturesque site. Játiva also makes a pleasant inland excursion.

- **Costa del Azahar**
- **Morella**
- **Valencia**

Alicante/ Alacant★

The Greeks called Alicante *Akra Leuka* (white citadel), the Romans *Lucentum* (city of light). It combines provincial calm with the bustle of tourism.

🐾 WALKING TOUR
OLD TOWN

▷ *Follow the route marked on the town plan.*

Explanada de España★

The most pleasant promenade in the region, running past the marina, is shaded by magnificent palms. Sunday concerts are held on the bandstand.

Catedral de San Nicolás

Pl. Abad Penalva. ⏰ *Open daily 7.30am–12.30pm, 5.30–8.30pm.* 🎫*No charge.* ✆*965 21 26 62.*

The 17C building on the site of a mosque – the city was only reconquered in 1296 – has a well-proportioned cupola, 45m/148ft high, over a Herreran nave. On calle Labradores, with its terraces, are the 18C Palacio Maisonnave, no. 9 (now the Municipal Archives; ⏰*open Mon–Fri Sept–Jun 9am–2pm; Jul–Aug 9am–1.30pm*); and an 18C mansion, no. 14, now a cultural centre.

Ayuntamiento (Town Hall)

Pl. del Ayuntamiento 1. ⏰ *Open Mon–Fri 9am–2pm.* ✆*965 14 91 10. www.alicante-ayto.es.*

This imposing 18C palace of golden stone, with two tiers of balconies, is flanked by two towers. Visit the Rococo **capilla** (chapel) with *azulejos* from Manises, and reception rooms with blue silk hangings.

Nearby on calle Gravina is the early 18C palace of the Museo de Bellas Artes Gravina (art museum; ⏰*open Oct–Apr Tue–Sat 10am–2pm, 4–8pm, Sun and public holidays 10am–2pm; May–Sept Tue–Sat 10am–2pm, 5–9pm, Sun and public holidays 10am–2pm;* 🎫*no charge;* ✆*965 14 67 80; www.mubag.org*), with 16C–19C works.

▶ **Population:** 331 750
⚐ **Michelin Map:** 577 Q 28 (town plan) – map 123 COSTA BLANCA.
🔲 **Info:** Avenida Rambla Mendez Nuñez 23. ✆965 20 00 00. www.alicanteturismo.com.
▶ **Location:** Alicante is the midpoint of Spain's Mediterranean coast, 110km/69mi from Cartagena. ▭Avenida de Salamanca 1
⊘ **Don't Miss:** A stroll along the Explanada by the harbour.
🕐 **Timing:** Start with a view from the Castillo de Santa Bárbara.
👫 **Kids:** They will love the castles; the Castillo de Santa Bárbara is a must.

Iglesia de Santa María

Pl. de Santa María. ⏰ *Open daily 10am–1pm, 5–9pm.* 🎫*No charge.* ✆*965 21 60 26.*

The church is in a square below Santa Bárbara Castle. The 18C Baroque **façade**★ has wreathed columns, pillars and breaks in its cornices. Once a mosque, it altered in the 17C when Churrigueresque decoration was added. Note the graceful Renaissance marble fonts and a painting of John the Baptist and John the Apostle by Rodrigo de Osuna the Younger.

Museo de la Asegurada★

Pl. de Santa María 3. ⏰ *Call for opening times.* ✆*965 14 07 68.*

On the same plaza, in a 17C granary, this museum exhibits 20C painting and sculpture donated by sculptor Eugenio Sempere. There are works by artists both Spanish (Miró, Picasso, Gargallo, Tàpies and Dalí) and foreign (Vasarely, Braque, Chagall and Kandinsky).

Capital of the Costa Blanca

Because of its mild climate and proximity to vast beaches (El Postiguet, La Albufereta and San Juan), Alicante has developed into the tourist capital of the Costa Blanca (*see COSTA BLANCA*), with seaside resorts such as Santa Pola, Guardamar del Segura, Torrevieja, and Campoamor springing up all along the southern part of this flat, sandy coastline.

Castillo de Santa Bárbara

Frente Playa Postiguet.
Ascend by lift and walk down, either all the way (good views) or to the halfway stop.
Open daily 24 Sept–20 Mar 9am–7pm; 21 Mar–23 Sept 10am–8pm.
2.40€ (child same price) by lift; free to drive or walk up. 965 16 21 28.

This fortress atop Benacantil hill dates from the 9C in Muslim times, though outbuildings were raised in the 16C. The Revellín del Bon Repós rampart was built in the 18C. The Philip II hall is a worthy highlight.

The Plaza de la Torreta is surrounded by the oldest buildings. A platform commands a fine **view**★ of the harbour and town. The 16C section is at the halfway stop on the lift; the 17C perimeter is lower down. A footpath leads into the medieval streets and tiny squares of the working-class Santa Cruz quarter.

SIGHTS

MARQ (Museo Arqueológico Provincial de Alicante)★★

Pl. Doctor Gómez Ulla. Open Sept–mid-Jun Tue–Sat 10am–7pm, Sun and public holidays 10am–2pm. 3€. 965 14 90 00. www.marqalicante.com.

MARQ opens archaeology to all, with a magnificent presentation focused on the ancients of this area.

The museum is organised into large halls (Prehistory, Iberian, Roman, Middle Ages and Modern) around a space devoted to archaeology itself. Here you can get right into excavations in a cave, a church and an underwater site.

EXCURSIONS

ELCHE/ELX★

24km/15mi SW. Pl. del Parc 3. 966 65 81 96. www.turismedelx.com. Avenida del Ferrocarril Este.

Elche (Valencian: Elx) lies along the Vinalopó river. The **Dama de Elche** (4C BC), a masterpiece of Iberian art now in the Museo Arqueológico de Madrid, was discovered in **La Alcudia** *(2km/1.2mi S)*.

El Misteri is a medieval verse drama with an all-male cast. It recounts the Dormition, Assumption and Coronation of the Virgin. It is on UNESCO's Oral and Intangible Heritage of Humanity list. *(played in the Basílica de Santa María; 29 Oct and1 Nov; www.misteridelx.com)*

El Palmeral (Palm Grove) ★★ *(Porta de la Morera 49; open daily Apr–Oct 9am–8.30pm; Nov–Mar 9am–6pm; 5€; 956 45 19 36)* – The groves, planted by the Phoenicians and expanded by the Arabs, are the largest

El Palmeral

©Turespaña

in Europe with more than 200 000 trees, and are a UNESCO World Heritage Site. The palms flourish with the aid of a remarkable irrigation system. Female trees produce dates, and the fronds from the male trees are used in Palm Sunday processions and handicrafts.

Huerta del Cura★★ (○ *open daily Apr–Oct 9am–8.30pm; Nov–Mar 9am–6pm;* ⊜*5€.* ℘*965 45 19 36*) – This delightful garden of Mediterranean and subtropical plants lies under magnificent palm trees; one, with seven trunks, is said to be 160 years old.

Parque Municipal★(*pas. de l'Estació*) – A well-tended garden covered with palm trees.

Museo Arqueológico y de Historia de Elche (MAHE) (*Diagonal del Palau;* ○ *open Mon–Fri noon–9pm, Sat–Sun 10am–9pm;*⊜*no charge;* ℘*966 661 53 82*) – The museum is in the Moorish Palacio de Altamira. The archaeological section traces Elche from its origins to the Visigoth era. Notable are sculpture and ceramics from the Iberian period and the *Venus of Illicis*, a delicately carved white marble Roman sculpture.

Basílica de Santa María (*pl. del Congreso Eucarístico;* ○ *open daily 7am–1.30pm, 5.30–9pm;* ⊜*2€;* ℘*965 45 15 40*) – This monumental 17C–18C Baroque basilica with a beautiful portal by Nicolás de Bussi is the setting for the annual mystery play. View the palm groves from the tower.

Nearby are the 17C–18C Almohad tower, **La Calahorra** (*Uberna 14*), and the Baños árabes.

Baños árabes (*pas. de Santa Llucía; access by a side door of the Convento de la Merced.* ○ *open Tue–Sat 10am–1.30pm, 4.30–8pm, Sun and public holidays 10.30am–1.30pm;*⊜*1€;* ℘ *965 45 28 87*) – A well-prepared exhibition details the culture of the bath in the 12C.

La Alcudia: archaeological site and museum (*ctra. Dolores; 2km/1.2mi S;* ○*open daily 10am–8pm;*⊜*2.50€;*℘*966 61 15 06*) – The remains and museum reveal the story of a city from the Neolithic period to its decline in Visigoth times.

TOUR INLAND
176km/110mi N.

▷ *Take the N 340 in San Juan, then the Alcoi road and then turn right.*

Cuevas de Canalobre

◄⋯*Guided tours (40min) mid-Sept–Jun Mon–Fri 10.30am–4.50pm, Sat–Sun and public holidays 10.30am–5.50pm; Jul–mid-Sept and Holy Week daily 10.30am–7.30pm.* ○*Closed 1 Jan, Mon after Easter Monday, 25 Dec.* ⊜*5€.* ℘*965 69 92 50. www.cuevasdecanalobre.com.*

The caves are at 700m/2 296.5ft up Mount Cabezón de Oro, with candelabra *(canalobre)* formations.

▷ *Return to the N 340.*

Cross dry country of figs and carobs.

Jijona/Xixona

The speciality of this town is *turrón*, an almond-honey sweet. Visit a **museum** (El Lobo; *ctra Jijona-Busot;* ○ *open Mon–Sat 10am–2pm, 4–8pm, Sun 10am–2pm, 5–8pm;* ⊜*1€;* ℘ *965 61 02 25; www.museodelturron.com*) and factories. Beyond Jijona (Valencian: Xixona) the road twists up through almond terraces to the **Puerto de la Carrasqueta★** (1 024m/3 360ft), a pass with a view towards Alicante.

Alcoy/Alcoi

▭▭*Plaza Estación.*

Alcoy is an industrial town in a mountain setting. Every year, between 22 and 24 April, **Moors and Christians★** (Moros y Cristianos) **festival** (*www.ajualcoi.org*) celebrates a Christian victory in 1276. It is the biggest, most colourful and noisiest of Spain's many Moors and Christians events.

▷ *Take the CV 795 to Barxell, then follow the CV 794.*

Bocairent

▭▭*Camino de la Estación, Ontiyent 10km/7mi N.*

The church in this hilltop market village has an interesting **Museo Parroquial** (Parish Museum; *Abadía 36;*

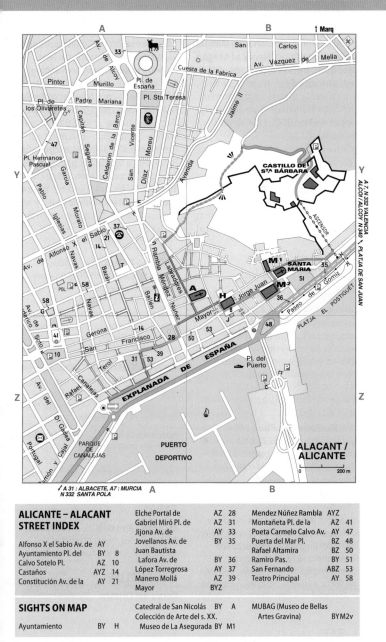

guided tours (45min) by appointment only; 1.80€; 962 35 00 62) with works by **Juan de Juanes** (1523–79) – who died here – and his school, and a 14C Last Supper by Marcial de Sax.

Take the CV81.

Villena

Ronda de la Estación

Castillo de la Atalaya (guided tours every hour Tue–Fri 10.30am–1.30pm, Sat–Sun and public holidays 11am–2pm; 965 80 38 04) – This castle of Arabic origin dominates its former feudal domain. Among its owners have been famed men of letters: **Don Juan Manuel** in the 14C and Prince **Henry of Aragon** (**Marqués de Villena,** 1384–1434), poet and magic fan. Its keep survives, with circular towers in the corners, and large Homenaje (homage) tower (upper section 15C). Fine views from the walls.

Iglesia de Santiago *(pl. de Santiago;* ⏰ *open Tue–Thu, Sat 11am–1pm, Fri 11am–11.30am, Sun and public holidays 10am–11am;* 📞 *965 81 39 19)* – This Gothic-Renaissance church (14C–17C) with notable bell tower stands near the town hall. Note unusual **spiral pillars**★ supporting Gothic vaults, and a Renaissance-style baptismal font.

Museo Arqueológico (Archaeological Museum) – *(pl. de Santiago 1;* ⏰ *open Tue–Fri 10am–2pm, Sat–Sun and public holidays 11am–2pm;* ⏰ *closed 1, 6 Jan, 25 Dec;* 🚫 *no charge;* 📞 *965 80 11 50; www. museovillena.com)* – The museum, in the town hall (*Palacio Municipal* , fine Renaissance façade and patio), displays solid gold from the Bronze Age (1500– 1000 BC). The outstanding **Villena Treasure**★★ includes jewellery and gourds decorated with sea urchin shell patterns.

ADDRESSES

🏨 STAY

🛏 **Hostal Les Monges Palace –** *San Agustín 4.* 📞 *965 21 50 46. www. lesmonges.net. 22 rooms.* 🍴 *6€.* An excellent location in the heart of old Alicante, with a standard not normally found in a *pensión*. Features of this charming 18C building include a marble staircase and large mirrors and windows.

🛏🛏 **Mediterránea Plaza** – *Pl. de Ayuntamiento 6.* 📞 *965 21 01 88. www. eurostarshotels.com. 50 rooms.* 🍴 *11€.* Located in the historical centre by the town hall, the ample facilities provided here makes this a good place to explore the city.

🛏🛏🛏 **Huerto del Cura** – *Porta de la Morera 14, Elche.* 📞 *966 61 00 11. www. huertodelcura.com. 81 rooms.* 🍴 *12€. Restaurant*🍴🍴🍴. Marvellous location right in a palm grove, opposite the famous Huerto del Cura. Bungalow-style rooms combine complete comfort with attention to all details.

🍴 EAT

🍴🍴🍴 **Asador Ilicitano** – *Maestro Giner 9, Elche.* 📞 *965 43 58 64. www. asadorilicitano.com. Closed Sun, fortnight in Aug.* A well-run steak house with rustic decor and modern embellishments. The pork dishes are exquisite and the service congenial.

🍴🍴🍴 **La Goleta** – *Explanada de España 8, bajos.* 📞 *965 21 43 92. www. restaurantelagoleta.es.* On a busy street near the marina, this restaurant has a pleasant covered terrace and marine decor inside. It offers regional sausages, fried seafood, faultless paella, and good home-made desserts.

🍴🍴🍴 **Nou Manolín** – *Villegas 3.* 📞 *965 20 03 68. www.noumanolin.com.* A classic restaurant with a rustic feel. The lovely banqueting room is the highlight of this three floor establishment.

Horchateria Azul – *Calderón de la Barca 38.* 📞 *965 21 63 10. Closed Sun.* A tiny shop without pretension, specialising in *horchata*, a drink made from barley and almonds. Friendly staff.

TAPAS

El Canto – *Alemania 26.* 📞 *965 92 56 50.* A delicious menu of *pinchos* and *raciones* offered in a bar atmosphere.

🌙 NIGHTLIFE

Barrio del Carmen – Alicante's old quarter is pleasant by day, and after 11pm, the whole district is transformed into one huge disco.

Puerto de Alicante – One of the liveliest areas on summer nights. On one side are locales with Latin and Spanish rhythms, on the other the shops and cafés and terraces of the Panoramis complex.

🛒 SHOPPING

Mercado Central – *Av. Alfonso X El Sabio. Open daily 6am–1pm.* This large covered market sells meat on the first floor and fish in the basement.

FIESTAS

Alicante celebrates **Hogueras de San Juan** *(www.hogueras.org)* from the 20–24 June, when giant pasteboard figures are set alight around the city, and the sky is lit up by a huge firework display.

Costa del Azahar

The mountain-sheltered Orange Blossom Coast is one of Spain's major tourist centres, marked by high-rise blocks and hotels along sandy beaches and orange groves. A number of small towns and villages preserve old quarters redolent of history.

🚗 DRIVING TOURS

From Vinaròs to Castellón
72km/45mi.

▶ *Follow either the N 340 or the AP 7 toll motorway.*

The northern coast of the province of Castellón is separated from the interior by the Maestrazgo mountains, recalling knights from the Templar and Montesa orders who controlled this area during the Middle Ages. Large resorts include Peñíscola and Benicàssim.

Vinaròs
🚉 *Plaza de la Estación.*
Vinaròs has the 16C **Iglesia de Nuestra Señora de la Asunción** *(pl. Parroquial; ℰ964 45 19 33)*, and a pleasant promenade close to the fishing port.

Peñíscola★★
🚉 *Plaza de la Estación, Benicarló. 10km/6.2mi N.*
The **old quarter★**, surrounded by walls, sits on a small rocky peninsula in the shadow of an imposing fortress, while its sandy beaches extend to either side. A small **fishing port** is still active.

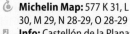

- 👤 **Michelin Map:** 577 K 31, L 30, M 29, N 28-29, O 28-29
- ℹ **Info:** Castellón de la Plana: Plaza María Agustina 5. ℰ964 35 86 88; Gandía: Avenida Marqués de Campo. ℰ964 287 77 88; Peñíscola: Paseo Marítimo. ℰ964 48 02 08. www.castellon-costaazahar.com.
- ▶ **Location:** Costa del Azahar stretches along the Mediterranean coast in eastern Spain, from Valencia. The AP 7 Autopista connects the beaches.
- 👥 **Kids:** Sand, surf and kids go together; apply the sunblock.

Castillo★
Castillo. 🕐 *Open daily Holy Week–15 Oct 9.30am–9.30pm; 16 Oct–Holy Week 10.30am–5.30pm.* 🎫*2.50€. ℰ964 48 00 21.*
Built by Templars in the early 14C, the castle was subsequently modified by Pope Luna, whose coat of arms, featuring a crescent moon in allusion to his name, can be seen on a gate. Grouped around the parade ground are the vast church, with pointed vaulting and a free-standing tower containing the conclave room and the study of the learned antipope who confirmed the foundation in 1411 of the University of St Andrew's in Scotland (⬥*see The Michelin Green Guide Scotland).*
The terrace offers a **panorama★** of the village and coastline. The castle is the setting for events such as the Festival of

Baroque and Ancient Music, in the first fortnight of August.
The castal road passes through an arid landscape. The resort of Alcossebre, popular with Spanish families, stands between Peñíscola and Benicàssim.

Benicàssim
🚌 *Plaza Estación.*
The other major tourist centre in the province of Castellón is separated from the interior by the **Desierto de las Palmas** (Palm Desert), which has suffered badly from fire in the past few years. Benicàssim has excellent beaches, lined by villas and apartments. The quieter town of Oropesa is located to the north. It also hosts an internationally renowned rock music festival every July (*www.fiberfib.com*).

Castellón de la Plana
🚌 *Pintor Oliet 2.*
Just a couple of miles separate Benicàssim from the port of Castellón, whose origins date back to the 13C. The capital of the province is situated in La Plana, an extensive fertile area irrigated by the River Mijares. On the main square is the **Catedral de Santa María** (*Arcipreste Balaguer 1;* ⏰*open daily 7.30am–1pm, 5–8pm;* ⇨*no charge;*

A Legendary Siege

Sagunto has a place in Spain's heroic history. In 218 BC the Carthaginian general **Hannibal** besieged Sagunto, then a small seaport allied to Rome, for a period of eight months. Seeing only one alternative to surrender, the local inhabitants lit a huge fire and women, children, the sick and the old then proceeded to throw themselves into the furnace while soldiers and menfolk made a suicidal sortie against the enemy. The event marked the beginning of the Second Punic War. Five years later, Scipio Africanus Major rebuilt the city, which became an important Roman town.

🖉*964 22 34 63*), rebuilt after the Spanish Civil War; the octagonal bell tower is from the late 16C. The town hall (*ayuntamiento*) is from the late 17C.
Other sights include paintings attributed to Zurbarán in the Convento de las Madres Capuchinas, and the Museo Provincial de Bellas Artes (*av. Hermanos Bou 28;* ⏰*open Tue–Sat 10am–8pm, Sun and public holidays 10am–2pm;* ⇨*no charge;* 🖉*964 72 75 00*), with prehistoric objects and local canvases and ceramics.

From Castellón to Valencia
69km/43mi.
22km/14mi NW on the CV 10 and CV 160.

Vilafamés
Vilafamés is an attractive town of Moorish origin with whitewashed houses and artists' workshops extending below the ruins of a castle.

Museo Popular de Arte Contemporáneo
Diputación 20. ⏰*Open Oct–May Tue–Fri 10am–1.30pm, 4–7pm, Sat–Sun 10.30am–2pm, 4–7pm; Jun–Sept Tue–Fri 10am–1.30pm, 5–8pm, Sat–Sun 10.30am–2pm, 5–8pm.* ⇨*1.80€.* 🖉*964 32 91 52.*
The museum, in a 15C palace, displays works by Miró, Barjola, Serrano, Genovés, Chillida and Grupo Crónica.

▶ *Return to Castellón; continue along the A 7 for 25km/15mi to Vall d'Uxo.*

Cuevas de San José
In Vall d'Uxo, follow signs to the caves (grutas). 🚶*Guided tours (35min) daily Oct–May 11am–1.15pm, 3.30–5.45pm; Jun–Jul and Sept 11am–1.15pm, 3.30–6.30pm; Aug 11am–1.15pm, 3.30–7.15pm.* ⏰ *Closed 1, 6 Jan, 25 Dec.* ⇨*9€.* 🖉*964 69 67 61. www. riosubterraneo.com.*
An underground river hollowed out these caves at the foot of the Parque Natural de La Sierra de Espadán. Tours by boat cover a distance of around 1.2km/0.75mi.

▶ *Continue for 20km/12.4mi along the CV 230, then follow the N 234.*

Segorbe
🚃 *Explanada Estación 2.*

The **cathedral** (*pl. de San Cristóbal*) is chiefly important for its **museum** (*museo;* 🕐 *open Tue–Sun 11am–1.30pm, 5–7pm;* 🕐 *closed 1 Jan, Good Friday, 25 Dec;* 🎫*3€;* ✆*964 71 10 14*), which contains a large **collection of altarpieces** painted by the **Valencia School**★. There are several paintings by **Vicente Macip** (d. 1545), who was influenced by the Italian Renaissance style. An *Ecce Homo* by his son **Juan de Juanes** bears the gentle touch favoured by Leonardo da Vinci. There are also works by Rodrigo de Osona and Jacomart and a 15C marble low relief of a Madonna by Donatello.

▶ *Continue along the N 234, towards the coast.*

Sagunto
🚃 *Vía Férrea.*

Historic Sagunto sits at the foot of a hill occupied by the ruins of a castle and Roman theatre. The port is 5km/3mi to the east.

Ruins
Castillo. 🕐 *Open Apr–Oct Tue–Sat 10am–8pm, Sun and public holidays 10am–2pm; Nov–Mar Tue–Sat 10am–6pm, Sun and public holidays 10am–2pm.* 🕐 *Closed 1 Jan, Good Friday, 25 Dec.* 🎫*No charge.* ✆*962 66 55 81. Access the ruins by the alleyways of the old Jewish quarter.*

The 1C **theatre**, restored and still in use, with fine acoustics,was built into the hillside by the Romans. The **Acropolis** consists of the ruins and remains of ramparts, temples and houses built by Iberians, Phoenicians, Carthaginians, Romans, Visigoths and Moors. Buildings to the west date from the War of Independence, when the French general Suchet besieged the town. The **view**★ encompasses the town, countryside and sea.

Valencia ✆*See VALENCIA*

From Valencia to Játiva/Xàtiva
122km/76mi.

▶ *Leave Valencia along the coast road S.*

Parque Natural de La Albufera
This vast body of water (*albufera*, "small sea" in Arabic) south of Valencia is the largest freshwater lagoon in Spain, separated from the sea by an offshore bar, the Dehesa, that has been planted with rice since the 13C. Its eels appear on typical menus in restaurants in **El Palmar** (*to the S*) which also serve Valencia's famous dish, **paella**.

🔢*For further details on the park, contact the* **Centro de Interpretación del Racó de l'Olla** (🕐 *open Mon, Wed, Fri 9am–2pm, Tue, Thu 9am–2pm, 4–5.30pm (6.30pm summer), Sat–Sun and public holidays 9am–2pm, 3–5.30pm;* 🕐 *closed 1, 6 Jan, 25 Dec;* ✆*961 62 73 45).*

The novel *Cañas y Barro*, by **Vicente Blasco Ibáñez** (1867–1928), was set in the Albufera.

▶ *Continue along the CV 500.*

Cullera
This resort is at the mouth of the River Júcar; its bay is demarcated to the north by a lighthouse, the Faro de Cullera (*www.culleraturismo.com*). In the town are remains of a 13C castle.

▶ *Head 27km/17mi S along the N 332.*

Gandia
🚃 *Parc de L'estacio.*

Gandia is at the centre of a *huerta* which produces large quantities of oranges. A resort has developed near the harbour along a 3km/1.8mi-long sandy **beach**.

Palacio Ducal
Duc Alfons El Vell 1. 🕐 *Open May–Oct Tue–Sat 10am–2pm, 5–7pm, Sun 9.30am–1.30pm; Nov–Apr Tue–Sat 10am–2pm, 4–6pm, Sun 9.30am–1.30pm.* 🕐 *Closed public holidays in*

afternoon. ⊚*4.50€.* ℘*962 87 14 65.*
www.palauducal.com.

The mansion in which St Francis
Borja was born, now a Jesuit college,
underwent considerable modification
between the 16C and 18C. Only the
patio remains Gothic in appearance
and typical of those along this coast.
Colegiata de Santa María (*open
daily 9am–noon, 6–8pm;* ⊚*no charge;*
℘*962 87 19 51*), a collegiate church in
nearby Plaza Mayor, built in the 14C–15C
and expanded in the 16C, is one of the
finest Gothic structures in Valencia
province.

○ *Head inland along the CV 60.*
Before Palomar, bear right on the A 7.

Játiva/Xàtiva

🚌 *Plaza de la Estación.*
Known as "the town of the thousand
fountains", Xàtiva stands in a plain
covered with a Mediterranean landscape
of vineyards, orchards and cypress
trees. The town was the birthplace of
two members of the Borja family who
became popes, Calixtus III (1455–58)
and Alexander VI, and, in 1591, of the
painter **José Ribera**. The 16C **colegiata**
(collegiate church; *pl. Calixto III;* *open
daily 10.30am–1pm;* ℘*962 27 38 36*),
modified in the 18C, faces the former
Hospital Royal, which has an ornate
Gothic-Plateresque façade.

Museo de l'Almodí

Corretgeria 46. ○ *Open 16 Sept–14 Jun
Tue–Fri 10am–2pm, 4–6pm, Sat–Sun
10am–2pm; 15 Jun–15 Sept Tue–Fri
9.30am–2.30pm, Sat–Sun 10am–2pm.
2.10€; free Sun.* ℘*962 27 65 97.
www.xativa.es/museu/cas/museo.htm.*
The Almudin, a Renaissance-style former
granary with a Gothic façade, houses
fine Moorish-era artefacts, along with
gold and silverwork and paintings. An
11C **Moorish fountain** (*pila*) of pink
marble is exceptional for its depiction
of human figures, extremely rare in
Islamic art.

Ermita de Sant Feliu

○ *On the castle road.* ○ *Open Nov–
Mar Mon–Sat 10am–1pm, 3–6pm,
Sun and public holidays 10am–1pm;
Apr–Oct Mon–Sat 10am–1pm, 4–7pm,
Sun and public holidays 10am–1pm.*
℘*962 27 33 46.*
Built on the flank of the hill, this chapel
contains a group of 15C–16C Valencian
primitives. At the entrance is a white
marble **stoup**★ hollowed out of a
former capital.

Castillo

Subida al Castillo. ○ *Open Tue–Sun
Apr–Sept 10am–7pm; Oct–Mar 10am–
6pm.* ○ *Closed 1 Jan, 25 Dec.* ⊚*2.10€.*
℘*962 27 42 74.*

ADDRESSES

🛏 STAY

⊜⊜ **Albatros** –*Clot de la Mota 11 (near
beach), Gandia.* ℘*982 84 56 00. www.
hotel-albatros.com. 46 rooms.* �*5.60€.*
This hotel's sharp style and amenities
are rare in the beach area. Limited menu
served in the evening.

⊜⊜⊜⊜ **Hostería del Mar** – *Av. Papa
Luna 18, Peñíscola.* ℘*902 48 06 00. www.
hosteriadelmar.net. 85 rooms.* ⊏吕*8.56€.*
This smart modern hotel maintains a
traditional Castillan atmosphere. The
restaurant specialises in fish and rice
dishes as well as grilled meats.

🍴 EAT

⊜⊜ **El Peñón** – *Santos Mártires 22,
Peñíscola. On the way up to the castle,
next to the Ermita de la Virgen.* ℘*964 48
07 16. Closed Christmas–Feb and Wed.*
Half-hidden in one of the narrow streets
of the old town, the Peñón is a friendly
restaurant with attractive decor and a
pleasant small terrace, where you can
enjoy excellent fish dishes.

⊜⊜⊜⊜ **Salvia** – *Ctra Subida al Castillo, Cullera.* ℘*961 72 03 98. www.salvia
restaurant.com. Closed Mon for dinner, Tue
and a fortnight in Nov.* Enjoy traditional
cuisine along with the panoramic views
of the sea and the town.

Costa Blanca★

The White Coast stretches south from Valencia to Murcia. It is flat and sandy, with occasional highlands where the sierras drop to the sea. A hot climate, low rainfall, dazzling light, long beaches and turquoise water attract vast numbers of tourists.

 DRIVING TOUR

From Denia to Guadalest
115km/71mi – allow 2 days

Denia (Dénia)
The former Greek colony became Roman *Dianium*. Denia today is a fishing harbour, toy manufacturing centre and seaside resort. In the fortress (*2.15€, including museum; 966 42 06 56*) above town is an archaeological museum. The coast south of Denia becomes steep and rocky with pine forests.

Cap de Sant Antoni★
Near the lighthouse on this headland, a last foothill of the Sierra del Mongó, is a good **view**★ towards Xàbia and the Cabo de la Nao headland.

Jávea (Xàbia)
The old quarter is on high ground around a fortified 14C Gothic church. The modern quarter is near the harbour, beach and parador.

Cabo de la Nao★
The climb affords views over Jávea at the foot of the Sierra del Mongó; then enter thick pinewoods where villas stand in clearings. Cabo de la Nao is an eastern extension of the Sierras Béticas (Baetic Cordillera) that continues under the sea to reappear as the island of Ibiza. There is a beautiful **view**★ south from the point down the coast to the Penyal d'Ifac. Sea caves (approached by boat) and charming creeks such as **La Granadella** (south) and **Cala Blanca** (north) are excellent for diving.

Michelin Map: 577 P 29-30, Q 29-30 – COMMUNIDAD VALENCIANA (ALICANTE/ ALACANT), MURCIA

Info: Altea: San Pedro 9. 965 84 41 14; Denia: Plaza Oculista Buigues 9. 966 42 23 67. www.costablanca.org.

Location: Costa Blanca towns are linked by the N 332 and the AP 7 toll motorway.

Don't Miss: Beaches, sun, villages.

Kids: Tierra Mítica amusement park at Benidorm.

Calp (Calpe)
The **Penyal d'Ifac**★, a rocky outcrop 332m/1 089ft high, is the setting of Calp. A path leads to the top of the Penyal (*about 1hr walk*) with views along the coast of Calp and its salt pans, of the dark mountain chains, and northwards of the coast as far as Cabo de la Nao. The Sierra de Bernia road twists and turns before crossing the spectacular Barranco de Mascarat (Mascarat Ravine) in the hinterland to Cabo de la Nao.

Altea
Altea's white walls, rose-coloured roofs and glazed blue tile domes rise in tiers up a hillside overlooking the sea – a symphony of colour and reflected light below the Sierra de Bernia. A walk through the alleys to the church and then the view from the square over the village and beyond to the Penyal d'Ifac will reveal the attraction of so many painters towards Altea.

Benidorm
The excellent climate, cheap packaged holidays from Britain and Germany, and two immense beaches (the Levante and the Poniente), curving away on either side of a small rock promontory, are the elements of Benidorm's incredible growth from a modest fishing village in the 1950s to a Mediterranean Manhattan.

From the lookout on **El Castillo** point, there are **views**★ of the beaches and sea. The old quarter stands behind the point, close to the blue domed church.

♨ Terra Mítica

3km/2mi from Benidorm.
Exit the AP 7 at exit 65 A. ◷*Open daily 10am–8pm (please check website for changes).* ◉*34€/1 day (48€/2 days; 21€/evenings); child 25.50€/35€/ 16.50€.* ℘*902 02 02 20.*
www.terramiticapark.com.
This vast theme park is based upon ancient Egypt, Greece, Rome and Iberia, Terra Mítica has attractions for visitors of all ages and tastes, as well as shows and a choice of shops and restaurants.

Main attractions – In Ancient Egypt, enter the Pyramid of Terror, or descend the Cataracts of the Nile on an exciting white-water roller coaster ride. In Greece, emulate Theseus in the Labyrinth of the Minotaur, or experience the sensation of falling down a waterfall in the Fury of Triton. The Magnus Colossus in Rome is a spectacular wooden roller coaster. In the Flight of the Phoenix, enjoy the excitement of a free fall from 54m/177ft, or battle against currents and whirlpools in the Rapids of Argos, in the Islands section.

ADDRESSES

🏠 STAY

◉◉ **Hostal L'Ánfora** – *Expl. Cervantes 8, Denia.* ℘*966 43 01 01. www.hostal lanfora.com. 20 rooms.* This small building with its distinctive green façade is located at the fishing port in Denia. Although small and basic, the rooms here are bright and clean. In the mornings, guests can also enjoy the sight of local fishing boats from their windows.

🍴 EAT

◉◉ **Casa Modesto Vivero de Lan-gostas** – *Cala de Finestrat. 4km/2.5mi W of Benidorm along the Playa de Poniente.* ℘*965 85 86 37. Closed 15 Jan–15 Mar.* The menu at this beach restaurant revolves around fish and seafood. The views from this cove are splendid, although

▶ *Take the CV 70 to Callosa d'En Sarrià then head along the CV 755 to Alcoi.*

On the drive inland, you pass through small valleys cloaked in all sorts of fruit trees, including citrus and medlars. The village of **Polop** stretches up a hillside in a picturesque mountain setting. Beyond, the landscape becomes more arid but the views more extensive, the mountains more magnificent.

Guadalest★

Guadalest stands out from the terraced valleys of olive and almond trees to face the harsh limestone escarpments of the Sierra de Aitana. The **site**★ is impressive. The village, forced halfway up a ridge of rock, is a stronghold accessible only through an archway cut into stone. Walk round the **Castillo de San José** (now a cemetery; *Iglesia 2;* ◷*open daily Holy Week–Oct 10.15am–1.45pm, 3.15–8pm; Nov–Holy Week 10.15am–1.45pm, 3.15–6pm;* ◷*closed 1 Jan, 25 Dec;* ◉*3€;* ℘*965 88 53 93*) where ruins remain of fortifications wrecked by an earthquake in 1744. The splendid view takes in the Guadalest reservoir with its reflections of surrounding mountain crests, the amazing site of the old village, and, in the distance, the sea.

the high-rise towers of Benidorm are something of a blot.

◉◉◉ **Racó de Toni** – *La Mar 127, Altea.* ℘*965 84 17 63. Closed Nov.* A traditional menu is served in a warm atmosphere with friendly service. Can get overcrowded.

TAPAS

La Cava Aragonesa – *Pl. de la Constitución (also entry on Callejón Santo Domingo), Benidorm Old Town.* ℘*966 80 12 06. www.lacavaaragonesa.es.* This typical bar makes a refreshing change from the dozens of neighbouring tower blocks, with its cured hams hanging from the ceiling and its good choice of tapas. Also on the attractive alleyway of Callejón de Santo Domingo, try the tapas at **Bar Aurrerá**.

Morella

Morella has an amazing site★: 14C ramparts, punctuated by towers, form a mile-long girdle round a 1 004m/3 294ft hill which the town ascends in tiers to castle ruins.

SIGHTS

A stroll around Morella's concentric streets reveals a number of mansions and religious buildings. One of the gateways, the Puerta de San Miguel, houses a small **museum** dedicated to the age of dinosaurs (○*open Tue–Sun 11am–2pm, 4–6pm (7pm in summer);* ○*closed public holidays;* ☞*2€;* ℘*964 17 31 17).*

Iglesia de Santa María la Mayor★

Placeta de la Iglesia. ○*Open daily Jul–Aug 11am–2pm, 4–7pm; Sept–Jun noon–2pm, 4–6pm.* ○ *Closed 1, 6 Jan, 25, 31 Dec.* ☞*No charge.* ℘*964 16 03 79.*
The basilica is one of the most interesting Gothic churches in the Levante.
It has two fine portals, the 14C Apostle Doorway, and the Virgins' Doorway with an openwork tympanum. The unusual raised Renaissance *coro* at the nave centre has a spiral staircase magnificently carved with biblical scenes and a delicate balustrade with a frieze illustrating the Last Judgement. The sanctuary was sumptuously decorated in Baroque style in the 17C and an elegant organ loft introduced in the 18C.
There is a small **museum** with a beautiful Valencian *Descent from the Cross* and a 14C *Madonna* by Sassoferrato.

Castillo

Pl. San Francisco. ○ *Open daily Apr–Oct 10am–7.30pm; Nov–Mar 9am–6.30pm.* ○ *Closed 1 Jan, 24–26 Dec.* ☞*1.50€.* ℘*964 17 31 28.*
On the way up there are good **views**★ of the town, the 13C–14C ruins of the Convento de San Francisco with its Gothic cloisters, the 14C–15C aqueduct and the reddish heights of the surrounding sierras.

▶ **Population:** 2 854
⚒ **Michelin Map:** 577 K 29
🚩 **Info:** Avenida Vilafranca. ℘964 16 10 71. www.morella.net.
◐ **Location:** Morella nestles in the Maestrazgo of Valenciana, linked to the coast by the N 232 to Peñíscola (78km/49mi) and Castellón de la Plana (98km/61mi).

EXCURSIONS

Santuario de la Balma

25km/15.5mi NW along the CV 14.
This unusual Marian sanctuary is built into a rock wall overlooking the River Bergantes. The cave in which the Virgin appeared is enclosed by a 13C side wall and a 17C façade. Access is via a narrow gallery excavated into the rock.

Mirambel

30km/19mi W on the CS 840.
◐ *Bear left after 11km/7mi.*

This small, well-preserved mountain village retains its medieval character. A number of houses bear coats of arms.

ADDRESSES

🏠 STAY

▭▭ **Del Pastor** – *San Julián 12, Morella.* ℘*964 16 10 16. www.hoteldelpastor.com. 12 rooms. Closed 17–26 Dec. 26 rooms. Restaurant*▭▭. A small, family-run establishment, with a lovely stone façade. The rooms are well decorated and maintained. The excellent restaurant serves local cuisine in a rustic ambience.

Murcia★

Murcia, an historic but also booming university town, lies along the Segura in a fertile market-gardening area *(huerta)*.

A BIT OF HISTORY
The city, founded in the reign of Abd ar-Rahman II in 825 as Madina Mursiya, was reconquered in 1266. Up to the 18C, Murcia prospered from agriculture and silk weaving.

SIGHTS
Catedral★
Pl. Cardenal Belluga. Open 7am–1pm, 5–8.30pm. No charge. Closed during the Virgen de la Fuensanta pilgrimage (twice per year in Lent and September). 968 22 13 71.
The original 14C cathedral is camouflaged beneath Renaissance and Baroque additions. The **façade**★, with an arrangement of columns and curves, is a brilliant example of Baroque. The impressive belfry, 95m/311ft in height, was completed by Ventura Rodríguez in the 18C. The interior, beyond the entry cupola, is preponderantly Gothic, apart from the 16C **Capilla de los Junterones** *(fourth south chapel)*, which has rich Renaissance decoration.
The **Capilla de los Vélez**★ *(off the ambulatory)* is sumptuous Late Gothic with splendid star vaulting, and wall decoration with Renaissance and Mudéjar motifs.
The sacristy, approached through two successive Plateresque doors (beautiful panels on the first), is covered by an unusual radiating dome. The walls are richly panelled with Plateresque carving below and Baroque above.

Museo Salzillo★
Pl. San Agustín 3. Open Tue–Sat 9.30am–2pm, 5–8pm, Sun and public holidays 11am–2pm. Closed 1, 6 Jan, Holy Week, 1 May, 9 Jun, 25 Dec. 3€. 968 29 18 93. www.museosalzillo.es.
The museum possesses Salzillo's masterpieces including the eight polychrome wood sculptures of **pasos**

- **Population:** 430 571
- **Michelin Map:** 123 COSTA BLANCA
- **Info:** Plaza Cardenal Belluga. 968 35 87 49. www.murciaturistica.es.
- **Location:** 50km/31mi from the coast. Plaza de la Industria.

carried in the Good Friday procession during Holy Week, kept in side chapels off the nave of the Church of Jesus. The deep emotion on the faces is impressive. The museum also contains vivid terracotta pieces used to create scenes from the life of Jesus.

EXCURSIONS
Orihuela★
24km/15mi NE on the A 7. Avenida Teodomiro 68.
This peaceful town, with its many churches, lies along the Segura, which provides water for market gardens *(huertas)* and for the local **palm grove**. For centuries, Orihuela was a university town. The house of poet and dramatist Miguel Hernández is now a museum *(Miguel Hernández 73; open Jun–Sept Tue–Sat 10am–2pm, 5–8pm, Sun and public holidays 10am–2pm; Oct–May 10am–2pm, 4–7pm, Sun and public holidays 4–7pm; closed 1, 6 Jan, 25 Dec; no charge; 965 30 63 27).*

Catedral del Salvador★
Mayor. Open Mon–Fri 10.30am–1pm, 4–6.30pm, Sat 10.30am–1pm. No charge. 965 30 06 38.
Constructed in the 14C–16C, the cathedral has a Renaissance north doorway. The interior has three cruciform Gothic naves, ambulatory, and unusual vaulting with spiral ribs.
The stalls of the choir are carved in Baroque style. There are notable Renaissance **grilles** around the choir and presbitery. The **Museo de la Catedral** houses a *Temptation of St Thomas Aquinas* by Velázquez, a *Christ* by Morales and a *Mary Magdalene* by Ribera.

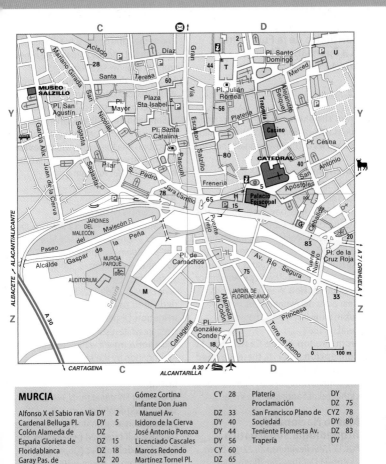

The **Palacio del Obispo** on calle Ramón y Cajal behind the cathedral has a magnificent 18C patio.

Convento de Santo Domingo

Adolfo Clavarana (north of the city).
🕐 *Open Tue–Fri 10am–1.30pm, 5–8pm, Sat 10am–2pm, 5–7pm, Sun 10am–2pm.* 🕐 *Closed 1, 6 Jan, 17 Jul, 25 Dec.* ⊛*No charge.* 📞*965 30 02 40.* This monumental building (16C–18C), formerly the university, started out in Renaissance style and transformed into Baroque. The long college façade conceals two sober cloisters (17C–18C). The 18C **church**★ is covered with murals and exuberant stucco mouldings.

Museo de la Muralla

Río. 🕐 *Open Tue–Sat 10am–2pm, 4–5pm, Sun and public holidays 10am–2pm.* ⊛*No charge.* 📞*965 30 46 98.* Descend below street level to the remains of the city wall, dwellings and baths from the Moorish era, and a Gothic palace and a Baroque building.

The **Iglesia de Santiago** (*pl. de Santiago 2;* 🕐*open daily Jul–Sept 10am–2pm, 5–8pm; Oct–Jun 10am–2pm, 4.30–7pm;* ⊛*1€;* 📞*965 30 13 60*), near the town hall, is Gothic in style, with Renaissance transept and apse. It was founded by the Catholic Monarchs whose yoke and arrow emblems, together with a statue of St James, are on the Gothic portal; the doorway on the right is Baroque. In the interior, note statues attributed to Salzillo in the side chapels.

Santuario de la Fuensanta (La Fuensanta Shrine)
7km/4.3mi S.

▷ *Follow the signs from Puente Viejo.*

From the shrine of the Virgen de la Fuensanta, patron saint of Murcia, enjoy fine **views** of the town and the *huerta*.

Cartagena
62km/39mi SE along the N 301.
Plaza de México 2.

In 223 BC this bay settlement was captured by the Carthaginians; it was subsequently colonised by the Romans, as *Cartago Nova*. Philip II fortified the surrounding hilltops, and Charles III built the Arsenal. The city is known for its dramatic Holy Week processions.
Near plaza del Ayuntamiento is the early **submarine** invented by native son Isaac Peral, in 1888.
From the top of the **Castillo de la Concepción** *(Gisbert)*, there is a good general **view** of the harbour and the ruins of the former Romanesque cathedral of Santa María la Vieja.

Museo Nacional de Arqueología Subacuática
Pas. del Muelle Alfonso XII 22. ⏰ *Open 15 Apr–15 Oct Tue–Thu 10am–9pm, Fri–Sat 10am–10pm, Sun and public holidays 10am–3pm; 16 Oct–14 Apr Tue–Sat 10am–7.30pm, Sun and public holidays 10am–3pm.* ⏰ *Closed 1, 6 Jan, 1 May, 24–25, 31 Dec.* ✉*3€; no charge Sat (from 3pm), Sun.* ✆*968 12 11 66. http://museoarqua.mcu.es.*
This museum displays underwater finds, notably Phoenician, Punic and Roman amphorae. Maps and models of vessels (galleys, biremes and triremes) illustrate seafaring in times past.

Mar Menor
At La Manga: 81km/51mi SE via the N 301 and MU 312 and 33km/21mi from Cartagena.
Mar Menor, or Little Sea, is a lagoon separated from the open Mediterranean by **La Manga**, a sand bar 500m/1 640ft wide which extends from the eastern

end of the Cabo de Palos headland. Gilt-head, mullet and king prawns are fished from its shallow salt-water.
La Manga del Mar Menor is a large, elongated seaside resort with surrealistic tower blocks stretching for miles.
In **Santiago de la Ribera**, where there is no natural beach, pontoons with changing cabins line the seafront. **San Javier**, nearby, is the seat of the Academia General del Aire (Air Academy).

Alcantarilla
9km/5.6mi W on the N 340.
The **Museo de la Huerta** *(av. Príncipe;* ⏰*open 1 Apr–26 Oct Tue–Fri 1am–8pm, Sat–Sun 10am–1.30pm, 4–6pm; 27 Oct–30 Mar Tue–Fri 10am–6.30pm, Sat–Sun 10am–1pm;* ⏰*closed public holidays;* ✉*no charge;* ✆*968 89 25 86)* is a museum dedicated to local **agriculture and irrigation**. Dispersed among the orange trees are white rustic dwellings *(barracas)* and a **noria**, a giant waterwheel devised for irrigation by the Moors.

Lorca
67km/42mi SW along the N 340-E 12.
Alameda de Menchirón.
Lorca lies in an irrigated valley at the foot of a hill crowned by a **castle**, the **Fortaleza del Sol** *(*⏰*open Mar–Dec daily 10.30am–6.30pm;* ✉*10€, child 7€;* ✆*902 40 00 47)*, where visitors may spend the day back in the Middle Ages.
The main sights are the **plaza de España**, surrounded by the Baroque façades of the **ayuntamiento** (town hall), the **Juzgado** (Law Courts), embellished with a corner sculpture, and the **Colegiata de San Patricio** *(*✆*968 46 99 66)*, a collegiate church built in the 16C and 18C, and the **Palacio de Guevara**. Its doorway, although in poor condition, is a fine example of Baroque sculpture (1694; *now the tourist office;* ✆*968 44 19 14; http://lorcatallerdeltiempo.es)*.

Caravaca de la Cruz
70km/44mi W along the C 415. Tourist Office, calle de Las Monjas, 17. ✆*968 70 10 03. /www.turismocaravaca.org..*
This attractive town is topped by its castle of Muslim origin, which was

extended in the 15C by the Knights Templars. Within the comppund the **Santuario de la Santa Cruz** is an impressive Baroque monument. Below, the town also retains many fine examples of superb Renaissance architecture, the jewel in the crown being the **Iglesia de San Salvador**, which has been declared a Historic-Artistic Site.

ADDRESSES

STAY

Hispano 2 – *Radio Murcia 3. 968 21 61 52. www.hotelhispano.net. 35 rooms. 5€. Restaurant*.
A local classic, known for its excellent location by the cathedral among the winding lanes and pedestrian streets. Rooms are of a basic comfort level, and public areas are limited but cosy.

EAT

Acuario – *Pl. Puxmarina 3. 968 21 99 55. Closed Sun, Mon eve, a fortnight in Aug and Holy Week.* This established family restaurant offers regional cuisine with contemporary touches, based on local recipes and produce. Good for the price.

Valencia★★

Spain's third-largest city, Valencia is unprepossessing at first glance with anonymous high-rise suburbs at its outer limits. However, wide palm-lined avenues encircle the old quarter with its fortified gateways, quaint shops and Gothic houses. This is a city reborn, thanks to works by Santiago Calatrava and Sir Norman Foster and by its hosting the America's Cup in 2007. To top it off, superb beaches are easily reached by tram.

THE CITY TODAY

Over the last five years Valencia has become a popular city break to rank alongside Barcelona, and like its Catalan cousin, it too has turned its face back to the sea with its beach and particularly its port area revitalised since 2007. The eating, drinking and nightlife, both here and in the Old Town are excellent.

A BIT OF HISTORY

2 000 years of history – The city founded by the Greeks in 138 BC passed into the hands of Carthaginians, Romans, Visigoths and Arabs, was briefly reconquered in 1094 by **El Cid**, and taken definitively in 1238 by James the

- ▶ **Population:** 807 200
- **Michelin Map:** 577 N28 (town plan) or 574 N 28
- **Info:** Plaza de la Reina 19. 963 15 39 31. www.turisvalencia.es.
- **Location:** Valencia is the main city of the Levante region. Avenida Blasco Ibáñez (Cabanyal); Xàtiva 24 (Estaciò Nord).
- **Parking:** Don't try to find a space in the old quarter.
- **Don't Miss:** A walk in the old quarter and the Ciudad de las Artes y las Ciències.
- **Timing:** Start with unmissable modern architecture (Santiago Calatrava's City of Arts and Sciences and the convention centre) and Sir Norman Foster's Turia bridge; or with the heritage section of the city.
- **Kids:** L' Oceanogràfic is one of the world's great aquariums.

Conqueror. Valencia prospered until the discovery of America, and again with a silk renaissance in the 17C.

Valencia sided with Charles of Austria in the War of the Spanish Succession, and lost its privileges. In 1808, it rose against the French. In 1939 it was the last Republican redoubt.

Art in Valencia – Valencia flourished economically in the 15C, and artistically as well, as seen in the Gothic architecture of palaces, the Cathedral and the Lonja (Exchange). Among painters were **Luis Dalmau**, who developed a Hispano-Flemish style; **Jaime Baço** (**Jacomart**), **Juan Reixach** and the **Osonas**, father and son. Notable 15C decorative arts were wrought ironwork, gold- and silversmithing, and ceramics *(see the Museo Nacional de Cerámica in Sights).*

The Valencia huerta and Albufera – The Roman irrigation system around Valencia was improved by the Moors. Orchards and market gardens produce fruit and early vegetables for Europe. South of Valencia lies a vast lagoon, the **Parque Natural de La Albufera** *(see COSTA DEL AZAHAR).*

SIGHTS
Ciudad de las Artes y las Ciències★★
This cultural and recreational complex (350 000sq m/420 000sq yd) is a series of spectacular avant-garde white buildings that reflect onto sheets of water. The following sights are based at this Ciy of Arts and Sciences.

Tribunal de las Aguas
Since the Middle Ages disputes in the *huerta* have been settled by the Water Tribunal: every Thursday at noon, representatives of the areas irrigated by the eight canals, accompanied by an *alguazil* (officer of justice), meet in front of the Portada de los Apóstoles (Apostles' Door) of the Cathedral; the offence is read out, judged (the judges all in black) and the sentence pronounced immediately (a fine, deprivation of water) by the most senior judge. The proceedings are oral and there is no appeal.

L'Oceanogràfic★★
(*Estación de El Cabanyal and Estación del Norte; av. Autopista del Saler 5; open Jan–May and 16 Sept–Dec Sun–Fri 10am–6pm, Sat 10am–8pm; Jun–15 Jul and 1–15 Sept Sun–Fri 10am–8pm, Sat 10am–8pm; 16 Jul–Aug daily 10am–midnight. 22.80€ (25€ with L'Hemisfèric and Museu de les Ciències Príncipe Felipe), child 17.20€/19€. 902 10 00 31. www.cac.es)*
– Part of Valencia's City of Arts and Sciences, the facilities of this, the largest maritime centre of Europe, are set around a lake and joined by gardens and tunnels. The exhibit focuses on marine life in the Mediterranean, marshland, temperate and tropical zones (turtles and grey seals outside and a great 70m/230ft tunnel-aquarium below), the Arctic, the Antarctic (penguins) and Oceans (including a 30m/100ft aquarium-tunnel with sharks and rays). The dolphin centre hosts performances all day.

L'Umbracle★
– White parabolic arches shelter this pleasant palm garden on a terrace facing the Museu de las Ciències.

Museu de les Ciències Príncipe Felipe★★
(*av. Autopista del Saler 1–7; open daily 15 Sept–Jun 10am–7pm; Jul–14 Sept 10am–9pm; closed 1 Jan, 31 Dec; 7.50€; 902 10 00 31; www.cac.es)*
Based at Valencia's City of Arts and Sciences, the largest interactive science museum in Europe, designed by Santiago Calatrava, is a hands-on encounter with the human genome, space travel, astronomy and more.

L'Hemisfèric★
(*Autopista del Saler; check programmes and prices by calling 902 10 00 31; www.cac.es)* – Also the work of Calatrava, this building – at Valencia's City of Arts and Sciences – symbolises a human eye open to the world. Set in a huge pool, it houses a planetarium and Omnimax cinema.

The World's Largest Food Fight

The town of **Buñol** *(40km/25mi W of Valencia off the A 3)*, numbering some 10 000 inhabitants, lies in the tranquil setting of the Sierra de Las Cabrillas. Yet, at the end of every August, the town swells beyond all proportion for the celebration of one of the most famous festivals in Spain, **La Tomatina** *(www.tomatina.es)*. A week-long festival of parades honour the town's patron, San Luis Bertràn. This culminates on the Wednesday, when at 10am, the crowds are challenged to snatch a ham placed on a greasy pole. The feat achieved, the firing of water cannons mark the release of over a hundred metric tons of tomatoes and one hour of chaotic tomato throwing. Legend has it that this helter-skelter celebration has its roots from when a food fight among the town's youths broke out in 1945. It has now become one of the defining images of the Spanish lust for life.

Palau de les Arts Reina Sofía *(Autopista del Saler 1. ℘961 97 58 00. www.lesarts.com)* – The four halls here host classical and modern opera, music, theatre and dance.

Museo Nacional de Cerámica y de las Artes Suntuarias González Martí★★ (National Museum of Ceramics and Decorative Art)

Poeta Querol 2. ⓞ *Open Tue–Sat 10am–2pm, 4–8pm; Sun and public holidays 10am–2pm.* ⓞ *Closed 1 Jan, 1 May, 24, 25, 31 Dec.* ◎*3€; free Sat afternoon, Sun, 18 Apr, 18 May, 12 Oct, 6 Dec.* ℘*963 51 63 92. http://mnceramica.mcu.es.*

This museum occupies the lovely Baroque **Palacio del Marqués de Dos Aguas**★★. On the **ground floor** is the richly decorated **carriage**★ of the Marquis of Dos Aguas (1753). Rooms on the **first floor** include the Chinese salon, the *fumoir*, and the chapel.

The **ceramic collection** on the **second floor** includes Moorish ceramics (the basis of the craft in Spain), green and black porcelain, and later pieces from Málaga, Murcia and Manises. Christian ceramics of the 13C and 14C evidence continuity from the Moorish. Outstanding are green and manganese ceramics from **Paterna** *(6km/3.7mi N of Valencia)*. The golden age of ceramics in **Manises** *(8km/5mi N of Valencia)* is represented by lovely pieces.

Also on display are Chinese porcelain and European imitations, and an impressive Toledo urn.

The **Real Fábrica de Alcora**, established in 1727, became the centre of innovation in Spain, spreading the Louis XIV, Classic and Baroque styles. Pieces from 19C **Manises** evidence later styles that spread through southern and eastern Spain. There is also a Valencian kitchen with 18C and 19C tiles.

Colegio del Patriarca o del Corpus Christi★ (Patriarch or Corpus Christi College)

Nave 1. ⓞ *Open daily 11am–1.30pm.* ⓞ *Closed Good Fri.* ◥*Guided tours available Mon–Fri.* ℘*963 51 41 76.* ◎*1.50€.*

This ex-seminary dates back to the 16C. The **church** *(enter by left door)* is one of the few Renaissance churches in Spain with frescoes; on the lower wall sections are Manises tiles. The seminary is built around a harmonious patio decorated with Talavera *azulejo* friezes.

The small **museum** of 15C–17C art includes paintings by Juan de Juanes, a **triptych of the Passion**★ by Dirk Bouts, a 14C Byzantine crucifix from the Monastery of Athos, a 13C Romanesque *Christ* and a portrait of the founder, Ribera, by Ribalta, and paintings by Ribalta, Morales and El Greco.

In the same plaza is the **Universidad** (University; *www.uv.es*).

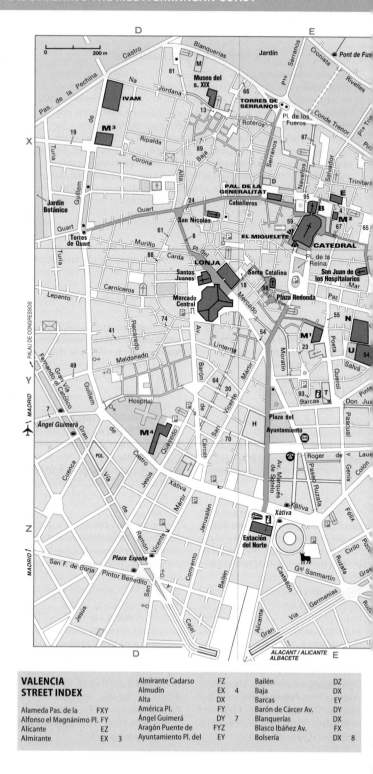

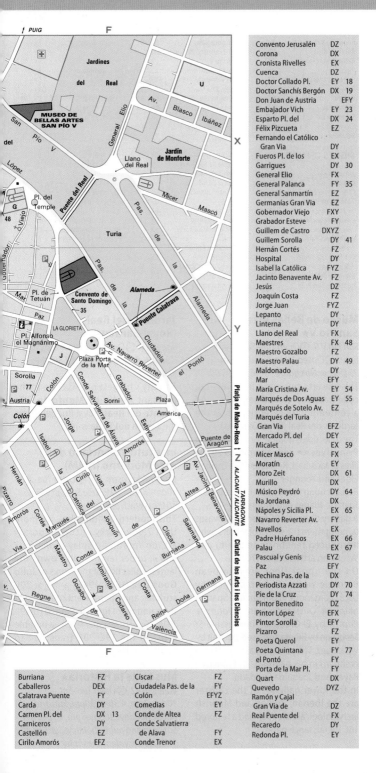

Regne de València Av.	FZ		Salvador Giner	DX	81	Temple Pl. del	FX	
Reina Pl. de la	EY		San Francisco de Borja	DZ		Tetuán Pl. de	FY	
Reina Doña Germana	FZ		San Pío V	FX		Transits	EY	93
Ripalda	DX		San Vicente Ferrer Pl.	EY	83	Trinidad Puente	EX	
Roger de Lauria	EZ		San Vicente Mártir	DEYZ		Trinitarios	EX	
Roteros	EX		Santa Ana Muro	EX	87	Turia	DXY	
Ruzafa	EZ		Santa Teresa	DY	88	Universidad	EY	94
Ruzafa Pas.	EZ		Santo Tomás	DX	89	Virgen Pl. de la	EX	95
Salamanca	FZ		Serranos	EX		Virgen de la Paz Pl.	EY	98
Salvá	EY		Serranos Puente	EX		Xàtiva	DEZ	
Salvador	EX		Sorni	FY				

SIGHTS ON MAP			de los Hospitalarios	EY		Cerámica	EY	M¹
			Iglesia de San Nicolás	DX		Museo Valenciano de		
Almudín	EX	E	Iglesia de Santa Catalina	EY		la Ilustración y		
Catedral	EX		Iglesia de los			la Modernidad	DY	M⁴
Centro de la Beneficencia,			Santos Juanes	DY		Museo de Bellas		
Museo de Prehistoria			IVAM	DX		Artes San Pío V	FX	
y Ethnologia	DX	M³	Jardines del Real	FX		Nuestra Señora de		
Ciudad de las Artes y			Jardín Botánico	DX		los Desamparados	EX	B
las Ciències	FZ		Jardín de Montforte	FX		Palau de Congressos	DY	
Colegio del Patriarca			Lonja	DY		Palau de la Generalitat	EX	
o del Corpus Christi	EY	N	Mercado Central	DY		Platja de la Malva-Rosa	FYZ	
Convento de Santo			El Miguelete	EX		Torres de Quart	DX	
Domingo	FY		Museo de la Ciudad	EX	M²	Torres de Serranos	EX	
Estación del Norte	EZ		Museo del S. XIX	DX		Universidad	EY	U
Iglesia de San Juan			Museo Nacional de					

Museo de Bellas Artes San Pío V★

San Pío V 9. ⊙Open Tue–Sun 10am–8pm. ⊙Closed 1 Jan, Good Friday, 25 Dec. ∞No charge. ℘963 87 03 00.

This fine arts museum is in an 18C–19C collegiate church and seminary, and a contemporary extension, near the Jardines del Real (Royal Gardens).

The collection is notable for its **Valencian Primitives**★★ with altarpieces by the likes of Jacomart, Reixac and the Osonas, Elder and Younger.

Representing the Renaissance are Macip, Juan de Juanes and others.

A gallery displays 16C Spanish canvases (among them the works of Ribalta, who introduced tenebrism to Spain) and Valencian artists of the 17C.

On the upper floor are European Baroque works (*St Bartholomew* by Luca Giordano) and Golden Age Spanish painting. Outstanding are *St John the Baptist* by El Greco, an impressive *St Sebastian* by Ribera and a self-portrait by Velázquez. The portrait mastery of Goya is shown in his paintings of Francisco Bayeu and Joaquina Candado.

In the lower galleries of the cloister are the Iberian, Roman and Moorish archaeological collection and a restored 16C Renaissance patio.

Jardines del Real (Royal Gardens)★

San Pío V. ⊙Open daily Nov–Mar 7.30am–8.30pm; Apr–Oct 7.30am–9.30pm.

The city's biggest park is close to the pleasant **Jardín de Monforte**. The **Puente del Real** (Royal Bridge) across the **Jardín del Turia** is 16C.

Instituto Valenciano de Arte Moderno (IVAM)

Guillem de Castro 118. ⊙Open Tue–Sun 10am–8pm. ∞2€; free Sun. ℘963 86 30 00. www.ivam.es.

This modern building houses more than 7 000 works of contemporary art, on rotating display (*Galleries 3 and 4, upper level*). It also owns the largest collection of the works of **Julio González** (1876–1942), a major 20C sculptor; and a permanent collection of the paintings of **Ignacio Pinazo** (1849–1916) (*Gallery 5, upper level*) , a notable artist of the 19C–20C transition to modern styles.

Museo de la Historia★

Valencia 42. ⊙Open Tue–Sat 10am–2pm, 4.30–8.30pm, Sun and public holidays 10am–3pm. ∞2€; free Sat–Sun and public holidays. ℘963 70 11 05. www.valencia.es/mhv.

Located in a 19C water works, this museum tells the story of Valencia from its beginnings to the end of the 20C. Most evocative are the dramatised audiovisual presentations of each era.

ADDITIONAL SIGHTS

Museo Valenciano de la Ilustración y la Modernidad (Museum of Illustration and Modernism) (*Guillém de Castro 8*)

Museo de la Prehistoria (La Beneficencia) (*Corona 36*)

Convento de Santo Domingo (*pl. de Tetuán 22*)

Jardín Botánico de la Universidad (Botanical Garden) (*Quart 80*)

WALKING TOUR
CIUDAD VIEJA★ (OLD TOWN)

Allow 3hr. Follow route on town plan. The best starting point is El Miguelete, the bell tower of the Cathedral.

El Miguelete★

Pl. de la Reina. Open daily 10am–1pm, 4.30–7pm. 2€. 963 91 81 27. "Little Michael" (Micalet in Valencian) is the main bell of this octagonal Gothic tower, consecrated on St Michael's day in 1418. Climb up for a view of the cathedral and the town's glazed roofs.

Catedral★

Pl. de la Reina. Open Mon–Sat 10am–6pm, Sun and public holidays 2–5.30pm. 3€. 963 91 81 27. www.catedraldevalencia.es.

Work began in 1262; most of the building is Gothic from the 14C and 15C. The elegant and slender early 18C west face imitates Italian Baroque style. The Assumption on the pediment is by Ignacio Vergara and Esteve.

The south door is Romanesque; the north, the **Portada de los Apóstoles** (Apostles' Door), is Gothic, decorated with time-worn sculptures. A statue of the Virgin and Child on the tympanum is surrounded by angel musicians.

Inside, light filters through the alabaster windows in the beautiful Flamboyant Gothic **lantern**. The **retable** in the

capilla mayor (chancel), the work of Fernando de Llanos and Yáñez de la Almedina (early 16C), influenced by Leonardo, illustrates the Lives of Christ and the Virgin.

In the ambulatory, a Renaissance portico protects an alabaster relief of the Resurrection (1510). Opposite is the 15C late Gothic Virgen del Coro (Chancel Virgin) in polychrome alabaster. In a chapel is a Baroque Cristo de la Buena Muerte (Christ of Good Death).

Capilla del Santo Cáliz or Sala Capitular★ (Chapel of the Holy Grail or Chapter house)

Last chapel along the north aisle.

The chamber has elegant star vaulting. Behind the altar, 12 alabaster low reliefs are by Poggibonsi. In the centre, a magnificent 1C carnelian agate cup is said to be the Holy Grail, brought to Spain in the 3C. The **museum** beyond contains a monumental modern monstrance, works of Juan de Juanes and Vicente Macip and original statues of the Apostles' Door (*open Mon–Sat 10am–5.30pm, Sun 2–5.30pm; 963 91 81 27*).

Exit at the right of the transept; continue to plaza del Arzobispo.

At the left are ruins dating from the Roman era up to medieval times.

Take Palau to plaza de Nápols y Sicilia and turn right onto Trinquete de Caballeros.

Iglesia de San Juan del Hospital (Church of St John of the Hospital)★

Trinquete de Caballeros 5 (access through courtyard). Open Mon–Fri 7am–8am, 9.30am–1.30pm, 5–9.30pm, Sat 9.30am–1.30pm, 5–9pm, Sun 11am–2pm, 5–9.30pm. 963 92 29 65. www.sanjuandelhospital.es.

This early 13C Gothic church consists of a single nave with pointed barrel vault. In the first chapel are beautiful 13C murals.

▶ *Return to the Plaza del Arzobispo.*

Cripta Arqueológica de la Cárcel de San Vicente (San Vicente Jail Archaeological Crypt)

Pl. del Arzobispo 1. ⏰ *Open Tue–Sat 9.30am–2pm, 5.30–8pm, Sun and public holidays 9.30am–2pm.* 💶*2€; free Sun and hols.* ☎*963 94 14 17.*
The remains of a Visigothic funerary chapel with four finely worked screens and a 6C burial; and two Visigothic stone sarcophagi.

Almudín

Pl. San Luis Bertrán. ⏰ *Open Tue–Sat 10am–2pm, 4.30–8.30pm, Sun and public holidays 10am–3pm.* 💶*No charge.* ☎*963 52 54 78.*
This is a 14C–16C granary with primitive frescoes and two 19C *azulejos* altars.

▶ *Continue to plaza de la Virgen.*

Plaza de la Virgen★

The basilica of the Virgen de los Desamparados and the Apostle Doorway of the Cathedral face this pleasant plaza.

Real Basílica de Nuestra Señora la Virgen de los Desamparados

Pl. de la Virgen s/n. ⏰ *Open daily 7am–2pm, 4.30–9pm.* 💶*No charge.* ☎*963 91 86 11. www.basilicadesamparados.org.*

This late 17C church is linked to the apse of the Cathedral by a Renaissance arch. The floor plan is oval. Beneath the painted cupola is the venerated statue of the patron of Valencia, the Virgin of the Abandoned (*desamparados*), which receives a steady flow of devotees.

Palacio de la Generalitat★

Pl. de Manises. ⏰ *Open Mon–Fri 10am–2pm.* 💶*No charge.* ☎*963 86 34 61.*
A tower was added to this fine 15C Gothic palace in the 17C and an identical one in the 20C. It was until 1707 the meeting place of the Valencia Cortes. In the Gothic patio is Benlliure's sculpture of Dante's *Inferno* (1900).
A golden salon has a wonderful gilt and multicoloured **artesonado ceiling**★ and a large painting of the Tribunal de las Aguas (Water Tribunal, 🔎*see entry*). On the first floor are the Sala de los Reyes (Royal Hall) with portraits of the Valencian kings, and the Gran Salón de las Cortes Valencianas (Grand Council Chamber). The *azulejos* frieze and the coffered ceiling are 16C. The rear façade and the Palau de la Batlia (the provincial administration) give onto the pleasant **plaza de Manises**.

Torres de Serranos★

Pl. Fueros. ⏰ *Open Tue–Sat 10.30am–2pm, 4.30–8.30pm, Sun and public holidays 10am–3pm.* 💶*2€; free*

Las Fallas

The origins of this festival date back to the Middle Ages when on St Joseph's Day, the carpenters' brotherhood, one of the town's traditional crafts, burned their accumulated wood shavings in bonfires known as *Fallas* (from the Latin *fax*: torch). The name became synonymous with a festival for which, in time, objects were made solely for burning – particularly effigies of less popular members of the community! In the 17C single effigies were replaced by pasteboard groups or floats produced by quarters of the town – rivalry is such that the figures today are fantastic in size, artistry and satirical implication. Prizes are awarded during the general festivities, which include fireworks, processions, bullfights, etc., before everything goes up in the fires or *cremá* on the evening of 19 March. Figures (*ninots*) dating from 1934 to the present day which have been spared from the bonfires are on display in the interesting **Museo Fallero** (*pl. Monteolivete 4; open Tue–Sat 10am–3pm, 4.30–8.30pm, Sun and public holidays 10am–3pm; closed 1 Jan, 1 May, 25 Dec;* 💶*2€; no charge Sat–Sun;* ☎*963 52 54 78; www.fallas.com*).

Sat–Sun and public holidays.
℘963 91 90 70.
The towers are a good example of late 14C military architecture; they guarded one of the city entrances. Note the flowing lines of the battlements and the delicate tracery above the gateway.

▶ *Return to plaza de Manises.*

Calle Caballeros

The most important street of the old city heads from plaza de la Virgen into the traditional Carmen district. Some of the houses preserve their Gothic patios (nos. 22, 26 and 33).

▶ *Follow the lane opposite no. 26.*

Iglesia de San Nicolás de Bari

Caballeros 35. ⏰ *Open Tue–Sat 9.30am–11am, 6.30–8pm. Sun and public holidays 10am–1pm.*
℘963 91 33 17.
In one of the town's oldest churches, in Churrigueresque style, are an altarpiece by Juan de Juanes *(to the left)* and, by the font, a *Calvary* by Osona the Elder.

▶ *Continue to plaza del Esparto, then follow Quart.*

Torres de Quart

Av. Guillem de Castro.
These 15C towers were damaged in the 19C by Napoleon's cannons.

▶ *From plaza del Esparto, take Bolsería.*

Lonja★ (Silk Exchange)

Pl. del Mercado. ⏰ *Open Tue–Sat 10am–2pm, 4.30–8.30pm, Sun and public holidays 10am–3pm.* ◉*2€; free Sat–Sun and public holidays.* *℘963 52 54 78.*
This 15C Flamboyant Gothic building replaced an earlier exchange outgrown by prosperous merchants.
The left wing, separated from the entrance by a tower, is crowned by a gallery with a medallion frieze. The old commercial silk **hall**★★ is lofty, with

Detail of the façade of
Palacio del Marqués de Dos Aguas
J. Malburet/MICHELIN

ogival arches supported on slender, elegantly cabled columns; the bays are filled with delicate tracery.

Iglesia de los Santos Juanes

Pl. del Mercado. ⏰ *Open Mon–Tue, Thu–Fri 7.30am–10am, 7–8pm, Wed 7.30am–1pm, 7–8pm, Sat 6–8pm, Sun and public holidays 8am–1pm, 6–8pm.* ◉*No charge.* *℘963 91 63 54.*
This is a vast church with a Baroque façade. The single aisle, originally Gothic, was modified in the 17C and 18C with exuberant Baroque stuccowork.

Mercado Central

Pl. del Mercado. ⏰ *Open Mon–Sat 8am–3pm.* *℘963 82 91 00.*
www.mercadocentralvalencia.es.
The enormous metal and glass 1928 Central Market, a fine example of Modernist architecture, is busiest in the mornings with stalls full of fish and local produce.

Iglesia de Santa Catalina

Pl. de Santa Catalina. ⏰ *Open daily 10.30am–1.30pm, 5.30–7.30pm.* ◉*No charge.* *℘963 91 77 13.*
The church is notable for its magnificent 17C **Baroque belfry**★. The interior is soberly Gothic.

▶ *From San Vicente Mártir, turn left by the Abadía de San Martín.*

Palacio del Marqués de Dos Aguas★★
Poeta Querol 2.
This magnificent Baroque building houses the Museo Nacional de Cerámica y de las Artes Suntuarias González Martí (&*see Sights*). The 18C marble portal was once covered by paintings.

ADDRESSES

🏠 STAY

⊜🛏 **Hostal Antigua Morellana** – *En Bou 2.* 🖉*963 91 57 73. www.hostalam. com. 18 rooms.* A stone's throw from the Lonja and main market, this family-run hotel offers excellent value for money. The comfortable and bright rooms provide the best views of the picturesque narrow streets in the Carmen district.

⊜🛏 **Hotel Reina Victoria** – *Barcas 4–6.* 🖉*963 52 04 87. www. husareinavictoria.com. 95 rooms.* ⊇*12€. Restaurant*⊜🛏. It's worth making a journey here if only to admire the immaculate white stone Baroque façade. The interior lives up to expectations, with its charming entry hall set with marble and mirrors, elegant English bar, and classic rooms with modern comforts.

⊜🛏🍴 **Hotel Ad-Hoc** – *Boix 4.* 🖉*963 91 91 40. www.adhochoteles. com. 28 rooms.* ⊇*10€. Restaurant*⊜🛏. This 19C mansion on a quiet street retains such features as a mosaic floor and exposed beams. Rooms are well-decorated and comfortable. Try for an upstairs room with balcony.

⊜🛏🍴 **Hostal Residencia Venecia** – *Pl. Ayuntamiento (enter through Llop 5).* 🖉*963 52 42 67. www.hotelvenecia. com. 54 rooms.* ⊇*6.50€.* The building is outstanding, with classic façade and balconies facing the plaza del Ayuntamiento, Valencia's social and cultural centre. Rooms are well furnished and the breakfast room enjoys fine views.

▶ *From San Vicente Mártir, continue to the plaza del Ayuntamiento*

Plaza del Ayuntamiento
This great square is the meeting point of *Valencianos,* with a showy flower market always in bloom.

🍽 EAT

⊜🛏 **Asador del Carme** – *Pl. del Carme 6.* 🖉*963 92 24 48. www.asadordelcarme. com. Closed Mon Oct–May.* Customers are attracted by the pleasant covered terrace, extensive menu of grilled meats and copious salads, the quiet of the square and the lovely views of the Iglesia del Carmen.

⊜🛏 **Montes** – *Pl. Obispo Amigó 5.* 🖉*963 85 50 25. Closed Holy Week, Aug, Sun for dinner, Mon and Tue for dinner.* Great value service for a budget restaurant. The lengthy dining room complements the entrance bar.

⊜🛏🍴 **Palace Fesol** – *Hernán Cortés 7.* 🖉*963 52 93 23. www.palacefesol. com. Closed Holy Week, a fortnight in Aug, Sat–Sun in summer and Sun eve, Mon in winter.* A well-established family enterprise, with glaze tiled walls and a maritime decor. The menu features Valencian cuisine including rice dishes.

⊜🛏🍴🍴 **Torrijos** – *Dr Sumsi 4.* 🖉*963 73 29 49. www.restaurantetorrijos.com. CloSun for dinner and fortnights in Jan, Mar, Aug, Sept.* Elegantly modern decor complements the attentive service, in what is a gem of Valencian cuisine. Specialities include creative squid and tuna dishes.

TAPAS

Las Cuevas – *Samaniego 9.* 🖉*963 91 71 96. Closed Sun and Aug.* It's just like a cave: tiny windows, narrow doors and beams. Nothing but tapas are served here, prepared in the Valencian way: mussels, stuffed red peppers, sardines etc. At weekends, Las Cuevas fills up with the city's youngsters.

Bar Pilar – *Moro Zeit 13.* 📞*963 91 04 97. Open daily noon–midnight.* Founded in 1917, Pilar is one of the best tapas bars in the city. The house speciality is mussels-based *clochinas*. Another tapas institution, *El Molinón,* is directly opposite, making this a good area in which to discover Valencian nightlife.

Sagardi Euskal Taberna – *San Vicente Mártir 6.* 📞*963 91 06 68. www.sagardi. com.* Enjoy Basque skewers and cider in the downstairs bar, or go up one flight for a more relaxed meal amid minimalist décor.

🍽 CAFÉS

El Siglo – *Pl. Santa Catalina 11.* 📞*963 91 84 66. Closed Sat.* Founded in 1836, El Siglo (The Century) is a chocolate maker, ice-cream producer and horchata specialist rolled into one. The extensive building is adorned with *azulejos* from Manises. Another confectioner, Santa Catalina, less-frequented, is just 10m/3ft away.

🎭 NIGHTLIFE

Calle Caballeros – This street is the hub of Valencia's nightlife. Between plaza de la Virgen, with its numerous outdoor cafés, and plaza Tossal, a popular square for tapas, you'll pass by the *Johnny Maracas* salsa bar (*no 39*), the *Bab al Hanax* disco (no 36), and the fashion *Café Bolsería (www.bolseriavalencia.com)* with its jet-set clientele.

Café de las Horas – *Conde de Almodóvar 1.* 📞*963 91 73 36.* This café with a 19C atmosphere is just steps from the Plaza de la Virgen. The high point is the decor, including trompe-l'œil scenes on the walls, a little fountain, and finely tuned lighting that goes with the music to create an intimate atmosphere.

Café del Negrito – *Pl. Negrito 1.* 📞*963 91 42 33.* This artists' café, situated in a small square in the old town, is a popular meeting-place for friends who come here to enjoy the best "Valencian water" and to enjoy the Negrito's

famous orange juice and champagne cocktails. Note the bar opposite, the *Ghecko (*📞*963 91 07 79)*, which is completely covered in shells.

La Marxa – *Cocinas 5.* 📞*963 91 70 65.* At the heart of the famous Carmen district, La Marxa is the emblem of Valencian nightlife, and has been instrumental in developing Valencia's reputation as a city with a vibrant club scene.

🛒 SHOPPING

Lladró – *Poeta Querol 9.* 📞*963 51 16 25. www.lladro.com. Open Mon–Sat 10am–2pm, 4–8pm.* This famous porcelain manufacturer has boutiques around the world selling stunning works of art across a broad price range.

Mercadillo de la Plaza Redonda – *Open daily 9am–1pm, 4–9pm.* This typical small market in plaza Redonda is the place to buy a whole range of clothes and bric-a-brac, or else simply to watch the world go by over a coffee. On Sundays, animals and pets can also be bought here.

Turrones Ramos – *Sombrerería 11 (next to Pl. Redonda).* 📞*963 92 33 98. Closed Sat–Sun and in Aug.* This shop has sold hand-made *turrón* since 1890. The marzipan is worth trying too, especially *casca de batata* and *casca de yema* made with sweet potato or egg yolk."

FESTIVALS

During the week of 12–19 March, the city celebrates the annual festival of St Joseph, with its famous **Las Fallas** *(www.fallasfromvalencia. com;* 🔖*see sidebar).* The 9th October commemorates the end of Moorish rule in 1238 and is celebrated as a national day for the region. Among religious festivals, the solemn **Corpus Christi** procession, dating from 1355 and the festival of the **Virgen de los Desamparados**, patroness of the city (second Sunday in May; *www. basilicadesamparados.org*) are notable.

Playa de Portals Nous, Mallorca
B. Perousse/ MICHELIN

Balearic Islands★★★

▸ **Population:** 1 071 221
◔ **Michelin Map:** 579

The Balearics evoke summer sunshine and frenetic nightlife, yet their history and beauty are as impressive as those of any island in the Mediterranean. Although the archipelago is one of the most popular destinations in the world, over 40 per cent of its verdant landscapes are protected by law.

The **Balearic archipelago** lies off Spain's Levante, in the Mediterranean, and covers 5 000sq km/1 900sq mi. It includes three large islands – **Mallorca**, **Menorca** and **Ibiza** – each with a distinctive character, two smaller inhabited isles – Formentera and Cabrera – and many uninhabited islets. All three larger islands have airports and inter-island ferries link them together.

Palma, capital of Mallorca, and the only real city in the archipelago, is also administrative capital of the Comunidad Autónoma Balear (Balearic Autonomous Community). The language, Balearic, is derived from Catalan and runs alongside Castilian.

The Balearics took off as **holiday islands** in the 1950s and Mallorca in particular was in the vanguard of mass tourism.

Initially a fashionable "jet-set" destination, **Majorca** (as it is known in English) had by the 1980s become synonymous with the worst excesses of holiday commercialisation and badly behaved tourists. In order to reverse this trend, during the late 1990s the island was rebranded by the island authorities both from a marketing perspective (for example, the anglicised "Majorca", replete with its old-fashioned downmarket associations, was proscribed), and also physically, as the island infrastructure was moved upmarket. Old hotels, in notorious concrete-canyon package holiday resorts such as Magaluf, were demolished with great ceremony, and new policies to encourage visitors to discover inland **Mallorca** were put in place. Today mass tourism is still very much alive but the island also now attracts the kind of fashionable visitors who, not so very long ago, would have steered well clear; consequently a whole new range of designer-chic hotels, attractive modernised rural retreats, and upmarket restaurants, bars and nightclubs have sprung up to grace the island, particularly in and around the capital of Palma which has become virtually a city break destination in its own right.

The situation is similar in **Ibiza**. It, too, has long suffered from charmless mass-market tourist centres, like San António, but these contrast with its charming hippy-chic **Eivissa** (Ibiza Town) and, away from the noisy centres, much of the island is undisturbed and surprisingly rural. The music scene remains of prime importance and ensures an annual "pilgrimage" of young tourists from all over the world.

Menorca meanwhile is the quietest of the developed islands, relying on its beautiful sandy beaches, prehistoric sites and natural attractions to bring a constant stream of UK and German visitors to its low-key family-orientated resorts.

Eivissa

M. Lemaire/MICHELIN

Mallorca★★★

Mallorca, the largest and by far the most popular of the Balearic Islands, is a holiday paradise for north Europeans, particularly popular with British and German visitors. The dramatic, steep cliff landscapes of the north coast, indented with coves, contrast with the beaches of the gentle south coast with their crystalline turquoise waters. Concrete seaside developments are offset by Mallorca's picturesque inland towns and villages.

LANDSCAPE AND TRADITION

The **Serra de Tramuntana** in the north-west rises in limestone crests – the highest is **Puig Major** (1 445m/4 740ft) – parallel to the coast. Spectacular cliffs plunging into the sea are high enough to block winds from the mainland.

Pines, junipers and holm oaks cover the slopes, interspersed with Mallorca's famous olive trees. Terraces of vegetables and fruit trees surround hillside villages.

The central plain, **Es Pla**, is divided by low walls into fields and fig and almond orchards; market towns, with outlying windmills to pump water, retain the regular medieval fortress plan.

The **Serra de Levant** to the east is hollowed out into wonderful caves. The rocky coast is indented with sheltered, sand-carpeted coves.

A BIT OF HISTORY

A Short-lived kingdom (1262–1349) – James (Jaume) I of Aragón recaptured Mallorca from the Muslims in 1229. Thirty years later James united Mallorca-Baleares, Roussillon and Montpellier in a kingdom which he presented to his son, James II. He and his successor, Sancho, founded new Catalan towns. Pedro IV seized the archipelago in 1343 to reunite it with Aragón. A merchant navy was established which brought prosperity, and a school of cartography rapidly became famous.

The Mallorcan Primitives (14C–15C) – Gothic Mallorcan painting, characterised

- ▶ **Population:** 790 763
- ⚅ **Michelin Map:** 579 – BALEARES
- 🛈 **Info:** Palma: Plaza de la Reina 2. ℘971 71 22 16. www.illesbalears. es/ing/majorca/home.jsp. Airport: ℘971 78 90 00.
- 👥 **Kids:** Marineland; Palma Aquarium.

by a gentleness of expression, was open to external influences: the so-called **Master of Privileges** (Maestro de los Privilegios) showed a Sienese preference for miniaturisation and warm colours; later, **Joan Daurer** and the **Maestro de Obispo Galiana** were inspired by Catalan painting.

15C artists included **Gabriel Moger**, **Miguel de Alcanyis** and **Martí Torner**, who had studied in Valencia. The **Maestro de Predelas** is distinguishable by his attention to detail, **Rafael Moger** by his realism. **Pedro (Pere) Nisart** and **Alonso de Sedano** introduced the Flemish style (⚅ see Museo de Mallorca).

Famous Mallorcans and visitors – **Ramón Llull** (1232–1315) personifies the cosmopolitan 13C outlook of Mallorca. He learned languages and studied philosophy, theology and alchemy, and was beatified. **Fray Junípero Serra** (1713–84) founded missions in California. He was beatified in 1988.

Among the foreign artists to visit in the 19C were **Frédéric Chopin** and **George Sand**. **Robert Graves** (1895–1985), the English poet and author, lived here from 1929. The Austrian archduke **Ludwig Salvator** (1847–1915) compiled the most detailed study of the archipelago. He was patron to the French speleologist E A Martel.

SIGHTS
PALMA DE MALLORCA★★

🚄 Estació Intermodal (Palma to Sa Pobla) ℘971 75 22 45.

Palma spreads along a wide bay. Residential quarters with hotels stretch on either side of the historic centre, in avinguda Gabriel Roca, shaded by palms. The old harbour, bordered by passeig Sagrera, serves passenger and merchant ships. The new harbour at the southern tip of El Terreno accommodates the largest liners.

The Bahía de Palma
The bay, protected from north and west winds by the highest peak on Mallorca, Puig Major, has a mild climate all year. To the west, hotels stand along the indented Bendinat coastline where there is little sand, except at **Palmanova** and **Magaluf**. The coast to the east is less sheltered, but has mile upon mile of fine sand with a series of resorts – **Can Pastilla**, **Ses Meravelles** and **S'Arenal**.

The "Ciutat de Mallorca"
Palma was known by this name after its liberation on 31 December 1229. Trade links were forged with the mainland, Africa and northern Europe; Jews and Genoese established themselves. James II (Jaume II) and his successors endowed the city with beautiful Gothic buildings. Aragonese expansion to Naples and Sicily enabled Palma to extend her commerce.

Palma's old mansions
In the 15C and 16C, the great families of Palma favoured the Italian style. They built elegant residences with stone façades, relieved by windows with Renaissance decoration. In the 18C a characteristic Mallorcan *casa* (house) appeared, with an inner court of massive marble columns, wide shallow arches and a high and graceful loggia.

Modern Palma
Palma is home to a large proportion of the population of the island and is one of the most popular cities in Spain to visit. Tourists congregate in and around **El Terreno** – especially in plaza Gomila – and **Cala Major** quarters in the west of town. The native heart of the city remains the **passeig des Born**. Shops sell pearls, glassware and leather in the old town east of El Born, in pedestrian streets around Plaça Major and in avinguda Jaume III.

BARRIO DE LA CATEDRAL★ (CATHEDRAL QUARTER)
Allow 3hr

Catedral★★
Pl. Almoina. Open Apr–May and Oct Mon–Fri 10am–5.15pm, Sat 10am–2.15pm; Jun–Sept Mon–Fri 10am–6.15pm, Sat 10am–2.15pm; Nov–Mar Mon–Fri 10am–3.15pm, Sat 10am–2.15pm. *4€. 971 72 31 30. www.catedraldemallorca.info.*

The bold yet elegant Cathedral, its buttresses surmounted by pinnacles, rises above the sea. The Santanyí limestone of its walls changes colour according to the time of day: ochre, golden or pink. Begun in the early 14C, it is one of the great late-Gothic constructions.

The west face was rebuilt in neo-Gothic style in the 19C after an earthquake; its 16C Renaissance portal remains intact. The south door, the **Portada del Mirador** (Viewpoint Doorway), overlooks the sea, the delicate Gothic decoration dating from the 15C. Statues of St Peter and St Paul on either side prove that Sagrera, architect of the Llotja (Exchange), was a talented sculptor.

The **interior** is large and light, measuring 121m x 55m (397ft x 180ft) and 44m/144ft to the top of the vaulting. Slender octagonal pillars divide the nave from the aisles. The Capilla Mayor or Real (Royal Chapel) contains an enormous wrought-iron baldaquin by Gaudí (1912) with Renaissance choir stalls on either side. Tombs of the kings of Mallorca, James II and Jaume III, lie in the Capilla de la Trinidad (Trinity Chapel).

Museo de la Seu
Almoina house, next to the cathedral bell tower. Open same hours as cathedral. *971 72 31 30. www.catedraldemallorca.info/principal.*

In the Gothic chapterhouse is the Santa Eulàlia altarpiece by the Maestro de los Privilegios (1335). In the oval Baroque chapter house are reliquaries including one of the True Cross.

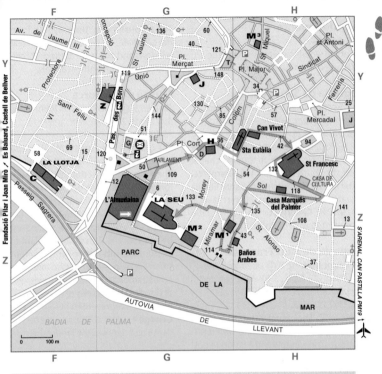

WALKING TOURS
Allow 2hr – see town plan.

L'Almudaina
Palau Reial. Open Apr–Sept Mon–Fri 10am–5.45pm, Sat and public holidays 10am–1.15pm; Oct–Mar Mon–Fri 10am–1.15pm, 4–5.15pm, Sat and public holidays 10am–1.15pm. 4€. 971 71 91 45.

This fortress of the Córdoba caliphate was converted in the 14C and 15C into a royal palace. Today, as a residence of the King of Spain, several rooms have been restored and furnished with Flemish tapestries and paintings. In the courtyard, note the carved eaves and the doorway of the Iglesia de Santa Ana (St Anne's Church), a rare Romanesque structure in the Balearics.

Ayuntamiento
Pl. Cort 1.
Carved wooden eaves overhang the 17C façade of the town hall.

Iglesia de Santa Eulàlia
Pl. Santa Eulàlia 2. ◷ *Open Mon–Sat 9am–10.30am, 5–8pm.* ⊕*No charge.* ℘*971 71 46 25.*
13C–15C. The tall nave is unusually bare for a Gothic church. In the first chapel off the south aisle is a 15C altarpiece. Between the churches of Santa Eulàlia and Sant Francesc, at no 2 Carrer Savellà, is the 18C **Can Vivot**, its beautiful patio decorated with marble columns.

Iglesia de Sant Francesc
Pl. Sant Francesc 7. ◷ *Open Mon–Sat 9.30am–12.30pm, 3.10–6pm; Sun and public holidays 9am–12.30pm.* ⊕*1€.* ℘*971 71 26 95.*
13C–14C. The church façade, rebuilt in the late 17C, has an immense Plateresque rose window and a Baroque portal with a beautifully carved tympanum by Francisco Herrera. The first apsidal chapel on the left contains the tomb of Ramón Llull.
The **cloisters**★ *(claustro)*, begun in 1286, are elegant. Apart from one side of trefoil openings, the architect divided the remaining galleries into multifoil bays on slender columns in varied diameters. The ceiling is painted.

Casa Marqués del Palmer
Sol 7.
In Carrer del Sol stands Casa Marqués del Palmer (Can Catlar), a mansion built in 1556 in stone now blackened by age. Renaissance decoration around the upper-floor windows mellows the austerity of Gothic walls. The upper gallery, under deep eaves, is a replica of that on the Llotja.
The old Jewish quarter, **La Portella**, lies close against the town wall.

Baños Árabes
Can Serra 7. ◷ *Open daily Apr–Nov 9am–7.30pm; Dec–Mar 9am–6pm.* ⊕*2€.* ℘*971 72 15 49.*

The Moorish baths, the only relic from the caliphate, are beneath small circular windows and a classical dome on 12 columns with rudimentary capitals.

Museo de Mallorca
Portella 5. ◷ *Open Tue–Sat 10am–7pm, Sun 10am–2pm.* ⊕*2.40€.* ℘*971 71 75 40.*
The ground floor displays Muslim capitals, *artesonado* ceilings and ceramics. The **Fine Arts**★ section displays Mallorcan Gothic paintings. Works from the early 14C show clear Italian influence. Catalan works begin to appear after 1349 when Mallorca was annexed by Aragón: the *Crucifixion* by Ramón Destorrents, interesting for its composition and expression, was to influence other paintings. Francesch Comes, one of the most prestigious of the early 15C painters, is represented here by his **St George**★ *(room 3)*, remarkable for the depth and detail of the landscape.

Museo Diocesano (Diocesan Museum)
Mirador 5. ◷ *Open Mon–Sat 10am–2pm.* ⊕*3€.* ℘*971 72 38 60.*
Among the many Gothic works is Pere Nisart's outstanding **St George**★ (1568) which shows the saint slaying the dragon against a backdrop of 16C Palma.

TO THE WEST OF EL BORN
La Llotja (La Lonja)★
Pas. Sagrera. ◷ *Open for exhibitions: Tue–Sat 11am–2pm, 5–9pm, Sun 11am–1.30pm.* ℘*971 71 17 05.*
Guillermo Sagrera designed this 15C commodities exchange. The Llotja's military features are only for appearances, to distract the eye from the buttresses and austerity of the walls. The interior, with pointed arches on spirally fluted columns, is quite elegant.

Antiguo Consulado del Mar (Former Maritime Consulate)
Pas. Sagrera. ℘*971 71 60 92.*
The early 17C building with a Renaissance balcony was the meeting-place of the Tribunal de Comercio Marítimo

(Merchant Shipping Tribunal). Today it houses the regional administration.

▷ *Walk up the passeig des Born.*

Palau Solleric
Pas. des Born 27. ⏱*Open Tue–Sat 10.30am–1.30pm, 5.30–8.30pm, Sun and public holidays 10.30am–1.30pm.* ☎*971 72 20 92.*
This 18C palace overlooking the Born is completed by an elegant loggia; follow the narrow covered way to the most perfect **patio**★ in Palma, along with a double staircase with delicate ironwork.

Es Baluard Museu d'Art Modern i Contemporani de Palma (Museum of Modern and Contemporary Art of Palma)
Pl. Porta Santa Catalina 10. ⏱ *Open Oct–15 Jun Tue–Sun 10am–8pm; 16 Jun–Sept Tue–Sun 10am–10pm.* ⏱ *Closed 1 Jan, 25 Dec.* 💶*6€, Fri by donation (minimum 0.10€).* ☎*971 90 82 00. www.esbaluard.org.*
Occupying part of a medieval fortress this gallery occupies a stunning angular white concrete-and-glass building. The permanent collection includes: Mediterranean landscapes by the likes of Joaquín Sorolla, Santiago Rusiñol and Joan Miró; ceramics by Picasso; drawings by Chagall ,Toulouse-Lautrec, and Barceló; a Miró gallery. High-quality temporary exhibitions feature international artists.

OUTSIDE THE CENTRE
Museu d'Art Espanyol Contemporani – Colecció March★ (Museum of Modern Spanish Art – March Collection)
San Miguel 11. ⏱ *Open Mon–Fri 10am–6.30pm, Sat 10.30am–2pm.* ⏱ *Closed public holidays.* 💶*No charge.* ☎*971 71 35 15. www.march.es.*
In this 18C mansion is a **permanent collection**★ of contemporary Spanish artists, from the Avant-Garde (Picasso, Miró, Dalí and J González) to recent figures.

Casa Berga
Pl. Mercat 12.
This 1712 mansion is the Palacio de Justicia (Law Courts). The façade is encumbered with stone balconies but the vast inner courtyard is typically Mallorcan.

Poble Español★ (Spanish Village)
Off the town plan, along pas. de Sagrera. ☎*971 73 70 75. www.congress-palace-palma.com.*
The buildings are exact reproductions of famous houses or monuments: the Myrtle Court from the Alhambra in Granada, the Casa de El Greco in Toledo, etc. Craftsmen and folk troupes bring the village to life.
Features of all major Roman sites in Spain have been incorporated in the monumental **Palacio de Congresos** (Convention Centre) facing the village.

▷ *Leave Palma along passeig de Sagrera*

Castillo de Bellver★
Camilo José Cela 17. ⏱*Open Apr–Sept Mon–Sat 8am–8.25pm, Sun and public holidays 10am–7pm; Oct–Mar Mon–Sat 8am–7.15pm, Sun and public holidays 10am–5pm.* 💶*2€.* ☎*971 73 06 57.*
The castle, built by the Mallorcan kings of the 14C as a summer residence, served as a prison until 1915.
The round buildings and circular perimeter and court are highly original; a freestanding keep dominates all. The Roman statues belong to the **Museo Municipal de Historia** (City History Museum; 💶*2.50€*). Also displayed are finds from excavations in Pollença. View a **panorama**★★ of the bay from the terrace.

▷ *Leave the centre via pas. de Sagrera.*

Fundació Pilar i Joan Miró (Pilar and Joan Miró Foundation).
Joan de Saridakis 29. ⏱ *Open 16 May–15 Sept Tue–Sat 10am–7pm, Sun and public holidays 10am–3pm; 16 Sept–15 May Tue–Sat 10am–6pm, Sun and public holidays 10am–3pm.*

Closed 1 Jan & 25 Dec. ✆5€.
🖉 971 70 14 20.
http://miro.palmademallorca.es.
The museum is the legacy of Joan Miró (1893–1983) and his wife. In the shadow of Son Abrines, Miró's residence from 1956, works donated by the artist are displayed in a part of the building called the Espacio Estrella.

EXCURSIONS
👥 Palma Aquarium
Manuela De Los Herreros i Sora 21.
Open year-round; call or see website for details. Ticket office closes 1hr before park. ✆19.50€; child 15€. 🖉971 26 42 75. www.palmaaquarium.com.
Located near the airport, but in lovely grounds, this spectacular new aquarium is one of the finest in Europe. It comprises over 50 different viewing areas with 8 000 specimens from 700 species – from seahorses to sharks – plucked from the Mediterranean and more exotic waters.

👥 Marineland
Calle Garcilaso de la Vega 9, Costa d'en Blanes. *Open 23 Feb–16 Nov daily 9.30am–6pm (ticket office closes Mon–Fri 4.30pm, Sat–Sun 5pm).* ✆22€; child 16€. 🖉971 675 125. www.marineland.es.
This huge dolphinarium is rated among the best in Europe and also includes Californian Sea Lions. There are many other attractions on site including an exotic birds show, an aquarium with penguins and sharks, a tropical bird house and aviary, and a children's water park.

🚗 DRIVING TOURS
See map of island.

1 LA COSTA ROCOSA★★★ (THE ROCKY COAST)
From Palma to Alcúdia
264km/165mi. Allow 2 days.

Mallorca's west coast is dominated by the limestone Serra de Tramuntana, rising to 1 445m/4 740ft at Puig Major. In the south, around Estellencs and Banyalbufar, slopes are terraced into *marjades* of olives, almonds and vines.

▷ *Leave Palma along passeig Sagrera.*

Port d'Andratx★
32km/18.6mi W of Palma.
The small fishing port is now also used by pleasure craft.
The C 710 from Andratx to Sóller is an extremely **scenic road**★★★, mostly along a cliff. It commands outstanding views and is shaded by pine trees.

Mirador Ricardo Roca★★
18km/11.2mi NE of Port d'Andratx.
The **view** from this lookout drops sheer to tiny coves lapped by the limpid sea.

Mirador de Ses Ànimes★★
28km/17.4mi NE of Port d'Andratx.
The **panorama** from the watchtower stretches south from the Isla de Dragonera and north to Port de Sóller.

Cartuja de Valldemossa (Valldemossa Carthusian Monastery)
Pl. de la Cartuja, Valldemossa.
45km/28mi NE of Port d'Andratx.
Open daily from 10am till 3pm or 5.30pm (depending upon month.
Closed 1 Jan, 25 Dec. ✆8.50€.
🖉971 61 21 06. www.museochopin.com.
The monastery was made famous by the visit George Sand and Chopin paid in the winter of 1838–39. Bad weather and local hostility left Sand disenchanted, although she invoked the countryside in *A Winter in Majorca.* From the monks' cells there are pleasant **views** of the surrounding olive groves. An 18C **pharmacy** has a collection of jars and boxes. A small **museum** displays xylographs (wood engravings).
Valldemossa is one of the prettiest villages on Mallorca and is well worth a wander but do arrive either early or late to avoid the coach parties who come to visit the monastery.

Son Marroig

Ctra de Valldemossa-Deià. 7km/4.3mi N of Valldemossa. 🕐 *Open Oct–May Mon–Sat 10am–6pm; Apr–Sept 10am–8pm.* ⊚3€. 🖉971 63 91 58. *www.sonmarroig.com.*

The former residence of Archduke Ludwig Salvator includes an exhibition of archaeological finds and Mallorcan furniture. A belvedere in the garden affords a view of the **Foradada**, a pierced rock rising out of the sea.

Deià

4km/2.5mi E of Son Marroig.
Another charming typical Mallorcan village, enjoying a beautiful setting in the Tramuntana, Deià has maintained its character despite the hordes of visitors it receives. The writer and poet Robert Graves made it his home from 1929, on and off, until his death in 1985, and is buried here (Deià Cemetery).

Sóller

11km/6.8mi NE of Deià.
The delightful 19C houses of Sóller spread in a quiet valley of market gardens, orange trees and olives groves. The charming vintage narrow-gauge **Tren de Sóller**, also known as the Orange Blossom train *(tickets payable on board;* ⊚10€; 🖉971 63 01 30; *www. trendesoller.com)* has been running the 27km/17 miles from Palma direct to Sóller since 1913.

Port de Sóller

5km/3mi N of Sóller.
Port de Sóller, in the curve of an almost circular bay which shelters pleasure boats, is the major seaside resort of the west coast. A tram *(tranvía;* ⊚4€; *www. trendesoller.com)* runs between Port de Sóller and Sóller. Coastal boat trips operate from the harbour.

▷ *Take the C 711 from Sóller to Alfàbia.*

Jardines de Alfàbia (Alfàbia Gardens)

🕐 *Open Apr–Oct Mon–Sat 9.30am–6.30pm; Nov–Mar Mon–Fri 9.30am–5.30pm, Sat 9.30am–1pm.* ⊚4.50€.

🖉*971 61 31 23.*
www.jardinesdealfabia.com.
Only the *artesonado* ceiling over the porch remains from a 14C Moorish residence. Follow the path through the gardens to the **library** for a taste of a traditional seigniorial residence.

▷ *Return to Sóller. Take the narrow mountain road via the picturesque villages of Biniaraix and Fornalutx, then follow the C 710.*

Mirador de Ses Barques

From this viewpoint there is an interesting **panorama** of Port de Sóller. The road heads through a long tunnel before following the upper valley of the Pareis. The land is dominated by **Puig Major**.

▷ *After skirting the Gorg Blau reservoir, take the Sa Calobra road.*

Sa Calobra road★★★

The magnificently planned road plunges 900m/2 953ft in 14km/8.7mi through steep, jagged rocks.

Sa Calobra★

Near the village is the mouth of the **Pareis river**★, its clear water pouring over round white shingle. The river bed is accessible along a track through two underground galleries; a 2–3km/1.2–1.8mi walk along the course gives an idea of how enclosed the stream is.

▷ *Return to the C 710.*

About 1km/0.6mi north of the Sa Calobra fork, a small **mirador**★ *(lookout, alt 664m/2 178ft)* gives a good view over the cleft hollowed out by the Pareis.

Monasterio de Nuestra Señora de Lluc

🕐 *Open daily 10am–1.30pm, 2.30–5pm.* ⊚4€ *(museum).* 🖉971 87 15 25. *www.lluc.net.*
The monastery dates from the 13C when a young shepherd found a statue of the Virgin. *La Moreneta*, the dark stone statue, is patron of Mallorca.

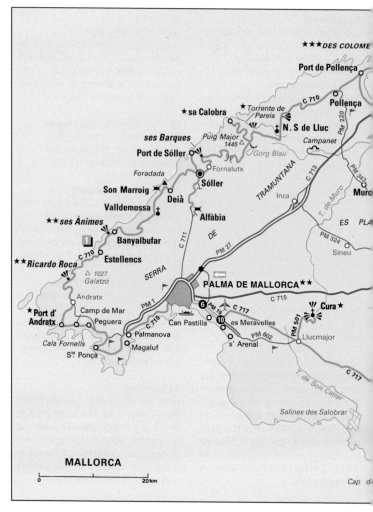

MALLORCA

0 _____ 20km

From a pass 5km/3mi north of Lluc, you can see the Bahía de Pollença.

Port de Pollença

This large resort has a perfect **setting**★ in a sheltered bay between the Cabo Formentor headland to the north and Cabo del Pinar to the south, and provides a vast expanse of calm water for waterskiing and sailing.

Cabo de Formentor road★

The road commands spectacular views as it twists upward. The **Mirador des Colomer viewpoint**★★★ *(access along a stepped path)* overlooks great rock promontories. The **Platja de Formentor** is a sheltered beach. The grand Hotel Formentor was once famous for its casino and millionaire guests. The road continues through a tunnel and a steep and arid landscape. **Cabo de Formentor**★, with its lighthouse, is the most northerly point of the island.

Return to Port de Pollença, then skirt the bay until you reach Alcúdia.

Alcúdia

Alcúdia, encircled by 14C ramparts, guards the promontory which divides the bays of Pollença and Alcúdia. Two

⏱ *Closed holidays.* ✎*2€.*
📞*971 54 70 04.*
A chapel in Alcúdia's old quarter houses statues, oil lamps, bronzes and jewellery from the ancient city of Pollentia.

Port d'Alcúdia
2km/1.2mi E.
The port of Alcúdia overlooks a vast bay built up with hotels. A beach stretches to the south as far as Can Picafort. The marsh of La Albufera is a nature reserve.

Coves de Campanet
17km/10.5mi SW along the C 713 and a secondary, signposted road. 🔊*Guided tours (45min) daily Nov–Mar 10am–6pm; Apr–Oct 10am–7pm.* ✎*9.50 €.* 📞*971 51 61 30. www.covesde campanet.com.*
About half of these caves along the 1.3km/0.8mi-long path have ceased formation. In the waterlogged area, the most common features are straight and delicate stalactites.

Muro
▶ *Follow the C 713 SW for 11km/6.8mi and then bear left for another 7km/4mi via Sa Pobla.*

The road crosses countryside bristling with windmills. The **ethnological section** of the **Museo de Mallorca** *(Major 15;* ⏱*open Tue–Wed and Fri–Sat 10am–3pm;* ✎*2.40€;* 📞*971 86 06 47),* in a large 17C noble residence, displays exhibits on traditional furniture, dress, farming and many island trades.

② East Coast And Caves★★
From Artà to Palma
165km/102.5mi. Allow 1 day.

Artà
The high rock site is crowned by the Iglesia de Sant Salvador and the ruins of an ancient fortress. The Artà region

gates (**Puerta del Muelle** to the harbour, and the **Puerta de San Sebastián** across town) from early walls were incorporated into 14C ramparts. The streets in the shadow of the walls have a distinctive medieval air.
About 2km/1.2mi south is the site of Roman **Pollentia** founded in the 2C BC. Only the theatre ruins remain.

Museo Monográfico de Pollentia
Sant Jaume 30, Alcúdia. ⏱ *Open Nov–Mar Tue–Fri 10am–3pm, Sat–Sun 10am–2pm; Apr–Oct Tue–Fri 10am–2pm, 4–6.30pm, Sat–Sun 10am–2pm.*

is rich in **megalithic remains** (👣*see MENORCA*), particularly *talayots*, sometimes spied over low walls in the fields.

▷ *Continue along the C 715.*

Capdepera
Access to the fortress: by car, along narrow streets; on foot, up steps.
The remains of a 14C fortress give Capdepera an angular silhouette of crenellated walls and square towers. The buttressed ramparts enclose only a restored **chapel** (𝄞*971 81 87 46*). Walk the old sentry path to **view**★ the sea and the nearby coves.

Cala Rajada
3km/1.8mi NE of Capdepera.
Cala Rajada is a delightful fishing village and pleasure boat harbour.
Across the pinewood towards the lighthouse are two rocky inlets, relatively wild; 2km/1.2mi further north is **Cala Agulla**, with a sandy beach.

▷ *Return to Capdepera and follow the signs to the Coves d'Artà.*

Coves d'Artà★★★
🐾*Guided tours (40min) daily May–Cot 10am–6pm; Nov–Apr 10am–5pm; last admission 30min before closing.*
🕐 *Closed 1 Jan, 25 Dec.* 👁10€. 𝄞*971 84 12 93. www.cuevasdearta.com.*
The caves, in the cape closing Canyamel bay to the north, were largely hollowed out by the sea – the giant mouth overlooks the sea from 35m/115ft. The lofty chambers contain massive concretions. The vestibule is blackened by smoke from 19C torches. Inside are the **Reina de las Columnas** (Queen of Columns), 22m/72ft tall, Dantesque surroundings cleverly highlighted in the **Sala del Infierno** (Chamber of Hell) and a fantasy of forms in the **Sala de las Banderas** (Hall of Flags), 45m/148ft high.

▷ *Return to the PM 404 and bear left. At Portocristo, take the Manacor road; turn shortly for the Coves dels Hams.*

Coves dels Hams
🐾*Guided tours (40min) Nov 11am–5pm; Dec–Feb 11am–4.30pm; Mar 10.30am–5pm; Apr, May & Oct 10.30am–5.30pm; Jun–Sept 10am–6pm.* 🕐 *Closed 25 Dec.* 👁10€. 𝄞*971 82 09 88. www.cuevas-hams.com.*
The caves join with the sea; the water level in several pools rises and falls with the Mediterranean tide. Some concretions in the **Sala de los Anzuelos**★ (Fish-hook Chamber) are snow white.

▷ *Return to Portocristo and bear right.*

Coves del Drach★★★
🐾*Guided tours (1hr) daily Apr–Oct hourly 10am–5pm; Nov–Mar 10.45am, noon, 2pm, 3.30pm, 4.30pm.* 🕐 *Closed 1 Jan, 25 Dec.* 👁10.50€. 𝄞*971 82 07 53. www.cuevasdrach.com.*
Four chambers succeed one another over a distance of 2km/1.2mi. The cave **roofs**, are amazing, glittering with countless sharply pointed icicles. **Lago Martel** is vast and limpid, a lake in a chamber used by musicians as they glide across the water in boats.

▷ *Continue along the road towards Santanyí then right onto the PM 401.*

Monasterio de Sant Salvador★
🕐 *Open daily 8am–9pm.* 👁*No charge.* 𝄞*971 93 61 36.*
The monastery, on a rise 500m/1 640ft above the plain (🚗*tight hairpin bends*), commands a wide **panorama**★★. It was founded in the 14C. In the church, behind the Baroque high altar, is a venerated **Virgin and Chil,** in the south chapels are three **Nativities** set in dioramas and a multicoloured 14C stone **altarpiece** carved with the Passion.

▷ *Return to the Santanyí road.*

Secondary roads lead to resorts built up in the creeks along the coast, namely **Cala d'Or**★, **Cala Figuera**★, which is still a delightful little fishing village, and **Cala Santanyí**★.

▶ *From Santanyí follow the C 717 towards Palma. In Llucmajor, bear right onto the PM 501.*

Santuario de Cura★

🕐 *Open daily 10am–1pm, 3.30–6pm. ☎971 12 02 60. www.santuariode cura.com.*

The road climbs to the monastery. The buildings have been restored and modernised by the Franciscans and include the 17C **church**, Sala de Gramática (Grammar Room) and a small **museum**. From the terrace on the west side there is a **panorama**★★ of Palma, the bay, the Puig Major and, in the northeast, Cabo de Formentor headland.

▶ *Return to Llucmajor and continue W along the C 717 to Palma.*

ADDRESSES

▲ STAY

🍽 **Hotel Born** – *Sant Jaume 3, Palma. ☎971 71 29 42. www.hotelborn.com. 25 rooms.* This hotel occupies a former 16C palace with a delightful Ibizan-style patio. The rooms are quiet with tasteful decor.

🍽 **Hotel Mar i Vent** – *Major 49, Banyalbufar. ☎971 61 80 00. www. hotelmarivent.com. Restaurant🍽. Closed Dec–Jan. 29 rooms.* A charming hotel converted from an old stone house with views of the wooded mountains and the Mediterranean.

🍽 **Hotel San Lorenzo** – *San Lorenzo 14, Palma. ☎971 72 82 00. www. hotelsanlorenzo.com. 9 rooms. ⊐14€.* An attractive 17C stately mansion with an inviting atmosphere. Beautifully decorated rooms are complemented by the swimming pool and garden.

🍽 **Hotel Son Trobat** – *Ctra Manacor-Sant Llorenç, Sant Llorenç des Cardassar. 4.8km/3mi NE of Manacor on the C 715. ☎971 56 96 74. www.sontrobat. com. 25 rooms. Restaurant🍽.* This large property in the countryside combines the rustic charm of a period property with all mod cons including two swimming pools, jacuzzi and sauna.

♀ EAT

🍽 **Ca's Cuiner** – *Pl. Cort 5, Palma. ☎971 72 12 62. Closed Sun.* Both a shop selling ready-made meals, and bona fide restaurant, Ca's Cuiner is considered the temple of Mallorcan cuisine.

🍽 **La Bodeguilla** – *Sant Jaume 1, Palma. ☎971 71 82 74. www.la-bodeguilla.com. Closed a week in Jul, Sun.* A restaurant spread over two floors with an adjoining wine shop, Large barrels are used as dining tables to enjoy dinner or tapas.

🍽 **Ca'n Cuarassa** – *Carretera Port de Pollença, Alcúdia. ☎971 86 42 66. www.cancuarassa.com.* Fine location on the beach overlooking the Bay of Pollensa, and modern decor with minimalist details that fit in well. The Mediterranean menu is best enjoyed on the terraces.

🍽 **Sa Plaça Petra** – *Pl. Ramón Llull 4, Petra. About 10km/6.2mi E of Manacor. ☎971 56 16 46. Closed Nov and Tue.* This attractive tranquil restaurant is a combination of old and new. It has a pleasant terrace, as well as three guest rooms (🍽).

🍽 **Son Tomás** – *Baronia 17, Banyalbufar. ☎971 61 81 49. Closed mid-Dec–Jan and Tue.* A wonderful, family-run restaurant with an open kitchenwhose staff take great care over a traditional seafood menu.

🍽 **Tristán** – *Puerto Portais, Portais Nous. ☎971 67 55 47. www. grupotristan.com.* A creative tasting and gourmet tapas menu served in an elegant dining room, overlooking the harbour.

Menorca★★

Menorca, with an area of 669sq km/ 258sq mi, has managed to avoid the rampant development that has blighted its neighbours and its coastline is dotted with sandy coves of crystal-clear water, excellent for diving. The island is also famous for its prehistoric monuments.

▶ **Population:** 88 434
⏱ **Michelin Map:** 579
▯ **Info:** Ciutadella: Plaça Catedral 5. Maó: Cós de Gràcia 30. ✆902 92 90 15. www.visitmenorca.com. www.e-menorca.org.
◗ **Location:** Menorca is the second-largest of the Balearic islands and the furthest from the mainland.

LANDSCAPE AND TRADITION

Menorca's highest point, Monte Toro, 358m/1 175ft, is in the north of the island, known as the Tramuntana, where there are outcrops of dark slate rock. Along the coast, these ancient, eroded cliffs have been cut into a saw's edge of *rías* (inlets) and deep coves. South of the Maó-Ciutadella line, the Migjorn limestone platform forms cliffs along the coast.

Vegetation is typically Mediterranean: pinewoods, gnarled and twisted wild olives, heather and aromatic herbs such as rosemary, camomile and thyme. Dry-stone walls divide fields, punctuated by gates of twisted olive branches.

Megalithic monuments – In the second millennium BC, the cavernous nature of the Minorcan countryside offered shelter for both the living and the dead; some of the caves, such as **Calascoves**, are even decorated. At the same time, **talayots** began to appear (over 200 have been identified), great cones of stones, possibly covering a funeral chamber and forming the base for a wooden house. Other monuments of the civilisation include **taulas**, consisting of two huge stone blocks placed one on top of the other in the shape of a T, possibly serving as altars, and **navetas**, which take the form of upturned boats and contain funeral chambers.

⊙ A locally available map shows the monument sites: Mapa Arqueológico de Menorca, by J Mascaró Pasarius.

Architecture – The walls and even the roofs of Minorcan houses are brightly whitewashed; low dividing walls have a white band along the top. Tiles are used for roofing, chimneys and guttering. Houses face south, their fronts characterised by wide, open bays. Northern walls, exposed to fierce *tramontana* winds, have small windows.

English influence on architecture is evident. Many houses in towns have sash windows and some mansions are in the Palladian style of 18C Britain.

The fields around Ciutadella are scattered with *barracas*, curious stone constructions with false ceilings, which served as shelters for shepherds.

A BIT OF HISTORY

Prehistoric peoples have left monuments throughout the island. Menorca was colonised by the Romans, conquered by Vandals in 427, and came under Muslim control in 903. In the 13C, Alfonso III of Aragón invaded, made Ciutadella capital and encouraged settlers from Catalunya and Aragón.

In the 16C, Barbary pirates left Maó and Ciutadella in virtual ruin.

In 1713, Menorca, which had begun to prosper through trade in the late 17C, was ceded to the English crown by the Treaty of Utrecht. Maó became England's stronghold in the Mediterranean. Apart from a short period of French rule from 1756 to 1763, the island remained throughout the 18C under the British. The first road, between Maó and Ciutadella, still exists (north of the C 721), known as camino Kane for a British governor. At the beginning of the 19C, Menorca was restored to Spain.

The island's economy has gradually been orientated towards the leather

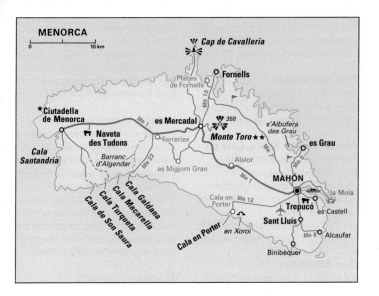

industry and jewellery-making while cattle raising provides the island with its well-known cheeses.

SIGHTS
CIUTADELLA/CIUDADELA★
In the Middle Ages, Ciutadella, citadel and capital of Menorca, was ringed with walls. The fortified aspect of the city becomes evident when viewed from the harbour. Sacked by Turkish pirates in the 16C, Ciutadella was partly rebuilt in the late 17C and 18C.

The **Midsummer's Day festivities**, or **Fiestas de San Juan** (24 Jun), are celebrated in traditional fashion. On the preceding Sunday, a man representing John the Baptist, dressed in skins and carrying a lamb, runs to the sound of *fabiols* (flutes) and *tambourins*. On 24 and 25 June, over 100 horsemen take part in jousting tournaments and processions.

Barrio Antiguo (Old Quarter)
Plaza del Born, the ex-parade ground, is flanked by the eclectic 19C **ayuntamiento** (town hall) and the early 19C **Palacio de Torre-Saura**, a palace with side loggias. An obelisk commemorates resistance against the Turks in the 16C.

Catedral
Plaça de la Catedral. ☎971 38 07 39.
The late-14C fortified church retains a minaret from Islamic days. The single aisle is ogival and the apse pentagonal. View the Baroque doorway from calle del Rosario. At the end of the street, turn left into calle del Santísimo. **Palacio Saura** has a Baroque façade with a cornice. **Palacio Martorell** across the street is more sober.

Take calle del Obispo Vila, passing the Claustro de Socorro (Socorro Cloisters) and the Iglesia de Santo Cristo (Church of the Holy Christ) to the main street which leads to **plaza de España** and the arcaded **carrer de Ses Voltes**.

Puerto (Harbour)
The ramp approach to the harbour, which serves pleasure craft, is along a former counterscarp. Quayside cafés and restaurants bustle with life. The esplanade, plaça de Sant Joan, the centre for Midsummer's Day festivities, is bordered by boat shelters hollowed out of rock. The area comes alive at night.

EXCURSIONS
Nau or Naveta des Tudons
5km/3mi E of Ciutadella.
☎902 92 90 15.

This funerary monument, shaped like an upturned ship, is notable for the vast stones in the walls and lining the floor.

Cala Santandria
3km/1.8mi S of Citadella.
This is a small sheltered beach in a creek, a local resort popular with locals.

Arenal de Son Saura, Cala en Turqueta, Cala Macarella
SE of Ciutadella. Son Saura: 12km/7.4mi via Torre Saura; Turqueta: 12km/7.4mi via Sant Joanet; Macarella: 14km/8.7mi via Sant Joan Gran.
The three beaches are set in small, beautifully unspoilt creeks fringed by pines.

Maó/Mahón
45km/28mi E of Ciutadella along Me 1.
Maó's **site**★ is most striking when approached from the sea, atop a cliff in the curve of a deep, 5km/3mi long natural harbour.
Maó was endowed with Palladian-style mansions during English occupation. On the north side of the harbour is the Finca de San Antonio – the Golden Farm – where Admiral Nelson put the finishing touches to his book, *Sketches of My Life* (October 1799). Maó gave its name to mayonnaise.
Most of Maó's shops are between **plaza del Ejército**, a large, lively square lined with cafés and restaurants, and the quieter **plaza de España** with its two churches: **Santa María**, with a beautiful Baroque organ, and **Carmen**, the Carmelite church, whose cloisters now hold the municipal market.

Museo de Menorca
Av. Dr Guardia, Maó. ⏲ *Open Apr–Oct Tue–Sat 10am–2pm, 6–8.30pm, Sun 10am–2pm; Nov–Mar Tue–Fri 9.30am–2pm, Sat–Sun 10am–2pm.* ⏲ *Closed public holidays.* 🎫*2.40€.* ☏*971 35 09 55.*
The museum is a former Franciscan monastery. Rooms around a sober 18C cloister display prehistoric and other objects relating to Menorcan history. A room is dedicated to *talayot* culture.

Puerto (Harbour)
Walk down the steep ramp from carrer de Ses Voltes, cut by a majestic flight of steps, and follow the quay to the north side. From here is the classic view of the town lining the top of the cliff.

La Rada★ (Roadstead)
On the south side are coves and villages, among them Cala Figuera with its fishing harbour and restaurants. **Es Castell** was an English garrison named Georgetown. It has a grid plan, with a parade ground at its centre. The islands in the harbour include Lazareto and Cuarentena, which was a quarantine hospital for sailors. A road follows the northern shore to the lighthouse affording views of Maó.

Talayot de Trepucó
1km/0.6mi S of Maó.
This megalithic site is famous for its 4.80m/16ft *taula.*

Sant Lluís
4km/2.5mi S.
This town with narrow streets was founded by the French. Small resorts have grown up nearby at **Alcaufar** and **Binibèquer**, a new village made to look like a fishing hamlet.

Es Grau
8km/5mi N.
Beside the attractive white village with its long beach is a vast lagoon, **Albufera de es Grau,** 2km/1.2mi long and 400m/437yd wide. It is an ideal spot to watch migrant birds (rails, ducks and herons).

Cala en Porter
12km/7.4mi W.
Promontories protect a narrow estuary, lined by a sandy beach. Houses perch upon the left cliff. Ancient troglodyte dwellings, the **Coves d'en Xoroi** (*www.covadenxoroi.com*), overlook the sea.

Mercadal
19km/11.8mi NW of Cala en Porter.
Mercadal, a village of brilliantly white-washed houses halfway between Maó

and Ciutadella, is where roads to the coast meet on the north–south axis.

Monte Toro
3.5km/2mi along a narrow road.
On a clear day, the **view**★★ from the church-crowned summit (358m/1 175ft) is of the entire island.

Fornells
8.5km/5.3mi N on the C 723.
Fornells, a fishing village of whitewashed houses with green shutters, lies at the mouth of a deep inlet, surrounded on all sides by bare moorland. The village lives off crayfish. The local speciality, crayfish soup or *caldereta*, is a delight.

Cap de Cavalleria
12km/7.4mi N along the PM 722.
The drive to the cape, northernmost point on the island, is through windswept moorland, battered by the *tra-montana*, with large, elegant country houses, like that at Finca Santa Teresa. The **view** from the lighthouse is of a rocky, indented coast, more Atlantic than Mediterranean.

Cala (Santa) Galdana
16km/10mi SW via Ferreries.
This cove set in a limpid bay flanked by tall cliffs has been marred by large hotels.

🚶 It is possible to walk to the cove from **the Algendar ravine** (on leaving Ferreries, take the track left towards Ciutadella; 3hr there and back).
Within walking distance of Cala Galdana are the idyllic Caribbean-like **white-sand coves** of Cala Mitjana, Cala Turqueta, Cala Macarella and Cala Trébaluger. Beware that they get very busy in peak season. Small boats also service these beaches, running from Cala Galdana and Cala n'Bosch.

Ibiza★

Ibiza, with an area of 572sq km/221sq mi, is renowned for nightlife and visiting hedonists, yet parts of the island remain a natural paradise. There are stunning beaches, hidden coves and delightful villages with narrow streets lined by white-washed houses all of which forge a personality that is unique in the Balearics.

- ▶ **Population:** 113 908
- ⏱ **Michelin Map:** 579
- ℹ **Info:** Eivissa: Passeig Vara de Rey 1. ☏ 971 30 19 00. www.ibiza.travel.
- ▶ **Location:** Ibiza is the closest island to the Spanish mainland (83km/52mi).

LANDSCAPE AND TRADITION
Ibiza, the **Isla Blanca** (White Island), 72.4km/45mi southwest of Mallorca, is 41km/25mi in length.
Dazzling whitewashed walls, flat roof terraces, tortuous alleys and an atmosphere similar to that of a Greek island give Ibiza its unique character. It is mountainous, with little space for cultivation. Among pines and junipers on the hillsides stand the cube-shaped houses of many small villages. The shore appears wild and indented; promontories are marked by rocks out to sea, some as high as the limestone needle known as **Vedrá**★ (almost 400m/1 300ft).
Traditional architecture – The typical Ibizan cottage, or **casament**, now largely found inland, is made up of several white cubes with few windows. Arcaded porches provide shade and a sheltered area for storing crops.
Country churches are equally plain with gleaming white exteriors and dark interiors. Façades are square, surmounted by narrow bell gables, pierced by wide porches. Fortified churches once provided shelter from pirates in Sant Carles, Sant Joan, Sant Jordi and Sant Miquel.

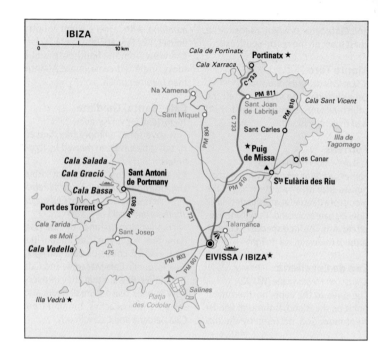

IBIZA

0 ———— 10 km

Cala de Portinatx
Cala Xarraca
Portinatx ★
C 733
Na Xamena
PM 811
Sant Joan de Labritja
Cala Sant Vicent
PM 810
Sant Miquel
Illa de Tagomago
PM 804
C 733
Sant Carles
★ **Puig de Missa**
Cala Salada
Cala Gració
es Canar
Sant Antoni de Portmany
Cala Bassa
S¹ᵃ Eulària des Riu
PM 810
Port des Torrent
PM 803
C 731
Cala Tarida
es Molí
Sant Josep
Talamanca
Cala Vedella
△ 475
PM 803
PM 801
EIVISSA / IBIZA ★
Salines
Illa Vedrà ★
Platja des Codolar

Folklore and traditional costume
– Ibiza's uncomplicated folklore lives
on. Women still wear the traditional
long gathered skirt and dark shawl. At
festivals the costume is brightened with
fine gold filigree necklaces or **empren-
dades**. Dances are performed to the
accompaniment of flute, tambourine
and castanets.

A BIT OF HISTORY

In the 10C BC, Phoenicians made the
island a staging-post for ships loaded
with Spanish ores; in the 7C BC, Carthage
founded a colony; under the Romans the
capital grew in size and prosperity.

SIGHTS
EIVISSA★

Eivissa's colourful beauty and impressive
site★★ are best appreciated from the
sea; alternatively, take the **Talamanca**
road and look back *(3km/1.8mi NE)*. The
town, built on a hill, consists of an old
quarter ringed by walls, the lively Marina
district near the harbour, and, further
out, residential and shopping areas.
Along the shore are large hotels.

UPPER TOWN★ (DALT VILA)

Allow 1hr30min.
The Dalt Vila, enclosed by the 16C walls
built under Emperor Charles V, is the
heart of the old city and retains even
today a rustic, medieval character. There
remain many noble houses worth looking at particularly for their vast patios
and Gothic windows.
Enter the quarter through the **Porta
de Taules**, a gateway surmounted by
Philip II's crest. Continue by car up a
steep slope to the Cathedral square or
stroll the quiet meandering streets with
their shops and art galleries.

Catedral

Pl. de la Catedral. ◷ *Open Apr–Oct
Mon–Sat 9.30am–1.30pm, 5–8pm;
Nov–Mar Mon–Sat 9.30am–1.30pm,
5–7pm.* ⊘*No charge.* ☏*971 39 92 32.*
The Cathedral's massive 13C belfry,
which resembles a keep but for its two
storeys of Gothic bays, dominates the
town. The nave was rebuilt in the 17C.
An ancient bastion behind the east end
affords a **panoramic view**★.

Museo Arqueológico de Ibiza y Formentera★

Pl. de la Catedral 3. ○ *Open Apr–Sept Tue–Sat 10am–2pm, 6–8pm, Sun 10am–2pm; Oct–Mar Tue–Sat 9am–3pm, Sun 10am–2pm.* ○ *Closed public holidays.* ∞2.40€. ℘971 30 12 31. www.aamaef.org.

The most impressive exhibits are its Punic art, which developed around the Mediterranean from the 7C BC to the 3C AD. Particularly impressive are the ex-votos discovered on Ibiza and Formentera, predominantly from excavations at Illa Plana and the Es Cuiram cave. The cave is believed to have been a temple to the goddess **Tanit**, who was venerated from the 5C BC to the 2C BC. Also worthy of note are the polychrome moulded glass and Punic, Roman and Moorish ceramics.

LOWER TOWN
Necrópolis Puig des Molins★

Vía Romana 31. ○ *Open Oct–Mar Tue–Sat 9am–3pm, Sun 10am–2pm; Apr–Sept Tue–Sat 10am–2pm, 6–8pm, Sun 10am–2pm.* ○ *Closed public holidays.* ∞2.40€. ℘971 30 17 71.

The Puig des Molins hillside necropolis was a burial ground for the Phoenicians from the 7C BC and for the Romans until the 1C AD. There is a model of the site; some of the hypogea, or funerary chambers, of which over 3 000 have been discovered, may be visited. The objects displayed were found in the tombs and include everyday and ritual articles. The outstanding, partly coloured, 5C BC **bust of the goddess Tanit**★, a Punic version of the Phoenician Astarte, exemplifies Greek beauty. A second bust is more Carthaginian.

La Marina

The Marina district near the market and harbour, with its restaurants, bars and shops, stands in lively contrast to the quieter Dalt Vila.

Sa Penya★

The former fishermen's quarter, now the centre of Ibiza's nightlife, is built on a narrow rock promontory at the harbour mouth. White cubic houses overlap in picturesque chaos, completely blocking streets forcing bypasses via steps cut out of the rock.

SANT ANTONI DE PORTMANY/ SAN ANTONIO ABA

Sant Antoni with its vast, curved bay has been extensively developed. The old quarter, hidden behind modern apartment blocks, centres on a fortified 14C church rebuilt in the 16C. There is a large pleasure boat harbour. Several coves and creeks are within easy reach.

EXCURSIONS
Cala Gració

2km/1.2mi N.

A lovely, easily accessible, sheltered creek.

Cala Salada

5km/3mi N.

The road descends through pines to a sheltered beach in a cove.

Port des Torrent and Cala Bassa

5km/3mi SW.

Port des Torrent is all rocks; Cala Bassa a long, pine-fringed beach. Rocks are smooth and separate and just above or just below the water line, providing perfect underwater swimming conditions.

Cala Vedella

15km/9.3mi S.

A road skirts the shoreline through pine trees between the beaches of Cala Tarida (rather built-up), Es Molí (unspoiled) and Cala Vedella in its enclosed creek. You can return to Sant Antoni along a mountain road cut into the cliffs as far as Sant Josep.

SANTA EULÀRIA DES RIU/ SANTA EULÀLIA DEL RÍO

Santa Eulària des Riu, in a fertile plain watered by Ibiza's only river, is a large seaside resort. Nearby beaches such as **Es Canar** have also been developed.

Puig de Missa★

Bear right off the Eivissa/Ibiza road 50m/55yd after the petrol station (on the left).

This minute, fortified town crowning the hilltop provides a remarkable overview of the island's traditional peasant architecture; in times of danger, the church (16C) served as a refuge.

Portinatx★

27km/17mi N on the PM 810, PM 811 and C 733.

The road passes through **Sant Carles**, which has a fine church and is a departure point for quiet local beaches. It descends to the vast **Sant Vicent** creek *(cala)* with its sandy beach and opposite, the Isla de Togomago, then crosses a landscape covered in pines. The last section threads between holm oaks and almond trees looking down on **Cala Xarraca**. Creeks sheltered by cliffs and pine-fringed beaches make **Cala de Portinatx** one of the island's most attractive areas.

ADDRESSES

🏨 STAY

Hostal La Marina – *Barcelona 7. ℰ971 31 01 72. www.hostal-lamarina. com. 30 rooms. ☞2€. Restaurant.* A friendly and colouristic hostel established since the 19C. Centrally located by the port. The rooms have been recently renovated with the best looking out to sea. The tavern restaurant has a neo-rustic decor with a very agreeable terrace.

Hostal Parque – *Pl. del Parque 4. ℰ971 30 13 58. www.hostalparque.com. 30 rooms.* Small but pleasing rooms with excellent sound-proofing to block out the noise from the plaça del Parque, a popular meeting point for local youngsters.

Hotel Montesol – *Pas.Vara de Rei 2. ℰ971 31 01 61. www.hotelmont esol.com. 55 rooms. ☞5€.* Nothing in the town can compare with this large, mustard-coloured building dating from the beginning of the last century, with its comfortable rooms overlooking the streets of the old quarter. Make sure you enjoy a drink on the hotel's terrace café, which continues to be one of Ibiza's famous locations.

Agroturismo Can Jondal – *Ctra de San José a Ibiza. ℰ971 18 72 70. www.canjondal.com. 6 rooms.* A pleasant Ibizan house with whitewashed walls, numerous terraces and tastefully decorated rooms, all on an eco-farm using renewable energy, it is also a holistic meditation centre. A haven of peace and quiet on the slopes of a hill in the midst of nature. A friendly welcome guaranteed.

La Colina – *Sangha Colina, ctra Ibiza a Santa Eulària. 5.5km/3.5mi SW of Santa Eulària des Ríu. ℰ971 33 27 67. www.lacolina-ibiza.com. Closed Nov–Jan. 13 rooms. ☞.* This traditional, Ibizan-style country house stands on the side of a small hill. Now a quiet, family-run hotel, it is increasingly popular with foreign visitors. Pleasant outdoor areas, including a swimming pool.

Hotel Rural Es Cucons – *Santa Agnès de Corona. 1km/0.6mi along Corona, Camí des Plà de Corona. ℰ971 80 55 01. www.escucons.com. 14 rooms. Restaurant. Closed Nov–Mar.* The family who own this hotel have succeeded in converting this former Ibizan farm into an architectural jewel that has been magnificently decorated in keeping with its origins. A superb combination of luxury and simplicity at the heart of an expansive valley.

🍽/EAT

Ca's Milà – *Playa de Cala Tarida, Sant Josep. ℰ971 80 61 93. www.ibiza-restaurants.com/casmila. Closed Jan–Mar, weekdays Nov–Dec.* A privileged location by the seafront with wonderful views of the coastline. A very good seafood menu, with specialities such as rolled smoked salmon with avocado. Try to get a table on the terrace.

La Masía d'en Sort – *Ctra de Sant Miquel de Balansat, Santa Eulària. ℰ971 31 02 28. Closed Mon (Sept–Jul),* *lunch.* Beautiful farm with lovely island architecture and a rustic, Iberian interior. This well-known institution serves enjoyable local cuisine, complemented by a terrace as well as an art gallery on the first floor.

El Cigarral – *Fray Vicente Nicolás 9.* 𝄐 *971 31 12 46. Closed Sun, fortnight in May.* An elegant restaurant decorated with an array of plants and Castilian decorations. The superb menu has traditional cuisine served in a modern way with the finest market produce.

Formentera

Formentera, the Roman Island of Wheat (from *frumentum*), smallest in the archipelago (area 84sq km/ 32sq mi), is ideal for those in search of peace and quiet, impressive scenery and beautiful beaches lapped by crystal-clear water.

▶ **Population:** 7 461
◔ **Michelin Map:** 579
▯ **Info:** Sant Francesc: Port de Savina (Obras del Puerto building). 𝄐971 32 20 57. www. turismoformentera.com.
◗ **Location:** Formentera lies just 7km/4.3mi S of Ibiza.

LANDSCAPE AND TRADITION

Formentera is two islets and a sandy isthmus, 14km/8.7mi long. The capital, Sant Francesc de Formentera, the passenger port, Cala Savina, the salt pans, Cabo de Barbaria and the dry open expanse where cereals, figs, almonds and a few vines grow, are on the western islet; the island's 192m/630ft mountain rises from the **Mola** promontory on the eastern islet. Rock cliffs and sand dunes alternate along the shore. Access to the island is exclusively by sea, and the best way of exploring Formentera is by bicycle.

A BIT OF HISTORY

Formentera's inhabitants arrived comparatively recently, the island having been abandoned in the Middle Ages in the face of marauding Barbary pirates and only repopulated at the end of the 17C. Most of the present population consists of fishermen and farmers, shipping figs and fish to Ibiza and salt to Barcelona.

SIGHTS

The Beaches (Playas or Platjas)

White sandy beaches with clear water are the main attraction. Long beaches stretch along either side of the isthmus, the rocky Tramuntana to the north and the sheltered, sandy Migjorn to the south. Smaller beaches include Es Pujòls (the most developed), Illetas and Cala Saona.

Cala Savina

Your landing point is in the main harbour: a few white houses stand between two big lagoons, salt marshes glisten in the distance on the left.

Sant Francesc (San Francisco Javier)

3km/1.8mi SE of Savina.
Chief town on the island. Its houses are clustered around the 18C church-fortress.

El Pilar de la Mola

14km/8.7mi SE of Sant Francesc.
The hamlet at the centre of the Mola promontory has this geometrically designed church which is similar to those on Ibiza, only smaller.

Far de la Mola

2km/1.2mi SE of Pilar de la Mola.
The lighthouse overlooks an impressive cliff. There is a monument to Jules Verne who mentioned this spot in *Off on a Comet* (1877).

Canary Islands ★★★

These volcanic islands, where nature is at its most generous, provide visitors with many contrasts: from exuberant vegetation to desert landscapes; steep cliffs to endless beaches; picturesque villages to overcommercialised resorts. All this, coupled with a fantastic climate, has turned the Canaries into one of the world's leading holiday destinations, particularly in the European winter. The Canaries have a combined area of 7 273sq km/2 808sq mi and a total population of over two million.

The Canary Islands – seven in total with six smaller isles – lie between 100km/62mi and 300km/186.4mi off the northwest coast of North Africa. Ferries and inter-island flights connect the islands, though (unlike in Greece) there is no "island-hopping" culture.

Volcanic creation – The islands were thrust up from the Atlantic seabed by volcanic eruptions. La Gomera and Gran Canaria have a conic silhouette and most of the islands, except Fuerteventura and Lanzarote, are hilly and end in steep cliffs. Crowning Tenerife, Pico del Teide at 3 718m/12 195ft is the highest point in Spain, exceeding the average depth of the sea round the islands (3 000m/1 640.4 fathoms).

La Palma rises to 2 426m/7 959ft and because of its relatively small area is said to be the steepest island in the world. It features the world's largest *caldera* (volcanic crater) too. Here, and elsewhere, lava, slag fields and cinder cones form what is known as *malpaís*, most extensive and most spectacular on Lanzarote where huge areas resemble a moonscape.

The Conquest – The Spanish Conquistadores found a native Stone Age population known as the **Guanches**, who lived in caves, practised trepanning and mummified their dead. The Guanches had little answer to the invaders and were decimated, not least as a result of common illnesses introduced inadvertently by the Spaniards, to which they had no natural resistance. By the end of the century the islands were taken and most Guanches were either dead or had assimilated into the new order.

The Fortunate Islands – Ancient mariners nicknamed the archipelago The Fortunate Islands on account of their year-round mild climate. While El Teide is snow-capped for several months of the year, the coastal temperature rarely drops below 18°C/65°F.

The climate varies, however, sometimes quite dramatically, between the north and south of the larger islands, most notably on Tenerife and Gran Canaria. This has encouraged sun-and-fun resorts (such as Playa de las Américas and Playa del Inglés respectively) to develop in the south, which remains sun-kissed almost all year round. By contrast the northern coasts of Tenerife and Gran Canaria respectively can be (relatively) chilly and wet in winter and as a result have been less commercialised for the holiday trade.

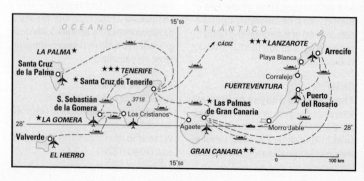

Tenerife★★★

The snow-capped silhouette of El Teide, the highest peak in Spain, is the symbol of this beautiful island, literally "snow-covered mountain" in Guanche. The spectacular Las Cañadas crater is witness to Tenerife's volcanic past. Year-round sun draws package tourists and youngsters to the brash man-made resorts of the parched south, while natural beauty and a mild climate attracts more mature holidaymakers to the north of the island.

PICO DEL TEIDE★★★
Clouds often enshroud Mount Teide and the superb panoramas from its viewpoints.

Ensure that you have comfortable footwear and a warm jacket. Temperature and weather can change dramatically in a short time.

La Esperanza Approach★
The road climbs to the crest which divides the island.

Pinar de la Esperanza★
The road runs for several miles through this extensive pinewood. In a clearing at **Las Raíces**, an obelisk commemorates the rebellion in July 1936 against the Republican government by Francisco Franco, who was stationed here.

▶ **Population:** 886 033

Info: Santa Cruz de Tenerife: Plaza de España. *922 23 98 11; Puerto de la Cruz: Las Lonjas. *922 38 60 00. www.webtenerifeuk.co.uk. www.todotenerife.es.

Location: Tenerife is the largest of the Canary Islands, with an area of 2 036sq km/786sq mi.

Kids: Loro Parque, Lago Martiánez, Siam Park, Parque Ecológico de las Aguilas del Teide, Aqualand.

Belvederes★★
When the cloud disperses, admire the stark contrast between the lush north coast and the aridity of the Güimar Valley from roadside belvederes. After La Crucita, the road enters a high-mountain landscape. The Astronomical Observatory at Izaña is visible *(left)*.

El Portillo
Alt 2 030m/6 660ft. This pass is the gateway to the extraordinary geological world of the Las Cañadas crater.

Parque Nacional del Teide★★★
There are two visitor centres (*both open daily 9am–4pm; *922 29 01 29). the El Portillo Centre has exhibits on

---

GETTING TO THE CANARY ISLANDS

By plane– Each island has an airport (Tenerife has two), offering easy, rapid access to the Spanish mainland and the rest of Europe. A number of inter-island routes also operate throughout the year. The two major airports are Tenerife and Gran Canaria; the airports at El Hierro and La Gomera
Iberia *902 40 05 00; www.iberia.com
Binter Canarias: Inter-island flights only. *902 39 13 92;

www.bintercanarias.com.
Spanair *902 13 14 15; www.spanair.com.
Air Europa *902 40 15 01; www.air-europa.com (flights to Gran Canaria, Tenerife and Lanzarote).
By ferry – From mainland Spain there is a two-day boat trip leaving from Cádiz and travelling to Santa Cruz de Tenerife and Las Palmas de Gran Canaria. There are also ferry, jet-foil and hydrofoil services to travel from one island to the other. **Trasmediterránea** *902 45 46 45; www.trasmediterranea.es.

volcanism, and trail information, the geological history of the park and its flora and fauna; the Cañada Blanca Visitor Centre is next to the parador hotel.

About 350m/1 150ft below the summit lies Las Cañadas plateau, a spectacular crater at over 2 000m/6 560ft which fell in on itself before El Teide was created. The peak rises from its northern side. In the centre of the park, opposite the *parador*, are **Los Roques**, a spectacular outcrop of lava boulders, laid bare by erosion. Another geological feature is **Los Azulejos**, boulders covered with copper oxide, which glint blue-green in the sun.

Pico del Teide★★★

🚠*Ascent by **cable car** from La Rambleta (2 356m/7 728ft): not suitable for those with respiratory or heart problems (the cable car climbs 1 199m/3 932ft in 10min).*
🕐 *Operates daily 9am–4pm, weather permitting.* 🕐 *Closed 1 Jan, 25 Dec.* 🚠*25€ round-trip.* 📞*922 01 04 45. www.telefericoteide.com.*
🚶*From the top (3 555m/11 660ft), a steep 30min walk across scree leads to the summit (🚷the path is closed).*
The crater at the summit is almost 25m/82ft deep and 50m/164ft across, swathed in wisps of sulphurous smoke. On a clear day, the view covers the whole Canaries archipelago.

La Orotava Approach★

The vegetation on the north coast (bananas, fruit trees and vines) is visible during the climb. Pinewoods begin in **Aguamansa**. Beyond the village at the side of the road, a huge basalt formation resembles a daisy.

Guía Approach

The climb via Guía is more mountainous. The narrow road crosses two defiles, Las Narices del Teide (last eruption in 1798) and the Chinyero volcano (1909).

Vilaflor Approach

Vilaflor is the highest town on the island (1 466m/4 806ft). The road crosses a beautiful pinewood and then, at the **Boca de Tauce pass**★★ (2 055m/6 742ft), reveals a striking view of Las Cañadas dominated by El Teide.

SAN CRISTÓBAL DE LA LAGUNA★

La Laguna, the former island capital and now seat of the university, was founded in 1496. Its centre features fine Spanish colonialist architecture.

Plaza del Adelantado

Fronting this pleasant, tree-lined square are the old **Convent of Santa Catalina**, which retains its original upper gallery, a feature rarely seen nowadays; the 17C **Palacio de Nava** with stone façade, reminiscent of the Bishop's Palace, and the town hall, or **ayuntamiento**, with Neoclassical façade (*Obispo Rey Redondo 1;* 🕐 *open Mon–Fri 10am–1.30pm; www.aytolalaguna.com).* The last is a combination of several buildings. The 16C and 18C portals on calle Obispo Rey Redondo are impressive.

▶ *Follow calle Obispo Rey Redondo.*

Catedral

Pl. Fray Albino. 🕐 *Call for opening times.* 📞*902 00 31 21.*
The elegant Neoclassical façade was erected in 1819; the nave and four aisles were rebuilt in neo-Gothic style in 1905. In the Capilla de los Remedios (*right transept*), note the retable, a 16C Virgin and 17C Flemish panels.

Iglesia de la Concepción★

Pl. Doctor Olivera. 🕐*Open Mon–Fri 8.30am–1.45pm, 5.30–7.30pm, Sat 8.30am–1.45pm, 5–7.30pm, Sun and public holidays 7.30am–1.45pm, 4.30–8.30pm.* 🚠*No charge.* 📞*922 25 91 30.*
A 17C grey stone tower rises over this 16C church, typical of the time of the conquest. The interior retains several Mudéjar ceilings, a ceiling with Portuguese influence, a Baroque pulpit

and choir stalls, and a beaten silver altar (*Capilla del Santísimo*).

▶ *Take Belén, then head down San Agustín.*

Palacio Episcopal or Antigua Casa de Salazar
San Agustín 28.
The Bishop's Palace has a beautiful 17C stone façade and attractive patio.

Museo de Historia de Tenerife
San Agustín 22. 🕐 *Open Tue–Sun 9am–7pm.* 🕐 *Closed 1, 6 Jan, 24–25, 31 Dec.* ✆*3€, no charge Sun.* 🖉*922 82 59 49.*
In the late-16C **Casa Lercano**, with its fine patio, exhibits provide an overview of the island's history from the 15C.

SANTA CRUZ DE TENERIFE★
The capital began as a port serving La Laguna. An oil refinery, tobacco factory and other industries operate here.
From the harbour breakwater there is a **view**★ of the stepped semicircle of high-rise buildings against the backdrop of the Pico del Teide. The Guimera Theatre – the oldest theatre in the Canaries inaugurated in 1851 – and the stunning, space-age Auditorio de Tenerife, designed by Santiago Calatrava, witness the city's strong cultural tradition. Santa Cruz is also famous for its **Carnival** *(last week in Feb;* 🖉*922 60 60 06)*, arguably the most colourful and certainly the largest in all Spain.

Iglesia de la Concepción
Tomás Pérez. 🕐 *Open daily 9am–1pm, 4.30–8pm.* ✆*No charge.* 🖉*922 33 01 87.*
A few houses with balconies around the 16C–18C church (fine Baroque retables) are all that remains of the old city.

Museo de la Naturaleza y el Hombre★ (Museum of Nature and Man)
Fuente Morales. 🕐 *Open Tue–Sun 9am–7pm.* 🕐 *Closed 1, 6 Jan, Carnival Tue, 24–25, 31 Dec.* ✆*3€; no charge Sun.* 🖉*922 53 58 16. www.museos detenerife.org.*

In the ex-Hospital Civil, a large Neo-classical building, are archaeology and natural science collections.

Palacio de Carta
Pl. de la Candelaria. ⚊ *Closed to the public.*
This 18C palace on plaza de la Candelaria, now a bank, retains its delightful wooden arches, galleries and patio.

Iglesia de San Francisco
San Francisco 13. 🕐 *Open for Mass.* 🖉*922 24 45 62. www.parroquia sanfrancisco.org.*
The 17C–18C church displays the characteristics of Canary Island churches from this period: naves with wooden roofs and cylindrical pillars.

Parque Municipal García Sanabria★
🖉*922 60 60 99.*
This alluring tropical and Mediterranean garden is close to La Rambla Genral Franco, a landscaped boulevard.

Museo Militar
Castillo de Almeida, San Isidro 1. 🕐 *Open Tue–Sat 10am–2pm.* ✆*No charge.* 🖉*922 84 35 00. Nelson lost both the battle and his right arm when attacking the castle on 24 July 1797.*

Parque Marítimo César Manrique★
Avenida Constitución 5. Leave by ② on the town plan. 🕐 *Open daily 10am–6pm (7pm in summer). Last admission 1hr before closing.* ✆*2.50€.* 🖉*922 20 32 44.*
This lido, designed by the great Lanzarote artist, César Manrique, combines water, volcanic rock and vegetation.

PUERTO DE LA CRUZ★
Puerto de la Cruz is the principal resort on the north coast with black beaches and several first-class visitor attractions. It attracts an older clientele than the resorts in the south but is still very lively, particularly at Carnival time. The old town, between the plaza de la

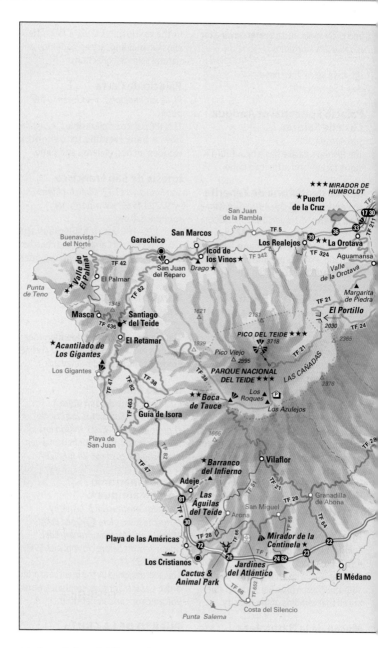

Iglesia and plaza del Charco, features many attractive 17C and 18C balconied houses and, unlike the other resorts on the island, retains a genuine Canarian atmosphere.

Just east of town the **Mirador de Humboldt**★★★offers a magnificent view of the town and the verdant sweep of the **Orotava Valley** running down to the sea from the slopes of mighty Mount Teide.

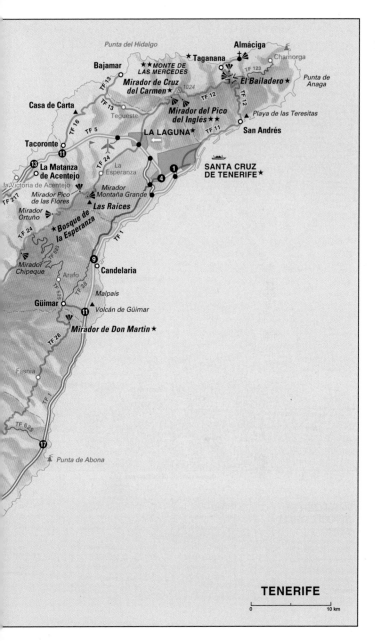

TENERIFE

0   10 km

🏊‍♂️ Costa Martiánez★

Av. de Colon. ⏰ *Open daily 10am–5pm.*
⏰ *Closed fortnight in May.* 🎫 *3.50€;*
child 1.20€; parasols available 1.50€.
✆ *922 38 59 55.*

This beautifully designed landmark
lido (also known as the Lido or Lago

Martiánez), famous for its fountains, is
another example of the work of César
Manrique, using vernacular architectures
and local natural features to maximum
visual effect.

The **Casino Taoro** is located within the
Costa Martiánez complex.

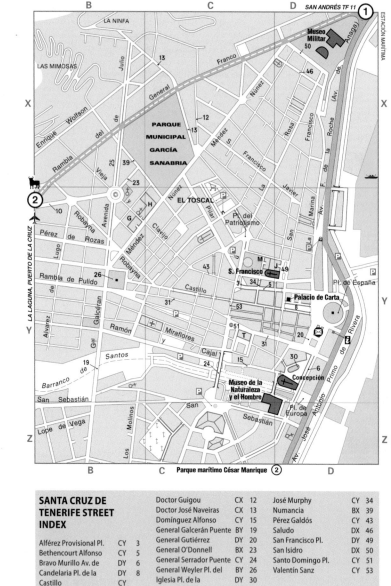

Jardín de Aclimatación de la Orotava★★

Retama 2. ⏰ *Open daily Apr–Sept 9am–7pm; Oct–Mar 9am–6pm.* ⏰ *Closed 1 Jan, Good Fri, 25 Dec.* ⌾*3€.* ✆*922 38 35 72.*
This 2ha/5-acre botanical garden, created in the 18C, contains trees and flowers from the Canary Islands and elsewhere, some of which are over 200 years old.

Playa Jardín★ (Garden Beach)

This black-sand beach is surrounded by gardens designed by César Manrique. The **Castillo de San Felipe** (✆*922*

38 36 63), a watchtower now used for cultural functions, can be seen at its eastern end.

👥 Loro Parque (Parrot Park)

Avenida Loro Parque. 🕐 Open daily 8.30am–6.45pm; last admission at 4pm. ⌾31.50€; child 20.50€; combined ticket with Siam Park 49€/33€. 𝄞922 37 38 41. www.loroparque.com.
Originally just a bird park, this is now one of the finest animal and marine theme parks in the world outside Florida, and is the island's most popular destination after Mount Teide. It features a world-class dolphinarium, killer whales, sea lions, a penguinarium, a large aquarium, tigers, gorillas, chimps and one of the world's finest collections of birds, all set in beautiful grounds. Kinderlandia is a mini-African theme park for little ones.

LA OROTAVA★★

This ancient town is arranged in terraces at the foot of Mount Teide. It boasts elegant balconied mansions and is famous for its Corpus Christi festival.

Plaza de la Constitución

The square is fronted by the 17C Baroque church of San Agustín and the Liceo Taoro cultural centre.

Iglesia de la Concepción

Tomás Pérez. 🕐 Open daily 9am–1pm, 4.30–8pm. ⌾No charge. 𝄞922 33 01 87.
The 18C church has a graceful Baroque façade. Visit the treasury.

Calle Carrera

Pass the **plaza del Ayuntamiento**, with its Neoclassical Palacio Municipal. Behind here the lush **Jardín de Aclimatación** (*Retama 2; 🕐 open daily Apr–Sept 9am–7pm; Oct–Mar 9am–6pm; 🕐closed 1 Jan, Good Friday & 25 Dec; ⌾3€; 𝄞922 38 35 72)* began life as a nursery for the botanical gardens in Puerto de la Cruz

Calle de San Francisco★

This street is adorned with some of the town's most beautiful balconies.

La Casa de los Balcones y la Casa Molina

San Francisco 3 & 5. 🕐 Casa de los Balcones (no 3): open Mon–Fri 8.30am–6.30pm, Sat 8.30am–4.30pm, Casa Molina (no 5): open Mon–Fri 9.30am–6.30pm. ⌾1.50€ (museum). 922 33 06 29. www.casa-balcones.com.
These two 17C houses feature delightful patios, a handicraft shop and a small museum which shows the inside of a local bourgeois house

Museo de Artesanía Iberoamericana

Tomás Zerolo 34. 🕐 Open Mon–Fri 9.30am–6pm, Sat 9.30am–2pm. ⌾2€. 𝄞922 35 29 06.
Set in the ex-Convento de San Benito Abad (17C) this displays Spanish and Latin-American handicrafts.

🚗 DRIVING TOUR

TOUR OF THE ISLAND

310km/194mi. See pp356–7 for map.

Garachico

Set on a picturesque stretch of rocky coast with natural pools Garachico was the finest harbour on the north coast until in 1706 the lava slick, clearly visible today, destroyed the old town. Its elegant 16C Castillo de San Miguel (*Avenida de Tomé Cano; 🕐 open for temporary exhibitions; ⌾0.50€; 𝄞922 83 00 00)* was the most notable survivor and is now home to a museum. The Iglesia de San Francisco also dates from the 16C while the 17C Convento de Santo Domingo houses a museum of contemporary art.

Masca

This remote hamlet is well worth the detour, set in lovely **countryside**★ where the houses are set on narrow ridges which plunge down into a verdant valley of dramatic rock formations.

Los Gigantes★

The Teno mountain range ends in black cliffs called Los Gigantes, "the giants", for their 400m/1 300ft vertical drop.

Adeje

Close to the village lies the **Barranco del Infierno (Hell Canyon)**★ which is justifiably popular with walkers.

Playa de las Américas

This large sprawling man-made resort is the most popular destination on the island. It features beaches of black sand, several family attractions on its outskirts, and a raucous nightlife. Neighbouring **Los Cristianos** is a busy port (ferries depart to La Gomera; *www.fredolsen. es*), which has been subsumed into the tourist sprawl.

 Follow the TF 28 in the Valle de San Lorenzo.

Mirador de la Centinela★

Like a sentinel, the viewpoint on a rocky projection commands a vast area.

Return to the inland road.

Mirador de Don Martín★

The belvedere provides a view of the Güimar rift valley and its plantations.

Güimar

A major town near the east coast.

Candelaria

This coastal town is a well-known place of pilgrimage. Its **basílica** *(pl. de la Basílica; 922 50 01 00) Can*houses a statue of the Virgin to which islanders make a pilgrimage on 14 and 15 August.

EXCURSIONS
MONTE DE LAS MERCEDES★★

Round trip of 49km/30mi from La Laguna. Allow 3hr.

The Anaga headland traps clouds from the north; tree laurel, giant heather and *fayas*, a local species, flourish.

Mirador de Cruz del Carmen★

See the La Laguna Valley from this viewpoint in Parque Rural de Anaga. *Visitor centre open daily 9.30am–3pm (4pm in winter). 922 82 20 56.*

Mirador del Pico del Inglés★★

A marvellous panorama spreads from the 1 024m/3 360ft peak of the Anaga headland to distant Pico del Teide.

El Bailadero★

The road crossing this pass commands good views in both directions.

Taganana★

On the way down to this coastal village are magnificent **views**★★. Visit the **Iglesia parroquial de Nuestra Señora de Las Nieves** for its Hispano-Flemish altarpiece *(pl. de la Virgen de las Nieves; open 10am–7pm; no visits during religious services; 922 59 01 86).*

ADDRESSES

STAY

Hotel Aguere – *Obispo Rey Redondo (Calle Carrera) 55, La Laguna. 922 25 94 90. www.hotelaguere.es. 23 rooms.* One of the few hotels on the island to retain its seigniorial charm. The wooden door provides access to a large, patio-style open hall area around which are all the rooms. The wooden floors, antique furniture and somewhat antiquated bathrooms provide further old-world charm. Highly recommended.

Hotel Monopol – *Quintana 15, Puerto de la Cruz. 922 38 46 11. www. monopoltf.com. 92 rooms. Restaurant.* This attractive four-storey whitewashed building adorned with wooden balconies stands in a pedestrianised street in a lively shopping district near the seafront. Comfortable rooms, arranged around a Canarian-style patio.
Senderos de Abona – *La Iglesia 5, Granadilla de Abona. 922 77 02 00. www.senderosdeabona.com. 17 rooms. Restaurant.* Rustic atmosphere, with serene patios. Friendly and polite staff.

◔◷◷◷ **Hotel San Roque** – *Esteban de Ponte 32, Garachico.* ℘*922 13 34 35. www.hotelsanroque.com. 32 rooms. Restaurant*◔◷◷◷. This luxury desgner-boutique hotel is tucked away in a quiet street in the centre of Garachico. It combines traditional Canarian design with contemporary style, fittings and all mod cons.

⊘ EAT

◔◷ **Régulo** – *San Felipe 16, Puerto de la Cruz.* ℘*922 38 45 06. www. restauranteregulo.com. Closed Sun, Mon lunch, fortnights in Jun and Jul.* This traditional island house retains all its charm, with a lovely patio and dining areas on two floor. Antiques and plants are prominent in the decor.

◔◷◷ **La Tasca de la Bodega** – *Av. San Sebastián 57, Santa Cruz de Tenerife.* ℘*922 22 39 09. Closed a week in Feb, Sat for dinner, Sun.* A renovated restaurant in an antique building, with a tapas bar by the entrance, a wine shop and various cosy dining rooms decorated with farming and wine growing equipment, noted for its Canarian cuisine.

Gran Canaria★★

Gran Canaria is often described as a continent in miniature on account of its many diverse landscapes. Almost half of its area is a UNESCO Biosphere Reserve. From the Pozo de las Nieves (1 949m/6 393ft) at its centre, ravines fan out in all directions. The mountain barrier divides the wetter landscapes of the north and west from extensive semi-desert-like areas in the south. The north and west coast is steep and rocky; on the accessible south coast are long golden sand beaches and throbbing man-made resorts.

SIGHTS
Las Palmas de Gran Canaria★

Las Palmas de Gran Canaria, founded in a palm grove in 1478, is nowadays the biggest city in the Canaries and also one of Spain's major ports. It was the most fashionable resort on the island for many decades but over the past 20 years or so it has lost its position to the burgeoning resorts of the sunnier south. Nonetheless, it is still easily the most interesting place to stay on Gran Canaria. The old city, **Vegueta**, dates from the Conquest; **Puerto de la Luz** and **Las Palmas** compose the tourist district, flanked by the harbour and Alcaravaneras beach on the east and Canteras beach on the west; between them lies residential **Ciudad Jardín**.

▸ **Population:** 829 597

▪ **Info:** Las Palmas: León y Castillo 17. ℘928 21 96 00; Playa del Inglés: Avenida España. ℘928 77 15 50. www.grancanaria.com.

▶ **Location:** Gran Canaria, the third-largest Canary Island (area: 560sq km/602sq mi), is wedged between Tenerife and Fuerteventura.

Vegueta – Triana★

Allow 2hr – ⬤ *see Vegueta, Triana p543..* These two districts form the historic centre of Las Palmas.

Plaza de Santa Ana

The palm-bordered square is overlooked by the town hall (1842) on one side, and the Cathedral on the other. To the side are the Bishop's Palace (Palacio Episcopal, 17C), with an *alfiz*-decorated portal showing clear Mudéjar influence, the Renaissance-style Casa del Regente and the Archivo Histórico Provincial (archives). During the Corpus Christi procession, the square is carpeted with flowers, sawdust and salt.

Catedral – *Pl. de Santa Ana.* ◷ *Open for Mass Mon–Fri 7.15am–10am, Sat 10am–2pm, Sun and public holidays 8am–2pm, 6–8pm.* ◔*No charge.* ℘*928 33 14 30.*

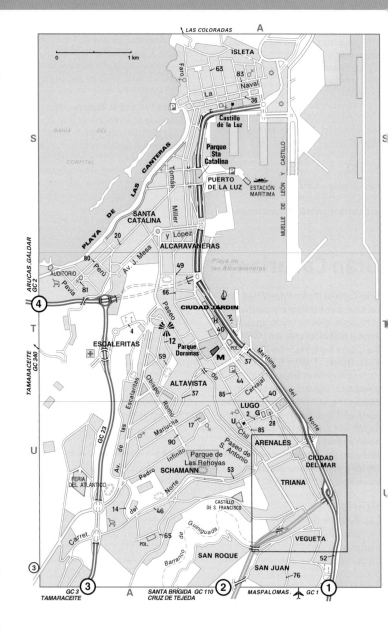

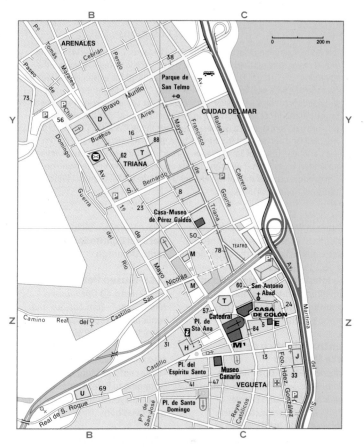

The Cathedral, begun in the early 16C, was not completed until the 19C. It has three elegant aisles with tierceron vaulting. In the transept are statues by Canarian sculptor **José Luján Pérez** (1756–1815).

Museo Diocesano de Arte Sacro

Entrance in pl. Espíritu Santo. ○ *Open Mon–Fri 10am–5pm, Sat 10am–1.30pm.* ☞*3€.* ℘*928 31 49 89.*

The museum of sacred art, in buildings around the 16C Patio de los Naranjos, contains 16C–19C engravings and gold and silverwork. In the chapterhouse is a mosaic from Manises (Valencia).

Casa de Colón★

Colón 1. ○*Open Mon–Fri 9am–7pm, Sat–Sun 9am–3pm.* ○*Closed public holidays.* ☞*No charge.* ℘*928 31 23 84. www.casadecolon.com.*

The palace of the island's first governors, where Columbus stayed in 1502, houses

Christopher Columbus

It is often maintained that, but for the Canary Islands, Columbus (1451–1506) would never have reached America. His persistence in trying to convince the sovereigns of Portugal, England, France and Castile of the existence of a westerly passage to Asia is well known. Eventually their Catholic Majesties of Castile provided three ships – the *Niña*, the *Pinta* and the *Santa María* – for an expedition to the Indies. He set sail westward from Palos in August 1492 but was forced to put into Las Palmas and La Gomera for repairs to the *Pinta*. On 12 October 1492 he spied land and set foot for the first time on the American continent – on the Caribbean Island of San Salvador. On each of his three subsequent voyages he landed at Las Palmas de Gran Canaria or on La Gomera before going on to discover the other islands of the Antilles (1493), the Orinoco delta (1498) and the shores of Honduras (1502).

a museum. Maps and instruments evoke Columbus' expeditions. Note the fine *artesonado* ceilings. On the upper floor are 16C–19C paintings.

The **Iglesia de San Antonio Abad** (*pl. San Antonio Abad 4*), on the site where Columbus attended Mass, has a fine Baroque interior.

Centro Atlántico de Arte Moderno

Balcones 9–11. Open Tue–Sat 10am–9pm, Sun 10am–2pm. Closed public holidays. No charge. 902 31 18 00. www.caam.net.

Along **calle de los Balcones** in one of several 18C buildings with fine doorways is this art centre, renovated by the architect Sáenz de Oíza, with works by 20C artists from the Canary Islands, the Spanish mainland and abroad.

Museo Canario★

Doctor Verneau 2. Open Mon–Fri 10am–8pm, Sat–Sun and public holidays 10am–2pm. Closed 1 Jan, 25 Dec. 3€. 928 33 68 00. www. elmuseocanario.com.

This museum displays a collection of artefacts from pre-Hispanic culture, including mummies, idols and skins. **Don't miss:** the collection of Guanche skulls some of which have been trepanned; terracotta seals *(pintaderas)* found only on Gran Canaria, whose purpose remains a mystery; a recreation of Gáldar's Cueva Pintada (see below).

Adjacent are two picturesque squares, **plaza del Espíritu Santo** and **plaza de Santo Domingo**.

Casa-Museo Pérez Galdós

Cano 2 and 6. Open Tue–Fri 10am–2pm, 4–8pm, Sat–Sun and public holidays 10am–2pm. Closed 1 Jan, Shrove Tue, 22 May, 25 Dec. No charge. 928 36 69 76. www. casamuseoperezgaldos.com.

Manuscripts, photographs and objects belonging to Pérez Galdós (1843–1920) are displayed in the house where the writer was born.

Parque de San Telmo

Calle Mayor de Triana, leading from this park, is the main street in the old town. The small **Iglesia de San Bernardo** is full of character with its Baroque altars and paintings. An unusual Modernist kiosk stands in a corner of the park.

MODERN TOWN

Allow 2hr – see plan of city.

Drive along avenida Marítima del Norte, skirting the town.

Parque Doramas

In this park are the Santa Catalina Hotel with its casino, and **Pueblo Canario**, a Canary Island village created by painter Néstor de la Torre (1887–1938; open Tue–Sat 10am–8pm, Sun 10.30am–2.30pm; closed 1 Jan, Holy Thu, Good Fri, 25 Dec; 2€; 928 24 51 35). Folklore festivals are held in the complex, which includes craft shops and the **Museo Néstor** (🕐 open Tue–Sat 10am–8pm, Sun and public holidays 10.30am–2.30pm; 🎫2€; 📞928 24 51 35; www.museonestor.com).

Parque Santa Catalina

The park, in **Puerto de la Luz**, includes the Museo de la Ciencia (Science Museum; 🕐open Tue–Sun 10am–8pm; 🎫5€ (including cinema and planetarium); 1€ robocoaster; www.museoelder.org) and the Miller cultural centre. Nearby streets are lined with restaurants and bars. Bazaars sell electronics at duty-reduced prices.

Playa de las Canteras★

This superb 3.5km/2mi beach is sheltered by a line of rocks offshore and backed by a pleasant promenade with restaurants and cafés. At its southeastern end, the **Auditorio Alfredo Kraus** (👣 guided tours (50min) Mon–Fri noon, Sun 11.30am; 🎫3€; www.auditorio-alfredokraus.com) hosts an opera season. It is the site of the Canaries Music Festival (www.festivaldecanarias.com).

Castillo de la Luz

Juan Rejón. ⊶Closed for restoration until 2010. 📞928 46 47 57.
The 15C fort is an exhibition locale.

Paseo Cornisa

This avenue in modern Escaleritas provides a fine **panorama**★ of Puerto de la Luz and La Isleta.

🚗 DRIVING TOURS

THE NORTH COAST
From Las Palmas to La Aldea de San Nicolás
128km/79mi – allow 1 day.

▷ Leave Las Palmas on the GC 2, 🚴 on the plan. Take exit 8.

Arucas

Arucas is the third-largest town on the island. A narrow road leads up **Montaña de Arucas**, shaped like a sugar loaf, offering a **panorama**★ to Las Palmas de Gran Canaria. The black-rock church below stands out against white houses.

▷ Take the C 813. At Buenlugar, 6km/3.7mi beyond Arucas, turn left.

Firgas

This is the source of a popular sparkling mineral water. The paseo de Gran Canaria pays a picturesque homage to the island's communities.

▷ Return to the main road.

Los Tilos de Moya

Los Tilos is a protected area with a wood of wild laurel trees.

▷ At Guía, turn right to join the C 810. Head towards Las Palmas for a few metres, then turn off to Cenobio de Valerón.

Cenobio de Valerón★

Cuesta de Silva, Santa María de Guía. 🕐Open Tue–Sun Oct–Mar 10am–5pm; Apr–Sept 10am–6pm. 🕐Closed 1, 6 Jan, 1 May, 25 Dec. 🎫2.50€. 📞618 60 78 96. www.cenobiodevaleron.com.
Tradition has it that native girls were prepared in caves hollowed out of tufa for their role as Sacred Virgins. In fact, this was merely a granary. Above it, chiefs met in council (tagoror).

▷ Return to the C 810 and head towards Gáldar.

Gáldar

At the foot of Mount Gáldar the Guanche king held his court (guanarteme).
Outside the heritage centre is the **Cueva Pintada**, a cave with **mural paintings**★. Guanche objects are displayed (Audiencia 2; 🕐 open Tue–Sat 9.30am–8pm, Sun 11am–8pm, 24, 31 Dec 9.30am–3pm; 🕐closed 1, 6 Jan, 1 May, 25 Dec; 🎫6€; booking required 📞928 89 57 46; 📞928 89 54 89; www.cuevapintada.org).

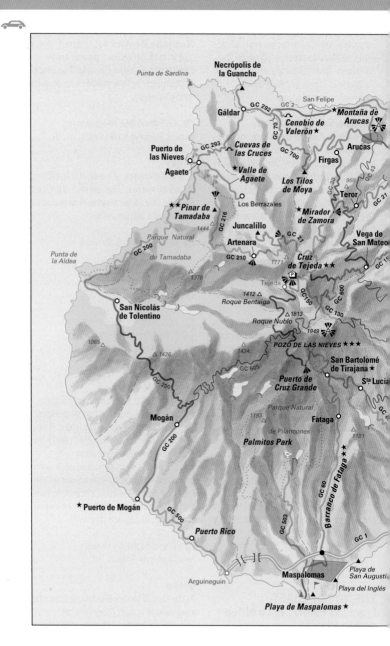

Necrópolis de la Guancha

2km/1.2mi N of Gáldar on coast.

For Info: ☎ 928 21 94 21.

Excavations have brought to light a Guanche settlement and a necropolis of circular constructions of great blocks of lava and a large burial mound.

▶ *Return to Gáldar; take the C 810 S.*

Cuevas de las Cruces

Halfway between Gáldar and Agaete.

These are attractive caves in the tufa.

GRAN CANARIA

Agaete

In this charming white-walled village is an important burial site, being readied for visitors. On 4 August the village celebrates the **Fiesta de la Rama**, one of the island's most popular festivals.

Los Berrazales Road★
SE of Agaete.
The road parallels the verdant **Agaete Valley**★ sheltered by mountains.

Puerto de las Nieves
1.3km0.8mi W of Agaete.
This little fishing harbour once shipped bananas. From the quay there is a good view of what remains of the **Finger of God** (Dedo de Dios), a heavily eroded pointed rock.
The hermitage **(ermita)** contains an interesting 15C Flemish triptych by Joos van Clave (🕐 *visits by prior arrangement;* 📞*928 55 43 82).*

La Aldea de San Nicolás
A spectacular road follows cliffs and crosses several ravines to La Aldea de San Nicolás, a village in a fertile basin growing sugar cane and tomatoes.

THE CENTRE OF THE ISLAND
156km/97mi – allow 1 day.

▶ *Leave Las Palmas de Gran Canaria on the C 811, N on the plan*

Tafira
A holiday resort favoured by islanders, the town is the site of a university.

Jardín Canario★
Camino del Palmeral. 🕐 *Open daily 9am–6pm.* 📞*928 21 95 80. www. jardincanario.org.*
The largest botanical garden in Spain (27ha/67 acres) is devoted to Canarian flora, with more than 500 species.

▶ *In Monte Lentiscal turn left.*

Mirador de Bandama★★
A road leads to the summit of Bandama (569m/1 867ft) and a superb view of the enormous Caldera de la Bandama, a crater with its eruption formations intact, and a small cultivated area. The **panorama** takes in Tafira, the Montaña de Arucas and Las Palmas to the north, the crater, and the Real Club de Golf (the oldest in Spain) and Telde to the south. In the caldera are old incised drawings.

▷ *Return to the C 811.*

Santa Brígida

This village sits close to a ravine planted with palms. A plant and flower market is held weekends. The Casa del Vino de Gran Canaria sells wines *(Calvo Sotelo 26;* ◷*open Tue–Fri 10am–6pm, Sat–Sun and public holidays 10am–3pm; ℘928 64 42 45; www.museosdelvino.es).*

Vega de San Mateo

A large fruit and vegetable market is held Saturdays and Sundays. The **Casa-Museo Cho Zacarías** *(av. Tinamar 17;* ◷*open Mon–Sat 9am–1pm; ⬭3.60€; ℘928 66 17 97)*, in a series of traditional houses, displays pottery, furniture, textiles, traditional implements, etc.

▷ *Continue along the C 811 for 6km/3.7mi, then bear left.*

Pozo de las Nieves★★★

From the summit (1 949m/6 394ft), which is sometimes snow-capped, there is a spectacular **panorama**★★★ of the island. On a clear day, Mount Teide (Tenerife) stands on the horizon.

Cruz de Tejeda★★

NW of Pozo de las Nieves.
Near the parador at the top of the pass (1 450m/4 757ft) lies the village of **Tejeda** in a huge volcanic basin. Out of the chaotic landscape rise the peaks of Roque Bentaiga and Roque Nublo, both venerated by the indigenous people.

▷ *Bear W to Artenara along the GC 110.*

The drive includes **views**★ of the troglodyte village of **Juncalillo** where most people live in lava caves.

Artenara

This village is the highest on the island (1 230m/4 035ft). In the enchanting **Ermita de la Cuevita**, a hermitage dug into the rock, is a statue of the Virgin with Child. The **panorama**★ is impressive. From the edge of the village, there is a superb **view**★ of Roque Bentayga. The most

comfortable place to view this from is the Mesón de la Silla restaurant *(℘928 66 61 08)* but there is also an adjacent viewing area.

Pinar de Tamadaba★★

The road passes through Canary pines extending to the edge of a cliff which drops sheer to the sea.

▷ *Continue to the end of a tarred road, to the Zona de Acampada, then park and walk 200m/220yd.*

On a clear day, the **view**★★ of Agaete, Gáldar and the coast, with the Pico del Teide on the horizon, is superb.

▷ *Return by the same road and turn left onto the GC 110 to Valleseco.*

Mirador de Zamora★

Just north of Valleseco there is an attractive **view**★ of Teror.

Teror

Teror has fine mansions with wooden balconies. The 18C **Basílica de Nuestra Señora del Pino** houses a statue of Our Lady of the Pine Tree, the island's patron, who is said to have appeared in 1481 *(pl. Nuestra Señora del Pino;* ◷*open Mon 1–8.30pm, Tue–Fri 9am–1pm, 3–8.30pm, Sat 9am–8.30pm, Sun 7.30–7.30pm; ⬭0.60€ (treasury); ℘928 63 01 18)*. Thousands gather on 8 September to present their gifts and join in worship.
On Sundays a lively market is held.

THE SOUTH COAST
Las Palmas to Maspalomas
59km/37mi – allow about 2hr.

▷ *Leave Las Palmas de Gran Canaria along the GC 1, ① on the plan, and then take exit 8 (Telde).*

Telde

This was a Guanche kingdom. In the lower town is the 15C **Iglesia de San Juan Bautista** *(Párroco Morales 2; ℘928 60 00 92)*, a church rebuilt in the 17C and 18C, which contains a 16C Flemish retable depicting the Life of the Virgin.

▷ *Take calle Inés Chimida.*

The road leads to the quiet **San Francisco district**, known for its traditional craftwork.

▷ *Follow the C 813 towards Ingenio. Beyond the junction with the C 816 turn left, immediately after some cottages, into a rough track; the last 250m/270yd is on foot.*

Yacimiento Arqueológico de Cuatro Puertas★

6km/3.7mi S of Telde. ℰ*928 68 13 36.* The cave, which has four openings *(cuatro puertas),* is where the indigenous council *(tagoror)* used to meet. The east face of the mountain is riddled with caves where the Guanche embalmed their dead. The summit (to the east) is a sacred site, Almogarén.

Maspalomas/Playa del Inglés/ Playa de San Agustín

This is one of Spain's largest resort areas, a sprawl of apartments and residential zones *(urbanizaciones)* with shopping/ recreation areas *(centros commerciales),* spread along the sandy coastline. Maspalomas has developed around its spectacular dunes and **beach**★, part of a 400ha/990-acre protected zone, including a palm grove.

Puerto de Mogán★

38km/24mi NW.
This is a picturesque man-made resort in typical Canarian style, built around an attractive marina.

San Bartolomé de Tirajana★

48km/30mi N on the GC 520. The way up passes through the **Barranco de Fataga**★★, a beautiful ravine. San Bartolomé is set in a magnificent green mountain cirque.

▷ *Return to San Bartolomé and take the C 815 going SE.*

ADDRESSES

🛏 STAY

🍽 **Tenesoya** – *Sagasta 98, Las Palmas de Gran Canaria.* ℰ*928 46 96 08. www. hoteltenesoya.com. 42 rooms.* ⊐*5€.* Just a step from the beach with comfortable rooms and updated, well-equipped bathrooms.

🍽🍽🍽 **Casa de Los Camellos** – *Progreso 12 (on the corner of Retama), Agüimes.* ℰ*928 78 50 03. www.hecansa. com. 11 rooms. Restaurant*🍽🍽🍽*.* This small hotel, in the old part of Agüimes, has been restored in a welcoming, rustic style, with wooden floors and furniture, and pleasant, attractive bedrooms. Good restaurant.

🍽🍽🍽 **Hotel Rural El Refugio** – *Cruz de Tejeda.* ℰ*928 66 65 13. www. hotelruralelrefugio.com. 10 rooms.* ⊐*6€. Restaurant*🍽🍽*.* Extraordinary setting in an area of lush vegetation deep in the interior. An excellent base for excursions through the centre of the island. Cosy bedrooms with wooden floors and attractive furniture.

🍴 EAT

🍽🍽🍽 **Casa de Galicia** – *Salvador Cuyás 8, Las Palmas de Gran Canaria.* ℰ*928 27 98 55.* High-quality Galician cuisine where the emphasis is on freshness. A good position between the Playa de las Canteras and the Parque de Santa Catalina

🍽🍽🍽 **Mesón de la Montaña** – *La montaña de Arucas.* ℰ*928 60 14 75. www.mesonarucas.es..* Traditional Canarian cuisine served at large round tables in a pleasant location offering good views.

Lanzarote★★★

Lanzarote, designated a Biosphere Reserve, is by far the most unusual and intriguing of the Canary Islands. With an area of 846sq km/326sq km, its lava-black landscape, dotted with oases of bright green vegetation and crops and dazzling white houses, has been likened to a giant modern artwork. Unlike many parts of Gran Canaria and Tenerife it has retained a vernacular style and local identity; there are no high-rise hotels, neither advertising boards nor pylons, nor many of the other familiar accretions of modern life and mass market tourism. This is mostly a result of the tireless conservation work of island champion César Manrique (1919–92), modern artist and landscaper extraordinaire. Wherever you go on Lanzarote you will be confronted with his works and philosophy.

LANDSCAPE AND TRADITION

In 1730, a massive series of eruptions occurred in the area now known as the **Montañas del Fuego** (Mountains of Fire). These lasted six years with 26 volcanoes covering one third of the island in lava. In 1824 a new volcano, Tinguatón, engulfed fields and houses.

Lava fields *(malpaís)* and thick black ash and pebbles are pitted with over 100 craters. In **La Geria**, where volcanic pebbles *(lapilli)* are plentiful, vines are protected by low semicircular walls. The grapes produce an excellent light white wine – Malvasía – with a distinctive bouquet. Throughout the island the fields are covered with a deep layer of the *lapilli* to retain moisture from the evening and morning dew, on an island where it rarely rains.

A BIT OF HISTORY

From the 14C to the present – The island owes its name to Lanceloto Malocello from Genoa, who landed in the 14C. In 1401 the Normans **Gadifer de la Salle** and **Jean de Bethencourt** captured the island for the King of Castile.

▶ **Population:** 127 457
🅸 **Info:** Arrecife: Blas Cabrera Felipe. ℘928 81 17 62. www.turismo lanzarote.com.
◐ **Location:** Lanzarote lies 100km/62mi from North Africa.

Lanzarote was a base for expeditions against the other islands and became prey to marauding slavers.

SIGHTS
Arrecife
This important port was originally defended from pirates by the **Castillo de San Gabriel** (◷*open Tue–Fri 10am–1pm, 4–7pm, Sat 10am–1pm*), built in the 16C on an islet and linked to the town by two bridges.

Recently given a makeover by the island authorities to entice more visitors to come here for a day trip, the island capital has good shopping, a pleasant beach, promenade and a picturesque lagoon, the Charco de San Ginés, where fisherman tie up small boats. To the north is the 18C **Castillo de San José**. Restored by César Manrique, it houses the **Museo Internacional de Arte Contemporáneo** (*Carretera de Naos;* ◷ *open daily 11am–9pm;* ⬬*2.50€;* ℘*928 81 23 21).*

EXCURSIONS
◔ *Each tour departs from Arrecife.*

THE CENTRE OF THE ISLAND
62km/39mi through the island's centre.

Fundación César Manrique★
Taro de Tahíche, Villa de Teguise.
◷ *Open Jul–Oct Tue–Sat 10am–7pm, Sun 10am–3pm; Nov–Jun Mon–Sat 10am–6pm, Sun 10am–3pm.* ◷ *Closed 1 Jan.* ⬬*8€.* ℘*928 84 31 38. www.fcmanrique.org.*
The foundation devoted to the greatest Lanzaroteño is in a remarkable and quite unique house that sits atop five volcanic bubbles. César Manrique chose this location to live – his extraordinary home is

open to the public – and to demonstrate the bond between architecture and nature.

Monumento al Campesino

This monument near **Mozaga**, by César Manrique, marks the centre of the island, and pays homage to the peasant farmers of Lanzarote. Next to it is the **Casa-Museo del Campesino** (🕐 *open daily 10am–6pm;* ⊘ *no charge;* ✆ *928 52 01 36),* a characteristic country house.

Museo Agrícola El Patio★

Echeyde 18, Tiagua. 🕐 *Open Mon–Fri 10am–5.30pm, Sat 10am–2.30pm.* ⊘ *5€ (including wine tasting and one tapa).* ✆ *928 52 91 34.*
The exhibits at this old farm highlight rural life on the island. A tasting of Malvasía wine is also offered.

Museo del Vino El Grifo

El Islote 121, San Bartolomé. 🕐 *Open daily 10.30am–6pm.* ⊘ *3€.* ✆ *928 52 49 51. www.elgrifo.com.*

The 18C El Grifo wine storehouses are a museum of traditional winemaking.

La Geria★★

La Geria lies between Yaiza and Mozaga in a blackish desert pockmarked with craters. The village is a wine centre.

THE SOUTH OF THE ISLAND

Round-trip of 124km/77mi from Arrecife.

Parque Nacional de Timanfaya★★★

🚌 *Guided tours of the park by coach are available from 9am; last tour at 5pm.* ⊘ *8€ (including volcano circuit).* ✆ *928 84 02 38.*
The range, which emerged in the 1730–36 eruptions, stands out sometimes red, sometimes black, above cinder and slag. It is the major natural attraction on the island. The **Montañas de Fuego** form the centre of this massif.
Dromedaries, once common beasts of burden on Lanzarote, wait by the roadside 5km/3mi north of Yaiza to provide a swaying and jolting ride up

the mountainside, from where there is a good view of the next crater. Although the volcanoes have not erupted since 1736, their fires burn and bubble still. To demonstrate the point, at the visitor centre, twigs are dropped into a shallow hole (by the park ranger) and instantly catch fire; water poured into a pipe set into the lava steams immediately because of the subsoil temperature (140°C/284°F at 10cm/4in, over 400°C/752°F at 6m/19.6ft), and in the El Diablo restaurant, food is cooked using the heat of the earth as a giant barbecue. There are fine views from the restaurant.

Buses from here follow the 14km/8.7mi **Ruta de los Volcanes**. A lookout affords a view over an immense lava field stretching to the sea.

Los Hervideros

In the caverns at the end of the tongue of lava, the sea boils (*hervir*: to boil) in an endlessly fascinating spectacle.

El Golfo★★

A lagoon is filled with vivid emerald-green water; a steep cliff of pitted black rock forms an impressive backdrop.

Salinas de Janubio★

Deep blue seawater entering a crater is harvested to leave gleaming white pyramids of salt in square pans.

Playa Blanca

This pleasant resort has a promenade between old fishermen's houses and the white beach.

Punta del Papagayo★

The Rubicón region is where Bethencourt settled. The only trace is the Castillo de las Coloradas, a tower on the cliff edge. Dusty roads lead from Playa Blanca to the protected **Reserva Natural de los Ajaches** (*open daily 9am–7pm; 3€ vehicle fee; 928 17 34 52*), which leads to the isolated uncommercialised white-sand Papagayo beaches, the finest on the island. From here there are fine **views**★ of Playa Blanca and Fuerteventura .

▷ *Take the LZ 2.*

Museo de Cetáceos de Canarias (Whale Museum)

Antiguo Varadero Building, Puerto Calero. ⏰ *Open Tue–Sat 10am–6pm, last admission at 5.15pm.* ⏰ *Closed 1, 6 Jan, 25 Dec.* 8€. 928 84 95 60. *www.museodecetaceos.org.*

One of the best European whale collections uses replicas, skeletons, explanatory panels, sound and images to tell the story of these mammals.

▷ *Return to Arrecife via the LZ 2.*

THE NORTH OF THE ISLAND
Round trip of 77km/47mi from Arrecife – about half a day

Jardín de Cactus★

Ctra General del Norte, Guatiza. ⏰ *Open daily 10am–7pm.* 5€. 928 52 93 97.

This cactus garden displays many species from the Canary Islands, America and Madagascar, on terraces in an old quarry. In this area are prickly pears, a cactus which attracts cochineal beetles, once crushed to obtain a crimson dye.

Cueva de los Verdes★★★

Haría. Guided tours (1hr) daily 10am–7pm, last admission 6pm. 8€. 928 84 84 84.

At the foot of the Corona volcano are volcanic galleries where the Guanches once took refuge from marauding pirates. There are 2km/1mi of illuminated passages at different levels.

Jameos del Agua★

Carretera de Orzola, Haría. ⏰ *Open daily 10am–7pm; Tue, Fri, Sat 7pm–2am, including a folklore show at 11pm.* 8€ (day), 9€ (evening). 928 84 80 20.

A *jameo* is a cavity formed when the top of a volcanic tube collapses. César Manrique has turned two *jameos* into an extraordinary fantasy grotto, regarded by most people as his *tour de force* on Lanzarote. Quite separately, a lagoon in the cave is the habitat of a minute, blind albino millenary crab, only found here. The **Casa de los Volcanes** on the upper level is an excellent exhibition and study centre on volcanism. By night the Jameos del Agua becomes a small stylish leisure complex with a restaurant, bar, dance floor and auditorium.

Mirador del Río★★

Carretera del norte, Ye. ◷ *Open daily 10am–7pm.* ◓*4.50€.* ☏*928 52 65 48.* At the north end of the island stands a steep isolated headland, **Riscos de Famara**. The belvedere commands a superb **panorama★★** across the azure waters of the **El Río** strait to La Graciosa and its neighbouring islands; immediately below are salt pans. A **passenger ferry** (⛴*Orzola to La Graciosa (25min): see website for schedule;* ◓*20€ round-trip;* ☏*902 40 16 66; www.lineas-romero. com)* operates between Orzola and La Graciosa.

♟ Tropical Park, Guinate

From Haría, take the LZ 202 via Mirador del Río. ◷*Open daily 10am–5pm. 14€; child 6€.* ☏*928 83 55 00. www. guinatepark.com.*

These gardens are devoted to exotic birds and feature parrot shows and penguins.

Haría

From afar Haría resembles a typical North African village, set in a lush valley replete with palm trees. The best view is from the Mirador de Haría★, some 5km/3mi south.

Teguise

Teguise, once the capital, is a beautifully restored and very atmospheric town with some of the finest colonial buildings in the archipelago. Several of these have been tastefully converted to restaurants, bars and shops. Teguise is most famous nowadays for its **Sunday Market** (◷*open 9am–2pm),* which draws coach tours from all over the island.
In the nearby **Castillo de Santa Bárbara,** built in the 16C on the Guanapay volcano, is the **Museo del Emigrante** (◷ *open Mon–Fri 10am–6pm, Sat–Sun 10am–4pm;* ◓*no charge;* ☏*928 84 59 13),* which documents the often poignant tales of emigration of Canary Islanders to America. There are excellent views of the town and surrounding countryside from here.

ADDRESSES

🛏 STAY

⬭ **Hotel Miramar** – *Coll 2, Arrecife.* ☏*928 81 26 00. www.hmiramar.com. 85 rooms.* ◓*5€. Restaurant* ⬭⬭. Although this 1980s-style building is lacking in architectural charm, its location, by the sea and opposite the Castillo de San Gabriel in the centre of Arrecife, couldn't be better. Bedroom balconies offer good sea views, although the bedrooms themselves are on the basic side with antiquated furniture.

⬭⬭⬭ **Finca de las Salinas** – *La Cuesta 17, Yaiza.* ☏*928 83 03 25. www. fincasalinas.com. 17 rooms. 2 Restaurants* ⬭⬭. An 18C mansion with an attractive façade and rustic rooms located in a lively neighbourhood.

🍴 EAT

⬭⬭⬭ **Amura** – *Pas. Marítimo, Puerto Calero.* ☏*928 51 31 81. www. restauranteamura.com. Closed Mon.* This restaurant in an attractive colonial-style octagonal building has a spectacular terrace. Its location opposite the marina, surrounded by palms, is outstanding.

⬭⬭⬭ **La Cañada** – *César Manrique 3, Puerto del Carmen.* ☏*928 51 04 15. Closed Sun.* A kitchen that takes pride in the quality of its ingredients. A lovely terrace and dining room, located on a small hill.

Fuerteventura

Fuerteventura has a captivating elemental beauty thanks to its bare landscape and beaches of white sand with turquoise water all around. Strong winds and a calm sea on the east coast make this island ideal for sailing, diving, fishing and, in particular, kitesurfing and windsurfing.

LANDSCAPE AND CLIMATE

Arid Fuerteventura is dotted with bare crests and extinct volcanoes. It was described as a "skeletal island" by its most famous native, the poet and writer **Miguel de Unamuno**, exiled here in 1924. The harsh terrain is only suitable for grazing goats, which outnumber humans. Villages are marked by palm trees and windmills.

Fuerteventura shares the climate of nearby Africa; sand, blown across the sea, formed an isthmus, El Jable, between the once-separate islets of Maxorata and Jandía.

🚗 DRIVING TOUR

NORTH TO SOUTH

Corralejo★

This likeable one-time fishing village, now the island's main tourist resort, is at the northern tip of the island beyond the *malpaís*.

Crystal-clear water laps at the immense beautiful white dune **beaches** of the Parque Natural Dunas de Corralejo and the Isla de Lobos, a Robinson Crusoe island, accessible by ferry. Lanzarote is visible north.

▷ Leave Corralejo along the FV 101.

La Oliva

The **Centro de Arte Canario** (🕐open Mon–Sat 10.30am–6pm, 5pm in winter; ✎admission charge; ☎928 86 82 33) is the island's best art gallery, devoted to Canarian art. Opposite stands the landmark **Casa de Coroneles**, a grand 18C house; once the residence of the gov-

▶ **Population:** 74 983
ℹ **Info:** Corralejo: Plaza Grande de Corralejo. ☎928 86 62 35. www.turismodecanarias. com/en/islas/fuerteventura.
◑ **Location:** Fuerteventura lies 100km/62mi NW of the coast of Africa. Immediately N is Lanzarote. Area: 1 731sq km/668sq mi.
👪 **Kids:** Oasis Park.

ernor of the island, it is now an arts and cultural centre.

▷ Continue on the FV 10 passing the Guanche's sacred Mount Tindaya on your right. Just before you turn right onto the FV 207 look for the large hillside statue of Miguel de Unamuno. Pass through Tefia.

Ecomuseo de la Alcogida

La Alcogida, Tefia. 🕐*Open Tue–Fri, Sun 9.30am–5.30pm.* ✎*5€.* ☎*928 85 14 00. www.majorero.com/laalcogida.*
This is the island's most engaging museum, depicting rural country life around 50 to 100 years ago, scattered among seven houses and farms.

Betancuria★

This pretty valley town (in fact no bigger than a small village), was once the island capital, founded in 1404 by island conqueror Jean de Bethencourt.
Betancuria retains a ruined Franciscan monastery and an ancient **cathedral**, with white walls and a picturesque wooden balcony, now called the **Iglesia de Santa María la Antigua**. The baptistery contains an interesting crucifix; the sacristy has a fine panelled ceiling.
On the south side, a small **Museo Arqueológico** displays Guanche artefacts (*Roberto Roldán;* 🕐*open Tue–Sat 10am–6pm;* 🕐*closed public holidays;* ✎*1.20€;* ☎*928 87 82 41).*
The road south provides an attractive contrast between the wide horizon of bare rose-tinted peaks and the village

of **Vega de Río Palmas** nestling in its green valley-oasis.

▷ *Head SW along the FV 617, turn left onto the FV2 coast road, then NE for a short distance.*

👥 **La Lajita Oasis Park**
Ctra General de Jandia, La Lajita.
🕐*Open daily from 10am.* 🚌*19.50€ (8.50€ camel ride); child 10.25€ (4.50€ camel ride).* 📞*902 40 04 34. www.lajitaoasispark.com.*
Located at the gateway to the Jandía Peninsula, Oasis Park is quite literally an oasis of beautiful botanical gardens and exotic animals amid the parched southern landscape. This zoo park includes over 200 species of birds and hundreds of small animals, and is most famous for its camel rides (these were common

beast of burden on the island as recently as the mid-20C). There are also shows featuring sea lions, birds of prey, parrots and crocodiles. Here you will also find a large African area with giraffes elephants, hippos, cheetahs etc.

▷ *Head back SW on the FV2.*

Península de Jandía
The leeward (southern) side of this protected southernmost part of the island is famous for its magnificent beaches. These are largely uncommercialised though a number of low-key resorts popular with German and Scandinvian visitors have grown up over the last three decades. This is the main centre for windsurfing and kitesurfing on the island and world championships are staged here.

La Gomera★

La Gomera, with an area of 378km/146sq mi, is ideal for visitors seeking peace, contact with nature and outdoor activities. This round island rises from coastal cliffs, cut by deep ravines, to a *meseta* with a single peak, Mount Garajonay (1 487m/4 880ft). Black beaches are reminders of volcanic activity as are the dramatic basalt cliffs known as Los Órganos, which are only visible by boat. The fertile red soil is carefully husbanded and picturesque terraces are a feature of the island.

SIGHTS
San Sebastián de la Gomera
Christopher Columbus stayed here during his first voyage. His route can be traced down the main street from the corner house where he took on water *(ask to see the well, el pozo, in the patio)*, past the **Iglesia de la Asunción** *(Medio; ☎922 87 03 03)*, where he heard Mass, to the **Casa de la Aguada**, a small house located before the post office, where he is said to have slept.

🚗 DRIVING TOUR

▶ *15km/9.3mi. Leave San Sebastián de la Gomera on the TF 711.*

The road emerges from the first tunnel in the **Hermigua Valley**★★ amid white houses, palms and banana plantations.

Agulo★
19km/11.8m NW from San Sebastián.
This small villages enjoys a picture-postcard seaside location with Tenerife clearly visible on the horizon.
In the adjacent pretty village of **Las Rosas** demonstration of *El Silbo*, the unique whistling language invented by the islanders in order to

- ▶ **Population:** 21 952
- **Info:** Calle Real 4, San Sebastián de La Gomera. ☎922 14 15 12. www. gomera-island.com.
- **Location:** La Gomera is a 35min ferry ride from Los Cristianos on Tenerife.

communicate with each other across Gomera's many ravines, are given at the Las Rosas restaurant.

Parque Nacional Garajonay★★
Juego de Bolas visitor centre. 🕐*Open daily 9.30am–4.30pm.* 🚶*Guided walking tours on Sat by prior arrangement.* ☎922 80 09 93. http:// reddeparquesnacionales.mma.es.
This national park is covered by laurels, traces of the Tertiary era, and giant heathers, punctuated by rocks. Mist caused by trade winds lends an air of mystery.

Valle Gran Rey★★
55km/34mi from San Sebastián de la Gomera on the TF 713.
The road ascends the slopes to the south; the climb to the central *meseta* in the park is less steep.
Chipude– Attractive potters' village.
Arure – After the bridge there is a good **panorama**★ of Taguluche.
Barranco del Valle Gran Rey★★ – The most ravine on the island.

El Hierro

This small remote windblown sland, just 278sq km/107sq mi, sees very few visitors. Those who come witness fertile farmland, spectacular cliffs plunging into the sea, volcanic cones, fields of lava carpeted in laurel, and an underwater world popular with divers.

▶ **Population:** 10 162
🄘 **Info:** Calle Dr Quintero 4, Valverde. ℘922 55 03 02. www.elhierro.es.
◐ **Location:** El Hierro is in the far southwest of the archipelago. Ferries run to neighbouring islands (℘902 100 107; www.fredolsen.es).

EXCURSIONS

The excursions below depart from **Valverde**, the capital of the island, at an altitude of 571m/1 873ft.

Tamaduste

8km/5mi NE.
A large sandbank by the small seaside resort forms a lagoon.

El Golfo★★

8km/5mi W.
There is a fine **view**★★ of El Golfo from the **Mirador de La Peña**. The rim of a crater is covered with laurels and giant heather; the level floor is cultivated. La Fuga de Gorreta, near the Salmor rocks *(NE)*, is the habitat of a primeval lizard.

TOUR THROUGH LA DEHESA

◐ *105km/65mi.*
Head S from Valverde along the TF 912.

Tiñor – Pyramid-shaped formations of ash among fertile fields denote this area. Until 1610, when it was blown down, a Garoé tree was venerated by natives.
Sabinosa – A spa-hotel treats skin and digestive diseases.
La Dehesa – A track from 3km/1.8mi on crosses the arid La Dehesa region and provides extensive **views**★ of the south coast where the fiery red earth, pitted with craters, slopes to the sea.
Punta de Orchilla – Orchilla Point was the zero meridian before Greenwich. Beyond the lighthouse are sabine trees, conifers with twisted trunks found only on El Hierro.

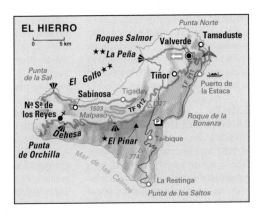

Ermita de Nuestra Señora de los Reyes – In this hermitage is a statue of the Virgen de Los Reyes, patron saint of the island. Every four years since 1741, it is carried in procession to Valverde *(Bajada Virgen de los Reyes)*. It will next take place on the 1st Saturday of July in 2009.
El Pinar – A pleasant **pine forest**★ extends all over this region.

La Palma★

With a surface of just 706sq km/272sq mi and its highest peak rising to 2 426m/7 962ft, La Palma has the highest average altitude of any island in the world. Rain is more abundant than in the rest of the Canaries, resulting in numerous streams and springs. It is called, justifiably on both counts, the "Beautiful Island" and the "Green Island" because of its woods of laurel and pine and numerous banana plantations. La Palma has distanced itself from major tourist development and appeals to nature-lovers, walkers, and those seeking peace and quiet.

A BIT OF HISTORY

The Caldera de Taburiente, a huge mountain arch curiously shaped like a crater, spreads over 10km/6.2mi. A chain of peaks, Las Cumbres, extends south; ravines produce an indented coastline. In the mountains, rainwater is collected to irrigate the lower terraces.

SIGHTS

SANTA CRUZ DE LA PALMA

The administrative centre was founded in 1493 by the conquistador Alonso Fernández de Lugo. In the 16C, with rising sugar exports and the expansion of the naval yards, Santa Cruz was one of the Spanish Empire's major ports (third only to Sevilla and Antwerp) and prey to pirates; now it is a peaceful city where elegant façades line the seafront. Its most famous native is Manolo Blahnik. At Playa de Los Cancajos *(5km/3mi S)* the beach and rocks are black.

Plaza de España

Several buildings date from the Renaissance. The 16C **Iglesia de El Salvador** has beautiful ceilings with **artesonado ornament**★; the sacristy has Gothic vaulting. Opposite stand the 16C town hall and houses in colonial style.

Walk uphill to the delightful **plaza de Santo Domingo**. Next to a college

▶ **Population:** 85 932
▪ **Info:** Avenida Blas Pérez Glez, Santa Cruz de la Palma. ☎922 41 21 06. www.lapalmaturismo.com.
◗ **Location:** La Palma is located in the far north west of the archipelago.

stands the **chapel** of a former monastery with beautiful Baroque altars. *To visit the chapel, ask for the keys at the Iglesia de El Salvador, ☎922 41 32 50.*

🚗 DRIVING TOURS

The two tours suggested below both depart from Santa Cruz de la Palma.

THE NORTH OF THE ISLAND
Observatorio Roque de los Muchachos★★★
36km/22.3mi NW. Allow about 1hr45min for the ascent.
Laurel bushes and pine trees line the winding road which offers extensive views as it climbs to the **astrophysical observatory**, at 2 432m/7 981ft, includes the William Herschel Telescope, one of the largest in the world with a 4.2m/13.7ft mirror (*Apartado de Correos 50; guided tours by prior arrangement; ☎922 405 500; www.iac.es).*
From the Roque de los Muchachos the **panorama**★★★ encompasses the Caldera, Los Llanos de Aridane, the islands of El Hierro and La Gomera, and Mount Teide on Tenerife.

Punta Cumplida
36km/22.3mi N.
There are fine views of the coast from the cliff road which crosses deep ravines *(barrancos)* in the Los Tilos Biosphere Reserve. Note the impressive number of craters.
La Galga *(15km/9.3mi N off LP 1)* – North of the village, after the tunnel, the road crosses a steep and well-wooded **ravine**★.

La Cumbrecita

J. Malburet/ MICHELIN

San Andrés *(22km/13.6mi N off LP 1)* – In the church is a beautiful Mudéjar ceiling in the chancel.

Charco Azul – Natural seawater pools.

Puerto Espíndola – A fishing village where boats are drawn up onto a shingle beach in a breach in the cliff face.

Punta Cumplida – Walk round the lighthouse to see waves breaking on basalt rock piles. The attractive Fajana swimming pools are north of here.

Los Sauces *(2km/1.2mi W of San Andrés)*– The main agricultural centre in the north of the island.

Los Tiles★ – Detour up Agua Ravine to the lime tree forest. **Los Tiles Interpretation and Investigation Centre** (🕒 *open daily Jul–Oct 9am– 5.30pm; Nov–Jun 9am–5pm; 🎧922 45 12 46)* interprets the flora in the reserve.

THE CENTRE AND SOUTH OF THE ISLAND

Via Los Llanos and Fuencaliente
190km/118mi.

▷ *Head N out of Santa Cruz. After the ravine, take the first left.*

On the seafront of Santa Cruz, stands the **Castillo de Santa Catalina**, built to fend off priate raiders in the 17C. In the **Barco de la Virgen** *(the Virgin's Boat)*, a curious cement reproduction of Columbus' Santa María, is a small **naval museum** *(Pérez Galdós 18; 🎧922 42 00*

07). The road passes the **Fuerte de la Virgen**, a 16C fortress.

Las Nieves

At the foot of Pico de las Nieves, shaded by laurel trees, the **Real Santuario de Nuestra Señora de las Nieves** houses the statue of the island's patron saint. Every five years (the next will be in 2010) it is the centrepiece of a grand parade.

La Concepción★

The summit of the Caldereta commands a wonderful **bird's-eye view**★ of Santa Cruz de la Palma, the harbour and the mountains.

▷ *Take the TF 812 westwards.*

Parque Nacional de la Caldera de Taburiente★★★

4km/2.5mi W of the tunnel on the right is the **Centro de Visitantes** *(Ctra, General de Padrón, nº 47, El Paso; 🎧922 49 72 77)*, with information on marked footpaths.

▷ *Ahead, turn right for La Cumbrecita.*

The **Cumbrecita Pass** (1 833m/6 014ft) and the **Lomo de las Chozas Pass** *(1km/0.6mi farther on)* provide a splendid **panorama**★★★ of the Caldera de Taburiente, dotted with Canary pines and crowned by rose-tinted peaks.

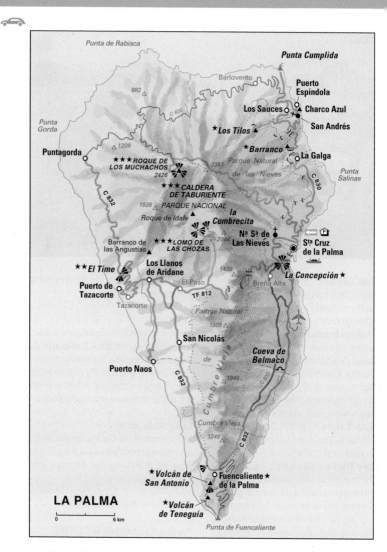

LA PALMA

0   6 km

Los Llanos de Aridane

The island's second largest town is in a plain of bananas and avocado trees.

El Time★★

The top of El Time cliff affords a remarkable **panorama**★★ of the Aridane plain, a sea of banana palms, and of the Barranco de las Angustias, a rock fissure which is the only outlet for the Caldera de Taburiente.

Puntagorda

This fine landscape is particularly beautiful in spring, when the almond trees are in blossom.

◗ *Return to El Time.*

Puerto de Tazacorte

Alonso Fernández de Lugo landed in this small harbour in 1492. In 1585, Francis Drake raided this town on his way to the Caribbean. Nicnamed 'París chiquito' (little Paris), the small beach is popular on Sundays.

Fuencaliente de la Palma

©Turespaña

Puerto Naos
Descend through lava fields from the 1949 eruption and then through thhe lush avocado and banana plantations irrigated by La Caldera de Taburiente, to the Puerto with its large beach of black volcanic sand.

San Nicolás
The lava stream from the Nambroque volcano cut the village in two in 1949.

Fuencaliente de la Palma★
Before reaching Fuencaliente, look back from the Mirador de las Indias for a **glimpse**★ of the coast through the pines. A hot water spring disappeared during the eruption of **San Antonio volcano**★ in 1677. Circle the volcano to see the craters of **Teneguía volcano**★, which appeared in October 1971, and the lava stream which separated the lighthouse from the village.

Cueva de Belmaco
5km/3mi from the airport fork.
The cave of Guanche King Belamaco. At the back of the cave are rocks with inscriptions.

ADDRESSES

STAY

⊜ **Hotel Edén** – *Pl. de España, Los Llanos de Aridane.* ✆*922 46 01 04. www.hoteledenlapalma.com. 19 rooms. ⚏4€. Closed May.* This small hotel in the island's second town, amid banana plantations, is good for those on a budget. Small, comfortable rooms.

⊜⊜⊜⊜ **Hotel La Palma Romántica** – *Las llanadas, Barlovento. 1km/0.6mi SW of Barlovento.* ✆*922 18 62 21. www.hotellapalmaromantica.com. 40 rooms. Restaurant⊜.* This rural hotel in the north has sweeping views of the coast. Large rooms, friendly staff and a reasonable restaurant. A good, quiet base.

🛒 SHOPPING
LOCAL PRODUCTS

Cheese – Smoked white goats' cheese is one of La Palma's specialities. The island's goat population numbers some 30 000.

Cigars – Tobacco was first introduced to the islands by Cuban Indians. The handmade palm cigars have a deserved reputation and are highly appreciated by cigar connoisseurs the world over.

Silk – La Palma's textile tradition dates back to the 17C. Today, a number of local artisans still work with natural silk.

INDEX

INDEX

INDEX

INDEX

INDEX

🏠 STAY

🍴 EAT

MAPS AND PLANS

MAP LEGEND

	Sight	Seaside resort	Winter sports resort	Spa
Highly recommended	★★★	�	✳✳✳	♯♯♯
Recommended	★★	addadd	✳✳	♯♯
Interesting	★	add	✳	♯

Selected monuments and sights

	Tour - Departure point
⚑ ⚑	Catholic church
⚑ ⚑	Protestant church, other temple
⬡ ⬟ ⬢	Synagogue - Mosque
	Building
▪	Statue, small building
⚵	Calvary, wayside cross
◎	Fountain
—•—■—	Rampart - Tower - Gate
✕	Château, castle, historic house
∴	Ruins
◡	Dam
✿	Factory, power plant
☆	Fort
⋒	Cave
▭	Troglodyte dwelling
⋔	Prehistoric site
▼	Viewing table
₩	Viewpoint
▲	Other place of interest

Sports and recreation

🏇	Racecourse
🏒	Skating rink
☳ ☳	Outdoor, indoor swimming pool
🎬	Multiplex Cinema
⛵	Marina, sailing centre
⛺	Trail refuge hut
□–■–■–□	Cable cars, gondolas
□–+++–□	Funicular, rack railway
🚂	Tourist train
◊	Recreation area, park
🎡	Theme, amusement park
☠	Wildlife park, zoo
⊛	Gardens, park, arboretum
☻	Bird sanctuary, aviary
🚶	Walking tour, footpath
☺	Of special interest to children

Abbreviations

G, POL	Police (Federale Politie)	**P**	Local government offices (Gouvernement provincial)
H	Town hall (Hôtel de ville ou maison communale)	**ℙ**	Provincial capital (Chef-lieu de provincial)
J	Law courts (Palais de justice)	**T**	Theatre (Théâtre)
M	Museum (Musée)	**U**	University (Université)

Additional symbols

Symbol	Description	Symbol	Description
🛈	Tourist information	✉	Post office
═══ ═	Motorway or other primary route	☎	Telephone
❶ ❶	Junction: complete, limited	⬓	Covered market
▭ ═	Pedestrian street	⁙	Barracks
I═══I	Unsuitable for traffic, street subject to restrictions	△	Drawbridge
▱▱▱ ----	Steps – Footpath	∪	Quarry
🚉 🚉	Train station – Auto-train station	✕	Mine
🚌 🚌	Coach (bus) station	Ⓑ Ⓕ	Car ferry (river or lake)
—•—	Tram	⛴	Ferry service: cars and passengers
Ⓜ	Metro, underground	⛵	Foot passengers only
🅿	Park-and-Ride	③	Access route number common to Michelin maps and town plans
♿	Access for the disabled	Bert (R.)...	Main shopping street
		AZ B	Map co-ordinates

Michelin Apa Publications Ltd

A joint venture between Michelin and Langenscheidt

58 Borough High Street, London SE1 1XF, United Kingdom

No part of this publication may be reproduced in any form
without the prior permission of the publisher.

© 2010 Michelin Apa Publications Ltd
ISBN 978-1-906261-92-4
Printed: November 2009
Printed and bound in Germany